THE GREAT PRAJNA PARAMITA SUTRA

Volume 1

Translated by
Naichen Chen

The Great Prajna Paramita Sutra, Volume 1

Copyright © 2017 Naichen Chen. All rights reserved. No part of this book may be reproduced or retransmitted in any form or by any means without the written permission of the publisher.

Published by Wheatmark®
2030 East Speedway Boulevard, Suite 106
Tucson, Arizona 85719 USA
www.wheatmark.com

Names: Chen, Naichen, translator.
Title: The Great Prajna Paramita Sutra / translated by Naichen Chen.
Other Titles: Tripiṭika. Sūtrapiṭika. Prajñāpāramitā. English. | Da bo re bo luo mi duo jing. English.
Description: Tucson, Arizona : Wheatmark, [2017-] | English translation of: Da bo re bo luo mi duo jing, which was a Chinese translation of the original Sanskrit title, Tripiṭika. Sūtrapiṭika. Prajñāpāramitā.
Identifiers: LCCN 2016952997 | ISBN 978-1-62787-456-4 (hardcover : vol. 1) | ISBN 978-1-62787-457-1 (ebook : vol. 1)
Subjects: LCSH: Nāgārjuna, active 2nd century. Mahāprajñāpāramitāśāstra. | Buddhism--Sacred books. | Religious life--Buddhism.
Classification: LCC BQ1882.E5 C44 2017 (print) | LCC BQ1882.E5 (ebook) | DDC 294.38--dc23

Contents

About the Translator
vii

Acknowledgments
ix

Translator's Introduction
xi

Fascicle 1
Chapter 1: The Causes and Conditions of the Assembly
Section 1
1

Fascicle 2
Chapter 1: The Causes and Conditions of the Assembly
Section 2
22

Fascicle 3
Chapter 2: Learning Contemplation
Section 1
51

Fascicle 4
Chapter 2: Learning Contemplation
Section 2
71

Chapter 3: In Accordance with Prajna Paramita
Section 1
86

Fascicle 5
Chapter 3: In Accordance with Prajna Paramita
Section 2
95

Fascicle 6
Chapter 3: In Accordance with Prajna Paramita
Section 3
115

Fascicle 7
Chapter 3: In Accordance with Prajna Paramita
Section 4
133

Chapter 4: Rebirth
Section 1
147

Fascicle 8
Chapter 4: Rebirth
Section 2
157

Fascicle 9
Chapter 4: Rebirth
Section 3
182

Contents

Fascicle 10
Chapter 5: Praising the Superior Virtues
209

Chapter 6: Appearance of the Shape of the Tongue
221

Fascicle 11
Chapter 7: The Cautions and the Teachings
Section 1
234

Fascicle 12
Chapter 7: The Cautions and the Teachings
Section 2
258

Fascicle 13
Chapter 7: The Cautions and the Teachings
Section 3
284

Fascicle 14
Chapter 7: The Cautions and the Teachings
Section 4
312

Fascicle 15
Chapter 7: The Cautions and the Teachings
Section 5
337

Fascicle 16
Chapter 7: The Cautions and the Teachings
Section 6
365

Fascicle 17
*Chapter 7: The Cautions and the Teachings
Section 7*
386

Fascicle 18
*Chapter 7: The Cautions and the Teachings
Section 8*
415

Fascicle 19
*Chapter 7: The Cautions and the Teachings
Section 9*
452

Fascicle 20
*Chapter 7: The Cautions and the Teachings
Section 10*
486

Glossary of Terms
527

About the Translator

THE TRANSLATOR, NAICHEN CHEN (1941–), HAS WORKED ON this sutra for eight years. He earned a PhD in philosophy of education at the University of Florida. He has served as a professor of philosophy, Buddhism, and education at universities in Taiwan and the United States. He has also served as the president of National Hua Lien Teachers College in Taiwan and the president of University of the West (formerly Hsi Lai University) in Los Angeles, California. He has authored essays and books on education, religion, and philosophy in both Chinese and English.

Acknowledgments

FOR THE FAVORS BESTOWED ON ME TO MAKE this translation and its publication possible, I would like to express my deepest and sincerest gratitude to the following:

The Buddhas, bodhisattvas, and dharma protectors for having always guided and kept me since beginning the translation in 2008 or even earlier;

Master Xuanzang for translating *The Great Prajna Paramita Sutra* from Sanskrit into Chinese;

Master Hsing Yun, the founder of Fo Guang Shan Monastery, and Venerable Tzu Hui and Venerable Tzu Jung for their instruction and inspiration and for the very useful *Fo Guang Buddhist Dictionary* that the monastery compiled and published;

Master Yin Shun for nurturing me with his extraordinary books on Buddhism;

Mr. Xiu Lin for introducing me to Buddhism in 1964, teaching me meditation and Taijiquan, and, with his wife, purchasing a brand-new set of Tripitaka, the edition first published in Taiwan in 1954, as a gift to me;

Dr. Robert R. Sherman for not only reading and editing most of the manuscript of this translation but also, along with his wife, Joy, supporting me and my family with love, friendship, and sustaining concern;

My high school teacher, Mr. An-Shun Yeh, for teaching me about compassion;

Dr. Richard Kimball for reading and editing some of my translation and offering suggestions about a few terms appearing in my English translation for the first time;

Alice and J. P. Wang for assisting me and generously offering me patronage and for their invaluable friendship to me and my family;

Good friends of mine—Han-chiang Chen, Tien-en Kao, Yao-fu Lin, Fred Fwu-Tyan Ho, Yi Hsiung Tsai, Chianan Tai, Tsu Shen Lu, Wan-yih Lin, Hsin-wu Liu, Chien Chin Chen, Sing-bor Tong, Chou Tien Chen, Cheng I Chen, Shin I Chen, Rong Yaw Tang, Ugur H. T. Wu, Teng-yi Feng, and Martin Lin—for their sustaining encouragement and friendship;

My father, Chiguang Chen, and my mother, Yunying Lee Chen, for giving me life, raising me, educating me with incomparable freedom and love, and showing me what a virtuous and meaningful life really is;

My wife, Meitze, and our son, Nan-kuei; our daughter-in-law, Ying-hui; our grandson, Derek; and our daughter, Nanyu, for bringing me a happy and prosperous family life, continuing support, unconditional love, and the unexhausted spring of wisdom and inspiration; and

Grael Norton, Lori Conser, and their esteemed colleagues of Wheatmark for their professional and graceful way of taking care of the publication of this sutra.

Translator's Introduction

THE GREAT PRAJNA PARAMITA SUTRA, WITH APPROXIMATELY FIVE million words in six hundred fascicles, is regarded as the largest canon in Buddhism. The present version is, so far, the only complete presentation of this great sutra in English and is the second version, translated and published unabridged, in addition to the Chinese one rendered from Sanskrit about 1,350 years ago (from 660 to 663) by Xuanzang (Hsüan-tsang, c. 602–664), from which the present English translation is made. This English translation will appear as a set of hardbound volumes; an extensive glossary of the terms will be included.

The Sanskrit word *prajna* means "wisdom." But it has a connotation beyond how that word commonly is understood. It includes wisdom of the world and beyond the world; the wisdom based on perfect knowledge; the wisdom of living daily life and viewing human life, sentient beings, and the world; and the wisdom attained through logical and experiential reasoning and intuitive contemplation of all existent beings and their phenomena.

The Sanskrit word *paramita* means "ferrying" over the ocean or the river to reach the other shore. It also means "perfection." The cultivation of wisdom to its perfection is called *prajna paramita* because it can ferry sentient beings from their existing shore of vexations and suffering to the other shore of liberation and happiness. Therefore, such wisdom is the great superior wisdom, "the great prajna paramita."

The Sanskrit word *bodhisattva* refers to ones who not only can be awakened to the truth and become enlightened themselves but also can assist others to become awakened and enlightened. The bodhisattvas serve as a "great vehicle" to liberate sentient beings from suffering, vexations, and bondage so they can attain freedom, easiness, peace, and happiness in body and mind. Bodhisattvas are called *mahasattva* (great) because they are so broad-minded, loving-kind, and compassionate that they care about other sentient beings more than themselves. The great bodhisattvas are those who aspire to the unsurpassed, perfect, and universal bodhi. They have not yet become a Buddha, but they are determined and have vowed to learn and cultivate diligently and perfectly superior actions and virtuous dharmas. They walk on the road leading to the great bodhi and the Buddhahood. This is the only way the great bodhisattvas are able to set free sentient beings.

The Great Prajna Paramita Sutra is important not only because of its extensive teaching but also because it demonstrates what the great bodhisattva, the great bodhisattva path of cultivation, and the great bodhisattva vehicle are. It also demonstrates the differences between the great bodhisattva vehicle, the so-called large vehicle, and the other two vehicles for voice-hearers and self-enlightened ones, as well as how one should cultivate and learn to become a bodhisattva, reaching the state of nonregression in the pursuit of the unsurpassed, perfect, and universal bodhi and finally becoming a Buddha. This sutra depicts, manifests, and elaborates an entire learning process that can lead to attaining Buddhahood.

The dialogues and dialectic conversations between the Buddha and his senior disciples—Subhuti (Well Appearing One), Sariputra, Ananda (Joyfully Celebrating One), and Purna (Fully Loving Kind One), as well as Bodhisattva Maitreya, Heavenly Emperor Indra, and others—manifest the essential meanings of the "large vehicle"; the cultivation and learning of the bodhisattva path; the perfect knowledge and wisdom of the Buddha; the thirty-two perfect major marks and the eighty distinguishing minor features of the Buddha; and the Buddha's abilities, wisdom, and powers not shared by other sentient beings. Demonic hindrances that the bodhisattvas might encounter in their cultivation also are revealed and warned of.

Translator's Introduction

Additionally, the ontology of Buddhism is broadly and thoroughly discussed in this sutra through the dialogues between the Buddha and his disciples. The "Being" of the world—named realness, dharma realm, dharma nature, and so forth in this sutra—contains the characteristics of emptiness, selflessness, nonarising, nonextinction, nongoing, noncoming, nonmaking, nondoing, nondifferentiation, and formlessness. These concepts and names, along with other concepts and names, are established provisionally as indicators of all beings, namely the existents of the world, or as they are described in this sutra, the dharmas. Other establishments, either caused by mental images or other factors, are based on causes and conditions that are not real because they have no fixed "natures." All dharmas of the world and their relationships comprise the phenomenal realm of the world, the "conditioned realm." They are not separate from the realness or the "Being" of the world, the "unconditioned realm." The phenomena and the realness are neither the same nor separate. They are rather the two sides of the reality of the world as well as of sentient beings. The original natures of all dharmas, resembling empty space, are like dreams, illusions, mirror images, echoes, illusory images of water under sunlight, flowers in the sky, transformed things, and mirages. These ontological discussions suggest, reasonably and step by step, a metaphysical basis for the fathomless prajna paramita, the main concern and focus of the entire sutra.

To realize the truth of the phenomena of the world accurately and as it really is can awaken one to the reality of the world. But knowledge alone is not sufficient for the realization and attainment of the unsurpassed, perfect, and universal enlightenment. The perfect knowledge of all perfect knowledge that assimilates the perfect knowledge of everything, the perfect knowledge of the forms of all paths, and the perfect knowledge of all phenomena can be fulfilled in its ultimate state not only through the learning and absorption of all dharmas and their principles, but also through the cultivation of virtuous roots. This process appears at the outset to be on a dual track based on accurate cognition and the cultivation of the virtuous roots, but it will not become nondualistic and a single form until all virtues gained here and produced elsewhere, and initiated by the holy ones, are transferred joyfully by bodhisattvas along with sentient beings equally toward the unsurpassed, perfect, and universal bodhi.

This is the "large vehicle," in contrast to smaller ones in which only self-interest is concerned. The great bodhisattva path thus is formed in the progress of cultivation. It is based on emptiness, selflessness, nonattainment, nonattachment, nondifferentiation, nonaspiration, and formlessness; that is, it adopts nonattainment as a secure expedient not to stop at the self-interest stages of the voice-hearer and the self-enlightened one in order to enter correctly onto the bodhisattva path of nonarising, which is the only access to attaining Buddhahood. According to the sutra, it is because of prajna paramita that all the Buddhas in the past, future, and present in the worlds of the ten directions are able to understand and attain the unsurpassed, perfect, and universal bodhi and become the Buddha. Thus, prajna paramita is the mother of all Buddhas.

But why do the great bodhisattvas work so hard to pursue the unsurpassed bodhi when they realize that all dharmas are empty, and, as with dreams and so forth, nothing really can be attained? Because the great bodhisattvas develop great loving-kindness, great compassion, great joy, and great equanimity when seeing that sentient beings suffer severely in the reincarnation of birth and death because of their incorrect knowledge and views of the world. The only way the great bodhisattvas can relieve sentient beings from suffering and bring them freedom, peace, and happiness is to help them cultivate the bodhisattva path and become Buddhas themselves.

The bodhisattva path is difficult because one needs to cultivate many virtuous dharmas, learn to be patient when teaching sentient beings, and be accepted by them. Bodhisattvas should take great vows, learn everything to its perfection, and get to know how to teach sentient beings expediently and skillfully. The armors that bodhisattvas must wear for this purpose are the six paramitas: giving, pure precept, forbearance, diligence, meditation, and prajna paramitas.

The perfect fulfillment of these six ways is named *paramita* because it serves to ferry sentient beings from one shore to the other. The first five practices are based on prajna paramita, the perfect knowledge and wisdom, since no one really can be free from attachment and attainment in their cultivation without it. The expedient skillfulness of prajna paramita always plays the most important role for the correct cultivation of all virtuous dharmas. Realizing that all dharmas are empty in the final analysis, without arising and extinction and without differentiation and forms, the great bodhisattvas joyfully refrain from turning away from sentient beings and persevere in pursuing the great bodhi in order to benefit and bring happiness to all sentient beings. They thus practice all virtuous dharmas without being attached to them by adopting nonattainment as expedience.

In addition to the cultivation of the six paramitas, the great bodhisattvas also learn to dwell peacefully in all kinds of emptiness: internal emptiness, external emptiness, internal-external emptiness, and so forth, as well as emptiness of selfless self-nature. They will dwell peacefully in realness, dharma realm, dharma nature, the nature of equality, and so forth, as well as the realm of the inconceivable. They also will dwell peacefully in the four noble truths: suffering, the cause of suffering, the cessation of suffering, and the path for the cessation of suffering. They will cultivate the thirty-seven factors for enlightenment: the four bases of mindfulness, four correct endeavors, four bases of power, five roots, five powers, seven factors for enlightenment, and the noble eightfold path; the four meditations, four immeasurable minds, and four formless concentrations; the eight liberations, eight vexation-overcoming meditations, nine concentrations in sequence, and the ten universal contemplations; the liberation gates of emptiness, formlessness, and nonaspiration; all dharani gates and all samadhi gates; the ten stages of bodhisattva; the five eyes and the six supernatural powers; staying in correct mindfulness and dwelling in equanimity at all times; the Buddha's ten abilities, four kinds of fearlessness, four unhindered understandings, great loving-kindness, great compassion, great joy, and great equanimity, and eighteen distinctive features of Buddha's wisdom and power; the perfect knowledge of everything, the perfect knowledge of the forms of the paths, and the perfect knowledge of all phenomena; and the rest of innumerable and boundless Buddha dharma. These are all virtuous dharmas that the great bodhisattvas will learn and cultivate to their perfection before they become perfectly and universally enlightened.

The Sakyamuni Buddha became perfectly and universally enlightened at the age of twenty-nine. Within the first three weeks, he taught directly about his own inner mental process of realizing perfect enlightenment, as recorded in *Hua Yen Sutra* (*The Magnificent and Dignified Flowers Sutra*). It was the view of the world as viewed from a Buddha's eye. His inner experience was subtle, glorious, and exquisite, but when he was teaching at that time, only a few highly enlightened bodhisattvas could understand him, and most in the audience were like the dumb and the deaf. They could not understand what the Buddha said.

From the fourth week on, the Buddha turned to teach the *Agamas*, which were more suitable for voice-hearing practitioners. The teachings during this period, given at Deer Park, focused on but were not limited to the four noble truths, twelve chains of dependent origination, and the precepts for monks and nuns. This period of teaching lasted for twelve years until he knew that most of his disciples were well equipped and ready to expand beyond the cultivation and learning for self-interest and could assist sentient beings to cultivate, learn, and attain the perfect enlightenment. These self-benefactors would learn to be teachers and counselors and then signified the dawn of the path of the bodhisattva for the voice-hearers.

Then came a period for the larger-vehicle sutras that lasted for eight years. The Buddha taught more sutras in accord with the large vehicle to turn the voice-hearers into great bodhisattvas and teachings such as *Vimalakirti, Golden Light, Srimala, Lankavatara,* and *Suraṃgama* were given.

Next came the Prajna Period. The Buddha spent the next twenty-two years teaching prajna paramita, the foundation of the bodhisattva path for attaining the unsurpassed, universal, and perfect bodhi of the Buddha. The *Diamond Sutra* and the *Heart Sutra*, which became very popular in later days, were taught as parts of *The Great Prajna Paramita Sutra*. These teachings were given in sixteen assemblies at four places: Vulture Peak at Rajagriha,

Jetavana Vihara at Sravasti, the Heaven of Enjoying Other-Made Changes, and Kalandaka Veṇuvana (Bamboo Grove) at Rajagriha.

In his last eight years, the Buddha taught the *Lotus Sutra* (*Wonderful Dharma Lotus Sutra*) at Vulture Peak and then the *Nirvana Sutra* on the last day before entering nirvana.

The Buddha developed efficient methods and models for teaching. On the one hand, he conversed with his disciples, and they challenged each other. In their conversations, truth was revealed through logical reasoning and clarification. On the other hand, he used similes and analogies to make abstract ideas understandable, vivid, and easy to remember. Because of his supernatural powers, the Buddha could read his disciples' minds and guide them according to their individual differences. He suggested the method of dharani for incorporating various ideas into a few crucial words and sentences so that learners could memorize and retain what they had learned. He always was tranquil and graceful in demeanor when speaking with students and others. He guided students by adopting nonattainment as expedience out of the fathomless and pure wisdom based on perfect knowledge. Prajna paramita thus should also be regarded as the most superior philosophy of education for all educators in this regard.

FASCICLE 1

Chapter 1
The Causes and Conditions of the Assembly

Section 1

(In the First Assembly)

THIS IS WHAT I HEARD.

At one time, the Bhagavat lived on the top of Mount Vulture Peak in Rajagriha. He stayed with 1,250 senior monks, who were all arhats. All of these monks had eliminated all flaws and had no more vexations. They had attained genuine freedom, peace, and easiness. Their minds were well liberated and their wisdom was well released. They had been as well tamed as smart horses and the great dragons. They had accomplished all that should be done, abandoned all that should be renounced, and attained the real self-benefit. They had ended all bonds and gained liberation through correct knowledge. They had achieved ultimate, uppermost easiness in their minds. All of these monks were led by Mahakasyapa. Among them, Ananda was the only one who had not yet achieved the stage of arhat; he was still in the stream-entry stage at that time. There were also five hundred arhat nuns present in the assembly, led by Mahaprajapati. In addition, there were innumerable laypersons present in the assembly; all had gained an insight into the noble truths.

There were also countless bodhisattvas present in the meeting. They had all attained the complete dharani gates and samadhi gates; dwelled in emptiness, formlessness, and aspiration of nondiscrimination; attained equality-forbearance for all beings; fully achieved four unhindered understandings; possessed limitless ability in teaching and debating the dharma; mastered the five supernatural powers freely and completely; and attained the wisdom of correct judgment with no mistakes and regression. They all spoke and behaved in solemnity and dignity, and thus were highly respected. They worked diligently and bravely and stayed away from laziness. They had renounced their families and wealth and were willing to renounce their life if it was necessary. They had gotten rid of arrogance and pride and were both contamination-free and craving-free. They always maintained a mind of equality toward all sentient beings when teaching the correct dharma to them. They had fully understood the deepest meaning of dharma forbearance.

They had attained a fearless and carefree mind. They had overcome various demonic delusions, broken through the bondage of karma, and destroyed all adversaries of mental distress. They created and raised high the flag of dharma to correct all faulty visions, and what they did could not be measured by voice-hearers and self-enlightened ones. Their minds were free, and their understanding of dharma was unobstructed. They had been relieved from the obstacles of karma, problems, and wrong views. They mastered the expedient skills in correct choice, lecturing, and debate. They had entered the deep dharma gate of dependent origination of arising and extinction.

They had stayed away from incorrect views and hidden roots of vexations and had discarded various kinds of wound and twisted bondages. They had fully understood the ultimate meanings of the noble truths. They had made great vows for numberless kalpas and had decided that they would greet people with kind and joyful appearance before talking to them. They would speak without frowning and in clear words with harmonious rhythm. They would praise others skillfully and properly and debate without hindrance; when facing crowds of people, they would appear with solemnity and the power of virtue; and they would always be fearless and carefree no matter whether they were admired or criticized. Besides, they would be able to speak skillfully and endlessly for numberless kalpas.

They had observed various dharma gates and understood very well that all existent beings were illusory. They were like the images of water under sunlight, the dreams, the moon in the water, the echoes, the flowers in the sky, the images, the shadows, the transformed things, and the mirages. All these things look real, but actually they are not. These bodhisattvas had departed from inferior mind and spoke the truth fearlessly because they could enter numberless dharma gates freely.

They knew well the minds and personalities of the sentient beings and could adopt subtle and wonderful wisdom to free them. They had great concern over all sentient beings but never felt any burden. They had attained unsurpassed forbearance of nonarising. They could enter the perfect knowledge of equality in various dharmas very well and knew the very deep dharma natures as they really were. They guided people skillfully in accordance with their special needs. They understood the truth and could lecture wonderfully about the dharma gate of dependent origination. They embraced a great aspiration dedicated to absorbing boundless Buddha lands. The numberless Buddhas in the ten directions often appeared before them as they practiced correct mindfulness in deep concentration.

The Buddhas were born and lived lives as ordinary people did. These bodhisattvas would ask the Buddhas to turn the dharma wheel in order to relieve innumerable sentient beings. But they deliberately did not enter into nirvana. They assisted the sentient beings with eliminating the bondage caused by incorrect views and the flames of afflictions. They could play freely and instantaneously get into and out of hundreds of thousands of deep concentrations and thus initiate limitless superior merits and virtues.

All of these bodhisattvas had accumulated wonderful, vast, oceanlike merits and virtues, so one could not help admiring them ceaselessly for innumerable kalpas. Among these bodhisattvas were Sage-Keeping Great Bodhisattva, Treasure Nature Great Bodhisattva, Treasure Storage Great Bodhisattva, Treasure Conferred Great

Bodhisattva, Mentor Great Bodhisattva, Humanity Conferred Great Bodhisattva, Star Conferred Great Bodhisattva, God Conferred Great Bodhisattva, Emperor Conferred Great Bodhisattva, Broad Wisdom Great Bodhisattva, Superior Wisdom Great Bodhisattva, Higher Wisdom Great Bodhisattva, Growing Wisdom Great Bodhisattva, Boundless Wisdom Great Bodhisattva, Nonvoid View Great Bodhisattva, Unhindered Wisdom Great Bodhisattva, Well Initiating Great Bodhisattva, Very Brave Great Bodhisattva, Extreme Diligence Great Bodhisattva, Constant Diligence Great Bodhisattva, Constant Effort Great Bodhisattva, Nondeserting Effort Great Bodhisattva, Sun Storage Great Bodhisattva, Moon Storage Great Bodhisattva, Incomparable Wisdom Great Bodhisattva, Contemplating-in-Freedom Great Bodhisattva, Attaining Great Power Great Bodhisattva, Wonderful Auspiciousness Great Bodhisattva (Manjusri Great Bodhisattva), Treasure Seal Hand Great Bodhisattva, Destroying Devils Power Great Bodhisattva, Diamond Wisdom Great Bodhisattva, Diamond Storage Great Bodhisattva, Often Raising Hand Great Bodhisattva, Great Compassion Great Bodhisattva, Great Solemnity Great Bodhisattva, Solemnity King Great Bodhisattva, Peak Great Bodhisattva, Treasure Mountain Great Bodhisattva, Virtue King Great Bodhisattva, and Maitreya Great Bodhisattva. All the numberless hundreds of thousands of koti nayuta great bodhisattvas were dharma princes, were ready to succeed to the thrones of the Buddhas, and constituted the leading group of the meeting.

At that time, the World-Honored One spread a mat on the lion throne, sitting straight up on it with his legs crossed. In correct mindfulness of aspiration for nirvana, he entered a wonderful samadhi-king state into which various kinds of samadhi were attracted to flow.

After a while, the World-Honored One, in correct knowledge and correct mindfulness, rose up peacefully from a samadhi-king state and used his pure heavenly eyes to look at as many Buddha worlds in the ten directions as the sands of the Ganges River. He felt so comfortable and enjoyable. There was a pattern of one thousand wheels in the bottom of each of his feet from which six million koti nayuta rays emitted. Six million rays emitted from each of his toes, two insteps, two heels, four ankles, two shins, two buttocks, two knees, two thighs, two haunches, waist, the flank of his trunk, belly, back, navel, heart, chest with auspicious symbol of perfect virtues, breast, armpits, shoulders, upper arms, elbows, lower arms, wrists, hands, palms, fingers, neck, throat, cheeks, chin, forehead, the top of his head, eyebrows, eyes, ears, nose, four front teeth, the forty teeth, and the very fine hairs between his two brows. Each and all of these rays shined over the large threefold thousand-world, and from there the lights extended to spread all over the Buddha lands, which were as many as the sands of the Ganges River. Any sentient being in these lands, when meeting the lights, would definitely attain the unsurpassed, perfect, and universal bodhi.

At that time, the World-Honored One felt comfort and joy even in all his pores. From each of them, six million koti nayuta rays emitted, and the lights shined over the large threefold thousand-world, and from there the lights extended to spread all over the Buddha lands, which were as many as the sands of the Ganges River. Any sentient being in these lands, when meeting the lights, would definitely attain the unsurpassed, perfect, and universal bodhi.

At that time, the World-Honored One allowed the constant light of his body to shine over the large threefold thousand-world, and from there the lights extended to spread all over the Buddha lands, which were as many as the sands of the Ganges River. Any sentient being in these lands, when meeting the lights, would definitely attain the unsurpassed, perfect, and universal bodhi.

In the meantime, the World-Honored One extended his wide, long tongue to cover the entire large threefold thousand-world, and smiled. Innumerable millions of koti nayuta rays emitted from the Buddha's tongue, and from each of the mixed colors of lights a treasure lotus emerged. The flowers and their thousand leaves were all golden and decorated with various kinds of treasures, which were beautiful, solemn, fresh, vivid, lovely, and attractive. Sweet and strong fragrances of the lotuses permeated everywhere. All the lotuses were very thin, soft, and smooth; any light touch of them would bring one a wonderful pleasure. On each lectern of the lotus, a Buddha sat and taught the wonderful dharma in accordance with prajna paramita. Any sentient being who heard it would definitely attain the unsurpassed, perfect, and universal bodhi. From there the Buddha's voice spread all over various Buddha lands in the ten directions, which were as many as the sands of the Ganges River, and the benefits produced by the teaching were also as many as the sands of the Ganges River.

At that time, the World-Honored One again entered the Samadhi of Lion's Play without rising from his seat and exhibited his supernatural powers to make the large threefold thousand-world move in six different ways: move, powerful move, most powerful move; rise, powerful rise, most powerful rise; shake, powerful shake, most powerful shake; beat, powerful beat, most powerful beat; roar, powerful roar, most powerful roar; and explosion, powerful explosion, most powerful explosion. His powers further made this realm rise in the east and sink in the west, rise in the west and sink in the east, rise in the south and sink in the north, rise in the north and sink in the south, rise in the middle and sink at the border, and rise at the border and sink in the middle. The whole land was pure, clean, bright, and soft and brought benefits, peace, and comfort to the sentient beings. At that time, all sentient beings living in the hells, the realm of the animals, the realm of the ghosts, and other perilous and inferior realms of the large threefold thousand-world were relieved from suffering and were reborn in the human realm or in the six heavens of the realm of desire. Still remembering where they were from, these sentient beings went to the Buddha's residence, full of joy, knelt down, and bowed with respect at the Buddha's feet. From there the Buddha's powers extended to cover the Buddha lands in the ten directions, which were as many as the sands of the Ganges River, and once more made the lands quake in six ways. All sentient beings in the inferior realms were relieved from suffering and were reborn in the human realm or the six heavens of the realm of desire. Still remembering where they were from, these sentient beings went to the Buddha's residence, full of joy, and knelt down and bowed with respect at the Buddha's feet.

In the meantime, in this large threefold thousand-world as well as in the rest of the worlds of the ten directions, which were as many as the sands of the Ganges River, the blind could see, the deaf could hear, the dumb could speak, those with wandering thought could concentrate, the mind in turmoil could rest, the poor became rich, the naked were dressed, the hungry had food, the thirsty had drinks, the ill were cured, the ugly became pretty, the physically disabled became healthy, the deficient sense organs became perfect, the confused awoke, and the tired now rested in peace and comfort. Meanwhile, all sentient beings were with one heart and treated each other like father and mother, brother and sister, friend and relative. They all stepped away from vicious words, actions, and occupations and learned to speak correct words, do right things, and engage in beneficial jobs. They walked away from the path of ten negative karmas and turned toward the path of ten positive karmas. They learned to think positively and let go of all negative thinking. They discarded noncelibacy and turned to pure celibacy. They loved purity and let go of impurity. They loved quietness and stayed away from noise, and instantly they felt a wonderful joy in body and mind, a feeling of concentration a practitioner could experience when staying in the third stage of meditation. They suddenly had a definitive wisdom arise in mind: "Isn't it wonderful to practice giving, taming, forbearance, diligence, tranquillity, and insightful investigation, get away from laziness; practice celibacy; and have loving-kindness, compassion, joy, and equanimity toward all sentient beings without disturbing each other?"

At that time, when the World-Honored One was sitting on the lion-seat, some unique bright lights caused by powerful dignity and great virtues appeared to shine over the large threefold thousand-world and as many Buddha lands as the sands of the Ganges River in the ten directions. The lights were so bright that all these lands were overshadowed and turned dim. Mount Sumeru, Great Circular Iron Enclosure (Mount Cakravada-parvata), the heavenly palaces of dragon gods, and the heavens of purity all became invisible. It was like the lights of the full moon in autumn that overshadowed the stars, the sunlight in summer that outshined all colors, and the four treasured Wonderful High King Mountains that eclipsed the lights of smaller mountains. The Buddha used supernatural powers to show his original physical body so that all the sentient beings in the large threefold thousand-world could see him.

Meanwhile, all heavenly beings, human beings, and nonhuman beings in the innumerable heavens of this threefold thousand-world, including the heavens in the Heaven of Pure Residence, and so forth, as well as the Heaven of Four Great Kings in the realm of desire, witnessed the Buddha who was sitting on the lion-seat. The Buddha's powerful lights were so bright and significant that they looked like a large golden mountain. When the sentient beings saw this, they celebrated, cheered up, and exclaimed in excitement because they had never seen this before. They went to the Buddha's place, and each of them carried a variety of numberless heavenly flowers, wreaths, spread perfume, burning incense, powdered incense, clothes, jewelry necklaces, treasure banners, canopies, entertainment and music, various rarities and valuable things, and countless species of heavenly lotuses, including heavenly blue lotus, heavenly scarlet lotus, heavenly white lotus, heavenly yellow lotus, heavenly red lotus, heavenly gold money flower, heavenly fragrance flower, as well as numberless flowers grown in waters and in grounds. They made all of these wonderful things as offerings to the Buddha. The Buddha used his supernatural powers to lift all the flower ornaments up in the air and turn them into as many flower tables as the number of the large threefold thousand-world and made all the beautiful canopies, treasure bells, pearl banners, and colorful decoration of silks and ribbons fall from the sky. All were so attractive and enjoyable.

At that moment, this Buddha land was so completely glorified that it looked like the extremely joyful world in the west. The Buddha's lights shined brilliantly on all species and all kinds of things in the large threefold thousand-world; the entire empty space turned golden in color, and so did the other Buddha lands of the ten directions, which were as many as the sands of the Ganges River.

Meanwhile, all the humans living on the continents of Jambudvipa, Purvavideha, Aparagodaniya, and Uttarakuru in this large threefold thousand-world, owing to the Buddha's supernatural powers, could see the Buddha sitting in front of them and teaching the dharma to them. All the heavenly beings living in the heavens of the Four Great Kings, the Heaven of Thirty-Three Smaller Heavens, Heaven of Yama, Heaven of Tusita, Heaven of Enjoying Self-Made Changes, Heaven of Enjoying Other-Made Changes, Heaven of Brahma Followers, Heaven of Brahma Associates, Heaven of Brahma Family, Heaven of Great Brahma, Heaven of Light, Heaven of Lesser Light, Heaven of Infinite Light, Heaven of Extremely Great Brightness and Purity, Heaven of Purity, Heaven of Lesser Purity, Heaven of Infinite Purity, Heaven of Universal Purity, Heaven of Expansion, Heaven of Lesser Expansion, Heaven of Infinite Expansion, Heaven of Extensive Rewards, Heaven of No Aspiration, Heaven of No Affliction, Heaven of Good Appearance, Heaven of Good Sight, and the Heaven of Ultimate Form, because of the Buddha's supernatural powers, could also see the Buddha sitting in front of them and teaching the dharma to them.

At that time, without rising from his seat, the World-Honored One smiled in joy; great lights emitted from his face to shine all over the large threefold thousand-world and as many Buddha lands in the ten directions as the sands of the Ganges River. In the meantime, all the sentient beings in this large threefold thousand-world followed the direction of the Buddha's lights so they could see universally all the Thus-Comers, the Ones Worthy of Offerings, the Perfectly and Universally Enlightened Ones in as many Buddha lands as the sands of the Ganges. They could see the voice-hearers and the bodhisattvas gathering in circles around the Thus-Comers and the rest of the sentient and insentient beings of various species and kinds in these Buddha lands. All the sentient beings in as many Buddha lands in the ten directions as the sands of the Ganges River also followed the direction of the Buddha's lights in this land and saw the Sakyamuni Thus-Comer, the One Worthy of Offerings, the Perfectly and Universally Enlightened One; the voice-hearers and the bodhisattvas gathering together in circles; and the rest of the sentient and insentient beings of various species and kinds.

In the meantime, in the last world of the east, at the end of as many worlds as the sands of the Ganges, named Lots of Treasures, there was a Buddha whose name was Treasure Nature, and he had these names: Thus-Comer, One Worthy of Offerings, Perfectly and

Universally Enlightened One, One Perfect in Wisdom and Actions, Well Gone One, One Who Knows the World, Unsurpassed Great Person, Taming and Guiding One, Teacher of Heavenly and Human Beings, Buddha, and Bhagavat. He was guiding the world in peace and stability and was going to teach great prajna paramita to the great bodhisattvas.

A bodhisattva named Universal Light in that land witnessed the great lights, the changes in the earth, and the form of the Buddha's body. He was in wonder, so he went to the Buddha's place, bowed down before the Buddha's feet, and asked, "Why are there such auspicious phenomena?"

Treasure Nature Buddha replied, "Good gentleman, at the end of the western worlds, which are as many as the sands of the Ganges, there is a world named Barely Tolerable. The Buddha in that land is named Sakyamuni Thus-Comer, One Worthy of Offerings, Perfectly and Universally Enlightened One, One Perfect in Wisdom and Actions, Well Gone One, One Who Knows the World, Unsurpassed Great Person, Taming and Guiding One, Teacher of Heavenly and Human Beings, Buddha, and Bhagavat. He is guiding the world in peace and stability and is going to teach great prajna paramita to the great bodhisattvas. It is because of the Buddha's supernatural powers that such auspicious signs appeared."

Hearing what the Buddha said, Universal Light rejoiced and was excited. He said, "World-Honored One! May I have your permission to go to the Barely Tolerable World to attend the assembly and make offerings to the Sakyamuni Thus-Comer and all the great bodhisattvas in order to attain the unhindered understandings, dharani gates, samadhi gates, and self-ease and freedom in playing supernatural powers so that I will be able to reach the last stage before ascending to the highest throne? I beg your kind and compassionate permission!"

The Treasure Nature Buddha said, "It is very good! It is very good! It is now the right time. You may go as you wish."

The Buddha handed Universal Light Bodhisattva a golden thousand-stem lotus with a thousand leaves of varied, beautiful treasures and said, "You bring this flower to Sakyamuni Buddha's residence and say, 'The Treasure Nature Thus-Comer is sending his limitless regards: Are you less ill and worried? Are you having a pleasant and easy daily life? Are your energy and strength in good harmony? Are you staying in rest and comfort? Are the worldly affairs endurable? Are the sentient beings easy to guide and teach? I am bringing you, World-Honored One, this lotus on my Buddha's behalf to wish you well in doing Buddhist service.' When you go there, you must live with correct knowledge and try to learn more about the land and its people. You should not be rash and arrogant and thus get hurt. Why do I say so? Because the great bodhisattvas there all have incomparable virtues and dignity. They are wholeheartedly compassionate, and their rebirth in that land was caused by great causes and conditions."

Universal Light Bodhisattva received the flower and the message, bowed down before the Buddha's feet, and walked around the Buddha clockwise, together with innumerable hundreds of thousands of koti nayuta monastic and lay bodhisattvas as well as numberless, hundreds of thousands of boys and girls, to say goodbye. Each one was carrying numberless various species of flowers, treasure banners, canopies, clothes, treasure decorations, and many other offerings when they started their journey. They passed as many lands in the east as the sands of the Ganges and stopped at each Buddha land on the way to make offerings and pay homage to each Buddha with praise and respect. Finally, they arrived at the Barely Tolerable World. They bowed down before the Buddha's feet, walked around the Buddha a hundred thousand times, and then stood to one side.

Universal Light Bodhisattva stepped forward and said to the Buddha, "World-Honored One! From this land to the east, at the end of as many Buddha lands as the sands of the Ganges, there is a world with the name Lots of Treasures. The Buddha there is named Treasure Nature Thus-Comer, One Worthy of Offerings, Perfectly and Universally Enlightened One, One Perfect in Wisdom and Actions, Well Gone One, One Who Knows the World, Unsurpassed Great Person, Taming and Guiding One, Teacher of Heavenly and Human Beings, Buddha, and Bhagavat. He is sending his limitless regards to you, World-Honored One: Are you less ill and worried? Are you having a pleasant and easy daily life? Are your energy and strength in good harmony? Are you staying in rest and comfort? Are the worldly affairs endurable? Are the sentient beings easy to guide and teach? I am bringing you, the World-Honored One, this golden, thousand-stem lotus on my Buddha's behalf to wish you well in doing Buddhist service."

Sakyamuni Buddha received the lotus and threw it back to as many Buddha lands as the sands of the Ganges in the east. Because of the Buddha's supernatural powers, the lotus spread through all the Buddha lands. On each flower lectern, a transformed Buddha was sitting with his legs crossed and was teaching the dharma in accordance with great prajna paramita to the great bodhisattvas. All the sentient beings who heard the teachings would definitely attain the unsurpassed, perfect, and universal bodhi. In the meantime, when Universal Light and all his associates witnessed this, they rejoiced and were excited and appreciated what they had never experienced before. They thus made offerings of what they had, in accordance with their individual roots of goodness, to the Buddha and the bodhisattvas with respect and admiration. They then sat back and spoke about the wonderful dharma.

Thus, in each of these Buddhas' places in the east there was also one leading bodhisattva, who witnessed the great lights, the earthquakes, and the form of the Buddha's body, and went to ask the Buddha, "World-Honored One! Why are there such auspicious signs?"

Then each Buddha in each land replied, "In the west is a world named Barely Tolerable. The Buddha there is named Sakyamuni and is going to teach great prajna paramita to the bodhisattvas. It is because of the Buddha's supernatural powers that those auspicious phenomena were caused."

Each of the leading bodhisattvas in each of the Buddha lands rejoiced after hearing this reply and asked the Buddha's permission to go to the Barely Tolerable World to pay homage and make offerings to the Buddha and the bodhisattvas there. Each of the Buddhas said yes to the request with admiration and gave each a golden lotus made of a thousand treasures, along with this message: "You may bring this to that Buddha's place and say to him on my behalf, 'My Buddha is sending you limitless regards: Are you less ill and worried? Are you having a pleasant and easy daily life? Are your energy and strength in perfect harmony? Are you living in rest and comfort? Are the worldly affairs endurable? Are the sentient beings easy to guide and teach? I am bringing you, World-Honored One, this lotus on my Buddha's behalf to wish you well in doing Buddhist service.' When you go there, you must dwell in correct knowledge and try to learn more about the land and the people. You should not be rash and arrogant and thus get hurt. Why? Because the bodhisattvas there all have incomparable virtues and dignity, they are wholeheartedly compassionate, and their rebirth in that land was caused by great causes and conditions."

Each leading bodhisattva received the flower and the message and started the journey with innumerable bodhisattvas and boys and girls. They stopped at each Buddha land they passed, made offerings to the Buddhas and bodhisattvas, and finally arrived in the land they sought. They bowed down before the Buddha's feet, walked around the Buddha a hundred thousand times, and presented the lotus and the message. The Buddha received the flower and threw it back to the east. Because of his supernatural powers, the flower spread throughout all Buddha lands, and on each flower lectern a transformed Buddha sat, teaching the great prajna paramita to the bodhisattvas, and all hearers would definitely attain the unsurpassed, perfect, and universal bodhi. Each of the leading bodhisattvas and his associates were rejoicing and excited and appreciated what they had never experienced before. They then made offerings of all they had in accordance with individual roots of goodness to the Buddha and the bodhisattvas with respect and admiration and then sat themselves to the side.

At that time, at the end of as many worlds as the sands of the Ganges in the south, there was a world that was named Leaving All Worries. The Buddha in that world was named Virtue of Nonworry Thus-Comer, One Worthy of Offerings, Perfectly and Universally Enlightened One, One Perfect in Wisdom and Actions, Well Gone One, One Who Knows the World, Unsurpassed Great Person, Taming and Guiding One, Teacher of Heavenly and Human Beings, Buddha, Bhagavat, who was overseeing the land in peace and stability and teaching great prajna paramita to the bodhisattvas.

A bodhisattva in that land was named Leaving Worry and witnessed the great lights, the earthquakes, and the form of the Buddha's body. He was in wonder, so he went to the Buddha's place, bowed down before the Buddha's feet, and asked, "World-Honored One! Why are there such auspicious phenomena?"

The Virtue of Nonworry Buddha replied, "Good gentleman! At the end of as many worlds in the north as the sands of the Ganges, there is a world that is named Barely Tolerable, and the Buddha in that land is named Sakyamuni Thus-Comer, One Worthy of Offerings, Perfectly and Universally Enlightened One, One Perfect in Wisdom and Actions, Well Gone One, One Who Knows the World, Unsurpassed Great Person, Taming and Guiding One, Teacher of Heavenly and Human Beings, Buddha, Bhagavat. He is guiding the world in peace and stability and is going to teach great prajna paramita. It is because of the Buddha's supernatural powers that such auspicious signs appeared."

Leaving Worry rejoiced and was excited after hearing this, and said, "World-Honored One! May I ask your permission to go to Barely Tolerable World to attend the assembly, pay homage and make offerings to Sakyamuni Buddha and the bodhisattvas there in order to attain the unhindered understanding, dharani gates, samadhi gates, and the freedom and self-ease in playing supernatural powers so that I will be able to reach the last stage before ascending to the highest throne? I beg your kind and compassionate permission!"

The Virtue of Nonworry Buddha replied, "Very good! Very good! It is now the right time. You may go as you wish." The Buddha handed Leaving Worry Bodhisattva a golden thousand-stem lotus with a thousand leaves of varied beautiful treasures and said, "You bring this flower to Sakyamuni Buddha's residence and say, 'The Virtue of Nonworry Thus-Comer is sending his limitless regards: Are you less ill and worried? Are you having a pleasant and easy daily life? Are your energy and strength in good harmony? Are you abiding in rest and comfort? Are the worldly affairs endurable? Are the sentient beings easy to guide and teach? I am bringing you, World-Honored Buddha, this lotus on my Buddha's behalf to wish you well in doing Buddhist service.' When you go there, you must dwell in correct knowledge and try to learn more about the land and the people. You should not be rash and arrogant and thus get into trouble. Why do I say so? Because the bodhisattvas there all have incomparable virtues and dignity, they are wholeheartedly compassionate, and their rebirth in that land was caused by great causes and conditions."

Leaving Worry Bodhisattva then received the flower and the message, bowed down before the Buddha's feet, and walked around the Buddha clockwise, together with innumerable hundreds of thousands of koti nayuta monastic and lay bodhisattvas as well as numberless hundreds of thousands of boys and girls, to say goodbye. Each one was carrying numberless various species of flowers, treasure banners, canopies, clothes, treasure decorations, and many other offerings, and then started their journey. They passed as many lands as the sands of the Ganges in the south, stopped at each Buddha land on the way, and made offerings and paid homage to each Buddha with respect and admiration. Finally, they arrived at the Barely Tolerable World. They bowed down before the Buddha's feet, walked around the Buddha for a hundred thousand times, and then stood to the side.

Leaving Worry Bodhisattva stepped forward and said to the Buddha, "World-Honored One, from this land to the south, at the end of as many Buddha lands as the sands of the Ganges, there is a world which is named Leaving All Worries, and the Buddha there is named Virtue of Nonworry Thus-Comer, One Worthy of Offerings, Perfectly and Universally Enlightened One, One Perfect in Wisdom and Actions, Well Gone One, One Who Knows the World, Unsurpassed Great Person, Taming and Guiding One, Teacher of Heavenly and Human Beings, Buddha, and Bhagavat. He is sending his limitless regards to you, World-Honored One: Are you less ill and worried? Are you having a pleasant and easy daily life? Are your energy and strength in good harmony? Are you staying in rest and comfort? Are the worldly affairs endurable? Are the sentient beings easy to guide and teach? I am bringing you, World-Honored One, this golden thousand-stem lotus on my Buddha's behalf to wish you well in doing Buddhist service."

Meanwhile, Sakyamuni Buddha received the lotus and then

threw it back to as many Buddha lands as the sands of the Ganges in the south. Because of the Buddha's supernatural powers, the lotus spread through all the Buddha lands, and on each flower lectern, a transformed Buddha was sitting with his legs crossed and teaching the dharma in correspondence with great prajna paramita to the bodhisattvas. The sentient beings who heard this would definitely attain the unsurpassed, perfect, and universal bodhi. In the meantime, Leaving Worry and all his associates rejoiced and were excited and appreciated what they had never experienced before. They then made offerings of whatever they had, in accord with their individual inner goodness, to the Buddha and bodhisattvas with respect and admiration, and then sat to one side.

Thus, in each of all the Buddha lands in the south of this world, there was a Buddha who was teaching the wonderful dharma to the sentient beings, and there was also a leading bodhisattva who, after witnessing the great lights, the earthquakes, and the Buddha's appearance, went to the Buddha's place and said, "World-Honored One! Why are there such auspicious phenomena?"

Then each Buddha replied, "In the north of this land, there is a world that is named Barely Tolerable, and the Buddha there is named Sakyamuni and is going to teach great prajna paramita to the bodhisattvas. It is because of his supernatural powers that these auspicious phenomena appeared."

Each leading bodhisattva rejoiced after hearing this and asked his Buddha's permission to attend the assembly and pay respect and make offerings to the Buddha and bodhisattvas in Barely Tolerable World. Each Buddha approved the request with admiration, gave a golden thousand-treasure lotus to the leading bodhisattva, and said, "Please bring this lotus to the Buddha's place and say to the Buddha, 'My Buddha is sending limitless regards: Are you less ill and worried? Are you having a pleasant and easy daily life? Are your energy and strength in good harmony? Are you staying in rest and comfort? Are the worldly affairs endurable? Are the sentient beings easy to guide and teach? I am bringing you, World-Honored One, this lotus on my Buddha's behalf to wish you well in doing Buddhist service.' When you go there, you must stay in correct knowledge and try to learn more about the land and the people. You should not be rash and arrogant and thus get hurt. Why do I say so? Because the bodhisattvas there all have incomparable virtues and dignity, they are wholeheartedly compassionate, and their rebirth in that land was caused by great causes and conditions."

Each leading bodhisattva received the flower and the message and started his journey with innumerable bodhisattvas and boys and girls. They stopped at each Buddha land they passed, made offerings to the Buddhas and bodhisattvas in each land, and finally arrived in the land they sought. They bowed down before the Buddha's feet, walked around the Buddha a hundred thousand times, presented the lotus, and passed on the message.

The Buddha received the flower and threw it back to the south. Because of his supernatural powers, the flower spread through all Buddha lands, and on each flower lectern there was one transformed Buddha, who was sitting and teaching great prajna paramita to the bodhisattvas. All hearers would definitely attain the unsurpassed, perfect, and universal bodhi. Each leading bodhisattva and his associates were excited. They rejoiced and appreciated what they had never experienced before. They then made offerings with respect and admiration to the Buddha and the bodhisattvas of all they had in accordance with their individual roots of goodness, and then sat to one side.

At that time, at the end of as many worlds in the west as the sands of the Ganges, there was a world named Quietude. The Buddha in that world was named Treasure Flame Thus-Comer, One Worthy of Offerings, Perfectly and Universally Enlightened One, One Perfect in Wisdom and Actions, Well Gone One, One Who Knows the World, Unsurpassed Great Person, Taming and Guiding One, Teacher of Heavenly and Human Beings, Buddha, and Bhagavat. He was guiding the world in peace and stability and was teaching great prajna paramita to the bodhisattvas.

A bodhisattva in that land was named Act Wisely. After seeing the great lights, the earthquakes, and the Buddha's appearance, he was so awestruck that he went to the Buddha's place, bowed down before the Buddha's feet, and asked, "World-Honored One! Why are there such auspicious phenomena?"

Treasure Flame Buddha replied, "Good gentleman, at the end

of as many worlds in the east as the sands of the Ganges, there is a world named Barely Tolerable, and the Buddha in that land is named Sakyamuni Thus-Comer, One Worthy of Offerings, Perfectly and Universally Enlightened One, One Perfect in Wisdom and Actions, Well Gone One, One Who Knows the World, Unsurpassed Great Person, Taming and Guiding One, Teacher of Heavenly and Human Beings, Buddha, and Bhagavat. He is guiding the world in peace and stability and is going to teach great prajna paramita to the bodhisattvas. It is because of the Buddha's supernatural powers that such auspicious phenomena appeared."

Act Wisely Bodhisattva rejoiced and was excited after hearing this and said, "World-Honored One! May I have your permission to go to Barely Tolerable World to attend the assembly, pay homage, and make offerings to Sakyamuni Buddha and the bodhisattvas there in order to attain the unhindered understanding, dharani gates, samadhi gates, and the freedom and self-ease in supernatural powers so that I will be able to reach the last stage before ascending to the highest throne? I beg your kind and compassionate permission!"

Treasure Flame Buddha then said to Act Wisely, "Very good! Very good! It is the right time! You may go as you wish."

The Buddha handed Act Wisely Bodhisattva a golden thousand-stem lotus with a thousand leaves of varied beautiful treasures and said, "You bring this flower to Sakyamuni Buddha's residence and say, 'The Treasure Flame Buddha is sending his limitless regards: Are you less ill and worried? Are you having a pleasant and easy daily life? Are your energy and strength in good harmony? Are you staying in rest and comfort? Are the worldly affairs endurable? Are the sentient beings easy to guide and teach? I am bringing you, World-Honored One, this lotus on my Buddha's behalf to wish you well in doing Buddhist service.' When you go there, you must dwell in correct knowledge and try to learn more about the land and the people. You should not be rash and arrogant and thus get in trouble. Why do I say so? Because the bodhisattvas there all have incomparable virtues and dignity, they are wholeheartedly compassionate, and their rebirth in that land was caused by great causes and conditions."

Act Wisely Bodhisattva then received the flower and the message, bowed down before the Buddha's feet, and walked around the Buddha clockwise along with innumerable hundreds of thousands of koti nayuta monastic and lay bodhisattvas, as well as numberless hundreds of thousands of boys and girls, to say goodbye. Each one was carrying numberless various species of flowers, treasure banners, canopies, clothes, treasure decorations, and many other offerings and started the journey. They passed as many lands in the west as the sands of the Ganges and stopped at each Buddha land on the way and made offerings and paid homage to each Buddha with praise and respect. Finally they arrived at the Barely Tolerable World. They bowed down before the Buddha's feet, walked around the Buddha for a hundred thousand times, and then stood aside.

Act Wisely Bodhisattva stepped forward and said to the Buddha, "World-Honored One! From this land to the west, at the end of as many Buddha lands as the sands of the Ganges, there is a world that is named Quietude. The Buddha there is named Treasure Flame Thus-Comer, One Worthy of Offerings, Perfectly and Universally Enlightened One, One Perfect in Wisdom and Actions, Well Gone One, One Who Knows the World, Unsurpassed Great Person, Taming and Guiding One, Teacher of Heavenly and Human Beings, Buddha, and Bhagavat. He is sending his limitless regards to you, World-Honored One: Are you less ill and worried? Are you having a pleasant and easy daily life? Are your energy and strength in good harmony? Are you staying in rest and comfort? Are the worldly affairs endurable? Are the sentient beings easy to guide and teach? I am bringing you, World-Honored One, this golden thousand-stem lotus on my Buddha's behalf to wish you well in doing Buddhist service."

Meanwhile, Sakyamuni Buddha received the lotus and then threw it back to as many Buddha lands as the sands of the Ganges in the west. Because of the Buddha's supernatural powers, the lotus spread throughout all the Buddha lands, and on each flower lectern, a transformed Buddha was sitting with his legs crossed and teaching the dharma in correspondence with great prajna paramita to the bodhisattvas. The sentient beings who heard this would definitely attain the unsurpassed, perfect, and universal bodhi. In the meantime, Act Wisely and all his associates were excited. They rejoiced and appreciated what they had never experienced before. They then made offerings of all they had, in accordance with their roots of goodness, to the Buddha and bodhisattvas with respect and admiration, and then sat to one side.

Thus in each of all the Buddha lands in the west of this world, there was a Buddha who was teaching the wonderful dharma to the sentient beings, and there was also a leading bodhisattva who, after witnessing the great lights, the earthquakes, and the Buddha's appearance, went to the Buddha's place and said, "World-Honored One! Why are there these auspicious phenomena?"

Then each Buddha replied, "In the east of this land, there is a world that is named Barely Tolerable, and the Buddha there is named Sakyamuni, and is going to teach great prajna paramita to the bodhisattvas. It is because of his supernatural powers that these auspicious phenomena appeared."

Each leading bodhisattva rejoiced after hearing this and asked his Buddha's permission to attend the assembly and pay respect and make offerings to the Buddha and bodhisattvas in Barely Tolerable World. Each Buddha approved the request with admiration, gave a golden thousand-treasure lotus to the leading bodhisattva, and said, "Please bring this lotus and say to the Buddha, 'My Buddha is sending his limitless regards: Are you less ill and worried? Are you having a pleasant and easy daily life? Are your energy and strength in good harmony? Are you staying in rest and comfort? Are the worldly affairs endurable? Are the sentient beings easy to guide and teach? I am bringing you, World-Honored One, this lotus on my Buddha's behalf to wish you well in doing Buddhist service.' When you go there, you must dwell in correct knowledge and try to learn more about the land and the people. You should not be rash and arrogant and thus get hurt. Why do I say so? Because the bodhisattvas there all have incomparable virtues and dignity, they are wholeheartedly compassionate, and their rebirth in that land was caused by great causes and conditions."

Each leading Bodhisattva received the flower and the message and started their journey with innumerable bodhisattvas and boys and girls. They stopped at each Buddha land they passed, made offerings to the Buddhas and bodhisattvas in each land, and finally arrived in the land they sought. They bowed down before the Buddha's feet, walked around the Buddha a hundred thousand times, presented the lotus, and passed on their Buddha's message. The Buddha received the flower and threw it back to the west. Because of his supernatural powers, the flower spread through all Buddha lands, and on each flower lectern one transformed Buddha was sitting and teaching the great prajna paramita to the bodhisattvas. All hearers would definitely attain the unsurpassed, perfect, and universal bodhi. Each leading bodhisattva and his associates were excited. They rejoiced and appreciated what they had never experienced before. They then made offerings to the Buddha and the bodhisattvas of all they had with respect and praises in accord with their individual roots of goodness. Then they sat to the side.

Fascicle 2

Chapter 1
The Causes and Conditions of the Assembly

Section 2

(In the First Assembly)

At that time, at the end of as many worlds as the sands of the Ganges in the north, there was a world named Most Superior, and the Buddha in that world was named Superior Emperor Thus-Come-er, One Worthy of Offerings, Perfectly and Universally Enlightened One, One Perfect in Wisdom and Actions, Well Gone One, One Who Knows the World, Unsurpassed Great Person, Taming and Guiding One, Teacher of Heavenly and Human Beings, Buddha, and Bhagavat. He was guiding the world in peace and stability and teaching great prajna paramita for the great bodhisattvas.

A bodhisattva in that land named Superior Conferring witnessed the great lights, the earthquakes, and the image of the Buddha's body. He was so awestruck that he went to the Buddha's place, bowing down before the Buddha's feet, and asked, "World-Honored One! Why are there such auspicious phenomena?"

Superior Emperor Buddha replied, "Good gentleman, at the end of as many worlds as the sands of the Ganges in the south, there is a world named Barely Tolerable. The Buddha in that land is named

Sakyamuni Thus-Comer, One Worthy of Offerings, Perfectly and Universally Enlightened One, One Perfect in Wisdom and Actions, Well Gone One, One Who Knows the World, Unsurpassed Great Person, Taming and Guiding One, Teacher of Heavenly and Human Beings, Buddha, and Bhagavat. He is guiding the world in peace and stability and going to teach great prajna paramita to the great bodhisattvas. It is because of the Buddha's supernatural powers that such auspicious phenomena appeared."

Superior Conferring rejoiced and was excited after hearing this and said, "World-Honored One! May I ask your permission to go to the Barely Tolerable World to attend the assembly, pay homage, and make offerings to Sakyamuni Thus-Comer and the bodhisattvas there in order to attain the unhindered understanding, dharani gates, samadhi gates, and the freedom and self-ease in playing supernatural powers so that I will be able to reach the last stage before ascending to the highest throne? I beg your kind and compassionate permission!"

Superior Emperor Buddha said to Superior Conferring Bodhisattva, "Very good, very good! It is the right time. You may go as you wish."

The Buddha thus handed him a golden thousand-stem lotus with a thousand leaves decorated with a variety of pretty treasures and said, "You bring this flower to Sakyamuni Buddha's place and say, 'The Superior Emperor Thus-Comer is sending his limitless regards: Are you having few ills and worries? Are you having a pleasant and easy daily life? Are your energy and strength in good harmony? Are you staying in rest and happiness? Are the worldly affairs endurable? Are the sentient beings easy to guide and teach? I am bringing you, World-Honored One, this lotus on my Buddha's behalf to wish you well in doing Buddhist service.' When you go there, you must dwell in correct vision and try to learn more about the land and the people. You should not be rash and arrogant and thus get in trouble. Why do I say so? Because the bodhisattvas there all have incomparable virtues and dignity, they are wholeheartedly compassionate, and their rebirth in that land was the result of great causes and conditions."

Superior Conferring Bodhisattva then received the flower and the message, bowed down before the Buddha's feet, and walked around the Buddha clockwise, together with innumerable hundreds of thousands of koti nayuta monastic and lay bodhisattvas, as well as numberless hundreds of thousands of boys and girls, to say goodbye. Each one was carrying numberless, various species of flowers, treasure flags, canopies, clothes, treasure decorations and many other offerings and started their journey. They passed as many lands as the sands of the Ganges in the north and stopped at each Buddha land on the way to make offerings and pay homage to each Buddha with praise and respect. Finally, they arrived at the Barely Tolerable World. They bowed down before the Buddha's feet, walked around the Buddha for a hundred thousand times, and then stood to the side.

Superior Conferring Bodhisattva stepped forward and said to the Buddha, "World-Honored One! From this land to the north, at the end of as many Buddha lands as the sands of the Ganges, there is a world with the name Most Superior. The Buddha there is named Superior Emperor Thus-Comer, One Worthy of Offerings, Perfectly and Universally Enlightened One, One Perfect in Wisdom and Actions, Well Gone One, One Who Knows the World, Unsurpassed Great Person, Taming and Guiding One, Teacher of Heavenly and Human Beings, Buddha, and Bhagavat. He is sending his limitless regards to you, World-Honored One: Are you having few ills and worries? Are you having a pleasant and easy daily life? Are your energy and strength in good harmony? Are you staying in rest and comfort? Are the worldly affairs endurable? Are the sentient beings easy to guide and teach? I am bringing you, World-Honored One, this golden thousand-stem lotus on my Buddha's behalf to wish you well in doing Buddhist service."

Sakyamuni Buddha received the lotus and then threw it back to the many Buddha lands as the sands of the Ganges in the north. Because of the Buddha's supernatural powers, the lotus spread through all the Buddha lands, showing on each flower lectern a transformed Buddha sitting with his legs crossed and teaching the dharma in accordance with great prajna paramita to the bodhisattvas. All the sentient beings who heard the teachings would definitely attain the unsurpassed, perfect, and universal bodhi. In the meantime, when Superior Conferring and all his associates witnessed this, they rejoiced and appreciated what they had never seen before. They thus made offerings of what they had, in accordance with their individual roots of goodness, to the Buddha and bodhisattvas with respect and admiration and then sat to one side.

Thus, in each of the Buddha lands in the north of this world, there was a Buddha who was teaching the wonderful dharma to the sentient beings, and there was also a leading bodhisattva who, after witnessing the great lights, the earthquakes, and the form of the Buddha's body, went to the Buddha's place and said, "World-Honored One! Why are there such auspicious phenomena?"

Then each Buddha replied, "In the south of this land, there is a world that is named Barely Tolerable, and the Buddha there is named Sakyamuni and is going to teach great prajna paramita to the bodhisattvas. It is because of the Buddha's supernatural powers that these auspicious phenomena appeared."

Each of the leading bodhisattvas rejoiced after hearing this and asked the Buddha's permission to go to the Barely Tolerable World to attend the assembly, pay homage, and make offerings to the Buddha and bodhisattvas there. Each Buddha approved their request with admiration, handed a golden thousand-treasure lotus to the leading bodhisattva, and said, "You may bring this to the Buddha's place along with this message: 'My Buddha is sending you limitless regards: Are you having few ills and worries? Are you having a pleasant and easy daily life? Are your energy and strength in good harmony? Are you staying in rest and comfort? Are the worldly affairs endurable? Are the sentient beings easy to guide and teach? I am bringing you, World-Honored One, this lotus on my Buddha's behalf to wish you well in doing Buddhist service.' When you go there, you must stay in correct vision and try to learn more about the land and the people. You should not be rash and arrogant and thus get into trouble. Why do I say so? Because the bodhisattvas there all have incomparable virtues and dignity, they are wholeheartedly compassionate, and their rebirth in that land was the result of great causes and conditions."

Each leading bodhisattva received the flower and the message and started the journey with innumerable bodhisattvas and boys and girls. They stopped at each Buddha land they passed, made offerings to the Buddhas and bodhisattvas, and finally arrived in the land they sought. They bowed down before the Buddha's feet, walked around the Buddha a hundred thousand times, and presented the lotus and the message. The Buddha received the flower and threw it back to the north. Because of his supernatural powers, the flower spread throughout all Buddha lands, and on each flower lectern there was one transformed Buddha sitting and teaching great prajna paramita to the bodhisattvas. All hearers would definitely attain unsurpassed, perfect, and universal bodhi. Each of the leading bodhisattvas and his associates rejoiced and were excited and appreciated what they had never experienced before. They then made offerings of all they had, in accord with their individual roots of goodness, to the Buddha and the bodhisattvas with respect and praises, and then sat to one side.

At that time, at the end of the many northeastern worlds as the sands of the Ganges, there was a world named Glory of Concentration. The Buddha in that world was named Concentration Elephant Superior Virtue Thus-Comer, One Worthy of Offerings, Perfectly and Universally Enlightened One, One Perfect in Wisdom and Actions, Well Gone One, One Who Knows the World, Unsurpassed Great Person, Taming and Guiding One, Teacher of Heavenly and Human Beings, Buddha, and Bhagavat. He was guiding the world in peace and stability and teaching great prajna paramita to the great bodhisattvas.

A bodhisattva in that land was named Leaving Dust Bravery and witnessed the great lights, the earthquakes, and the image of the Buddha's body and was in wonder. He went to the Buddha's place, bowed down before the Buddha's feet, and asked, "World-Honored One! Why are there such auspicious phenomena?"

Concentration Elephant Superior Virtue Buddha replied to Leaving Dust Bravery Bodhisattva, "Good gentleman, at the end of as many worlds in the southwest as the sands of the Ganges, there is a world named Barely Tolerable, and the Buddha in that land is named Sakyamuni Thus-Comer, One Worthy of Offerings, Perfectly and Universally Enlightened One, One Perfect in Wisdom and Actions, Well Gone One, One Who Knows the World, Unsurpassed Great Person, Taming and Guiding One, Teacher of Heavenly and Human Beings, Buddha, and Bhagavat. He is guiding the world in peace and stability and is going to teach great prajna paramita to the bodhisattvas. It is because of the Buddha's supernatural powers that such auspicious signs appeared."

Leaving Dust Bravery rejoiced and was excited after hearing this and said, "World-Honored One! May I ask your permission to go to the Barely Tolerable World to attend the assembly, pay homage, and make offerings to Sakyamuni Buddha and the bodhisattvas there in order to attain the unhindered understanding, dharani gates, samadhi gates, and the freedom and self-ease in supernatural powers so that I will be able to reach the last stage before ascending to the highest throne? I beg your kind and compassionate permission!"

Concentration Elephant Superior Virtue Buddha replied to Leaving Dust Bravery Bodhisattva, "Very good! Very good! It is now the right time. You may go as you wish."

The Buddha handed Leaving Dust Bravery Bodhisattva a golden thousand-stem lotus with a thousand leaves of varied beautiful treasures and said, "You bring this flower to Sakyamuni Buddha's place, and say, 'The Concentration Elephant Superior Virtue Thus-Comer is sending his limitless regards. Are you having few ills and worries? Are you having a pleasant and easy daily life? Are your energy and strength in good harmony? Are you staying in rest and comfort? Are the worldly affairs endurable? Are the sentient beings easy to guide and teach? I am bringing you, World-Honored One, this lotus on my Buddha's behalf to wish you well in doing Buddhist service.' When you go there, you must dwell in correct knowledge and try to learn more about the land and the people. You should not be rash and arrogant and thus get into trouble. Why do I say so? Because the bodhisattvas there all have incomparable virtues and dignity, they are wholeheartedly compassionate, and their rebirth in that land was the result of great causes and conditions."

Leaving Dust Bravery Bodhisattva then received the flower and the message, bowed down before the Buddha's feet, and walked around the Buddha clockwise, together with innumerable hundreds of thousands of koti nayuta monastic bodhisattvas and lay bodhisattvas, as well as numberless hundreds of thousands boys and girls, as a way of saying good-bye. Each one was carrying numberless species of flowers, treasure banners, canopies, clothes, treasure decorations, and many other offerings and then started their journey.

They passed as many lands as the sands of the Ganges in the northeast, stopped at each Buddha land on the way and made offerings and paid homage to each Buddha with praise and respect. Finally, they arrived at the Barely Tolerable World. They bowed down before the Buddha's feet, walked around the Buddha for a hundred thousand times, and then stood aside.

Leaving Dust Bravery Bodhisattva stepped forward and said to the Buddha, "World-Honored One! From this land to the northeast, at the end of many Buddha lands as the sands of the Ganges, there is a world named Concentration Glory, and the Buddha there is named Concentration Elephant Superior Virtue Thus-Comer, One Worthy of Offerings, Perfectly and Universally Enlightened One, One Perfect in Wisdom and Actions, Well Gone One, One Who Knows the World, Unsurpassed Great Person, Taming and Guiding One, Teacher of Heavenly and Human Beings, Buddha, and Bhagavat. He is sending his limitless regards to you, World-Honored One: Are you having few ills and worries? Are you having a pleasant and easy daily life? Are your energy and strength in good harmony? Are you staying in rest and comfort? Are the worldly affairs endurable? Are the sentient beings easy to guide and teach? I am bringing you, World-Honored One, this golden thousand-stem lotus on my Buddha's behalf to wish you well in doing Buddhist service."

Sakyamuni Buddha received the lotus and then threw it back to as many Buddha lands as the sands of the Ganges in the northeast. Because of the Buddha's supernatural powers, the lotus spread throughout all the Buddha lands, and on each flower lectern a transformed Buddha was sitting with legs crossed and teaching the dharma in accordance with great prajna paramita to the bodhisattvas. The sentient beings who heard this would definitely attain the unsurpassed, perfect, and universal bodhi. In the meantime, Leaving Dust Bravery and all his associates rejoiced and were excited and appreciated what they had never experienced before. They then made offerings of all they had, in accord with their individual roots of goodness, to the Buddha and bodhisattvas with respect and admiration, and then sat to one side.

Thus, in each of the Buddha lands in the northeast of this world, there was a Buddha who was teaching the wonderful dharma to all sentient beings, and there was also a leading bodhisattva who, after witnessing the great lights, the earthquakes, and the Buddha's appearance, went to the Buddha's place and asked, "World-Honored One! Why are there such auspicious phenomena?"

Then each Buddha replied, "In the southwest of this land there is a world named Barely Tolerable, and the Buddha there is named Sakyamuni and is going to teach great prajna paramita to the bodhisattvas. It is because of his supernatural powers that these auspicious phenomena appeared."

Each leading bodhisattva rejoiced after hearing this and asked his Buddha's permission to attend the assembly, pay respect, and make offerings to the Buddha and bodhisattvas in Barely Tolerable World. Each Buddha approved the request with admiration, gave a golden thousand-treasure lotus to the leading bodhisattva, and said, "Please bring this lotus to the Buddha's place and say, 'My Buddha is sending his limitless regards: Are you having few ills and worries? Are you having a pleasant and easy daily life? Are your energy and strength in good harmony? Are you staying in rest and comfort? Are the worldly affairs endurable? Are the sentient beings easy to guide and teach? I am bringing you, World-Honored One, this lotus on my Buddha's behalf to wish you well in doing Buddhist service.' When you go there, you must stay in a correct mind and try to learn more about the land and the people. You should not be rash and arrogant and thus get into trouble. Why do I say so? Because the bodhisattvas there all have incomparable virtues and dignity, they are wholeheartedly compassionate, and their rebirth in that land was the result of great causes and conditions."

Each leading bodhisattva received the flower and the message and started the journey with innumerable bodhisattvas and boys and girls. They stopped at each Buddha land they passed, made offerings to the Buddhas and bodhisattvas, and finally arrived in the land they sought. They bowed down before the Buddha's feet, walked around the Buddha a hundred thousand times, presented the lotus, and passed on the message. The Buddha received the flower and threw it back to the northeast. Because of his supernatural powers, the flower spread through all Buddha lands, and on each lectern one transformed Buddha was sitting and teaching great prajna paramita to the bodhisattvas. All hearers would definitely attain the unsurpassed, perfect, and universal bodhi. Each leading bodhisattva and his associates rejoiced and were excited and appreciated what they had never experienced before. They then made offerings of all they had, in accord with their individual roots of goodness, to the Buddha and the bodhisattvas with respect and praises, and then sat to one side.

At that time, at the end of as many worlds in the southeast as the sands of the Ganges, there was a world that was named Wonderfully Enlightened Glory and Delight. The Buddha in that world was named Lotus Superior Virtue Thus-Comer, One Worthy of Offerings, Perfectly and Universally Enlightened One, One Perfect in Wisdom and Actions, Well Gone One, One Who Knows the World, Unsurpassed Great Person, Taming and Guiding One, Teacher of Heavenly and Human Beings, Buddha, and Bhagavat. He was guiding the world in peace and stability and was teaching great prajna paramita to the great bodhisattvas.

A bodhisattva in that land was named Lotus Hand. After witnessing the great lights, the earthquakes, and the image of the Buddha's body, he was so awestruck that he went to the Buddha's place, bowed down before the Buddha's feet, and asked, "World-Honored One! Why are there such auspicious phenomena?"

Lotus Superior Virtue Buddha replied to Lotus Hand Bodhisattva, "Good gentleman, at the end of as many worlds in the northwest as the sands of the Ganges, there is a world named Barely Tolerable, and the Buddha in that land is named Sakyamuni Thus-Comer, One Worthy of Offerings, Perfectly and Universally Enlightened One, One Perfect in Wisdom and Actions, Well Gone One, One Who Knows the World, Unsurpassed Great Person, Taming and Guiding One, Teacher of Heavenly and Human Beings, Buddha, and Bhagavat. He is guiding the world in peace and stability and is going to teach great prajna paramita to the great bodhisattvas. It is because of the Buddha's supernatural powers that such auspicious phenomena appeared."

Lotus Hand rejoiced and was excited after hearing this and said, "World-Honored One! May I have your permission to go to Barely Tolerable World to attend the assembly, pay homage, and make offerings to Sakyamuni Buddha and the bodhisattvas there in order to attain the unhindered understanding, dharani gates, samadhi gates, and the freedom and self-ease in supernatural powers so that I will be able to reach the last stage before ascending to the highest throne? I beg your kind and compassionate permission!"

Lotus Superior Virtue Buddha said to Lotus Hand Bodhisattva, "Very good! Very good! Now it is the right time. You may go as you wish."

The Buddha then handed Lotus Hand Bodhisattva a golden thousand-stem lotus with a thousand leaves of varied pretty treasures and said to him, "You take this flower to Sakyamuni Buddha's place and say, 'The Lotus Superior Virtue Thus-Comer is sending his limitless regards: Are you having few ills and worries? Are you having a pleasant and easy daily life? Are your energy and strength in good harmony? Are you staying in rest and comfort? Are the worldly affairs endurable? Are the sentient beings easy to guide and teach? I am bringing you, World-Honored One, this lotus on my Buddha's behalf to wish you well in doing Buddhist service.' When you go there, you must dwell in correct knowledge and try to learn more about the land and the people. You should not be rash and arrogant and thus get in trouble. Why do I say so? Because the bodhisattvas there all have incomparable virtues and dignity, they are wholeheartedly compassionate, and their rebirth in that land was the result of great causes and conditions."

Lotus Hand Bodhisattva received the flower and the message, bowed down before the Buddha's feet, and walked around the Buddha clockwise, together with innumerable hundreds of thousands of koti nayuta monastic and lay bodhisattvas, as well as numberless hundreds of thousands of boys and girls, as a way of saying good-bye. Each one was carrying numberless varied species of flowers, treasure banners, canopies, clothes, treasure decorations, and many other offerings, and started their journey. They passed as many lands as the sands of the Ganges in the southeast and stopped at each Buddha land on the way to make offerings and pay homage to each Buddha with praise and respect. Finally they arrived at the Barely Tolerable World. They bowed down before the Buddha's feet, walked around the Buddha for a hundred thousand times, and then stood to one side.

Lotus Hand Bodhisattva stepped forward and said to the Buddha, "World-Honored One! From this land to the southeast, at the end of as many Buddha lands as the sands of the Ganges, there is a world named Wonderfully Enlightened Glory and Delight. The Buddha there is named Lotus Superior Virtue Thus-Comer, One Worthy of Offerings, Perfectly and Universally Enlightened One, One Perfect in Wisdom and Actions, Well Gone One, One Who Knows the World, Unsurpassed Great Person, Taming and Guiding One, Teacher of Heavenly and Human Beings, Buddha, and Bhagavat. He is sending his limitless regards to you, World-Honored One: Are you having few ills and worries? Are you having a pleasant and easy daily life? Are your energy and strength in good harmony? Are you staying in rest and comfort? Are the worldly affairs endurable? Are the sentient beings easy to guide and teach? I am bringing you, World-Honored One, this golden thousand-stem lotus on my Buddha's behalf to wish you well in doing Buddhist service."

Sakyamuni Buddha received the lotus and then threw it back to as many Buddha lands as the sands of the Ganges in the southeast. Because of the Buddha's supernatural powers, the lotus spread through all the Buddha lands, and on each flower lectern, a transformed Buddha was sitting with his legs crossed and teaching the dharma, in accordance with great prajna paramita, to the bodhisattvas. The sentient beings who heard this would definitely attain the unsurpassed, perfect, and universal bodhi. In the meantime, Lotus Hand and all his associates rejoiced and were excited and appreciated what they had never experienced before. They then made offerings of all they had in accord with their individual roots of goodness to the Buddha and bodhisattvas with respect and admiration, and then sat to one side.

Thus in each of all the Buddha lands in the southeast of this world, there was a Buddha who was teaching the wonderful dharma to the sentient beings. And there was also a leading bodhisattva who, after witnessing the great lights, the earthquakes, and the Buddha's appearance, went to the Buddha's place and said, "World-Honored One! Why are there such auspicious phenomena?"

Then each Buddha replied, "In the northwest of this land, there is a world named Barely Tolerable, and the Buddha there is named Sakyamuni and is going to teach great prajna paramita to the bodhisattvas. It is because of his supernatural powers that these auspicious phenomena appeared."

Each of the leading bodhisattvas rejoiced after hearing this and asked his Buddha's permission to go to the Barely Tolerable World to attend the assembly, pay respect, and make offerings to the Buddha and bodhisattvas. Each Buddha approved the request with admiration, gave a golden thousand-treasure lotus to the leading bodhisattva, and said, "You may bring this to the Buddha's place and say, 'My Buddha is sending his limitless regards: Are you having few ills and worries? Are you having a pleasant and easy daily life? Are your energy and strength in good harmony? Are you staying in rest and comfort? Are the worldly affairs endurable? Are the sentient beings easy to guide and teach? I am bringing you, World-Honored One, this lotus on my Buddha's behalf to wish you well in doing Buddhist service.' When you go there, you must dwell in correct knowledge and try to learn more about the land and the people. You should not be rash and arrogant and thus get in trouble. Why do I say so? Because the bodhisattvas there all have incomparable virtues and dignity, they are wholeheartedly compassionate, and their rebirth in that land was the result of great causes and conditions."

Each leading bodhisattva received the flower and the message and started the journey with innumerable bodhisattvas and boys and girls. They stopped at each Buddha land they passed, made offerings to the Buddhas and bodhisattvas in each land, and finally arrived in the land they sought. They bowed down before the Buddha's feet, walked around the Buddha a hundred thousand times, presented the lotus, and passed on the message.

The Buddha received the flower and threw it back to the southeast. Because of his supernatural powers, the flower spread through all the Buddha lands, and on each lectern one transformed Buddha was sitting and teaching great prajna paramita to the bodhisattvas. All hearers would definitely attain the unsurpassed, perfect, and universal bodhi. Each leading bodhisattva and his associates rejoiced and were excited and appreciated what they had never experienced before. They then made offerings of all they had, in accordance with their individual roots of goodness, to the Buddha and the bodhisattvas with respect and praises, and then sat to one side.

At that time, at the end of as many worlds in the southwest as the sands of the Ganges, there was a world named Leaving Dust Gathering. The Buddha in that world was named Universal Sunshine Superior Virtue Thus-Comer, One Worthy of Offerings, Perfectly and Universally Enlightened One, One Perfect in Wisdom and Actions, Well Gone One, One Who Knows the World, Unsurpassed Great Person, Taming and Guiding One, Teacher of Heavenly and Human Beings, Buddha, and Bhagavat. He was guiding the world in peace and stability and teaching great prajna paramita to the bodhisattvas.

A bodhisattva in that land was named Bright Sunlight. After witnessing the great lights, the earthquakes, and the image of the Buddha's body, he was so awestruck that he went to the Buddha's place, bowed down before the Buddha's feet, and asked, "World-Honored One! Why are there such auspicious phenomena?"

Universal Sunshine Superior Virtue Buddha replied to Bright Sunlight Bodhisattva, "Good gentleman, at the end of as many worlds in the northeast as the sands of the Ganges, there is a world named Barely Tolerable, and the Buddha in that land is named Sakyamuni Thus-Comer, One Worthy of Offerings, Perfectly and Universally Enlightened One, One Perfect in Wisdom and Actions, Well Gone One, One Who Knows the World, the Unsurpassed Great Person, Taming and Guiding One, Teacher of Heavenly and Human beings, Buddha, and Bhagavat. He is guiding the world in peace and stability and is going to teach great prajna paramita to the great bodhisattvas. It is because of the Buddha's supernatural powers that such auspicious signs appeared."

Bright Sunlight rejoiced and was excited after hearing this and said, "World-Honored One! May I have your permission to go to Barely Tolerable World to attend the assembly, pay homage, and make offerings to Sakyamuni Buddha and the bodhisattvas there in order to attain the unhindered understanding, dharani gates, samadhi gates, and freedom and self-ease in supernatural powers so that I will be able to reach the last stage before ascending to the highest throne? I beg your kind and compassionate permission!"

Universal Sunshine Superior Virtue Buddha replied to Bright Sunlight Bodhisattva, "Very good! Very good! It is the right time. You may go now as you wish."

The Buddha then handed Bright Sunlight Bodhisattva a golden thousand-stem lotus with a thousand leaves of varied pretty treasures and advised him. "You bring this flower to Sakyamuni Buddha's place and say, 'The Universal Sunshine Superior Virtue Thus-Comer is sending his limitless regards: Are you having few ills and worries? Are you having a pleasant and easy daily life? Are your energy and strength in good harmony? Are you staying in rest and comfort? Are the worldly affairs endurable? Are the sentient beings easy to guide and teach? I am bringing you, World-Honored One, this lotus on my Buddha's behalf to wish you well in doing Buddhist service.' When you go there, you must dwell in correct knowledge and try to learn more about the land and the people. You should not be rash and arrogant and thus get in trouble. Why do I say so? Because the bodhisattvas there all have incomparable virtues and dignity, they are wholeheartedly compassionate, and their rebirth in that land was the result of great causes and conditions."

Bright Sunlight Bodhisattva then received the flower and the message, bowed down before the Buddha's feet, and walked around the Buddha clockwise, together with innumerable hundreds of thousands of koti nayuta monastic and lay bodhisattvas, as well as numberless hundreds of thousands of boys and girls, as a way of saying good-bye. Each one was carrying numberless varied species of flowers, treasure banners, canopies, clothes, treasure decorations, and many other offerings and started their journey. They passed as many lands as the sands of the Ganges in the southwest and stopped at each Buddha land on the way to make offerings and pay homage to each Buddha with praise and respect. Finally, they arrived at the Barely Tolerable World. They bowed down before the Buddha's feet, walked around the Buddha for a hundred thousand times, and then stood to the side.

Bright Sunlight Bodhisattva stepped forward and said to the Buddha, "World-Honored One! From this land to the southwest at the end of as many Buddha lands as the sands of the Ganges, there is a world named Leaving Dust Gathering. The Buddha there is named Sunshine Superior Virtue Thus-Comer, One Worthy of Offerings, Perfectly and Universally Enlightened One, One Perfect in Wisdom and Actions, Well Gone One, One Who Knows the World, Unsurpassed Great Person, Taming and Guiding One, Teacher of Heavenly and Human Beings, Buddha, and Bhagavat. He is sending his limitless regards to you, World-Honored One: Are you having few ills and worries? Are you having a pleasant and easy daily life? Are your energy and strength in good harmony? Are you staying in rest and comfort? Are the worldly affairs endurable? Are the sentient beings easy to guide and teach? I am bringing you, World-Honored One, this golden thousand-stem lotus on my Buddha's behalf to wish you well in doing Buddhist service."

Sakyamuni Buddha received the lotus and then threw it back to as many Buddha lands as the sands of the Ganges in the southwest. Because of the Buddha's supernatural powers, the lotus spread through all the Buddha lands, and on each flower lectern, a transformed Buddha was sitting with his legs crossed and teaching the dharma, in accordance with great prajna paramita, to the bodhisattvas. The sentient beings who heard this would definitely attain the unsurpassed, perfect, and universal bodhi. In the meantime, Bright Sunlight and all his associates rejoiced and were excited and appreciated what they had never experienced before. They then made offerings of all they had in accord with their individual roots of goodness to the Buddha and bodhisattvas with respect and admiration, and then sat to one side.

Thus in each of all the Buddha lands in the southwest of this world, there was a Buddha who was teaching the wonderful dharma to the sentient beings, and there was also a leading bodhisattva who, after witnessing the great lights, the earthquakes, and the Buddha's appearance, went to the Buddha's place and said, "World-Honored One! Why are there such auspicious phenomena?"

Then each Buddha replied, "In the northeast of this land, there is a world named Barely Tolerable, and the Buddha there is named Sakyamuni and is going to teach great prajna paramita to the bodhisattvas. It is because of his supernatural powers that these auspicious phenomena appeared."

Each leading bodhisattva rejoiced after hearing this and asked his Buddha's permission to go to the Barely Tolerable World to attend the assembly, pay respect, and make offerings to the Buddhas and bodhisattvas. Each Buddha approved the request with admiration, gave a golden thousand-treasure lotus to the leading bodhisattva, and said, "You may bring this to the Buddha's place and say, 'My Buddha is sending his limitless regards: Are you having few ills and worries? Are you having a pleasant and easy daily life? Are your energy and strength in good harmony? Are you staying in rest and comfort? Are the worldly affairs endurable? Are the sentient beings easy to guide and teach? I am bringing you, World-Honored One, this lotus on my Buddha's behalf to wish you well in doing Buddhist service.' When you go there, you must dwell in correct knowledge and try to learn more about the land and the people. You should not be rash and arrogant and thus get in trouble. Why do I say so? Because the bodhisattvas there all have incomparable virtues and dignity, they are wholeheartedly compassionate, and their rebirth in that land was the result of great causes and conditions."

Each leading bodhisattva received the flower and the message and started the journey with innumerable bodhisattvas and boys and girls. They stopped at each Buddha land they passed, made offerings to the Buddhas and bodhisattvas in each land, and finally arrived in the land they sought. They bowed down before the Buddha's feet, walked around the Buddha a hundred thousand times, presented the lotus, and passed on the message.

The Buddha received the flower and threw it back to the southwest. Because of his supernatural powers, the flower spread through all Buddha lands, and on each lectern one transformed Buddha was sitting and teaching great prajna paramita to the bodhisattvas. All hearers would definitely attain the unsurpassed, perfect, and universal bodhi. Each leading bodhisattva and his associates rejoiced and were excited and appreciated what they had never experienced before. They then made offerings of all they had, in accordance with their individual roots of goodness, to the Buddha and the bodhisattvas with respect and praises, and then sat to the side.

At that time, at the end of as many worlds in the northwest as the sands of the Ganges, there was a world named Genuine Freedom. The Buddha in that world was named One Treasure Canopy Superior Thus-Comer, One Worthy of Offerings, Perfectly and Universally Enlightened One, One Perfect in Wisdom and Actions, Well Gone One, One Who Knows the World, Unsurpassed Great Person, Taming and Guiding One, Teacher of Heavenly and Human Beings, Buddha, and Bhagavat. He was guiding the world in peace and stability and teaching great prajna paramita to the great bodhisattvas.

A bodhisattva in that land was named Treasure Superior. After witnessing the great lights, the earthquakes, and the image of the Buddha's body, he was so awestruck that he went to the Buddha's place, bowed down before the Buddha's feet, and asked, "World-Honored One! Why are there such auspicious phenomena?"

One Treasure Canopy Superior Buddha replied to Treasure Superior Bodhisattva, "Good gentleman, at the end of as many worlds in the southeast as the sands of the Ganges, there is a world named Barely Tolerable, and the Buddha in that land is named Sakyamuni Thus-Comer, One Worthy of Offerings, Perfectly and Universally Enlightened One, One Perfect in Wisdom and Actions, Well Gone One, One Who Knows the World, Unsurpassed Great Person, Taming and Guiding One, Teacher of Heavenly and Human beings, Buddha, and Bhagavat. He is guiding the world in peace and stability and is going to teach great prajna paramita to the great bodhisattvas. It is because of the Buddha's supernatural powers that such auspicious signs appeared."

Treasure Superior rejoiced and was excited after hearing this, and said, "World-Honored One! May I have your permission to go to Barely Tolerable World to attend the assembly, pay homage, and make offerings to Sakyamuni Buddha and the bodhisattvas there in order to attain the unhindered understanding, dharani gates, samadhi gates, and the freedom and self-ease in playing supernatural powers so that I will be able to reach the last stage before ascending to the highest throne? I beg your kind and compassionate permission!"

One Treasure Canopy Superior Buddha replied to Treasure Superior Bodhisattva, "Very good! Very good! It is the right time. You may go now as you wish!"

The Buddha then handed Treasure Superior Bodhisattva a golden thousand-stem lotus with a thousand leaves of varied pretty treasures and advised him, "You bring this flower to Sakyamuni Buddha's place and say, 'The One Treasure Canopy Superior Thus-Comer is sending his limitless regards: Are you having few ills and worries? Are you having a pleasant and easy daily life? Are your energy and strength in good harmony? Are you staying in rest and comfort? Are the worldly affairs endurable? Are the sentient beings easy to guide and teach? I am bringing you, World-Honored One, this lotus on my Buddha's behalf to wish you well in doing Buddhist service.' When you go there, you must dwell in correct knowledge and try to learn more about the land and the people. You should not be rash and arrogant and thus get in trouble. Why do I say so? Because the bodhisattvas there all have incomparable virtues and dignity, they are wholeheartedly compassionate, and their rebirth in that land was the result of great causes and conditions."

Treasure Superior Bodhisattva then received the flower and the message, bowed down before the Buddha's feet, and walked around the Buddha clockwise, together with innumerable hundreds of thousands of koti nayuta monastic and lay bodhisattvas, as well as numberless hundreds of thousands of boys and girls, to say goodbye. Each one was carrying numberless varied species of flowers, treasure banners, canopies, clothes, treasure decorations, and many other offerings and started their journey. They passed as many lands as the sands of the Ganges in the northwest, and stopped at each Buddha land on the way to make offerings and pay homage to each Buddha with praise and respect. Finally they arrived at the Barely Tolerable World. They bowed down before the Buddha's feet, walked around the Buddha for a hundred thousand times, and then stood to the side.

Treasure Superior Bodhisattva stepped forward and said to the Buddha, "World-Honored One! From this land to the northwest, at the end of as many Buddha lands as the sands of the Ganges, there is a world named Genuine Freedom. The Buddha there is named One Treasure Canopy Superior Thus-Comer, One Worthy of Offerings, Perfectly and Universally Enlightened One, One Perfect in Wisdom and Actions, Well Gone One, One Who Knows the World, Unsurpassed Great Person, Taming and Guiding One, Teacher of Heavenly and Human Beings, Buddha, and Bhagavat. He is sending his limitless regards to you, World-Honored One: Are you having few ills and worries? Are you having a pleasant and easy daily life? Are your energy and strength in good harmony? Are you staying in rest and comfort? Are the worldly affairs endurable? Are the sentient beings easy to guide and teach? I am bringing you, World-Honored One, this golden thousand-stem lotus on my Buddha's behalf to wish you well in doing Buddhist service."

Sakyamuni Buddha received the lotus and then threw it back to as many Buddha lands as the sands of the Ganges in the northwest. Because of the Buddha's supernatural powers, the lotus spread through all the Buddha lands, and on each flower lectern, a transformed Buddha was sitting with his legs crossed and teaching the dharma, in accordance with great prajna paramita, to the bodhisattvas. The sentient beings who heard this would definitely attain the unsurpassed, perfect, and universal bodhi. In the meantime, Treasure Superior and all his associates rejoiced and were excited and appreciated what they had never experienced before. They then made offerings of all they had in accord with their individual roots of goodness to the Buddha and bodhisattvas with respect and admiration, and then sat to one side.

Thus in each of the Buddha lands in the northwest of this world, there was a Buddha who was teaching the wonderful dharma to the sentient beings. And there was also a leading bodhisattva who, after witnessing the great lights, the earthquakes, and the Buddha's appearance, went to the Buddha's place and said, "World-Honored One! Why are there such auspicious phenomena?"

Then each Buddha replied, "In the southeast of this land, there is a world named Barely Tolerable, and the Buddha there is named

Sakyamuni and is going to teach great prajna paramita to the bodhisattvas. It is because of his supernatural powers that these auspicious phenomena appeared."

Each leading bodhisattva rejoiced after hearing this and asked his Buddha's permission to go to the Barely Tolerable World to attend the assembly, pay respect, and make offerings to the Buddha and bodhisattvas. Each Buddha approved the request with admiration, gave a golden thousand-treasure lotus to the leading bodhisattva, and said, "You may bring this to the Buddha's place, and say, 'My Buddha is sending his limitless regards: Are you having few ills and worries? Are you having a pleasant and easy daily life? Are your energy and strength in good harmony? Are you staying in rest and comfort? Are the worldly affairs endurable? Are the sentient beings easy to guide and teach? I am bringing you, World-Honored One, this lotus on my Buddha's behalf to wish you well in doing Buddhist service.' When you go there, you must dwell in correct knowledge and try to learn more about the land and the people. You should not be rash and arrogant and thus get into trouble. Why do I say so? Because the bodhisattvas there all have incomparable virtues and dignity, they are wholeheartedly compassionate, and their rebirth in that land was caused by great causes and conditions."

Each leading bodhisattva received the flower and the message and started the journey with innumerable bodhisattvas and boys and girls. They stopped at each Buddha land they passed, and made offerings to the Buddhas and bodhisattvas in each land, and finally arrived in the land they sought. They bowed down before the Buddha's feet, walked around the Buddha a hundred thousand times, presented the lotus, and passed on the message. The Buddha received the flower and threw it back to the northwest. Because of his supernatural powers, the flower spread through all Buddha lands, and on each lectern one transformed Buddha was sitting and teaching great prajna paramita to the bodhisattvas. All hearers would definitely attain the unsurpassed, perfect, and universal bodhi. Each leading bodhisattva and his associates rejoiced and were excited and appreciated what they had never experienced before. They then made offerings of all they had in accordance with their individual roots of goodness to the Buddha and the bodhisattvas with respect and praises, and then sat to one side.

At that time, at the nadir of as many worlds as the sands of the Ganges, there was a world named Lotus. The Buddha in that world was named Lotus Virtue Thus-Comer, One Worthy of Offerings, Perfectly and Universally Enlightened One, One Perfect in Wisdom and Actions, Well Gone One, One Who Knows the World, Unsurpassed Great Person, Taming and Guiding One, Teacher of Heavenly and Human Beings, Buddha, and Bhagavat. He was guiding the world in peace and stability and teaching great prajna paramita to the great bodhisattvas.

A bodhisattva in that land was named Lotus Superior. After witnessing the great lights, the earthquakes, and the image of the Buddha's body, he was so awestruck that he went to the Buddha's place, bowed down before the Buddha's feet, and asked, "World-Honored One! Why are there such auspicious phenomena?"

Lotus Virtue Buddha replied to Lotus Superior Bodhisattva, "Good gentleman, at the end of as many worlds as the sands of the Ganges above, there is a world named Barely Tolerable, and the Buddha in that land is named Sakyamuni Thus-Comer, One Worthy of Offerings, Perfectly and Universally Enlightened One, One Perfect in Wisdom and Actions, Well Gone One, One Who Knows the World, the Unsurpassed Great Person, Taming and Guiding One, Teacher of Heavenly and Human beings, Buddha, and Bhagavat. He is guiding the world in peace and stability and is going to teach great prajna paramita to the bodhisattvas. It is because of the Buddha's supernatural powers that such auspicious signs appeared."

Lotus Superior rejoiced and was excited after hearing this, and said, "World-Honored One! May I have your permission to go to Barely Tolerable World to attend the assembly, pay homage, and make offerings to Sakyamuni Buddha and the bodhisattvas there in order to attain the unhindered understanding, dharani gates, samadhi gates, and the freedom and self-ease in playing supernatural powers so that I will be able to reach the last stage before ascending to the highest throne? I beg your kind and compassionate permission!"

Lotus Virtue Buddha answered Lotus Superior Bodhisattva, "Very good! Very good! It is exactly the right time. You may go now as you wish."

The Buddha then handed Lotus Superior Bodhisattva a golden thousand-stem lotus with a thousand leaves of varied pretty treasures and advised him, "You bring this flower to Sakyamuni Buddha's place and say, 'The Lotus Virtue Thus-Comer is sending his limitless regards: Are you having few ills and worries? Are you having a pleasant and easy daily life? Are your energy and strength in good harmony? Are you staying in rest and comfort? Are the worldly affairs endurable? Are the sentient beings easy to guide and teach? I am bringing you, World-Honored One, this lotus on my Buddha's behalf to wish you well in doing Buddhist service.' When you go there, you must dwell in correct knowledge and try to learn more about the land and the people. You should not be rash and arrogant and thus get in trouble. Why do I say so? Because the bodhisattvas there all have incomparable virtues and dignity, they are wholeheartedly compassionate, and their rebirth in that land was the result of great causes and conditions."

Lotus Superior Bodhisattva then received the flower and the message, bowed down before the Buddha's feet, and walked around the Buddha clockwise, together with innumerable hundreds of thousands of koti nayuta monastic and lay bodhisattvas, and numberless hundreds of thousands of boys and girls, as a way of saying good-bye. Each one was carrying numberless varied species of flowers, treasure banners, canopies, clothes, treasure decorations, and many other offerings and started their journey. They passed as many lands as the sands of the Ganges in the nadir and stopped at each Buddha land on the way to make offerings and pay homage to each Buddha with praise and respect. Finally, they arrived at the Barely Tolerable World. They bowed down before the Buddha's feet, walked around the Buddha for a hundred thousand times, and then stood to the side.

Lotus Superior Bodhisattva stepped forward and said to the Buddha, "World-Honored One! From this land to the nadir at the end of as many Buddha lands as the sands of the Ganges, there is a world that is named Lotus. The Buddha there is named Lotus

Virtue Thus-Comer, One Worthy of Offerings, Perfectly and Universally Enlightened One, One Perfect in Wisdom and Actions, Well Gone One, One Who Knows the World, Unsurpassed Great Person, Taming and Guiding One, Teacher of Heavenly and Human Beings, Buddha, and Bhagavat. He is sending his limitless regards to you, World-Honored One: Are you having few ills and worries? Are you having a pleasant and easy daily life? Are your energy and strength in good harmony? Are you staying in rest and comfort? Are the worldly affairs endurable? Are the sentient beings easy to guide and teach? I am bringing you, World-Honored One, this golden thousand-stem lotus on my Buddha's behalf to wish you well in doing Buddhist service."

Sakyamuni Buddha received the lotus and then threw it back to as many Buddha lands as the sands of the Ganges underneath. Because of the Buddha's supernatural powers, the lotus spread through all the Buddha lands, and on each flower lectern a transformed Buddha was sitting with his legs crossed and teaching the dharma in accordance with great prajna paramita to the bodhisattvas. The sentient beings who heard this would definitely attain the unsurpassed, perfect, and universal bodhi. In the meantime, Lotus Superior and all his associates rejoiced and were excited and appreciated what they had never experienced before. They then made offerings of all they had in accord with their individual roots of goodness to the Buddha and bodhisattvas with respect and admiration, and then sat to one side.

Thus in each of the Buddha lands under this world, there was a Buddha who was teaching the wonderful dharma to the sentient beings. And there was also a leading bodhisattva who, after witnessing the great lights, the earthquakes, and the Buddha's appearance, went to the Buddha's place and said, "World-Honored One! Why are there such auspicious phenomena?"

Then each Buddha replied, "Above this land there is a world named Barely Tolerable, and the Buddha there is named Sakyamuni and is going to teach great prajna paramita to the bodhisattvas. It is because of his supernatural powers that these auspicious phenomena appeared."

Each leading bodhisattva rejoiced after hearing this and asked his Buddha's permission to go to the Barely Tolerable World to attend the assembly, pay respect, and make offerings to the Buddha and bodhisattvas. Each Buddha approved the request with admiration, gave a golden thousand-treasure lotus to the leading bodhisattva, and said, "You may bring this to the Buddha's place, and say, 'My Buddha is sending his limitless regards: Are you having few ills and worries? Are you having a pleasant and easy daily life? Are your energy and strength in good harmony? Are you staying in rest and comfort? Are the worldly affairs endurable? Are the sentient beings easy to guide and teach? I am bringing you, World-Honored One, this lotus on my Buddha's behalf to wish you well in doing Buddhist service.' When you go there, you must dwell in correct knowledge and try to learn more about the land and the people. You should not be rash and arrogant and thus get in trouble. Why do I say so? Because the bodhisattvas there all have incomparable virtues and dignity, they are wholeheartedly compassionate, and their rebirth in that land was the result of great causes and conditions."

Each leading bodhisattva received the flower and the message and started the journey with innumerable bodhisattvas and boys and girls. They stopped at each Buddha land they passed, made offerings to the Buddhas and bodhisattvas in each land, and finally arrived in the land they sought. They bowed down before the Buddha's feet, walked around the Buddha a hundred thousand times, presented the lotus, and passed on the message. The Buddha received the flower and threw it back to the worlds below. Because of his supernatural powers, the flower spread through all Buddha lands, and on each lectern one transformed Buddha was sitting and teaching great prajna paramita to the bodhisattvas. All hearers would definitely attain the unsurpassed, perfect, and universal bodhi. Each leading bodhisattva and his associates rejoiced and were excited and appreciated what they had never experienced before. They then made offerings of all they had, in accordance with their individual roots of goodness, to the Buddha and the bodhisattvas with respect and praises, and then sat to one side.

At that time, at the zenith of as many worlds as the sands of the Ganges, there was a world that was named Delight. The Buddha in that world was named Delight Virtue Thus-Comer, One Worthy of Offerings, Perfectly and Universally Enlightened One, One Perfect in Wisdom and Actions, Well Gone One, One Who Knows the World, Unsurpassed Great Person, Taming and Guiding One, Teacher of Heavenly and Human Beings, Buddha, and Bhagavat. He was guiding the world in peace and stability and teaching great prajna paramita to the great bodhisattvas.

A bodhisattva in that land was named Delight Conferring. After witnessing the great lights, the earthquakes, and the image of the Buddha's body, he was so awestruck that he went to the Buddha's place, bowed down before the Buddha's feet, and asked, "World-Honored One! Why are there such auspicious phenomena?"

Delight Virtue Buddha replied to Delight Conferring Bodhisattva, "Good gentleman, at the end of as many worlds as the sands of the Ganges below, there is a world named Barely Tolerable, and the Buddha in that land is named Sakyamuni Thus-Comer, One Worthy of Offerings, Perfectly and Universally Enlightened One, One Perfect in Wisdom and Actions, Well Gone One, One Who Knows the World, Unsurpassed Great Person, Taming and Guiding One, Teacher of Heavenly and Human beings, Buddha, and Bhagavat. He is guiding the world in peace and stability and is going to teach great prajna paramita to the great bodhisattvas. It is because of the Buddha's supernatural powers that such auspicious signs appeared."

Delight Conferring rejoiced and was excited after hearing this and said, "World-Honored One! May I have your permission to go to Barely Tolerable World to attend the assembly, pay homage, and make offerings to Sakyamuni Buddha and the bodhisattvas there in order to attain the unhindered understanding, dharani gates, samadhi gates, and the freedom and self-ease in playing supernatural powers so that I will be able to reach the last stage before ascending to the highest throne? I beg your kind and compassionate permission!"

Delight Virtue Buddha replied to Delight Conferring Bodhisattva, "Very good! Very good! It is the right time. You may go now as you wish."

The Buddha then handed Delight Conferring Bodhisattva a golden thousand-stem lotus with a thousand leaves of varied pretty treasures and advised him, "You bring this flower to Sakyamuni Buddha's place and say, 'The Delight Virtue Thus-Comer is sending his limitless regards: Are you having few ills and worries? Are you having a pleasant and easy daily life? Are your energy and strength in good harmony? Are you staying in rest and comfort? Are the worldly affairs endurable? Are the sentient beings easy to guide and teach? I am bringing you, World-Honored One, this lotus on my Buddha's behalf to wish you well in doing Buddhist service.' When you go there, you must dwell in correct knowledge and try to learn more about the land and the people. You should not be rash and arrogant and thus get in trouble. Why do I say so? Because the bodhisattvas there all have incomparable virtues and dignity, they are wholeheartedly compassionate, and their rebirth in that land was the result of great causes and conditions."

Delight Conferring Bodhisattva then received the flower and the message, bowed down before the Buddha's feet, and walked around the Buddha clockwise, together with innumerable hundreds of thousands of koti nayuta monastic and lay bodhisattvas, and numberless hundreds of thousands of boys and girls, as a way of saying good-bye. Each one was carrying numberless varied species of flowers, treasure banners, canopies, clothes, treasure decorations, and many other offerings and started their journey. They passed as many lands as the sands of the Ganges in the zenith, and stopped at each Buddha land on the way to make offerings and pay homage to each Buddha with praise and respect. Finally they arrived at the Barely Tolerable World. They bowed down before the Buddha's feet, walked around the Buddha for a hundred thousand times, and then stood to the side.

Delight Conferring Bodhisattva stepped forward and said to the Buddha, "World-Honored One! From this land to the zenith at the end of as many Buddha lands as the sands of the Ganges, there is a world named Delight. The Buddha there is named Delight Virtue Thus-Comer, One Worthy of Offerings, Perfectly and Universally Enlightened One, One Perfect in Wisdom and Actions, Well Gone One, One Who Knows the World, Unsurpassed Great Person, Taming and Guiding One, Teacher of Heavenly and Human Beings, Buddha, and Bhagavat. He is sending his limitless regards to you,

World-Honored One: Are you having few ills and worries? Are you having a pleasant and easy daily life? Are your energy and strength in good harmony? Are you staying in rest and comfort? Are the worldly affairs endurable? Are the sentient beings easy to guide and teach? I am bringing you, World-Honored One, this golden thousand-stem lotus on my Buddha's behalf to wish you well in doing Buddhist service."

Sakyamuni Buddha received the lotus and then threw it back to as many Buddha lands as the sands of the Ganges above. Because of the Buddha's supernatural powers, the lotus spread through all the Buddha lands, and on each flower lectern, a transformed Buddha was sitting with his legs crossed and teaching the dharma in accordance with great prajna paramita to the bodhisattvas. The sentient beings who heard the teaching would definitely attain the unsurpassed, perfect, and universal bodhi. In the meantime, Delight Conferring and all his associates rejoiced and were excited and appreciated what they had never experienced before. They then made offerings of all they had, in accord with their individual roots of goodness, to the Buddha and bodhisattvas with respect and admiration, and then sat to one side.

Thus in each of all the Buddha lands above this world, there was a Buddha who was teaching the wonderful dharma to the sentient beings, and there was also a leading bodhisattva, after witnessing the great lights, the earthquakes, and the Buddha's appearance, who went to the Buddha's place and said, "World-Honored One! Why are there such auspicious phenomena?"

Then each Buddha replied, "Below this land, there is a world named Barely Tolerable, and the Buddha there is named Sakyamuni and is going to teach great prajna paramita to the bodhisattvas. It is because of his supernatural powers that these auspicious phenomena appeared."

Each leading bodhisattva rejoiced after hearing this and asked his Buddha's permission to go to the Barely Tolerable World to attend the assembly, pay respect, and make offerings to the Buddha and bodhisattvas. Each Buddha approved the request with admiration, gave a golden thousand-treasure lotus to the leading bodhisattva, and said, "You may bring this to the Buddha's place, and say, 'My Buddha is sending his limitless regards: Are you having few ills and worries? Are you having a pleasant and easy daily life? Are your energy and strength in good harmony? Are you staying in rest and comfort? Are the worldly affairs endurable? Are the sentient beings easy to guide and teach? I am bringing you, World-Honored One, this lotus on my Buddha's behalf to wish you well in doing Buddhist service.' When you go there, you must dwell in correct knowledge and try to learn more about the land and the people. You should not be rash and arrogant and thus get into trouble. Why do I say so? Because the bodhisattvas there all have incomparable virtues and dignity, they are wholeheartedly compassionate, and their rebirth in that land was the result of great causes and conditions."

Each leading bodhisattva received the flower and the message and started the journey with innumerable bodhisattvas and boys and girls. They stopped at each Buddha land they passed, made offerings to the Buddhas and bodhisattvas in each land, and finally arrived in the land they sought. They bowed down before the Buddha's feet, walked around the Buddha a hundred thousand times, presented the lotus, and passed on the message. The Buddha received the flower and threw it back to the worlds above. Because of his supernatural powers, the flower spread through all Buddha lands, and on each lectern one transformed Buddha was sitting and teaching great prajna paramita to the bodhisattvas. All hearers would definitely attain the unsurpassed, perfect, and universal bodhi. Each leading bodhisattvas and his associates rejoiced and were excited and appreciated what they had never experienced before. They then made offerings of all they had, in accordance with their individual roots of goodness, to the Buddha and the bodhisattvas with respect and praises, and then sat to one side.

At that time, the large threefold thousand-world of the Buddhas was filled with a variety of treasures. Various species of wonderful flowers bloomed everywhere. Treasure banners, flags, and canopies stood in rows all over the places. Trees of flowers, trees of fruits, trees of fragrance, trees of garlands, trees of treasures, trees of clothes, and the trees of other varied ornaments spread amid them. All were so beautiful, glorious, and attractive. It was like in various lotus worlds and the pure floral lands of the Thus-Comers, where the Wonderfully Auspicious Bodhisattva, Dwelling Well in Wisdom Bodhisattva, and the rest of numberless great bodhisattvas of great powers have lived long.

FASCICLE 3

Chapter 2
Learning Contemplation

Section 1

(In the First Assembly)

AT THAT TIME, KNOWING THAT ALL THE SENTIENT beings from various worlds, including the heavenly beings, demons, Brahmas, sramanas, Brahmans, gandharvas, asuras, dragons, the bodhisattvas who had reached the last stage before ascending to the highest throne, and the humans and nonhumans who were interested in the dharma, had gathered together, the World-Honored One said to the long-lived sage Sariputra, "If the great bodhisattvas would like to become awakened perfectly and universally to all phenomena of all dharmas, they should learn prajna paramita."

After hearing what the Buddha said, Sariputra jumped up from his seat with great joy and bowed down to the Buddha's feet. He knelt down with his right knee touching the ground and his left shoulder covered and said, "World-Honored One! How should the bodhisattvas learn prajna paramita in order to perfectly and universally become awakened to the phenomena of all dharmas?"

The Buddha said to the long-lived sage Sariputra, "Sariputra! The great bodhisattvas should dwell peacefully in prajna paramita by adopting nondwelling as expedience because both dwelling and the ones who dwell are unattainable. The great bodhisattvas should fulfill perfectly giving paramita by adopting nonrenunciation as expedience because the giver, the receiver, and the things given are all unattainable. The great bodhisattvas should fulfill perfectly pure-precept paramita by adopting nonprotection as expedience because the forms of violation and nonviolation are unattainable. The great bodhisattvas should fulfill perfectly forbearance paramita by adopting nongrasping as expedience because the forms of motion and motionlessness are unattainable. The great bodhisattvas should fulfill perfectly diligence paramita by adopting noneffort as expedience because both effort and laziness in body and mind are unattainable. The great bodhisattvas should fulfill perfectly meditation paramita by adopting nonreflection as expedience because both taste and nontaste in dharma are unattainable. The great bodhisattvas should fulfill perfectly prajna paramita by adopting nonattachment as expedience because both dharma natures and dharma forms are unattainable.

"Furthermore, Sariputra, the great bodhisattvas should dwell peacefully in prajna paramita and adopt nonattainment as expedience to perfectly fulfill the four bases of mindfulness, four correct endeavors, four bases of powers, five roots, five powers, seven factors for enlightenment, and the noble eightfold path only because these thirty-seven ways for enlightenment are unattainable. The great bodhisattvas should dwell peacefully in prajna paramita and adopt nonattainment as expedience to perfectly fulfill the liberation gates of emptiness, formlessness, and nonaspiration because these three gates are unattainable. The great bodhisattvas should dwell peacefully in prajna paramita and adopt nonattainment as expedience to perfectly fulfill the four meditations, four immeasurable minds, and four formless concentrations because all these meditations, immeasurable minds, and formless concentrations are unattainable. The great bodhisattvas should dwell peacefully in prajna paramita and adopt nonattainment as expedience to perfectly fulfill the eight liberations, eight vexation-overcoming meditations, nine concentrations in sequence, and the ten universal contemplations because all these liberations, meditations, concentrations, and contemplations are unattainable. The great bodhisattvas should dwell peacefully in prajna paramita and adopt nonattainment as expedience to perfectly fulfill the nine reflections: the physical body is swelling, it has pus and festering wounds, its skin and flesh are eaten and peeled off, its appearance turns blue owing to bruises, it is eaten by pecking, it is separated and scattered around, it has only bones and skeleton remained, it is burned, and the reflection that nothing in the world can endure forever. This is because all these reflections are unattainable.

"When dwelling peacefully in prajna paramita, the great bodhisattvas should adopt nonattainment as expedience to perfectly fulfill the ten kinds of mindfulness: the mindfulness of the Buddha, the dharma, the sangha, the precepts, equanimity, the heaven, inhalation and exhalation, a disgust of the world, a disgust of death, and a disgust of the body because all these kinds of mindfulness are unattainable. When dwelling peacefully in prajna paramita, the great bodhisattvas should adopt nonattainment as expedience to perfectly fulfill the reflection on the ten things, namely impermanence, suffering, selflessness, impurity, death, the condition that all worldly things are undesirable, the disgust of food, correct termination, correct departure, and correct extinction, because all these reflections are unattainable. When dwelling peacefully in prajna paramita, the great bodhisattvas should adopt nonattainment as expedience to perfectly fulfill eleven kinds of perfect knowledge: the perfect knowledge of suffering, the cause of suffering, the cessation of suffering, the path for the cessation of suffering, exhaustion, nonarising, the dharma, the classes of the dharma, the world, knowing others' minds, and the perfect knowledge as it is taught by the Buddha. This is because all these kinds of perfect knowledge are unattainable. When dwelling peacefully in prajna paramita, the great bodhisattvas should adopt nonattainment as expedience to perfectly fulfill the samadhi with both contemplation and investigation, the samadhi with investigation only, and the samadhi without contemplation and investigation because these three conditions of samadhi are unattainable.

"When dwelling peacefully in prajna paramita, the great bodhisattvas should perfectly fulfill the three flawless roots by adopting nonattainment as expedience to learn the four noble truths that one should know but has not yet known, to learn and get to know more about the four noble truths, and to learn all aspects of the four noble truths and finally succeed to cease suffering. This is because all these three roots are unattainable. When dwelling peacefully in prajna paramita, the great bodhisattvas should adopt nonattainment as expedience to perfectly fulfill the contemplation on impure body, the universal contemplation, the perfect knowledge of all perfect knowledge, samatha, and vipasyana because these five things are all unattainable. When dwelling peacefully in prajna paramita, the great bodhisattvas should adopt nonattainment as expedience to perfectly fulfill the four approaches of absorption, four superior dwellings, three supernatural powers, five eyes, six supernatural powers, and the six paramitas because all these things are unattainable. When dwelling peacefully in prajna paramita, the great bodhisattvas should adopt nonattainment as expedience to perfectly fulfill the seven holy treasures, eight factors for awakening, the knowledge shared by the sentient beings of the nine realms, the dharani gates, and the samadhi gates because these five things are all unattainable. When dwelling peacefully in prajna paramita, the great bodhisattvas should adopt nonattainment as expedience to perfectly fulfill the ten stages, ten practices, ten forbearances, and twenty ways of reinforcing motivation because all these are unattainable.

"When dwelling in prajna paramita, the great bodhisattvas should adopt nonattainment as expedience to perfectly fulfill the Buddha's ten abilities, four kinds of fearlessness, four unhindered understandings, eighteen distinctive features of Buddha's wisdom and power, thirty-two perfect major marks, and eighty distinguishing minor features of physical body because all of these six spheres are unattainable. When dwelling in prajna paramita, the great bodhisattvas should adopt nonattainment as expedience to perfectly fulfill staying in correct mindfulness, dwelling in equanimity at all times, the perfect knowledge of everything, the perfect knowledge of the forms of the paths, the perfect knowledge of all phenomena, and the exquisite and subtle knowledge of all phenomena because all these six spheres are unattainable. When dwelling in prajna paramita, the great bodhisattvas should adopt nonattainment as expedience to perfectly fulfill great loving-kindness, great compassion, great joy, great equanimity, and the rest of innumerable, boundless Buddha dharmas because all these are unattainable.

"Furthermore, Sariputra, in order to attain quickly the perfect knowledge of all perfect knowledge, the great bodhisattvas should learn prajna paramita. In order to fulfill quickly the perfect knowledge of everything, the perfect knowledge of the forms of the paths, and the perfect knowledge of all phenomena, the great bodhisattvas should learn prajna paramita. In order to fulfill quickly the perfect knowledge of the images of the minds of the sentient beings and the exquisite and subtle knowledge of all phenomena, the great bodhisattvas should learn prajna paramita. In order to quickly eliminate all vexations and the rooted hidden negative disposition, the great bodhisattvas should learn prajna paramita. In order to quickly enter onto the correct path of bodhisattva and depart from arising, the great bodhisattvas should learn prajna paramita. In order to surpass the stage of the voice-hearer and the stage of the self-enlightened one, the great bodhisattvas should learn prajna paramita. In order to dwell in the stage of bodhisattva of nonregression, the great bodhisattvas should learn prajna paramita. In order to attain the six superior supernatural powers, the great bodhisattvas should learn prajna paramita. In order to know different orientations of the minds and the actions of all sentient beings, the great bodhisattvas should learn prajna paramita.

"In order to surpass the wisdom of the voice-hearers and self-enlightened ones, the great bodhisattvas should learn prajna paramita. In order to attain all dharani gates and samadhi gates, the great bodhisattvas should learn prajna paramita. In order to surpass the giving practiced by the voice-hearers and self-enlightened ones with a mind of joyful participation, the great bodhisattvas should learn parajna paramita. In order to surpass the pure precepts practiced by the voice-hearers and self-enlightened ones who possess a mind of joyful participation, the great bodhisattvas should learn prajna paramita. In order to surpass the concentrations, wisdom, liberations, and the knowledge and views of liberations practiced by the voice-hearers and self-enlightened ones who possess a mind of joyful participation, the great bodhisattvas should learn prajna paramita. In order to surpass all meditations, liberations, samadhi, samapatti, and the rest of the virtuous dharmas practiced by the voice-hearers and self-enlightened ones who possess a mind of joyful participation, the great bodhisattvas should learn prajna paramita. In order to surpass all virtuous dharmas practiced by ordinary people, voice-hearers, and self-enlightened ones who possess a mind of joyful participation, the great bodhisattvas should learn prajna paramita. In order to practice a little giving, pure precept, forbearance, diligence, meditation, and prajna, and transfer expediently and skillfully the merits and virtues thus derived toward the unsurpassed, perfect, and universal bodhi for the sake of the sentient beings, the great bodhisattvas should learn prajna paramita.

"Furthermore, Sariputra, in order to remove obstacles and fulfill quickly the practice of giving, pure precept, forbearance, diligence, meditation, and prajna, the great bodhisattvas should learn prajna paramita. In order to frequently see the Buddhas in each of one's lives and always hear correct teachings and be inspired, awakened, taught, and guided by the Buddhas, the great bodhisattvas should learn prajna paramita. In order to attain a Buddha body with thirty-two perfect major marks and eighty distinguishing minor features, the great bodhisattvas should learn prajna paramita. In order to be able to memorize previous lives in generations to come, never discontinue aspiration to the great bodhi, stay away from evil friends, stay close to virtuous and beneficial friends, and constantly practice bodhisattva way, the great bodhisattvas should learn prajna paramita. In order to attain great dignity and virtues in generations to come, destroy the devils of enmity, and subjugate other-path practitioners, the great bodhisattvas should learn prajna paramita. In order to stay away from all vexations and karmic obstacles for the generations to come, and thoroughly understand the dharmas without difficulty, the great bodhisattvas should learn prajna paramita. In order to sustain incessantly a virtuous mind, virtuous aspiration, and virtuous conduct in generations to come without laziness and tiredness, the great bodhisattvas should learn prajna paramita. In order to be reborn in a Buddha family as a dharma prince, enter into the stage of pure-child, and never stay

Fascicle 3, Chapter 2, Section 1   57

away from the Buddhas and bodhisattvas, the great bodhisattvas should learn prajna paramita. In order to grow up with distinguishing features of appearance as glorious and dignified as that of a Buddha in the generations to come and make sentient beings happy when looking at them so that the sentient beings will be inspired to pursue the unsurpassed, perfect, and universal enlightenment and fulfill quickly the merits and virtues of the Buddhas, the great bodhisattvas should learn prajna paramita. In order to make the most wonderful offerings respectfully as they wish based on superior virtuous roots, to esteem and acclaim all Thus-Comers, Ones Worthy of Offerings, Perfectly and Universally Enlightened Ones so that their virtuous roots will be fulfilled quickly, the great bodhisattvas should learn prajna paramita. In order to satisfy the needs of all sentient beings in food, clothes, beds, bedding, medicines, flowers, lights, vehicles, gardens, houses, properties, cereals, treasures, jewels, entertainment, and other most wonderful things, the great bodhisattvas should learn prajna paramita.

"Furthermore, Sariputra, in order to establish well the sentient beings in all empty space realms, dharma realms, and the worlds so that they will be able to dwell peacefully in giving paramita, pure-precept paramita, forbearance paramita, diligence paramita, meditation paramita, and prajna paramita, the great bodhisattvas should learn prajna paramita. In order to obtain the merits and virtues produced by a single virtuous mind and let them sustain without exhaustion until sitting peacefully on the throne of the wonderful bodhi and attaining the unsurpassed, perfect, and universal bodhi, the great bodhisattvas should learn prajna paramita. In order to obtain the admirations conferred by all Thus-Comers, Ones Worthy of Offerings, Perfectly and Universally Enlightened Ones, as well as by the bodhisattvas in the Buddha worlds of the ten directions, the great bodhisattvas should learn prajna paramita. In order to be able to reach everywhere, by making a wish, in as many worlds of the ten directions as the sands of the Ganges, make offerings to the Buddhas, and bring benefits and happiness to all sentient beings, the great bodhisattvas should learn prajna paramita. In order to spread one voice of admiring various Buddhas and teaching the sentient beings to permeate as many worlds of the ten directions as the sands of the Ganges, the great bodhisattvas should learn prajna paramita. In order to establish well all sentient beings, with an instantaneous thought, in as many Buddha worlds of the ten directions as the sands of the Ganges and assist them to learn the path of the ten virtuous karmas, take triple refuge, and observe the precepts, the great bodhisattvas should learn prajna paramita. In order to establish well all sentient beings, with an instantaneous thought, in as many Buddha worlds of the ten directions as the sands of the Ganges, so that they will be able to cultivate the four meditations, four immeasurable minds, and four formless concentrations, and acquire the five supernatural powers, the great bodhisattva should learn prajna paramita. In order to establish well all sentient beings, with an instantaneous thought, in as many Buddha worlds of the ten directions as the sands of the Ganges, and assist them with cultivating the bodhisattva actions of the large vehicle without destroying other vehicles, the great bodhisattvas should learn prajna paramita. In order to maintain the Buddhist lineage, prevent its development from discontinuation and protect the family of bodhisattva from regression but quickly achieve in dignifying and purifying the Buddha lands, the great bodhisattvas should learn prajna paramita.

"Furthermore, Sariputra, in order to thoroughly understand internal emptiness, external emptiness, internal-external emptiness, emptiness of emptiness, emptiness of space, emptiness of ultimate truth, emptiness of conditioned phenomena, emptiness of unconditioned reality, emptiness in the final analysis, emptiness of nontemporality, emptiness of deconstruction, emptiness of changelessness, emptiness of original nature, emptiness of particular characteristics, emptiness of common characteristics, emptiness of all dharmas, emptiness of nonattainment, emptiness of selflessness, emptiness of self-nature, and emptiness of selfless self-nature, the great bodhisattvas should learn prajna paramita. In order to thoroughly understand realness, dharma realm, dharma nature, the nature of nonillusion, the nature of changelessness, the nature of equality, the nature of nonarising, dharma concentration, dharma dwelling, reality, the realm of empty space, and the realm of the inconceivable, the great bodhisattvas should learn prajna paramita. In order to thoroughly understand all characteristics of all dharmas as they really are, the great bodhisattvas should learn prajna paramita. In order to thoroughly understand the natures of cause and condition, consecutive thoughts in sequence, the conditions that stimulate the mind, and the conditions that reinforce main causes, the great bodhisattvas should learn prajna paramita. In order to thoroughly understand that all dharmas are like the illusions, the dreams, echoes, images, shadows, illusory images of water under sunlight, flowers in the sky, mirages, and the transformed things; that all dharmas are only the manifestation of the mind; and that both their natures and phenomena are empty, the great bodhisattvas should learn prajna paramita.

"In order to know the large threefold thousand-world, the empty space, vast earth, mountains, oceans, rivers, ponds, valleys, lakes, and the ultimate particles of the earth, water, fire, and wind, the great bodhisattvas should learn prajna paramita. In order to use one hundredth of a hair to lift up and move all the waters in oceans, rivers, ponds, valleys, and the lakes of the whole large threefold thousand-world to a most remote world without disturbing the aquatic animals in them, the great bodhisattvas should learn prajna paramita. In order to put off instantly the conflagration, by blowing a breath of air, at the end of the kalpa that will burn up the entire large threefold thousand-world, the great bodhisattvas should learn prajna paramita. In order to stop the hurricane, using one finger, from swirling up the large threefold thousand-world and all the big mountains, such as Sumeru, Large Sumeru, Circular Iron Enclosure, and Large Circular Iron Enclosure, as well as the smaller mountains and the vast grounds in it, and from breaking and squeezing them into chaffs, the great bodhisattvas should learn prajna paramita.

"In order to fill up the entire empty space of the large threefold thousand-world through crossed-legs meditative sitting, the great bodhisattvas should learn prajna paramita. In order to throw away, with a hair, the entire large threefold thousand-world, including the mountains Sumeru, Large Sumeru, Circular Iron Enclosure, Large Circular Iron Enclosure, other smaller mountains, as well as many other things on the earth, to immeasurable, innumerable, and boundless worlds on the other side of the universe, without disturbing sentient beings in them, the great bodhisattvas should learn prajna paramita. In order to make merely one food, one flower, one incense, one banner, one flag, one canopy, one tent, one lamp, one piece of clothing, one song and so forth, as offerings to present in respect and admiration to the Thus-Comers, Ones Worthy of Offerings, the Perfectly and Universally Enlightened Ones, and their disciples in as many worlds of the ten directions as the sands of the Ganges River, and for the offerings to always remain sufficient, the great bodhisattvas should learn prajna paramita. In order to establish well the sentient beings in as many worlds of the ten directions as the sands of the Ganges River and let them dwell in the aggregates of pure precept, concentration, wisdom, liberation, and the knowledge and views of liberation; dwell in stream-entry effect, once-return effect, nonreturn effect, arhat effect, and self-enlightenment bodhi; or even enter into the nirvana without remainder, the great bodhisattvas should learn prajna paramita.

"Furthermore, Sariputra, if the great bodhisattvas cultivate prajna paramita, they will be able to know accurately what great rewards giving will bring about. They will know accurately that such a giving will enable one to be reborn in a noble family of Ksatriya, Brahman, elder, or layperson; be reborn in the Heaven of Four Great Kings, the Heaven of Thirty-Three Smaller Heavens, the Heaven of Yama, the Heaven of Tusita, the Heaven of Enjoying Self-Made Changes, or the Heaven of Enjoying Other-Made Changes; achieve the first meditation, the second meditation, the third meditation, or the fourth meditation; attain the concentration of boundless emptiness, boundless consciousness, nothingness, or nonthinking and not nonthinking. They will be able to know accurately that, because of such a giving, one will initiate the four bases of mindfulness, and so forth, as well as the noble eightfold path; one will attain the thirty-seven factors for enlightenment, three liberation gates, eight liberations, eight vexation-overcoming meditations, nine concentrations in sequence, and ten universal contemplations; one will attain the dharani gates and the samadhi gates; and one will enter onto the bodhisattva path of nonarising. They will know accurately that, because of such a giving, one will achieve the stages of ecstasy, freedom from defilements, emitting light, flaming wisdom, being extremely difficult to be surpassed, manifestation of pure realness, going far away, the unmovable, expedient wisdom, and dharma cloud; one will obtain the five eyes and the six supernatural powers; one will attain the Buddha's ten abilities, four kinds of fearlessness, four unhindered understandings, eighteen distinctive features of Buddha's wisdom and power, great loving-kindness, great compassion, great joy, and great equanimity. They will accurately know that, because of such a giving, one will obtain the thirty-two perfect major marks or the eighty distinguishing minor marks; one will obtain the way of staying in correct mindfulness or the nature of dwelling in equanimity at all times; one will obtain stream-entry effect, once-return effect, nonreturn effect, arhat effect, self-enlightenment bodhi, or the unsurpassed, perfect, and universal bodhi. They will be able to know accurately that what great rewards pure precept, forbearance, diligence, meditation, and prajna will also bring about.

"Furthermore, Sariputra, if the great bodhisattvas cultivate prajna paramita, they will be able to know accurately that the expedient and skillful practice of giving can fulfill perfectly giving paramita, pre-precept paramita, forbearance paramita, diligence paramita, meditation paramita, and prajna paramita. They will be able to know accurately that the expedient and skillful practice of pure precept can fulfill perfectly pure-precept paramita, forbearance paramita, diligence paramita, meditation paramita, prajna paramita, and giving paramita. They will be able to know accurately that the expedient and skillful practice of forbearance can fulfill perfectly forbearance paramita, diligence paramita, meditation paramita, prajna paramita, giving paramita, and pure-precept paramita. They will be able to know accurately that the expedient and skillful practice of diligence can fulfill perfectly diligence paramita, meditation paramita, prajna paramita, giving paramita, pure-precept paramita, and forbearance paramita. They will be able to know accurately that the expedient and skillful practice of meditation can fulfill perfectly meditation paramita, prajna paramita, giving paramita, pure-precept paramita, forbearance paramita, and diligence paramita. They will also be able to know accurately that the expedient and skillful practice of prajna can fulfill perfectly prajna paramita, giving paramita, pure-precept paramita, forbearance paramita, diligence paramita, and meditation paramita."

At that time, Sariputra asked the Buddha, "World-Honored One! How can the great bodhisattvas, when cultivating prajna paramita, know accurately that giving, pure precept, forbearance, diligence, meditation, and prajna practiced in expedient skillfulness can fulfill perfectly giving paramita, pure-precept paramita, forbearance paramita, diligence paramita, meditation paramita, and prajna paramita?"

The Buddha replied to the long-lived sage Sariputra, "The great bodhisattvas who cultivate prajna paramita will know accurately that if great bodhisattvas adopt nonattainment as expedience to cultivate giving paramita and thoroughly understand that all givers, receivers, and the things given are unattainable, then such giving will be able to fulfill giving paramita, pure-precept paramita, forbearance paramita, diligence paramita, meditation paramita, and prajna paramita to their perfection. The great bodhisattvas who cultivate prajna paramita will know accurately that if the great bodhisattvas adopt nonattainment as expedience to cultivate pure-precept paramita, and thoroughly understand that all the phenomena of violation and nonviolation of precepts are unattainable, then such pure precept will be able to fulfill pure-precept paramita, forbearance paramita, diligence paramita, meditation paramita, prajna paramita, and giving paramita to their perfection. The great bodhisattvas who cultivate prajna paramita will know accurately that if the great bodhisattvas adopt nonattainment as expedience to cultivate forbearance paramita and thoroughly understand that all phenomena of motion and motionlessness are unattainable, then such forbearance will be able to fulfill forbearance, diligence, meditation, prajna, giving, and pure-precept paramitas to their perfection. The great bodhisattvas who cultivate prajna paramita will know accurately that if the great bodhisattvas adopt nonattainment as expedience to cultivate diligence and thoroughly understand that both industry and laziness in body and mind are unattainable, then such diligence will be able to fulfill diligence paramita, meditation paramita, prajna paramita, giving paramita, pure-precept paramita, and forbearance paramita to their perfection. The great bodhisat-

Fascicle 3, Chapter 2, Section 1   63

tvas who cultivate prajna paramita will know accurately that if the great bodhisattvas adopt nonattainment as expedience to cultivate meditation, and thoroughly understand that both the good taste of the dharma and the not good taste of the dharma are unattainable, then such meditation will be able to fulfill meditation paramita, prajna paramita, giving paramita, pure-precept paramita, forbearance paramita, and diligence paramita to their perfection. The great bodhisattvas who cultivate prajna paramita will know accurately that if the great bodhisattvas adopt nonattainment as expedience to cultivate prajna and thoroughly understand that the natures and phenomena of all dharmas are unattainable, then such prajna will be able to fulfill prajna paramita, giving paramita, pure-precept paramita, forbearance paramita, diligence paramita, and meditation paramita to their perfection.

"Furthermore, Sariputra, if the great bodhisattvas would like to attain all the merits and virtues of the Thus-Comers, Ones Worthy of Offerings, and Perfectly and Universally Enlightened Ones in the past, future, and present, they should learn prajna paramita. If the great bodhisattvas would like to go to the other shore by crossing all conditioned and unconditioned dharmas, they should learn prajna paramita. If the great bodhisattvas would like to study thoroughly realness, dharma realm, dharma nature, nonarising, and the reality of various dharmas in the past, future, and present, they should learn prajna paramita. If the great bodhisattvas would like to become the leaders of all voice-hearers and self-enlightened ones, they should learn prajna paramita. If the great bodhisattvas would like to become the intimate attendants of various Buddhas, they should learn prajna paramita. If the great bodhisattvas would like to become the intimate associates of various Buddhas, they should learn prajna paramita. If the great bodhisattvas would like to have a large group of associates for every generation to come, they should learn prajna paramita. If the great bodhisattvas would like to have other bodhisattvas as their family and associates, they should learn prajna paramita.

"If the great bodhisattvas would like to purify their bodies and make themselves worthy of respect and offerings made by the world, they should learn prajna paramita. If the great bodhisattvas would like to destroy and overcome the mind of stinginess and greediness forever, they should learn prajna paramita. If the great bodhisattvas are determined never to have a single idea arise to violate the precepts again, they should learn prajna paramita. If the great bodhisattvas would like to remove all kinds of anger and hatred forever, they should learn prajna paramita. If the great bodhisattvas would like to get rid of various kinds of slack and laziness forever, they should learn prajna paramita. If the great bodhisattvas would like to end all kinds of restless and distracted minds forever, they should learn prajna paramita. If the great bodhisattvas would like to stay far away from all kinds of wisdom abuse forever, they should learn prajna paramita. If the great bodhisattvas would like to establish all sentient beings in beneficial works leading to happiness through practicing giving, through cultivation, by making offerings, or by providing a base of reliance, they should learn prajna paramita. If the great bodhisattvas would like to attain the five eyes, namely the physical eyes, heavenly eyes, wisdom eyes, dharma eyes, and the Buddha eyes, they should learn prajna paramita.

"Furthermore, Sariputra, if the great bodhisattvas would like to use their heavenly eyes to see all the Buddhas in as many worlds of the ten directions as the sands of the Ganges, they should learn prajna paramita. If the great bodhisattvas would like to hear by using their heavenly ears all the correct dharma taught by the Buddhas in as many worlds of the ten directions as the sands of the Ganges, they should learn prajna paramita. If the great bodhisattvas would like to know accurately the minds and the associated images of the Buddhas in as many worlds of the ten directions as the sands of the Ganges, they should learn prajna paramita. If the great bodhisattvas would like to hear, tirelessly and constantly, the dharma teachings given by the Buddhas in as many worlds of the ten directions as the sands of the Ganges and never forget what they have heard until attaining the unsurpassed, perfect, and universal bodhi, they should learn prajna paramita. If the great bodhisattvas would like to see all Buddha lands of the ten directions in the past, future, and present, they should learn prajna paramita. If the great bodhisattvas would like to hear the sutras, teachings partially given in verses, prophecies, teachings all given in verses, teachings initiated by Buddha, cause and condition, accomplishment, previous lives, elaborated teachings, unusual conducts, similes, and discourses, which are taught by the Buddhas of the ten directions in the past, future, and present and which have either been heard or have not been heard by the voice-hearers, and would like to understand thoroughly their essential, profound meanings, they should learn prajna paramita. If the great bodhisattvas would like to accept, embrace, read, and recite the dharma gates taught by the Buddhas of the ten directions in the past, future, and present and further understand them thoroughly, explain their essential meanings perfectly, and teach them extensively to others, they should learn prajna paramita. If the great bodhisattvas would like not only to cultivate all the dharma gates taught by the Buddhas of the ten directions in the past, future, and present, but also encourage expediently others to practice them down to the ground, they should learn prajna paramita.

"The great bodhisattvas should learn prajna paramita if they would like to bring lights to as many dark hells or the worlds without sun and moon in the ten directions as the sands of the Ganges. The great bodhisattvas should learn prajna paramita if they would like to enlighten expediently as many ignorant worlds of the ten directions as the sands of the Ganges, where incorrect views flourish; the sentient beings do not know about the evil and the virtuous deeds. They do not believe in causality. They do not believe that there are lives in the past and future. They do not believe in the four noble truths of suffering, the cause of suffering, the cessation of suffering, and the path for the cessation of suffering. They do not believe that the practice of giving, pure precept, forbearance, diligence, meditation, and prajna can bring about positive results in the world and beyond the world; and they have never heard about the Buddha, the dharma, and the sangha. The great bodhisattvas should learn prajna paramita if they intend to educate the sentient beings there expediently so they will greatly rejoice upon hearing the names of the triple gem, practice the virtuous conducts, and stay away from the evil conducts. The great bodhisattvas should learn prajna paramita if they would like to assist, with their own virtues and powers, the sentient beings in as many worlds of the ten directions as the sands of the Ganges, so that the blind can see, the deaf can hear, the dumb can speak, the insane can be in peace, the wandering minds concentrate, the poor become rich, the naked are given clothes, the hungry are fed, the thirsty drink, the ills are healed, the ugly become pretty, the handicapped are recovered, the deficiency in organs are perfected, the lost minds are awakened, and the tired have rest. The great bodhisattvas should learn prajna paramita if they would like to guide, with their own virtues and powers, the sentient beings in as many worlds of the ten directions as the sands of the Ganges so they will treat each other lovingly and kindly as parents, brothers, sisters, friends, and relatives, and never do anything to harm the others; rather, they will always do things beneficial to each other.

"The great bodhisattvas should learn prajna paramita if they would like to assist the sentient beings, with their own virtues and powers, in as many worlds of the ten directions as the sands of the Ganges, so that those in inferior destinies can be reborn in virtuous destinies and those already in virtuous destinies will never be reborn in inferior destinies. The great bodhisattvas should learn prajna paramita if they would like to assist the sentient beings, with their virtues and powers, in as many worlds of the ten directions so that those who are used to negative karma convert to positive karma and keep on this tirelessly. The great bodhisattvas should learn prajna paramita if they would like to assist the sentient beings, with their own virtues and powers, in as many worlds of the ten directions as the sands of the Ganges, so that those who are used to violating pure precept will dwell in precepts, the distracted and wandering minds will stay in concentration, the ignorant will dwell in wisdom, the fettered will dwell in freedom, and those who know nothing of liberation will dwell in the knowledge and views of liberation. The great bodhisattvas should learn prajna paramita if they would like to assist the sentient beings, with their own virtues and powers, in as many worlds of the ten directions as the sands of the Ganges, so that those who have not grasped the truth will grasp it and are able to dwell in stream-entry effect, once-return effect, or nonreturn effect and will attain arhat effect, self-enlightenment bodhi, or the unsurpassed, perfect, and universal bodhi. The great bodhisattvas should learn prajna paramita if they would like to have the same superior appearance and demeanors as the Buddha does, which the sentient beings are delighted to watch tirelessly and by which all are inspired to stop evils and do all kinds of virtuous things.

"Furthermore, Sariputra, the great bodhisattvas once thought, 'When can I teach the dharma to the public in a solemn demeanor as with the gaze of an elephant king?' In order to achieve this purpose, they should learn prajna paramita.

"The great bodhisattvas once thought, 'When can I attain pure action, speech, and mind in accordance with wisdom at all times?' In order to achieve this purpose, they should learn prajna paramita.

"The great bodhisattvas once thought, 'When can I walk freely with my feet off the ground with a four-finger distance?' In order to achieve this purpose, they should learn prajna paramita.

"The great bodhisattvas once thought, 'When can I be worthy of the offerings made with respect and admiration by innumerable hundreds of thousands of koti nayuta of heavenly beings and the dragons in the heavens, namely the Heaven of Four Great Kings, the Heaven of Thirty-Three Smaller Heavens, the Heaven of Yama, the Heaven of Tusita, the Heaven of Enjoying Self-Made Changes, the Heaven of Enjoying Other-Made Changes, the Heaven of Brahma Followers, the Heaven of Brahma Subordinates, the Heaven of Brahma Family, the Heaven of Great Brahma, the Heaven of Light, the Heaven of Lesser Light, the Heaven of Infinite Light, the Heaven of Extremely Great Brightness and Purity, the Heaven of Purity, the Heaven of Lesser Purity, the Heaven of Infinite Purity, the Heaven of Universal Purity, the Heaven of Expansion, the Heaven of Lesser Expansion, the Heaven of Infinite Expansion, the Heaven of Extensive Rewards, the Heaven of No Aspiration, the Heaven of No Affliction, the Heaven of Good Appearance, the Heaven of Good Sight, and the Heaven of Ultimate Form, and be ushered and surrounded by them when I walk toward the bodhi tree?' If the great bodhisattva would like to fulfill this wish, they should learn prajna paramita.

"The great bodhisattvas once thought, 'When can I sit under the bodhi tree on the mattress made of treasured cloths provided by immeasurable hundreds of thousands of koti nayuta of heavenly beings from the Heaven of Four Great Kings, the Heaven of Thirty-Three Smaller Heavens, and so forth, as well as the Heaven of Ultimate Form, and by the dragons?' If the great bodhisattvas would like to fulfill this wish, they should learn prajna paramita.

"The great bodhisattvas once thought, 'When can I sit with the legs crossed under the bodhi tree, soothe and comfort the vast land with my graceful hands that are glorified by wonderful features, and inspire the earth gods and their family members to rise from underground to witness what I am doing?' If the great bodhisattvas would like to fulfill this wish, they should learn prajna paramita.

"The great bodhisattvas once thought, 'When can I sit under the bodhi tree, subjugate all evil demons, and attain the unsurpassed, perfect, and universal bodhi?' If the great bodhisattvas would like to fulfill this wish, they should learn prajna paramita.

"The great bodhisattvas once thought, 'Will the places around me turn into diamonds when I walk, stay, sit, or lie after I attain the unsurpassed, perfect, and universal enlightenment?' In order to achieve this purpose, they should learn prajna paramita.

"The great bodhisattvas once thought, 'Can I attain the unsurpassed, perfect, and universal enlightenment the day when I renounce the high position in my country and become a monk? Can I start to turn the wonderful dharma wheel the same day when I become a monk, so I am able to immediately assist immeasurable sentient beings to get far away from dusts and defilements and obtain pure dharma eye? Can I further assist immeasurable sentient beings to eliminate flaws permanently and obtain the liberation of wisdom? Can I again assist immeasurable sentient beings to persevere in the pursuit of the unsurpassed bodhi without regression?' In order to achieve all these purposes, they should learn prajna paramita.

"The great bodhisattvas once thought, 'When can I attain the unsurpassed bodhi and have immeasurable voice-hearers and bodhisattvas as my disciples, and whenever I teach the dharma, immeasurable sentient beings will attain arhat effect even without rising from their seats? And moreover, will immeasurable sentient beings achieve nonregression in the pursuit of the unsurpassed bodhi even

Fascicle 3, Chapter 2, Section 1   69

without rising from their seats?' In order to achieve these purposes, they should learn prajna paramita.

"The great bodhisattvas once thought, 'When can I acquire an endless longevity, boundless brightness, and glorious and dignified appearance so that whoever sees me will not be bored? So that as I walk, a thousand-leaf lotus will support my feet, and the sign of a thousand-spoke wheel from my soles will remain on the ground? So that as I raise my leg to walk, the earth will be greatly shocked, and the sentient beings living underground will not be disturbed? So that as I look around, my whole body will turn accordingly, and wherever I walk, the ground around me will turn into diamonds and the earth about the size of a wheel will move accordingly?' In order to achieve these purposes, they should learn prajna paramita.

"The great bodhisattvas once thought, 'When can I have all my limbs emit lights to shine over boundless worlds of the ten directions and wherever the lights shine, the sentient beings will be greatly benefited?' In order to achieve these purposes, they should learn prajna paramita.

"The great bodhisattvas once thought, 'When can I attain the unsurpassed, perfect, and universal bodhi so that in my Buddha land there will be no names for greed, anger, and ignorance, nor are heard the inferior destinies such as the hells, the realm of the animals, and the realm of the ghosts?' If the great bodhisattvas would like to fulfill this wish, they should learn prajna paramita.

"The great bodhisattvas once thought, 'When can I attain the unsurpassed, perfect, and universal bodhi so that all the sentient beings in my Buddha land will obtain the wonderful wisdom as those in other Buddha lands do and always think, "Isn't it wonderful to practice giving, taming and overcoming, forbearance, brave progress, tranquility, and insightful contemplation; stay away from laziness and slack; practice celibacy, loving-kindness, compassion, joy, equanimity; and all will not annoy each other?' If the great bodhisattvas would like to fulfill this wish, they should learn prajna paramita.

"The great bodhisattvas once thought, 'When can I attain the unsurpassed, perfect, and universal bodhi so that all the sentient beings in my Buddha land will achieve superior merits and virtues and will be admired by the Buddhas and bodhisattvas in the rest of the Buddha lands?' If the great bodhisattvas would like to fulfill this wish, they should learn prajna paramita.

"The great bodhisattvas once thought, 'When can I attain the unsurpassed, perfect, and universal bodhi so that after teaching as much as possible to the sentient beings, I will enter into nirvana, and afterward I will continue to do things to benefit the sentient beings so the correct dharma will go on without discontinuation?' If the great bodhisattvas would like to fulfill this wish, they should learn prajna paramita.

"The great bodhisattvas once thought, 'When can I attain the unsurpassed, perfect, and universal bodhi so that the sentient beings in as many worlds of the ten directions as the sands of the Ganges will also be able to definitely attain the unsurpassed, perfect, and universal bodhi, if they have only ever heard my name?' If the great bodhisattvas would like to fulfill this wish, they should learn prajna paramita.

"Sariputra! In order to attain these immeasurable, countless, and inconceivable rare merits and virtues, the great bodhisattvas should learn prajna paramita."

FASCICLE 4

Chapter 2
Learning Contemplation

Section 2

(In the First Assembly)

THE BUDDHA SAID TO SARIPUTRA, "IF THE GREAT bodhisattvas cultivate prajna paramita, they will be able to fulfill all these merits and virtues. At that time, the four heavenly kings of the large threefold thousand-world will be thrilled and will think, 'Now we should present four bowls to the bodhisattvas, as our ancient heavenly kings did to the Buddha in the past.' Right at this moment, the Heaven of Thirty-Three Smaller Heavens, the Heaven of Yama, the Heaven of Tusita, the Heaven of Enjoying Self-Made Changes, and the Heaven of Enjoying Other-Made Changes in the large threefold thousand-world will also be thrilled and will think, 'We should make offerings with respect and admiration to such great bodhisattvas so that the powers of vicious asuras gangs will be diminished and the heavenly sentient beings will benefit.' It is right at this moment, the Heaven of Brahma Followers, the Heaven of Brahma Subordinates, the Heaven of Brahma Family, the Heaven of Great Brahma, the Heaven of Light, the Heaven of Lesser Light, the Heaven of Infinite Light, the Heaven of Extremely

Great Brightness and Purity, the Heaven of Purity, the Heaven of Lesser Purity, the Heaven of Infinite Purity, the Heaven of Universal Purity, the Heaven of Expansion, the Heaven of Lesser Expansion, the Heaven of Infinite Expansion, the Heaven of Extensive Rewards, the Heaven of No Aspiration, the Heaven of No Affliction, the Heaven of Good Appearance, the Heaven of Good Sight, and the Heaven of Ultimate Form will all be thrilled and will think, 'We must plead these bodhisattvas to attain the unsurpassed, perfect, and universal bodhi very soon, and turn the dharma wheel to benefit all sentient beings.'

"Sariputra! When seeing the great bodhisattvas cultivate prajna paramita and work to develop the six paramitas, the good gentlemen, gentlewomen, and so forth, will be thrilled and will think, 'We would like to become the parents, brothers, sisters, wives, family, and virtuous and knowledgeable friends of these great bodhisattvas. Because of the convenience caused by this close relationship, it will become easier for us to cultivate various good karmas and so we will be able to attain the unsurpassed, perfect, and universal bodhi.' In the meantime, the heavenly beings in the Heaven of Four Great Kings, and so forth, as well as the Heaven of Ultimate Form in that world will see and hear this. They will be also thrilled and will think, 'We would like to do anything helpful to assist these great bodhisattvas so they will stay away from impure actions and always practice celibacy from the time of beginning to aspire to pursue the great bodhi until becoming a Buddha. Why? Anything contaminated by desires will stand in the way for one to be reborn in the heaven, let alone for one to attain the unsurpassed, perfect, and universal bodhi.' Therefore, only if the great bodhisattvas cut off desires, renounce family, and cultivate celibacy will they be able to attain the unsurpassed, perfect, and universal bodhi. Those who do not cultivate this way will not."

Sariputra then asked the Buddha, "World-Honored One! Should great bodhisattvas have parents, wives, relatives, and friends?"

The Buddha replied to the long-lived sage Sariputra, "Some bodhisattvas who cultivate great bodhisattva actions do have parents, wives, and family, while some have no wife and always practice celibacy since the day of beginning to aspire to the great bodhi until finally becoming a Buddha. Some great bodhisattvas have demonstrated to live a life containing the five desires in an expedient way, and later they will renounce the family, practice celibacy, and finally attain the unsurpassed, perfect, and universal bodhi. Sariputra! It is like a master magician who makes a trick of showing people the illusion that he is indulged in the pleasure of five desires. What do you think about this? Is the illusion real?"

Sariputra replied, "No, World-Honored One! No, Well Gone One!"

The Buddha said, "Sariputra! The same is with the great bodhisattvas. In order to assist the sentient beings with maturing, they show expediently and skillfully a transformed life of enjoying the five desires. But it is not real. These great bodhisattvas find the five desires distasteful. They are not contaminated. Besides, they also scold the five desires by using negative words: desire is a burning fire that destroys one's mind and body; desire is filthy and should be avoided before it contaminates oneself and others; desire as the chief criminal is always harmful in the past, the future, and the present; desire is an enemy who has waited long enough to do destructive things; desire is like a torch made out of grasses; desire is like a bitter fruit; desire is like a sharp sword; desire is like a whirling fire in a circle; desire is like a poisoned arrow or something like that; desire is like a puzzling illusion; desire is like a dark well; desire is like a deceiving person or a violent person. Sariputra, the bodhisattvas use numberless negative phrases to rebuke all kinds of desire, make people know all the faults that desire may cause, and show that desire is an illusion and is not real. In order to teach and benefit the sentient beings, they adopt expedient methods to show that they get involved in desires, but actually they do not."

At that time, Sariputra asked the Buddha, "World-Honored One, how should great bodhisattvas practice prajna paramita?"

The Buddha said to the long-lived sage Sariputra, "Sariputra, when cultivating prajna paramita, the great bodhisattvas should contemplate this way: 'A bodhisattva actually does not see a bodhisattva or the name of a bodhisattva; he or she does not see prajna paramita or the name of prajna paramita; he or she does not see action or nonaction.' Why? Sariputra, the self-nature of bodhisattva is empty, while the name of bodhisattva is empty too. Why? The self-nature of matter is empty, but it is not because of emptiness. The emptiness of matter is not matter. Matter is not apart from emptiness, while emptiness is not apart from matter. Matter is emptiness, while emptiness is matter. The self-natures of feeling, thinking, action, and consciousness are empty, but it is not because of emptiness. The emptiness of feeling, thinking, action, and consciousness is not feeling, thinking, action, and consciousness. Feeling, thinking, action, and consciousness are not apart from emptiness, while emptiness is not apart from feeling, thinking, action, and consciousness. Feeling, thinking, action, and consciousness are emptiness, while emptiness is feeling, thinking, action, and consciousness. Why? Sariputra, bodhi is only a name, sattva is only a name, bodhisattva is only a name, and emptiness is only a name. Feeling, thinking, action, and consciousness are only the names. Such self-nature has no arising, extinction, contamination, or purification. When cultivating prajna paramita this way, the great bodhisattvas do not see arising, extinction, contamination, or purification. Why? These are only provisionally established names used to indicate different dharmas, and based on these names, the differentiation of the dharmas appears. These are then followed by the languages, and because of such and such languages, attachment is produced. When cultivating prajna paramita, the great bodhisattvas do not see all of these, and thus they have no attachment.

"Furthermore, Sariputra, when cultivating prajna paramita, the great bodhisattvas should contemplate this way: 'Bodhisattva is just a name, Buddha is just a name, and prajna paramita is just a name. Matter is just a name; feeling, thinking, intention, or consciousness are just names. The eye sphere is just a name; the ear, nose, tongue, body or the conscious sphere are just names. The sight sphere is just a name; the sound, smell, taste, touch or mental-image sphere are just names. The eye realm is just a name; the ear, nose, tongue, body, or conscious realm are just names. The sight realm is just a name; the sound, smell, taste, contact, or mental-image realm are just names. The eye consciousness realm is just a name; the ear consciousness realm, nose consciousness realm, tongue consciousness realm, body consciousness realm, and the conscious consciousness realm are just names. The eye contact is just a name; the ear contact, nose contact, tongue contact, body contact, and conscious contact are just names. The feelings produced by the eye contact is just a name; the feelings produced by the ear contact, nose contact, tongue contact, body contact, or conscious contact is just a name. The earth realm is just a name; the water, fire, wind, space, and consciousness realms are just names. The concept of cause and condition is just a name; consecutive thoughts in sequence, the conditions that stimulate the mind, and the conditions that reinforce main causes are just names. All dharmas produced by conditions are just names. Ignorance is just a name; action, consciousness, name and form, six sense spheres, contact, reception, craving, grasping, existence, birth, old age, death, worry, sorrow, misery, anxiety, and upset are just names. Giving paramita is just a name; pure-precept paramita, forbearance paramita, diligence paramita, meditation paramita, and prajna paramita are just names. Internal emptiness is just a name; external emptiness, internal-external emptiness, emptiness of emptiness, emptiness of space, emptiness of ultimate truth, emptiness of the conditioned phenomena, emptiness of the unconditioned reality, emptiness in the final analysis, emptiness of nontemporality, emptiness of deconstruction, emptiness of changelessness, emptiness of original nature, emptiness of particular characteristics, emptiness of common characteristics, emptiness of all dharmas, emptiness of nonattainment, emptiness of selflessness, emptiness of self-nature, and emptiness of selfless self-nature are just names. The four bases of mindfulness are just names; the four correct endeavors, four bases of power, five roots, five powers, seven factors for enlightenment, and noble eightfold path are just names. The liberation gate of emptiness is just a name; the liberation gate of formlessness and the liberation gate of nonaspiration are just names. The noble truth of suffering is just a name; the noble truths of the cause of suffering, the cessation of suffering, and the path for the cessation of suffering are just names. The four meditations are just names; the four immeasurable minds and the four formless concentrations are just names. The eight liberations are just names; the eight vexation-overcoming meditations, nine concentrations in sequence, and the ten universal contemplations are just names.

Dharani gates is just a name; samadhi gates is just a name. The stage of ecstasy is just a name; the stage of freedom from defilements, of emitting light, of flaming wisdom, of being extremely difficult to be surpassed, of the manifestation of the pure realness, of going far away, of the unmovable, of expedient wisdom, and of dharma cloud are just names. The stage of ordinary sentient being is just a name; the stage of embryonic Buddha nature, the stage of eight-forbearance, the stage of insight, the stage of slight desire, the stage of freedom from desires, the stage of arhat, the stage of self-enlightened one, the stage of bodhisattva, and the stage of Thus-Comer are just names. The five eyes is just a name. The six supernatural powers is just a name. The Buddha's ten abilities is just a name; the four kinds of fearlessness, four unhindered understandings, great loving-kindness, great compassion, great joy, great equanimity, and the eighteen distinctive features of Buddha's wisdom and power are just names. The thirty-two perfect major marks is just a name; the eighty distinguishing minor features is just a name. Staying in correct mindfulness is just a name; dwelling in equanimity at all times is just a name. The perfect knowledge of everything is just a name; the perfect knowledge of the forms of the paths and the perfect knowledge of all phenomena are just names. The perfect knowledge of all perfect knowledge is just a name. Removing the long-rooted disposition of vexations forever is just a name. The stream-entry stage is just a name; the stages of once return, non-return, and arhat are just names; self-enlightenment bodhi is just a name; all bodhisattva actions are just names; the unsurpassed, perfect, and universal bodhi of the Buddhas is just a name. The dharma of the world is just a name; the dharma beyond the world is just a name. The flawed dharma is just a name; the flawless dharma is just a name. The conditioned dharma is just a name; and the unconditioned dharma is just a name too.'

"Sariputra, 'I' is just a name. The so-called 'I' is actually unattainable, so are the sentient being, the living one, the one who gives birth, the one who raises others, the gentleperson, the individual in reincarnation, the mentally born one, the learned child, the maker, the one who makes others make, the elicitor, the one who makes others elicit, the receiver, the one who makes others receive, the

Fascicle 4, Chapter 2, Section 2

knower, and the viewer are just names. They are unattainable and empty. They are provisionally established names, and so are all dharmas; therefore, one should not be attached to them. When cultivating prajna paramita, the great bodhisattvas do not see the 'I,' the sentient being, and so forth, as well as the viewer, nor do they see the dharma natures.

"Sariputra, if the great bodhisattvas cultivate prajna paramita this way, they will attain the wisdom inferior only to the Buddha, but much more superior to the wisdom owned by all voice-hearers and self-enlightened ones because of the emptiness of nonattainment. Why? The great bodhisattvas view the names and the objects named as unattainable. They do not see them, nor are they attached to them. Sariputra, if the great bodhisattvas cultivate prajna paramita this way, they are named good practitioners of prajna paramita. Sariputra, suppose that you and Mahamaudgalyayana practice wisdom that appears as many fields of rice, hemp, bamboo, reeds, and sugarcane as to fill the entire continent of Jambudvipa, while on the other hand the great bodhisattvas practice prajna paramita. In comparison, the former will be less than the latter by one hundredth, one thousandth, one hundred-thousandth, one kotith, one hundred kotith, one thousand kotith, one hundred thousand kotith, too little to be counted, reckoned, measured, and demonstrated, even as little as one upanisadam-api. Why? The bodhisattva wisdom will guide all sentient beings toward nirvana, while the wisdom of the voice-hearer and self-enlightened one will not. Moreover, Sariputra, the wisdom that the great bodhisattvas as prajna paramita practitioners cultivate in one day will be far ahead of what all voice-hearers and self-enlightened ones can reach.

"Sariputra, let us put Jambudvipa aside. Suppose that you and Mahamaudgalyayana practice wisdom that appears as many fields of rice, hemp, bamboo, reeds, and sugarcane as to fill all the four continents, while on the other hand the great bodhisattvas practice prajna paramita. In comparison, the former will be less than the latter by one hundredth, one thousandth, one hundred thousandth, one kotith, one hundred kotith, one thousand kotith, one hundred thousand kotith, too little to be counted, reckoned, measured, and demonstrated, even as little as one upanisadam-api. Why? The bodhisattva wisdom will guide all sentient beings toward nirvana, while the wisdom of the voice-hearer and self-enlightened one will not. Moreover, Sariputra, the wisdom that the great bodhisattvas as prajna paramita practitioners cultivate in one day will be far ahead of what all voice-hearers and self-enlightened ones can reach.

"Sariputra, let us put the four continents aside at this moment. Suppose that you and Mahamaudgalyayana practice wisdom that appears as many fields of rice, hemp, bamboo, reeds, and sugarcane as to fill the entire large threefold thousand-world, while on the other hand the great bodhisattvas practice prajna paramita. In comparison, the former will be less than the latter by one hundredth, one thousandth, one hundred thousandth, one kotith, one hundred kotith, one thousand kotith, one hundred thousand kotith, too little to be counted, reckoned, measured, and demonstrated, even as little as one upanisadam-api. Why? The bodhisattva wisdom will guide all sentient beings toward nirvana, while the wisdom of the voice-hearer and self-enlightened one will not. Moreover, Sariputra, the wisdom that the great bodhisattvas as prajna paramita practitioners cultivate in one day will be far ahead of what all voice-hearers and self-enlightened ones can reach.

"Sariputra, let us put the large threefold thousand-world aside. Suppose that you and Mahamaudgalyayana practice wisdom that appears as many fields of rice, hemp, bamboo, reeds, and sugarcane as to fill as many Buddha worlds in the ten directions as the sands of the Ganges, while on the other hand the great bodhisattvas practice prajna paramita. In comparison, the former will be less than the latter by one hundredth, one thousandth, one hundred thousandth, one kotith, one hundred kotith, one thousand kotith, one hundred thousand kotith, too little to be counted, reckoned, measured, and demonstrated, even as little as one upanisadam-api. Why? The bodhisattva wisdom will guide all sentient beings toward nirvana, while the wisdom of the voice-hearer and self-enlightened one will not. Moreover, Sariputra, the wisdom that the great bodhisattvas as prajna paramita practitioners practice in one day will be far ahead of what all voice-hearers and self-enlightened ones can reach."

At that time, Sariputra asked the Buddha, "World-Honored One, if there is no difference among the wisdom of stream-entry, once-return, nonreturn, and arhat; the wisdom of self-enlightenment bodhi; the wisdom of great bodhisattva; and the wisdom of the Thus-Comer, One Worthy of Offerings, Perfectly and Universally Enlightened One, if all these kinds of wisdom are not in conflict, they are without arising and extinction, and their self-natures are empty, and if the differences of all these dharmas are unattainable, then why does the World-Honored One say that the wisdom that the great bodhisattvas as prajna paramita practitioners cultivate in one day will be much higher than the wisdom that all voice-hearers and self-enlightened ones practice?"

The Buddha said to the long-lived sage Sariputra, "What do you think about this: do the superior things that happen when the great bodhisattvas as prajna paramita practitioners cultivate wisdom in one day also happen with the wisdom practiced by all voice-hearers and self-enlightened ones?"

Sariputra replied, "No, World-Honored One! No, Well Gone One!"

"Moreover, Sariputra, a great bodhisattva has cultivated prajna paramita for one day and thought, 'I must cultivate the exquisite and subtle knowledge of all phenomena, the perfect knowledge of everything, the perfect knowledge of the forms of the paths, and the perfect knowledge of all phenomena so that I can bring benefits, peace, and happiness to all sentient beings.' After being awakened to all phenomena in all dharmas, this great bodhisattva will establish all sentient beings in nirvana without remainder. What do you think about this: does the wisdom of voice-hearers and self-enlightened ones also inspire them to do so?"

Sariputra replied, "No, World-Honored One! No, Well Gone One!"

"Moreover, Sariputra, what do you think about this: do all voice-hearers and self-enlightened ones think, 'I must realize and attain the unsurpassed, perfect, and universal bodhi so that I can expediently establish all sentient beings in nirvana without remainder?'"

Sariputra replied, "No, World-Honored One! No, Well Gone One!"

"Furthermore, Sariputra, do all voice-hearers and self-enlightened ones think, 'I must cultivate giving, pure precept, forbearance, diligence, meditation, and prajna paramitas. I must cultivate the superior four bases of mindfulness, four correct endeavors, four bases of powers, five roots, five powers, seven factors for enlightenment, and the noble eightfold path. I must cultivate the superior four meditations, four immeasurable minds, and four formless meditations. I must cultivate the superior eight liberations, eight vexation-overcoming meditations, nine concentrations in sequence, and the ten universal contemplations. I must cultivate the superior liberation gates of emptiness, formlessness, and nonaspiration. I must dwell in internal emptiness, external emptiness, internal-external emptiness, emptiness of emptiness, emptiness of space, emptiness of ultimate truth, emptiness of conditioned phenomena, emptiness of unconditioned reality, emptiness in the final analysis, emptiness of nontemporality, emptiness of deconstruction, emptiness of changelessness, emptiness of original nature, emptiness of particular characteristics, emptiness of common characteristics, emptiness of all dharmas, emptiness of nonattainment, emptiness of selflessness, emptiness of self-nature, and emptiness of selfless self-nature. I must dwell in realness, dharma realm, dharma nature, nature of nonillusion, nature of changelessness, nature of equality, nature of nonarising, dharma concentration, dharma dwelling, reality, the realm of empty space, and the realm of the inconceivable. I must dwell in the superior noble truths of suffering, the cause of suffering, the cessation of suffering, and the path for the cessation of suffering. I must cultivate all dharani gates and all samadhi gates. I must cultivate the ten stages of bodhisattva, namely the stages of ecstasy, freedom from defilements, emitting light, flaming wisdom, being extremely difficult to be surpassed, manifestation of pure realness, going far away, the unmovable, expedient wisdom, and dharma cloud. I must fulfill the supernatural powers of bodhisattva to their perfection, assist the sentient beings to mature, and purify and dignify the Buddha lands. I must fulfill the five eyes and the six supernatural powers to their perfection. I must fulfill the Buddha's ten abilities, four kinds of fearlessness, four unhindered understandings, great loving-kindness, great compassion, great joy, great equanimity, and the eighteen distinctive features of Buddha's

Fascicle 4, Chapter 2, Section 2   81

wisdom and power to their perfection. I must fulfill the thirty-two perfect major marks and the eighty distinguishing minor features to their perfection. I must fulfill staying in correct mindfulness and dwelling in equanimity at all times to their perfection. I must fulfill the perfect knowledge of everything, the perfect knowledge of the forms of the paths, and the perfect knowledge of all phenomena to their perfection. I must remove the long-rooted disposition of vexations forever and attain the unsurpassed, perfect, and universal bodhi in order to guide expediently immeasurable, countless, and boundless sentient beings and establish them in the nirvana without remainder'?"

Sariputra replied, "No, World-Honored One! No, Well Gone One!"

The Buddha said, "Sariputra! All the great bodhisattvas who are cultivating prajna paramita will think, 'I must cultivate giving, pure precept, forbearance, diligence, meditation, and prajna paramitas, and so forth, as well as remove my long-rooted disposition of vexations forever, and finally attain the unsurpassed, perfect, and universal bodhi so that I can guide expediently immeasurable, countless, and boundless sentient beings and establish them well in the nirvana without remainder.'

"Sariputra, it is like the firefly who does not think, 'I hope my light will shine all over the entire continent of Jambudvipa and illuminate it.' So all the voice-hearers and self-enlightened ones will not think, 'I must cultivate giving, pure precept, forbearance, diligence, meditation, and prajna paramitas, and so forth, as well as eliminate the long-rooted disposition of vexations forever; I must realize insightfully the unsurpassed, perfect, and universal bodhi and expediently establish immeasurable, countless, and boundless sentient beings in the nirvana without remainder.' Sariputra, like the bright and flaming sun that illuminates the entire continent of Jambudvipa universally, so do the great bodhisattvas who cultivate prajna paramita and think, 'I must cultivate giving, pure precept, forbearance, diligence, meditation, and prajna paramitas, and so forth, as well as eliminate the long-rooted disposition of vexations forever; realize insightfully the unsurpassed, perfect, and universal bodhi; and expediently establish immeasurable, countless, and boundless sentient beings in the nirvana without remainder.'

"So, Sariputra, you must know that in comparing the wisdom practiced by all voice-hearers and self-enlightened ones with the wisdom practiced in one day by the great bodhisattvas who are cultivating prajna paramita, the former is less than the latter by one hundredth, one thousandth, one hundred-thousandth, too little to be counted, reckoned, measured, and demonstrated, and even as little as one upanisadam-api."

At that time, Sariputra asked the Buddha, "World-Honored One, how do the great bodhisattvas surpass all stages of voice-hearing and self-enlightenment, reach the stage of bodhisattva without regression, and purify the unsurpassed bodhi path of Buddha?"

The Buddha replied to the long-lived sage Sariputra, "Since the time of beginning to aspire to practice giving, pure precept, forbearance, diligence, meditation, prajna, expedient skillfulness, wonderful aspiration, abilities, and perfect knowledge paramitas, and to dwell in the liberation gates of emptiness, formlessness, and nonaspiration, the great bodhisattvas have already surpassed all voice-hearers and self-enlightened ones, achieved the stage of nonregression, and been able to purify the unsurpassed bodhi path of Buddha."

Meanwhile, Sariputra asked the Buddha again, "World-Honored One! In which stage do the great bodhisattvas work together with all voice-hearers and self-enlightened ones for making the real fields of bliss?"

The Buddha replied to the long-lived sage Sariputra, "Sariputra! From the beginning, when the great bodhisattvas are determined to practice giving, pure precept, forbearance, diligence, meditation, prajna, expedient skillfulness, wonderful aspiration, abilities, and perfect knowledge paramitas and dwell in the liberation gates of emptiness, formlessness, and nonaspiration and so forth until they sit steadily on the throne of wonderful bodhi, they have always worked with all voice-hearers and self-enlightened ones for making the real fields of bliss. Why? Sariputra! Because of the great bodhisattvas, all virtuous dharmas appear in the world, namely the path of the ten virtuous karmas, five precepts for lay believers, eight precepts for lay believers, four meditations, four immeasurable minds, four formless concentrations, and the bliss-inviting practice of giving, pure precept, and meditation. Because of the great bodhisattvas, the four bases of mindfulness, four correct endeavors, four bases of powers, five roots, five powers, seven factors for enlightenment, and the noble eightfold path; the liberation gates of emptiness, formlessness, and nonaspiration; and the noble truths of suffering, the cause of suffering, the cessation of suffering, and the path for the cessation of suffering appear in the world. Because of the great bodhisattvas, giving, pure precept, forbearance, diligence, meditation, and prajna paramitas appear in the world. Because of the great bodhisattvas, internal emptiness, external emptiness, internal-external emptiness, emptiness of emptiness, emptiness of space, emptiness of ultimate truth, emptiness of conditioned phenomena, emptiness of unconditioned reality, emptiness in the final analysis, emptiness of nontemporality, emptiness of deconstruction, emptiness of changelessness, emptiness of original nature, emptiness of particular characteristics, emptiness of common characteristics, emptiness of all dharmas, emptiness of nonattainment, emptiness of selflessness, emptiness of self-nature, and emptiness of selfless self-nature appear in the world. Because of the great bodhisattvas, realness, dharma realm, dharma nature, the nature of nonillusion, the nature of changelessness, the nature of equality, the nature of nonarising, dharma concentration, dharma dwelling, reality, the realm of empty space, and the realm of the inconceivable appear in the world. Because of the great bodhisattvas, the eight liberations, eight vexation-overcoming meditations, nine concentrations in sequence, and the ten universal contemplations appear in the world. Because of the great bodhisattvas, all dharani gates, all samadhi gates, and the ten stages of bodhisattva appear in the world. Because of the great bodhisattvas, the five eyes and the six supernatural powers appear in the world. Because of the great bodhisattvas, the Buddha's ten abilities, four kinds of fearlessness, four unhindered understandings, great loving-kindness, great compassion, great joy, great equanimity, and the eighteen distinctive features of Buddha's wisdom and power appear in the world. Because of the great bodhisattvas, staying in correct mindfulness and dwelling in equanimity at all times appear in the world. Because of the great bodhisattvas, the perfect knowledge of everything, the perfect knowledge of the forms of the paths, and the perfect knowledge of all phenomena appear in the world. Because of the great bodhisattvas, immeasurable, countless, and boundless virtuous dharmas appear in the world, so to assist the sentient beings to mature and purify and dignify the Buddha lands.

"It is because of these virtuous dharmas of bodhisattva that the noble family of Ksatriya, noble family of Brahman, noble family of the elder, noble family of layperson, the Heaven of Four Great Kings, Heaven of Thirty-Three Smaller Heavens, Heaven of Yama, Heaven of Tusita, Heaven of Enjoying Self-Made Changes, Heaven of Enjoying Other-Made Changes, Heaven of Brahma Followers, Heaven of Brahma Subordinates, Heaven of Brahma Family, Heaven of Great Brahma, Heaven of Light, Heaven of Lesser Light, Heaven of Infinite Light, Heaven of Extremely Great Brightness and Purity, Heaven of Purity, Heaven of Lesser Purity, Heaven of Infinite Purity, Heaven of Universal Purity, Heaven of Expansion, Heaven of Lesser Expansion, Heaven of Infinite Expansion, Heaven of Extensive Rewards, Heaven of Sentient Beings without Thinking, Heaven of No Aspiration, Heaven of No Affliction, Heaven of Good Appearance, Heaven of Good Sight, Heaven of Ultimate Form, Heaven of Boundless Emptiness, Heaven of Boundless Consciousness, Heaven of Nothingness, and the Heaven of Nonthinking and Not Nonthinking appear in the world. It is again because of the virtuous dharmas of bodhisattva that stream-enterers, once-returners, nonreturners, arhats, self-enlightened ones, great bodhisattvas, and the Thus-Comers, Ones Worthy of Offerings, the Perfectly and Universally Enlightened Ones appear in the world."

At that time, Sariputra asked the Buddha, "World-Honored One, should the great bodhisattvas repay the ones who had once bestowed favors to them?"

The Buddha replied to the long-lived sage Sariputra, "They don't need to repay because they have already done more than that. Why do I say so? The great bodhisattvas have brought immeasurable virtuous dharmas to the sentient beings, so the great bodhisattvas themselves are great givers also. They bring sentient beings the path of the ten virtuous karmas, five precepts for lay believers, eight precepts for lay believers, four meditations, four immeasurable minds, four formless concentrations, and the bliss-inviting practice of giving, pure precept, and cultivation. They bring sentient beings the four bases of mindfulness, four correct endeavors, four bases of powers, five roots, five powers, seven factors for enlightenment, and the noble eightfold path; the liberation gates of emptiness, formlessness, and nonaspiration; and the noble truths of suffering, the cause of suffering, the cessation of suffering, and the path for the cessation of suffering. They bring the sentient beings giving, pure precept, forbearance, diligence, meditation, prajna, expedient skillfulness, wonderful aspiration, abilities, and knowledge paramitas. They also bring sentient beings internal emptiness, external emptiness, internal-external emptiness, emptiness of emptiness, emptiness of space, emptiness of ultimate truth, emptiness of conditioned phenomena, emptiness of unconditioned reality, emptiness in the final analysis, emptiness of nontemporality, emptiness of deconstruction, emptiness of changelessness, emptiness of original nature, emptiness of particular characteristics, emptiness of common characteristics, emptiness of all dharmas, emptiness of nonattainment, emptiness of selflessness, emptiness of self-nature, and the emptiness of selfless self-nature. They also bring all sentient beings realness, dharma realm, dharma nature, the nature of nonillusion, the nature of changelessness, the nature of equality, the nature of nonarising, dharma concentration, dharma dwelling, reality, the realm of empty space, and the realm of the inconceivable. They again bring all sentient beings the eight liberations, eight vexation-overcoming meditations, nine concentrations in sequence, and the ten universal contemplations. They bring sentient beings all dharani gates, all samadhi gates, and the ten stages of bodhisattva cultivation. They bring sentient beings the five eyes and the six supernatural powers. They further bring sentient beings the Buddha's ten abilities, four kinds of fearlessness, four unhindered understandings, great loving-kindness, great compassion, great joy, great equanimity, and the eighteen distinctive features of Buddha's wisdom and power. They again bring sentient beings staying in correct mindfulness and dwelling in equanimity at all times. They also bring all sentient beings the perfect knowledge of everything, the perfect knowledge of the forms of the paths, and the perfect knowledge of all phenomena. They also bring sentient beings unconditioned giving, speaking good and kind words, doing actions beneficial to others, getting along with others in harmony and empathy, assisting the sentient beings to mature, and dignifying and purifying the Buddha lands expediently and skillfully. They bring sentient beings the stream-entry effect, once-return effect, nonreturn effect, arhat effect, and the self-enlightenment bodhi. They also bring sentient beings all bodhisattva actions and the unsurpassed, perfect, and universal bodhi of the Buddhas.

"Sariputra, because the great bodhisattvas have given the sentient beings immeasurable, countless, and boundless virtuous dharmas, they are great givers. It is through this way that they have repaid the ones who bestow favors to them by giving them a good field in which superior blessings are planted and grow."

Chapter 3
In Accordance with Prajna Paramita

Section I

(In the First Assembly)

AT THAT TIME, SARIPUTRA ASKED THE BUDDHA, "WORLD-HONORED One, with what dharmas do the great bodhisattvas correspond when they are cultivating prajna paramita so they are said to be in accordance with prajna paramita?"

The Buddha said to the long-lived sage Sariputra, "Sariputra,

Fascicle 4, Chapter 3, Section I 87

as the great bodhisattvas who are cultivating prajna paramita correspond with the emptiness of matter, they are said to be in accordance with prajna paramita; as they correspond with the emptiness of feeling, thinking, action, and consciousness, they are said to be in accordance with prajna paramita.

"Sariputra, as the great bodhisattvas who are cultivating prajna paramita correspond with the emptiness of the eye sphere, they are said to be in accordance with prajna paramita; as they correspond with the emptiness of the ear, nose, tongue, body, and conscious spheres, they are said to be in accordance with prajna paramita.

"Sariputra, as the great bodhisattvas who are cultivating prajna paramita correspond with the emptiness of the sight sphere, they are said to be in accordance with prajna paramita; as they correspond with the emptiness of the sound, smell, taste, touch, and mental-image spheres, they are said to be in accordance with prajna paramita.

"Sariputra, as the great bodhisattvas who are cultivating prajna paramita correspond with the emptiness of the eye realm, they are said to be in accordance with prajna paramita; as they correspond with the emptiness of the ear, nose, tongue, body, and conscious realms, they are said to be in accordance with prajna paramita.

"Sariputra, as the great bodhisattvas who are cultivating prajna paramita correspond with the emptiness of the sight realm, they are said to be in accordance with prajna paramita; as they correspond with the emptiness of the sound, smell, taste, touch, and mental-image realms, they are said to be in accordance with prajna paramita.

"Sariputra, as the great bodhisattvas who are cultivating prajna paramita correspond with the emptiness of the eye consciousness realm, they are said to be in accordance with prajna paramita; as they correspond with the emptiness of the ear, nose, tongue, body, and conscious consciousness realms, they are said to be in accordance with prajna paramita.

"Sariputra, as the great bodhisattvas who are cultivating prajna paramita correspond with the emptiness of the eye contact, they are said to be in accordance with prajna paramita; as they correspond with the emptiness of the ear, nose, tongue, body, and conscious contacts, they are said to be in accordance with prajna paramita.

"Sariputra, as the great bodhisattvas who are cultivating prajna paramita correspond with the emptiness of the feelings produced by eye contact, they are said to be in accordance with prajna paramita; as they correspond with the emptiness of the feelings produced by ear, nose, tongue, body, and conscious contacts, they are said to be in accordance with prajna paramita.

"Sariputra, as the great bodhisattvas who are cultivating prajna paramita correspond with the emptiness of the earth realm, they are said to be in accordance with prajna paramita; as they correspond with the emptiness of the water, fire, wind, space, and consciousness realms, they are said to be in accordance with prajna paramita.

"Sariputra, as the great bodhisattvas who are cultivating prajna paramita correspond with the emptiness of cause and condition, they are said to be in accordance with prajna paramita; as they correspond with the emptiness of consecutive sequence of thoughts, conditions that stimulate the mind, the conditions that reinforce main causes, and the dharmas produced by conditions, they are said to be in accordance with prajna paramita.

"Sariputra, as the great bodhisattvas who are cultivating prajna paramita correspond with the emptiness of ignorance, they are said to be in accordance with prajna paramita; as they correspond with the emptiness of action, consciousness, name and form, six sense spheres, contact, reception, craving, grasping, existence, birth, old age, death, worry, sorrow, misery, anxiety, and upset, they are said to be in accordance with prajna paramita.

"Sariputra, as the great bodhisattvas who are cultivating prajna paramita correspond with the emptiness of giving paramita, they are said to be in accordance with prajna paramita; as they correspond with the emptiness of pure precept, forbearance, diligence, meditation, and prajna paramitas, they are said to be in accordance with prajna paramita.

"Sariputra, as the great bodhisattvas who are cultivating prajna paramita correspond with internal emptiness, they are said to be in accordance with prajna paramita; as they correspond with external

Fascicle 4, Chapter 3, Section I 89

emptiness, internal-external emptiness, emptiness of emptiness, emptiness of space, emptiness of ultimate truth, emptiness of conditioned phenomena, emptiness of unconditioned reality, emptiness in the final analysis, emptiness of nontemporality, emptiness of deconstruction, emptiness of changelessness, emptiness of original nature, emptiness of particular characteristics, emptiness of common characteristics, emptiness of all dharmas, emptiness of nonattainment, emptiness of selflessness, emptiness of self-nature, and emptiness of selfless self-nature, they are said to be in accordance with prajna paramita.

"Sariputra, as the great bodhisattvas who are cultivating prajna paramita correspond with the emptiness of realness, they are said to be in accordance with prajna paramita; as they correspond with the emptiness of dharma realm, dharma nature, the nature of nonillusion, the nature of changelessness, the nature of equality, the nature of nonarising, dharma concentration, dharma dwelling, reality, the realm of empty space, and the realm of the inconceivable, they are said to be in accordance with prajna paramita.

"Sariputra, as the great bodhisattvas who are cultivating prajna paramita correspond with the emptiness of the four bases of mindfulness, they are said to be in accordance with prajna paramita; as they correspond with the emptiness of the four correct endeavors, four bases of power, five roots, five powers, seven factors for enlightenment, and the noble eightfold path, they are said to be in accordance with prajna paramita.

"Sariputra, as the great bodhisattvas who are cultivating prajna paramita correspond with the emptiness of the noble truth of suffering, they are said to be in accordance with prajna paramita; as they correspond with the emptiness of the noble truths of the cause of suffering, the cessation of suffering, and the path for the cessation of suffering, they are said to be in accordance with prajna paramita.

"Sariputra, as the great bodhisattvas who are cultivating prajna paramita correspond with the emptiness of the path of the ten virtuous karmas, they are said to be in accordance with prajna paramita; as they correspond with the emptiness of the five precepts for lay believers and the eight precepts for lay believers, they are said to be in accordance with prajna paramita.

"Sariputra, as the great bodhisattvas who are cultivating prajna paramita correspond with the emptiness of bliss-inviting giving practice, they are said to be in accordance with prajna paramita; as they correspond with the emptiness of bliss-inviting precepts and cultivation, they are said to be in accordance with prajna paramita.

"Sariputra, as the great bodhisattvas who are cultivating prajna paramita correspond with the emptiness of the four meditations, they are said to be in accordance with prajna paramita; as they correspond with the emptiness of the four immeasurable minds and the four formless concentrations, they are said to be in accordance with prajna paramita.

"Sariputra, as the great bodhisattvas who are cultivating prajna paramita correspond with the emptiness of the eight liberations, they are said to be in accordance with prajna paramita; as they correspond with the emptiness of the eight vexation-overcoming meditations, nine concentrations in sequence, and the ten universal contemplations, they are said to be in accordance with prajna paramita.

"Sariputra, as the great bodhisattvas who are cultivating prajna paramita correspond with the emptiness of the liberation gate of emptiness, they are said to be in accordance with prajna paramita; as they correspond with the emptiness of the liberation gates of formlessness and nonaspiration, they are said to be in accordance with prajna paramita.

"Sariputra, as the great bodhisattvas who are cultivating prajna paramita correspond with the emptiness of all dharani gates, they are said to be in accordance with prajna paramita; as they correspond with the emptiness of all samadhi gates, they are said to be in accordance with prajna paramita.

"Sariputra, as the great bodhisattvas who are cultivating prajna paramita correspond with the emptiness of the stage of ecstasy, they are said to be in accordance with prajna paramita; as they correspond with the emptiness of the stages of freedom from defilements, emitting light, flaming wisdom, being extremely difficult to be surpassed, manifestation of pure realness, going far away, the unmovable, expedient wisdom, and dharma cloud, they are said to be in accordance with prajna paramita.

Fascicle 4, Chapter 3, Section I 91

"Sariputra, as the great bodhisattvas who are cultivating prajna paramita correspond with the emptiness of the five eyes, they are said to be in accordance with prajna paramita; as they correspond with the emptiness of the six supernatural powers, they are said to be in accordance with prajna paramita.

"Sariputra, as the great bodhisattvas who are cultivating prajna paramita correspond with the emptiness of the Buddha's ten abilities, they are said to be in accordance with prajna paramita; as they correspond with the emptiness of the four kinds of fearlessness, four unhindered understandings, great loving-kindness, great compassion, great joy, great equanimity, and the eighteen distinctive features of Buddha's wisdom and power, they are said to be in accordance with prajna paramita.

"Sariputra, as the great bodhisattvas who are cultivating prajna paramita correspond with the emptiness of the thirty-two perfect major marks, they are said to be in accordance with prajna paramita; as they correspond with the emptiness of the eighty distinguishing minor features, they are said to be in accordance with prajna paramita.

"Sariputra, as the great bodhisattvas who are cultivating prajna paramita correspond with the emptiness of staying in correct mindfulness, they are said to be in accordance with prajna paramita; as they correspond with the emptiness of dwelling in equanimity at all times, they are said to be in accordance with prajna paramita.

"Sariputra, as the great bodhisattvas who are cultivating prajna paramita correspond with the emptiness of the perfect knowledge of everything, they are said to be in accordance with prajna paramita; as they correspond with the emptiness of the perfect knowledge of the forms of the paths and the perfect knowledge of all phenomena, they are said to be in accordance with prajna paramita.

"Sariputra, as the great bodhisattvas who are cultivating prajna paramita correspond with the emptiness of the perfect knowledge of all perfect knowledge, they are said to be in accordance with prajna paramita; as they correspond with the emptiness of eliminating the long-rooted disposition of vexations, they are said to be in accordance with prajna paramita.

"Sariputra, as the great bodhisattvas who are cultivating prajna paramita correspond with the emptiness of the stream-entry effect, they are said to be in accordance with prajna paramita; as they correspond with the emptiness of the once-return effect, nonreturn effect, arhat effect, and the self-enlightenment bodhi, they are said to be in accordance with prajna paramita.

"Sariputra, as the great bodhisattvas who are cultivating prajna paramita correspond with the emptiness of all great bodhisattva actions, they are said to be in accordance with prajna paramita; as they correspond with the emptiness of the unsurpassed, perfect, and universal bodhi of the Buddhas, they are said to be in accordance with prajna paramita.

"Sariputra, as the great bodhisattvas who are cultivating prajna paramita correspond with the emptiness of the 'I,' they are said to be in accordance with prajna paramita; as they correspond with the emptiness of the sentient being, the living one, the one who gives birth, the one who rears others, the gentleperson, the individual in reincarnation, the mentally born one, the learned child, the maker, the one who makes others make, the initiator, the one who makes others initiate, the receiver, the one who makes others receive, the knower, and the viewer, they are said to be in accordance with prajna paramita.

"Sariputra, as the great bodhisattvas who are cultivating prajna paramita correspond with all these kinds of emptiness, they are said to be in accordance with prajna paramita.

"Sariputra, as the great bodhisattvas who are cultivating prajna paramita correspond with prajna paramita, they do not see if matter is correspondent or not correspondent, nor do they see if feeling, thinking, action, and consciousness are correspondent or not correspondent. Why? Sariputra! These great bodhisattvas do not see if matter is a dharma of arising or extinction, nor do they see if feeling, thinking, action, and consciousness are the dharmas of arising or extinction. They do not see if matter is a dharma of contamination or purity, nor do they see if feeling, thinking, action, and consciousness are the dharmas of contamination or purity. Sariputra! These great bodhisattvas do not see matter and feeling accord, feeling and thinking accord, thinking and action accord, or action and consciousness accord. Why? Sariputra! There is not a dharma that really accords with the other because of the emptiness of original nature. Why? Sariputra! All kinds of matter are empty. They are not matter at all. All kinds of feeling, thinking, action, and consciousness are empty. They are not feeling, thinking, action, and consciousness at all. Why? All kinds of matter are empty. They are not the phenomena of changeable substance. All kinds of feeling are empty. They are not the phenomena of reception. All kinds of thinking are empty. They are not the phenomena of forming images. All kinds of action are empty. They are not the phenomena of initiating karmas. All kinds of consciousness are empty. They are not the phenomena of cognition. Why? Sariputra! Matter is not different from emptiness, and emptiness is not different from matter; matter is emptiness, and emptiness is matter. Feeling, thinking, action, and consciousness are not different from emptiness, and emptiness is not different from feeling, thinking, action, and consciousness. Feeling, thinking, action, and consciousness are emptiness, and emptiness is feeling, thinking, action, and consciousness. Why? Sariputra! All these dharmas are empty phenomena. They are without birth and extinction, contamination and purity, addition and subtraction, and the past, future, and present.

"Therefore, Sariputra, in emptiness there is no matter, feeling, thinking, action, and consciousness; there are no earth, water, fire, wind, space, and consciousness realms; there are no eye, ear, nose, tongue, body, and conscious spheres; there are no sight, sound, smell, taste, touch, and mental-image spheres; there are no eye, ear, nose, tongue, body, and conscious realms; there are no sight, sound, smell, taste, touch, or mental-image realms; there are no eye, ear, nose, tongue, body, and conscious consciousness realms; there are no eye, ear, nose, tongue, body, and conscious contacts; there are no feelings produced by the eye, ear, nose, tongue, body, and conscious contacts; there is no arising and extinction of ignorance; there is no arising and extinction of action, consciousness, name and form, six sense spheres, contact, reception, craving, grasping, existence, birth, old age, death, worry, sorrow, misery, anxiety, and upset; there are no noble truths of suffering, the cause of suffering, the cessation of suffering, and of the path for the cessation of suffering; there is no attainment and intuitive contemplation; there is no stream-enterer and stream-entry effect; there is no once-returner and once-return effect; there is no nonreturner and nonreturn effect; there is no arhat and arhat effect; there is no self-enlightened one and self-enlightenment bodhi; there are no bodhisattva and bodhisattva actions; and there is no Buddha and the bodhi of the Buddha. Sariputra! As the great bodhisattvas who are cultivating prajna paramita correspond with all these dharmas, they are in accordance with prajna paramita.

FASCICLE 5

Chapter 3
In Accordance with Prajna Paramita

Section 2

(In the First Assembly)

"FURTHERMORE, SARIPUTRA, WHEN CULTIVATING PRAJNA PARAMITA, THE GREAT bodhisattvas do not see matter as correspondent or not correspondent. They do not see feeling, thinking, action, and consciousness as correspondent or not correspondent. They do not see the eye sphere as correspondent or not correspondent. They do not see the ear, nose, tongue, body, and consciousness spheres as correspondent or not correspondent. They do not see the sight sphere as correspondent or not correspondent. They do not see the sound, smell, taste, touch, and mental-image spheres as correspondent or not correspondent. They do not see the eye realm as correspondent or not correspondent. They do not see the ear, nose, tongue, body, and conscious realms as correspondent or not correspondent. They do not see the sight realm as correspondent or not correspondent. They do not see the sound, smell, taste, touch, and mental-image realms as correspondent or not correspondent. They do not see the eye consciousness realm as correspondent or not correspondent. They do not see the ear, nose, tongue, body, and conscious consciousness realms as correspondent or not correspondent. They do not see the eye contact as correspondent or not correspondent. They do not see the ear, nose, tongue, body, and conscious contacts as correspondent or not correspondent. They do not see the feelings produced by eye contact as correspondent or not correspondent. They do not see the feelings produced by ear, nose, tongue, body, and conscious contacts as correspondent or not correspondent. They do not see the earth realm as correspondent or not correspondent. They do not see the water, fire, wind, space, and consciousness realms as correspondent or not correspondent. They do not see cause and condition as correspondent or not correspondent. They do not see consecutive thoughts in sequence, conditions that stimulate the mind, and the conditions that reinforce main causes as correspondent or not correspondent. They do not see the dharmas produced by conditions as correspondent or not correspondent. They do not see ignorance as correspondent or not correspondent. They do not see action, consciousness, name and form, six sense spheres, contact, reception, craving, grasping, existence, birth, old age, death, worry, sorrow, misery, anxiety, and upset as correspondent or not correspondent. They do not see the realm of desire as correspondent or not correspondent. They do not see the realm of form and the realm of formlessness as correspondent or not correspondent. They do not see giving paramita as it is correspondent or not correspondent. They do not see pure precept, forbearance, diligence, meditation, and prajna paramitas as correspondent or not correspondent. They do not see internal emptiness as correspondent or not correspondent. They do not see external emptiness, internal-external emptiness, emptiness of emptiness, emptiness of space, emptiness of ultimate truth, emptiness of the conditioned phenomena, emptiness of the unconditioned reality, emptiness in the final analysis, emptiness of nontemporality, emptiness of deconstruction, emptiness of changelessness, emptiness of original nature, emptiness of particular characteristics, emptiness of common characteristics, emptiness of all dharmas, emptiness of nonattainment, emptiness of selflessness, emptiness of self-nature, and emptiness of selfless self-nature as correspondent or not correspondent. They do not see realness as correspondent or not correspondent. They do not see dharma realm, dharma nature, the nature of nonillusion, the nature of changelessness, the nature of equality, the nature of nonarising, dharma concentration, dharma dwelling, reality, the realm of empty space, and the realm of the inconceivable as correspondent or not correspondent. They do not see the four bases of mindfulness as correspondent or not correspondent. They do not see the four correct endeavors, four bases of power, five roots, five powers, seven factors for enlightenment, and the noble eightfold path as correspondent or not correspondent. They do not see the noble truth of suffering as correspondent or not correspondent. They do not see the noble truths of the cause of suffering, the cessation of suffering, and the path for the cessation of suffering as correspondent or not correspondent. They do not see the path of the ten virtuous karmas as correspondent or not correspondent. They do not see the five precepts for lay believers and the eight precepts for lay believers as correspondent or not correspondent. They do not see bliss-inviting giving practice as correspondent or not correspondent. They do not see bliss-inviting precepts observing and cultivation as correspondent or not correspondent. They do not see the four meditations as correspondent or not correspondent. They do not see the four immeasurable minds and the four formlessness concentrations as correspondent or not correspondent. They do not see the eight liberations as correspondent or not correspondent. They do not see the eight vexation-overcoming meditations, nine concentrations in sequence, and the ten universal contemplations as correspondent or not correspondent. They do not see the liberation gate of emptiness as correspondent or not correspondent. They do not see the liberation gates of formlessness and nonaspiration as correspondent or not correspondent. They do not see all dharani gates as correspondent or not correspondent. They do not see all samadhi gates as correspondent or not correspondent. They do not see the stage of ecstasy as correspondent or not correspondent. They do not see the stages of freedom from defilements, flaming wisdom, being extremely difficult to be surpassed, manifestation of pure realness, going far away, the unmovable, expedient wisdom, and dharma cloud as correspondent or not correspondent. They do not see the five eyes as correspondent or not correspondent. They do not see the six supernatural powers as correspondent or not correspondent. They do not see the Buddha's ten abilities as correspondent or not correspondent. They do not see the four kinds of fearlessness, four unhindered understandings, great loving-kindness, great compassion, great joy, great equanimity, and the eighteen distinctive features of Buddha's wisdom and power as correspondent or not correspondent. They do not see the thirty-two perfect major marks as correspondent or not correspondent. They do not see the eighty distinguishing minor features as correspondent or not correspondent. They do not see staying in correct mindfulness as correspondent or not correspondent. They do not see dwelling in equanimity at all times as correspondent or not correspondent. They do not see the perfect knowledge of everything as correspondent or not correspondent. They do not see the perfect knowledge of the forms of the paths and the perfect knowledge of all phenomena as correspondent or not correspondent. They do not see the perfect knowledge of all perfect knowledge as correspondent or not correspondent. They do not see the permanent removal of the long-rooted disposition of vexations as correspondent or not correspondent. They do not see the stream-entry effect as correspondent or not correspondent. They do not see the once-return effect, nonreturn effect, and arhat effect as correspondent or not correspondent. They do not see the self-enlightenment bodhi as correspondent or not correspondent. They do not see all great bodhisattva actions and the unsurpassed, perfect, and universal bodhi of the Buddhas as correspondent or not correspondent. They do not see the 'I' as correspondent or not correspondent. They do not see the sentient being, the living one, the one who gives birth, the one who raises others, the gentleperson, the individual in reincarnation, the mentally born one, the learned child, the maker, the one who makes others make, the one who creates reward or punishment, the one who makes others create reward or punishment, the one who receives reward or punishment, the one who makes others receive reward or punishment, the knower, and the viewer as correspondent or not correspondent. Sariputra, it is based on this cause and condition to say that the great bodhisattvas are correspondent with prajna paramita when cultivating prajna paramita.

"Furthermore, Sariputra, when cultivating prajna paramita, the great bodhisattvas do not contemplate whether emptiness is correspondent with emptiness; whether formlessness is correspondent with formlessness; and whether nonaspiration is correspondent with nonaspiration. Why? It is because emptiness, formlessness, and nonaspiration have nothing to do with correspondence or noncorrespondence. Sariputra! As the great bodhisattvas who cultivate prajna paramita correspond with these dharmas, they correspond with prajna paramita.

"Furthermore, Sariputra, as the great bodhisattvas cultivate prajna paramita and enter into the emptiness of particular characteristics of all dharma, they will not contemplate whether matter is correspondent; whether feeling, thinking, action, and consciousness are correspondent. These great bodhisattvas will not contemplate whether matter is correspondent with the past. Why? It is because the past cannot be seen. They will not contemplate whether feeling, thinking, action, and consciousness are correspondent with the past. Why? It is because the past cannot be seen. They will not contemplate whether matter is correspondent with the future. Why? It is because the future cannot be seen. They will not contemplate whether feeling, thinking, action, and consciousness are correspondent with the future. Why? It is because the future cannot be seen. They will not contemplate whether matter is correspondent with the present. Why? It is because the present cannot be seen. They will not contemplate whether feeling, thinking, action, and consciousness are correspondent with the present. Why? It is because the present cannot be seen.

"Furthermore, Sariputra, as the great bodhisattvas cultivate prajna paramita, they do not contemplate if the past is correspondent with the future, if the past is correspondent with the present, if the future is correspondent with the present, if the present is correspondent with the past, if the present is correspondent with the future, if the past is correspondent with the future and the present, if the future is correspondent with the past and the present, if the present is correspondent with the past and the future, or if the past, future, and present are correspondent. Why? Sariputra, because the three phases of time are empty. Sariputra, as the great bodhisattvas who are cultivating parajna paramita correspond with these dharmas, they correspond with prajna paramita.

"Furthermore, Sariputra, as the great bodhisattvas cultivate prajna paramita, they do not contemplate if the perfect knowledge of everything corresponds with the past. Why? As the past cannot be seen, how can one contemplate if the perfect knowledge of everything corresponds with the past? They do not contemplate if the perfect knowledge of everything corresponds with the future. Why? As the future cannot be seen, how can one contemplate if the perfect knowledge of everything corresponds with the future? They do not contemplate if the perfect knowledge of everything corresponds with the present. Why? As the present cannot be seen, how can one contemplate if the perfect knowledge of everything corresponds with the present? Sariputra, as the great bodhisattvas who are cultivating prajna paramita correspond with these dharmas, they correspond with prajna paramita.

"Furthermore, Sariputra, when the great bodhisattvas cultivate prajna paramita, they do not contemplate if the perfect knowledge of everything corresponds with matter. Why? As matter cannot be seen, how can one contemplate if the perfect knowledge of everything corresponds with matter? They do not contemplate if the perfect knowledge of everything corresponds with feeling, thinking, action, and consciousness. Why? As feeling, thinking, action, and consciousness cannot be seen, how can one contemplate if the perfect knowledge of everything corresponds with feeling, thinking, action, and consciousness? Sariputra, as the great bodhisattvas who are cultivating prajna paramita correspond with these dharmas, they are named in accordance with prajna paramita.

"Furthermore, Sariputra, when cultivating prajna paramita, the great bodhisattvas do not contemplate if the perfect knowledge of everything corresponds with matter. Why? As matter cannot be seen, how can one contemplate if the perfect knowledge of everything corresponds with matter? They do not contemplate if the perfect knowledge of everything corresponds with feeling, thinking, action, and consciousness. Why? As feeling, thinking, action, and consciousness cannot be seen, how can one contemplate if the perfect knowledge of everything corresponds with feeling, thinking, action, and consciousness? Sariputra, as the great bodhisattvas who are cultivating prajna paramita correspond with these dharmas, they correspond with prajna paramita.

"Furthermore, Sariputra, when cultivating prajna paramita, the great bodhisattvas do not contemplate if the perfect knowledge of everything corresponds with the eye sphere. Why? As the eye sphere cannot be seen, how can one contemplate if the perfect knowledge of everything corresponds with the eye sphere? They do not contemplate if the perfect knowledge of everything corresponds with the ear, nose, tongue, body, and conscious spheres. Why? As the ear, nose, tongue, body, and conscious spheres cannot be seen, how can one contemplate if the perfect knowledge of everything corresponds with the ear, nose, tongue, body, and conscious spheres? Sariputra, as the great bodhisattvas who are cultivating prajna paramita correspond with these dharmas, they correspond with prajna paramita.

"Furthermore, Sariputra, when cultivating prajna paramita, the great bodhisattvas do not contemplate if the perfect knowledge of everything corresponds with the sight sphere. Why? As the sight sphere cannot be seen, how can one contemplate if the perfect knowledge of everything corresponds with the sight sphere? They do not contemplate if the perfect knowledge of everything corresponds with the sound, smell, taste, touch, and mental-image spheres. Why? As the sound, smell, taste, touch, and mental-image spheres cannot be seen, how can one contemplate if the perfect knowledge of everything corresponds with the sound, smell, taste, touch, and mental-image spheres? Sariputra, as the great bodhisattvas who are cultivating prajna paramita correspond with these dharmas, they correspond with prajna paramita.

"Furthermore, Sariputra, when cultivating prajna paramita, the great bodhisattvas do not contemplate if the perfect knowledge of everything corresponds with the eye realm. Why? As the eye realm cannot be seen, how can one contemplate if the perfect knowledge of everything corresponds with the eye realm? They do not contemplate if the perfect knowledge of everything corresponds with the ear, nose, tongue, body, and conscious realms. Why? As the ear, nose, tongue, body, and conscious realms cannot be seen, how can one contemplate if the perfect knowledge of everything corresponds with the ear, nose, tongue, body, and conscious realms? Sariputra, as the great bodhisattvas who are cultivating prajna paramita correspond with these dharmas, they correspond with prajna paramita.

"Furthermore, Sariputra, when cultivating prajna paramita, the great bodhisattvas do not contemplate if the perfect knowledge of everything corresponds with the sight realm. Why? As the sight realm cannot be seen, how can one contemplate if the perfect knowledge of everything corresponds with the sight realm? They do not contemplate if the perfect knowledge of everything corresponds with the sound, smell, taste, touch, and mental-image realms. Why? As the sound, smell, taste, touch, and mental-image realms cannot be seen, how can one contemplate if the perfect knowledge of everything corresponds with the sound, smell, taste, touch, and mental-image realms? Sariputra, as the great bodhisattvas who are cultivating prajna paramita correspond with these dharmas, they correspond with prajna paramita.

"Furthermore, Sariputra, when cultivating prajna paramita, the great bodhisattvas do not contemplate if the perfect knowledge of everything corresponds with the eye consciousness realm. Why? As the eye consciousness realm cannot be seen, how can one contemplate if the perfect knowledge of everything corresponds with the eye consciousness realm? They do not contemplate if the perfect knowledge of everything corresponds with the ear, nose, tongue, body, and conscious consciousness realms. Why? As the ear, nose, tongue, body, and conscious consciousness realms cannot be seen, how can one contemplate if the perfect knowledge of everything corresponds with the ear, nose, tongue, body, and conscious consciousness realms? Sariputra, as the great bodhisattvas who are cultivating prajna paramita correspond with these dharmas, they correspond with prajna paramita.

"Furthermore, Sariputra, when cultivating prajna paramita, the great bodhisattvas do not contemplate if the perfect knowledge of everything corresponds with the eye contact. Why? As the eye

Fascicle 5, Chapter 3, Section 2   103

contact cannot be seen, how can one contemplate if the perfect knowledge of everything corresponds with the eye contact? They do not contemplate if the perfect knowledge of everything corresponds with the ear, nose, tongue, body, and conscious contacts. Why? As the ear, nose, tongue, body, and conscious contacts cannot be seen, how can one contemplate if the perfect knowledge of everything corresponds with the ear, nose, tongue, body, and conscious contacts? Sariputra, as the great bodhisattvas who are cultivating prajna paramita correspond with these dharmas, they correspond with prajna paramita.

"Furthermore, Sariputra, when cultivating prajna paramita, the great bodhisattvas do not contemplate if the perfect knowledge of everything corresponds with the earth realm. Why? As the earth realm cannot be seen, how can one contemplate if the perfect knowledge of everything corresponds with the earth realm? They do not contemplate if the perfect knowledge of everything corresponds with the water, fire, wind, space, and consciousness realms. Why? As the water, fire, wind, space, and consciousness realms cannot be seen, how can one contemplate if the perfect knowledge of everything corresponds with the water, fire, wind, space, and consciousness realms? Sariputra, as the various great bodhisattvas who are cultivating prajna paramita correspond with these dharmas, they correspond with prajna paramita.

"Furthermore, Sariputra, when cultivating prajna paramita, the great bodhisattvas do not contemplate if the perfect knowledge of everything corresponds with cause and condition. Why? As cause and condition cannot be seen, how can one contemplate if the perfect knowledge of everything corresponds with cause and condition? They do not contemplate if the perfect knowledge of everything corresponds with consecutive thoughts in sequence, conditions that stimulate the mind, conditions that reinforce main causes, and the dharmas caused by conditions. Why? As consecutive thoughts in sequence, conditions that stimulate the mind, conditions that reinforce main causes, and the dharmas caused by conditions cannot be seen, how can one contemplate if the perfect knowledge of everything corresponds with consecutive thoughts in sequence, conditions that stimulate the mind, conditions that reinforce main causes, and the dharmas caused by conditions? Sariputra, as the various great bodhisattvas who are cultivating prajna paramita correspond with such dharmas, they correspond with prajna paramita.

"Furthermore, Sariputra, when cultivating prajna paramita, the great bodhisattvas do not contemplate if the perfect knowledge of everything corresponds with ignorance. Why? As ignorance cannot be seen, how can one contemplate if the perfect knowledge of everything corresponds with ignorance? They do not contemplate if the perfect knowledge of everything corresponds with action, name and form, six sense spheres, contact, reception, craving, grasping, existence, birth, old age, death, worry, sorrow, misery, anxiety, and upset. Why? As action, and so forth, as well as old age, death, worry, sorrow, misery, anxiety, and upset cannot be seen, how can one contemplate if the perfect knowledge of everything corresponds with action, and so forth, as well as old age, death, worry, sorrow, misery, anxiety, and upset? Sariputra, as the great bodhisattvas who are cultivating prajna paramita correspond with these dharmas, they correspond with prajna paramita.

"Furthermore, Sariputra, when cultivating prajna paramita, the great bodhisattvas do not contemplate if the perfect knowledge of everything corresponds with giving paramita. Why? As giving paramita cannot be seen, how can one contemplate if the perfect knowledge of everything corresponds with giving paramita? They do not contemplate if the perfect knowledge of everything corresponds with pure precept, forbearance, diligence, meditation, and prajna paramitas. Why? As pure precept, forbearance, diligence, meditation, and prajna paramitas cannot be seen, how can one contemplate if the perfect knowledge of everything corresponds with pure precept, forbearance, diligence, meditation, and prajna paramitas? Sariputra, as the great bodhisattvas who are cultivating prajna paramita correspond with such dharmas, they correspond with prajna paramita.

"Furthermore, Sariputra, when cultivating prajna paramita, the great bodhisattvas do not contemplate if the perfect knowledge of everything corresponds with internal emptiness. Why? As internal emptiness cannot be seen, how can one contemplate if the perfect knowledge of everything corresponds with internal emptiness? They do not contemplate if the perfect knowledge of everything corresponds with external emptiness, internal-external emptiness, emptiness of emptiness, emptiness of space, emptiness of ultimate truth, emptiness of conditioned phenomena, emptiness of unconditioned reality, emptiness in the final analysis, emptiness of nontemporality, emptiness of deconstruction, emptiness of changelessness, emptiness of original nature, emptiness of particular characteristics, emptiness of common characteristics, emptiness of all dharmas, emptiness of nonattainment, emptiness of selflessness, emptiness of self-nature, and emptiness of selfless self-nature. Why? As external emptiness, and so forth, as well as emptiness of selfless self-nature cannot be seen, how can one contemplate if the perfect knowledge of everything corresponds with external emptiness, and so forth, as well as emptiness of selfless self-nature? Sariputra, as the great bodhisattvas who are cultivating prajna paramita correspond with such dharmas, they correspond with prajna paramita.

"Furthermore, Sariputra, when cultivating prajna paramita, the great bodhisattvas do not contemplate if the perfect knowledge of everything corresponds with the four bases of mindfulness. Why? As the four bases of mindfulness cannot be seen, how can one contemplate if the perfect knowledge of everything corresponds with the four bases of mindfulness? They do not contemplate if the perfect knowledge of everything corresponds with the four correct endeavors, four bases of power, five roots, five powers, seven factors for enlightenment, and the noble eightfold path. Why? As the four correct endeavors, and so forth, as well as the noble eightfold path cannot be seen, how can one contemplate if the perfect knowledge of everything corresponds with the four correct endeavors, and so forth, as well as the noble eightfold path? Sariputra, as the great bodhisattvas who are cultivating prajna paramita correspond with such dharmas, they correspond with prajna paramita.

"Furthermore, Sariputra, when cultivating prajna paramita, the great bodhisattvas do not contemplate if the perfect knowledge of everything corresponds with the noble truth of suffering. Why? As the noble truth of suffering cannot be seen, how can one contemplate if the perfect knowledge of everything corresponds with the noble truth of suffering? They do not contemplate if the perfect knowledge of everything corresponds with the noble truths of the cause of suffering, the cessation of suffering, and the path for the cessation of suffering. Why? As the noble truths of the cause of suffering, the cessation of suffering, and the path for the cessation of suffering cannot be seen, how can one contemplate if the perfect knowledge of everything corresponds with the noble truths of the cause of suffering, the cessation of suffering, and the path for the cessation of suffering? Sariputra, as the great bodhisattvas who are cultivating prajna paramita correspond with such dharmas, they correspond with prajna paramita.

"Furthermore, Sariputra, when cultivating prajna paramita, the great bodhisattvas do not contemplate if the perfect knowledge of everything corresponds with the four meditations. Why? As the four meditations cannot be seen, how can one contemplate if the perfect knowledge of everything corresponds with the four meditations? They do not contemplate if the perfect knowledge of everything corresponds with the four immeasurable minds and the four formless concentrations. Why? As the four immeasurable minds and the four formless concentrations cannot be seen, how can one contemplate if the perfect knowledge of everything corresponds with the four immeasurable minds and the four formless concentrations? Sariputra, as the great bodhisattvas who are cultivating prajna paramita correspond with such dharmas, they correspond with prajna paramita.

"Furthermore, Sariputra, when cultivating prajna paramita, the great bodhisattvas do not contemplate if the perfect knowledge of everything corresponds with the eight liberations. Why? As the eight liberations cannot be seen, how can one contemplate if the perfect knowledge of everything corresponds with the eight liberations? They do not contemplate if the perfect knowledge of everything corresponds with the eight vexation-overcoming meditations, nine concentrations in sequence, and ten universal contemplations. Why? As the eight vexation-overcoming meditations, nine concentrations in sequence, and ten universal contemplations cannot be seen, how can one contemplate if the perfect knowledge of everything corresponds with the eight vexation-overcoming meditations, nine concentrations in sequence, and ten universal contemplations? Sariputra, as the great bodhisattvas who are cultivating prajna paramita correspond with such dharmas, they correspond with prajna paramita.

"Furthermore, Sariputra, when cultivating prajna paramita, the great bodhisattvas do not contemplate if the perfect knowledge of everything corresponds with the liberation gate of emptiness. Why? As the liberation gate of emptiness cannot be seen, how can one contemplate if the perfect knowledge of everything corresponds with the liberation gate of emptiness? They do not contemplate if the perfect knowledge of everything corresponds with the liberation gates of formlessness and nonaspiration. Why? As the liberation gates of formlessness and nonaspiration cannot be seen, how can one contemplate if the perfect knowledge of everything corresponds with the liberation gates of formlessness and nonaspiration? Sariputra, as the great bodhisattvas who are cultivating prajna paramita correspond with such dharmas, they correspond with prajna paramita.

"Furthermore, Sariputra, when cultivating prajna paramita, the great bodhisattvas do not contemplate if the perfect knowledge of everything corresponds with all dharani gates. Why? As all dharani gates cannot be seen, how can one contemplate if the perfect knowledge of everything corresponds with all dharani gates? They do not contemplate if the perfect knowledge of everything corresponds with all samadhi gates. Why? As all samadhi gates cannot be seen, how can one contemplate if the perfect knowledge of everything corresponds with all samadhi gates? Sariputra, as the great bodhisattvas who are cultivating prajna paramita correspond with such dharmas, they correspond with prajna paramita.

"Furthermore, Sariputra, when cultivating prajna paramita, the great bodhisattvas do not contemplate if the perfect knowledge of everything corresponds with the stage of ecstasy. Why? As the stage of ecstasy cannot be seen, how can one contemplate if the perfect knowledge of everything corresponds with the stage of ecstasy? They do not contemplate if the perfect knowledge of everything corresponds with the stages of freedom from defilements, emitting light, flaming wisdom, being extremely difficult to be surpassed, manifestation of pure realness, going far away, the unmovable, expedient wisdom, and dharma cloud. Why? As the stage of freedom from defilements and so forth as well as the stage of dharma cloud cannot be seen, how can one contemplate if the perfect knowledge of everything corresponds with the stage of freedom from defilements and so forth as well as the stage of dharma cloud? Sariputra, as the great bodhisattvas who are cultivating prajna paramita correspond with such dharmas, they correspond with prajna paramita.

"Furthermore, Sariputra, when cultivating prajna paramita, the great bodhisattvas do not contemplate if the perfect knowledge of everything corresponds with the five eyes. Why? As the five eyes cannot be seen, how can one contemplate if the perfect knowledge of everything corresponds with the five eyes? They do not contemplate if the perfect knowledge of everything corresponds with the six supernatural powers. Why? As the six supernatural powers cannot be seen, how can one contemplate if the perfect knowledge of everything corresponds with the six supernatural powers? Sariputra, as the great bodhisattvas who are cultivating prajna paramita correspond with such dharmas, they correspond with prajna paramita.

"Furthermore, Sariputra, when cultivating prajna paramita, the great bodhisattvas do not contemplate if the perfect knowledge of everything corresponds with the Buddha's ten abilities. Why? As the Buddha's ten abilities cannot be seen, how can one contemplate if the perfect knowledge of everything corresponds with the Buddha's ten abilities? They do not contemplate if the perfect knowledge of everything corresponds with the four kinds of fearlessness, four unhindered understandings, great loving-kindness, great compassion, great joy, great equanimity, and the eighteen distinctive features of Buddha's wisdom and power. Why? As the four kinds of fearlessness and so forth as well as the eighteen distinctive features of Buddha's wisdom and power cannot be seen, how can one contemplate if the perfect knowledge of everything corresponds with the four kinds of fearlessness, and so forth, as well as the eighteen distinctive features of Buddha's wisdom and power? Sariputra, as the great bodhisattvas who are cultivating

Fascicle 5, Chapter 3, Section 2 109

prajna paramita correspond with such dharmas, they correspond with prajna paramita.

"Furthermore, Sariputra, when cultivating prajna paramita, the great bodhisattvas do not contemplate if the perfect knowledge of everything corresponds with the thirty-two perfect major marks. Why? As the thirty-two perfect major marks cannot be seen, how can one contemplate if the perfect knowledge of everything corresponds with the thirty-two perfect major marks? They do not contemplate if the perfect knowledge of everything corresponds with the eighty distinguishing minor features. Why? As the eighty distinguishing minor features cannot be seen, how can one contemplate if the perfect knowledge of everything corresponds with the eighty distinguishing minor features? Sariputra, as the great bodhisattvas who are cultivating prajna paramita correspond with such dharmas, they correspond with prajna paramita.

"Furthermore, Sariputra, when cultivating prajna paramita, the great bodhisattvas do not contemplate if the perfect knowledge of everything corresponds with staying in correct mindfulness. Why? As staying in correct mindfulness cannot be seen, how can one contemplate if the perfect knowledge of everything corresponds with staying in correct mindfulness? They do not contemplate if the perfect knowledge of everything corresponds with dwelling in equanimity at all times. Why? As dwelling in equanimity at all times cannot be seen, how can one contemplate if the perfect knowledge of everything corresponds with dwelling in equanimity at all times? Sariputra, as the great bodhisattvas who are cultivating prajna paramita correspond with such dharmas, they correspond with prajna paramita.

"Furthermore, Sariputra, when cultivating prajna paramita, the great bodhisattvas do not contemplate if the perfect knowledge of everything corresponds with the perfect knowledge of everything. Why? As the perfect knowledge of everything cannot be seen, how can one contemplate if the perfect knowledge of everything corresponds with the perfect knowledge of everything? They do not contemplate if the perfect knowledge of everything corresponds with the perfect knowledge of the forms of the paths and the perfect knowledge of all phenomena. Why? As the perfect

110   *The Great Prajna Paramita Sutra*

knowledge of the forms of the paths and the perfect knowledge of all phenomena cannot be seen, how can one contemplate if the perfect knowledge of everything corresponds with the perfect knowledge of the forms of the paths and the perfect knowledge of all phenomena? Sariputra, as the great bodhisattvas who are cultivating prajna paramita correspond with such dharmas, they correspond with prajna paramita.

"Furthermore, Sariputra, when cultivating prajna paramita, the great bodhisattvas do not contemplate if the perfect knowledge of everything corresponds with the Buddha. Why? As the Buddha cannot be seen, how can one contemplate if the perfect knowledge of everything corresponds with the Buddha? They do not contemplate if the perfect knowledge of everything corresponds with bodhi. Why? As bodhi cannot be seen, how can one contemplate if the perfect knowledge of everything corresponds with bodhi? Sariputra, as the great bodhisattvas who are cultivating prajna paramita correspond with such dharmas, they correspond with prajna paramita.

"Furthermore, Sariputra, when cultivating prajna paramita, the great bodhisattvas do not contemplate if the perfect knowledge of everything corresponds with the Buddha or if the Buddha corresponds with the perfect knowledge of everything. Why? It is because the perfect knowledge of everything is the Buddha, and the Buddha is the perfect knowledge of everything. They do not contemplate if the perfect knowledge of everything corresponds with the bodhi or if the bodhi corresponds with the perfect knowledge of everything. Why? It is because the perfect knowledge of everything is the bodhi, and the bodhi is the perfect knowledge of everything. As the great bodhisattvas who are cultivating prajna paramita correspond with such dharmas, they correspond with prajna paramita.

"Furthermore, Sariputra, when cultivating prajna paramita, the great bodhisattvas are not attached to thinking that matter is existent or nonexistent or that feeling, thinking, action, and consciousness are existent or nonexistent. They are not attached to thinking that matter is permanent or impermanent or that feeling, thinking, action, and consciousness are permanent or impermanent.

Fascicle 5, Chapter 3, Section 2

They are not attached to thinking that matter is pleasant or painful or that feeling, thinking, action, and consciousness are pleasant or painful. They are not attached to thinking that matter is with or without selfness or that feeling, thinking, action, and consciousness are with or without selfness. They are not attached to thinking that matter is tranquil or not tranquil or that feeling, thinking, action, and consciousness are tranquil or not tranquil. They are not attached to thinking that matter is empty or not empty or that feeling, thinking, action, and consciousness are empty or not empty. They are not attached to thinking that matter is with or without form or that feeling, thinking, action, and consciousness are with or without form. They are not attached to thinking that matter is with or without aspiration or that feeling, thinking, action, and consciousness are with or without aspiration. Sariputra! As the great bodhisattvas who are cultivating prajna paramita correspond with these dharmas, they correspond with prajna paramita.

"Furthermore, Sariputra, when cultivating prajna paramita, the great bodhisattvas are not attached to thinking that the eye sphere is existent or nonexistent or that the ear, nose, tongue, body, and conscious spheres are existent or nonexistent. They are not attached to thinking that the eye sphere is permanent or impermanent or that the ear, nose, tongue, body, and conscious spheres are permanent or impermanent. They are not attached to thinking that the eye sphere is pleasant or painful or that the ear, nose, tongue, body, and conscious spheres are pleasant or painful. They are not attached to thinking that the eye sphere is with or without selfness or that the ear, nose, tongue, body, and conscious spheres are with or without selfness. They are not attached to thinking that the eye sphere is tranquil or not tranquil or that the ear, nose, tongue, body, and conscious spheres are tranquil or not tranquil. They are not attached to thinking that the eye sphere is empty or not empty or that the ear, nose, tongue, body, and conscious spheres are empty or not empty. They are not attached to thinking that the eye sphere is with or without form or that the ear, nose, tongue, body, and conscious spheres are with or without form. They are not attached to thinking that the eye sphere is with or without aspiration or that the ear, nose, tongue, body, and conscious spheres are with or without aspiration. Sariputra! As the great bodhisattvas who are cultivating prajna paramita correspond with these dharmas, they correspond with prajna paramita.

"Furthermore, Sariputra, when cultivating prajna paramita, the great bodhisattvas are not attached to thinking that the sight sphere is existent or nonexistent or that the sound, smell, taste, touch, and mental-image spheres are existent or nonexistent. They are not attached to thinking that the sight sphere is permanent or impermanent or that the sound, smell, taste, touch, and mental-image spheres are permanent or impermanent. They are not attached to thinking that the sight sphere is pleasant or painful or that sound, smell, taste, touch, and mental-image spheres are pleasant or painful. They are not attached to thinking that the sight sphere is with or without selfness or that the sound, smell, taste, touch, and mental-image spheres are with or without selfness. They are not attached to thinking that the sight sphere is tranquil or not tranquil or that the sound, smell, taste, touch, and mental-image spheres are tranquil or not tranquil. They are not attached to thinking that the sight sphere is empty or not empty or that the sound, smell, taste, touch, and mental-image spheres are empty or not empty. They are not attached to thinking that the sight sphere is with or without form or that the sound, smell, taste, touch, and mental-image spheres are with or without form. They are not attached to thinking that the sight sphere is with or without aspiration or that the sound, smell, taste, touch, and mental-image spheres are with or without aspiration. Sariputra! As the great bodhisattvas who are cultivating prajna paramita correspond with these dharmas, they correspond with prajna paramita.

"Furthermore, Sariputra, when cultivating prajna paramita, the great bodhisattvas are not attached to thinking that the eye realm is existent or nonexistent or that the ear, nose, tongue, body, and conscious realms are existent or nonexistent. They are not attached to thinking that the eye realm is permanent or impermanent or that the ear, nose, tongue, body, and conscious realms are permanent or impermanent. They are not attached to thinking that the eye realm is pleasant or painful or that the ear, nose, tongue, body, and conscious realms are pleasant or painful. They are not attached to thinking that the eye realm is with or without selfness or that the ear, nose, tongue, body, and conscious realms are with or without selfness. They are not attached to thinking that the eye realm is tranquil or not tranquil or that the ear, nose, tongue, body, and conscious realms are tranquil or not tranquil. They are not attached to thinking that the eye realm is empty or not empty or that the ear, nose, tongue, body, and conscious realms are empty or not empty. They are not attached to thinking that the eye realm is with or without form or that the ear, nose, tongue, body, and conscious realms are with or without form. They are not attached to thinking that the eye realm is with or without aspiration or that the ear, nose, tongue, body, and conscious realms are with or without aspiration. Sariputra! As the great bodhisattvas who are cultivating prajna paramita correspond with these dharmas, they correspond with prajna paramita.

"Furthermore, Sariputra, when cultivating prajna paramita, the great bodhisattvas are not attached to thinking that the sight realm is existent or nonexistent or that the sound, smell, taste, touch, and mental-image realms are existent or nonexistent. They are not attached to thinking that the sight realm is permanent or impermanent or that the sound, smell, taste, touch, and mental-image realms are permanent or impermanent. They are not attached to thinking that the sight realm is pleasant or painful or that sound, smell, taste, touch, and mental-image realms are pleasant or painful. They are not attached to thinking that the sight realm is with or without selfness or that the sound, smell, taste, touch, and mental-image realms are with or without selfness. They are not attached to thinking that the sight realm is tranquil or not tranquil or that the sound, smell, taste, touch, and mental-image realms are tranquil or not tranquil. They are not attached to thinking that the sight realm is empty or not empty or that the sound, smell, taste, touch, and mental-image realms are empty or not empty. They are not attached to thinking that the sight realm is with or without form or that the sound, smell, taste, touch, and mental-image realms are with or without form. They are not attached to thinking that the sight realm is with or without aspiration or that the sound, smell, taste, touch, and mental-image realms are with or without aspiration. Sariputra! As the great bodhisattvas who are cultivating prajna paramita correspond with these dharmas, they correspond with prajna paramita.

"Furthermore, Sariputra, when cultivating prajna paramita, the great bodhisattvas are not attached to thinking that the eye consciousness realm is existent or nonexistent or that the ear, nose, tongue, body, and conscious consciousness realms are existent or nonexistent. They are not attached to thinking that the eye consciousness realm is permanent or impermanent or that the ear, nose, tongue, body, and conscious consciousness realms are permanent or impermanent. They are not attached to thinking that the eye consciousness realm is pleasant or painful or that the ear, nose, tongue, body, and conscious consciousness realms are pleasant or painful. They are not attached to thinking that the eye consciousness realm is with or without selfness or that the ear, nose, tongue, body, and conscious consciousness realms are with or without selfness. They are not attached to thinking that the eye consciousness realm is tranquil or not tranquil or that the ear, nose, tongue, body, and conscious consciousness realms are tranquil or not tranquil. They are not attached to thinking that the eye consciousness realm is empty or not empty or that the ear, nose, tongue, body, and conscious consciousness realms are empty or not empty. They are not attached to thinking that the eye consciousness realm is with or without form or that the ear, nose, tongue, body, and conscious consciousness realms are with or without form. They are not attached to thinking that the eye consciousness realm is with or without aspiration or that the ear, nose, tongue, body, and conscious consciousness realms are with or without aspiration. Sariputra! As the great bodhisattvas who are cultivating prajna paramita correspond with these dharmas, they correspond with prajna paramita.

FASCICLE 6

Chapter 3
In Accordance with Prajna Paramita

Section 3

(In the First Assembly)

"FURTHERMORE, SARIPUTRA, WHEN CULTIVATING PRAJNA PARAMITA, THE GREAT bodhisattvas are not attached to thinking that the eye contact is existent or nonexistent or that the ear, nose, tongue, body, and conscious contacts are existent or nonexistent. They are not attached to thinking that the eye contact is permanent or impermanent or that the ear, nose, tongue, body, and conscious contacts are permanent or impermanent. They are not attached to thinking that the eye contact is pleasant or painful or that the ear, nose, tongue, body, and conscious contacts are pleasant or painful. They are not attached to thinking that the eye contact is with or without selfness or that the ear, nose, tongue, body, and conscious contacts are with or without selfness. They are not attached to thinking that the eye contact is tranquil or not tranquil or that the ear, nose, tongue, body, and conscious contacts are tranquil or not tranquil. They are not attached to thinking that the eye contact is empty or not empty or that the ear, nose, tongue, body, and conscious contacts are empty or not empty. They are not attached to thinking that the eye contact is with or without form or that the ear, nose, tongue, body, and conscious contacts are with or without form. They are not attached to thinking that the eye contact is with or without aspiration or that the ear, nose, tongue, body, and conscious contacts are with or without aspiration. Sariputra, as the great bodhisattvas who are cultivating prajna paramita correspond with these dharmas, they are correspondent with prajna paramita.

"Furthermore, Sariputra, when cultivating prajna paramita, the great bodhisattvas are not attached to thinking that the feelings produced by eye contact are existent or nonexistent or that the feelings produced by ear, nose, tongue, body, and conscious contacts are existent or nonexistent. They are not attached to thinking that the feelings produced by eye contact are permanent or impermanent or that the feelings produced by ear, nose, tongue, body, and conscious contacts are permanent or impermanent. They are not attached to thinking that the feelings produced by eye contact are pleasant or painful or that the feelings produced by ear, nose, tongue, body, and conscious contacts are pleasant or painful. They are not attached to thinking that the feelings produced by eye contact are with or without selfness or that the feelings produced by ear, nose, tongue, body, and conscious contacts are with or without selfness. They are not attached to thinking that the feelings produced by eye contact are tranquil or not tranquil or that the feelings produced by ear, nose, tongue, body, and conscious contacts are tranquil or not tranquil. They are not attached to thinking that the feelings produced by eye contact are empty or not empty or that the feelings produced by ear, nose, tongue, body, and conscious contacts are empty or not empty. They are not attached to thinking that the feelings produced by eye contact are with or without form or that the feelings produced by ear, nose, tongue, body, and conscious contacts are with or without form. They are not attached to thinking that the feelings produced by eye contact are with or without aspiration or that the feelings produced by ear, nose, tongue, body, and conscious contacts are with or without aspiration. Sariputra, as the great bodhisattvas who are cultivating prajna paramita correspond with these dharmas, they are correspondent with prajna paramita.

Fascicle 6, Chapter 3, Section 3

"Furthermore, Sariputra, when cultivating prajna paramita, the great bodhisattvas are not attached to thinking that the earth realm is existent or nonexistent or that the water, fire, wind, space, and consciousness realms are existent or nonexistent. They are not attached to thinking that the earth realm is permanent or impermanent or that the water, fire, wind, space, and consciousness realms are permanent or impermanent. They are not attached to thinking that the earth realm is pleasant or painful or that the water, fire, wind, space, and consciousness realms are pleasant or painful. They are not attached to thinking that the earth realm is with or without selfness or that the water, fire, wind, space, and consciousness realms are with or without selfness. They are not attached to thinking that the earth realm is tranquil or not tranquil or that the water, fire, wind, space, and consciousness realms are tranquil or not tranquil. They are not attached to thinking that the earth realm is empty or not empty or that the water, fire, wind, space, and consciousness realms are empty or not empty. They are not attached to thinking that the earth realm is with or without form or that the water, fire, wind, space, and consciousness realms are with or without form. They are not attached to thinking that the earth realm is with aspiration or without aspiration or that the water, fire, wind, space, and consciousness realms are with or without aspiration. Sariputra, as the great bodhisattvas who are cultivating prajna paramita correspond with these dharmas, they are correspondent with prajna paramita.

"Furthermore, Sariputra, when cultivating prajna paramita, the great bodhisattvas are not attached to thinking that cause and condition is existent or nonexistent or that consecutive thoughts in sequence, conditions that stimulate the mind, conditions that reinforce main causes, and the dharmas produced by conditions are existent or nonexistent. They are not attached to thinking that cause and condition is permanent or impermanent or that consecutive thoughts in sequence, conditions that stimulate the mind, conditions that reinforce main causes, and the dharmas produced by conditions are permanent or impermanent. They are not attached to thinking that cause and condition is pleasant or painful or that consecutive thoughts in sequence, conditions that stimulate the mind, conditions that reinforce main causes, and the dharmas produced by conditions are pleasant or painful. They are not attached to thinking that cause and condition is with or without selfness or that consecutive thoughts in sequence, conditions that stimulate the mind, conditions that reinforce main causes, and the dharmas produced by conditions are with or without selfness. They are not attached to thinking that cause and condition is tranquil or not tranquil or that consecutive thoughts in sequence, conditions that stimulate the mind, conditions that reinforce main causes, and the dharmas produced by conditions are tranquil or not tranquil. They are not attached to thinking that cause and condition is empty or not empty or that consecutive thoughts in sequence, conditions that stimulate the mind, conditions that reinforce main causes, and the dharmas produced by conditions are empty or not empty. They are not attached to thinking that cause and condition is with or without form or that consecutive thoughts in sequence, conditions that stimulate the mind, conditions that reinforce main causes, and the dharmas produced by conditions are with or without form. They are not attached to thinking that cause and condition is with or without aspiration or that consecutive thoughts in sequence, conditions that stimulate the mind, conditions that reinforce main causes, and the dharmas produced by conditions are with or without aspiration. Sariputra, as the great bodhisattvas who are cultivating prajna paramita correspond with these dharmas, they are correspondent with prajna paramita.

"Furthermore, Sariputra, when cultivating prajna paramita, the great bodhisattvas are not attached to thinking that ignorance is existent or nonexistent or that action, consciousness, name and form, six sense spheres, contact, reception, craving, grasping, existence, birth, old age, death, worry, sorrow, misery, anxiety, and upset are existent or nonexistent. They are not attached to thinking that ignorance is permanent or impermanent or that action, and so forth, as well as old age, death, worry, sorrow, misery, anxiety, and upset are permanent or impermanent. They are not attached to thinking that ignorance is pleasant or painful or that action, and so forth, as well as old age, death, worry, sorrow, misery, anxiety, and upset are pleasant or painful. They are not attached to thinking that ignorance is with or without selfness or that action, and so forth, as well as old age, death, worry, sorrow, misery, anxiety, and upset are with or without selfness. They are not attached to thinking that ignorance is tranquil or not tranquil or that action, and so forth, as well as old age, death, worry, sorrow, misery, anxiety, and upset are tranquil or not tranquil. They are not attached to thinking that ignorance is empty or not empty or that action, and so forth, as well as old age, death, worry, sorrow, misery, anxiety, and upset are empty or not empty. They are not attached to thinking that ignorance is with or without form or that action, and so forth, as well as old age, death, worry, sorrow, misery, anxiety, and upset are with or without form. They are not attached to thinking that ignorance is with or without aspiration or that action, and so forth, as well as old age, death, worry, sorrow, misery, anxiety, and upset are with or without aspiration. Sariputra, as the great bodhisattvas who are cultivating prajna paramita correspond with these dharmas, they correspond with prajna paramita.

"Furthermore, Sariputra, when cultivating prajna paramita, the great bodhisattvas are not attached to thinking that giving paramita is existent or nonexistent or that pure precept, forbearance, diligence, meditation, and prajna paramitas are existent or nonexistent. They are not attached to thinking that giving paramita is permanent or impermanent or that pure precept, forbearance, diligence, meditation, and prajna paramitas are permanent or impermanent. They are not attached to thinking that giving paramita is pleasant or painful or that pure precept, forbearance, diligence, meditation, and prajna paramitas are pleasant or painful. They are not attached to thinking that giving paramita is with or without selfness or that pure precept, forbearance, diligence, meditation, and prajna paramitas are with or without selfness. They are not attached to thinking that giving paramita is tranquil or not tranquil or that pure precept, forbearance, diligence, meditation, and prajna paramitas are tranquil or not tranquil. They are not attached to thinking that giving paramita is empty or not empty or that pure precept, forbearance, diligence, meditation, and prajna paramitas are empty or not empty. They are not attached to thinking that giving paramita is with or without form or that pure precept, forbearance, diligence, meditation, and prajna paramitas are with or without form. They are not attached to thinking that giving paramita is with or without aspiration or that pure precept, forbearance, diligence, meditation, and prajna paramitas are with or without aspiration. Sariputra, as the great bodhisattvas who are cultivating prajna paramita correspond with these dharmas, they correspond with prajna paramita.

"Furthermore, Sariputra, when cultivating prajna paramita, the great bodhisattvas are not attached to thinking that internal emptiness is existent or nonexistent or that external emptiness, internal-external emptiness, emptiness of emptiness, emptiness of space, emptiness of ultimate truth, emptiness of conditioned phenomena, emptiness of unconditioned reality, emptiness in the final analysis, emptiness of nontemporality, emptiness of deconstruction, emptiness of changelessness, emptiness of original nature, emptiness of particular characteristics, emptiness of common characteristics, emptiness of all dharmas, emptiness of nonattainment, emptiness of selflessness, emptiness of self-nature, and emptiness of selfless self-nature are existent or nonexistent. They are not attached to thinking that internal emptiness is permanent or impermanent or that external emptiness, and so forth, as well as emptiness of selfless self-nature are permanent or impermanent. They are not attached to thinking that internal emptiness is pleasant or painful or that external emptiness, and so forth, as well as emptiness of selfless self-nature are pleasant or painful. They are not attached to thinking that internal emptiness is with or without selfness or that external emptiness, and so forth, as well as emptiness of selfless self-nature are with or without selfness. They are not attached to thinking that internal emptiness is tranquil or not tranquil or that external emptiness, and so forth, as well as emptiness of selfless self-nature are tranquil or not tranquil. They are not attached to thinking that internal emptiness is empty or not empty or that external emptiness, and so forth, as well as emptiness of selfless self-nature are empty or not empty. They are not attached to thinking that internal emptiness is with or without form or that external emptiness, and so forth, as well as emptiness of selfless self-nature are with or without form. They are not attached to thinking that internal emptiness is with or without aspiration or that external

Fascicle 6, Chapter 3, Section 3   121

emptiness, and so forth, as well as emptiness of selfless self-nature are with or without aspiration. Sariputra, as the great bodhisattvas who are cultivating prajna paramita correspond with these dharmas, they correspond with prajna paramita.

"Furthermore, Sariputra, when cultivating prajna paramita, the great bodhisattvas are not attached to thinking that realness is existent or nonexistent or that dharma realm, dharma nature, the nature of nonillusion, the nature of changelessness, the nature of equality, the nature of nonarising, dharma concentration, dharma dwelling, reality, the realm of empty space, and the realm of the inconceivable are existent or nonexistent. They are not attached to thinking that realness is permanent or impermanent or that dharma realm, and so forth, as well as the realm of the inconceivable are permanent or impermanent. They are not attached to thinking that realness is pleasant or painful or that dharma realm, and so forth, as well as the realm of the inconceivable are pleasant or painful. They are not attached to thinking that realness is with or without selfness or that dharma realm, and so forth, as well as the realm of the inconceivable are with or without selfness. They are not attached to thinking that realness is tranquil or not tranquil or that dharma realm, and so forth, as well as the realm of the inconceivable are tranquil or not tranquil. They are not attached to thinking that realness is empty or not empty or that dharma realm, and so forth, as well as the realm of the inconceivable are empty or not empty. They are not attached to thinking that realness is with or without form or that dharma realm, and so forth, as well as the realm of the inconceivable are with or without form. They are not attached to thinking that realness is with or without aspiration or that dharma realm, and so forth, as well as the realm of the inconceivable are with or without aspiration. Sariputra, as the great bodhisattvas who are cultivating prajna paramita correspond with these dharmas, they correspond with prajna paramita.

"Furthermore, Sariputra, when cultivating prajna paramita, the great bodhisattvas are not attached to thinking that the four bases of mindfulness are existent or nonexistent or that the four correct endeavors, four bases of power, five roots, five powers, seven factors for enlightenment, and the noble eightfold path are existent or nonexistent. They are not attached to thinking that the four bases of mindfulness are permanent or impermanent or that the four correct endeavors, and so forth, as well as the noble eightfold path are permanent or impermanent. They are not attached to thinking that the four bases of mindfulness are pleasant or painful or that the four correct endeavors, and so forth, as well as the noble eightfold path are pleasant or painful. They are not attached to thinking that the four bases of mindfulness are with or without selfness or that the four correct endeavors, and so forth, as well as the noble eightfold path are with or without selfness. They are not attached to thinking that the four bases of mindfulness are tranquil or not tranquil or that the four correct endeavors, and so forth, as well as the noble eightfold path are tranquil or not tranquil. They are not attached to thinking that the four bases of mindfulness are empty or not empty or that the four correct endeavors, and so forth, as well as the noble eightfold path are empty or not empty. They are not attached to thinking that the four bases of mindfulness are with or without form or that the four correct endeavors, and so forth, as well as the noble eightfold path are with or without form. They are not attached to thinking that the four bases of mindfulness are with or without aspiration or that the four correct endeavors, and so forth, as well as the noble eightfold path are with or without aspiration. Sariputra, as the great bodhisattvas who are cultivating prajna paramita correspond with these dharmas, they correspond with prajna paramita.

"Furthermore, Sariputra, when cultivating prajna paramita, the great bodhisattvas are not attached to thinking that the noble truth of suffering is existent or nonexistent or that the noble truths of the cause of suffering, the cessation of suffering, and the path for the cessation of suffering are existent or nonexistent. They are not attached to thinking that the noble truth of suffering is permanent or impermanent or that the noble truths of the cause of suffering, the cessation of suffering, and the path for the cessation of suffering are permanent or impermanent. They are not attached to thinking that the noble truth of suffering is pleasant or painful or that the noble truths of the cause of suffering, the cessation of suffering, and the path for the cessation of suffering are pleasant or painful.

They are not attached to thinking that the noble truth of suffering is with or without selfness or that the noble truths of the cause of suffering, the cessation of suffering, and the path for the cessation of suffering are with or without selfness. They are not attached to thinking that the noble truth of suffering is tranquil or not tranquil or that the noble truths of the cause of suffering, the cessation of suffering, and the path for the cessation of suffering are tranquil or not tranquil. They are not attached to thinking that the noble truth of suffering is empty or not empty or that the noble truths of the cause of suffering, the cessation of suffering, and the path for the cessation of suffering are empty or not empty. They are not attached to thinking that the noble truth of suffering is with or without form or that the noble truths of the cause of suffering, the cessation of suffering, and the path for the cessation of suffering are with or without form. They are not attached to thinking that the noble truth of suffering is with or without aspiration or that the noble truths of the cause of suffering, the cessation of suffering, and the path for the cessation of suffering are with or without aspiration. Sariputra, as the great bodhisattvas who are cultivating prajna paramita correspond with these dharmas, they correspond with prajna paramita.

"Furthermore, Sariputra, when cultivating prajna paramita, the great bodhisattvas are not attached to thinking that the four meditations are existent or nonexistent or that the four immeasurable minds and the four formless concentrations are existent or nonexistent. They are not attached to thinking that the four meditations are permanent or impermanent or that the four immeasurable minds and the four formless concentrations are permanent or impermanent. They are not attached to thinking that the four meditations are pleasant or painful or that the four immeasurable minds and the four formless concentrations are pleasant or painful. They are not attached to thinking that the four meditations are with or without selfness or that the four immeasurable minds and the four formless concentrations are with or without selfness. They are not attached to thinking that the four meditations are tranquil or not tranquil or that the four immeasurable minds and the four formless concentrations are tranquil or not tranquil. They are not attached to thinking that the four meditations are empty or not empty or that the four immeasurable minds and the four formless concentrations are empty or not empty. They are not attached to thinking that the four meditations are with or without form or that the four immeasurable minds and the four formless concentrations are with or without form. They are not attached to thinking that the four meditations are with or without aspiration or that the four immeasurable minds and the four formless concentrations are with or without aspiration. Sariputra, as the great bodhisattvas who are cultivating prajna paramita correspond with these dharmas, they correspond with prajna paramita.

"Furthermore, Sariputra, when cultivating prajna paramita, the great bodhisattvas are not attached to thinking that the eight liberations are existent or nonexistent or that the eight vexation-overcoming meditations, nine concentrations in sequence, and the ten universal contemplations are existent or nonexistent. They are not attached to thinking that the eight liberations are permanent or impermanent or that the eight vexation-overcoming meditations, nine concentrations in sequence, and the ten universal contemplations are permanent or impermanent. They are not attached to thinking that the eight liberations are pleasant or painful or that the eight vexation-overcoming meditations, nine concentrations in sequence, and the ten universal contemplations are pleasant or painful. They are not attached to thinking that the eight liberations are with or without selfness or that the eight vexation-overcoming meditations, nine concentrations in sequence, and the ten universal contemplations are with or without selfness. They are not attached to thinking that the eight liberations are tranquil or not tranquil or that the eight vexation-overcoming meditations, nine concentrations in sequence, and the ten universal contemplations are tranquil or not tranquil. They are not attached to thinking that the eight liberations are empty or not empty or that the eight vexation-overcoming meditations, nine concentrations in sequence, and the ten universal contemplations are empty or not empty. They are not attached to thinking that the eight liberations are with or without form or that the eight vexation-overcoming meditations, nine concentrations in sequence, and the ten universal contemplations are with or without form. They are not attached to thinking that the eight liberations are with or without aspiration or that the eight vexation-overcoming meditations, nine concentrations in sequence, and the ten universal contemplations are with or without aspiration. Sariputra, as the great bodhisattvas who are cultivating prajna paramita correspond with these dharmas, they correspond with prajna paramita.

"Furthermore, Sariputra, when cultivating prajna paramita, the great bodhisattvas are not attached to thinking that the liberation gate of emptiness is existent or nonexistent or that the liberation gates of formlessness and nonaspiration are existent or nonexistent. They are not attached to thinking that the liberation gate of emptiness is permanent or impermanent or that the liberation gates of formlessness and nonaspiration are permanent or impermanent. They are not attached to thinking that the liberation gate of emptiness is pleasant or painful or that the liberation gates of formlessness and nonaspiration are pleasant or painful. They are not attached to thinking that the liberation gate of emptiness is with or without selfness or that the liberation gates of formlessness and nonaspiration are with or without selfness. They are not attached to thinking that the liberation gate of emptiness is tranquil or not tranquil or that the liberation gates of formlessness and nonaspiration are tranquil or not tranquil. They are not attached to thinking that the liberation gate of emptiness is empty or not empty or that the liberation gates of formlessness and nonaspiration are empty or not empty. They are not attached to thinking that the liberation gate of emptiness is with or without form or that the liberation gates of formlessness and nonaspiration are with or without form. They are not attached to thinking that the liberation gate of emptiness is with or without aspiration or that the liberation gates of formlessness and nonaspiration are with or without aspiration. Sariputra, as the great bodhisattvas who are cultivating prajna paramita correspond with these dharmas, they correspond with prajna paramita.

"Furthermore, Sariputra, when cultivating prajna paramita, the great bodhisattvas are not attached to thinking that all dharani gates are existent or nonexistent or that all samadhi gates are existent or nonexistent. They are not attached to thinking that all dharani gates are permanent or impermanent or that all samadhi gates are permanent or impermanent. They are not attached to thinking that all dharani gates are pleasant or painful or that all samadhi gates are pleasant or painful. They are not attached to thinking that all dharani gates are with or without selfness or that all samadhi gates are with or without selfness. They are not attached to thinking that all dharani gates are tranquil or not tranquil or that all samadhi gates are tranquil or not tranquil. They are not attached to thinking that all dharani gates are empty or not empty or that all samadhi gates are empty or not empty. They are not attached to thinking that all dharani gates are with or without form or that all samadhi gates are with or without form. They are not attached to thinking that all dharani gates are with or without aspiration or that all samadhi gates are with or without aspiration. Sariputra, as the great bodhisattvas who are cultivating prajna paramita correspond with these dharmas, they correspond with prajna paramita.

"Furthermore, Sariputra, when cultivating prajna paramita, the great bodhisattvas are not attached to thinking that the stage of ecstasy is existent or nonexistent or that the stages of freedom from defilements, emitting lights, flaming wisdom, being extremely difficult to be surpassed, manifestation of pure realness, going far away, the unmovable, expedient wisdom, and dharma cloud are existent or nonexistent. They are not attached to thinking that the stage of ecstasy is permanent or impermanent or that the stage of freedom from defilements, and so forth, as well as the stage of dharma cloud are permanent or impermanent. They are not attached to thinking that the stage of ecstasy is pleasant or painful or that the stage of freedom from defilements, and so forth, as well as the stage of dharma cloud are pleasant or painful. They are not attached to thinking that the stage of ecstasy is with or without selfness or that the stage of freedom from defilements, and so forth, as well as the stage of dharma cloud are with or without selfness. They are not attached to thinking that the stage of ecstasy is tranquil or not tranquil or that the stage of freedom from defilements, and so forth, as well as the stage of dharma cloud are tranquil or not tranquil. They are not attached to thinking that the stage of ecstasy is empty or not empty or that the stage of freedom from defilements, and so forth, as well as the stage of dharma cloud are empty or not empty. They are not attached to thinking that the stage of ecstasy is with or without form or that the stage of freedom from defilements, and so forth, as well as the stage of dharma cloud are with or without form. They are not attached to thinking that the stage of ecstasy is with or without aspiration or that the stage of freedom from defilements, and so forth, as well as the stage of dharma cloud are with or without aspiration. Sariputra, as the great bodhisattvas who are cultivating prajna paramita correspond with these dharmas, they correspond with prajna paramita.

"Furthermore, Sariputra, when cultivating prajna paramita, the great bodhisattvas are not attached to thinking that the five eyes are existent or nonexistent or that the six supernatural powers are existent or nonexistent. They are not attached to thinking that the five eyes are permanent or impermanent or that the six supernatural powers are permanent or impermanent. They are not attached to thinking that the five eyes are pleasant or painful or that the six supernatural powers are pleasant or painful. They are not attached to thinking that the five eyes are with or without selfness or that the six supernatural powers are with or without selfness. They are not attached to thinking that the five eyes are tranquil or not tranquil or that the six supernatural powers are tranquil or not tranquil. They are not attached to thinking that the five eyes are empty or not empty or that the six supernatural powers are empty or not empty. They are not attached to thinking that the five eyes are with or without form or that the six supernatural powers are with or without form. They are not attached to thinking that the five eyes are with or without aspiration or that the six supernatural powers are with or without aspiration. Sariputra, as the great bodhisattvas who are cultivating prajna paramita correspond with these dharmas, they correspond with prajna paramita.

"Furthermore, Sariputra, when cultivating prajna paramita, the great bodhisattvas are not attached to thinking that the Buddha's ten abilities are existent or nonexistent or that the four kinds of fearlessness, four unhindered understandings, great loving-kindness, great compassion, great joy, great equanimity, and the eighteen distinctive features of Buddha's wisdom and power are existent or nonexistent. They are not attached to thinking that the Buddha's ten abilities are permanent or impermanent or that the four kinds of fearlessness, and so forth, as well as the eighteen distinctive features of Buddha's wisdom and power are permanent or impermanent. They are not attached to thinking that the Buddha's ten abilities are pleasant or painful or that the four kinds of fearlessness, and so forth, as well as the eighteen distinctive features of Buddha's wisdom and power are pleasant or painful. They are not attached to thinking that the Buddha's ten abilities are with or without selfness or that the four kinds of fearlessness, and so forth, as well as the eighteen distinctive features of Buddha's wisdom and power are with or without selfness. They are not attached to thinking that the Buddha's ten abilities are tranquil or not tranquil or that the four kinds of fearlessness, and so forth, as well as the eighteen distinctive features of Buddha's wisdom and power are tranquil or not tranquil. They are not attached to thinking that the Buddha's ten abilities are empty or not empty or that the four kinds of fearlessness, and so forth, as well as the eighteen distinctive features of Buddha's wisdom and power are empty or not empty. They are not attached to thinking that the Buddha's ten abilities are with or without form or that the four kinds of fearlessness, and so forth, as well as the eighteen distinctive features of Buddha's wisdom and power are with or without form. They are not attached to thinking that the Buddha's ten abilities are with or without aspiration or that the four kinds of fearlessness, and so forth, as well as the eighteen distinctive features of Buddha's wisdom and power are with or without aspiration. Sariputra, as the great bodhisattvas who are cultivating prajna paramita correspond with these dharmas, they correspond with prajna paramita.

"Furthermore, Sariputra, when cultivating prajna paramita, the great bodhisattvas are not attached to thinking that the thirty-two perfect major marks are existent or nonexistent or that the eighty distinguishing minor features are existent or nonexistent. They are not attached to thinking that the thirty-two perfect major marks are permanent or impermanent or that the eighty distinguishing minor features are permanent or impermanent. They are not attached to thinking that the thirty-two perfect major marks are pleasant or painful or that the eighty distinguishing minor features are pleasant or painful. They are not attached to thinking that the thirty-two perfect major marks are with or without selfness or that the eighty distinguishing minor features are with or without selfness. They are not attached to thinking that the thirty-two perfect major marks are tranquil or not tranquil or that the eighty distinguishing minor features are tranquil or not tranquil. They are not attached to thinking that the thirty-two perfect major marks are empty or not empty or that the eighty distinguishing minor features are empty or not empty. They are not attached to thinking that the thirty-two perfect major marks are with or without form or that the eighty distinguishing minor features are with or without form. They are not attached to thinking that the thirty-two perfect major marks are with or without aspiration or that the eighty distinguishing minor features are with or without aspiration. Sariputra, as the great bodhisattvas who are cultivating prajna paramita correspond with these dharmas, they correspond with prajna paramita.

"Furthermore, Sariputra, when cultivating prajna paramita, the great bodhisattvas are not attached to thinking that staying in correct mindfulness is existent or nonexistent or that dwelling in equanimity at all times is existent or nonexistent. They are not attached to thinking that staying in correct mindfulness is permanent or impermanent or that dwelling in equanimity at all times is permanent or impermanent. They are not attached to thinking that staying in correct mindfulness is pleasant or painful or that dwelling in equanimity at all times is pleasant or painful. They are not attached to thinking that staying in correct mindfulness is with or without selfness or that dwelling in equanimity at all times is with or without selfness. They are not attached to thinking that staying in correct mindfulness is tranquil or not tranquil or that dwelling in equanimity at all times is tranquil or not tranquil. They are not attached to thinking that staying in correct mindfulness is empty or not empty or that dwelling in equanimity at all times is empty or not empty. They are not attached to thinking that staying in correct mindfulness is with or without form or that dwelling in equanimity at all times is with or without form. They are not attached to thinking that staying in correct mindfulness is with or without aspiration or that dwelling in equanimity at all times is with or without aspiration. Sariputra, as the great bodhisattvas who are cultivating prajna paramita correspond with these dharmas, they correspond with prajna paramita.

"Furthermore, Sariputra, when cultivating prajna paramita, the great bodhisattvas are not attached to thinking that the perfect knowledge of everything is existent or nonexistent or that the perfect knowledge of the forms of the paths and the perfect knowledge of all phenomena are existent or nonexistent. They are not attached to thinking that the perfect knowledge of everything is permanent or impermanent or that the perfect knowledge of the forms of the paths and the perfect knowledge of all phenomena are permanent or impermanent. They are not attached to thinking that the perfect knowledge of everything is pleasant or painful or that the perfect knowledge of the forms of the paths and the perfect knowledge of all phenomena are pleasant or painful. They are not attached to thinking that the perfect knowledge of everything is with or without selfness or that the perfect knowledge of the forms of the paths and the perfect knowledge of all phenomena are with or without selfness. They are not attached to thinking that the perfect knowledge of everything is tranquil or not tranquil or that the perfect knowledge of the forms of the paths and the perfect knowledge of all phenomena are tranquil or not tranquil. They are not attached to thinking that the perfect knowledge of everything is empty or not empty or that the perfect knowledge of the forms of the paths and the perfect knowledge of all phenomena are empty or not empty. They are not attached to thinking that the perfect knowledge of everything is with or without form or that the perfect knowledge of the forms of the paths and the perfect knowledge of all phenomena are with or without form. They are not attached to thinking that the perfect knowledge of everything is with or without aspiration or that the perfect knowledge of the forms of the paths and the perfect knowledge of all phenomena are with or without aspiration. Sariputra, as the great bodhisattvas who are cultivating prajna paramita correspond with these dharmas, they correspond with prajna paramita.

"Furthermore, Sariputra, when cultivating prajna paramita, the great bodhisattvas are not attached to thinking that the stream-entry effect is existent or nonexistent or that the once-return effect, nonreturn effect, arhat effect, and the self-enlightenment bodhi are existent or nonexistent. They are not attached to thinking that the stream-entry effect is permanent or impermanent or that the once-return effect, nonreturn effect, arhat effect, and the self-enlightenment bodhi are permanent or impermanent. They are not attached to thinking that the stream-entry effect is pleasant or painful or that the once-return effect, nonreturn effect, arhat effect, and the self-enlightenment bodhi are pleasant or painful. They are not attached to thinking that the stream-entry effect is with or without selfness or that the once-return effect, nonreturn effect, arhat effect, and the self-enlightenment bodhi are with or without selfness. They are not attached to thinking that the stream-entry effect is tranquil or not tranquil or that the once-return effect, nonreturn effect, arhat effect, and the self-enlightenment bodhi are tranquil or not tranquil. They are not attached to thinking that the stream-entry effect is empty or not empty or that the once-return effect, nonreturn effect, arhat effect, and the self-enlightenment bodhi are empty or not empty. They are not attached to thinking that the stream-entry effect is with or without form or that the once-return effect, nonreturn effect, arhat effect, and the self-enlightenment bodhi are with or without form. They are not attached to thinking that the stream-entry effect is with or without aspiration or that the once-return effect, nonreturn effect, arhat effect, and the self-enlightenment bodhi are with or without aspiration. Sariputra, as the great bodhisattvas who are cultivating prajna paramita correspond with these dharmas, they correspond with prajna paramita.

"Furthermore, Sariputra, when cultivating prajna paramita, the great bodhisattvas are not attached to thinking that all great bodhisattva actions are existent or nonexistent or that the unsurpassed, perfect, and universal bodhi is existent or nonexistent. They are not attached to thinking that all great bodhisattva actions are permanent or impermanent or that the unsurpassed, perfect, and universal bodhi is permanent or impermanent. They are not attached to thinking that all great bodhisattva actions are pleasant or painful or that the unsurpassed, perfect, and universal bodhi is pleasant or painful. They are not attached to thinking that all great bodhisattva actions are with or without selfness or that the unsurpassed, perfect, and universal bodhi is with or without selfness. They are not attached to thinking that all great bodhisattva actions are tranquil or not tranquil or that the unsurpassed, perfect, and universal bodhi is tranquil or not tranquil. They are not attached to thinking that all great bodhisattva actions are empty or not empty or that the unsurpassed, perfect, and universal bodhi is empty or not empty. They are not attached to thinking that all great bodhisattva actions are with or without form or that the unsurpassed, perfect, and universal bodhi is with or without form. They are not attached to thinking that all great bodhisattva actions are with or without aspiration or that the unsurpassed, perfect, and universal bodhi is with or without aspiration. Sariputra, as the great bodhisattvas who are cultivating prajna paramita correspond with these dharmas, they correspond with prajna paramita.

"Sariputra, when cultivating prajna paramita, the great bodhisattvas do not think, 'I am practicing prajna paramita.' Nor do they think, 'I am not practicing prajna paramita.' They do not think, 'I am practicing and not practicing prajna paramita.' Nor do they think, 'I am not practicing and not nonpracticing prajna paramita.' Sariputra, as the great bodhisattvas who are cultivating prajna paramita correspond with these dharmas, they correspond with prajna paramita."

FASCICLE 7

Chapter 3
In Accordance with Prajna Paramita

Section 4

(In the First Assembly)

"FURTHERMORE, SARIPUTRA, WHEN CULTIVATING PRAJNA PARAMITA, THE GREAT bodhisattvas do not cultivate prajna paramita for the sake of giving paramita or of pure precept, forbearance, diligence, meditation, and prajna paramitas.

"When cultivating prajna paramita, the great bodhisattvas do not cultivate prajna paramita for the sake of internal emptiness or of external emptiness, internal-external emptiness, emptiness of emptiness, emptiness of space, emptiness of ultimate truth, emptiness of conditioned phenomena, emptiness of unconditioned reality, emptiness in the final analysis, emptiness of nontemporality, emptiness of deconstruction, emptiness of changelessness, emptiness of original nature, emptiness of particular characteristics, emptiness of common characteristics, emptiness of all dharmas, emptiness of nonattainment, emptiness of selflessness, emptiness of self-nature, and emptiness of selfless self-nature.

"When cultivating prajna paramita, the great bodhisattvas do not cultivate prajna paramita for the sake of realness or of dharma realm, dharma nature, nature of nonillusion, the nature of changelessness, the nature of equality, the nature of nonarising, dharma concentration, dharma dwelling, reality, the realm of empty space, and the realm of the inconceivable.

"When cultivating prajna paramita, the great bodhisattvas do not cultivate prajna paramita for the sake of entering onto the correct path of nonarising or achieving the stage of nonregression, assisting the sentient beings to mature, and dignifying and purifying the Buddha lands.

"When cultivating prajna paramita, the great bodhisattvas do not cultivate prajna paramita for the sake of the four bases of mindfulness or the four correct endeavors, four bases of power, five roots, five powers, seven factors for enlightenment, and noble eightfold path. They do not cultivate prajna paramita for the sake of the noble truth of suffering or the noble truths of the cause of suffering, the cessation of suffering, and the path for the cessation of suffering.

"When cultivating prajna paramita, the great bodhisattvas do not cultivate prajna paramita for the sake of the four meditations or the four immeasurable minds and the four formless concentrations.

"When cultivating prajna paramita, the great bodhisattvas do not cultivate prajna paramita for the sake of the eight liberations or the eight vexation-overcoming meditations, nine concentrations in sequence, and the ten universal contemplations.

"When cultivating prajna paramita, the great bodhisattvas do not cultivate prajna paramita for the sake of the liberation gate of emptiness or the liberation gates of formlessness and nonaspiration.

"When cultivating prajna paramita, the great bodhisattvas do not cultivate prajna paramita for the sake of all dharani gates or all samadhi gates.

"When cultivating prajna paramita, the great bodhisattvas do not cultivate prajna paramita for the sake of the stage of ecstasy or the stages of freedom from defilements, emitting light, flaming wisdom, being extremely difficult to be surpassed, manifestation of pure realness, going far away, the unmovable, expedient wisdom, and dharma cloud.

"When cultivating prajna paramita, the great bodhisattvas do not cultivate prajna paramita for the sake of the physical eyes or the heavenly eyes, wisdom eyes, dharma eyes, and Buddha eyes.

"When cultivating prajna paramita, the great bodhisattvas do not cultivate prajna paramita for the sake of the Buddha's ten abilities or the four kinds of fearlessness, four unhindered understandings, great loving-kindness, great compassion, great joy, great equanimity, and the eighteen distinctive features of Buddha's wisdom and power.

"When cultivating prajna paramita, the great bodhisattvas do not cultivate prajna paramita for the sake of the thirty-two perfect major marks or the eighty distinguishing minor features.

"When cultivating prajna paramita, the great bodhisattvas do not cultivate prajna paramita for the sake of staying in correct mindfulness or dwelling in equanimity at all times.

"When cultivating prajna paramita, the great bodhisattvas do not cultivate prajna paramita for the sake of the perfect knowledge of everything or the perfect knowledge of the forms of the paths, the perfect knowledge of all phenomena, and the exquisite and subtle knowledge of all phenomena.

"When cultivating prajna paramita, the great bodhisattvas do not cultivate prajna paramita to transcend stream-entry effect or to transcend once-return effect, nonreturn effect, arhat effect, and self-enlightenment bodhi.

"When cultivating prajna paramita, the great bodhisattvas do not cultivate prajna paramita for the sake of all great bodhisattva actions or the unsurpassed, perfect, and universal bodhi of the Buddhas.

"Why? Sariputra, it is because when cultivating prajna paramita, the great bodhisattvas do not see any difference among the dharma natures.

"Sariputra, as the great bodhisattvas who are cultivating prajna paramita correspond with these dharmas, they correspond with prajna paramita.

"Furthermore, Sariputra, when cultivating prajna paramita, the great bodhisattvas do not cultivate prajna paramita for the sake of the supernatural power of the heavenly eyes or the supernatural powers of the heavenly ears, of knowing others' minds, of knowing previous lives, of making transformation, and of flawless knowledge. Why? When cultivating prajna paramita, the great bodhisattvas do not see the prajna paramita that they cultivate, let alone the six supernatural powers that great bodhisattva and Thus-Comer have cultivated.

"Sariputra, as the great bodhisattvas who are cultivating prajna paramita correspond with these dharmas, they correspond with prajna paramita.

"Furthermore, Sariputra, when practicing prajna paramita, the great bodhisattvas do not have this thought in their minds: 'I can use my supernatural power of heavenly eyes to see universally how all the sentient beings in as many Buddha lands of the ten directions as the sands of the Ganges to be reborn from this land to that land.' Nor will they think, 'I can use my supernatural power of heavenly ears to hear all the dharma voices taught by the Buddhas and great bodhisattvas in as many Buddha lands of the ten directions as the sands of the Ganges.' Nor will they think, 'I can use my supernatural power of knowing others' minds to read all sentient beings' minds in as many Buddha lands of the ten directions as the sands of the Ganges.' Nor will they think, 'I can use my supernatural power of knowing previous lives to know what the previous lives of all sentient beings in as many Buddha lands of the ten directions as the sands of the Ganges were.' Nor will they think, 'I can use my supernatural power of making transformation to travel to as many Buddha lands of the ten directions as the sands of the Ganges to admire and pay respect and homage to all Buddhas and great bodhisattvas.' Nor will they think, 'I can use my supernatural power of flawless knowledge to see the sentient beings in as many Buddha lands of the ten directions as the sands of the Ganges, and get to know whether they still have flaws or are completely free from flaws.'

"Sariputra, as the great bodhisattvas who are cultivating prajna paramita correspond with these dharmas, they correspond with prajna paramita.

"Furthermore, Sariputra, if the great bodhisattvas who are cultivating prajna paramita correspond with prajna paramita, they will be able to establish well immeasurable, countless, and boundless

Fascicle 7, Chapter 3, Section 4   137

sentient beings in nirvana without remainder, and no evil demon can take advantage to harm them. Their vexations will be eliminated, and all affairs of the world can be done as they wish. All Thus-Comers, Ones Worthy of Offerings, Perfectly and Universally Enlightened Ones and the great bodhisattvas in as many realms of the ten directions as the sands of the Ganges will keep and protect these bodhisattvas, prevent them from falling into the stages of the voice-hearer and self-enlightened one. All heavenly beings from the Heaven of Four Great Kings, Heaven of Thirty-Three Smaller Heavens, Heaven of Yama, Heaven of Tusita, Heaven of Enjoying Self-Made Changes, Heaven of Enjoying Other-Made Changes, Heaven of Brahma Followers, Heaven of Brahma Subordinates, Heaven of Brahma Family, Heaven of Great Brahma, Heaven of Light, Heaven of Lesser Light, Heaven of Infinite Light, Heaven of Extremely Great Brightness and Purity, Heaven of Purity, Heaven of Lesser Purity, Heaven of Infinite Purity, Heaven of Universal Purity, Heaven of Expansion, Heaven of Lesser Expansion, Heaven of Infinite Expansion, Heaven of Extensive Rewards, Heaven of No Aspiration, Heaven of No Affliction, Heaven of Good Appearance, Heaven of Good Sight, and the Heaven of Ultimate Form, as well as all voice-hearers and self-enlightened ones in as many realms of the ten directions as the sands of the Ganges, will embrace and guard these bodhisattvas, remove all obstacles in whatever they do, and heal their physical and mental diseases. The enormous pains caused by guilty karmas they are supposed to suffer as retribution in the lives to come will be present in this life but greatly alleviated in painfulness. Why? Sariputra, it is because these great bodhisattvas have bestowed loving-kindness and compassion on all sentient beings universally.

"Sariputra, because of the mighty supernatural powers caused by the cultivation of prajna paramita, the great bodhisattvas are able to initiate quickly the most carefree dharani gates and samadhi gates with less effort and make them manifest. Wherever they are reborn, they will be able to make offerings to and serve and will never stay away from all Thus-Comers, Ones Worthy of Offerings, and Perfectly and Universally Enlightened Ones until attaining the unsurpassed, perfect, and universal bodhi that they are pursuing.

"Sariputra, as the great bodhisattvas who are cultivating prajna paramita correspond with prajna paramita, they are able to attain such immeasurable, countless, inconceivable, subtle, and exquisite merits and virtues.

"Furthermore, Sariputra, when cultivating prajna paramita, the great bodhisattvas do not think, 'There are the dharmas that are correspondent or not correspondent with other dharmas, equivalent or not equivalent to other dharmas.' Why? Sariputra, it is because the great bodhisattvas do not see any dharma correspondent or not correspondent with other dharmas, equivalent or not equivalent to other dharmas.

"When cultivating prajna paramita, the great bodhisattvas do not think, 'I will be perfectly and universally enlightened in dharma realm quickly or not quickly.' Why? Sariputra, it is because these great bodhisattvas do not see any dharma manifesting perfect and universal enlightenment in dharma realm. When cultivating prajna paramita, the great bodhisattvas do not see any dharma apart from dharma realm, or dharma realm apart from the dharmas. They do not see the dharmas being with dharma realm, or dharma realm being with the dharmas.

"When cultivating prajna paramita, the great bodhisattvas do not think, 'Dharma realm can serve as the cause and condition of the dharmas.' Nor do they think, 'The dharmas can serve as the cause and condition for dharma realm.' When cultivating prajna paramita, the great bodhisattvas do not think, 'This dharma can realize dharma realm, and that dharma cannot realize dharma realm.' Why? Sariputra, as these great bodhisattvas do not see the dharma, how can they see any dharma that can or cannot realize dharma realm?

"Sariputra, as the great bodhisattvas who are cultivating prajna paramita correspond with these dharmas, they correspond with prajna paramita.

"Furthermore, Sariputra, when cultivating prajna paramita, the great bodhisattvas do not see that matter is correspondent with emptiness or emptiness is correspondent with matter, nor do they see that feeling, thinking, action, and consciousness are correspondent with emptiness or that emptiness is correspondent with feeling, thinking, action, and consciousness.

"When cultivating prajna paramita, the great bodhisattvas do not see that the eye sphere is correspondent with emptiness or that emptiness is correspondent with the eye sphere, nor do they see that the ear, nose, tongue, body, and conscious spheres are correspondent with emptiness or that emptiness is correspondent with the ear, nose, tongue, body, and conscious spheres.

"When cultivating prajna paramita, the great bodhisattvas do not see that the sight sphere is correspondent with emptiness or emptiness is correspondent with the sight sphere, nor do they see that the sound, smell, taste, touch, and mental-image spheres are correspondent with emptiness or that emptiness is correspondent with the sound, smell, taste, touch, and mental-image spheres.

"When cultivating prajna paramita, the great bodhisattvas do not see that the eye realm is correspondent with emptiness or that emptiness is correspondent with the eye realm, nor do they see that the ear, nose, tongue, body, and conscious realms are correspondent with emptiness or that emptiness is correspondent with the ear, nose, tongue, body, and conscious realms.

"When cultivating prajna paramita, the great bodhisattvas do not see that the sight realm is correspondent with emptiness or that emptiness is correspondent with the sight realm, nor do they see that the sound, smell, taste, touch, and mental-image realms are correspondent with emptiness or that emptiness is correspondent with the sound, smell, taste, touch, and mental-image realms.

"When cultivating prajna paramita, the great bodhisattvas do not see that the eye consciousness realm is correspondent with emptiness or that emptiness is correspondent with the eye consciousness realm, nor do they see that the ear, nose, tongue, body, and conscious consciousness realms are correspondent with emptiness or that emptiness is correspondent with the ear, nose, tongue, body, and conscious consciousness realms.

"When cultivating prajna paramita, the great bodhisattvas do not see that the eye contact is correspondent with emptiness or that emptiness is correspondent with the eye contact, nor do they see that the ear, nose, tongue, body, and conscious contacts are correspondent with emptiness or that emptiness is correspondent with the ear, nose, tongue, body, and conscious contacts.

"When cultivating prajna paramita, the great bodhisattvas do not see that the feelings produced by eye contact are correspondent with emptiness or that emptiness is correspondent with the feelings produced by eye contact, nor do they see that the feelings produced by ear, nose, tongue, body, and conscious contacts are correspondent with emptiness or that emptiness is correspondent with the feelings produced by ear, nose, tongue, body, and conscious contacts.

"When cultivating prajna paramita, the great bodhisattvas do not see that the earth realm is correspondent with emptiness or that emptiness is correspondent with the earth realm, nor do they see that the water, fire, wind, space, and consciousness realms are correspondent with emptiness or that emptiness is correspondent with the water, fire, wind, space, and consciousness realms.

"When cultivating prajna paramita, the great bodhisattvas do not see that cause and condition is correspondent with emptiness or that emptiness is correspondent with cause and condition, nor do they see that consecutive thoughts in sequence, conditions that stimulate the mind, conditions that reinforce main causes, and the dharmas caused by conditions are correspondent with emptiness or that emptiness is correspondent with consecutive thoughts in sequence, conditions that stimulate the mind, conditions that reinforce main causes, and the dharmas caused by conditions.

"When cultivating prajna paramita, the great bodhisattvas do not see that ignorance is correspondent with emptiness or that emptiness is correspondent with ignorance, nor do they see that action, consciousness, name and form, six sense spheres, contact, reception, craving, grasping, existence, birth, old age, death, worry, sorrow, misery, anxiety, and upset are correspondent with emptiness or that emptiness is correspondent with action, and so forth, as well as old age, death, worry, sorrow, misery, anxiety, and upset.

"When cultivating prajna paramita, the great bodhisattvas do not see that giving paramita is correspondent with emptiness or that emptiness is correspondent with giving paramita, nor do they see that pure precept, forbearance, diligence, meditation, and prajna paramitas are correspondent with emptiness or that emptiness is correspondent with pure precept, forbearance, diligence, meditation, and prajna paramitas.

"When cultivating prajna paramita, the great bodhisattvas do not see that internal emptiness is correspondent with emptiness or that emptiness is correspondent with internal emptiness, nor do they see that external emptiness, internal-external emptiness, emptiness of emptiness, emptiness of space, emptiness of ultimate truth, emptiness of conditioned phenomena, emptiness of unconditioned reality, emptiness in the final analysis, emptiness of nontemporality, emptiness of deconstruction, emptiness of changelessness, emptiness of original nature, emptiness of particular characteristics, emptiness of common characteristics, emptiness of all dharmas, emptiness of nonattainment, emptiness of selflessness, emptiness of self-nature, and emptiness of selfless self-nature are correspondent with emptiness or that emptiness is correspondent with external emptiness and so forth as well as emptiness of selfless self-nature.

"When cultivating prajna paramita, the great bodhisattvas do not see that realness is correspondent with emptiness or that emptiness is correspondent with realness, nor do they see that dharma realm, dharma nature, the nature of nonillusion, the nature of changelessness, the nature of equality, the nature of nonarising, dharma concentration, dharma dwelling, reality, the realm of empty space, and the realm of the inconceivable are correspondent with emptiness or that emptiness is correspondent with dharma realm, and so forth, as well as the realm of the inconceivable.

"When cultivating prajna paramita, the great bodhisattvas do not see that the four bases of mindfulness are correspondent with emptiness or that emptiness is correspondent with the four bases of mindfulness, nor do they see that the four correct endeavors, four bases of power, five roots, five powers, seven factors for enlightenment, and the noble eightfold path are correspondent with emptiness or that emptiness is correspondent with the four correct endeavors, and so forth, as well as the noble eightfold path.

"When cultivating prajna paramita, the great bodhisattvas do not see that the noble truth of suffering is correspondent with emptiness or that emptiness is correspondent with the noble truth of suffering, nor do they see that the noble truths of the cause of suffering, the cessation of suffering, and the path for the cessation of suffering are correspondent with emptiness or that emptiness is correspondent with the noble truths of the cause of suffering, the cessation of suffering, and the path for the cessation of suffering.

"When cultivating prajna paramita, the great bodhisattvas do not see that the four meditations are correspondent with emptiness or that emptiness is correspondent with the four meditations, nor do they see that the four immeasurable minds and the four formless concentrations are correspondent with emptiness or that emptiness is correspondent with the four immeasurable minds and the four formless concentrations.

"When cultivating prajna paramita, the great bodhisattvas do not see that the eight liberations are correspondent with emptiness or that emptiness is correspondent with the eight liberations, nor do they see that the eight vexation-overcoming meditations, nine concentrations in sequence, and ten universal contemplations are correspondent with emptiness or that emptiness is correspondent with the eight vexation-overcoming meditations, nine concentrations in sequence, and ten universal contemplations.

"When cultivating prajna paramita, the great bodhisattvas do not see that the liberation gate of emptiness is correspondent with emptiness or that emptiness is correspondent with the liberation gate of emptiness, nor do they see that the liberation gates of formlessness and nonaspiration are correspondent with emptiness or that emptiness is correspondent with the liberation gates of formlessness and nonaspiration.

"When cultivating prajna paramita, the great bodhisattvas do not see that all dharani gates are correspondent with emptiness or that emptiness is correspondent with all dharani gates, nor do they see that all samadhi gates are correspondent with emptiness or that emptiness is correspondent with all samadhi gates.

"When cultivating prajna paramita, the great bodhisattvas do not see that the stage of ecstasy is correspondent with emptiness or that emptiness is correspondent with the stage of ecstasy, nor do they see that the stages of freedom from defilements, emitting light, flaming wisdom, being extremely difficult to be surpassed, manifestation of pure realness, going far away, the unmovable, expedient wisdom, and dharma cloud are correspondent with emptiness or that emptiness is correspondent with the stage of freedom from defilements, and so forth, as well as the stage of dharma cloud.

"When cultivating prajna paramita, the great bodhisattvas do not see that the five eyes are correspondent with emptiness or that emptiness is correspondent with the five eyes, nor do they see that the six supernatural powers are correspondent with emptiness or that emptiness is correspondent with the six supernatural powers.

"When cultivating prajna paramita, the great bodhisattvas do not see that the Buddha's ten abilities are correspondent with emptiness or that emptiness is correspondent with the Buddha's ten abilities, nor do they see that the four kinds of fearlessness, four unhindered understandings, great loving-kindness, great compassion, great joy, great equanimity, and the eighteen distinctive features of Buddha's wisdom and power are correspondent with emptiness or that emptiness is correspondent with the four kinds of fearlessness, and so forth, as well as the eighteen distinctive features of Buddha's wisdom and power.

"When cultivating prajna paramita, the great bodhisattvas do not see that the thirty-two perfect major marks are correspondent with emptiness or that emptiness is correspondent with the thirty-two perfect major marks, nor do they see that the eighty distinguishing minor features are correspondent with emptiness or that emptiness is correspondent with the eighty distinguishing minor features.

"When cultivating prajna paramita, the great bodhisattvas do not see that staying in correct mindfulness is correspondent with emptiness or that emptiness is correspondent with staying in correct mindfulness, nor do they see that dwelling in equanimity at all times is correspondent with emptiness or that emptiness is correspondent with dwelling in equanimity at all times.

"When cultivating prajna paramita, the great bodhisattvas do not see that the perfect knowledge of everything is correspondent with emptiness or that emptiness is correspondent with the perfect knowledge of everything, nor do they see that the perfect knowledge of the forms of the paths and the perfect knowledge of all phenomena are correspondent with emptiness or that emptiness is correspondent with the perfect knowledge of the forms of the paths and the perfect knowledge of all phenomena.

"When cultivating prajna paramita, the great bodhisattvas do not see that stream-entry effect is correspondent with emptiness or that emptiness is correspondent with stream-entry effect, nor do they see that once-return effect, nonreturn effect, arhat effect, and self-enlightenment bodhi are correspondent with emptiness or that emptiness is correspondent with once-return effect, nonreturn effect, arhat effect, and self-enlightenment bodhi.

"When cultivating prajna paramita, the great bodhisattvas do not see that all great bodhisattva actions are correspondent with emptiness or that emptiness is correspondent with all great bodhisattva actions, nor do they see that the unsurpassed, perfect, and universal bodhi of the Buddhas is correspondent with emptiness or that emptiness is correspondent with the unsurpassed, perfect, and universal bodhi of the Buddhas.

"Sariputra, as the great bodhisattvas who are cultivating prajna paramita correspond with these dharmas, they are the first ones to be correspondent with prajna paramita.

"Sariputra, since the great bodhisattvas who are cultivating prajna paramita correspond with such emptiness, they will not fall into the stages of the voice-hearer and the self-enlightened one. They will, rather, be able to dignify and purify the Buddha lands, assist the sentient beings to grow and mature, and realize insightfully the unsurpassed, perfect, and universal bodhi soon.

"Sariputra, for the great bodhisattvas who are cultivating prajna paramita, the correspondence with prajna paramita is the very first, the noblest, the most superior, the uppermost, the most wonderful, the highest, the unexcelled, and the unequaled one among all kinds of correspondence. Why? Sariputra, being correspondent with prajna paramita is to be correspondent with emptiness, formlessness, and nonaspiration. It is because of this cause and condition that the correspondence with prajna paramita is the very first one among all kinds of correspondence.

"Sariputra, as the great bodhisattvas, who are cultivating prajna paramita, correspond with such prajna paramita, they will be definitely approved with a prophecy by the Buddha of becoming a

Fascicle 7, Chapter 3, Section 4 145

Buddha in the future soon, or they are very close to that prophecy the Buddha will confer.

"Sariputra, because the great bodhisattvas have such a correspondence, they are able to bring great benefits to immeasurable, countless, and boundless sentient beings.

"Sariputra, these great bodhisattvas will not think, 'I am correspondent with prajna paramita.' Or think, 'I will be conferred or am very close to being conferred the prophecy of becoming a Buddha.' Or think, 'I can dignify and purify the Buddha lands.' Or think, 'I will assist the sentient beings to grow and mature.' Or think, 'I will realize insightfully and attain the unsurpassed, perfect, and universal bodhi in order to turn the wonderful dharma wheel and liberate immeasurable sentient beings.' Why? Sariputra! These great bodhisattvas do not see any dharma apart from the dharma realm or the dharma realm apart from the dharmas or any dharma that is with dharma realm or dharma realm that is with the dharmas. They do not see that any dharma can cultivate prajna paramita or that any dharma can be conferred the prophecy of becoming a Buddha by the Buddha or that any dharma will definitely attain the unsurpassed, perfect, and universal bodhi or that any dharma can dignify and purify the Buddha lands or that any dharma can help the sentient beings mature.

"Why? Sariputra, as cultivating prajna paramita, the great bodhisattvas do not have the thought of 'I,' or the thought of the sentient being, the living one, the one who gives birth, the one who raises others, the gentleperson, the individual in reincarnation, the mentally born one, the learned child, the maker, the one who makes others make, the initiator, the one who makes others initiate, the receiver, the one who makes others receive, the knower, or the viewer. Why? Because in the final analysis, the 'I,' the sentient being, and so forth, are without arising and extinction. As they are without arising and extinction, how can we say that one should cultivate prajna paramita in order to gain various kinds of virtues, merits, and triumphs?

"Sariputra, because these great bodhisattvas do not see the arising of the sentient beings, they cultivate prajna paramita; because they do not see the extinction of the sentient beings, they cultivate prajna paramita; because they know that the sentient beings are empty, they cultivate prajna paramita; because they know that the sentient beings are without selfness, they cultivate prajna paramita; because they know that the sentient beings are unattainable, they cultivate prajna paramita; because they know that the sentient beings are far away, they cultivate prajna paramita; and because they know that the original nature of the sentient beings is nonexistent, they cultivate prajna paramita.

"Sariputra, for the great bodhisattvas who are cultivating prajna paramita, the best correspondence is the one correspondent with emptiness; the noblest, most superior, and unequaled correspondence is the one correspondent with prajna paramita.

"Sariputra, as the great bodhisattvas achieve such a correspondence, they will be able to activate the Buddha's ten abilities, four kinds of fearlessness, four unhindered understandings, great loving-kindness, great compassion, great joy, great equanimity, eighteen distinctive features of Buddha's wisdom and power, the thirty-two perfect major marks, the eighty distinguishing minor features, staying in correct mindfulness, dwelling in equanimity at all times, the perfect knowledge of everything, the perfect knowledge of the forms of the paths, the perfect knowledge of all phenomena, and the rest of immeasurable, countless, and boundless Buddha dharma.

"Sariputra, as the great bodhisattvas who are cultivating prajna paramita correspond with such prajna paramita, they will ultimately stay away from the obstacles caused by greed, stinginess, violation of precepts, anger, hatred, laziness, tiredness, restlessness, and evil thoughts in mind. At the same time, giving, pure precept, forbearance, diligence, meditation, and prajna paramitas will be present before them effortlessly and without interruption."

Chapter 4
Rebirth

Section 1

(In the First Assembly)

AT THAT TIME, SARIPUTRA ASKED THE BUDDHA, "WORLD-HONORED One! Where are the great bodhisattvas who dwell peacefully in prajna paramita reborn from? Where will they be reborn after passing away from the present life?"

The Buddha replied to the long-lived sage Sariputra, "Some of the great bodhisattvas who dwell peacefully in prajna paramita are reborn here from other Buddha lands, some from the Heaven of Tusita, and some are from the human realm.

"Sariputra, the great bodhisattvas who dwell peacefully in prajna paramita and are from other Buddha lands are able to conform with prajna paramita quickly. Because they are correspondent with prajna paramita, the profound and wonderful dharma gate will be present for them at the moment of their rebirth. From that time on, they will always be correspondent with prajna paramita. Wherever they are reborn in the future, they will always encounter the Buddhas and be able to make offerings to the Buddhas and respect and admire them. Because of this cause and condition, they will fulfill prajna paramita gradually, but perfectly.

"Sariputra, the great bodhisattvas who dwell peacefully in prajna paramita and are from the Heaven of Tusita now have come to the final phase of cultivation before becoming a Buddha. For them, giving, pure precept, forbearance, diligence, meditation, and prajna paramitas will always be present effortlessly. They will never lose correct mindfulness, all dharani gates, and all samadhi gates.

"Sariputra, the great bodhisattvas who dwell peacefully in

prajna paramita and are from the human realm have the roots that are not sharp. They are not smart, but they work diligently in cultivating prajna paramita and have already achieved the stage of nonregression. Nevertheless, they are still unable to correspond with prajna paramita quickly. Besides, they cannot master all dharani gates and all samadhi gates freely.

"Again, Sariputra, in regard to the second part of your question, where will the great bodhisattvas who dwell peacefully in prajna paramita go after passing away from here? Sariputra, I will reply that because these great bodhisattvas are always correspondent with prajna paramita, they will be reborn after this life into other Buddha lands, from one to the other, and wherever they are reborn, they will always be privileged to encounter the Buddhas, make offerings, and pay acclamation and admiration to them. They will never stay away from the Buddhas until finally attaining the unsurpassed, perfect, and universal bodhi.

"Furthermore, Sariputra, some great bodhisattvas do not have expedient skillfulness, but they have practiced the first, second, third, and fourth stages of meditation and have practiced giving, pure precept, forbearance, diligence, meditation, and prajna paramitas. These great bodhisattvas will be reborn after this life into the heaven of longevity owing to their achievement in meditation. At the end of that long lifespan, they will be reborn into the human realm, in which they will encounter Buddhas, make offerings to them, and admire and acclaim them. Although they will practice giving, pure precept, forbearance, diligence, meditation, and prajna paramitas, their sense roots remain dull and slow, and their minds are not sharp and smart enough. Whatever they do is not done very expediently and skillfully.

"Furthermore, Sariputra, some great bodhisattvas have entered into the first, second, third, and the fourth stages of meditation and have also cultivated giving, pure precept, forbearance, diligence, meditation, and prajna paramitas. But they have no expedient skillfulness. It turns out that they stay away from meditations and are destined to be reborn in the realm of desire. These great bodhisattvas have dull sensation and slow minds and cannot act very expediently and skillfully either.

"Furthermore, Sariputra, some great bodhisattvas have entered into the first meditation and have also entered into the second, third, and fourth stages of meditation. They have entered into the mind of immeasurable loving-kindness, and have also entered into the minds of immeasurable compassion, joy, and equanimity. They have entered into the concentration of boundless emptiness and have also entered into the concentrations of boundless consciousness, nothingness, and nonthinking and not nonthinking. They have cultivated giving paramita and have also cultivated pure precept, forbearance, diligence, meditation, and prajna paramitas. They have dwelled peacefully in internal emptiness and have also dwelled peacefully in external emptiness, internal-external emptiness, emptiness of emptiness, emptiness of space, emptiness of ultimate truth, emptiness of conditioned phenomena, emptiness of unconditioned reality, emptiness in the final analysis, emptiness of nontemporality, emptiness of changelessness, emptiness of original nature, emptiness of particular characteristics, emptiness of common characteristics, emptiness of all dharmas, emptiness of nonattainment, emptiness of selflessness, emptiness of self-nature, and emptiness of selfless selfness. They have dwelled peacefully in realness and have also dwelled peacefully in dharma realm, dharma nature, nature of nonillusion, the nature of changelessness, the nature of equality, the nature of nonarising, dharma concentration, dharma dwelling, reality, the realm of empty space, and the realm of the inconceivable. They have cultivated the four bases of mindfulness and have also cultivated the four correct endeavors, four bases of power, five roots, five powers, seven factors for enlightenment, and noble eightfold path. They have dwelled peacefully in the noble truth of suffering and have also dwelled peacefully in the noble truths of the cause of suffering, the cessation of suffering, and the path for the cessation of suffering. They have cultivated the eight liberations and have also cultivated the eight vexation-overcoming meditations, nine concentrations in sequence, and ten universal contemplations. They have cultivated the liberation gate of emptiness and have also cultivated the liberation gates of formlessness and nonaspiration. They have cultivated all dharani gates and have also cultivated all samadhi gates. They have cultivated the five eyes and have also cultivated the six supernatural powers. They have cultivated the Buddha's ten abilities and have also cultivated the four kinds of fearlessness, four unhindered understandings, great loving-kindness, great compassion, great joy, great equanimity, and eighteen distinctive features of Buddha's wisdom and power. They have cultivated the way of staying in correct mindfulness and have also cultivated the nature of dwelling in equanimity at all times. They have cultivated the perfect knowledge of everything and have also cultivated the perfect knowledge of the forms of the paths and the perfect knowledge of all phenomena. Because these great bodhisattvas have the ability of doing things in expedient skillfulness, they will not allow the power of meditation, the immeasurable minds, or the formless concentration to lead them in rebirth; rather, they can go anywhere in rebirth at their own will, and wherever they are reborn, they are privileged to encounter the Buddhas, Ones Worthy of Offerings, the Perfectly and Universally Enlightened Ones; make offerings to them; and admire and acclaim them. They will never stay away from the profound prajna paramita. It is certain that these great bodhisattvas will attain the unsurpassed, perfect, and universal bodhi during the present Kalpa of the Sages.

"Furthermore, Sariputra, some great bodhisattvas have entered into the first meditation, as well as the second, third, and fourth meditations. They have entered into the mind of immeasurable loving-kindness, as well as the minds of immeasurable compassion, joy, and equanimity. They have entered into the concentration of boundless emptiness, as well as the concentrations of boundless consciousness, nothingness, and nonthinking and not nonthinking. Because these great bodhisattvas possess expedient skills, they will not let the power of meditation, the immeasurable minds, or the formless concentration dominate in rebirth; rather, they will choose to be reborn in the realm of desire in a noble family of Ksatriya, Brahman, the elder, or a lay believer. Their rebirth is not contaminated by greed, but with an intention to assist sentient beings to grow and mature.

"Furthermore, Sariputra, some great bodhisattvas have entered into the first meditation and the second, third, and the fourth meditations. They have entered into the mind of immeasurable loving-kindness, and also the minds of immeasurable compassion, joy, and equanimity. They have entered into the concentration of boundless emptiness and also the concentrations of boundless consciousness, nothingness, and nonthinking and not nonthinking. Because these great bodhisattvas have possessed expedient skills, they will not let the power of meditation, the immeasurable minds, or the formless concentration dominate their rebirth; rather, they will choose to be reborn in the Heaven of Four Great Kings, the Heaven of Thirty-Three Smaller Heavens, the Heaven of Yama, the Heaven of Tusita, the Heaven of Enjoying Self-Made Changes, or the Heaven of Enjoying Other-Made Changes. They will be reborn with an intention to assist the sentient beings to grow and mature and will dignify and purify the various Buddha lands. They will be privileged to always encounter the Buddhas, make offerings respectfully to, admire, and acclaim them. They will never miss doing this, even once.

"Furthermore, Sariputra, some great bodhisattvas have entered into the first meditation and also the second, third, and the fourth meditations. They have entered into the mind of immeasurable loving-kindness, and also the minds of immeasurable compassion, immeasurable joy, and immeasurable equanimity. They have entered into the concentration of boundless emptiness and also the concentrations of boundless consciousness, nothingness, and nonthinking and not nonthinking. Because these great bodhisattvas possess expedient skills, they are able to be reborn in the Brahman world as a great Brahman king and so possess the virtues and powers that exceed the rest of the Brahman followers. They will come down from the heaven and travel from one Buddha land to the other, and during the trips, they encourage and advise the great bodhisattvas who have not realized the unsurpassed, perfect, and universal bodhi to work hard to realize it. They will also encourage and advise those who have realized the unsurpassed, perfect, and universal bodhi to begin turning the dharma wheel in order to bring tremendous happiness and benefits to the sentient beings.

"Furthermore, Sariputra, because some great bodhisattvas have reached the status of being in the final phase before becoming a

Buddha and possess expedient skillfulness, they will be able to enter into the first, second, third, and fourth meditations. They have entered into the minds of immeasurable loving-kindness, compassion, joy, and equanimity. They have entered into the concentrations of boundless emptiness, boundless consciousness, nothingness, and nonthinking and not nonthinking. They have cultivated giving, pure precept, forbearance, diligence, meditation, and prajna paramitas. They have dwelled peacefully in internal emptiness, external emptiness, internal-external emptiness, emptiness of emptiness, emptiness of space, emptiness of ultimate truth, emptiness of conditioned phenomena, emptiness of unconditioned reality, emptiness in the final analysis, emptiness of nontemporality, emptiness of deconstruction, emptiness of changelessness, emptiness of original nature, emptiness of particular characteristics, emptiness of common characteristics, emptiness of all dharmas, emptiness of nonattainment, emptiness of selflessness, emptiness of self-nature, and emptiness of selfless self-nature. They have dwelled peacefully in realness, the dharma realm, dharma nature, the nature of nonillusion, the nature of changelessness, the nature of equality, the nature of nonarising, dharma concentration, dharma dwelling, reality, the realm of empty space, and the realm of the inconceivable. They have cultivated the four bases of mindfulness, four correct endeavors, four bases of power, five roots, five powers, seven factors for enlightenment, and noble eightfold path. They have dwelled peacefully in the noble truths of suffering, the cause of suffering, the cessation of suffering, and the path for the cessation of suffering. They have cultivated the eight liberations, eight vexation-overcoming meditations, nine concentrations in sequence, and ten universal contemplations. They have cultivated the liberation gates of emptiness, formlessness, and nonaspiration. They have cultivated all dharani gates and all samadhi gates. They have cultivated the five eyes and the six supernatural powers. They have cultivated the Buddha's ten abilities, four kinds of fearlessness, four unhindered understandings, great loving-kindness, great compassion, great joy, great equanimity, and eighteen distinguishing features of Buddha's wisdom and power. They have cultivated the way of staying in correct mindfulness and the nature of dwelling in equanimity at all times. They have cultivated the perfect knowledge of everything, the perfect knowledge of the forms of the paths, and the perfect knowledge of all phenomena. These great bodhisattvas will not allow the power of meditation, the immeasurable minds, or the formless concentration to dominate their rebirth; rather, they will choose to be reborn in the Heaven of Tusita. Before that, they will stay close to the Thus-Comer, the One Worthy of Offerings, the Perfectly and Universally Enlightened One, make offerings to him and practice pure celibacy diligently in the Buddha's place. At the end of their lifespan in Tusita, they will return to this human world. But this time, they will be already with perfect roots and correct views and can play supernatural powers freely. They will be ushered and accompanied by immeasurable, countless hundreds of thousands of koti nayuta heavenly beings. They will cultivate ascetic practices and realize the unsurpassed, perfect, and universal bodhi in this human world, and turn the wonderful dharma wheel in order to liberate immeasurable sentient beings.

"Furthermore, Sariputra, some great bodhisattvas have gained the six supernatural powers, but they will choose not to be reborn in the realm of desire, the realm of form, or the realm of formlessness; instead, they enjoy traveling from one Buddha land to the other, make offerings to, admire, and acclaim innumerable Thus-Comers, the Ones Worthy of Offerings, the Perfectly and Universally Enlightened Ones. They will cultivate various great bodhisattva actions gradually, but finally they will realize insightfully and attain the unsurpassed, perfect, and universal bodhi that they have been pursuing.

"Furthermore, Sariputra, some bodhisattvas have attained the six supernatural powers and enjoy using them to teach and help sentient beings. They travel from one Buddha land to the other, wherein no names like voice-hearer or self-enlightened one are heard. The only one pure practice is the one-vehicle, the vehicle for the bodhisattvas. These bodhisattvas will make offerings to, esteem, and admire innumerable Thus-Comers, the Ones Worthy of Offerings, the Perfectly and Universally Enlightened Ones in many Buddha lands and cultivate prajna paramita. They will gradually fulfill the work of dignifying and purifying the Buddha lands and tirelessly assisting the sentient beings to grow and mature.

"Furthermore, Sariputra, some great bodhisattvas have attained freedom and self-ease in playing the six supernatural powers. They travel from one Buddha land to the other, in which the lifespan of the sentient beings is countless. These great bodhisattvas will make offerings to, esteem, and acclaim innumerable Thus-Comers, the Ones Worthy of Offerings, the Perfectly and Universally Enlightened Ones in many Buddha lands and cultivate prajna paramita. They will gradually fulfill dignifying and purifying the Buddha lands and tirelessly assisting the sentient beings to grow and mature.

"Furthermore, Sariputra, some great bodhisattvas have acquired the six supernatural powers and enjoy playing them freely. They will travel from one Buddha land to the other, in some of which the names of the Buddha, the dharma, and the sangha have never been heard. These great bodhisattvas will go to those lands to praise and propagate the triple gem of the Buddha, the dharma, and the sangha, so the sentient beings there will develop a deep and pure belief in them and thus gain benefits, peace, and happiness. These great bodhisattvas will be reborn after the present life into the world where there is the Buddha. They will cultivate all great bodhisattva actions, and gradually they will attain the unsurpassed, perfect, and universal bodhi and bring benefits, peace, and happiness to all sentient beings.

"Furthermore, Sariputra, some great bodhisattvas have from the beginning made great vows to cultivate diligently and bravely and have soon attained the first, second, third, and fourth meditations. They have attained the minds of immeasurable loving-kindness, compassion, joy, and equanimity. They have attained the concentrations of boundless emptiness, consciousness, nothingness, and nonthinking and not nonthinking. They have cultivated giving, pure precept, forbearance, diligence, meditation, and prajna paramitas; dwelled peacefully in internal emptiness, external emptiness, internal-external emptiness, emptiness of emptiness, emptiness of space, emptiness of ultimate truth, emptiness of conditioned phenomena, emptiness of unconditioned reality, emptiness in the final analysis, emptiness of nontemporality, emptiness of deconstruc-

Fascicle 7, Chapter 4, Section 1   155

tion, emptiness of changelessness, emptiness of original nature, emptiness of particular characteristics, emptiness of common characteristics, emptiness of all dharmas, emptiness of nonattainment, emptiness of selflessness, emptiness of self-nature, and emptiness of selfless self-nature; dwelled peacefully in realness, dharma realm, dharma nature, the nature of nonillusion, the nature of changelessness, the nature of equality, the nature of nonarising, dharma concentration, dharma dwelling, reality, the realm of space, and the realm of the inconceivable; cultivated the four bases of mindfulness, four correct endeavors, four bases of power, five roots, five powers, seven factors for enlightenment, and noble eightfold path; dwelled peacefully in the noble truths of suffering, the cause of suffering, the cessation of suffering, and the path for the cessation of suffering; cultivated the eight liberations, eight vexation-overcoming meditations, nine concentrations in sequence, and ten universal contemplations; cultivated the liberation gates of emptiness, formlessness, and nonaspiration; cultivated all dharani gates and all samadhi gates; cultivated the stages of ecstasy, freedom from defilements, emitting light, flaming wisdom, being extremely difficult to be surpassed, the manifestation of pure realness, going far away, the unmovable, expedient wisdom, and dharma cloud; cultivated the five eyes and the six supernatural powers; cultivated the Buddha's ten abilities, four kinds of fearlessness, four unhindered understandings, great loving-kindness, great compassion, great joy, great equanimity, and the eighteen distinctive features of Buddha's wisdom and power; cultivated the way of staying in correct mindfulness and the nature of dwelling in equanimity at all times; and cultivated the perfect knowledge of everything, perfect knowledge of the forms of the paths, and the perfect knowledge of all phenomena. These great bodhisattvas will not be reborn in the realm of desire, form, or formlessness. Rather, they will choose to be reborn into the lands where they can do things to bring great benefits and happiness to the sentient beings.

"Furthermore, Sariputra, some great bodhisattvas before had already cultivated giving, pure precept, forbearance, diligence, meditation, and prajna paramitas. Therefore, from the time of beginning to make great vows, they have directly entered onto the correct bodhisattva path of nonarising and remained on the path until attaining the stage of nonregression.

"Furthermore, Sariputra, some great bodhisattvas before had cultivated the six paramitas and the rest of immeasurable and boundless Buddha dharma. Therefore, from the time of beginning to make great vows, they have been able to realize the unsurpassed, perfect, and universal bodhi, turn the wonderful dharma wheel, and ferry innumerable sentient beings to the other shore of liberation. They will enter into the great nirvana without remainder. After passing into nirvana, the correct dharma that they once taught will remain effective and influential and continue to benefit the boundless sentient beings for one kalpa or even longer.

"Furthermore, Sariputra, some great bodhisattvas before had cultivated the six paramitas and the rest of great bodhisattva actions. Therefore, since the moment of beginning to make the great vows, their minds have been correspondent with prajna paramita. They then will be in company with immeasurable, countless hundreds of thousands of koti nayuta great bodhisattvas to travel from one Buddha land to the other, make offerings to the World-Honored Ones, esteem and acclaim them, assist the sentient beings to mature, and dignify and purify the Buddha lands.

Fascicle 8

Chapter 4
Rebirth

Section 2

(In the First Assembly)

"Furthermore, Sariputra, some great bodhisattvas have cultivated prajna paramita and attained the four meditations, four immeasurable minds, and four formless concentrations; they have also progressed through all the nine concentrations. They are able to enter into and get out of the concentrations as freely as enjoying a play and have already reached a level that all voice-hearers and self-enlightened ones cannot achieve. These great bodhisattvas will sometimes enter into the first meditation. Rising from the first meditation, they will enter into the concentration of extinction. Rising from the concentration of extinction, they will enter into the second meditation. Rising from the second meditation, they will enter into the concentration of extinction. Rising from the concentration of extinction, they will enter into the third meditation. Rising from the third meditation, they will enter into the concentration of extinction. Rising from the concentration of extinction, they will enter into the fourth meditation. Rising from the fourth meditation, they will enter into the concentration of extinction.

Rising from the concentration of extinction, they will enter into the concentration of boundless emptiness. Rising from the concentration of boundless emptiness, they will enter into the concentration of extinction. Rising from the concentration of extinction, they will enter into the concentration of boundless consciousness. Rising from the concentration of boundless consciousness, they will enter into the concentration of extinction. Rising from the concentration of extinction, they will enter into the concentration of nothingness. Rising from the concentration of nothingness, they will enter into the concentration of extinction. Rising from the concentration of extinction, they will enter into the concentration of nonthinking and not nonthinking. Rising from the concentration of nonthinking and not nonthinking, they will enter into the concentration of extinction. And rising from the concentration of extinction, they will enter into the first meditation.

"Sariputra! When cultivating prajna paramita, because these great bodhisattvas have expedient skillfulness in various kinds of samapatti, they are able to progress in sequence with joy and freedom but without contamination and attachment.

"Furthermore, Sariputra, some great bodhisattvas have attained the four bases of mindfulness, four correct endeavors, four bases of power, five roots, five powers, seven factors for enlightenment, and noble eightfold path. They have also attained the liberation gates of emptiness, formlessness, and nonaspiration. They have dwelled peacefully in the noble truths of suffering, the cause of suffering, the cessation of suffering, and the path for the cessation of suffering. They have also attained the eight liberations, eight vexation-overcoming meditations, nine concentrations in sequence, and the ten universal contemplations. But they will not grasp the stream-entry effect, once-return effect, nonreturn effect, arhat effect, or the self-enlightenment bodhi.

"These great bodhisattvas have cultivated the expedient skillfulness of prajna paramita, so they are able to guide the sentient beings to also cultivate the four bases of mindfulness, four correct endeavors, four bases of power, five roots, five powers, seven factors for enlightenment, and noble eightfold path; cultivate the liberation gates of emptiness, formlessness, and nonaspiration; dwell

Fascicle 8, Chapter 4, Section 2   159

peacefully in the noble truths of suffering, the cause of suffering, the cessation of suffering, and the path for the cessation of suffering; and cultivate the eight liberations, eight vexation-overcoming meditations, nine concentrations in sequence, and ten universal contemplations. These sentient beings then will be able to attain the stream-entry effect, once-return effect, nonreturn effect, arhat effect, or the self-enlightenment bodhi.

"Sariputra! Although these great bodhisattvas have cultivated giving, pure precept, forbearance, diligence, meditation, and prajna paramitas; dwelled peacefully in internal emptiness, external emptiness, internal-external emptiness, emptiness of emptiness, emptiness of space, emptiness of ultimate truth, emptiness of conditioned phenomena, emptiness of unconditioned reality, emptiness in the final analysis, emptiness of nontemporality, emptiness of deconstruction, emptiness of changelessness, emptiness of original nature, emptiness of particular characteristics, emptiness of common characteristics, emptiness of all dharmas, emptiness of nonattainment, emptiness of selflessness, emptiness of self-nature, and emptiness of selfless self-nature; dwelled peacefully in realness, the dharma realm, dharma nature, the nature of nonillusion, the nature of changelessness, the nature of equality, the nature of nonarising, dharma concentration, dharma dwelling, reality, realm of empty space, and the realm of the inconceivable; cultivated all dharani gates and all samadhi gates; cultivated the stages of ecstasy, freedom from defilements, emitting light, flaming wisdom, being extremely difficult to be surpassed, manifestation of pure realness, going far away, the unmovable, expedient wisdom, and dharma cloud; attained five eyes and the six supernatural powers; cultivated the Buddha's ten abilities, four kinds of fearlessness, four unhindered understandings, great loving-kindness, great compassion, great joy, great equanimity, and eighteen distinctive features of Buddha's wisdom and power; cultivated the way of staying in correct mindfulness and the nature of dwelling in equanimity at all times; cultivated the perfect knowledge of everything, the perfect knowledge of the forms of the paths, and the perfect knowledge of all phenomena, they will not rush to attain the unsurpassed, perfect, and universal bodhi.

"Because these bodhisattvas have cultivated the expedient skillfulness of prajna paramita, they are able to guide the sentient beings to also cultivate giving, pure precept, forbearance, diligence, meditation, and prajna paramitas, and so forth, as well as the perfect knowledge of everything, the perfect knowledge of the forms of the paths, and the perfect knowledge of all phenomena in order to realize insightfully the unsurpassed, perfect, and universal bodhi.

"Sariputra! All the perfect knowledge of voice-hearing effect and self-enlightenment bodhi is the great bodhisattva forbearance.

"Sariputra, you must know that these bodhisattvas have dwelled firmly in a stage of nonregression only because they have dwelled peacefully in prajna paramita.

"Furthermore, Sariputra, some great bodhisattvas have for a long time dwelled peacefully in giving, pure precept, forbearance, diligence, meditation, and prajna paramitas, as well as in other innumerable, boundless Buddha dharma, and have purified and dignified the palace in the Heaven of Tusita. Sariputra! You must know that these great bodhisattvas will definitely attain the unsurpassed, perfect, and universal bodhi during this Kalpa of the Sages.

"Furthermore, Sariputra, some great bodhisattvas have cultivated prajna paramita and have attained the four meditations, four immeasurable minds, and four formless concentrations; attained the four bases of mindfulness, four correct endeavors, four bases of power, five roots, five powers, seven factors for enlightenment, and noble eightfold path; cultivated the liberation gates of emptiness, formlessness, and nonaspiration; cultivated the eight liberations, eight vexation-overcoming meditations, nine concentrations in sequence, and ten universal contemplations; cultivated giving, pure precept, forbearance, diligence, meditation, and prajna paramitas; cultivated all dharani gates and all samadhi gates; cultivated the ten stages of bodhisattva; cultivated the five eyes and the six supernatural powers; cultivated the ten Buddha's abilities, four kinds of fearlessness, four unhindered understandings, great loving-kindness, great compassion, great joy, great equanimity, and the eighteen distinctive features of Buddha's wisdom and power; cultivated the way of staying in correct mindfulness and the nature of dwelling in equanimity at all times; cultivated the perfect knowledge of

Fascicle 8, Chapter 4, Section 2   161

everything, the perfect knowledge of the forms of the paths, and the perfect knowledge of all phenomena, but they have not fully understood the noble truths. Sariputra! You must know that these great bodhisattvas have already reached the last lifetime before becoming a Buddha.

"Furthermore, Sariputra, some great bodhisattvas have cultivated giving, pure precept, forbearance, diligence, meditation, and prajna paramitas and have traveled from one Buddha land to the other. They have dignified and purified all those Buddha lands and have also established the sentient beings firmly on the path toward the unsurpassed enlightenment. Nevertheless, Sariputra, these great bodhisattvas will take immeasurable and boundless large kalpas before being able to attain the unsurpassed, perfect, and universal bodhi.

"Furthermore, Sariputra, some great bodhisattvas have dwelled peacefully in giving, pure precept, forbearance, diligence, meditation, and prajna paramitas and worked diligently to benefit the sentient beings. They have tried not to say nonsensical words, do nonsensical things, or hold nonsensical ideas and so will not cause nonsensical karmas.

"Furthermore, Sariputra, some great bodhisattvas have cultivated the six paramitas and kept working diligently to benefit the sentient beings. They have traveled from one Buddha land to the other, assisted the sentient beings with getting rid of the three inferior destinies of rebirth, and established them expediently and peacefully on the path leading to the good destinies of rebirth.

"Furthermore, Sariputra, some great bodhisattvas have dwelled in the six paramitas, but focused mostly on cultivating giving paramita bravely and diligently. They give all kinds of most desirable things to the sentient beings and do it tirelessly. They give food, drinks, vehicles, clothes, flower fragrances, jewel necklaces, houses, beds, beddings, lamps, money, cereals, entertainers and music players, guards, and whatever else to those in need. They practice such giving pleasantly, trying to satisfy the sentient beings. And after that, they will further advise the sentient beings and encourage them to cultivate the three bodhi paths.

"Furthermore, Sariputra, some great bodhisattvas have cultivated the six paramitas, but focused mostly on pure-precept paramita. They practiced it bravely and assiduously, and soon they realized the pure laws and obtained the pure demeanors of the body, language, and mind. They will advise and encourage the sentient beings to cultivate such pure laws and demeanors too so that they will be able to fulfill them perfectly before long.

"Furthermore, Sariputra, some great bodhisattvas have dwelled in the six paramitas, but focused mostly on forbearance paramita. They have practiced it bravely and assiduously and have gotten rid of anger and hatred. They will further advise the sentient beings and encourage them to cultivate forbearance too so that they will be able to fulfill it perfectly before long.

"Furthermore, Sariputra, some great bodhisattvas have dwelled in the six paramitas, but focused mostly on diligence paramita. They have practiced it bravely and assiduously and thus have fulfilled all kinds of virtuous dharmas. They furthermore advise and encourage the sentient beings to cultivate diligence too so that they will be able to fulfill it perfectly before long.

"Furthermore, Sariputra, some great bodhisattvas have dwelled in the six paramitas, but focused mostly on meditation paramita. They have practiced it bravely and assiduously and thus have fully fulfilled the cultivation of all kinds of superior samatha. They also advise and encourage the sentient beings to cultivate superior concentrations so that they will be able to fulfill them perfectly before long.

"Furthermore, Sariputra, some great bodhisattvas have dwelled in the six paramitas, but focused mostly on prajna paramita. They have practiced it bravely and assiduously and thus have fully fulfilled the cultivation of all kinds of vipasyana. They will also advise and encourage the sentient beings to cultivate such superior wisdom so that they are able to fulfill it perfectly before long.

"Furthermore, Sariputra, some great bodhisattvas have cultivated prajna paramita and expediently and skillfully transformed themselves to appear as a Buddha in order to go to the realms of the hells, animals, ghosts, humans, and heavenly beings and teach them correct dharma in accordance with their individual differences and languages so to bring superior benefits, peace, and happiness to all of them.

"Furthermore, Sariputra, some great bodhisattvas have dwelled in giving, pure precept, forbearance, diligence, meditation, and prajna paramitas, and transformed themselves to appear as a Buddha in order to travel to as many Buddha lands as the sands of the Ganges, in which they will teach the sentient beings correct dharma, make offerings to the Buddhas, and admire and acclaim them. They will hear and learn correct teachings from the Buddhas at each Buddha's place and work to dignify and purify the Buddha lands. After looking around the most wonderful and purest forms of Buddha lands in the ten directions, they will try to build their own most dignified and purest Buddha lands. All the bodhisattvas who are already in the final lifetime before becoming a Buddha will be invited to live in those Buddha lands. They will do this with an attempt to assist the bodhisattvas to realize insightfully and attain the unsurpassed, perfect, and universal bodhi very soon.

"Furthermore, Sariputra, some great bodhisattvas have cultivated giving, pure precept, forbearance, diligence, meditation, and prajna paramita, and thus have attained the thirty-two perfect major marks and the eighty distinguishing minor features. They look magnificent and perfect. Their sense organs are sharp and efficient, the most superior and purest of all. When looking at these great bodhisattvas, the sentient beings will adore them with respect so that their pure minds will also be inspired. These great bodhisattvas will guide and encourage the sentient beings according to their individual dispositions and motivations to realize and attain step by step the nirvana of the three vehicles.

"Therefore, Sariputra, when cultivating prajna paramita, the great bodhisattvas should learn how to purify their body, speech, and mind karmas.

"Furthermore, Sariputra, some great bodhisattvas have cultivated giving, pure precept, forbearance, diligence, meditation, and prajna paramitas, and have thus sharpened and brightened their sense organs, but they are not arrogant and do not look down on others with a pride of feeling that they have achieved this.

"Furthermore, Sariputra, some great bodhisattvas have dwelled in giving paramita and pure-precept paramita at all times since the moment of initially making great vows until reaching the stage of nonregression. They have not and will never fall in any of the inferior destinies of rebirth.

"Furthermore, Sariputra, some great bodhisattvas have never stayed away from the path of the ten virtuous karmas since the moment of beginning to make great vows until reaching the stage of nonregression.

"Furthermore, Sariputra, some great bodhisattvas have dwelled peacefully in giving paramita and pure-precept paramita and thus become the wheel-turning kings who possess the seven treasures. They teach correct dharma instead of incorrect dharma. They establish the sentient beings peacefully on the path of the ten virtuous karmas and also give properties and treasures to the ones in need.

"Furthermore, Sariputra, some great bodhisattvas have dwelled peacefully in giving paramita and pure-precept paramita and thus gained the rewards of becoming the wheel-turning kings for hundreds of thousands of times. They have encountered immeasurable hundreds of thousands of Buddhas, made offerings to them, esteemed and acclaimed them, and never missed any single opportunity to do this.

"Furthermore, Sariputra, some great bodhisattvas have dwelled peacefully in giving, pure precept, forbearance, diligence, meditation, and prajna paramitas and taught correct views to the sentient beings in order to illuminate their blindness and ignorance in truth. They have also used such a brightness of the truth to illuminate themselves. They will never be apart from this brightness until attaining the unsurpassed, perfect, and universal bodhi. Sariputra! These great bodhisattvas will always have the Buddha dharma present before them owing to this cause and condition.

"Therefore, Sariputra, when the great bodhisattvas are cultivating prajna paramita, no guilty karma of the body, speech, and the mind will be allowed to arise."

At that time, Sariputra asked the Buddha, "World-Honored One, what is meant by saying that the great bodhisattvas have committed the guilty body karma, guilty speech karma, and guilty mind karma?"

Fascicle 8, Chapter 4, Section 2

The Buddha replied to the long-lived sage Sariputra, "Sariputra, as the great bodhisattvas have this kind of thought—'This is the body, and my body karma arises from it; this is the speech, and my speech karma arises from it; this is the mind, and my mind karma arises from it'—then these great bodhisattvas have committed the guilty body karma, guilty speech karma, and the guilty mind karma. Furthermore, Sariputra, when the great bodhisattvas cultivate prajna paramita, they cannot attain the body and the body karma, the speech and the speech karma, and the mind and the mind karma. Sariputra, if the great bodhisattvas who are cultivating prajna paramita attain the body, speech, and mind and their karmas, they will have stinginess, greed, precept-violation, anger, hatred, tiredness, laziness, distraction, restlessness, and wisdom abuse in their minds. Once any of these happens, they will not be qualified the name of great bodhisattva anymore. Therefore, Sariputra, when cultivating prajna paramita, the great bodhisattvas should not allow these thoughts to arise. Furthermore, Sariputra, when cultivating giving, pure precept, forbearance, diligence, meditation, and prajna paramitas, the great bodhisattvas should not allow these heavy afflictions of body, speech, and mind to arise. Why? Sariputra, when cultivating the six paramitas, the great bodhisattvas will be able to purify all heavy afflictions of the body, speech, and the mind."

At that time, Sariputra asked the Buddha, "World-Honored One, how can the great bodhisattvas purify the heavy afflictions of the body, speech, and the mind?"

The Buddha replied to the long-lived sage Sariputra, "Sariputra, when cultivating the six paramitas, the great bodhisattvas do not attain the body and the heavy afflictions of the body, the speech and the heavy afflictions of the speech, or the mind and the heavy afflictions of the mind. Sariputra! This is how the great bodhisattvas are able to purify the heavy afflictions of the body, speech, and the mind when they are cultivating the six paramitas. Furthermore, Sariputra, some great bodhisattvas, from the time of beginning to make the great vows, have enjoyed practicing and embracing the path of the ten virtuous karmas, but they do not intend to aspire to the path of voice-hearing or self-enlightenment; rather, they always have compassion over the sentient beings and attempt to alleviate their suffering and have loving-kindness over the sentient beings and attempt to bring them happiness. Sariputra, I will also say that these great bodhisattvas are able to remove the three heavy afflictions of the body, speech, and the mind only because their powers of loving-kindness for benefiting sentient beings are so compelling. Furthermore, Sariputra, there are some great bodhisattvas who have cultivated giving, pure precept, forbearance, diligence, meditation, and prajna paramitas, and purified the path of the bodhi."

Sariputra asked the Buddha, "World-Honored One, what is the path of the bodhi for great bodhisattva?"

The Buddha replied to the long-lived sage Sariputra, "Sariputra, when cultivating the six paramitas, the great bodhisattvas do not attain the body karma and the heavy afflictions of the body, the speech karma and the heavy afflictions of the speech, or the mind karma and the heavy afflictions of the mind. They do not attain giving paramita, pure-precept paramita, forbearance paramita, diligence paramita, meditation paramita, or prajna paramita. They do not attain the voice-hearer, self-enlightened one, bodhisattva, or the Thus-Comer. Sariputra! This is named the path of the bodhi for great bodhisattva. Why? It is because in the path of the bodhi, all dharmas are unattainable. Furthermore, Sariputra, some great bodhisattvas have cultivated giving, pure precept, forbearance, diligence, meditation, and prajna paramitas, and as they move toward the path of the bodhi, nothing can hinder them."

At that time, Sariputra asked the Buddha, "World-Honored One, why is it said that as the great bodhisattvas who are cultivating the six paramitas move toward the path of the bodhi, nothing can hinder them?"

The Buddha replied to the long-lived sage Sariputra, "Sariputra, when cultivating the six paramitas, the great bodhisattvas are not attached to matter or to feeling, thinking, action, and consciousness. They are not attached to the eye sphere or to the ear, nose, tongue, body, and conscious spheres. They are not attached to the sight sphere or to the sound, smell, taste, touch, and mental-image spheres. They are not attached to the eye realm or to the ear, nose, tongue, body, and conscious realms. They are not attached to the eye consciousness realm or to the ear, nose, tongue, body, and conscious consciousness realms. They are not attached to the eye contact or to the ear, nose, tongue, body, and conscious contacts. They are not attached to the feelings produced by eye contact or to the feelings produced by ear, nose, tongue, body, or conscious contact. They are not attached to the earth realm or to the water, fire, wind, space, and consciousness realms. They are not attached to cause and condition or to consecutive thoughts in sequence, conditions that stimulate one's mind, conditions that reinforce the main causes, and the dharmas produced by conditions. They are not attached to ignorance or to action, consciousness, name and form, six sense spheres, contact, reception, craving, grasping, existence, birth, old age, death, worry, sorrow, misery, anxiety, and upset. They are not attached to giving paramita or to pure precept, forbearance, diligence, meditation, and prajna paramitas. They are not attached to internal emptiness or to external emptiness, internal-external emptiness, emptiness of emptiness, emptiness of space, emptiness of ultimate truth, emptiness of conditioned phenomena, emptiness of unconditioned reality, emptiness in the final analysis, emptiness of nontemporality, emptiness of deconstruction, emptiness of changelessness, emptiness of original nature, emptiness of particular characteristics, emptiness of common characteristics, emptiness of all dharmas, emptiness of nonattainment, emptiness of selflessness, emptiness of self-nature, and emptiness of selfless self-nature. They are not attached to realness or to dharma realm, dharma nature, the nature of nonillusion, the nature of changelessness, the nature of equality, the nature of nonarising, dharma concentration, dharma dwelling, reality, the realm of empty space, and the realm of the inconceivable. They are not attached to the four bases of mindfulness or to the four correct endeavors, four bases of power, five roots, five powers, seven factors for enlightenment, and the noble eightfold path. They are not attached to the noble truth of suffering or to the noble truths of the cause of suffering, the cessation of suffering, and the path for the cessation of suffering. They are not attached to the four meditations or to the four immeasurable minds and the four formless concentrations. They are not attached to the eight liberations or to the eight vexation-overcoming meditations, nine concentrations in sequence, and the ten universal contemplations. They are not attached to the liberation gate of emptiness or to the liberation gates of formlessness and nonaspiration. They are not attached to all dharani gates or to all samadhi gates. They are not attached to the stage of ecstasy or to the stages of freedom from defilements, emitting light, flaming wisdom, being extremely difficult to be surpassed, manifestation of pure realness, going far away, the unmovable, expedient wisdom, and dharma cloud. They are not attached to the five eyes or to the six supernatural powers. They are not attached to the Buddha's ten abilities or to the four kinds of fearlessness, four unhindered understandings, great loving-kindness, great compassion, great joy, great equanimity, and the eighteen distinctive features of Buddha's wisdom and power. They are not attached to the thirty-two perfect major marks or to the eighty distinguishing minor features. They are not attached to the way of staying in correct mindfulness or to the nature of dwelling in equanimity at all times. They are not attached to the perfect knowledge of everything or to the perfect knowledge of the forms of the paths and the perfect knowledge of phenomena. They are not attached to stream-entry effect or to once-return effect, nonreturn effect, arhat effect, and self-enlightenment bodhi. They are not attached to all great bodhisattva actions or to the unsurpassed, perfect, and universal bodhi of the Buddhas.

"Sariputra, it is because of these reasons that the great bodhisattvas who are cultivating prajna paramita will become more powerful and enthusiastic and will not be hindered on their way toward the bodhi.

"Furthermore, Sariputra, some great bodhisattvas have dwelled peacefully in prajna paramita and are able to attain the perfect knowledge of all perfect knowledge before long. Because of their perfect fulfillment of this superior perfect knowledge, all perilous and vicious destinies of rebirth will be closed for them, and no more poverty of heavenly and human lives fall on them. Their sense roots and physical appearance will be perfect and magnificent. All heavenly beings, human beings, asuras, and so forth, will esteem them and make offerings to them with great respect."

At that time, Sariputra asked the Buddha, "World-Honored

One! What is the superior perfect knowledge achieved by the great bodhisattva?"

The Buddha replied to the long-lived sage Sariputra, "Sariputra! Because the great bodhisattvas have achieved this perfect knowledge, they are able to see the Thus-Comers, Ones Worthy of Offerings, Perfectly and Universally Enlightened Ones in as many Buddha worlds of the ten directions as the sands of the Ganges. They are also able to hear the correct dharma taught by the Buddhas universally. They are able to witness all the voice-hearers, the monastic bodhisattvas, and so forth who assemble there to listen to the Buddha's teaching. They can also see how magnificent and pure the merits and virtues of those lands are. Sariputra! Because the great bodhisattvas have achieved such a perfect knowledge, they will not have the thought of the world, the thought of the Thus-Comer, the thought of the correct dharma, the thought of the bodhisattva, the thought of the voice-hearer, the thought of the self-enlightened one, the thought of themselves, the thought of others, and the thought of the Buddha land.

"Again, Sariputra, because of this perfect knowledge, the great bodhisattvas are able to practice giving paramita without attaining giving paramita, and practice pure precept, forbearance, diligence, meditation, and prajna paramitas without attaining pure precept, forbearance, diligence, meditation, and prajna paramitas.

"Because of this perfect knowledge, the great bodhisattvas are able to dwell in internal emptiness without attaining internal emptiness and also dwell in external emptiness, internal-external emptiness, emptiness of emptiness, emptiness of space, emptiness of ultimate truth, emptiness of conditioned phenomena, emptiness of unconditioned reality, emptiness in the final analysis, emptiness of nontemporality, emptiness of deconstruction, emptiness of changelessness, emptiness of original nature, emptiness of particular characteristics, emptiness of common characteristics, emptiness of all dharmas, emptiness of nonattainment, emptiness of selflessness, emptiness of self-nature, and emptiness of selfless self-nature without attaining external emptiness, and so forth, as well as emptiness of selfless self-nature.

"Because of this perfect knowledge, the great bodhisattvas are able to dwell in realness without attaining realness and also dwell in dharma realm, dharma nature, the nature of nonillusion, the nature of changelessness, the nature of equality, the nature of nonarising, dharma concentration, dharma dwelling, reality, the realm of empty space, and the realm of the inconceivable without attaining dharma realm, and so forth, as well as the realm of the inconceivable.

"Because of this perfect knowledge, the great bodhisattvas are able to cultivate the four bases of mindfulness without attaining the four bases of mindfulness and also cultivate the four correct endeavors, four bases of power, five roots, five powers, seven factors for enlightenment, and the noble eightfold path without attaining the four correct endeavors, and so forth, as well as the noble eightfold path.

"Because of this perfect knowledge, the great bodhisattvas are able to dwell in the noble truth of suffering without attaining the noble truth of suffering and also dwell in the noble truths of the cause of suffering, the cessation of suffering, and the path for the cessation of suffering without attaining the noble truths of the cause of suffering, the cessation of suffering, and the path for the cessation of suffering.

"Because of this perfect knowledge, the great bodhisattvas are able to cultivate the four meditations without attaining the four meditations and also cultivate the four immeasurable minds and the four formless concentrations without attaining the four immeasurable minds and the four formless concentrations.

"Because of this perfect knowledge, the great bodhisattvas are able to cultivate the eight liberations without attaining the eight liberations and also cultivate the eight vexation-overcoming meditations, nine concentrations in sequence, and the ten universal contemplations without attaining the eight vexation-overcoming meditations, nine concentrations in sequence, and the ten universal contemplations.

"Because of this perfect knowledge, the great bodhisattvas are able to cultivate the liberation gate of emptiness without attaining the liberation gate of emptiness and also cultivate the liberation gates of formlessness and nonaspiration without attaining the liberation gates of formlessness and nonaspiration.

"Because of this perfect knowledge, the great bodhisattvas are able to cultivate all dharani gates without attaining all dharani gates and also cultivate all samadhi gates without attaining all samadhi gates.

"Because of this perfect knowledge, the great bodhisattvas are able to cultivate the stage of ecstasy without attaining the stage of ecstasy and cultivate the stages of freedom from defilements, emitting light, flaming wisdom, being extremely difficult to be surpassed, manifestation of pure realness, going far away, the unmovable, expedient wisdom, and dharma cloud without attaining the stage of freedom from defilements, and so forth, as well as the stage of dharma cloud.

"Because of this perfect knowledge, the great bodhisattvas are able to cultivate the five eyes without attaining the five eyes and cultivate the six supernatural powers without attaining the six supernatural powers.

"Because of this perfect knowledge, the great bodhisattvas are able to cultivate the Buddha's ten abilities without attaining the Buddha's ten abilities and cultivate the four kinds of fearlessness, four unhindered understandings, great loving-kindness, great compassion, great joy, great equanimity, and the eighteen distinctive features of Buddha's wisdom and power without attaining the four kinds of fearlessness, and so forth, as well as the eighteen distinctive features of Buddha's wisdom and power.

"Because of this perfect knowledge, the great bodhisattvas cultivate the thirty-two perfect major marks without attaining the thirty-two perfect major marks and cultivate the eighty distinguishing minor features without attaining the eighty distinguishing minor features.

"Because of this perfect knowledge, the great bodhisattvas cultivate the way of staying in correct mindfulness without attaining the way of staying in correct mindfulness and cultivate the nature of dwelling in equanimity at all times without attaining the nature of dwelling in equanimity at all times.

"Because of this perfect knowledge, the great bodhisattvas cultivate the perfect knowledge of everything without attaining the perfect knowledge of everything and cultivate the perfect knowledge of the forms of the paths and the perfect knowledge of all phenomena without attaining the perfect knowledge of the forms of the paths and the perfect knowledge of all phenomena.

"Because of this perfect knowledge, the great bodhisattvas cultivate all great bodhisattva actions without attaining all great bodhisattva actions and cultivate the unsurpassed, perfect, and universal bodhi of the Buddhas without attaining the unsurpassed, perfect, and universal bodhi of the Buddhas.

"Sariputra, this is named the superior perfect knowledge achieved by the great bodhisattva. Because of this perfect knowledge, the great bodhisattvas are able to fulfill all kinds of Buddha dharma perfectly and quickly. Although they are able to fulfill all kinds of Buddha dharma perfectly, they are not attached to the dharmas. It is because the self-natures of all dharmas are empty.

"Furthermore, Sariputra, some great bodhisattvas have cultivated giving, pure precept, forbearance, diligence, meditation, and prajna paramitas and thus acquired the five pure eyes. What are the five eyes? They are the physical eye, heavenly eye, wisdom eye, dharma eye, and the Buddha eye."

At that time, Sariputra asked the Buddha, "World-Honored One, what will happen when the great bodhisattvas obtain the pure physical eyes?"

The Buddha replied to the long-lived sage Sariputra, "Sariputra, some great bodhisattvas have acquired the pure physical eyes. As this happens, they can see clearly as far as one hundred yojanas. Some can see clearly as far as two hundred yojanas. Some can see clearly as far as three hundred yojanas. Some can see clearly as far as four, five, six hundred, or even one thousand yojanas. Some great bodhisattvas acquire the pure physical eyes and can see clearly as far as the entire continent of Jambudvipa, some can see clearly as far as two continents, some can see clearly as far as three continents, and some can see clearly as far as four continents. Some great bodhisattvas acquire the pure physical eyes and can see clearly as far as the entire small thousand-world, some can see clearly as far as the entire middle thousand-world, and some can see clearly as far as the entire large thousand-world. Sariputra, these are what happen as great bodhisattvas acquire the pure physical eyes."

Fascicle 8, Chapter 4, Section 2   173

At that time, Sariputra again asked the Buddha, "World-Honored One, what will happen when the great bodhisattvas acquire the pure heavenly eyes?"

The Buddha replied to the long-lived sage Sariputra, "Sariputra, the great bodhisattvas have acquired the heavenly eyes and can see exactly as the heavenly beings of the Heaven of Four Great Kings do. They can see exactly as the heavenly beings of the Heaven of Thirty-Three Smaller Heavens, the Heaven of Yama, the Heaven of Tusita, the Heaven of Enjoying Self-Made Changes, and the Heaven of Enjoying Other-Made Changes do. Some great bodhisattvas have acquired the pure heavenly eyes and can see exactly as the heavenly beings of the Heaven of Brahman Followers do. They can see exactly as the heavenly beings of the Heaven of Brahma Subordinates, the Heaven of Brahma Family, and the Heaven of Great Brahma do. Some great bodhisattvas have acquired the pure heavenly eyes and can see exactly as the heavenly beings of the Heaven of Light do. They can see exactly as the heavenly beings of the Heaven of Lesser Light, the Heaven of Infinite Light, the Heaven of Extremely Great Brightness and Purity do. Some great bodhisattvas have acquired the pure heavenly eyes and can see exactly as the heavenly beings of the Heaven of Expansion do. They can see exactly as the heavenly beings of the Heaven of Lesser Expansion, the Heaven of Infinite Expansion, and the Heaven of Extensive Rewards do. Some great bodhisattvas have acquired the pure heavenly eyes and can see exactly as the thoughtless sentient beings do. Some great bodhisattvas have acquired the pure heavenly eyes and can see exactly as the heavenly beings of the Heaven of No Aspiration do. They can see exactly as the heavenly beings of the Heaven of No Affliction, the Heaven of Good Appearance, the Heaven of Good Sight, and the Heaven of Ultimate Form do.

"Sariputra, some great bodhisattvas have acquired the pure heavenly eyes and can see and know what the heavenly beings of the Heaven of Four Great Kings, and so forth, as well as the Heaven of Ultimate Form cannot see or know. Sariputra, some great bodhisattvas have acquired the pure heavenly eyes and can see exactly how all sentient beings in as many worlds of the ten directions as the sands of the Ganges die in these lands and how they are to be reborn in other lands. Sariputra, these are the great bodhisattvas who have acquired the pure heavenly eyes."

At that time, Sariputra again asked the Buddha, "World-Honored One, what will happen when the great bodhisattvas acquire the pure wisdom eyes?"

The Buddha replied to the long-lived sage Sariputra, "Sariputra! After acquiring the pure wisdom eyes, the great bodhisattvas do not see that the dharma is conditioned or unconditioned; the dharma is flawed or flawless; the dharma belongs to the world or beyond the world; the dharma is guilty or not guilty; the dharma is contaminated or purified; the dharma is with form or without form; the dharma is material or immaterial; the dharma is in the past, future, or the present; the dharma belongs to the realm of desire, the realm of form, or the realm of formlessness; the dharma is virtuous, not virtuous, or neutral; the dharma is at the stage of seeing the truth, the stage of cultivation, or the stage of perfection; the dharma is the one who needs more learning, the one who needs no more learning, or the one who neither needs learning nor needs no more learning; and so forth, as well as the self-natures and differences of all dharmas. Sariputra, as the great bodhisattvas acquire the pure wisdom eyes, they will neither see nor not see all dharmas. They will neither hear nor not hear all dharmas. They will neither awake nor not awake to all dharmas; they will neither know nor not know all dharmas. Sariputra! This is what will happen when the great bodhisattvas acquire the pure wisdom eyes."

At that time, Sariputra again asked the Buddha, "World-Honored One, what will happen when the great bodhisattvas acquire the pure dharma eyes?"

The Buddha replied to the long-lived sage Sariputra, "Sariputra, when the great bodhisattvas acquire the pure dharma eyes, they are able to know what differences among individual human beings really are. They know accurately that this is the action taken in accordance with one's faith, this is the action taken in accordance with the dharma, this is the action that is formless, this one has dwelled in emptiness, this one has dwelled in formlessness, and this one has dwelled in nonaspiration.

"They also accurately know that from the liberation gate of

emptiness, the five roots arise; from the five roots, consecutive concentration without interruption arises; and from consecutive concentration, the knowledge and views of liberation arise. Because of the knowledge and views of liberation, the three bonds of the mind are terminated forever, and stream-entry effect is thus obtained. They also accurately know that the three bonds of the mind comprise the wrong view, thinking that selfness is permanent and real; the invalid belief thinking that some kinds of 'precepts' will lead to liberation; and the skepticism about the truth. They also know accurately that as one reaches the initial stage of cultivation, his or her desire, greed, and anger will become slight and thus attains once-return effect. As one progresses further to a higher level of cultivation, his or her desire, greed, and anger will be completely eliminated, and thus acquires nonreturn effect. As one reaches the next higher level through additional effort, his or her five upper bonds will be eliminated, and thus acquires arhat effect. They know that the five upper bonds indicate the five wrong views and conducts in the realm of form and the realm of formlessness, which comprise the greed for form, greed for formlessness, ignorance, arrogance, and the wandering and restless mind.

"They also accurately know that from the liberation gate of formlessness, the five roots arise; from the five roots, the consecutive concentration arises; from the consecutive concentration, the knowledge and correct views of liberation arise; because of the knowledge and correct views of liberation, the three bonds are terminated permanently, and thus stream-entry effect is attained. They also accurately know that as one reaches the initial stage of cultivation, his or her desire, greed, and anger become slight, and once-return effect is thus acquired; as one progresses higher in cultivation, his or her desire, greed, and anger are eliminated completely, and nonreturn effect is thus acquired; as one progresses even higher through additional effort, his or her five upper bonds are terminated forever, and arhat effect is thus acquired.

"They also accurately know that from the liberation gate of nonaspiration, the five roots arise; from the five roots, the consecutive concentration arises; from the consecutive concentration, the knowledge and correct views of liberation arise; because of the knowledge and correct views of liberation, the three bonds are terminated forever, and stream-entry effect is thus acquired. They accurately know that as one reaches the initial stage of cultivation, his or her desire, greed, and anger become slight, and thus once-return effect is acquired; as one progresses to a higher level of cultivation, his or her desire, greed, and anger are terminated permanently, and nonreturn effect is thus acquired; as one progresses even to a higher level of cultivation through additional effort, his or her five upper bonds are eliminated forever, and arhat effect is thus acquired.

"They also accurately know that from the liberation gates of emptiness and formlessness, the five roots arise; from the five roots, the consecutive concentration arises; from the consecutive concentration, the knowledge and correct views of liberation arise; and because of the knowledge and correct views of liberation, the three bonds are terminated forever, and stream-entry effect is thus acquired. They also accurately know that as one reaches the initial stage of cultivation, his or her desire, greed, and anger become slight, and once-return effect is thus acquired; as one progresses higher in cultivation, his or her desire, greed, and anger are eliminated permanently, and nonreturn effect is thus acquired; as one progresses even higher in cultivation through additional effort, his or her five upper bonds are terminated forever, and arhat effect is thus acquired.

"They also accurately know that from the liberation gates of emptiness and nonaspiration, the five roots arise; from the five roots, the consecutive concentration arises; from the consecutive concentration, the knowledge and correct views of liberation arise; and because of the knowledge and correct views of liberation, the three bonds are terminated forever, and stream-entry effect is thus acquired. They also know accurately that as one reaches the initial stage of cultivation, his or her desire, greed, and anger become slight, and once-return effect is thus acquired. As one progresses higher in cultivation, his or her desire, greed, and anger are completely eliminated, and nonreturn effect is thus acquired. As one progresses even higher in cultivation through additional effort, his or her five upper bonds are terminated forever, and arhat effect is thus acquired.

"They also accurately know that from the liberation gates of formlessness and nonaspiration, the five roots arise; from the five roots, the consecutive concentration arises; from the consecutive concentration, the knowledge and correct views of liberation arise; and because of the knowledge and correct views of liberation, the three bonds are terminated forever, and stream-entry effect is thus acquired. They also accurately know that as one reaches the initial stage of cultivation, his or her desire, greed, and anger become slight, and once-return effect is thus acquired. As one progresses higher in cultivation, his or her desire, greed, and anger are eliminated permanently, and nonreturn effect is thus acquired. As one progresses even higher in cultivation through additional effort, his or her five upper bonds are terminated forever, and arhat effect is thus acquired.

"They also accurately know that from the liberation gates of emptiness, formlessness and nonaspiration, the five roots arise; from the five roots, the consecutive concentration arises; from the consecutive concentration, the knowledge and correct views of liberation arise; and because of the knowledge and correct views of liberation, the three bonds are terminated forever, and stream-entry effect is thus acquired. As one reaches the initial stage of cultivation, his or her desire, greed, and anger become slight, and once-return effect is thus acquired. As one progresses higher in cultivation, his or her desire, greed, and anger are completely eliminated, and nonreturn effect is thus acquired. As one progresses even higher in cultivation through additional effort, his or her five upper bonds are terminated forever, and arhat effect is thus acquired.

"Sariputra, this is the pure dharma eye that the great bodhisattvas will obtain.

"Furthermore, Sariputra, as the great bodhisattvas acquire the pure dharma eye, they know accurately that there is a group of individuals in reincarnation whose five roots arise from the liberation gates of emptiness, formlessness, and nonaspiration. From the five roots, their consecutive concentrations arise; from the consecutive concentrations, their knowledge and correct views of liberation arise; and because of the knowledge and correct views of liberation, they are able to know accurately that the arising of all dharmas is the extinction of all dharmas. Owing to this knowledge, they are able to acquire the superior five roots, terminate various vexations, and indirectly attain the self-enlightenment bodhi. Sariputra, this is the dharma eye that the great bodhisattvas will acquire.

"Furthermore, Sariputra, as the great bodhisattvas acquire the pure dharma eye, they will accurately know, for instance, a certain great bodhisattva has, since the time of beginning to make great vows, cultivated giving, pure precept, forbearance, diligence, meditation, and prajna paramitas and thus achieved the root of faith, the root of diligence, and expedient skillfulness. This bodhisattva then thinks that he or she needs a physical body so that he or she can cultivate virtuous dharmas and improve him or herself. With such a purpose in mind, this great bodhisattva will be reborn either in the noble family of Ksatriya, Brahman, the elder, or the lay believer or will be reborn in the Heaven of Four Great Kings, the Heaven of Thirty-Three Smaller Heavens, the Heaven of Yama, the Heaven of Tusita, the Heaven of Enjoying Self-Made Changes, or in the Heaven of Enjoying Other-Made Changes, in which he or she will do the things beneficial to sentient beings, assist them to grow and mature, and provide them with the best entertainments as they wish. He or she will also dignify and purify the Buddha lands, make the best offerings to the Buddhas, the World-Honored Ones, and admire and acclaim them. He or she will never fall in the stage of the voice-hearer or the stage of the self-enlightened one, nor will he or she regress in the pursuit of the unsurpassed, perfect, and universal bodhi. Sariputra, this is what will happen as the great bodhisattvas acquire the pure dharma eye.

"Furthermore, Sariputra, as the great bodhisattvas acquire the pure dharma eye, they will know accurately, for instance, that a certain great bodhisattva had been conferred, is conferred, or will be conferred by the Buddha the prophecy of attaining the unsurpassed, perfect, and universal bodhi in the future. They know accurately that this great bodhisattva has attained nonregression or has not attained nonregression in the pursuit of the unsurpassed, perfect, and universal bodhi. They know accurately that this great bodhisattva has dwelled or has not yet dwelled in the state of nonregression and that this great bodhisattva has or has not fulfilled the

Fascicle 8, Chapter 4, Section 2 179

supernatural powers perfectly. They know accurately that because this great bodhisattva has fulfilled the supernatural powers perfectly, he or she is able to go to as many Buddha lands in the ten directions as the sands of the Ganges; make offerings to the Thus-Comers, Ones Worthy of Offerings, the Perfectly and Universally Enlightened Ones, as well as the great bodhisattvas; and admire and pay homage to them. Or because this great bodhisattva has not fulfilled the supernatural powers perfectly, he or she is unable to go to as many Buddha lands in the ten directions as the sands of the Ganges; make offerings to the Thus-Comers, Ones Worthy of Offerings, the Perfectly and Universally Enlightened Ones, as well as the great bodhisattvas; and admire and pay homage to them. They know accurately that this great bodhisattva has acquired the supernatural powers, while the other one has not yet; that this great bodhisattva has attained the dharma forbearance of nonarising, while the other one has not yet; that this great bodhisattva has attained the superior roots, while the other one has not yet; that this great bodhisattva has dignified and purified the Buddha lands, while the other one has not yet; that this great bodhisattva has assisted the sentient beings to grow and mature, while the other one has not yet; that this great bodhisattva has realized his or her great aspiration, while the other one has not yet; that this great bodhisattva has been praised by all the Buddhas, while the other one has not yet; that this great bodhisattva has kept in close connection with the Buddhas, while the other one has not; that this great bodhisattva has an unlimited lifespan, while the other one has a limited lifespan; that this great bodhisattva will have immeasurable bhiksu followers when finally attaining the unsurpassed, perfect, and universal bodhi, while the other one will have measurable bhiksu followers when attaining the unsurpassed, perfect, and universal bodhi; that this great bodhisattva will have monastic bodhisattvas in his or her company when attaining the unsurpassed, perfect, and universal bodhi, while the other one has none; that this great bodhisattva is dedicated to the actions beneficial to others only, while the other one is dedicated to the actions beneficial to both others and him or herself; that this great bodhisattva is practicing difficult, ascetic actions, while the other one is not; that this great bodhisattva has now come to the last lifetime before becoming a Buddha, while the other one still has a lot of lifetimes to go; that this great bodhisattva has no more rebirth, while the other one has more rebirths; that this great bodhisattva has now sat on the throne of the wonderful bodhi, while the other one has not; and that this great bodhisattva is not disturbed by the demons, while the other one is. Sariputra! This is what will happen as the great bodhisattvas acquire the dharma eye."

At that time, Sariputra again asked the Buddha, "World-Honored One, what will happen as the great bodhisattvas acquire the Buddha eye?"

The Buddha replied to the long-lived sage Sariputra, "Sariputra, as the great bodhisattvas have possessed the bodhi mind in a constant condition and entered into the diamond-like concentration, they will attain the perfect knowledge of all phenomena and fulfill the Buddha's ten abilities, four kinds of fearlessness, four unhindered understandings, great loving-kindness, great compassion, great joy, great equanimity, eighteen distinctive features of Buddha's wisdom and power, and so forth, as well as other immeasurable, boundless, and incredible superior merits and virtues. It is at this moment that they will accomplish the unhindered, unobstructed, liberated Buddha eye. Because of attaining such pure Buddha eye, the great bodhisattvas will surpass all voice-hearers and self-enlightened ones in wisdom. Namely, there is nothing that they cannot see, nothing that they cannot hear, nothing that they cannot be awakened to, and nothing that they cannot know. They can see all phenomena in all dharmas. Sariputra, this is what will happen when the great bodhisattvas acquire the pure Buddha eye. Sariputra, because the great bodhisattvas have aspired to the unsurpassed, perfect, and universal bodhi, they are able to acquire such pure Buddha eye.

"Sariputra, in order to attain such pure five eyes, the great bodhisattvas should diligently cultivate giving, pure precept, forbearance, diligence, meditation, and prajna paramitas. Why? Sariputra, it is because these six paramitas comprise all pure, virtuous dharmas, namely the virtuous dharma of voice-hearing, virtuous dharma of self-enlightenment bodhi, virtuous dharma of bodhisattva, and the virtuous dharma of the Thus-Comer. Sariputra, to the question, what dharma comprises all virtuous dharmas? The correct answer is 'the profound prajna paramita.' Why? Sariputra, prajna paramita is a real mother and a foster mother of all virtuous dharmas; it gives birth to and fosters giving, pure precept, forbearance, diligence, meditation, and prajna paramitas, as well as the five eyes and other immeasurable, boundless, and incredible superior virtues and merits. Sariputra, in order to attain the pure five eyes, the great bodhisattvas should learn prajna paramita. In order to attain the unsurpassed, perfect, and universal bodhi, the great bodhisattvas should learn the pure five eyes. Sariputra, if the great bodhisattvas learn such pure five eyes, they will definitely attain the unsurpassed, perfect, and universal bodhi.

FASCICLE 9

Chapter 4
Rebirth

Section 3

(In the First Assembly)

"FURTHERMORE, SARIPUTRA, SOME GREAT BODHISATTVAS ARE ABLE TO activate the six supernatural powers when they cultivate prajna paramita. What are the six supernatural powers? The first is the supernatural power of transformation paramita, the second is the supernatural power of heavenly ear paramita, the third is the supernatural power of knowing others' minds paramita, the fourth is the supernatural power of knowing previous lives freely paramita, the fifth is the supernatural power of heavenly eye paramita, and the sixth is the supernatural power of flawless perfect knowledge paramita."

At that time, Sariputra asked the Buddha, "World-Honored One, what is the supernatural power of transformation paramita that the great bodhisattvas activate when they cultivate prajna paramita?"

The Buddha replied to the long-lived sage Sariputra, "Sariputra, in performing supernatural power of transformation, the great bodhisattvas may activate immeasurable tremendous magical changes, for instance, shake the objects in as many lands of the ten directions as the sands of the Ganges River; transform one thing into many things, transform many things into one thing, in visible or invisible ways, instantaneously, without hindrance and difficulty; pass through the mountains as if penetrating into air; fly to and fro as birds; dig oneself into and emerge out of the earth as if diving and surfing in water; walk on water as if walking on the ground; make fire shoot out of the body and be capable of burning the plateau; make water flow from the body into many streams and be capable of melting the snowy hills; cover the brightness of sun and moon with one hand, although the powers and the virtues of the sun and moon are irresistible; turn around in the Heaven of Pure Residence in freedom and comfort; and numberless and boundless other magical changes like these.

"Sariputra, although these great bodhisattvas have possessed such incredible power of transformation, they do not boast about it, nor are they attached to its nature and the use of it or to the one who possesses it. They even are not attached to the attachment and the nonattachment. Why? Because these great bodhisattvas understand that the self-natures of all dharmas are empty, the so-called self-natures are apart, and the self-natures are inherently unattainable. Sariputra, these great bodhisattvas will not think, 'I am activating the supernatural powers in order to entertain myself and others.' They will do it only for the sake of pursuing the perfect knowledge of all perfect knowledge. Sariputra! This is the supernatural power of transformation paramita that the great bodhisattvas activate when they cultivate prajna paramita."

At that time, Sariputra asked the Buddha again, "World-Honored One, what is the supernatural power of heavenly ear paramita that the great bodhisattvas activate when they cultivate prajna paramita?"

The Buddha replied to the long-lived sage Sariputra, "Sariputra, the great bodhisattvas who have acquired the supernatural power of heavenly ear can hear better and more pure than normal human and heavenly ears do. They can hear accurately all kinds of voices made by the sentient and nonsentient beings in as many realms of the ten directions as the sands of the Ganges. They can hear the voices of the hells, animals, ghosts, human beings, heavenly beings, voice-hearers, self-enlightened ones, bodhisattvas, and the Thus-Comers; the voices that deprecate birth and death, admire nirvana, abandon the conditioned beings, and the voices that aspire to the bodhi; the voices in disgust at the flawed things and the voices that enjoy the flawless things, praise the triple gem, and defeat the other paths; and the arguments and discussion to make decisions, the voices of chanting the sutras, advice given to stop bad conduct, persuasions and encouragements given to do good conduct, the voices to terminate suffering, the voices that rejoice and celebrate, and many other voices, high or low, that can be heard everywhere without hindrance and obstacles.

"Sariputra, although possessing the supernatural power of hearing, the great bodhisattvas do not boast about it, nor are they attached to its nature and the use of it, or to the one who possesses it. They even are not attached to the attachment and the nonattachment. Why? Because these great bodhisattvas know that the self-natures of all dharmas are empty, the so-called self-natures are not in the dharmas, and the self-natures are inherently unattainable. Sariputra, these great bodhisattvas will not have this thought in mind, 'I am activating the supernatural power of the heavenly ear in order to entertain myself and others.' Rather, they activate the supernatural power of the heavenly ear only for the sake of attaining the perfect knowledge of all perfect knowledge. Sariputra, this is the supernatural power of heavenly ear paramita that the great bodhisattvas activate when they cultivate prajna paramita."

At that time, Sariputra asked the Buddha again, "World-Honored One, what is the supernatural power of reading others' minds paramita that the great bodhisattvas activate when they cultivate prajna paramita?"

The Buddha replied to the long-lived sage Sariputra, "Sariputra, some great bodhisattvas have acquired the supernatural power of reading others' minds and know accurately the sentient beings in as many realms of the ten directions as the sands of the Ganges, including their minds and the associated mental images, namely knowing universally all sentient beings and knowing who, among them, has a greedy mind and who has a mind already getting rid of greed; who has an angry mind and who has a mind getting rid of anger; who has an ignorant mind and who has a mind getting rid of ignorance; who has a craving mind and who has no craving mind; who has a grasping mind and who has no grasping mind; who has an absorbing mind and who has a restless mind; who has a narrow mind and who has a broad mind; who has a boasting mind and who has a humble mind; whose mind is in tranquility and whose mind is not in tranquility; whose mind is wandering and whose mind is not wandering; whose mind is concentrative and whose mind is not concentrative; whose mind is liberated and whose mind is not liberated; whose mind is flawed and whose mind is flawless; whose mind is provocative and whose mind is not provocative; who is high-minded and who is not high-minded; and who has an unsurpassed mind and who has no unsurpassed mind.

"Sariputra, although these great bodhisattvas have possessed the supernatural power of knowing others' minds, they do not boast about it, nor are they attached to its nature and the use of it, or to the one who possesses it. They even are not attached to the attachment and the nonattachment. Why? Because these great bodhisattvas know that the self-natures of all dharmas are empty, the so-called self-natures are apart from the dharma, and the self-natures are inherently unattainable. Sariputra, these great bodhisattvas will not have this thought in their minds: 'I am activating the supernatural power of knowing others' minds in order to entertain myself and others.' They activate this supernatural power only for the sake of attaining the perfect knowledge of all perfect knowledge. Sariputra, this is the supernatural power of knowing others' minds paramita that the great bodhisattvas activate when they cultivate prajna paramita."

At that time, Sariputra asked the Buddha again, "World-Honored One, what is the supernatural power of knowing previous lives of all sentient beings paramita that the great bodhisattvas will activate when they cultivate prajna paramita?"

The Buddha replied to the long-lived sage Sariputra, "Sariputra, some great bodhisattvas have acquired the supernatural power of knowing previous lives of all sentient beings and know accurately the things that happened in the past lives of the sentient beings in as many realms of the ten directions as the sands of the Ganges. They know all the things that happened in the past lives of themselves and others, through one mindfulness instantaneously, ten-mindfulness instantaneously, one hundred-mindfulness instantaneously, one thousand-mindfulness or hundreds of thousands of mindfulness instantaneously, as they wish. They know the things that happened one day, ten days, one hundred days, one thousand days, or hundreds of thousands of days ago, as they wish. They know the things that happened one month, ten months, one hundred months, one thousand months, or hundreds of thousands of months ago, as they wish. They know the things that happened one year, ten years, one hundred years, one thousand years, or hundreds of thousands of years ago, as they wish. They know the things that happened one kalpa, ten kalpas, one hundred kalpas, one thousand kalpas, hundreds of thousands of kalpas, even numberless and countless hundreds of thousands of koti nayuta kalpas ago, as they wish. They know, as they wish, the things that happened in previous lives in regard to, for instance, when and where the things happened; who were involved, including their first and last names; what kind they were; the food they ate; the period of time they stayed; their life spans; the pleasures and sufferings they experienced; where they were reborn from and where they were to be reborn to; their appearances, speeches; and all those things in brief or in detail, of themselves and of others.

"Sariputra, although these great bodhisattvas have acquired the supernatural power of knowing previous lives of all sentient beings, they do not boast about it, nor are they attached to its nature and the use of it, or the one who possesses it. They even are not attached to the attachment and the nonattachment. Why? Because these great bodhisattvas know that the self-natures of all dharmas are empty, the so-called self-natures are not in the dharmas, and the self-natures are inherently unattainable. Sariputra, these great bodhisattvas will not have this thought in their minds: 'I am activating supernatural power of knowing previous lives of all sentient beings in order to entertain myself and others.' They activate this supernatural power only for the sake of attaining the perfect knowledge of all perfect knowledge. Sariputra, this is the supernatural power of knowing previous lives of all sentient beings paramita that the great bodhisattvas activate when they cultivate prajna paramita."

At that time, Sariputra again asked the Buddha, "World-Honored Buddha, what is the supernatural power of heavenly eye that the great bodhisattvas activate when they cultivate prajna paramita?"

The Buddha replied to the long-lived sage Sariputra, "Sariputra, some great bodhisattvas have acquired the supernatural power of heavenly eye and are able to see the images of all sentient beings and nonsentient beings in as many realms of the ten directions as the sands of the Ganges. They are able to see universally various sentient beings: some are dying while some are alive; some are good looking while some are not good looking; some are superior while some are inferior; some are reborn into the good destinies while some are into the inferior destinies; and so forth. They also see that various sentient beings were reborn in accordance with individual differences of karmas. Some of them had achieved wonderful actions in body, speech, and mind. They liked to admire the saints and the sages, and because of this cause and condition, they were reborn into the good destinies, either into the heavens or the human world to enjoy all kinds of wonderful pleasures. Some sentient beings had bad actions in body, speech, and mind. They slandered the saints and the sages, and because of this cause and condition, they were reborn into the inferior destinies, either into the hells, or the realm of animals, the realm of ghosts, the marginal areas of the world, or very low social classes, in which they suffered poor and filthy life. They are able to see accurately all these different kinds of karmas made by the sentient beings and the results thus derived.

"Sariputra, although these great bodhisattvas have acquired the supernatural power of heavenly eye, they do not boast about it, nor are they attached to its nature and the use of it, or to the one who possesses it. They even are not attached to the attachment and the nonattachment. Why? Because these great bodhisattvas know that the self-natures of all dharmas are empty, the so-called self-natures are not in the dharma, and the self-natures are inherently unattainable. Sariputra, these great bodhisattvas will not have this thought in their minds: 'I am activating supernatural power of heavenly eye in order to entertain myself and others.' They activate this supernatural power only for the sake of attaining the perfect knowledge of all perfect knowledge. Sariputra, this is the supernatural power of heavenly eye paramita that the great bodhisattvas will activate when they cultivate prajna paramita."

At that time, Sariputra asked the Buddha again, "World-Honored One, what is the supernatural power of the extinction of flaws paramita that the great bodhisattvas will activate when they cultivate prajna paramita?"

The Buddha replied to the long-lived sage Sariputra, "Sariputra, some great bodhisattvas have acquired the supernatural power of the extinction of flaws and are able to know accurately the sentient beings, including themselves, in as many realms of the ten directions as the sands of the Ganges, whether they are flawless or not. This supernatural power is caused by a diamond-like concentration, in which one's rooted obstacles and disposition are completely cut off. When one achieves the bodhisattva stage of nonregression, he or she is also named at the extinction of the flaws, because no more flawed action will be present. Once the great bodhisattvas have acquired the supernatural power of flawlessness, they will not fall back into the stage of the voice-hearer or that of the self-enlightened one, but keep moving straight toward the unsurpassed, perfect, and universal bodhi. They will not go astray or look for other kinds of justice and benefits.

"Sariputra, although these great bodhisattvas have acquired the supernatural power of flawlessness, they do not boast about it, nor are they attached to its nature and the use of it or to the one who possesses it. They even are not attached to the attachment and the nonattachment. Why? Because these great bodhisattvas know that the self-natures of all dharmas are empty, the so-called self-natures are not in the dharmas, and the self-natures are inherently unattainable. Sariputra, these great bodhisattvas will not have this thought in their minds: 'I am activating supernatural power of the extinction of flaws in order to entertain myself and others.' They activate this supernatural power only for the sake of attaining the perfect knowledge of all perfect knowledge. Sariputra, this is the supernatural power of the extinction of flaws paramita that the great bodhisattvas will activate when they cultivate prajna paramita."

"Therefore, Sariputra, this is how the great bodhisattvas are capable of completely purifying the six supernatural powers paramitas when cultivating prajna paramita. Because the six supernatural powers paramitas are purified perfectly, they are able to fulfill perfectly the perfect knowledge of all perfect knowledge, namely the perfect knowledge of everything and the perfect knowledge of the forms of the paths.

"Furthermore, Sariputra, some great bodhisattvas have dwelled peacefully in giving paramita and dignified and purified the path of the perfect knowledge of everything and the path of the perfect knowledge of all phenomena when they cultivated prajna paramita. Because of the emptiness in the final analysis, the mind of greed and stinginess will not arise anymore.

"Furthermore, Sariputra, some great bodhisattvas have dwelled peacefully in pure-precept paramita and dignified and purified the path of the perfect knowledge of everything and the path of the perfect knowledge of all phenomena when they cultivated prajna paramita. Because of the emptiness in the final analysis, the mind of observing the precepts and violating the precepts will not arise anymore.

"Furthermore, Sariputra, some great bodhisattvas have dwelled peacefully in forbearance paramita and dignified and purified the path of the perfect knowledge of everything and the path of the perfect knowledge of all phenomena when they cultivated prajna paramita. Because of the emptiness in the final analysis, the mind of loving-kindness and compassion and the mind of hatred and anger will not arise anymore.

"Furthermore, Sariputra, some great bodhisattvas have dwelled peacefully in diligence paramita and dignified and purified the path of the perfect knowledge of everything and the path of the perfect knowledge of all phenomena when they cultivated prajna paramita. Because of the emptiness in the final analysis, the mind of diligence and bravery and the mind of laziness and tiredness will not arise anymore.

"Furthermore, Sariputra, some great bodhisattvas have dwelled peacefully in meditation paramita and dignified and purified the path of the perfect knowledge of everything and the path of the perfect knowledge of all phenomena when they cultivated prajna paramita. Because of the emptiness in the final analysis, the mind of tranquility and the mind of restlessness will not arise anymore.

"Furthermore, Sariputra, when cultivating prajna paramita, some great bodhisattvas have dwelled peacefully in prajna paramita and dignified and purified the path of the perfect knowledge of everything and the path of the perfect knowledge of all phenomena. Because of the emptiness in the final analysis, the mind of wisdom and the mind of ignorance will not arise anymore.

"Furthermore, Sariputra, when cultivating prajna paramita, some great bodhisattvas have dwelled peacefully in giving paramita and pure-precept paramita and dignified and purified the path of the perfect knowledge of everything and the path of the perfect knowledge of all phenomena. Because of the emptiness in the final analysis, the mind of generous giving, greediness and stinginess, and the mind of observing and violating precepts will not arise anymore.

"Furthermore, Sariputra, when cultivating prajna paramita, some great bodhisattvas have dwelled peacefully in giving paramita and forbearance paramita and dignified and purified the path of the perfect knowledge of everything and the path of the perfect knowledge of all phenomena. Because of the emptiness in the final analysis, the minds of generous giving, greediness and stinginess, loving-kindness, compassion, hatred, and anger will not arise anymore.

"Furthermore, Sariputra, when cultivating prajna paramita, some great bodhisattvas have dwelled peacefully in giving paramita and diligence paramita and dignified and purified the path of the perfect knowledge of everything and the path of the perfect knowledge of all phenomena. Because of the emptiness in the final analysis, the minds of generous giving, greediness, stinginess, diligence, bravery, laziness, and tiredness will not arise anymore.

"Furthermore, Sariputra, when cultivating prajna paramita, some great bodhisattvas have dwelled peacefully in giving paramita and meditation paramita and dignified and purified the path of the perfect knowledge of everything and the path of the perfect knowledge of all phenomena. Because of the emptiness in the final analysis, the minds of generous giving, greediness, stinginess, tranquility, and restlessness will not arise anymore.

"Furthermore, Sariputra, when cultivating prajna paramita, some great bodhisattvas have dwelled peacefully in giving paramita and prajna paramita and dignified and purified the path of the perfect knowledge of everything and the path of the perfect knowledge of all phenomena. Because of the emptiness in the final analysis, the minds of generous giving, greediness, stinginess, wisdom, and ignorance will not arise anymore.

"Furthermore, Sariputra, when cultivating prajna paramita, some great bodhisattvas have dwelled peacefully in pure-precept paramita and forbearance paramita and dignified and purified the path of the perfect knowledge of everything and the path of the perfect knowledge of all phenomena. Because of the emptiness in the final analysis, the minds of observing precepts, violating precepts, loving-kindness, compassion, hatred, and anger will not arise anymore.

"Furthermore, Sariputra, when cultivating prajna paramita, some great bodhisattvas have dwelled peacefully in pure-precept paramita and diligence paramita and dignified and purified the path of the perfect knowledge of everything and the path of the perfect knowledge of all phenomena. Because of the emptiness in the final analysis, the minds of observing precepts, violating precepts, diligence, bravery, laziness, and tiredness will not arise anymore.

"Furthermore, Sariputra, when cultivating prajna paramita, some great bodhisattvas have dwelled peacefully in pure-precept paramita and meditation paramita and dignified and purified the path of the perfect knowledge of everything and the path of the perfect knowledge of all phenomena. Because of the emptiness in the final analysis, the minds of observing precepts, violating precepts, tranquility, and restlessness will not arise anymore.

"Furthermore, Sariputra, when cultivating prajna paramita, some great bodhisattvas have dwelled peacefully in pure-precept paramita and prajna paramita and dignified and purified the path of the perfect knowledge of everything and the path of the perfect knowledge of all phenomena. Because of the emptiness in the final analysis, the minds of observing precepts, violating precepts, wisdom, and ignorance will not arise anymore.

"Furthermore, Sariputra, when cultivating prajna paramita, some great bodhisattvas have dwelled peacefully in forbearance paramita and diligence paramita and dignified and purified the path of the perfect knowledge of everything and the path of the perfect knowledge of all phenomena. Because of the emptiness in the final analysis, the minds of loving-kindness, compassion, hatred, anger, diligence, bravery, laziness, and tiredness will not arise anymore.

"Furthermore, Sariputra, when cultivating prajna paramita, some great bodhisattvas have dwelled peacefully in forbearance paramita and meditation paramita and dignified and purified the path of the perfect knowledge of everything and the path of the perfect knowledge of all phenomena. Because of the emptiness in the final analysis, the minds of loving-kindness, compassion, hatred, anger, tranquility, and restlessness will not arise anymore.

"Furthermore, Sariputra, when cultivating prajna paramita, some great bodhisattvas have dwelled peacefully in forbearance paramita and prajna paramita and dignified and purified the path of the perfect knowledge of everything and the path of the perfect knowledge of all phenomena. Because of the emptiness in the final analysis, the minds of loving-kindness, compassion, hatred, anger, wisdom, and ignorance will not arise anymore.

"Furthermore, Sariputra, when cultivating prajna paramita, some great bodhisattvas have dwelled peacefully in diligence paramita and meditation paramita and dignified and purified the path of the perfect knowledge of everything and the path of the perfect knowledge of all phenomena. Because of the emptiness in the final analysis, the minds of diligence, bravery, laziness, tiredness, tranquility, and restlessness will not arise anymore.

"Furthermore, Sariputra, when cultivating prajna paramita, some great bodhisattvas have dwelled peacefully in diligence paramita and prajna paramita and dignified and purified the path of the perfect knowledge of everything and the path of the perfect knowledge of all phenomena. Because of the emptiness in the final analysis, the minds of diligence, bravery, laziness, tiredness, wisdom, and ignorance will not arise anymore.

Fascicle 9, Chapter 4, Section 3   193

"Furthermore, Sariputra, when cultivating prajna paramita, some great bodhisattvas have dwelled peacefully in meditation paramita and prajna paramita and dignified and purified the path of the perfect knowledge of everything and the path of the perfect knowledge of all phenomena. Because of the emptiness in the final analysis, the minds of tranquility, restlessness, wisdom, and ignorance will not arise anymore.

"Furthermore, Sariputra, when cultivating prajna paramita, some great bodhisattvas have dwelled peacefully in giving, pure precept, and forbearance paramitas and dignified and purified the path of the perfect knowledge of everything and the path of the perfect knowledge of all phenomena. Because of the emptiness in the final analysis, the minds of generous giving, greediness, stinginess, observing precepts, violating precepts, loving-kindness, compassion, hatred, and anger will not arise anymore.

"Furthermore, Sariputra, when cultivating prajna paramita, some great bodhisattvas have dwelled peacefully in giving, pure precept, and diligence paramitas and dignified and purified the path of the perfect knowledge of everything and the path of the perfect knowledge of all phenomena. Because of the emptiness in the final analysis, the minds of generous giving, greediness, stinginess, observing precepts, violating precepts, diligence, bravery, laziness, and tiredness will not arise anymore.

"Furthermore, Sariputra, when cultivating prajna paramita, some great bodhisattvas have dwelled peacefully in giving, pure precept, and meditation paramitas and dignified and purified the path of the perfect knowledge of everything and the path of the perfect knowledge of all phenomena. Because of the emptiness in the final analysis, the minds of generous giving, greediness, stinginess, observing precepts, violating precepts, tranquility, and restlessness will not arise anymore.

"Furthermore, Sariputra, when cultivating prajna paramita, some great bodhisattvas have dwelled peacefully in giving, pure precept, and prajna paramitas and dignified and purified the path of the perfect knowledge of everything and the path of the perfect knowledge of all phenomena. Because of the emptiness in the final analysis, the minds of generous giving, greediness, stinginess, observing precepts, violating precepts, wisdom, and ignorance will not arise anymore.

"Furthermore, Sariputra, when cultivating prajna paramita, some great bodhisattvas have dwelled peacefully in giving, forbearance, and diligence paramitas and dignified and purified the path of the perfect knowledge of everything and the path of the perfect knowledge of all phenomena. Because of the emptiness in the final analysis, the minds of generous giving, greediness, stinginess, loving-kindness, compassion, hatred, anger, diligence, bravery, laziness, and tiredness will not arise anymore.

"Furthermore, Sariputra, when cultivating prajna paramita, some great bodhisattvas have dwelled peacefully in giving, forbearance, and meditation paramitas and dignified and purified the path of the perfect knowledge of everything and the path of the perfect knowledge of all phenomena. Because of the emptiness in the final analysis, the minds of generous giving, greediness, stinginess, loving-kindness, compassion, hatred, anger, tranquility, and restlessness will not arise anymore.

"Furthermore, Sariputra, when cultivating prajna paramita, some great bodhisattvas have dwelled peacefully in giving, forbearance, and prajna paramitas and dignified and purified the path of the perfect knowledge of everything and the perfect knowledge of all phenomena. Because of the emptiness in the final analysis, the minds of generous giving, greediness, stinginess, loving-kindness, compassion, hatred, anger, wisdom, and ignorance will not arise anymore.

"Furthermore, Sariputra, when cultivating prajna paramita, some great bodhisattvas have dwelled peacefully in giving, diligence, and meditation paramitas and dignified and purified the path of the perfect knowledge of everything and the path of the perfect knowledge of all phenomena. Because of the emptiness in the final analysis, the minds of generous giving, greediness, stinginess, diligence, bravery, laziness, tranquility, and restlessness will not arise anymore.

"Furthermore, Sariputra, when cultivating prajna paramita, some great bodhisattvas have dwelled peacefully in giving, diligence, and prajna paramitas and dignified and purified the path of the perfect knowledge of everything and the path of the perfect knowledge of all phenomena. Because of the emptiness in the final analysis, the minds of generous giving, greediness, stinginess, diligence, bravery, laziness, tiredness, wisdom, and ignorance will not arise anymore.

"Furthermore, Sariputra, when cultivating prajna paramita, some great bodhisattvas have dwelled peacefully in giving, meditation, and prajna paramitas and dignified and purified the path of the perfect knowledge of everything and the path of the perfect knowledge of all phenomena. Because of the emptiness in the final analysis, the minds of generous giving, greediness, stinginess, tranquility, restlessness, wisdom, and ignorance will not arise anymore.

"Furthermore, Sariputra, when cultivating prajna paramita, some great bodhisattvas have dwelled peacefully in pure precept, forbearance, and diligence paramitas and dignified and purified the path of the perfect knowledge of everything and the path of the perfect knowledge of all phenomena. Because of the emptiness in the final analysis, the minds of observing precepts, violating precepts, loving-kindness, compassion, hatred, anger, diligence, bravery, laziness, and tiredness will not arise anymore.

"Furthermore, Sariputra, when cultivating prajna paramita, some great bodhisattvas have dwelled peacefully in pure precept, forbearance, and meditation paramitas and dignified and purified the path of the perfect knowledge of everything and the path of the perfect knowledge of all phenomena. Because of the emptiness in the final analysis, the minds of observing precepts, violating precepts, loving-kindness, compassion, hatred, anger, tranquility, and restlessness will not arise anymore.

"Furthermore, Sariputra, when cultivating prajna paramita, some great bodhisattvas have dwelled peacefully in pure precept, forbearance, and prajna paramitas and dignified and purified the path of the perfect knowledge of everything and the path of the perfect knowledge of all phenomena. Because of the emptiness in the final analysis, the minds of observing precepts, violating precepts, loving-kindness, compassion, hatred, anger, wisdom, and ignorance will not arise anymore.

"Furthermore, Sariputra, when cultivating prajna paramita,

some great bodhisattvas have dwelled peacefully in pure precept, diligence, and meditation paramitas and dignified and purified the path of the perfect knowledge of everything and the path of the perfect knowledge of all phenomena. Because of the emptiness in the final analysis, the minds of observing precepts, violating precepts, diligence, bravery, laziness, tiredness, tranquility, and restlessness will not arise anymore.

"Furthermore, Sariputra, when cultivating prajna paramita, some great bodhisattvas have dwelled peacefully in pure precept, diligence, and prajna paramitas and dignified and purified the path of the perfect knowledge of everything and the path of the perfect knowledge of all phenomena. Because of the emptiness in the final analysis, the minds of observing precepts, violating precepts, diligence, bravery, laziness, tiredness, wisdom, and ignorance will not arise anymore.

"Furthermore, Sariputra, when cultivating prajna paramita, some great bodhisattvas have dwelled peacefully in pure precept, meditation, and prajna paramitas and dignified and purified the path of the perfect knowledge of everything and the path of the perfect knowledge of all phenomena. Because of the emptiness in the final analysis, the minds of observing precepts, violating precepts, tranquility, restlessness, wisdom, and ignorance will not arise anymore.

"Furthermore, Sariputra, when cultivating prajna paramita, some great bodhisattvas have dwelled peacefully in forbearance, diligence, and meditation paramitas and dignified and purified the path of the perfect knowledge of everything and the path of the perfect knowledge of all phenomena. Because of the emptiness in the final analysis, the minds of loving-kindness, compassion, hatred, anger, diligence, bravery, laziness, tiredness, tranquility, and restlessness will not arise anymore.

"Furthermore, Sariputra, when cultivating prajna paramita, some great bodhisattvas have dwelled peacefully in forbearance, diligence, and prajna paramitas and dignified and purified the path of the perfect knowledge of everything and the path of the perfect knowledge of all phenomena. Because of the emptiness in the final analysis, the minds of loving-kindness, compassion, hatred, anger,

Fascicle 9, Chapter 4, Section 3 197

diligence, bravery, laziness, tiredness, wisdom, and ignorance will not arise anymore.

"Furthermore, Sariputra, when cultivating prajna paramita, some great bodhisattvas have dwelled peacefully in forbearance, meditation, and prajna paramitas and dignified and purified the path of the perfect knowledge of everything and the path of the perfect knowledge of all phenomena. Because of the emptiness in the final analysis, the minds of loving-kindness, compassion, hatred, anger, tranquility, restlessness, wisdom, and ignorance will not arise anymore.

"Furthermore, Sariputra, when cultivating prajna paramita, some great bodhisattvas have dwelled peacefully in diligence, meditation, and prajna paramitas and dignified and purified the path of the perfect knowledge of everything and the path of the perfect knowledge of all phenomena. Because of the emptiness in the final analysis, the minds of diligence, bravery, laziness, tiredness, tranquility, restlessness, wisdom, and ignorance will not arise anymore.

"Furthermore, Sariputra, when cultivating prajna paramita, some great bodhisattvas have dwelled peacefully in giving, pure precept, forbearance, and diligence paramitas and dignified and purified the path of the perfect knowledge of everything and the path of the perfect knowledge of all phenomena. Because of the emptiness in the final analysis, the mind of generous giving, greediness, and stinginess; the mind of observing and violating precepts; the mind of loving-kindness, compassion, hatred, and anger; and the mind of diligence, bravery, laziness, and tiredness will not arise anymore.

"Furthermore, Sariputra, when cultivating prajna paramita, some great bodhisattvas have dwelled peacefully in giving, pure precept, forbearance, and meditation paramitas and dignified and purified the path of the perfect knowledge of everything and the path of the perfect knowledge of all phenomena. Because of the emptiness in the final analysis, the mind of generous giving, greediness, and stinginess; the mind of observing and violating precepts; the mind of loving-kindness, compassion, hatred, and anger; and the mind of tranquility and restlessness will not arise anymore.

"Furthermore, Sariputra, when cultivating prajna paramita,

some great bodhisattvas have dwelled peacefully in giving, pure precept, forbearance, and prajna paramitas and dignified and purified the path of the perfect knowledge of everything and the path of the perfect knowledge of all phenomena. Because of the emptiness in the final analysis, the mind of generous giving, greediness, and stinginess; the mind of observing and violating precepts; the mind of loving-kindness, compassion, hatred, and anger; and the mind of wisdom and ignorance will not arise anymore.

"Furthermore, Sariputra, when cultivating prajna paramita, some great bodhisattvas have dwelled peacefully in giving, pure precept, diligence, and meditation paramitas and dignified and purified the path of the perfect knowledge of everything and the path of the perfect knowledge of all phenomena. Because of the emptiness in the final analysis, the mind of generous giving, greediness, and stinginess; the mind of observing and violating precepts; the mind of diligence, bravery, laziness, and tiredness; and the mind of tranquility and restlessness will not arise anymore.

"Furthermore, Sariputra, when cultivating prajna paramita, some great bodhisattvas have dwelled peacefully in giving, pure precept, diligence, and prajna paramitas and dignified and purified the path of the perfect knowledge of everything and the path of the perfect knowledge of all phenomena. Because of the emptiness in the final analysis, the mind of generous giving, greediness, and stinginess; the mind of observing and violating precepts; the mind of diligence, bravery, laziness, and tiredness; and the mind of wisdom and ignorance will not arise anymore.

"Furthermore, Sariputra, when cultivating prajna paramita, some great bodhisattvas have dwelled peacefully in giving, pure precept, meditation, and prajna paramitas and dignified and purified the path of the perfect knowledge of everything and the path of the perfect knowledge of all phenomena. Because of the emptiness in the final analysis, the mind of generous giving, greediness, and stinginess; the mind of observing and violating precepts; the mind of tranquility and restlessness; and the mind of wisdom and ignorance will not arise anymore.

"Furthermore, Sariputra, when cultivating prajna paramita, some great bodhisattvas have dwelled peacefully in giving, forbear-

Fascicle 9, Chapter 4, Section 3   199

ance, diligence, and meditation paramitas and dignified and purified the path of the perfect knowledge of everything and the path of the perfect knowledge of all phenomena. Because of the emptiness in the final analysis, the mind of generous giving, greediness, and stinginess; the mind of loving-kindness, compassion, hatred, and anger; the mind of diligence, bravery, laziness, and tiredness; and the mind of tranquility and restlessness will not arise anymore.

"Furthermore, Sariputra, when cultivating prajna paramita, some great bodhisattvas have dwelled peacefully in giving, forbearance, diligence, and prajna paramitas and dignified and purified the path of the perfect knowledge of everything and the path of the perfect knowledge of all phenomena. Because of the emptiness in the final analysis, the mind of generous giving, greediness, and stinginess; the mind of loving-kindness, compassion, hatred, and anger; the mind of diligence, bravery, laziness, and tiredness; and the mind of wisdom and ignorance will not arise anymore.

"Furthermore, Sariputra, when cultivating prajna paramita, some great bodhisattvas have dwelled peacefully in giving, forbearance, meditation, and prajna paramitas and dignified and purified the path of the perfect knowledge of everything and the path of the perfect knowledge of all phenomena. Because of the emptiness in the final analysis, the mind of generous giving, greediness, and stinginess; the mind of loving-kindness, compassion, hatred, and anger; the mind of tranquility and restlessness; and the mind of wisdom and ignorance will not arise anymore.

"Furthermore, Sariputra, when cultivating prajna paramita, some great bodhisattvas have dwelled peacefully in giving, diligence, meditation, and prajna paramitas and dignified and purified the path of the perfect knowledge of everything and the path of the perfect knowledge of all phenomena. Because of the emptiness in the final analysis, the mind of generous giving, greediness, and stinginess; the mind of diligence, bravery, laziness, and tiredness; the mind of tranquility and restlessness; and the mind of wisdom and ignorance will not arise anymore.

"Furthermore, Sariputra, when cultivating prajna paramita, some great bodhisattvas have dwelled peacefully in pure precept, forbearance, diligence, and meditation paramitas and dignified and purified the path of the perfect knowledge of everything and the path of the perfect knowledge of all phenomena. Because of the emptiness in the final analysis, the mind of observing and violating precepts; the mind of loving-kindness, compassion, hatred, and anger; the mind of diligence, bravery, laziness, and tiredness; and the mind of tranquility and restlessness will not arise anymore.

"Furthermore, Sariputra, when cultivating prajna paramita, some great bodhisattvas have dwelled peacefully in pure precept, forbearance, diligence, and prajna paramitas and dignified and purified the path of the perfect knowledge of everything and the path of the perfect knowledge of all phenomena. Because of the emptiness in the final analysis, the mind of observing and violating precepts; the mind of loving-kindness, compassion, hatred, and anger; the mind of diligence, bravery, laziness, and tiredness; and the mind of wisdom and ignorance will not arise anymore.

"Furthermore, Sariputra, when cultivating prajna paramita, some great bodhisattvas have dwelled peacefully in pure precept, forbearance, meditation, and prajna paramitas and dignified and purified the path of the perfect knowledge of everything and the path of the perfect knowledge of all phenomena. Because of the emptiness in the final analysis, the mind of observing and violating precepts; the mind of loving-kindness, compassion, hatred, and anger; the mind of tranquility and restlessness; and the mind of wisdom and ignorance will not arise anymore.

"Furthermore, Sariputra, when cultivating prajna paramita, some great bodhisattvas have dwelled peacefully in pure precept, diligence, meditation, and prajna paramitas and dignified and purified the path of the perfect knowledge of everything and the path of the perfect knowledge of all phenomena. Because of the emptiness in the final analysis, the mind of observing and violating precepts; the mind of diligence, bravery, laziness, and tiredness; the mind of tranquility and restlessness; and the mind of wisdom and ignorance will not arise anymore.

"Furthermore, Sariputra, when cultivating prajna paramita, some great bodhisattvas have dwelled peacefully in forbearance, diligence, meditation, and prajna paramitas and dignified and purified the path of the perfect knowledge of everything and the path of the perfect knowledge of all phenomena. Because of the emptiness in the final analysis, the mind of loving-kindness, compassion, hatred, and anger; the mind of diligence, bravery, laziness, and tiredness; the mind of tranquility and restlessness; and the mind of wisdom and ignorance will not arise anymore.

"Furthermore, Sariputra, when cultivating prajna paramita, some great bodhisattvas have dwelled peacefully in giving, pure precept, forbearance, diligence, and meditation paramitas and dignified and purified the path of the perfect knowledge of everything and the path of the perfect knowledge of all phenomena. Because of the emptiness in the final analysis, the mind of generous giving, greediness, and stinginess; the mind of observing and violating precepts; the mind of loving-kindness, compassion, hatred, and anger; the mind of diligence, bravery, laziness, and tiredness; and the mind of tranquility and restlessness will not arise anymore.

"Furthermore, Sariputra, when cultivating prajna paramita, some great bodhisattvas have dwelled peacefully in giving, pure precept, forbearance, diligence, and prajna paramitas and dignified and purified the path of the perfect knowledge of everything and the path of the perfect knowledge of all phenomena. Because of the emptiness in the final analysis, the mind of generous giving, greediness, and stinginess; the mind of observing and violating precepts; the mind of loving-kindness, compassion, hatred, and anger; the mind of diligence, bravery, laziness, and tiredness; and the mind of wisdom and ignorance will not arise anymore.

"Furthermore, Sariputra, when cultivating prajna paramita, some great bodhisattvas have dwelled peacefully in giving, pure precept, forbearance, meditation, and prajna paramitas and dignified and purified the path of the perfect knowledge of everything and the path of the perfect knowledge of all phenomena. Because of the emptiness in the final analysis, the mind of generous giving, greediness, and stinginess; the mind of observing and violating precepts; the mind of loving-kindness, compassion, hatred, and anger; the mind of tranquility and restlessness; and the mind of wisdom and ignorance will not arise anymore.

"Furthermore, Sariputra, when cultivating prajna paramita, some great bodhisattvas have dwelled peacefully in giving, pure precept, diligence, meditation, and prajna paramitas and dignified and purified the path of the perfect knowledge of everything and the path of the perfect knowledge of all phenomena. Because of the emptiness in the final analysis, the mind of generous giving, greediness, and stinginess; the mind of observing and violating precepts; the mind of diligence, bravery, laziness, and tiredness; the mind of tranquility and restlessness; and the mind of wisdom and ignorance will not arise anymore.

"Furthermore, Sariputra, when cultivating prajna paramita, some great bodhisattvas have dwelled peacefully in giving, forbearance, diligence, meditation, and prajna paramitas and dignified and purified the path of the perfect knowledge of everything and the path of perfect knowledge of all phenomena. Because of the emptiness in the final analysis, the mind of generous giving, greediness, and stinginess; the mind of loving-kindness, compassion, hatred, and anger; the mind of diligence, bravery, laziness, and tiredness; the mind of tranquility and restlessness; and the mind of wisdom and ignorance will not arise anymore.

"Furthermore, Sariputra, when cultivating prajna paramita, some great bodhisattvas have dwelled peacefully in pure precept, forbearance, diligence, meditation, and prajna paramitas and dignified and purified the path of the perfect knowledge of everything and the path of the perfect knowledge of all phenomena. Because of the emptiness in the final analysis, the mind of observing and violating precepts; the mind of loving-kindness, compassion, hatred, and anger; the mind of diligence, bravery, laziness, and tiredness; the mind of tranquility and restlessness; and the mind of wisdom and ignorance will not arise anymore.

"Furthermore, Sariputra, when cultivating prajna paramita, some great bodhisattvas have dwelled peacefully in giving, pure precept, forbearance, diligence, meditation, and prajna paramitas and dignified and purified the path of the perfect knowledge of everything and the path of the perfect knowledge of all phenomena. Because of the emptiness in the final analysis, the mind of generous giving, greediness, and stinginess; the mind of observing and violating precepts; the mind of loving-kindness, compassion, hatred, and anger; the mind of diligence, bravery, laziness, and tiredness; the mind of tranquility and restlessness; and the mind of wisdom and ignorance will not arise anymore.

"Furthermore, Sariputra, when cultivating prajna paramita, some great bodhisattvas have dwelled peacefully in the six paramitas and dignified and purified the path of the perfect knowledge of everything and the path of the perfect knowledge of all phenomena. Because of the emptiness in the final analysis that is without coming and going, there is no giving, stinginess, and greediness; they are provisionally established. There is no pure precept and the violation of precepts; they are provisionally established. There is no forbearance, hatred, and anger; they are provisionally established. There is no diligence and laziness; they are provisionally established. There is no tranquility and restlessness; they are provisionally established. There is no prajna and ignorance; they are provisionally established. These great bodhisattvas are attached to neither entering onto the correct path nor not entering onto the correct path. They are attached to neither ferrying themselves to the other shore nor not ferrying themselves to the other shore. They are attached to neither giving nor stinginess and greediness. They are attached to neither pure precept nor violating the precepts. They are attached to neither forbearance nor anger and hatred. They are attached to neither diligence nor laziness. They are attached to neither tranquility nor restlessness. They are attached to neither prajna nor ignorance.

"Sariputra, at that time, these great bodhisattvas are attached to neither the ones who give nor the ones who are greedy and stingy. They are attached to neither the ones who observe pure precepts nor the ones who violate the precepts. They are attached to neither the ones who are compassionate and patient nor the ones who are in hatred and anger. They are attached to neither the diligent ones nor the lazy ones. They are attached to neither the ones in meditation nor the ones in restlessness. They are attached to neither the ones who have prajna nor the ones who are ignorant. Sariputra, these great bodhisattvas are not even attached to attachment or nonattachment. Why? Sariputra, because these great bodhisattvas have understood that all dharmas are empty in the final analysis. Sariputra, these great bodhisattvas, at that time, are not attached to slander, reproach, admiration, damage, benefit, contempt, or respect. Why? Sariputra, because these great bodhisattvas have understood that all the dharmas are without arising in the final analysis. They have also understood that in the dharmas of nonarising, there is neither the dharma of slander nor the dharma of admiration, neither the dharma of damage nor the dharma of benefit, neither the dharma of contempt nor the dharma of respect. Sariputra, these great bodhisattvas, at that time, are not attached to the slanderers, the admirers, the damage producers, the benefactors, the ones with contempt, or the ones with respect, either. Why? Sariputra, these great bodhisattvas have fully understood that the original natures of all dharmas are empty, and in the emptiness of original natures there is no slanderer or admirer, damage producer or benefactor, one with contempt or one with respect. Sariputra, these great bodhisattvas, at that time, are attached to neither attachment nor nonattachment. Why? Sariputra, as the great bodhisattvas cultivate prajna paramita, they have terminated all kinds of attachment and nonattachment forever.

"Therefore, Sariputra, when cultivating prajna paramita, the merits and virtues gained by the great bodhisattvas are the highest, the most wonderful, and the most inconceivable ones. These are the merits and virtues that all voice-hearers and self-enlightened ones are unable to possess. Sariputra! After fulfilling these merits and virtues perfectly, the great bodhisattvas will further work hard to assist the sentient beings to mature by practicing the four approaches of absorption: superior giving, speaking good and kind words, doing actions beneficial to others, and getting along with others in harmony and empathy. They will further work hard to dignify and purify the Buddha lands with great, solid aspiration and brave diligence. Thus, they are able to realize insightfully the unsurpassed, perfect, and universal bodhi quickly.

"Furthermore, Sariputra, when cultivating prajna paramita, the great bodhisattvas will treat all sentient beings, inferior or superior, ugly or beautiful, equally. In addition, they will attempt to bring benefits and happiness to all sentient beings. Because of this kind intention, they view all dharma natures equally. Because of this view, they establish all sentient beings in peace and comfort uni-

Fascicle 9, Chapter 4, Section 3   205

versally and benefit them tremendously based on the equal natures of all dharmas. Sariputra! Because of this cause and condition, these great bodhisattvas will be always protected by and kept in the minds of all Thus-Comers, Ones Worthy of Offerings, Perfectly and Universally Enlightened Ones in the realms of the ten directions. They will be admired by all great bodhisattvas in the realms of the ten directions and adored and respected by all voice-hearers and self-enlightened ones who are practicing celibacy. They will also receive offerings and homage and admiration from all human beings, heavenly beings, and asuras. Because of this cause and condition, these great bodhisattvas will not see the undesirable sights, hear the undesirable sounds, smell the undesirable odors, taste the undesirable flavors, touch the undesirable matters, and think the undesirable ideas. Sariputra! Because of this cause and condition, the merits and virtues to be gained by these great bodhisattvas will increase and become more superior. They will never regress until attaining the unsurpassed, perfect, and universal bodhi."

When the Buddha was teaching the superior virtues and merits of the fathomless prajna paramita, immeasurable bhiksus stood up from their seats and made new and clean clothes as offerings to the Buddha. After that, they all made up their minds to aspire to the unsurpassed, perfect, and universal bodhi. At that time, the World-Honored One smiled and varied colorful lights emitted from his face.

In the meantime, Ananda stood up from his seat. He knelt down before the Buddha with his right leg touching the ground and left shoulder covered. He put his palms together and asked the Buddha, "World-Honored One! What are the causes and conditions that make you smile? I know that the Buddhas smile only when special causes and conditions appear. May the World-Honored One have pity and mercy on us and teach us!"

At that time, the Buddha said to Ananda, "All these bhiksus who just stood up from their seats will become the Buddhas sixty-one kalpas from now in the Kalpa of Constellation, and all will have the same name: Great Streamer Thus-Comer, One Worthy of Offerings, Perfectly and Universally Enlightened One, One Perfect in Wisdom and Conduct, Well Gone One, One Who Knows the

World, Unsurpassed Great Person, Taming and Guiding One, Teacher of Heavenly and Human Beings, Buddha, and Bhagavat. These bhiksus will be reborn in the country of Eastern Unmovable Buddha after this lifetime and will continue celibacy cultivation there."

Meanwhile, in the assembly, six million heavenly sons, inspired by the Buddha's teaching about the triumphant virtues and merits of the profound prajna paramita, decided to aspire to the unsurpassed, perfect, and universal enlightenment. The World-Honored One conferred on them the prophecy that they will renounce their families and practice celibacy diligently in the era of Maitreya Buddha and receive his teaching. The Maitreya Buddha will also confer on them the prophesy that they will attain the unsurpassed, perfect, and universal bodhi, turn the dharma wheel, deliver immeasurable sentient beings, and assist them to realize insightfully and attain the permanent and happy nirvana.

At that time, with the support of the Buddha's supernatural powers, all participants in the assembly witnessed the meetings in which the Buddhas were giving teachings to their disciples and other sentient beings in each of the thousand-worlds of the ten directions. In those worlds where the Buddhas were present, the virtues and merits were so magnificent and unique that this Barely Tolerable World could not catch up. Meanwhile, in this assembly, immeasurable hundreds of thousands of sentient beings were touched and vowed, "I would like to be reborn into those Buddha lands based on the pure karmas that I have cultivated."

At that time, the World-Honored One knew what they thought, so he smiled. As he smiled, lights of varied colors emitted from his face. Ananda rose up from his seat and in respect asked about the cause and condition of the Buddha's smile.

The Buddha said to Ananda, "Have you ever seen these immeasurable sentient beings rise up from their seats?"

Ananda replied, "Yes, I have."

The Buddha said to Ananda, "These sentient beings will be reborn after the present lifetime to each of those Buddha lands as each one wishes. They will continue to practice bodhisattva actions there until attaining the unsurpassed, perfect, and universal bodhi.

In those lands in which they are to be reborn, they will always be with the Buddha. They will make offerings to him and pay homage and admiration to him. They will diligently and assiduously cultivate giving, pure precept, forbearance, diligence, meditation, and prajna paramitas. They will dwell firmly in internal emptiness, external emptiness, internal-external emptiness, emptiness of emptiness, emptiness of space, emptiness of ultimate truth, emptiness of conditioned phenomena, emptiness of unconditioned reality, emptiness in the final analysis, emptiness of nontemporality, emptiness of deconstruction, emptiness of changelessness, emptiness of original nature, emptiness of particular characteristics, emptiness of common characteristics, emptiness of all dharmas, emptiness of nonattainment, emptiness of selflessness, emptiness of self-nature, and emptiness of selfless self-nature. They will also dwell firmly in realness, dharma realm, dharma nature, the nature of nonillusion, the nature of changelessness, the nature of equality, the nature of nonarising, dharma concentration, dharma dwelling, reality, the realm of empty space, and the realm of the inconceivable. They will cultivate the four bases of mindfulness, four correct endeavors, four bases of power, five roots, five powers, seven factors for enlightenment, and the noble eightfold path. They will dwell firmly in the noble truths of suffering, the cause of suffering, the cessation of suffering, and the path for the cessation of suffering. They will cultivate the four meditations, four immeasurable minds, and four formless concentrations. They will cultivate the eight liberations, eight vexation-overcoming meditations, nine concentrations in sequence, and the ten universal contemplations. They will cultivate the liberation gates of emptiness, formlessness, and nonaspiration. They will cultivate all dharani gates and all samadhi gates. They will cultivate the stages of bodhisattva. They will cultivate the five eyes and the six supernatural powers. They will cultivate the Buddha's ten abilities, four kinds of fearlessness, four unhindered understandings, great loving-kindness, great compassion, great joy, great equanimity, and the eighteen distinctive features of Buddha's wisdom and power. They will cultivate the way of staying in correct mindfulness and the nature of dwelling in equanimity at all times. They will cultivate the perfect knowledge of everything, the perfect knowledge of the forms of the paths, the perfect knowledge of all phenomena, and the rest of bodhisattva actions. Upon the completion of all these cultivations, they will become the Buddhas with the same name: Magnificent King Thus-Comer, One Worthy of Offerings, Perfectly and Universally Enlightened One, One Perfect in Wisdom and Conduct, Well Gone One, One Who Knows the World, Unsurpassed Great Person, Taming and Guiding One, Teacher of Heavenly and Human Beings, Buddha, and Bhagavat."

FASCICLE 10

Chapter 5
Praising the Superior Virtues

(In the First Assembly)

AT THAT TIME, THE LONG-LIVED SAGE SARIPUTRA, THE long-lived sage Mahamaudgalyayana, the long-lived sage Mahakasyapa, the long-lived sage Well Appearing One, the well-known and highly respected great bhiksus, bhiksunis, bodhisattvas, upasakas, and upasikas all stood up from their seats, joined their palms in respect, and said, "World-Honored One, the prajna paramita of the great bodhisattva is the great paramita.

"World-Honored One, the prajna paramita of the great bodhisattva is the broad paramita.

"World-Honored One, the prajna paramita of the great bodhisattva is the first paramita.

"World-Honored One, the prajna paramita of the great bodhisattva is the superior paramita.

"World-Honored One, the prajna paramita of the great bodhisattva is the wonderful paramita.

"World-Honored One, the prajna paramita of the great bodhisattva is the subtle paramita.

"World-Honored One, the prajna paramita of the great bodhisattva is the noble paramita.

"World-Honored One, the prajna paramita of the great bodhisattva is the high paramita.

"World-Honored One, the prajna paramita of the great bodhisattva is the utmost paramita.

"World-Honored One, the prajna paramita of the great bodhisattva is the paramita in the extreme.

"World-Honored One, the prajna paramita of the great bodhisattva is the upper paramita.

"World-Honored One, the prajna paramita of the great bodhisattva is the unsurpassed paramita.

"World-Honored One, the prajna paramita of the great bodhisattva is the unsurpassed uppermost paramita.

"World-Honored One, the prajna paramita of the great bodhisattva is the paramita of equality.

"World-Honored One, the prajna paramita of the great bodhisattva is the unequaled paramita.

"World-Honored One, the prajna paramita of the great bodhisattva is the unequaled paramita of equality.

"World-Honored One, the prajna paramita of the great bodhisattva is the paramita without counterpart.

"World-Honored One, the prajna paramita of the great bodhisattva is the paramita of empty space.

"World-Honored One, the prajna paramita of the great bodhisattva is the paramita of empty particular characteristics.

"World-Honored One, the prajna paramita of the great bodhisattva is the paramita of empty common characteristics.

"World-Honored One, the prajna paramita of the great bodhisattva is the paramita of the emptiness of all dharmas.

"World-Honored One, the prajna paramita of the great bodhisattva is the paramita of the emptiness of nonattainment.

"World-Honored One, the prajna paramita of the great bodhisattva is the paramita of the emptiness of selflessness.

"World-Honored One, the prajna paramita of the great bodhisattva is the paramita of the emptiness of self-nature.

Fascicle 10, Chapter 5

"World-Honored One, the prajna paramita of the great bodhisattva is the paramita of the emptiness of selfless self-nature.

"World-Honored One, the prajna paramita of the great bodhisattva is the paramita of the emptiness of changelessness.

"World-Honored One, the prajna paramita of the great bodhisattva is the paramita of nonarising.

"World-Honored One, the prajna paramita of the great bodhisattva is the paramita of nonextinction.

"World-Honored One, the prajna paramita of the great bodhisattva is uncontaminated paramita.

"World-Honored One, the prajna paramita of the great bodhisattva is the paramita without argument.

"World-Honored One, the prajna paramita of the great bodhisattva is the paramita of tranquility.

"World-Honored One, the prajna paramita of the great bodhisattva is the faraway paramita.

"World-Honored One, the prajna paramita of the great bodhisattva is the still and motionless paramita

"World-Honored One, the prajna paramita of the great bodhisattva is the paramita of tameness and subjugation.

"World-Honored One, the prajna paramita of the great bodhisattva is the paramita of bright dharani.

"World-Honored One, the prajna paramita of the great bodhisattva is the paramita of sincerity and truth.

"World-Honored One, the prajna paramita of the great bodhisattva is the paramita of exploring and opening up all merits and virtues.

"World-Honored One, the prajna paramita of the great bodhisattva is the paramita of fulfilling all merits and virtues.

"World-Honored One, the prajna paramita of the great bodhisattva is the paramita capable of defeating everything.

"World-Honored One, the prajna paramita of the great bodhisattva is the invincible paramita.

"World-Honored One, the great bodhisattvas who cultivate prajna paramita are the most venerable, most superior, highest, and most wonderful ones. They have great powers and are capable of cultivating the most unequaled giving of equality, fulfill it perfectly, and so are well equipped with the most unequaled equal giving paramita. Thus, they can acquire the most unequaled equal body, the so-called boundless, unique, perfect, wonderful, and magnificent body. They are able to realize and attain the most unequaled wonderful dharma of equality, namely the unsurpassed, perfect, and universal bodhi.

"World-Honored One, the great bodhisattvas who cultivate prajna paramita are the most venerable, most superior, highest, and most wonderful ones. They have great powers and are capable of cultivating the most unequaled pure precept of equality, fulfill it perfectly, and so are well equipped with the most unequaled equal pure-precept paramita. Thus, they can acquire the most unequaled equal body, the so-called boundless, unique, perfect, wonderful, and magnificent body; they are able to realize and attain the most unequaled wonderful dharma of equality, namely the unsurpassed, perfect, and universal bodhi.

"World-Honored One, the great bodhisattvas who cultivate prajna paramita are the most venerable, most superior, highest, and most wonderful ones. They have great powers and are capable of cultivating most unequaled forbearance of equality and fulfill it perfectly and so are well equipped with the most unequaled equal forbearance paramita. Thus, they can acquire the most unequaled equal body, the so-called boundless, unique, perfect, wonderful, and magnificent body; they are able to realize and attain the most unequaled wonderful dharma of equality, namely the unsurpassed, perfect, and universal bodhi.

"World-Honored One, the great bodhisattvas who cultivate prajna paramita are the most venerable, most superior, highest, and most wonderful ones. They have great powers and are capable of cultivating the most unequaled diligence of equality, fulfill it perfectly, and so are well equipped with the most unequaled equal diligence paramita. Thus, they can acquire the most unequaled equal body, the so-called boundless, unique, perfect, wonderful, and magnificent body; they are able to realize and attain the most unequaled wonderful dharma of equality, namely the unsurpassed, perfect, and universal bodhi.

Fascicle 10, Chapter 5   213

"World-Honored One, the great bodhisattvas who cultivate prajna paramita are the most venerable, most superior, highest, and most wonderful ones. They have great powers and are capable of cultivating the most unequaled meditation of equality, fulfill it perfectly, and so are well equipped with the most unequaled equal meditation paramita. Thus, they can acquire the most unequaled equal body, the so-called boundless, unique, perfect, wonderful, and magnificent body; they are able to realize and attain the most unequaled wonderful dharma of equality, namely the unsurpassed, perfect, and universal bodhi.

"World-Honored One, the great bodhisattvas who cultivate prajna paramita are the most venerable, most superior, highest, and most wonderful ones. They have great powers and are capable of cultivating the most unequaled prajna of equality, fulfill it perfectly, and so are well equipped with the most unequaled equal prajna paramita. Thus, they can acquire the most unequaled equal body, the so-called boundless, unique, perfect, wonderful, and magnificent body; they are able to realize and attain the most unequaled wonderful dharma of equality, namely the unsurpassed, perfect, and universal bodhi.

"World-Honored One, the great bodhisattvas who cultivate prajna paramita are the most venerable, most superior, highest, and most wonderful ones. They have great powers and are capable of dwelling firmly in the most unequaled equal internal emptiness, external emptiness, internal-external emptiness, emptiness of emptiness, emptiness of space, emptiness of ultimate truth, emptiness of conditioned phenomena, emptiness of unconditioned reality, emptiness in the final analysis, emptiness of deconstruction, emptiness of changelessness, emptiness of original nature, emptiness of particular characteristics, emptiness of common characteristics, emptiness of all dharmas, emptiness of nonattainment, emptiness of selflessness, emptiness of self-nature, and emptiness of selfless self-nature; fulfill them perfectly; and so are well equipped with the most unequaled equal internal emptiness, and so forth, as well as emptiness of selfless self-nature. Thus, they can acquire the most unequaled equal body, the so-called boundless, unique, perfect, wonderful, and magnificent body; and they are able to realize and attain the most unequaled wonderful dharma of equality, namely the unsurpassed, perfect, and universal bodhi.

"World-Honored One, the great bodhisattvas who cultivate prajna paramita are the most venerable, most superior, highest, and most wonderful ones. They have great powers and are capable of dwelling firmly in the most unequaled equal realness, the dharma realm, dharma nature, the nature of nonillusion, the nature of changelessness, the nature of equality, the nature of nonarising, dharma concentration, dharma dwelling, the realm of empty space, and the realm of the inconceivable; fulfill them perfectly; and so are well equipped with the most unequaled equal realness, and so forth, as well as the realm of the inconceivable. Thus, they can acquire the most unequaled equal body, the so-called boundless, unique, perfect, wonderful, and magnificent body; and they are able to realize and attain the most unequaled wonderful dharma of equality, namely the unsurpassed, perfect, and universal bodhi.

"World-Honored One, the great bodhisattvas who cultivate prajna paramita are the most venerable, most superior, highest, and most wonderful ones. They have great powers and are capable of cultivating the most unequaled equal four bases of mindfulness, four correct endeavors, four bases of power, five roots, five powers, seven factors for enlightenment, and noble eightfold path; fulfill them perfectly; and so are well equipped with the most unequaled equal four bases of mindfulness, and so forth, as well as the noble eightfold path. Thus, they can acquire the most unequaled equal body, the so-called boundless, unique, perfect, wonderful, and magnificent body; and they are able to realize and attain the most unequaled wonderful dharma of equality, namely the unsurpassed, perfect, and universal bodhi.

"World-Honored One, the great bodhisattvas who cultivate prajna paramita are the most venerable, most superior, highest, and most wonderful ones. They have great powers and are capable of dwelling firmly in the most unequaled equal noble truths of suffering, the cause of suffering, the cessation of suffering, and the path for the cessation of suffering; fulfill them perfectly; and so are well equipped with the most unequaled equal noble truths of suffering, the cause of suffering, the cessation of suffering, and the path for the cessation of suffering. Thus, they can acquire the most unequaled equal body, the so-called boundless, unique, perfect, wonderful, and magnificent body, and they are able to realize and attain the most unequaled wonderful dharma of equality, namely the unsurpassed, perfect, and universal bodhi.

"World-Honored One, the great bodhisattvas who cultivate prajna paramita are the most venerable, most superior, highest, and most wonderful ones. They have great powers and are capable of cultivating the most unequaled equal four meditations, four immeasurable minds, and four formless concentrations; fulfill them perfectly; and so are well equipped with the most unequaled equal four meditations, four immeasurable minds, and four formless concentrations. Thus, they can acquire the most unequaled equal body, the so-called boundless, unique, perfect, wonderful, and magnificent body; they are able to realize and attain the most unequaled wonderful dharma of equality, namely the unsurpassed, perfect, and universal bodhi.

"World-Honored One, the great bodhisattvas who cultivate prajna paramita are the most venerable, most superior, highest, and most wonderful ones. They have great powers and are capable of cultivating the most unequaled equal eight liberations, eight vexation-overcoming meditations, nine concentrations in sequence, and ten universal contemplations; fulfill them perfectly; and so are well equipped with the most unequaled equal eight liberations, eight vexation-overcoming meditations, nine concentrations in sequence, and ten universal contemplations. Thus, they can acquire the most unequaled equal body, the so-called boundless, unique, perfect, wonderful, and magnificent body; and they are able to realize and attain the most unequaled wonderful dharma of equality, namely the unsurpassed, perfect, and universal bodhi.

"World-Honored One, the great bodhisattvas who cultivate prajna paramita are the most venerable, most superior, highest, and most wonderful ones. They have great powers and are capable of cultivating the most unequaled equal liberation gates of emptiness, formlessness, and nonaspiration; fulfill them perfectly; and so are well equipped with the most unequaled equal liberation gates of emptiness, formlessness, and nonaspiration. Thus, they can acquire the most unequaled equal body, the so-called boundless, unique, perfect, wonderful, and magnificent body; and they are able to realize and attain the most unequaled wonderful dharma of equality, namely the unsurpassed, perfect, and universal bodhi.

"World-Honored One, the great bodhisattvas who cultivate prajna paramita are the most venerable, most superior, highest, and most wonderful ones. They have great powers and are capable of cultivating the most unequaled equal dharani gates and samadhi gates, fulfill them perfectly, and so are well equipped with the most unequaled equal dharani gates and samadhi gates. Thus, they can acquire the most unequaled equal body, the so-called boundless, unique, perfect, wonderful, and magnificent body, and they are able to realize and attain the most unequaled wonderful dharma of equality, namely the unsurpassed, perfect, and universal bodhi.

"World-Honored One, the great bodhisattvas who cultivate prajna paramita are the most venerable, most superior, highest, and most wonderful ones. They have great powers and are capable of cultivating the most unequaled equal stages of bodhisattva, fulfill them perfectly, and so are well equipped with the most unequaled equal stages of bodhisattva. Thus, they can acquire the most unequaled equal body, the so-called boundless, unique, perfect, wonderful, and magnificent body, and they are able to realize and attain the most unequaled wonderful dharma of equality, namely the unsurpassed, perfect, and universal bodhi.

"World-Honored One, the great bodhisattvas who cultivate prajna paramita are the most venerable, most superior, highest, and most wonderful ones. They have great powers and are capable of cultivating the most unequaled equal five eyes and six supernatural powers, fulfill them perfectly, and so are well equipped with the most unequaled equal five eyes and six supernatural powers. Thus, they can acquire the most unequaled equal body, the so-called boundless, unique, perfect, wonderful, and magnificent body, and they are able to realize and attain the most unequaled wonderful dharma of equality, namely the unsurpassed, perfect, and universal bodhi.

"World-Honored One, the great bodhisattvas who cultivate prajna paramita are the most venerable, most superior, highest, and most wonderful ones. They have great powers and are capable of cultivating the most unequaled equal Buddha's ten abilities, four kinds of fearlessness, four unhindered understandings, great loving-kindness, great compassion, great joy, great equanimity, and eighteen distinctive features of Buddha's wisdom and power; fulfill them perfectly; and so are well equipped with the most unequaled equal Buddha's ten abilities, and so forth, as well as eighteen distinctive features of Buddha's wisdom and power. Thus, they can acquire the most unequaled equal body, the so-called boundless, unique, perfect, wonderful, and magnificent body, and they are able to realize and attain the most unequaled wonderful dharma of equality, namely the unsurpassed, perfect, and universal bodhi.

"World-Honored One, the great bodhisattvas who cultivate prajna paramita are the most venerable, most superior, highest, and most wonderful ones. They have great powers and are capable of cultivating the most unequaled equal way of staying in correct mindfulness and the nature of dwelling in equanimity at all times, fulfill them perfectly, and so are well equipped with the most unequaled equal way of staying in correct mindfulness and the nature of dwelling in equanimity at all times. Thus, they can acquire the most unequaled equal body, the so-called boundless, unique, perfect, wonderful, and magnificent body, and they are able to realize and attain the most unequaled wonderful dharma of equality, namely the unsurpassed, perfect, and universal bodhi.

"World-Honored One, the great bodhisattvas who cultivate prajna paramita are the most venerable, most superior, highest, and most wonderful ones. They have great powers and are capable of cultivating the most unequaled equal perfect knowledge of everything, perfect knowledge of the forms of the paths, and the perfect knowledge of all phenomena; fulfill them perfectly; and so are well equipped with the most unequaled equal perfect knowledge of everything, perfect knowledge of the forms of the paths, and the perfect knowledge of all phenomena. Thus, they can acquire the most unequaled equal body, the so-called boundless, unique, perfect, wonderful, and magnificent body, and they are able to realize and attain the most unequaled wonderful dharma of equality, namely the unsurpassed, perfect, and universal bodhi.

"World-Honored One, because the Thus-Comers had cultivated prajna paramita, and thus had been able to cultivate various merits and virtues, dwell firmly in them, realize them perfectly, and were well equipped with them, they were able to acquire the most unequaled matter, as well as the most unequaled feeling, thinking, action, and consciousness; realize the most unequaled bodhi; turn the most unequaled dharma wheel; liberate immeasurable sentient beings; and make them obtain the unique and superior benefits and happiness. Because the Buddhas in the past, future, and present had cultivated, will cultivate, and are cultivating prajna paramita diligently and thus had fulfilled, will fulfill, and are fulfilling various merits and virtues perfectly, they had realized, will realize, and are realizing the unsurpassed, perfect, and universal bodhi. They are thus able to turn the wonderful dharma wheel, liberate immeasurable sentient beings, and make them acquire the unique and superior benefits and happiness. Therefore, World-Honored One, in order to cross the river to the other shore of liberation, the great bodhisattvas should learn prajna paramita. World-Honored One, all the heavenly beings, human beings, asuras, and so forth should make offerings and pay homage to the great bodhisattvas who are cultivating prajna paramita. They should admire, value, and protect the great bodhisattvas and assist them to cultivate prajna paramita assiduously and diligently without encountering difficulties, troubles, and hindrances."

At that time, the Buddha said to all voice-hearers and great bodhisattvas, "Yes, it is as you say. All heavenly beings, human beings, asuras, and so forth should make offerings and pay homage to the great bodhisattvas who are cultivating prajna paramita. They should admire, value, and protect them, assist them to cultivate prajna paramita assiduously and diligently, and keep them from all kinds of hindrance and difficulty. Why? It is because of these great bodhisattvas, the heavenly beings and human beings appear in the world, namely the sentient beings from the noble families of Ksatriya, Brahman, elders, lay believers, wheel-turning kings, the Heaven of Four Great Kings, the Heaven of Thirty-Three Smaller Heavens, the Heaven of Yama, the Heaven of Tusita, the Heaven of Enjoying Self-Made Changes, the Heaven of Enjoying Other-Made

Fascicle 10, Chapter 5   219

Changes, the Heaven of Brahma Followers, the Heaven of Brahma Subordinates, the Heaven of Brahma Family, the Heaven of Great Brahma, the Heaven of Light, the Heaven of Lesser Light, the Heaven of Infinite Light, the Heaven of Extremely Great Brightness and Purity, the Heaven of Purity, the Heaven of Lesser Purity, the Heaven of Infinite Purity, the Heaven of Universal Purity, the Heaven of Expansion, the Heaven of Lesser Expansion, the Heaven of Infinite Expansion, the Heaven of Extensive Rewards, the Heaven of Nonthinking Sentient Beings, the Heaven of No Aspiration, the Heaven of No Affliction, the Heaven of Good Appearance, the Heaven of Good Sight, the Heaven of Ultimate Form, the Heaven of Boundless Emptiness, the Heaven of Boundless Consciousness, the Heaven of Nothingness, and the Heaven of Nonthinking and Not Nonthinking appear in the world. Because of the great bodhisattva, the stream-enterers, once-returners, non-returners, arhats, self-enlightened ones, great bodhisattvas, and the Thus-Comers, Ones Worthy of Offerings, Perfectly and Universally Enlightened Ones appear in the world. Because of the great bodhisattva, the triple gem appears in the world and thus brings great benefits to sentient beings. Because of the great bodhisattva, various nourishing materials, namely food, clothes, bed, bedding, house, lamp, jewel, pearl, crystal, shell, jade, coral, gold, and silver, appear in the world.

"In summary, all pleasures of the human and heavenly worlds as well as the pleasures of nirvana exist because of the great bodhisattva. Why? It is because the great bodhisattvas have not only correctly cultivated giving, pure precept, forbearance, diligence, meditation, and prajna paramitas themselves, but have also taught others to do so. They have not only correctly dwelled in internal emptiness, external emptiness, internal-external emptiness, emptiness of emptiness, emptiness of space, emptiness of ultimate truth, emptiness of conditioned phenomena, emptiness of unconditioned reality, emptiness in the final analysis, emptiness of nontemporality, emptiness of deconstruction, emptiness of changelessness, emptiness of original nature, emptiness of particular characteristics, emptiness of common characteristics, emptiness of all dharmas, emptiness of nonattainment, emptiness of selflessness, emptiness of self-nature, and emptiness of the selfless self-nature themselves, but have also taught others to do so. They have not only correctly dwelled in realness, the dharma realm, dharma nature, nature of nonillusion, the nature of changelessness, the nature of equality, the nature of nonarising, dharma concentration, dharma dwelling, reality, the realm of empty space, and the realm of the inconceivable, but have also taught others to do so. They have not only correctly cultivated the four bases of mindfulness, four correct endeavors, four bases of power, five roots, five powers, seven factors for enlightenment, and noble eightfold path themselves, but have also taught others to do so. They have not only correctly dwelled in the four noble truths of suffering, the cause of suffering, the cessation of suffering, and the path for the cessation of suffering themselves, but have also taught others to do so. They have not only correctly cultivated the four meditations, four immeasurable minds, and four formless concentrations themselves, but have also taught others to do so. They have not only correctly cultivated the eight liberations, eight vexation-overcoming meditations, nine concentrations in sequence, and ten universal contemplations themselves, but have also taught others to do so. They have not only correctly cultivated the liberation gates of emptiness, formlessness, and nonaspiration themselves, but have also taught others to do so. They have not only correctly cultivated the dharani gates and samadhi gates themselves, but have also taught others to do so. They have not only correctly cultivated the stages of bodhisattva themselves, but have also taught others to do so. They have not only correctly cultivated the five eyes and the six supernatural powers themselves, but have also taught others to do so. They have not only correctly cultivated the Buddha's ten abilities, four kinds of fearlessness, four unhindered understandings, great loving-kindness, great compassion, great joy, great equanimity, and the eighteen distinctive features of Buddha's wisdom and ability themselves, but have also taught others to do so. They have not only correctly cultivated the way of staying in correct mindfulness and the nature of dwelling in equanimity at all times themselves, but have also taught others to do so. They have not only correctly cultivated the perfect knowledge of everything, perfect knowledge of the forms of the paths, and the perfect knowledge of all phenomena themselves, but have also taught others to do so. Therefore, it is because of the great bodhisattvas who cultivate prajna paramita that all sentient beings acquire superior benefits and happiness."

Chapter 6
Appearance of the Shape of the Tongue

(In the First Assembly)

AT THAT TIME, THE WORLD-HONORED ONE DISPLAYED HIS expanding tongue, wide and long, to spread over the large threefold thousand-world. From his wide and long tongue, immeasurable and countless varied colored rays of light emitted and shone over as many Buddha lands in the ten directions as the sands of the Ganges River.

At this time, in as many Buddha lands in the east as the sands of the Ganges River, immeasurable and countless great bodhisattvas witnessed the light, and each went to his or her Buddha, bowed down to the Buddha's feet, and asked respectfully, "World-Honored One! From whose supernatural powers and upon what causes and conditions has the auspicious symbol appeared?"

Each of the Buddhas replied to his crowd of great bodhisattvas respectively, "Good gentlemen! In the west there is a Buddha land with the name Barely Tolerable; the Buddha there is named Sakyamuni Thus-Comer, One Worthy of Offerings, Perfectly and Universally Enlightened One, One Perfect in Wisdom and Conduct,

Well Gone One, One Who Knows the World, Unsurpassed Great Person, Taming and Guiding One, Teacher of Heavenly and Human Beings, Buddha, and Bhagavat and is now teaching prajna paramita to the great bodhisattvas and displaying the expanding wide and long tongue to spread over all the large three thousand-world. It is from this tongue that immeasurable and countless rays of light in varied colors are emitting to shine over as many Buddha lands in the ten directions as the sands of the Ganges River. The light that you are watching is the one coming out of his wide and long tongue."

Upon hearing this, the great bodhisattvas so rejoiced that they jumped and danced and said to the Buddha, "We would like to go to the world of Barely Tolerable to attend the assembly, make offerings to Sakyamuni Buddha and all the great bodhisattvas there, and listen to the teaching on prajna paramita. We are begging your kind and compassionate permission!"

Each of the Buddhas responded, "It is the right time. You may go as you wish!"

Each group of the great bodhisattvas from each Buddha land bowed down to the ground before the Buddha's feet respectively and walked around the Buddha clockwise seven times to say good-bye. They left the Buddha and carried in solemnity immeasurable treasure pennants, canopies, garlands, jewel necklaces, and the flowers made of gold and silver. They played various kinds of the most entertaining and wonderful music, and before long they arrived at the Sakyamuni Buddha's place. They made offerings and paid homage to the Buddha with admiration and respect, bowed down to the ground before the Buddha's feet, and stood to one side.

At that time, in the south in as many Buddha lands as the sands of the Ganges River, immeasurable and countless great bodhisattvas witnessed the light and went to their Buddha's place, bowed down to the ground before the Buddha, and asked respectfully, "World-Honored One, from whose supernatural powers and upon what cause and condition has this auspicious symbol appeared?"

Each Buddha in the south responded to the great bodhisattvas, "Good gentlemen! In the north there is a world with the name Barely Tolerable; the Buddha there is named Sakyamuni Thus-Comer, One Worthy of Offerings, Perfectly and Universally Enlightened One, One Perfect in Wisdom and Conduct, Well Gone One, One Who Knows the World, Unsurpassed Great Person, Taming and Guiding One, Teacher of Heavenly and Human Beings, Buddha, and Bhagavat and is now teaching prajna paramita to the great bodhisattvas, and displaying his expanding wide and long tongue to spread over the large three thousand-world. It is from the tongue that immeasurable and countless rays of light are emitting in varied colors to shine all over as many Buddha lands in the ten directions as the sands of the Ganges River. The light that you are watching is the one coming out of his wide and long tongue."

Upon hearing this, the great bodhisattvas so rejoiced that they jumped and danced and said to the Buddha, "We would like to go to the world of Barely Tolerable to attend the assembly, make offerings to Sakyamuni Buddha and all the great bodhisattvas there, and listen to the teaching on prajna paramita. We are begging your kind and compassionate permission!"

Each Buddha responded, "It is the right time. You may go as you wish!"

Each crowd of great bodhisattvas from each Buddha land bowed down to the Buddha's feet respectively and walked around the Buddha clockwise seven times to say good-bye. They left the Buddha and carried in solemnity immeasurable treasure pennants, canopies, garlands, jewel necklaces, and the flowers made of gold and silver. They played varied, most pleasing, and wonderful music, and before long they arrived at the Sakyamuni Buddha's place. They made offerings and paid homage with admiration to the Buddha, bowed down to his feet, and stood to one side.

At that time, in the west in as many Buddha lands as the sands of the Ganges River, immeasurable and countless great bodhisattvas witnessed the rays of light, went to their Buddha's place, bowed down to the ground before the Buddha's feet, and asked respectfully, "World-Honored One, from whose supernatural powers and upon what cause and condition has this auspicious symbol appeared?"

Each Buddha responded to each crowd of the great bodhisattvas, "Good gentlemen! In the east there is a world with the name Barely Tolerable; the Buddha there is named Sakyamuni Thus-Comer,

One Worthy of Offerings, Perfectly and Universally Enlightened One, One Perfect in Wisdom and Conduct, Well Gone One, One Who Knows the World, Unsurpassed Great Person, Taming and Guiding One, Teacher of Heavenly and Human Beings, Buddha, and Bhagavat and is now teaching prajna paramita to the great bodhisattvas and displaying his expanding wide and long tongue to spread over the large three thousand-world. The tongue is emitting immeasurable and countless rays of light in varied colors to shine all over as many Buddha lands in the ten directions as the sands of the Ganges River. The light that you are watching is the one coming out of his wide and long tongue."

After hearing this, the great bodhisattvas so rejoiced that they jumped and danced and said to the Buddha, "We would like to go to the world of Barely Tolerable to attend the assembly, make offerings to Sakyamuni Buddha and all the great bodhisattvas there, and listen to the teaching of prajna paramita. We are begging your kind and compassionate permission!"

Each Buddha responded, "It is the right time. You may go as you wish!"

Each crowd of the great bodhisattvas from each Buddha land bowed down to the Buddha's feet respectively and walked around the Buddha clockwise seven times to say good-bye. They left the Buddha and carried in solemnity immeasurable treasure pennants, canopies, garlands, jewel necklaces, and the flowers made of gold and silver. They played varied, most pleasing, and wonderful music, and before long they arrived at the Sakyamuni Buddha's place. They made offerings and paid homage with admiration to the Buddha, bowed down to the Buddha's feet, and stood to one side.

At that time, in the north in as many Buddha lands as the sands of the Ganges River, immeasurable and countless great bodhisattvas witnessed the rays of light, went to their Buddha's place, bowed down to the ground before the Buddha's feet, and asked respectfully, "World-Honored One, from whose supernatural powers and upon what cause and condition has this auspicious symbol appeared?"

Each Buddha responded to each crowd of the great bodhisattvas, "Good gentlemen! In the south there is a world with the name Barely Tolerable; the Buddha there is named Sakyamuni Thus-Comer, One Worthy of Offerings, Perfectly and Universally Enlightened One, One Perfect in Wisdom and Conduct, Well Gone One, One Who Knows the World, Unsurpassed Great Person, Taming and Guiding One, Teacher of Heavenly and Human Beings, Buddha, and Bhagavat and is now teaching prajna paramita to the great bodhisattvas, and displaying his expanding wide and long tongue to spread over the large three thousand-world. The tongue is emitting immeasurable and countless rays of light in varied colors that shine all over as many Buddha lands in the ten directions as the sands of the Ganges River. The light that you are watching is the one coming out of his wide and long tongue."

After hearing this, the great bodhisattvas so rejoiced that they jumped and danced and said to the Buddha, "We would like to go to the world of Barely Tolerable to attend the assembly, make offerings to Sakyamuni Buddha and all the great bodhisattvas there, and listen to the teaching of prajna paramita. We are begging your kind and compassionate permission!"

Each Buddha responded, "It is the right time. You may go as you wish!"

Each crowd of the great bodhisattvas from each Buddha land bowed down to the Buddha's feet respectively and walked around the Buddha clockwise seven times to say good-bye. They left the Buddha and carried in solemnity immeasurable treasure pennants, canopies, garlands, jewel necklaces, and the flowers made of gold and silver. They played varied, most pleasing, and wonderful music, and before long they arrived at the Sakyamuni Buddha's place. They made offerings and paid homage with admiration to the Buddha, bowed down to the Buddha's feet, and stood to one side.

At that time, in the northeast in as many Buddha lands as the sands of the Ganges River, immeasurable and countless great bodhisattvas witnessed the rays of light, went to their Buddha's place, bowed down to the ground before the Buddha's feet, and asked respectfully, "World-Honored One, from whose supernatural powers and upon what cause and condition has this auspicious symbol appeared?"

Each Buddha responded to each crowd of the great bodhisattvas, "Good gentlemen! In the southwest there is a world with the name Barely Tolerable; the Buddha there is named Sakyamuni Thus-Comer, One Worthy of Offerings, Perfectly and Universally Enlightened One, One Perfect in Wisdom and Conduct, Well Gone One, One Who Knows the World, Unsurpassed Great Person, Taming and Guiding One, Teacher of Heavenly and Human Beings, Buddha, and Bhagavat and is now teaching prajna paramita to the great bodhisattvas, and displaying his expanding wide and long tongue to spread over the large three thousand-world. The tongue is emitting immeasurable and countless rays of light in varied colors that shine all over as many Buddha lands in the ten directions as the sands of the Ganges River. The light that you are watching is the one coming out of his wide and long tongue."

After hearing this, the great bodhisattvas so rejoiced that they jumped and danced and said to the Buddha, "We would like to go to the world of Barely Tolerable to attend the assembly, make offerings to Sakyamuni Buddha and all the great bodhisattvas there, and listen to the teaching of prajna paramita. We are begging your kind and compassionate permission!"

Each Buddha responded, "It is the right time. You may go as you wish!"

Each crowd of the great bodhisattvas from each Buddha land bowed down to the Buddha's feet respectively and walked around the Buddha clockwise seven times to say good-bye. They left the Buddha and carried in solemnity immeasurable treasure pennants, canopies, garlands, jewel necklaces, and the flowers made of gold and silver. They played varied, most pleasing, and wonderful music, and before long they arrived at the Sakyamuni Buddha's place. They made offerings and paid homage with admiration to the Buddha, bowed down to the Buddha's feet, and stood to one side.

At that time, in the southeast in as many Buddha lands as the sands of the Ganges River, immeasurable and countless great bodhisattvas witnessed the rays of light, went to their Buddha's place, bowed down to the ground before the Buddha's feet, and asked respectfully, "World-Honored One, from whose supernatural powers and upon what cause and condition has this auspicious symbol appeared?"

Each Buddha responded to each crowd of the great bodhisattvas, "Good gentlemen! In the northwest there is a world with the name Barely Tolerable; the Buddha there is named Sakyamuni Thus-Comer, One Worthy of Offerings, Perfectly and Universally Enlightened One, One Perfect in Wisdom and Conduct, Well Gone One, One Who Knows the World, Unsurpassed Great Person, Taming and Guiding One, Teacher of Heavenly and Human Beings, Buddha, and Bhagavat and is now teaching prajna paramita to the great bodhisattvas, and displaying his expanding wide and long tongue to spread over the large three thousand-world. The tongue is emitting immeasurable and countless rays of light in varied colors that shine all over as many Buddha lands in the ten directions as the sands of the Ganges River. The light that you are watching is the one coming out of his wide and long tongue."

After hearing this, the great bodhisattvas so rejoiced that they jumped and danced and said to the Buddha, "We would like to go to the world of Barely Tolerable to attend the assembly, make offerings to Sakyamuni Buddha and all the great bodhisattvas there, and listen to the teaching of prajna paramita. We are begging your kind and compassionate permission!"

Each Buddha responded, "It is the right time. You may go as you wish!"

Each crowd of the great bodhisattvas from each Buddha land bowed down to the Buddha's feet respectively and walked around the Buddha clockwise seven times to say good-bye. They left the Buddha and carried in solemnity immeasurable treasure pennants, canopies, garlands, jewel necklaces, and the flowers made of gold and silver. They played varied, most pleasing, and wonderful music, and before long they arrived at the Sakyamuni Buddha's place. They made offerings and paid homage with admiration to the Buddha, bowed down to the Buddha's feet, and stood to one side.

At that time, in the southwest in as many Buddha lands as the sands of the Ganges River, immeasurable and countless great bodhisattvas witnessed the rays of light, went to their Buddha's place, bowed down to the ground before the Buddha's feet, and asked respectfully, "World-Honored One, from whose supernatural powers and upon what cause and condition has this auspicious symbol appeared?"

Each Buddha responded to each crowd of the great bodhisattvas, "Good gentlemen! In the northeast there is a world with the name Barely Tolerable; the Buddha there is named Sakyamuni Thus-Comer, One Worthy of Offerings, Perfectly and Universally Enlightened One, One Perfect in Wisdom and Conduct, Well Gone One, One Who Knows the World, Unsurpassed Great Person, Taming and Guiding One, Teacher of Heavenly and Human Beings, Buddha, and Bhagavat and is now teaching prajna paramita to the great bodhisattvas, and displaying his expanding wide and long tongue to spread over the large three thousand-world. The tongue is emitting immeasurable and countless rays of light in varied colors to shine all over as many Buddha lands in the ten directions as the sands of the Ganges River. The light that you are watching is the one coming out of his wide and long tongue."

After hearing this, the great bodhisattvas so rejoiced that they jumped and danced and said to the Buddha, "We would like to go to the world of Barely Tolerable to attend the assembly, make offerings to Sakyamuni Buddha and all the great bodhisattvas there, and listen to the teaching of prajna paramita. We are begging your kind and compassionate permission!"

Each Buddha responded, "It is the right time. You may go as you wish!"

Each crowd of the great bodhisattvas from each Buddha land bowed down to the Buddha's feet respectively and walked around the Buddha clockwise seven times to say good-bye. They left the Buddha and carried in solemnity immeasurable treasure pennants, canopies, garlands, jewel necklaces, and the flowers made of gold and silver. They played varied, most pleasing, and wonderful music, and before long they arrived at the Sakyamuni Buddha's place. They made offerings and paid homage with admiration to the Buddha, bowed down to the Buddha's feet, and stood to one side.

At that time, in the northwest in as many Buddha lands as the sands of the Ganges River, immeasurable and countless great bodhisattvas witnessed the rays of light, went to their Buddha's place, bowed down to the ground before the Buddha's feet, and asked respectfully, "World-Honored One, from whose supernatural powers and upon what cause and condition has this auspicious symbol appeared?"

Each Buddha responded to each crowd of the great bodhisattvas, "Good gentlemen! In the southeast there is a world with the name Barely Tolerable; the Buddha there is named Sakyamuni Thus-Comer, One Worthy of Offerings, Perfectly and Universally Enlightened One, One Perfect in Wisdom and Conduct, Well Gone One, One Who Knows the World, Unsurpassed Great Person, Taming and Guiding One, Teacher of Heavenly and Human Beings, Buddha, and Bhagavat and is now teaching prajna paramita to the great bodhisattvas, and displaying his expanding wide and long tongue to spread over the large three thousand-world. The tongue is emitting immeasurable and countless rays of light in varied colors that shine all over as many Buddha lands in the ten directions as the sands of the Ganges River. The light that you are watching is the one coming out of his wide and long tongue."

After hearing this, the great bodhisattvas so rejoiced that they jumped and danced and said to the Buddha, "We would like to go to the world of Barely Tolerable to attend the assembly, make offerings to Sakyamuni Buddha and all the great bodhisattvas there, and listen to the teaching of prajna paramita. We are begging your kind and compassionate permission!"

Each Buddha responded, "It is the right time. You may go as you wish!"

Each crowd of the great bodhisattvas from each Buddha land bowed down to the Buddha's feet respectively and walked around the Buddha clockwise seven times to say good-bye. They left the Buddha and carried in solemnity immeasurable treasure pennants, canopies, garlands, jewel necklaces, and the flowers made of gold and silver. They played varied, most pleasing, and wonderful music, and before long they arrived at the Sakyamuni Buddha's place. They made offerings and paid homage with admiration to the Buddha, bowed down to the Buddha's feet, and stood to one side.

At that time, underneath in as many Buddha lands as the sands of the Ganges River, immeasurable and countless great bodhisattvas witnessed the rays of light, went to their Buddha's place, bowed down to the ground before the Buddha's feet, and asked respectfully, "World-Honored One, from whose supernatural powers and upon what cause and condition has this auspicious symbol appeared?"

Each Buddha responded to each crowd of the great bodhisattvas, "Good gentlemen! In the above there is a world with the name Barely Tolerable; the Buddha there is named Sakyamuni Thus-Comer, One Worthy of Offerings, Perfectly and Universally Enlightened One, One Perfect in Wisdom and Conduct, Well Gone One, One Who Knows the World, Unsurpassed Great Person, Taming and Guiding One, Teacher of Heavenly and Human Beings, Buddha, and Bhagavat and is now teaching prajna paramita to the great bodhisattvas, and displaying his expanding wide and long tongue to spread over the large three thousand-world. The tongue is emitting immeasurable and countless rays of light in varied colors that shine all over as many Buddha lands in the ten directions as the sands of the Ganges River. The light that you are watching is the one coming out of his wide and long tongue."

After hearing this, the great bodhisattvas so rejoiced that they jumped and danced and said to the Buddha, "We would like to go to the world of Barely Tolerable to attend the assembly, make offerings to Sakyamuni Buddha and all the great bodhisattvas there, and listen to the teaching of prajna paramita. We are begging your kind and compassionate permission!"

Each Buddha responded, "It is the right time. You may go as you wish!"

Each crowd of the great bodhisattvas from each Buddha land bowed down to the Buddha's feet respectively and walked around the Buddha clockwise seven times to say good-bye. They left the Buddha and carried in solemnity immeasurable treasure pennants, canopies, garlands, jewel necklaces, and the flowers made of gold and silver. They played varied, most pleasing, and wonderful music, and before long they arrived at the Sakyamuni Buddha's place. They made offerings and paid homage with admiration to the Buddha, bowed down to the Buddha's feet, and stood to one side.

At that time, in the above in as many Buddha lands as the sands of the Ganges River, immeasurable and countless great bodhisattvas witnessed the rays of light, went to their Buddha's place, bowed down to the ground before the Buddha's feet, and asked respectfully, "World-Honored One, from whose supernatural powers and upon what cause and condition has this auspicious symbol appeared?"

Each Buddha responded to each crowd of the great bodhisattvas, "Good gentlemen! Below us there is a world with the name Barely Tolerable; the Buddha there is named Sakyamuni Thus-Comer, One Worthy of Offerings, Perfectly and Universally Enlightened One, One Perfect in Wisdom and Conduct, Well Gone One, One Who Knows the World, Unsurpassed Great Person, Taming and Guiding One, Teacher of Heavenly and Human Beings, Buddha, and Bhagavat and is now teaching prajna paramita to the great bodhisattvas, and displaying his expanding wide and long tongue to spread over the large three thousand-world. The tongue is emitting immeasurable and countless rays of light in varied colors that shine all over as many Buddha lands in the ten directions as the sands of the Ganges River. The light that you are watching is the one coming out of his wide and long tongue."

After hearing this, the great bodhisattvas so rejoiced that they jumped and danced and said to the Buddha, "We would like to go to the world of Barely Tolerable to attend the assembly, make offerings to Sakyamuni Buddha and all the great bodhisattvas there, and listen to the teaching of prajna paramita. We are begging your kind and compassionate permission!"

Each Buddha responded, "It is the right time. You may go as you wish!"

Each crowd of the great bodhisattvas from each Buddha land bowed down to the Buddha's feet respectively and walked around the Buddha clockwise seven times to say good-bye. They left the Buddha and carried in solemnity immeasurable treasure pennants, canopies, garlands, jewel necklaces, and the flowers made of gold and silver. They played varied, most pleasing, and wonderful music, and before long they arrived at the Sakyamuni Buddha's place. They made offerings and paid homage with admiration to the Buddha, bowed down to the Buddha's feet, and stood to one side.

At that time, the heavenly beings from the Heaven of Four Great Kings, and so forth, as well as the Heaven of Enjoying Other-Made Changes in the realm of desire, and the heavenly beings from the Heaven of Brahma Followers, and so forth, as well as the Heaven of Ultimate Form in the realm of form, had each carried immeasurable fragrant wreaths made of spreading perfumes, incense powders, burning incenses, tree perfumes, leaf perfumes, and mixed perfumes, as well as pleasant wreaths, fresh wreaths, dragon-coin wreaths, and numberless kinds of mixed wreaths as offerings to the Buddha. They also carried immeasurable kinds of heavenly flowers, such as the blue lotus, white lotus, red lotus, snow-white lotus, exquisite sound flower, great exquisite sound flower, and other numberless kinds of heavenly flowers as offerings to the Buddha. They bowed down to the Buddha's feet with respect and acclamation, and then stood to one side.

At that time, owing to the Buddha's supernatural powers, the various kinds of treasure pennants, canopies, garlands, jewel necklaces, and fragrant flowers presented by all the great bodhisattvas from the ten directions and from the heavens in the realm of desire and the realm of form all suddenly surged up to the sky. Combining together, all were transformed into a platform to cover the entire large three thousand-world. At the four corners of the platform, different kinds of treasure pennants stood. From the canopies of the platform and the treasure banners, jade and pearl necklaces, lovely small flags, colorful ribbons, as well as rare and unique floral decorations were hanging. They all looked so magnificent, attractive, and lovely.

Hundreds of thousands of koti nayuta of sentient beings in the assembly then stood up from their seats and said respectfully to the Buddha with their palms joined, "World-Honored One, we are vowing to become the Buddha in the future and attain the perfect appearance and virtues as World-Honored One does. We are aspiring to have a country land as glorious as yours, and in the land, voice-hearers, great bodhisattvas, and heavenly and human beings will gather together, and the dharma wheel that we will turn will be as the Buddha has now."

At that time, the World-Honored One read the attendees' minds, knowing that they were having an in-depth and insightful understanding of the dharma forbearance of nonarising. They had become aware that all existent beings are without arising and extinction, action and effort. So the Buddha smiled, and varied colorful lights emitted from his face.

The venerable Ananda rose from his seat, joined his palms, and asked, "World-Honored One, why did you smile?"

The Buddha said to Ananda, "Each of the hundreds of thousands of koti nayuta of sentient beings who just rose from their seats has become deeply aware of the dharma forbearance of nonarising and will become a Buddha after sixty-eight koti great kalpas of cultivation in bodhisattva actions in the coming era of Flower-Accumulation Kalpa. All will have the same name: Factors for Enlightenment Flower Thus-Comer, One Worthy of Offerings, Perfectly and Universally Enlightened One, One Perfect in Wisdom and Conduct, Well Gone One, One Who Knows the World, Unsurpassed Great Person, Taming and Guiding One, Teacher of Heavenly and Human Beings, Buddha, and Bhagavat."

FASCICLE 11

Chapter 7
The Cautions and the Teachings

Section 1

(In the First Assembly)

AT THAT TIME, THE BUDDHA SAID TO THE long-lived sage Well Appearing One, "Because you have an excellent talent in debate, you should teach the dharmas correspondent with prajna paramita to the great bodhisattvas and give them cautions and advice so that they are able to cultivate and learn prajna paramita thoroughly to its perfection."

In the meantime, all the great bodhisattvas, the senior voice-hearers, the heavenly beings, dragons, yaksas, humans, and non-humans in the assembly had this question in their minds: "The venerable Well Appearing One now is going to teach the great bodhisattvas the dharmas correspondent with prajna paramita and give them cautions and lessons about how to cultivate and learn prajna paramita thoroughly to its perfection. Does he do this based on the powers of his own wisdom and talent of debate, or is it based on the supernatural powers of the Buddha?"

The long-lived sage Well Appearing One knew the thought the great bodhisattvas, senior voice-hearers, heavenly beings, dragons, yaksas, humans, and nonhumans had in their minds, so he said to the long-lived sage Sariputra, "All Buddha's disciples teach the dharma based on the supernatural powers bestowed by the Buddha. Why? Sariputra! The Buddhas teach their disciples the most essential part of the dharma and the disciples receive the teachings, learn and cultivate them assiduously and tirelessly, and will finally attain the reality of all dharmas. These disciples then will teach the dharma to others. Whatever they teach will not be contrary to dharma nature. Therefore, the Buddha's teaching is like handing down the light through the lamp. Sariputra! I will teach great bodhisattvas the dharma correspondent with prajna paramita under the support of the Buddha's supernatural powers. I will give cautions and advice to them so that they are able to study and cultivate prajna paramita thoroughly to its perfection. All I am going to do is not based on my own wisdom and talent of debate. Why? It is because the dharma correspondent with the profound prajna paramita is not at the level of the voice-hearer or the self-enlightened one."

At that time, the long-lived sage Well Appearing One asked the Buddha, "World-Honored One! You have instructed, saying, 'Because you have excellent talent of debate, you should teach the dharma correspondent with prajna paramita to the great bodhisattvas and give them cautions and advice so that they will be able to study and learn prajna paramita thoroughly.' World-Honored One! Among all these dharmas, which dharma is named 'great bodhisattva'? And which dharma is named 'prajna paramita'? World-Honored One! I cannot see any dharma that is named 'great bodhisattva' or any dharma that is named 'prajna paramita.' I even cannot see that these two names exist. Why do you want me to teach the dharma in correspondence with prajna paramita to the great bodhisattvas and give cautions and advice to them so that they will be able to study and learn prajna paramita thoroughly?"

The Buddha said, "Well Appearing One! The great bodhisattva is just a name, and prajna paramita is just a name also. These two names are just names. Well Appearing One! These two names have no arising and extinction. They are just the concepts or kind of the concept expressed in a provisionally made language. These two provisional names are not inside, outside, or in between because they are unattainable.

"Well Appearing One! You must know that 'I' is a provisional name, and such a name has no arising and no extinction. It is only a concept expressed in language that is called 'I.' The other names, such as the sentient being, the living one, the one who gives birth, the one who raises others, the gentleperson, the individual in reincarnation, the mentally born one, the learned child, the maker, the one who makes others make, the initiator, the one who makes others initiate, the receiver, the one who makes others receive, the knower, and the viewer are just provisional names. They have no arising or extinction. They are just the concepts expressed in a created language and are given the names 'the sentient being,' and so forth, as well as 'the viewer.' Such provisional names are not inside, outside, or in between because they are unattainable. Therefore, Well Appearing One, great bodhisattva, prajna paramita, and two names are unreal dharmas. These unreal dharmas neither arise nor extinguish, but only exist in one's thinking and are given the created names as great bodhisattva, prajna paramita, and two names. These three concepts are merely provisional names, which are not inside, outside, or in between because they are unattainable.

"Furthermore, Well Appearing One, matter is merely a dharma that is unreal. The unreal dharma neither arises nor extinguishes, but exists only in one's thinking or the sort and is given a created name: matter. So feeling, thinking, intention, and consciousness are also merely dharmas that are unreal. The unreal dharmas neither arise nor extinguish, but exist only in one's thinking and are given the created names of feeling, thinking, intention, and consciousness. All these provisional names are not inside, outside, or in between because they are unattainable. Therefore, Well Appearing One, great bodhisattva, prajna paramita, and two names are unreal dharmas. These unreal dharmas neither arise nor extinguish, but exist in one's thinking and are given the created names of great bodhisattva, prajna paramita, and two names. These are merely provisional names, which are not inside, outside, or in between because they are unattainable.

"Furthermore, Well Appearing One, the eye sphere is just a dharma that is unreal. This unreal dharma neither arises nor extinguishes, but exists in one's thinking and is given a created name: eye sphere. So the ear, nose, tongue, body, and conscious spheres are unreal. These unreal dharmas neither arise nor extinguish, but exist in one's thinking and are given the created names of ear, nose, tongue, body, and conscious spheres. All these are merely provisional names, and provisional names are not inside, outside, or in between because they are unattainable. Therefore, Well Appearing One, great bodhisattva, prajna paramita, and two names are unreal dharmas. These unreal dharmas neither arise nor extinguish, but exist in one's thinking and are given the created names of great bodhisattva, prajna paramita, and two names. These three kinds of dharma are provisional names; they are not inside, outside, or in between because they are unattainable.

"Furthermore, Well Appearing One, the sight sphere is just an unreal dharma. This unreal dharma neither arises nor extinguishes, but exists in one's thinking and is given a created name: sight sphere. So are the sound, smell, taste, touch, and mental-image spheres that are also unreal. These unreal dharmas neither arise nor extinguish, but exist in one's thinking and are given the created names of sound, smell, taste, touch, and mental-image spheres. All these are merely provisional names, and the provisional names are not inside, outside, or in between because they are unattainable. Therefore, Well Appearing One, great bodhisattva, prajna paramita, and two names are unreal dharmas. These unreal dharmas neither arise nor extinguish, but only exist in one's thinking and are given the created names of great bodhisattva, prajna paramita, and two names. These three kinds of dharma are provisional names that are not inside, outside, or in between because they are unattainable.

"Furthermore, Well Appearing One, the eye realm is just an unreal dharma. This unreal dharma neither arises nor extinguishes, but exists in one's thinking and is given a created name: eye realm. So are the ear, nose, tongue, body, and conscious realms that are also unreal. These unreal dharmas neither arise nor extinguish, but exist in one's thinking and are given the created names of ear, nose, tongue, body, and conscious realms. All these are merely provisional names, and the provisional names are not inside, outside, or in between because they are unattainable. Therefore, Well Appearing One, great bodhisattva, prajna paramita, and two names are unreal dharmas that neither arise nor extinguish, but only exist in one's thinking and are given the created names of great bodhisattva, prajna paramita, and two names. These three kinds of dharma are provisional names that are not inside, outside, or in between because they are unattainable.

"Furthermore, Well Appearing One, the sight realm is just an unreal dharma that neither arises nor extinguishes, but exists in one's thinking and is given a created name: sight realm. So are the sound, smell, taste, touch, and mental-image realms that are also unreal. These unreal dharmas neither arise nor extinguish, but exist in one's thinking and are given the created names of the sound, smell, taste, touch, and mental-image realms. All these are merely provisional names, and the provisional names are not inside, outside, or in between because they are unattainable. Therefore, Well Appearing One, great bodhisattva, prajna paramita, and two names are unreal dharmas that neither arise nor extinguish, but only exist in one's thinking and are given the created names of great bodhisattva, prajna paramita, and two names. These three kinds of dharma are provisional names that are not inside, outside, or in between because they are unattainable.

"Furthermore, Well Appearing One, the eye consciousness realm is just an unreal dharma that neither arises nor extinguishes, but exists in one's thinking and is given a created name: the eye consciousness realm. So are the ear, nose, tongue, body, and conscious consciousness realms that are also unreal, and these unreal dharmas neither arise nor extinguish, but exist in one's thinking and are given the created names of the ear, nose, tongue, body, and conscious consciousness realms. All these are merely provisional names, and the provisional names are not inside, outside, or in between because they are unattainable. Therefore, Well Appearing One, great bodhisattva, prajna paramita, and two names are unreal dharmas that neither arise nor extinguish, but only exist in one's thinking and are given the created names of great bodhisattva, prajna paramita, and two names. These three kinds of dharma are provisional names that are not inside, outside, or in between because they are unattainable.

"Furthermore, Well Appearing One, the eye contact is just an unreal dharma that neither arises nor extinguishes, but exists in one's thinking and is given a created name: the eye contact. So are the ear, nose, tongue, body, and conscious contacts that are also unreal, and these unreal dharmas neither arise nor extinguish, but exist in one's thinking and are given the created names of the ear, nose, tongue, body, and contacts. All these are merely provisional names, and the provisional names are not inside, outside, or in between because they are unattainable. Therefore, Well Appearing One, great bodhisattva, prajna paramita, and two names are unreal dharmas that neither arise nor extinguish, but only exist in one's thinking and are given the created names of great bodhisattva, prajna paramita, and two names. These three kinds of dharma are provisional names that are not inside, outside, or in between because they are unattainable.

"Furthermore, Well Appearing One, the feelings produced by eye contact is just an unreal dharma that neither arises nor extinguishes, but exists in one's thinking and is given a created name: the feelings produced by eye contact. So are the feelings produced by ear, nose, tongue, body, and conscious contacts that are also unreal, and these unreal dharmas neither arise nor extinguish, but exist in one's thinking and are given the created names of the feelings produced by ear, nose, tongue, body, and contacts. All these are merely provisional names, and the provisional names are not inside, outside, or in between because they are unattainable. Therefore, Well Appearing One, great bodhisattva, prajna paramita, and two names are unreal dharmas that neither arise nor extinguish, but only exist in one's thinking and are given the created names of great bodhisattva, prajna paramita, and two names. These three kinds of dharma are provisional names that are not inside, outside, or in between because they are unattainable.

"Furthermore, Well Appearing One, the head, neck, shoulder, upper arm, forearm, stomach, back, chest, waist, spine, thigh, knee, calf, shin, and the foot are unreal dharmas that neither arise nor extinguish, but exist in one's thinking and are given the created names of the head, neck, and so forth, as well as the foot. All these are merely provisional names, and the provisional names are not inside, outside, or in between because they are unattainable. Therefore, Well Appearing One, great bodhisattva, prajna paramita, and two names are unreal dharmas that neither arise nor extinguish, but only exist in one's thinking and are given the created names of great bodhisattva, prajna paramita, and two names. These three kinds of dharma are provisional names that are not inside, outside, or in between because they are unattainable.

"Furthermore, Well Appearing One, all kinds of grasses, trees, roots, stems, branches, leaves, flowers, and fruits are unreal dharmas that neither arise nor extinguish, but exist in one's thinking and are given the names of the grass, tree, root, stem, branch, leaf, flower, and the fruit. All these are merely provisional names, and the provisional names are not inside, outside, or in between because they are unattainable. Therefore, Well Appearing One, great bodhisattva, prajna paramita, and two names are unreal dharmas that neither arise nor extinguish, but only exist in one's thinking and are given the created names of great bodhisattva, prajna paramita, and two names. These three kinds of dharma are provisional names that are not inside, outside, or in between because they are unattainable.

"Furthermore, Well Appearing One, all Thus-Comers, Ones Worthy of Offerings, Perfectly and Universally Enlightened Ones in the past, future, and present are just the unreal dharmas that neither arise nor extinguish, but exist in one's thinking and are given the created names of Thus-Comers, Ones Worthy of Offerings, Perfectly and Universally Enlightened Ones in the past, future, and the present. All these are merely provisional names, and provisional names are not inside, outside, or in between because they are unattainable. Therefore, Well Appearing One, great bodhisattva, prajna paramita, and two names are unreal dharmas that neither arise nor extinguish, but only exist in one's thinking and are given the created names of great bodhisattva, prajna paramita, and two names. These three kinds of dharma are provisional names that are not inside, outside, or in between because they are unattainable.

"Furthermore, Well Appearing One, the illusions, dreams, echoes, images, illusory images of water under sunlight, shadows,

Fascicle 11, Chapter 7, Section 1   241

mirages, and the transformed things are just unreal dharmas that neither arise nor extinguish, but exist in one's thinking and are given the created names of the illusions, and so forth, as well as the transformed things. All these are merely provisional names, and provisional names are not inside, outside, or in between because they are unattainable. Therefore, Well Appearing One, great bodhisattva, prajna paramita, and two names are unreal dharmas that neither arise nor extinguish, but only exist in one's thinking and are given the created names of great bodhisattva, prajna paramita, and two names. These three kinds of dharma are provisional names that are not inside, outside, or in between because they are unattainable.

"Furthermore, Well Appearing One, when cultivating prajna paramita, the great bodhisattvas should not contemplate matter as it is permanent or impermanent, nor should they contemplate feeling, thinking, action, and consciousness as they are permanent or impermanent. They should not contemplate matter as it is pleasant or painful, nor should they contemplate feeling, thinking, action, and consciousness as they are pleasant or painful. They should not contemplate matter as it is with or without selfness, nor should they contemplate feeling, thinking, action, and consciousness as they are with or without selfness. They should not contemplate matter as it is pure or impure, nor should they contemplate feeling, thinking, action, and consciousness as they are pure or impure. They should not contemplate matter as it is empty or not empty, nor should they contemplate feeling, thinking, action, and consciousness as they are empty or not empty. They should not contemplate matter as it is with or without form, nor should they contemplate feeling, thinking, action, and consciousness as they are with or without form. They should not contemplate matter as it is with or without aspiration, nor should they contemplate feeling, thinking, action, and consciousness as they are with or without aspiration. They should not contemplate matter as it is tranquil or not tranquil, nor should they contemplate feeling, thinking, action, and consciousness as they are tranquil or not tranquil. They should not contemplate matter as it is far away or not far away, nor should they contemplate feeling, thinking, action, and consciousness as they are far away or not far away. They should not contemplate matter as it is conditioned or unconditioned, nor should they contemplate feeling, thinking, action, and consciousness as they are conditioned or unconditioned. They should not contemplate matter as it is flawed or flawless, nor should they contemplate feeling, thinking, action, and consciousness as they are flawed or flawless. They should not contemplate matter as it has arising or extinction, nor should they contemplate feeling, thinking, action, and consciousness as they have arising or extinction. They should not contemplate matter as it is virtuous or not virtuous, nor should they contemplate feeling, thinking, action, and consciousness as they are virtuous or not virtuous. They should not contemplate matter as it is guilty or not guilty, nor should they contemplate feeling, thinking, action, and consciousness as they are guilty or not guilty. They should not contemplate matter as it has or has no vexations, nor should they contemplate feeling, thinking, action, and consciousness as they have or have no vexations. They should not contemplate matter as it is of the world or beyond the world, nor should they contemplate feeling, thinking, action, and consciousness as they are of the world or beyond the world. They should not contemplate matter as it is contaminated or purified, nor should they contemplate feeling, thinking, action, and consciousness as they are contaminated or purified. They should not contemplate matter as it belongs to birth and death or belongs to nirvana, nor should they contemplate feeling, thinking, action, and consciousness as they belong to birth and death or belong to nirvana. They should not contemplate matter as it is inside, outside, or in between, nor should they contemplate feeling, thinking, action, and consciousness as they are inside, outside, or in between. They should not contemplate matter as it is attainable or unattainable, nor should they contemplate feeling, thinking, action, and consciousness as they are attainable or unattainable.

"Furthermore, Well Appearing One, when cultivating prajna paramita, the great bodhisattvas should not contemplate the eye sphere as it is permanent or impermanent, nor should they contemplate the ear, nose, tongue, body, and conscious spheres as they are permanent or impermanent. They should not contemplate the eye sphere as it is pleasant or painful, nor should they contemplate the ear, nose, tongue, body, and conscious spheres as they are pleasant or painful. They should not contemplate the eye sphere as it is with or without selfness, nor should they contemplate the ear, nose, tongue, body, and conscious spheres as they are with or without selfness. They should not contemplate the eye sphere as it is pure or impure, nor should they contemplate the ear, nose, tongue, body, and conscious spheres as they are pure or impure. They should not contemplate the eye sphere as it is empty or not empty, nor should they contemplate the ear, nose, tongue, body, and conscious spheres as they are empty or not empty. They should not contemplate the eye sphere as it is with or without form, nor should they contemplate the ear, nose, tongue, body, and conscious spheres as they are with or without form. They should not contemplate the eye sphere as it is with or without aspiration, nor should they contemplate the ear, nose, tongue, body, and conscious spheres as they are with or without aspiration. They should not contemplate the eye sphere as it is tranquil or not tranquil, nor should they contemplate the ear, nose, tongue, body, and conscious spheres as they are tranquil or not tranquil. They should not contemplate the eye sphere as it is far away or not far away, nor should they contemplate the ear, nose, tongue, body, and conscious spheres as they are far away or not far away. They should not contemplate the eye sphere as it is conditioned or unconditioned, nor should they contemplate the ear, nose, tongue, body, and conscious spheres as they are conditioned or unconditioned. They should not contemplate the eye sphere as it is flawed or flawless, nor should they contemplate the ear, nose, tongue, body, and conscious spheres as they are flawed or flawless. They should not contemplate the eye sphere as it has arising or extinction, nor should they contemplate the ear, nose, tongue, body, and conscious spheres as they have arising or extinction. They should not contemplate the eye sphere as it is virtuous or not virtuous, nor should they contemplate the ear, nose, tongue, body, and conscious spheres as they are virtuous or not virtuous. They should not contemplate the eye sphere as it is guilty or not guilty, nor should they contemplate the ear, nose, tongue, body, and conscious spheres as they are guilty or not guilty. They should not contemplate the eye sphere as it has or has no vexations, nor should they contemplate the ear, nose, tongue, body, and conscious spheres as they have or have no vexations. They should not contemplate the eye sphere as it is of the world or beyond the world, nor should they contemplate the ear, nose, tongue, body, and conscious spheres as they are of the world or beyond the world. They should not contemplate the eye sphere as it is contaminated or purified, nor should they contemplate the ear, nose, tongue, body, and conscious spheres as they are contaminated or purified. They should not contemplate the eye sphere as it belongs to birth and death or belongs to nirvana, nor should they contemplate the ear, nose, tongue, body, and conscious spheres as they belong to birth and death or belong to nirvana. They should not contemplate the eye sphere as it is inside, outside, or in between, nor should they contemplate the ear, nose, tongue, body, and conscious spheres as they are inside, outside, or in between. They should not contemplate the eye sphere as it is attainable or unattainable, nor should they contemplate the ear, nose, tongue, body, and conscious spheres as they are attainable or unattainable.

"Furthermore, Well Appearing One, when cultivating prajna paramita, the great bodhisattvas should not contemplate the sight sphere as it is permanent or impermanent, nor should they contemplate the sound, smell, taste, touch, and mental-image spheres as they are permanent or impermanent. They should not contemplate the sight sphere as it is pleasant or painful, nor should they contemplate the sound, smell, taste, touch, and mental-image spheres as they are pleasant or painful. They should not contemplate the sight sphere as it is with or without selfness, nor should they contemplate the sound, smell, taste, touch, and mental-image spheres as they are with or without selfness. They should not contemplate the sight sphere as it is pure or impure, nor should they contemplate the sound, smell, taste, touch, and mental-image spheres as they are pure or impure. They should not contemplate the sight sphere as it is empty or not empty, nor should they contemplate the sound, smell, taste, touch, and mental-image spheres as they are empty or not empty. They should not contemplate the sight sphere as it is with or without form, nor should they contemplate the sound, smell, taste, touch, and mental-image spheres as they are with or without form. They should not contemplate the sight sphere as it is with or without aspiration, nor should they contemplate the sound, smell, taste, touch, and mental-image sphere as they are with or without aspiration. They should not contemplate the sight sphere as it is tranquil or not tranquil, nor should they contemplate the sound, smell, taste, touch, and mental-image spheres as they are tranquil or not tranquil. They should not contemplate the sight sphere as it is far away or not far away, nor should they contemplate the sound, smell, taste, touch, and mental-image spheres as they are far away or not far away. They should not contemplate the sight sphere as it is conditioned or unconditioned, nor should they contemplate the sound, smell, taste, touch, and mental-image spheres as they are conditioned or unconditioned. They should not contemplate the sight sphere as it is flawed or flawless, nor should they contemplate the sound, smell, taste, touch, and mental-image spheres as they are flawed or flawless. They should not contemplate the sight sphere as it has arising or extinction, nor should they contemplate the sound, smell, taste, touch, and mental-image spheres as they have arising or extinction. They should not contemplate the sight sphere as it is virtuous or not virtuous, nor should they contemplate the sound, smell, taste, touch, and mental-image spheres as they are virtuous or not virtuous. They should not contemplate the sight sphere as it is guilty or not guilty, nor should they contemplate the sound, smell, taste, touch, and mental-image spheres as they are guilty or not guilty. They should not contemplate the sight sphere as it has or has no vexations, nor should they contemplate the sound, smell, taste, touch, and mental-image spheres as they have or have no vexations. They should not contemplate the sight sphere as it is of the world or beyond the world, nor should they contemplate the sound, smell, taste, touch, and mental-image spheres as they are of the world or beyond the world. They should not contemplate the sight sphere as it is contaminated or purified, nor should they contemplate the sound, smell, taste, touch, and mental-image spheres as they are contaminated or purified. They should not contemplate the sight sphere as it belongs to birth and death or belongs to nirvana, nor should they contemplate the sound, smell, taste, touch, and mental-image spheres as they belong to birth and death or belong to nirvana. They should not contemplate the sight sphere as it is inside, outside, or in between, nor should they contemplate the sound, smell, taste, touch, and mental-image spheres as they are inside, outside, or in between. They should not contemplate the sight sphere as it is attainable or unattainable, nor should they contemplate the sound, smell, taste, touch, and mental-image spheres as they are attainable or unattainable.

"Furthermore, Well Appearing One, when cultivating prajna paramita, the great bodhisattvas should not contemplate the eye realm as it is permanent or impermanent, nor should they contemplate the ear, nose, tongue, body, and conscious realms as they are permanent or impermanent. They should not contemplate the eye realm as it is pleasant or painful, nor should they contemplate the ear, nose, tongue, body, and conscious realms as they are pleasant or painful. They should not contemplate the eye realm as it is with or without selfness, nor should they contemplate the ear, nose, tongue, body, and conscious realms as they are with or without selfness. They should not contemplate the eye realm as it is pure or impure, nor should they contemplate the ear, nose, tongue, body, and conscious realms as they are pure or impure. They should not contemplate the eye realm as it is empty or not empty, nor should they contemplate the ear, nose, tongue, body, and conscious realms as they are empty or not empty. They should not contemplate the eye realm as it is with or without form, nor should they contemplate the ear, nose, tongue, body, and conscious realms as they are with or without form. They should not contemplate the eye realm as it is with or without aspiration, nor should they contemplate the ear, nose, tongue, body, and conscious realms as they are with or without aspiration. They should not contemplate the eye realm as it is tranquil or not tranquil, nor should they contemplate the ear, nose, tongue, body, and conscious realms as they are tranquil or not tranquil. They should not contemplate the eye realm as it is far away or not far away, nor should they contemplate the ear, nose, tongue, body, and conscious realms as they are far away or not far away. They should not contemplate the eye realm as it is conditioned or unconditioned, nor should they contemplate the ear, nose, tongue, body, and conscious realms as they are conditioned or unconditioned. They should not contemplate the eye realm as it is flawed or flawless, nor should they contemplate the ear, nose, tongue, body, and conscious realms as they are flawed or flawless. They should not contemplate the eye realm as it has arising or extinction, nor should they contemplate the ear, nose, tongue, body, and conscious realms as they have arising or extinction. They should not contemplate the eye realm as it is virtuous or not virtuous, nor should they contemplate the ear, nose, tongue, body, and conscious realms as they are virtuous or not virtuous. They should not contemplate the eye realm as it is guilty or not guilty, nor should they contemplate the ear, nose, tongue, body, and conscious realms as they are guilty or not guilty. They should not contemplate the eye realm as it has or has no vexations, nor should they contemplate the ear, nose, tongue, body, and conscious realms as they have or have no vexations. They should not contemplate the eye realm as it is of the world or beyond the world, nor should they contemplate the ear, nose, tongue, body, and conscious realms as they are of the world or beyond the world. They should not contemplate the eye realm as it is contaminated or purified, nor should they contemplate the ear, nose, tongue, body, and conscious realms as they are contaminated or purified. They should not contemplate the eye realm as it belongs to birth and death or belongs to nirvana, nor should they contemplate the ear, nose, tongue, body, and conscious realms as they belong to birth and death or belong to nirvana. They should not contemplate the eye realm as it is inside, outside, or in between, nor should they contemplate the ear, nose, tongue, body, and conscious realms as they are inside, outside, or in between. They should not contemplate the eye realm as it is attainable or unattainable, nor should they contemplate the ear, nose, tongue, body, and conscious realms as they are attainable or unattainable.

"Furthermore, Well Appearing One, when cultivating prajna paramita, the great bodhisattvas should not contemplate the sight realm as it is permanent or impermanent, nor should they contemplate the sound, smell, taste, touch, and mental-image realms as they are permanent or impermanent. They should not contemplate the sight realm as it is pleasant or painful, nor should they contemplate the sound, smell, taste, touch, and mental-image realms as they are pleasant or painful. They should not contemplate the sight realm as it is with or without selfness, nor should they contemplate the sound, smell, taste, touch, and mental-image realms as they are with or without selfness. They should not contemplate the sight realm as it is pure or impure, nor should they contemplate the sound, smell, taste, touch, and mental-image realms as they are pure or impure. They should not contemplate the sight realm as it is empty or not empty, nor should they contemplate the sound, smell, taste, touch, and mental-image realms as they are empty or not empty. They should not contemplate the sight realm as it is with or without form, nor should they contemplate the sound, smell, taste, touch, and mental-image realms as they are with or without form. They should not contemplate the sight realm as it is with or without aspiration, nor should they contemplate the sound, smell, taste, touch, and mental-image realms as they are with or without aspiration. They should not contemplate the sight realm as it is tranquil or not tranquil, nor should they contemplate the sound, smell, taste, touch, and mental-image realms as they are tranquil or not tranquil. They should not contemplate the sight realm as it is far away or not far away, nor should they contemplate the sound, smell, taste, touch, and mental-image realms as they are far away or not far away. They should not contemplate the sight realm as it is conditioned or unconditioned, nor should they contemplate the sound, smell, taste, touch, and mental-image realms as they are conditioned or unconditioned. They should not contemplate the sight realm as it is flawed or flawless, nor should they contemplate the sound, smell, taste, touch, and mental-image realms as they are flawed or flawless. They should not contemplate the sight realm as it has arising or extinction, nor should they contemplate the sound, smell, taste, touch, and mental-image realms as they have arising or extinction. They should not contemplate the sight realm as it is virtuous or not virtuous, nor should they contemplate the sound, smell, taste, touch, and mental-image realms as they are virtuous or not virtuous. They should not contemplate the sight realm as it is guilty or not guilty, nor should they contemplate the sound, smell, taste, touch, and mental-image realms as they are guilty or not guilty. They should not contemplate the sight realm as it has or has no vexations, nor should they contemplate the sound, smell, taste, touch, and mental-image realms as they have or have no vexations. They should not contemplate the sight realm as it is of the world or beyond the world, nor should they contemplate the sound, smell, taste, touch, and mental-image realms as they are of the world or beyond the world. They should not contemplate the sight realm as it is contaminated or purified, nor should they contemplate the sound, smell, taste, touch, and mental-image realms as they are contaminated or purified. They should not contemplate the sight realm as it belongs to birth and death or belongs to nirvana, nor should they contemplate the sound, smell, taste, touch, and mental-image realms as they belong to birth and death or belong to nirvana. They should not contemplate the sight realm as it is inside, outside, or in between, nor should they contemplate the sound, smell, taste, touch, and mental-image realms as they are inside, outside, or in between. They should not contemplate the sight realm as it is attainable or unattainable, nor should they contemplate the sound, smell, taste, touch, and mental-image realms as they are attainable or unattainable.

"Furthermore, Well Appearing One, when cultivating prajna paramita, the great bodhisattvas should not contemplate the eye consciousness realm as it is permanent or impermanent, nor should they contemplate the ear, nose, tongue, body, and conscious consciousness realms as they are permanent or impermanent. They should not contemplate the eye consciousness realm as it is pleasant or painful, nor should they contemplate the ear, nose, tongue, body, and conscious consciousness realms as they are pleasant or painful. They should not contemplate the eye consciousness realm as it is with or without selfness, nor should they contemplate the ear, nose, tongue, body, and conscious consciousness realms as they are with or without selfness. They should not contemplate the eye consciousness realm as it is pure or impure, nor should they contemplate the ear, nose, tongue, body, and conscious consciousness realms as they are pure or impure. They should not contemplate the eye consciousness realm as it is empty or not empty, nor should they contemplate the ear, nose, tongue, body, and conscious consciousness realms as they are empty or not empty. They should not contemplate the eye consciousness realm as it is with or without form, nor should they contemplate the ear, nose, tongue, body, and conscious consciousness realms as they are with or without form. They should not contemplate the eye consciousness realm as it is with or without aspiration, nor should they contemplate the ear, nose, tongue, body, and conscious consciousness realms as they are with or without aspiration. They should not contemplate the eye consciousness realm as it is tranquil or not tranquil, nor should they contemplate the ear, nose, tongue, body, and conscious consciousness realms as they are tranquil or not tranquil. They should not contemplate the eye consciousness realm as it is far away or not far away, nor should they contemplate the ear, nose, tongue, body, and conscious consciousness realms as they are far away or not far away. They should not contemplate the eye consciousness realm as it is conditioned or unconditioned, nor should they contemplate the ear, nose, tongue, body, and conscious consciousness realms as they are conditioned or unconditioned. They should not contemplate the eye consciousness realm as it is flawed or flawless, nor should they contemplate the ear, nose, tongue, body, and conscious consciousness realms as they are flawed or flawless. They should not contemplate the eye consciousness realm as it has arising or extinction, nor should they contemplate the ear, nose, tongue, body, and conscious consciousness realms as they have arising or extinction. They should not contemplate the eye consciousness realm as it is virtuous or not virtuous, nor should they contemplate the ear, nose, tongue, body, and conscious consciousness realms as they are virtuous or not virtuous. They should not contemplate the eye consciousness realm as it is guilty or not guilty, nor should they contemplate the ear, nose, tongue, body, and conscious consciousness realms as they are guilty or not guilty. They should not contemplate the eye consciousness realm as it has or has no vexations, nor should they contemplate the ear, nose, tongue, body, and conscious consciousness realms as they have or have no vexations. They should not contemplate the eye consciousness realm as it is of the world or beyond the world, nor should they contemplate the ear, nose, tongue, body, and conscious consciousness realms as they are of the world or beyond the world. They should not contemplate the eye consciousness realm as it is contaminated or purified, nor should they contemplate the ear, nose, tongue, body, and conscious consciousness realms as they are contaminated or purified. They should not contemplate the eye consciousness realm as it belongs to birth and death or belongs to nirvana, nor should they contemplate the ear, nose, tongue, body, and conscious consciousness realms as they belong to birth and death or belong to nirvana. They should not contemplate the eye consciousness realm as it is inside, outside, or in between, nor should they contemplate the ear, nose, tongue, body, and conscious consciousness realms as they are inside, outside, or in between. They should not contemplate the eye consciousness realm as it is attainable or unattainable, nor should they contemplate the ear, nose, tongue, body, and conscious consciousness realms as they are attainable or unattainable.

"Furthermore, Well Appearing One, when cultivating prajna paramita, the great bodhisattvas should not contemplate the eye contact as it is permanent or impermanent, nor should they contemplate the ear, nose, tongue, body, and conscious contacts as they are permanent or impermanent. They should not contemplate the eye contact as it is pleasant or painful, nor should they contemplate the ear, nose, tongue, body, and conscious contacts as they are pleasant or painful. They should not contemplate the eye contact as it is with or without selfness, nor should they contemplate the ear, nose, tongue, body, and conscious contacts as they are with or without selfness. They should not contemplate the eye contact as it is pure or impure, nor should they contemplate the ear, nose, tongue, body, and conscious contacts as they are pure or impure. They should not contemplate the eye contact as it is empty or not empty, nor should they contemplate the ear, nose, tongue, body, and conscious contacts as they are empty or not empty. They should not contemplate the eye contact as it is with or without form, nor should they contemplate the ear, nose, tongue, body, and conscious contacts as they are with or without form. They should not contemplate the eye contact as it is with or without aspiration, nor should they contemplate the ear, nose, tongue, body, and conscious contacts as they are with or without aspiration. They should not contemplate the eye contact as it is tranquil or not tranquil, nor should they contemplate the ear, nose, tongue, body, and conscious contacts as they are tranquil or not tranquil. They should not contemplate the eye contact as it is far away or not far away, nor should they contemplate the ear, nose, tongue, body, and conscious contacts as they are far away or not far away. They should not contemplate the eye contact as it is conditioned or unconditioned, nor should they contemplate the ear, nose, tongue, body, and conscious contacts as they are conditioned or unconditioned. They should not contemplate the eye contact as it is flawed or flawless, nor should they contemplate the ear, nose, tongue, body, and conscious contacts as they are flawed or flawless. They should not contemplate the eye contact as it has arising or extinction, nor should they contemplate the ear, nose, tongue, body, and conscious contacts as they have arising or extinction. They should not contemplate the eye contact as it is virtuous or not virtuous, nor should they contemplate the ear, nose, tongue, body, and conscious contacts as they are virtuous or not virtuous. They should not contemplate the eye contact as it is guilty or not guilty, nor should they contemplate the ear, nose, tongue, body, and conscious contacts as they are guilty or not guilty. They should not contemplate the eye contact as it has or has not vexations, nor should they contemplate the ear, nose, tongue, body, and conscious contacts as they have or have no vexations. They should not contemplate the eye contact as it is of the world or beyond the world, nor should they contemplate the ear, nose, tongue, body, and conscious contacts as they are of the world or beyond the world. They should not contemplate the eye contact as it is contaminated or purified, nor should they contemplate the ear, nose, tongue, body, and conscious contacts as they are contaminated or purified. They should not contemplate the eye contact as it belongs to birth and death or belongs to nirvana, nor should they contemplate the ear, nose, tongue, body, and conscious contacts as they belong to birth and death or belong to nirvana. They should not contemplate the eye contact as it is inside, outside, or in between, nor should they contemplate the ear, nose, tongue, body, and conscious contacts as they are inside, outside, or in between. They should not contemplate the eye contact as it is attainable or unattainable, nor should they contemplate the ear, nose, tongue, body, and conscious contacts as they are attainable or unattainable.

"Furthermore, Well Appearing One, when cultivating prajna paramita, the great bodhisattvas should not contemplate the pleasant, painful, and neutral feelings produced by eye contact as they are permanent or impermanent, nor should they contemplate the pleasant, painful, and neutral feelings produced by ear, nose, tongue, body, and conscious contacts as they are permanent or impermanent. They should not contemplate the pleasant, painful, and neutral feelings produced by eye contact as they are pleasant or painful, nor should they contemplate the pleasant, painful, and neutral feelings produced by ear, nose, tongue, body, and conscious contact as they are pleasant or painful. They should not contemplate the pleasant, painful, and neutral feelings produced by eye contact as it is with or without selfness, nor should they contemplate the pleasant, painful, and neutral feelings produced by ear, nose, tongue, body, and conscious contacts as they are with or without selfness. They should not contemplate the pleasant, painful, and neutral feelings produced by eye contact as they are pure or impure, nor should they contemplate the pleasant, painful, and neutral feelings produced by ear, nose, tongue, body, and conscious contacts as they are pure or impure. They should not contemplate the pleasant, painful, and neutral feelings produced by eye contact as they are empty or not empty, nor should they contemplate the pleasant, painful, and neutral feelings produced by ear, nose, tongue, body, and conscious contacts as they are empty or not empty. They should not contemplate the pleasant, painful, and neutral feelings produced by eye contact as they are with or without form, nor should they contemplate the pleasant, painful, and neutral feelings produced by ear, nose, tongue, body, and conscious contacts as they are with or without form. They should not contemplate the pleasant, painful, and neutral feelings produced by eye contact as they are with or without aspiration, nor should they contemplate the pleasant, painful, and neutral feelings produced by ear, nose, tongue, body, and conscious contacts as they are with or without aspiration. They should not contemplate the pleasant, painful, and neutral feelings produced by eye contact as they are tranquil or not tranquil, nor should they contemplate the pleasant, painful, and neutral feelings produced by ear, nose, tongue, body, and conscious contacts as they are tranquil or not tranquil. They should not contemplate the pleasant, painful, and neutral feelings produced by eye contact as they far away or not far away from defilements, nor should they contemplate the pleasant, painful, and neutral feelings produced by ear, nose, tongue, body, and conscious contacts as they are far away or not far away from defilements. They should not contemplate the pleasant, painful, and neutral feelings produced by eye contact as they are conditioned or unconditioned, nor should not contemplate the pleasant, painful, and neutral feelings produced by ear, nose, tongue, body, and conscious contacts as they are conditioned or unconditioned. They should not contemplate the pleasant, painful, and neutral feelings produced by eye contact as they are flawed or flawless, nor should they contemplate the pleasant, painful, and neutral feelings produced by ear, nose, tongue, body, and conscious contacts as they are flawed or flawless. They should not contemplate the pleasant, painful, and neutral feelings produced by eye contact as they have arising or extinction, nor should they contemplate the pleasant, painful, and neutral feelings produced by ear, nose, tongue, body, and conscious contacts as they have arising or extinction. They should not contemplate the pleasant, painful, and neutral feelings produced by eye contact as they are virtuous or not virtuous, nor should they contemplate the pleasant, painful, and neutral feelings produced by ear, nose, tongue, body, and conscious contacts as they are virtuous or not virtuous. They should not contemplate the pleasant, painful, and neutral feelings produced by eye contact as they are guilty or not guilty, nor should they contemplate the pleasant, painful, and neutral feelings produced by ear, nose, tongue, body, and conscious contacts as they are guilty or not guilty. They should not contemplate the pleasant, painful, and neutral feelings produced by eye contact as they have or have no vexations, nor should they contemplate the pleasant, painful, and neutral feelings produced by ear, nose, tongue, body, and conscious contacts as they have or have no vexations. They should not contemplate the pleasant, painful, and neutral feelings produced by eye contact as they belong to the world or beyond the world, nor should they contemplate the pleasant, painful, and neutral feelings produced by ear, nose, tongue, body, and conscious contacts as they belong to the world or beyond the world. They should not contemplate the pleasant, painful, and neutral feelings produced by eye contact as they are contaminated or purified, nor should they contemplate the pleasant, painful, and neutral feelings produced by ear, nose, tongue, body, and conscious contacts as they are contaminated or purified. They should not contemplate the pleasant, painful, and neutral feelings produced by eye contact as they belong to birth and death or belong to nirvana, nor should they contemplate the pleasant, painful, and neutral feelings produced by ear, nose, tongue, body, and conscious contacts as they belong to birth and death or belong to nirvana. They should not contemplate the pleasant, painful, and neutral feelings produced by eye contact as they are inside, outside, or in between, nor should they contemplate the pleasant, painful, and neutral feelings produced by ear, nose, tongue, body, and conscious contacts as they are inside, outside, or in between. They should not contemplate the pleasant, painful, and neutral feelings produced by eye contact as they are attainable or unattainable, nor should they contemplate the pleasant, painful, and neutral feelings produced by ear, nose, tongue, body, and conscious contacts as they are attainable or unattainable.

"Furthermore, Well Appearing One, when cultivating prajna paramita, the great bodhisattvas should not contemplate the earth realm as it is permanent or impermanent, nor should they contemplate the water, fire, wind, space, and consciousness realms as they are permanent or impermanent. They should not contemplate the earth realm as it is pleasant or painful, nor should they contemplate the water, fire, wind, space, and consciousness realms as they are pleasant or painful. They should not contemplate the earth realm as it is with or without selfness, nor should they contemplate the water, fire, wind, space, and consciousness realms as they are with or without selfness. They should not contemplate the earth realm as it is pure or impure, nor should they contemplate the water, fire, wind, space, and consciousness realms as they are pure or impure. They should not contemplate the earth realm as it is empty or not empty, nor should they contemplate the water, fire, wind, space, and consciousness realms as they are empty or not empty. They should not contemplate the earth realm as it is with or without form, nor should they contemplate the water, fire, wind, space, and consciousness realms as they are with or without form. They should not contemplate the earth realm as it is with or without aspiration, nor should they contemplate the water, fire, wind, space, and consciousness realms as they are with or without aspiration. They should not contemplate the earth realm as it is tranquil or not tranquil, nor should they contemplate the water, fire, wind, space, and consciousness realms as they are tranquil or not tranquil. They should not contemplate the earth realm as it is far away or not far away, nor should they contemplate the water, fire, wind, space, and consciousness realms as they are far away or not far away. They should not contemplate the earth realm as it is conditioned or unconditioned, nor should they contemplate the water, fire, wind, space, and consciousness realms as they are conditioned or unconditioned. They should not contemplate the earth realm as it is flawed or flawless, nor should they contemplate the water, fire, wind, space, and consciousness realms as they are flawed or flawless. They should not contemplate the earth realm as it has arising or extinction, nor should they contemplate the water, fire, wind, space, and consciousness realms as they have arising or extinction. They should not contemplate the earth realm as it is virtuous or not virtuous, nor should they contemplate the water, fire, wind, space, and consciousness realms as they are virtuous or not virtuous. They should not contemplate the earth realm as it is guilty or not guilty, nor should they contemplate the water, fire, wind, space, and consciousness realms as they are guilty or not guilty. They should not contemplate the earth realm as it has or has no vexations, nor should they contemplate the water, fire, wind, space, and consciousness realms as they have or have no vexations. They should not contemplate the earth realm as it is of the world or beyond the world, nor should they contemplate the water, fire, wind, space, and consciousness realms as they are of the world or beyond the world. They should not contemplate the earth realm as it is contaminated or purified, nor should they contemplate the water, fire, wind, space, and consciousness realms as they are contaminated or purified. They should not contemplate the earth realm as it belongs to birth and death or nirvana, nor should they contemplate the water, fire, wind, space, and consciousness realms as they belong to birth and death or nirvana. They should not contemplate the earth realm as it is inside, outside, or in between, nor should they contemplate the water, fire, wind, space, and consciousness realms as they are inside, outside, or in between. They should not contemplate the earth realm as it is attainable or unattainable, nor should they contemplate the water, fire, wind, space, and consciousness realms as they are attainable or unattainable.

FASCICLE 12

Chapter 7
The Cautions and the Teachings

Section 2

(In the First Assembly)

"FURTHERMORE, WELL APPEARING ONE, WHEN CULTIVATING PRAJNA PARAMITA, the great bodhisattvas should not contemplate cause and condition as it is permanent or impermanent, nor should they contemplate consecutive sequence of thoughts, the conditions that stimulate one's mind, and the conditions that reinforce main causes as they are permanent or impermanent. They should not contemplate cause and condition as it is pleasant or painful, nor should they contemplate consecutive sequence of thoughts, the conditions that stimulate one's mind, and the conditions that reinforce main causes as they are pleasant or painful. They should not contemplate cause and condition as it is with or without selfness, nor should they contemplate consecutive sequence of thoughts, the conditions that stimulate one's mind, and the conditions that reinforce main causes as they are with or without selfness. They should not contemplate cause and condition as it is pure or impure, nor should they contemplate consecutive sequence of thoughts, the conditions that stimulate one's mind, and the conditions that reinforce main

Fascicle 12, Chapter 7, Section 2

causes as they are pure or impure. They should not contemplate cause and condition as it is empty or not empty, nor should they contemplate consecutive sequence of thoughts, the conditions that stimulate one's mind, and the conditions that reinforce main causes as they are empty or not empty. They should not contemplate cause and condition as it is with or without form, nor should they contemplate consecutive sequence of thoughts, the conditions that stimulate one's mind, and the conditions that reinforce main causes as they are with or without form. They should not contemplate cause and condition as it is with or without aspiration, nor should they contemplate consecutive sequence of thoughts, the conditions that stimulate one's mind, and the conditions that reinforce main causes as they are with or without aspiration. They should not contemplate cause and condition as it is tranquil or not tranquil, nor should they contemplate consecutive sequence of thoughts, the conditions that stimulate one's mind, and the conditions that reinforce main causes as they are tranquil or not tranquil. They should not contemplate cause and condition as it is far away or not far away, nor should they contemplate consecutive sequence of thoughts, the conditions that stimulate one's mind, and the conditions that reinforce main causes as they are far away or not far away. They should not contemplate cause and condition as it is conditioned or unconditioned, nor should they contemplate consecutive sequence of thoughts, the conditions that stimulate one's mind, and the conditions that reinforce main causes as they are conditioned or unconditioned. They should not contemplate cause and condition as it is flawed or flawless, nor should they contemplate consecutive sequence of thoughts, the conditions that stimulate one's mind, and the conditions that reinforce main causes as they are flawed or flawless. They should not contemplate cause and condition as it arises or extinguishes, nor should they contemplate consecutive sequence of thoughts, the conditions that stimulate one's mind, and the conditions that reinforce main causes as they arise or extinguish. They should not contemplate cause and condition as it is virtuous or not virtuous, nor should they contemplate consecutive sequence of thoughts, the conditions that stimulate one's mind, and the conditions that reinforce main causes as they are virtuous or not virtuous. They should not contemplate cause and condition as it is guilty or not guilty, nor should they contemplate consecutive sequence of thoughts, the conditions that stimulate one's mind, and the conditions that reinforce main causes as they are guilty or not guilty. They should not contemplate cause and condition as it has or has no vexations, nor should they contemplate consecutive sequence of thoughts, the conditions that stimulate one's mind, and the conditions that reinforce main causes as they have or have no vexations. They should not contemplate cause and condition as it is of the world or beyond the world, nor should they contemplate consecutive sequence of thoughts, the conditions that stimulate one's mind, and the conditions that reinforce main causes as they are of the world or beyond the world. They should not contemplate cause and condition as it is contaminated or purified, nor should they contemplate consecutive sequence of thoughts, the conditions that stimulate one's mind, and the conditions that reinforce main causes as they are contaminated or purified. They should not contemplate cause and condition as it belongs to birth and death or nirvana, nor should they contemplate consecutive sequence of thoughts, the conditions that stimulate one's mind, and the conditions that reinforce main causes as they belong to birth and death or nirvana. They should not contemplate cause and condition as it is inside, outside, or in between, nor should they contemplate consecutive sequence of thoughts, the conditions that stimulate one's mind, and the conditions that reinforce main causes as they are inside, outside, or in between. They should not contemplate cause and condition as it is attainable or unattainable, nor should they contemplate consecutive sequence of thoughts, the conditions that stimulate one's mind, and the conditions that reinforce main causes as they are attainable or unattainable.

"Furthermore, Well Appearing One, when cultivating prajna paramita, the great bodhisattvas should not contemplate the dharmas produced by conditions as they are permanent or impermanent, pleasant or painful, with or without selfness, pure or impure, empty or not empty, with or without form, with or without aspiration, tranquil or not tranquil, far away or not far away, conditioned or unconditioned, flawed or flawless, with arising or extinction, virtuous or not virtuous, guilty or not guilty, with or without vexations, of the world or beyond the world, contaminated or purified, belonging to birth and death or nirvana, inside, outside, or in between, and attainable or unattainable.

"Furthermore, Well Appearing One, when cultivating prajna paramita, the great bodhisattvas should not contemplate ignorance as it is permanent or impermanent, nor should they contemplate action, consciousness, name and form, the six sense spheres, contact, reception, craving, grasping, existence, birth, old age, death, worry, sorrow, misery, anxiety, and upset as they are permanent or impermanent. They should not contemplate ignorance as it is pleasant or painful, nor should they contemplate action, and so forth, as well as old age, death, worry, sorrow, misery, anxiety, and upset as they are pleasant or painful. They should not contemplate ignorance as it is with or without selfness, nor should they contemplate action, and so forth, as well as old age, death, worry, sorrow, misery, anxiety, and upset as they are with or without selfness. They should not contemplate ignorance as it is pure or impure, nor should they contemplate action, and so forth, as well as old age, death, worry, sorrow, misery, anxiety, and upset as they are pure or impure. They should not contemplate ignorance as it is empty or not empty, nor should they contemplate action, and so forth, as well as old age, death, worry, sorrow, misery, anxiety, and upset as they are empty or not empty. They should not contemplate ignorance as it is with or without form, nor should they contemplate action, and so forth, as well as old age, death, worry, sorrow, misery, anxiety, and upset as they are with or without form. They should not contemplate ignorance as it is with or without aspiration, nor should they contemplate action, and so forth, as well as old age, death, worry, sorrow, misery, anxiety, and upset as they are with or without aspiration. They should not contemplate ignorance as it is tranquil or not tranquil, nor should they contemplate action, and so forth, as well as old age, death, worry, sorrow, misery, anxiety, and upset as they are tranquil or not tranquil. They should not contemplate ignorance as it is far away or not far away, nor should they contemplate action, and so forth, as well as old age, death, worry, sorrow, misery, anxiety, and upset as they are far away or not far away. They should not contemplate ignorance as it is conditioned or unconditioned, nor should they contemplate action, and so forth, as well as old age, death, worry, sorrow, misery, anxiety, and upset as they are conditioned or unconditioned. They should not contemplate ignorance as it is flawed or flawless, nor should they contemplate action, and so forth, as well as old age, death, worry, sorrow, misery, anxiety, and upset as they are flawed or flawless. They should not contemplate ignorance as it arises or extinguishes, nor should they contemplate action, and so forth, as well as old age, death, worry, sorrow, misery, anxiety, and upset as they arise or extinguish. They should not contemplate ignorance as it is virtuous or not virtuous, nor should they contemplate action, and so forth, as well as old age, death, worry, sorrow, misery, anxiety, and upset as they are virtuous or not virtuous. They should not contemplate ignorance as it is guilty or not guilty, nor should they contemplate action, and so forth, as well as old age, death, worry, sorrow, misery, anxiety, and upset as they are guilty or not guilty. They should not contemplate ignorance as it has or has no vexations, nor should they contemplate action, and so forth, as well as old age, death, worry, sorrow, misery, anxiety, and upset as they have or have no vexations. They should not contemplate ignorance as it is of the world or beyond the world, nor should they contemplate action, and so forth, as well as old age, death, worry, sorrow, misery, anxiety, and upset as they are of the world or beyond the world. They should not contemplate ignorance as it is contaminated or purified, nor should they contemplate action, and so forth, as well as old age, death, worry, sorrow, misery, anxiety, and upset as they are contaminated or purified. They should not contemplate ignorance as it belongs to birth and death or nirvana, nor should they contemplate action, and so forth, as well as old age, death, worry, sorrow, misery, anxiety, and upset as they belong to birth and death or nirvana. They should not contemplate ignorance as it is inside, outside, or in between, nor should they contemplate action, and so forth, as well as old age, death, worry, sorrow, misery, anxiety, and upset as they are inside, outside, or in between. They should not contemplate ignorance as it is attainable or unattainable, nor should they contemplate action, and so forth, as well as old age, death, worry,

Fascicle 12, Chapter 7, Section 2   263

sorrow, misery, anxiety, and upset as they are attainable or unattainable.

"Furthermore, Well Appearing One, when cultivating prajna paramita, the great bodhisattvas should not contemplate giving paramita as it is permanent or impermanent, nor should they contemplate pure precept, forbearance, diligence, meditation, and prajna paramitas as they are permanent or impermanent. They should not contemplate giving paramita as it is pleasant or painful, nor should they contemplate pure precept, forbearance, diligence, meditation, and prajna paramitas as they are pleasant or painful. They should not contemplate giving paramita as it is with or without selfness, nor should they contemplate pure precept, forbearance, diligence, meditation, and prajna paramitas as they are with or without selfness. They should not contemplate giving paramita as it is pure or impure, nor should they contemplate pure precept, forbearance, diligence, meditation, and prajna paramitas as they are pure or impure. They should not contemplate giving paramita as it is empty or not empty, nor should they contemplate pure precept, forbearance, diligence, meditation, and prajna paramitas as they are empty or not empty. They should not contemplate giving paramita as it is with or without form, nor should they contemplate pure precept, forbearance, diligence, meditation, and prajna paramitas as they are with or without form. They should not contemplate giving paramita as it is with or without aspiration, nor should they contemplate pure precept, forbearance, diligence, meditation, and prajna paramitas as they are with or without aspiration. They should not contemplate giving paramita as it is tranquil or not tranquil, nor should they contemplate pure precept, forbearance, diligence, meditation, and prajna paramitas as they are tranquil or not tranquil. They should not contemplate giving paramita as it is far away or not far away, nor should they contemplate pure precept, forbearance, diligence, meditation, and prajna paramitas as they are far away or not far away. They should not contemplate giving paramita as it is conditioned or unconditioned, nor should they contemplate pure precept, forbearance, diligence, meditation, and prajna paramitas as they are conditioned or unconditioned. They should not contemplate giving paramita as it is flawed or flawless, nor should they contemplate pure precept, forbearance, diligence, meditation, and prajna paramitas as they are flawed or flawless. They should not contemplate giving paramita as it arises or extinguishes, nor should they contemplate pure precept, forbearance, diligence, meditation, and prajna paramitas as they arise or extinguish. They should not contemplate giving paramita as it is virtuous or not virtuous, nor should they contemplate pure precept, forbearance, diligence, meditation, and prajna paramitas as they are virtuous or not virtuous. They should not contemplate giving paramita as it is guilty or not guilty, nor should they contemplate pure precept, forbearance, diligence, meditation, and prajna paramitas as they are guilty or not guilty. They should not contemplate giving paramita as it has or has no vexations, nor should they contemplate pure precept, forbearance, diligence, meditation, and prajna paramitas as they have or have no vexations. They should not contemplate giving paramita as it is of the world or beyond the world, nor should they contemplate pure precept, forbearance, diligence, meditation, and prajna paramitas as they are of the world or beyond the world. They should not contemplate giving paramita as it is contaminated or purified, nor should they contemplate pure precept, forbearance, diligence, meditation, and prajna paramitas as they are contaminated or purified. They should not contemplate giving paramita as it belongs to birth and death or nirvana, nor should they contemplate pure precept, forbearance, diligence, meditation, and prajna paramitas as they belong to birth and death or nirvana. They should not contemplate giving paramita as it is inside, outside, or in between, nor should they contemplate pure precept, forbearance, diligence, meditation, and prajna paramitas as they are inside, outside, or in between. They should not contemplate giving paramita as it is attainable or unattainable, nor should they contemplate pure precept, forbearance, diligence, meditation, and prajna paramitas as they are attainable or unattainable.

"Furthermore, Well Appearing One, when cultivating prajna paramita, the great bodhisattvas should not contemplate internal emptiness as it is permanent or impermanent, nor should they contemplate external emptiness, internal-external emptiness, emptiness of emptiness, emptiness of space, emptiness of ultimate truth, emptiness of conditioned phenomena, emptiness of unconditioned reality, emptiness in the final analysis, emptiness of nontemporality, emptiness of deconstruction, emptiness of changelessness, emptiness of original nature, emptiness of particular characteristics, emptiness of common characteristics, emptiness of all dharmas, emptiness of nonattainment, emptiness of selflessness, emptiness of self-nature, and emptiness of selfless self-nature as they are permanent or impermanent. They should not contemplate internal emptiness as it is pleasant or painful, nor should they contemplate external emptiness, and so forth, as well as emptiness of selfless self-nature as they are pleasant or painful. They should not contemplate internal emptiness as it is with or without selfness, nor should they contemplate external emptiness, and so forth, as well as emptiness of selfless self-nature as they are with or without selfness. They should not contemplate internal emptiness as it is pure or impure, nor should they contemplate external emptiness, and so forth, as well as emptiness of selfless self-nature as they are pure or impure. They should not contemplate internal emptiness as it is empty or not empty, nor should they contemplate external emptiness, and so forth, as well as emptiness of selfless self-nature as they are empty or not empty. They should not contemplate internal emptiness as it is with or without form, nor should they contemplate external emptiness, and so forth, as well as emptiness of selfless self-nature as they are with or without form. They should not contemplate internal emptiness as it is with or without aspiration, nor should they contemplate external emptiness, and so forth, as well as emptiness of selfless self-nature as they are with or without aspiration. They should not contemplate internal emptiness as it is tranquil or not tranquil, nor should they contemplate external emptiness, and so forth, as well as emptiness of selfless self-nature as they are tranquil or not tranquil. They should not contemplate internal emptiness as it is far away or not far away, nor should they contemplate external emptiness, and so forth, as well as emptiness of selfless self-nature as they are far away or not far away. They should not contemplate internal emptiness as it is conditioned or unconditioned, nor should they contemplate external emptiness, and so forth, as well as emptiness of selfless self-nature as they are conditioned or unconditioned. They should not contemplate internal emptiness as it is flawed or flawless, nor should they contemplate external emptiness, and so forth, as well as emptiness of selfless self-nature as they are flawed or flawless. They should not contemplate internal emptiness as it arises or extinguishes, nor should they contemplate external emptiness, and so forth, as well as emptiness of selfless self-nature as they arise or extinguish. They should not contemplate internal emptiness as it is virtuous or not virtuous, nor should they contemplate external emptiness, and so forth, as well as emptiness of selfless self-nature as they are virtuous or not virtuous. They should not contemplate internal emptiness as it is guilty or not guilty, nor should they contemplate external emptiness, and so forth, as well as emptiness of selfless self-nature as they are guilty or not guilty. They should not contemplate internal emptiness as it has or has no vexations, nor should they contemplate external emptiness, and so forth, as well as emptiness of selfless self-nature as they have or have no vexations. They should not contemplate internal emptiness as it is of the world or beyond the world, nor should they contemplate external emptiness, and so forth, as well as emptiness of selfless self-nature as they are of the world or beyond the world. They should not contemplate internal emptiness as it is contaminated or purified, nor should they contemplate external emptiness, and so forth, as well as emptiness of selfless self-nature as they are contaminated or purified. They should not contemplate internal emptiness as it belongs to birth and death or nirvana, nor should they contemplate external emptiness, and so forth, as well as emptiness of selfless self-nature as they belong to birth and death or nirvana. They should not contemplate internal emptiness as it is inside, outside, or in between, nor should they contemplate external emptiness, and so forth, as well as emptiness of selfless self-nature as they are inside, outside, or in between. They should not contemplate internal emptiness as it is attainable or unattainable, nor should they contemplate external emptiness, and so forth, as well as emptiness of selfless self-nature as they are attainable or unattainable.

"Furthermore, Well Appearing One, when cultivating prajna paramita, the great bodhisattvas should not contemplate realness as it is permanent or impermanent, nor should they contemplate dharma realm, dharma nature, nature of nonillusion, the nature of changelessness, the nature of equality, the nature of nonarising, dharma concentration, dharma dwelling, reality, the realm of empty space, and the realm of the inconceivable as they are permanent or impermanent. They should not contemplate realness as it is pleasant or painful, nor should they contemplate dharma realm, and so forth, as well as the realm of the inconceivable as they are pleasant or painful. They should not contemplate realness as it is with or without selfness, nor should they contemplate dharma realm, and so forth, as well as the realm of the inconceivable as they are with or without selfness. They should not contemplate realness as it is pure or impure, nor should they contemplate dharma realm, and so forth, as well as the realm of the inconceivable as they are pure or impure. They should not contemplate realness as it is empty or not empty, nor should they contemplate dharma realm, and so forth, as well as the realm of the inconceivable as they are empty or not empty. They should not contemplate realness as it is with or without form, nor should they contemplate dharma realm, and so forth, as well as the realm of the inconceivable as they are with or without form. They should not contemplate realness as it is with or without aspiration, nor should they contemplate dharma realm, and so forth, as well as the realm of the inconceivable as they are with or without aspiration. They should not contemplate realness as it is tranquil or not tranquil, nor should they contemplate dharma realm, and so forth, as well as the realm of the inconceivable as they are tranquil or not tranquil. They should not contemplate realness as it is far away or not far away, nor should they contemplate dharma realm, and so forth, as well as the realm of the inconceivable as they are far away or not far away. They should not contemplate realness as it is conditioned or unconditioned, nor should they contemplate dharma realm, and so forth, as well as the realm of the inconceivable as they are conditioned or unconditioned. They should not contemplate realness as it is flawed or flawless, nor should they contemplate dharma realm, and so forth, as well as the realm of the inconceivable as they are flawed or flawless. They should not contemplate realness as it arises or extinguishes, nor should they contemplate dharma realm, and so forth, as well as the realm of the inconceivable as they arise or extinguish. They should not contemplate realness as it is virtuous or not virtuous, nor should they contemplate dharma realm, and so forth, as well as the realm of the inconceivable as they are virtuous or not virtuous. They should not contemplate realness as it is guilty or not guilty, nor should they contemplate dharma realm, and so forth, as well as the realm of the inconceivable as they are guilty or not guilty. They should not contemplate realness as it has or has no vexations, nor should they contemplate dharma realm, and so forth, as well as the realm of the inconceivable as they have or have no vexations. They should not contemplate realness as it is of the world or beyond the world, nor should they contemplate dharma realm, and so forth, as well as the realm of the inconceivable as they are of the world or beyond the world. They should not contemplate realness as it is contaminated or purified, nor should they contemplate dharma realm, and so forth, as well as the realm of the inconceivable as they are contaminated or purified. They should not contemplate realness as it belongs to birth and death or nirvana, nor should they contemplate dharma realm, and so forth, as well as the realm of the inconceivable as they belong to birth and death or nirvana. They should not contemplate realness as it is inside, outside, or in between, nor should they contemplate dharma realm, and so forth, as well as the realm of the inconceivable as they are inside, outside, or in between. They should not contemplate realness as it is attainable or unattainable, nor should they contemplate dharma realm, and so forth, as well as the realm of the inconceivable as they are attainable or unattainable.

"Furthermore, Well Appearing One, when cultivating prajna paramita, the great bodhisattvas should not contemplate the four bases of mindfulness as they are permanent or impermanent, nor should they contemplate the four correct endeavors, four bases of power, five roots, five powers, seven factors for enlightenment, and the noble eightfold path as they are permanent or impermanent. They should not contemplate the four bases of mindfulness as they are pleasant or painful, nor should they contemplate the four correct endeavors, and so forth, as well as the noble eightfold path as they are pleasant or painful. They should not contemplate the four bases of mindfulness as they are with or without selfness, nor should they contemplate the four correct endeavors, and so forth, as well as the noble eightfold path as they are with or without selfness. They should not contemplate the four bases of mindfulness as they are pure or impure, nor should they contemplate the four correct endeavors, and so forth, as well as the noble eightfold path as they are pure or impure. They should not contemplate the four bases of mindfulness as they are empty or not empty, nor should they contemplate the four correct endeavors, and so forth, as well as the noble eightfold path as they are empty or not empty. They should not contemplate the four bases of mindfulness as they are with or without form, nor should they contemplate the four correct endeavors, and so forth, as well as the noble eightfold path as they are with or without form. They should not contemplate the four bases of mindfulness as they are with or without aspiration, nor should they contemplate the four correct endeavors, and so forth, as well as the noble eightfold path as they are with or without aspiration. They should not contemplate the four bases of mindfulness as they are tranquil or not tranquil, nor should they contemplate the four correct endeavors, and so forth, as well as the noble eightfold path as they are tranquil or not tranquil. They should not contemplate the four bases of mindfulness as they are far away or not far away, nor should they contemplate the four correct endeavors, and so forth, as well as the noble eightfold path as they are far away or not far away. They should not contemplate the four bases of mindfulness as they are conditioned or unconditioned, nor should they contemplate the four correct endeavors, and so forth, as well as the noble eightfold path as they are conditioned or unconditioned. They should not contemplate the four bases of mindfulness as they are flawed or flawless, nor should they contemplate the four correct endeavors, and so forth, as well as the noble eightfold path as they are flawed or flawless. They should not contemplate the four bases of mindfulness as they arise or extinguish, nor should they contemplate the four correct endeavors, and so forth, as well as the noble eightfold path as they arise or extinguish. They should not contemplate the four bases of mindfulness as they

270 The Great Prajna Paramita Sutra

are virtuous or not virtuous, nor should they contemplate the four correct endeavors, and so forth, as well as the noble eightfold path as they are virtuous or not virtuous. They should not contemplate the four bases of mindfulness as they are guilty or not guilty, nor should they contemplate the four correct endeavors, and so forth, as well as the noble eightfold path as they are guilty or not guilty. They should not contemplate the four bases of mindfulness as they have or have no vexations, nor should they contemplate the four correct endeavors, and so forth, as well as the noble eightfold path as they have or have no vexations. They should not contemplate the four bases of mindfulness as they are of the world or beyond the world, nor should they contemplate the four correct endeavors, and so forth, as well as the noble eightfold path as they are of the world or beyond the world. They should not contemplate the four bases of mindfulness as they are contaminated or purified, nor should they contemplate the four correct endeavors, and so forth, as well as the noble eightfold path as they are contaminated or purified. They should not contemplate the four bases of mindfulness as they belong to birth and death or nirvana, nor should they contemplate the four correct endeavors, and so forth, as well as the noble eightfold path as they belong to birth and death or nirvana. They should not contemplate the four bases of mindfulness as they are inside, outside, or in between, nor should they contemplate the four correct endeavors, and so forth, as well as the noble eightfold path as they are inside, outside, or in between. They should not contemplate the four bases of mindfulness as they are attainable or unattainable, nor should they contemplate the four correct endeavors, and so forth, as well as the noble eightfold path as they are attainable or unattainable.

"Furthermore, Well Appearing One, when cultivating prajna paramita, the great bodhisattvas should not contemplate the noble truth of suffering as it is permanent or impermanent, nor should they contemplate the noble truths of the cause of suffering, the cessation of suffering, and the path for the cessation of suffering as they are permanent or impermanent. They should not contemplate the noble truth of suffering as it is pleasant or painful, nor should they contemplate the noble truths of the cause of suffering, the cessation of suffering, and the path for the cessation of suffering as they are pleasant or painful. They should not contemplate the noble truth of suffering as it is with or without selfness, nor should they contemplate the noble truths of the cause of suffering, the cessation of suffering, and the path for the cessation of suffering as they are with or without selfness. They should not contemplate the noble truth of suffering as it is pure or impure, nor should they contemplate the noble truths of the cause of suffering, the cessation of suffering, and the path for the cessation of suffering as they are pure or impure. They should not contemplate the noble truth of suffering as it is empty or not empty, nor should they contemplate the noble truths of the cause of suffering, the cessation of suffering, and the path for the cessation of suffering as they are empty or not empty. They should not contemplate the noble truth of suffering as it is with or without form, nor should they contemplate the noble truths of the cause of suffering, the cessation of suffering, and the path for the cessation of suffering as they are with or without form. They should not contemplate the noble truth of suffering as it is with or without aspiration, nor should they contemplate the noble truths of the cause of suffering, the cessation of suffering, and the path for the cessation of suffering as they are with or without aspiration. They should not contemplate the noble truth of suffering as it is tranquil or not tranquil, nor should they contemplate the noble truths of the cause of suffering, the cessation of suffering, and the path for the cessation of suffering as they are tranquil or not tranquil. They should not contemplate the noble truth of suffering as it is far away or not far away, nor should they contemplate the noble truths of the cause of suffering, the cessation of suffering, and the path for the cessation of suffering as they are far away or not far away. They should not contemplate the noble truth of suffering as it is conditioned or unconditioned, nor should they contemplate the noble truths of the cause of suffering, the cessation of suffering, and the path for the cessation of suffering as they are conditioned or unconditioned. They should not contemplate the noble truth of suffering as it is flawed or flawless, nor should they contemplate the noble truths of the cause of suffering, the cessation of suffering, and the path for the cessation of suffering as they are flawed or

272   *The Great Prajna Paramita Sutra*

flawless. They should not contemplate the noble truth of suffering as it arises or extinguishes, nor should they contemplate the noble truths of the cause of suffering, the cessation of suffering, and the path for the cessation of suffering as they arise or extinguish. They should not contemplate the noble truth of suffering as it is virtuous or not virtuous, nor should they contemplate the noble truths of the cause of suffering, the cessation of suffering, and the path for the cessation of suffering as they are virtuous or not virtuous. They should not contemplate the noble truth of suffering as it is guilty or not guilty, nor should they contemplate the noble truths of the cause of suffering, the cessation of suffering, and the path for the cessation of suffering as they are guilty or not guilty. They should not contemplate the noble truth of suffering as it has vexations or has no vexations, nor should they contemplate the noble truths of the cause of suffering, the cessation of suffering, and the path for the cessation of suffering as they have vexations or have no vexations. They should not contemplate the noble truth of suffering as it is of the world or beyond the world, nor should they contemplate the noble truths of the cause of suffering, the cessation of suffering, and the path for the cessation of suffering as they are of the world or beyond the world. They should not contemplate the noble truth of suffering as it is contaminated or purified, nor should they contemplate the noble truths of the cause of suffering, the cessation of suffering, and the path for the cessation of suffering as they are contaminated or purified. They should not contemplate the noble truth of suffering as it belongs to birth and death or to nirvana, nor should they contemplate the noble truths of the cause of suffering, the cessation of suffering, and the path for the cessation of suffering as they belong to birth and death or to nirvana. They should not contemplate the noble truth of suffering as it is inside, outside, or in between, nor should they contemplate the noble truths of the cause of suffering, the cessation of suffering, and the path for the cessation of suffering as they are inside, outside, or in between. They should not contemplate the noble truth of suffering as it is attainable or unattainable, nor should they contemplate the noble truths of the cause of suffering, the cessation of suffering, and the path for the cessation of suffering as they are attainable or unattainable.

"Furthermore, Well Appearing One, when cultivating prajna paramita, the great bodhisattvas should not contemplate the four meditations as they are permanent or impermanent, nor should they contemplate the four immeasurable minds and the four formless concentrations as they are permanent or impermanent. They should not contemplate the four meditations as they are pleasant or painful, nor should they contemplate the four immeasurable minds and the four formless concentrations as they are pleasant or painful. They should not contemplate the four meditations as they are with or without selfness, nor should they contemplate the four immeasurable minds and the four formless concentrations as they are with or without selfness. They should not contemplate the four meditations as they are pure or impure, nor should they contemplate the four immeasurable minds and the four formless concentrations as they are pure or impure. They should not contemplate the four meditations as they are empty or not empty, nor should they contemplate the four immeasurable minds and the four formless concentrations as they are empty or not empty. They should not contemplate the four meditations as they are with or without form, nor should they contemplate the four immeasurable minds and the four formless concentrations as they are with or without form. They should not contemplate the four meditations as they are with or without aspiration, nor should they contemplate the four immeasurable minds and the four formless concentrations as they are with or without aspiration. They should not contemplate the four meditations as they are tranquil or not tranquil, nor should they contemplate the four immeasurable minds and the four formless concentrations as they are tranquil or not tranquil. They should not contemplate the four meditations as they are far away or not far away, nor should they contemplate the four immeasurable minds and the four formless concentrations as they are far away or not far away. They should not contemplate the four meditations as they are conditioned or unconditioned, nor should they contemplate the four immeasurable minds and the four formless concentrations as they are conditioned or unconditioned. They should not contemplate the four meditations as they are flawed or flawless, nor should they contemplate the four immeasurable minds and the four formless concentrations as they are flawed or flawless. They should not contemplate the four meditations as they arise or extinguish, nor should they contemplate the four immeasurable minds and the four formless concentrations as they arise or extinguish. They should not contemplate the four meditations as they are virtuous or not virtuous, nor should they contemplate the four immeasurable minds and the four formless concentrations as they are virtuous or not virtuous. They should not contemplate the four meditations as they are guilty or not guilty, nor should they contemplate the four immeasurable minds and the four formless concentrations as they are guilty or not guilty. They should not contemplate the four meditations as they have vexations or have no vexations, nor should they contemplate the four immeasurable minds and the four formless concentrations as they have vexations or have no vexations. They should not contemplate the four meditations as they are of the world or beyond the world, nor should they contemplate the four immeasurable minds and the four formless concentrations as they are of the world or beyond the world. They should not contemplate the four meditations as they are contaminated or purified, nor should they contemplate the four immeasurable minds and the four formless concentrations as they are contaminated or purified. They should not contemplate the four meditations as they belong to birth and death or to nirvana, nor should they contemplate the four immeasurable minds and the four formless concentrations as they belong to birth and death or to nirvana. They should not contemplate the four meditations as they are inside, outside, or in between, nor should they contemplate the four immeasurable minds and the four formless concentrations as they are inside, outside, or in between. They should not contemplate the four meditations as they are attainable or unattainable, nor should they contemplate the four immeasurable minds and the four formless concentrations as they are attainable or unattainable.

"Furthermore, Well Appearing One, when cultivating prajna paramita, the great bodhisattvas should not contemplate the eight liberations as they are permanent or impermanent, nor should they contemplate the eight vexation-overcoming meditations, nine concentrations in sequence, and ten universal contemplations as they are permanent or impermanent. They should not contemplate the eight liberations as they are pleasant or painful, nor should they contemplate the eight vexation-overcoming meditations, nine concentrations in sequence, and ten universal contemplations as they are pleasant or painful. They should not contemplate the eight liberations as they are with or without selfness, nor should they contemplate the eight vexation-overcoming meditations, nine concentrations in sequence, and ten universal contemplations as they are with or without selfness. They should not contemplate the eight liberations as they are pure or impure, nor should they contemplate the eight vexation-overcoming meditations, nine concentrations in sequence, and ten universal contemplations as they are pure or impure. They should not contemplate the eight liberations as they are empty or not empty, nor should they contemplate the eight vexation-overcoming meditations, nine concentrations in sequence, and ten universal contemplations as they are empty or not empty. They should not contemplate the eight liberations as they are with or without form, nor should they contemplate the eight vexation-overcoming meditations, nine concentrations in sequence, and ten universal contemplations as they are with or without form. They should not contemplate the eight liberations as they are with or without aspiration, nor should they contemplate the eight vexation-overcoming meditations, nine concentrations in sequence, and ten universal contemplations as they are with or without aspiration. They should not contemplate the eight liberations as they are tranquil or not tranquil, nor should they contemplate the eight vexation-overcoming meditations, nine concentrations in sequence, and ten universal contemplations as they are tranquil or not tranquil. They should not contemplate the eight liberations as they are or they are not far away, nor should they contemplate the eight vexation-overcoming meditations, nine concentrations in sequence, and ten universal contemplations as they are or they are not far away. They should not contemplate the eight liberations as they are conditioned or unconditioned, nor should they contemplate the eight vexation-overcoming meditations, nine concentrations in sequence, and ten universal contemplations as they are conditioned or unconditioned. They should not contemplate the eight liberations as they are flawed or flawless, nor should they contemplate the eight vexation-overcoming meditations, nine concentrations in sequence, and ten universal contemplations as they are flawed or flawless. They should not contemplate the eight liberations as they arise or extinguish, nor should they contemplate the eight vexation-overcoming meditations, nine concentrations in sequence, and ten universal contemplations as they arise or extinguish. They should not contemplate the eight liberations as they are virtuous or not virtuous, nor should they contemplate the eight vexation-overcoming meditations, nine concentrations in sequence, and ten universal contemplations as they are virtuous or not virtuous. They should not contemplate the eight liberations as they are guilty or not guilty, nor should they contemplate the eight vexation-overcoming meditations, nine concentrations in sequence, and ten universal contemplations as they are guilty or not guilty. They should not contemplate the eight liberations as they have vexations or have no vexations, nor should they contemplate the eight vexation-overcoming meditations, nine concentrations in sequence, and ten universal contemplations as they have vexations or have no vexations. They should not contemplate the eight liberations as they are of the world or beyond the world, nor should they contemplate the eight vexation-overcoming meditations, nine concentrations in sequence, and ten universal contemplations as they are of the world or beyond the world. They should not contemplate the eight liberations as they are contaminated or purified, nor should they contemplate the eight vexation-overcoming meditations, nine concentrations in sequence, and ten universal contemplations as they are contaminated or purified. They should not contemplate the eight liberations as they belong to birth and death or to nirvana, nor should they contemplate the eight vexation-overcoming meditations, nine concentrations in sequence, and ten universal contemplations as they belong to birth and death or to nirvana. They should not contemplate the eight liberations as they are inside, outside, or in between, nor should they contemplate the eight vexation-overcoming meditations, nine concentrations in sequence, and ten universal contemplations as they are inside, outside, or in between. They should not contemplate the

Fascicle 12, Chapter 7, Section 2   277

eight liberations as they are attainable or unattainable, nor should they contemplate the eight vexation-overcoming meditations, nine concentrations in sequence, and ten universal contemplations as they are attainable or unattainable.

"Furthermore, Well Appearing One, when cultivating prajna paramita, the great bodhisattvas should not contemplate the liberation gate of emptiness as it is permanent or impermanent, nor should they contemplate the liberation gates of formlessness and nonaspiration as they are permanent or impermanent. They should not contemplate the liberation gate of emptiness as it is pleasant or painful, nor should they contemplate the liberation gates of formlessness and nonaspiration as they are pleasant or painful. They should not contemplate the liberation gate of emptiness as it is with or without selfness, nor should they contemplate the liberation gates of formlessness and nonaspiration as they are with or without selfness. They should not contemplate the liberation gate of emptiness as it is pure or impure, nor should they contemplate the liberation gates of formlessness and nonaspiration as they are pure or impure. They should not contemplate the liberation gate of emptiness as it is empty or not empty, nor should they contemplate the liberation gates of formlessness and nonaspiration as they are empty or not empty. They should not contemplate the liberation gate of emptiness as it is with or without form, nor should they contemplate the liberation gates of formlessness and nonaspiration as they are with or without form. They should not contemplate the liberation gate of emptiness as it is with or without aspiration, nor should they contemplate the liberation gates of formlessness and nonaspiration as they are with or without aspiration. They should not contemplate the liberation gate of emptiness as it is tranquil or not tranquil, nor should they contemplate the liberation gates of formlessness and nonaspiration as they are tranquil or not tranquil. They should not contemplate the liberation gate of emptiness as it is or it is not far away, nor should they contemplate the liberation gates of formlessness and nonaspiration as they are or they are not far away. They should not contemplate the liberation gate of emptiness as it is conditioned or unconditioned, nor should they contemplate the liberation gates of formlessness and nonaspiration as they are conditioned or unconditioned. They should not contemplate the liberation gate of emptiness as it is flawed or flawless, nor should they contemplate the liberation gates of formlessness and nonaspiration as they are flawed or flawless. They should not contemplate the liberation gate of emptiness as it arises or extinguishes, nor should they contemplate the liberation gates of formlessness and nonaspiration as they arise or extinguish. They should not contemplate the liberation gate of emptiness as it is virtuous or not virtuous, nor should they contemplate the liberation gates of formlessness and nonaspiration as they are virtuous or not virtuous. They should not contemplate the liberation gate of emptiness as it is guilty or not guilty, nor should they contemplate the liberation gates of formlessness and nonaspiration as they are guilty or not guilty. They should not contemplate the liberation gate of emptiness as it has or has no vexations, nor should they contemplate the liberation gates of formlessness and nonaspiration as they have vexations or have no vexations. They should not contemplate the liberation gate of emptiness as it is of the world or beyond the world, nor should they contemplate the liberation gates of formlessness and nonaspiration as they are of the world or beyond the world. They should not contemplate the liberation gate of emptiness as it is contaminated or purified, nor should they contemplate the liberation gates of formlessness and nonaspiration as they are contaminated or purified. They should not contemplate the liberation gate of emptiness as it belongs to birth and death or to nirvana, nor should they contemplate the liberation gates of formlessness and nonaspiration as they belong to birth and death or to nirvana. They should not contemplate the liberation gate of emptiness as it is inside, outside, or in between, nor should they contemplate the liberation gates of formlessness and nonaspiration as they are inside, outside, or in between. They should not contemplate the liberation gate of emptiness as it is attainable or unattainable, nor should they contemplate the liberation gates of formlessness and nonaspiration as they are attainable or unattainable.

"Furthermore, Well Appearing One, when cultivating prajna paramita, the great bodhisattvas should not contemplate the dharani gates as they are permanent or impermanent, nor should they contemplate the samadhi gates as they are permanent or impermanent. They should not contemplate the dharani gates as they are pleasant and painful, nor should they contemplate the samadhi gates as they are pleasant or painful. They should not contemplate the dharani gates as they are with or without selfness, nor should they contemplate the samadhi gates as they are with or without selfness. They should not contemplate the dharani gates as they are pure or impure, nor should they contemplate the samadhi gates as they are pure or impure. They should not contemplate the dharani gates as they are empty or not empty, nor should they contemplate the samadhi gates as they are empty or not empty. They should not contemplate the dharani gates as they are with or without form, nor should they contemplate the samadhi gates as they are with or without form. They should not contemplate the dharani gates as they are with or without aspiration, nor should they contemplate the samadhi gates as they are with or without aspiration. They should not contemplate the dharani gates as they are tranquil or not tranquil, nor should they contemplate the samadhi gates as they are tranquil or not tranquil. They should not contemplate the dharani gates as they are far away or not far away, nor should they contemplate the samadhi gates as they are far away or not far away. They should not contemplate the dharani gates as they are conditioned or unconditioned, nor should they contemplate the samadhi gates as they are conditioned or unconditioned. They should not contemplate the dharani gates as they are flawed or flawless, nor should they contemplate the samadhi gates as they are flawed or flawless. They should not contemplate the dharani gates as they arise or extinguish, nor should they contemplate the samadhi gates as they arise or extinguish. They should not contemplate the dharani gates as they are virtuous or not virtuous, nor should contemplate the samadhi gates as they are virtuous or not virtuous. They should not contemplate the dharani gates as they are guilty or not guilty, nor should they contemplate the samadhi gates as they are guilty or not guilty. They should not contemplate the dharani gates as they have or have no vexations, nor should they contemplate the samadhi gates as they have or have no vexations. They should not contemplate the dharani gates as they are of the world or beyond the world, nor should they contemplate the samadhi gates as they are of the world or beyond the world. They should not contemplate the dharani gates as they are contaminated or purified, nor should they contemplate the samadhi gates as they are contaminated or purified. They should not contemplate the dharani gates as they belong to birth and death or to nirvana, nor should they contemplate the samadhi gates as they belong to birth and death or to nirvana. They should not contemplate the dharani gates as they are inside, outside, or in between, nor should they contemplate the samadhi gates as they are inside, outside, or in between. They should not contemplate the dharani gates as they are attainable or unattainable, nor should they contemplate the samadhi gates as they are attainable or unattainable.

"Furthermore, Well Appearing One, when cultivating prajna paramita, the great bodhisattvas should not contemplate the stage of ecstasy as it is permanent or impermanent, nor should they contemplate the stages of freedom from defilements, emitting light, flaming wisdom, being extremely difficult to be surpassed, manifestation of pure realness, going far away, the unmovable, expedient wisdom, and dharma cloud as they are permanent or impermanent. They should not contemplate the stage of ecstasy as it is pleasant or painful, nor should they contemplate the stage of freedom from defilements, and so forth, as well as the stage of dharma cloud as they are pleasant or painful. They should not contemplate the stage of ecstasy as it is with or without selfness, nor should they contemplate the stage of freedom from defilements, and so forth, as well as the stage of dharma cloud as they are with or without selfness. They should not contemplate the stage of ecstasy as it is pure or impure, nor should they contemplate the stage of freedom from defilements, and so forth, as well as the stage of dharma cloud as they are pure or impure. They should not contemplate the stage of ecstasy as it is empty or not empty, nor should they contemplate the stage of freedom from defilements, and so forth, as well as the stage of dharma cloud as they are empty or not empty. They should not contemplate the stage of ecstasy as it is with or without form, nor should they contemplate the stage of freedom from defilements, and so forth, as well as the stage of dharma cloud as

Fascicle 12, Chapter 7, Section 2   281

they are with or without form. They should not contemplate the stage of ecstasy as it is with or without aspiration, nor should they contemplate the stage of freedom from defilements, and so forth, as well as the stage of dharma cloud as they are with or without aspiration. They should not contemplate the stage of ecstasy as it is tranquil or not tranquil, nor should they contemplate the stage of freedom from defilements, and so forth, as well as the stage of dharma cloud as they are tranquil or not tranquil. They should not contemplate the stage of ecstasy as it is or it is not far away, nor should they contemplate the stage of freedom from defilements, and so forth, as well as the stage of dharma cloud as they are or they are not far away. They should not contemplate the stage of ecstasy as it is conditioned or unconditioned, nor should they contemplate the stage of freedom from defilements, and so forth, as well as the stage of dharma cloud as they are conditioned or unconditioned. They should not contemplate the stage of ecstasy as it is flawed or flawless, nor should they contemplate the stage of freedom from defilements, and so forth, as well as the stage of dharma cloud as they are flawed or flawless. They should not contemplate the stage of ecstasy as it arises or extinguishes, nor should they contemplate the stage of freedom from defilements, and so forth, as well as the stage of dharma cloud as they arise or extinguish. They should not contemplate the stage of ecstasy as it is virtuous or not virtuous, nor should they contemplate the stage of freedom from defilements, and so forth, as well as the stage of dharma cloud as they are virtuous or not virtuous. They should not contemplate the stage of ecstasy as it is guilty or not guilty, nor should they contemplate the stage of freedom from defilements, and so forth, as well as the stage of dharma cloud as they are guilty or not guilty. They should not contemplate the stage of ecstasy as it has or has no vexations, nor should they contemplate the stage of freedom from defilements, and so forth, as well as the stage of dharma cloud as they have or have no vexations. They should not contemplate the stage of ecstasy as it is of the world or beyond the world, nor should they contemplate the stage of freedom from defilements, and so forth, as well as the stage of dharma cloud as they are of the world or beyond the world. They should not contemplate the stage of ecstasy as it is contaminated or purified, nor should they contemplate the stage of freedom from defilements, and so forth, as well as the stage of dharma cloud as they are contaminated or purified. They should not contemplate the stage of ecstasy as it belongs to birth and death or to nirvana, nor should they contemplate the stage of freedom from defilements, and so forth, as well as the stage of dharma cloud as they belong to birth and death or to nirvana. They should not contemplate the stage of ecstasy as it is inside, outside, or in between, nor should they contemplate the stage of freedom from defilements, and so forth, as well as the stage of dharma cloud as they are inside, outside, or in between. They should not contemplate the stage of ecstasy as it is attainable or unattainable, nor should they contemplate the stage of freedom from defilements, and so forth, as well as the stage of dharma cloud as they are attainable or unattainable.

"Furthermore, Well Appearing One, when cultivating prajna paramita, the great bodhisattvas should not contemplate the five eyes as they are permanent or impermanent, nor should they contemplate the six supernatural powers as they are permanent or impermanent. They should not contemplate the five eyes as they are pleasant and painful, nor should they contemplate the six supernatural powers as they are pleasant or painful. They should not contemplate the five eyes as they are with or without selfness, nor should they contemplate the six supernatural powers as they are with or without selfness. They should not contemplate the five eyes as they are pure or impure, nor should they contemplate the six supernatural powers as they are pure or impure. They should not contemplate the five eyes as they are empty or not empty, nor should they contemplate the six supernatural powers as they are empty or not empty. They should not contemplate the five eyes as they are with or without form, nor should they contemplate six supernatural powers as they are with or without form. They should not contemplate the five eyes as they are with or without aspiration, nor should they contemplate the six supernatural powers as they are with or without aspiration. They should not contemplate the five eyes as they are tranquil or not tranquil, nor should they contemplate the six supernatural powers as they are tranquil or not tranquil. They should not contemplate the five eyes as they are far away or not far away, nor should they contemplate the six supernatural powers as they are far away or not far away. They should not contemplate the five eyes as they are conditioned or unconditioned, nor should they contemplate the six supernatural powers as they are conditioned or unconditioned. They should not contemplate the five eyes as they are flawed or flawless, nor should they contemplate the six supernatural powers as they are flawed or flawless. They should not contemplate the five eyes as they arise or extinguish, nor should they contemplate the six supernatural powers as they arise or extinguish. They should not contemplate the five eyes as they are virtuous or not virtuous, nor should they contemplate the six supernatural powers as they are virtuous or not virtuous. They should not contemplate the five eyes as they are guilty or not guilty, nor should they contemplate the six supernatural powers as they are guilty or not guilty. They should not contemplate the five eyes as they have vexations or have no vexations, nor should they contemplate the six supernatural powers as they have vexations or have no vexations. They should not contemplate the five eyes as they are of the world or beyond the world, nor should they contemplate the six supernatural powers as they are of the world or beyond the world. They should not contemplate the five eyes as they are contaminated or purified, nor should they contemplate the six supernatural powers as they are contaminated or purified. They should not contemplate the five eyes as they belong to birth and death or to nirvana, nor should they contemplate the six supernatural powers as they belong to birth and death or to nirvana. They should not contemplate the five eyes as they are inside, outside, or in between, nor should they contemplate the six supernatural powers as they are inside, outside, or in between. They should not contemplate the five eyes as they are attainable or unattainable, nor should they contemplate the six supernatural powers as they are attainable or unattainable.

FASCICLE 13

Chapter 7
The Cautions and the Teachings

Section 3

(In the First Assembly)

"FURTHERMORE, WELL APPEARING ONE, WHEN CULTIVATING PRAJNA PARAMITA, the great bodhisattvas should not contemplate the Buddha's ten abilities as they are permanent or impermanent, nor should they contemplate the four kinds of fearlessness, four unhindered understandings, and the eighteen distinctive features of Buddha's wisdom and power as they are permanent or impermanent. They should not contemplate the Buddha's ten abilities as they are pleasant or painful, nor should they contemplate the four kinds of fearlessness, four unhindered understandings, and the eighteen distinctive features of Buddha's wisdom and power as they are pleasant or painful. They should not contemplate the Buddha's ten abilities as they are with or without selfness, nor should they contemplate the four kinds of fearlessness, four unhindered understandings, and the eighteen distinctive features of Buddha's wisdom and power as they are with or without selfness. They should not contemplate the Buddha's ten abilities as they are pure or impure, nor should they contemplate the four kinds of fearlessness, four unhindered understandings, and the eighteen distinctive features of Buddha's wisdom and power as they are pure or impure. They should not contemplate the Buddha's ten abilities as they are empty or not empty, nor should they contemplate the four kinds of fearlessness, four unhindered understandings, and the eighteen distinctive features of Buddha's wisdom and power as they are empty or not empty. They should not contemplate the Buddha's ten abilities as they are with or without form, nor should they contemplate the four kinds of fearlessness, four unhindered understandings, and the eighteen distinctive features of Buddha's wisdom and power as they are with or without form. They should not contemplate the Buddha's ten abilities as they are with or without aspiration, nor should they contemplate the four kinds of fearlessness, four unhindered understandings, and the eighteen distinctive features of Buddha's wisdom and power as they are with or without aspiration. They should not contemplate Buddha's ten abilities as they are tranquil or not tranquil, nor should they contemplate the four kinds of fearlessness, four unhindered understandings, and the eighteen distinctive features of Buddha's wisdom and power as they are tranquil or not tranquil. They should not contemplate the Buddha's ten abilities as they are far away or not far away, nor should they contemplate the four kinds of fearlessness, four unhindered understandings, and the eighteen distinctive features of Buddha's wisdom and power as they are far away or not far away. They should not contemplate the Buddha's ten abilities as they are conditioned or unconditioned, nor should they contemplate the four kinds of fearlessness, four unhindered understandings, and the eighteen distinctive features of Buddha's wisdom and power as they are conditioned or unconditioned. They should not contemplate the Buddha's ten abilities as they are flawed or flawless, nor should they contemplate the four kinds of fearlessness, four unhindered understandings, and the eighteen distinctive features of Buddha's wisdom and power as they are flawed or flawless. They should not contemplate the Buddha's ten abilities as they are with arising or extinction, nor should they contemplate the four kinds of fearlessness, four unhindered understandings, and the eighteen distinctive features of Buddha's wisdom and power as they are with arising or extinction. They should not contemplate the Buddha's ten abilities as they are virtuous or not virtuous, nor should they contemplate the four kinds of fearlessness, four unhindered understandings, and the eighteen distinctive features of Buddha's wisdom and power as they are virtuous or not virtuous. They should not contemplate the Buddha's ten abilities as they are guilty or not guilty, nor should they contemplate the four kinds of fearlessness, four unhindered understandings, and the eighteen distinctive features of Buddha's wisdom and power as they are guilty or not guilty. They should not contemplate the Buddha's ten abilities as they are with or without vexations, nor should they contemplate the four kinds of fearlessness, four unhindered understandings, and the eighteen distinctive features of Buddha's wisdom and power as they are with or without vexations. They should not contemplate the Buddha's ten abilities as they are of the world or beyond the world, nor should they contemplate the four kinds of fearlessness, four unhindered understandings, and the eighteen distinctive features of Buddha's wisdom and power as they are of the world or beyond the world. They should not contemplate the Buddha's ten abilities as they are contaminated or purified, nor should they contemplate the four kinds of fearlessness, four unhindered understandings, and the eighteen distinctive features of Buddha's wisdom and power as they are contaminated or purified. They should not contemplate the Buddha's ten abilities as they belong to birth and death or to nirvana, nor should they contemplate the four kinds of fearlessness, four unhindered understandings, and the eighteen distinctive features of Buddha's wisdom and power as they belong to birth and death or to nirvana. They should not contemplate the Buddha's ten abilities as they are inside, outside, or in between, nor should they contemplate the four kinds of fearlessness, four unhindered understandings, and the eighteen distinctive features of Buddha's wisdom and power as they are inside, outside, or in between. They should not contemplate the Buddha's ten abilities as they are attainable or unattainable, nor should they contemplate the four kinds of fearlessness, four unhindered understandings, and the eighteen distinctive features of Buddha's wisdom and power as they are attainable or unattainable.

Fascicle 13, Chapter 7, Section 3   287

"Furthermore, Well Appearing One, when cultivating prajna paramita, the great bodhisattvas should not contemplate great loving-kindness as it is permanent or impermanent, nor should they contemplate great compassion, great joy, and great equanimity as they are permanent or impermanent. They should not contemplate great loving-kindness as it is pleasant or painful, nor should they contemplate great compassion, great joy, and great equanimity as they are pleasant or painful. They should not contemplate great loving-kindness as it is with or without selfness, nor should they contemplate great compassion, great joy, and great equanimity as they are with or without selfness. They should not contemplate great loving-kindness as it is pure or impure, nor should they contemplate great compassion, great joy, and great equanimity as they are pure or impure. They should not contemplate great loving-kindness as it is empty or not empty, nor should they contemplate great compassion, great joy, and great equanimity as they are empty or not empty. They should not contemplate great loving-kindness as it is with or without form, nor should they contemplate great compassion, great joy, and great equanimity as they are with or without form. They should not contemplate great loving-kindness as it is with or without aspiration, nor should they contemplate great compassion, great joy, and great equanimity as they are with or without aspiration. They should not contemplate great loving-kindness as it is tranquil or not tranquil, nor should they contemplate great compassion, great joy, and great equanimity as they are tranquil or not tranquil. They should not contemplate great loving-kindness as it is far away or not far away, nor should they contemplate great compassion, great joy, and great equanimity as they are far away or not far away. They should not contemplate great loving-kindness as it is conditioned or unconditioned, nor should they contemplate great compassion, great joy, and great equanimity as they are conditioned or unconditioned. They should not contemplate great loving-kindness as it is flawed or flawless, nor should they contemplate great compassion, great joy, and great equanimity as they are flawed or flawless. They should not contemplate great loving-kindness as it is with arising or extinction, nor should they contemplate great compassion, great joy, and great equanimity as they are with arising or extinction. They should not contemplate great loving-kindness as it is virtuous or not virtuous, nor should they contemplate great compassion, great joy, and great equanimity as they are virtuous or not virtuous. They should not contemplate great loving-kindness as it is guilty or not guilty, nor should they contemplate great compassion, great joy, and great equanimity as they are guilty or not guilty. They should not contemplate great loving-kindness as it is with or without vexations, nor should they contemplate great compassion, great joy, and great equanimity as they are with or without vexations. They should not contemplate great loving-kindness as it is of the world or beyond the world, nor should they contemplate great compassion, great joy, and great equanimity as they are of the world or beyond the world. They should not contemplate great loving-kindness as it is contaminated or purified, nor should they contemplate great compassion, great joy, and great equanimity as they are contaminated or purified. They should not contemplate great loving-kindness as it belongs to birth and death or to nirvana, nor should they contemplate great compassion, great joy, and great equanimity as they belong to birth and death or to nirvana. They should not contemplate great loving-kindness as it is inside, outside, or in between, nor should they contemplate great compassion, great joy, and great equanimity as they are inside, outside, or in between. They should not contemplate great loving-kindness as it is attainable or unattainable, nor should they contemplate great compassion, great joy, and great equanimity as they are attainable or unattainable.

"Furthermore, Well Appearing One, when cultivating prajna paramita, the great bodhisattvas should not contemplate the thirty-two perfect major marks as they are permanent or impermanent, nor should they contemplate the eighty distinguishing minor features as they are permanent or impermanent. They should not contemplate the thirty-two perfect major marks as they are pleasant or painful, nor should they contemplate the eighty distinguishing minor features as they are pleasant or painful. They should not contemplate the thirty-two perfect major marks as they are with or without selfness, nor should they contemplate the eighty distinguishing minor features as they are with or without selfness.

Fascicle 13, Chapter 7, Section 3

They should not contemplate the thirty-two perfect major marks as they are pure or impure, nor should they contemplate the eighty distinguishing minor features as they are pure or impure. They should not contemplate the thirty-two perfect major marks as they are empty or not empty, nor should they contemplate the eighty distinguishing minor features as they are empty or not empty. They should not contemplate the thirty-two perfect major marks as they are with or without form, nor should they contemplate the eighty distinguishing minor features as they are with or without form. They should not contemplate the thirty-two perfect major marks as they are with or without aspiration, nor should contemplate the eighty distinguishing minor features as they are with or without aspiration. They should not contemplate the thirty-two perfect major marks as they are tranquil or not tranquil, nor should they contemplate the eighty distinguishing minor features as they are tranquil or not tranquil. They should not contemplate the thirty-two perfect major marks as they are far away or not far away, nor should they contemplate the eighty distinguishing minor features as they are far away or not far away. They should not contemplate the thirty-two perfect major marks as they are conditioned or unconditioned, nor should they contemplate the eighty distinguishing minor features as they are conditioned or unconditioned. They should not contemplate the thirty-two perfect major marks as they are flawed or flawless, nor should they contemplate the eighty distinguishing minor features as they are flawed or flawless. They should not contemplate the thirty-two perfect major marks as they are with arising or extinction, nor should they contemplate the eighty distinguishing minor features as they are with arising or extinction. They should not contemplate the thirty-two perfect major marks as they are virtuous or not virtuous, nor should contemplate the eighty distinguishing minor features as they are virtuous or not virtuous. They should not contemplate the thirty-two perfect major marks as they are guilty or not guilty, nor should they contemplate the eighty distinguishing minor features as they are guilty or not guilty. They should not contemplate the thirty-two perfect major marks as they are with or without vexations, nor should they contemplate the eighty distinguishing minor features as they are with or without vexations. They should not contemplate the thirty-two perfect major marks as they are of the world or beyond the world, nor should they contemplate the eighty distinguishing minor features as they are of the world or beyond the world. They should not contemplate the thirty-two perfect major marks as they are contaminated or purified, nor should they contemplate the eighty distinguishing minor features as they are contaminated or purified. They should not contemplate the thirty-two perfect major marks as they belong to birth and death or to nirvana, nor should they contemplate the eighty distinguishing minor features as they belong to birth and death or to nirvana. They should not contemplate the thirty-two perfect major marks as they are inside, outside, or in between, nor should they contemplate the eighty distinguishing minor features as they are inside, outside, or in between. They should not contemplate the thirty-two perfect major marks as they are attainable or unattainable, nor should they contemplate the eighty distinguishing minor features as they are attainable or unattainable.

"Furthermore, Well Appearing One, when cultivating prajna paramita, the great bodhisattvas should not contemplate staying in correct mindfulness as it is permanent or impermanent, nor should they contemplate dwelling in equanimity at all times as it is permanent or impermanent. They should not contemplate staying in correct mindfulness as it is pleasant or painful, nor should they contemplate dwelling in equanimity at all times as it is pleasant or painful. They should not contemplate staying in correct mindfulness as it is with or without selfness, nor should they contemplate dwelling in equanimity at all times as it is with or without selfness. They should not contemplate staying in correct mindfulness as it is pure or impure, nor should they contemplate dwelling in equanimity at all times as it is pure or impure. They should not contemplate staying in correct mindfulness as it is empty or not empty, nor should they contemplate dwelling in equanimity at all times as it is empty or not empty. They should not contemplate staying in correct mindfulness as it is with or without form, nor should they contemplate dwelling in equanimity at all times as it is with or without form. They should not contemplate staying in correct mindfulness as it is with or without aspiration, nor should they contemplate dwelling in equanimity at all times as it is with or without aspiration. They should not contemplate staying in correct mindfulness as it is tranquil or not tranquil, nor should they contemplate dwelling in equanimity at all times as it is tranquil or not tranquil. They should not contemplate staying in correct mindfulness as it is far away or not far away, nor should they contemplate dwelling in equanimity at all times as it is far away or not far away. They should not contemplate staying in correct mindfulness as it is conditioned or unconditioned, nor should they contemplate dwelling in equanimity at all times as it is conditioned or unconditioned. They should not contemplate staying in correct mindfulness as it is flawed or flawless, nor should they contemplate dwelling in equanimity at all times as it is flawed or flawless. They should not contemplate staying in correct mindfulness as it is with arising or extinction, nor should they contemplate dwelling in equanimity at all times as it is with arising or extinction. They should not contemplate staying in correct mindfulness as it is virtuous or not virtuous, nor should they contemplate dwelling in equanimity at all times as it is virtuous or not virtuous. They should not contemplate staying in correct mindfulness as it is guilty or not guilty, nor should they contemplate dwelling in equanimity at all times as it is guilty or not guilty. They should not contemplate staying in correct mindfulness as it is with or without vexations, nor should they contemplate dwelling in equanimity at all times as it is with or without vexations. They should not contemplate staying in correct mindfulness as it is of the world or beyond the world, nor should they contemplate dwelling in equanimity at all times as it is of the world or beyond the world. They should not contemplate staying in correct mindfulness as it is contaminated or purified, nor should they contemplate dwelling in equanimity at all times as it is contaminated or purified. They should not contemplate staying in correct mindfulness as it belongs to birth and death or to nirvana, nor should they contemplate dwelling in equanimity at all times as it belongs to birth and death or to nirvana. They should not contemplate staying in correct mindfulness as it is inside, outside, or in between, nor should they contemplate dwelling in equanimity at all times as it is inside, outside, or in between. They should not contemplate staying in correct mindfulness as it is attainable or unattainable, nor should they contemplate dwelling in equanimity at all times as it is attainable or unattainable.

"Furthermore, Well Appearing One, when cultivating prajna paramita, the great bodhisattvas should not contemplate the perfect knowledge of everything as it is permanent or impermanent, nor should they contemplate the perfect knowledge of the forms of the paths and the perfect knowledge of all phenomena as they are permanent or impermanent. They should not contemplate the perfect knowledge of everything as it is pleasant or painful, nor should they contemplate the perfect knowledge of the forms of the paths and the perfect knowledge of all phenomena as they are pleasant or painful. They should not contemplate the perfect knowledge of everything as it is with or without selfness, nor should they contemplate the perfect knowledge of the forms of the paths and the perfect knowledge of all phenomena as they are with or without selfness. They should not contemplate the perfect knowledge of everything as it is pure or impure, nor should they contemplate the perfect knowledge of the forms of the paths and the perfect knowledge of all phenomena as they are pure or impure. They should not contemplate the perfect knowledge of everything as it is empty or not empty, nor should they contemplate the perfect knowledge of the forms of the paths and the perfect knowledge of all phenomena as they are empty or not empty. They should not contemplate the perfect knowledge of everything as it is with or without form, nor should they contemplate the perfect knowledge of the forms of the paths and the perfect knowledge of all phenomena as they are with or without form. They should not contemplate the perfect knowledge of everything as it is with or without aspiration, nor should they contemplate the perfect knowledge of the forms of the paths and the perfect knowledge of all phenomena as they are with or without aspiration. They should not contemplate the perfect knowledge of everything as it is tranquil or not tranquil, nor should they contemplate the perfect knowledge of the forms of the paths and the perfect knowledge of all phenomena as they are tranquil or not tranquil. They should not contemplate the perfect knowl-

Fascicle 13, Chapter 7, Section 3

edge of everything as it is far away or not far away, nor should they contemplate the perfect knowledge of the forms of the paths and the perfect knowledge of all phenomena as they are far away or not far away. They should not contemplate the perfect knowledge of everything as it is conditioned or unconditioned, nor should they contemplate the perfect knowledge of the forms of the paths and the perfect knowledge of all phenomena as they are conditioned or unconditioned. They should not contemplate the perfect knowledge of everything as it is flawed or flawless, nor should they contemplate the perfect knowledge of the forms of the paths and the perfect knowledge of all phenomena as they are flawed or flawless. They should not contemplate the perfect knowledge of everything as it is with arising or extinction, nor should they contemplate the perfect knowledge of the forms of the paths and the perfect knowledge of all phenomena as they are with arising or extinction. They should not contemplate the perfect knowledge of everything as it is virtuous or not virtuous, nor should they contemplate the perfect knowledge of the forms of the paths and the perfect knowledge of all phenomena as they are virtuous or not virtuous. They should not contemplate the perfect knowledge of everything as it is guilty or not guilty, nor should they contemplate the perfect knowledge of the forms of the paths and the perfect knowledge of all phenomena as they are guilty or not guilty. They should not contemplate the perfect knowledge of everything as it is with or without vexations, nor should they contemplate the perfect knowledge of the forms of the paths and the perfect knowledge of all phenomena as with or without vexations. They should not contemplate the perfect knowledge of everything as it is of the world or beyond the world, nor should they contemplate the perfect knowledge of the forms of the paths and the perfect knowledge of all phenomena as they are of the world or beyond the world. They should not contemplate the perfect knowledge of everything as it is contaminated or purified, nor should they contemplate the perfect knowledge of the forms of the paths and the perfect knowledge of all phenomena as they are contaminated or purified. They should not contemplate the perfect knowledge of everything as it belongs to birth and death or to nirvana, nor should they contemplate the perfect knowledge of the forms of the paths and the perfect knowledge of all phenomena as they belong to birth and death or to nirvana. They should not contemplate the perfect knowledge of everything as it is inside, outside, or in between, nor should they contemplate the perfect knowledge of the forms of the paths and the perfect knowledge of all phenomena as they are inside, outside, or in between. They should not contemplate the perfect knowledge of everything as it is attainable or unattainable, nor should they contemplate the perfect knowledge of the forms of the paths and the perfect knowledge of all phenomena as they are attainable or unattainable.

"Furthermore, Well Appearing One, when cultivating prajna paramita, the great bodhisattvas should not contemplate stream-entry effect as it is permanent or impermanent, nor should they contemplate once-return effect, nonreturn effect, arhat effect, and self-enlightenment bodhi as they are permanent or impermanent. They should not contemplate stream-entry effect as it is pleasant or painful, nor should they contemplate once-return effect, nonreturn effect, arhat effect, and self-enlightenment bodhi as they are pleasant or painful. They should not contemplate stream-entry effect as it is with or without selfness, nor should they contemplate once-return effect, nonreturn effect, arhat effect, and self-enlightenment bodhi as they are with or without selfness. They should not contemplate stream-entry effect as it is pure or impure, nor should they contemplate once-return effect, nonreturn effect, arhat effect, and self-enlightenment bodhi as they are pure or impure. They should not contemplate stream-entry effect as it is empty or not empty, nor should they contemplate once-return effect, nonreturn effect, arhat effect, and self-enlightenment bodhi as they are empty or not empty. They should not contemplate stream-entry effect as it is with or without form, nor should they contemplate once-return effect, nonreturn effect, arhat effect, and self-enlightenment bodhi as they are with or without form. They should not contemplate stream-entry effect as it is with or without aspiration, nor should they contemplate once-return effect, nonreturn effect, arhat effect, and self-enlightenment bodhi as they are with or without aspiration. They should not contemplate stream-entry effect as it is tranquil or not tranquil, nor should they contemplate once-return effect, nonreturn effect, arhat effect, and self-enlightenment bodhi as they are tranquil or not tranquil. They should not contemplate stream-entry effect as it is far away or not far away, nor should they contemplate once-return effect, nonreturn effect, arhat effect, and self-enlightenment bodhi as they are far away or not far away. They should not contemplate stream-entry effect as it is conditioned or unconditioned, nor should they contemplate once-return effect, nonreturn effect, arhat effect, and self-enlightenment bodhi as they are conditioned or unconditioned. They should not contemplate stream-entry effect as it is flawed or flawless, nor should they contemplate once-return effect, nonreturn effect, arhat effect, and self-enlightenment bodhi as they are flawed or flawless. They should not contemplate stream-entry effect as it is with arising or extinction, nor should they contemplate once-return effect, nonreturn effect, arhat effect, and self-enlightenment bodhi as they are with arising or extinction. They should not contemplate stream-entry effect as it is virtuous or not virtuous, nor should they contemplate once-return effect, nonreturn effect, arhat effect, and self-enlightenment bodhi as they are virtuous or not virtuous. They should not contemplate stream-entry effect as it is guilty or not guilty, nor should they contemplate once-return effect, nonreturn effect, arhat effect, and self-enlightenment bodhi as they are guilty or not guilty. They should not contemplate stream-entry effect as it is with or without vexations, nor should they contemplate once-return effect, nonreturn effect, arhat effect, and self-enlightenment bodhi as they are with or without vexations. They should not contemplate stream-entry effect as it is of the world or beyond the world, nor should they contemplate once-return effect, nonreturn effect, arhat effect, and self-enlightenment bodhi as they are of world or beyond the world. They should not contemplate stream-entry effect as it is contaminated or purified, nor should they contemplate once-return effect, nonreturn effect, arhat effect, and self-enlightenment bodhi as they are contaminated or purified. They should not contemplate stream-entry effect as it belongs to birth and death or to nirvana, nor should they contemplate once-return effect, nonreturn effect, arhat effect, and self-enlightenment bodhi as they belong to birth and death or to nirvana. They should not contemplate stream-entry effect as it is inside, outside, or in between, nor should they contemplate once-return effect, nonreturn effect, arhat effect, and self-enlightenment bodhi as they are inside, outside, or in between. They should not contemplate stream-entry effect as it is attainable or unattainable, nor should they contemplate once-return effect, nonreturn effect, arhat effect, and self-enlightenment bodhi as they are attainable or unattainable.

"Furthermore, Well Appearing One, when cultivating prajna paramita, the great bodhisattvas should not contemplate all great bodhisattva actions as they are permanent or impermanent, nor should they contemplate the unsurpassed, perfect, and universal bodhi of the Buddhas as it is permanent or impermanent. They should not contemplate all great bodhisattva actions as they are pleasant or painful, nor should they contemplate the unsurpassed, perfect, and universal bodhi of the Buddhas as it is pleasant or painful. They should not contemplate all great bodhisattva actions as they are with or without selfness, nor should they contemplate the unsurpassed, perfect, and universal bodhi of the Buddhas as it is with or without selfness. They should not contemplate all great bodhisattva actions as they are pure or impure, nor should they contemplate the unsurpassed, perfect, and universal bodhi of the Buddhas as it is pure or impure. They should not contemplate all great bodhisattva actions as they are empty or not empty, nor should they contemplate the unsurpassed, perfect, and universal bodhi of the Buddhas as it is empty or not empty. They should not contemplate all great bodhisattva actions as they are with or without form, nor should they contemplate the unsurpassed, perfect, and universal bodhi of the Buddhas as it is with or without form. They should not contemplate all great bodhisattva actions as they are with or without aspiration, nor should they contemplate the unsurpassed, perfect, and universal bodhi of the Buddhas as it is with or without aspiration. They should not contemplate all great bodhisattva actions as they are tranquil or not tranquil, nor should they contemplate the unsurpassed, perfect, and universal bodhi of the Buddhas as it is tranquil or not tranquil. They should not contemplate all great bodhisattva actions as they are far away or not far away, nor should they contemplate the unsurpassed, perfect,

Fascicle 13, Chapter 7, Section 3   297

and universal bodhi of the Buddhas as it is far away or not far away. They should not contemplate all great bodhisattva actions as they are conditioned or unconditioned, nor should they contemplate the unsurpassed, perfect, and universal bodhi of the Buddhas as it is conditioned or unconditioned. They should not contemplate all great bodhisattva actions as they are flawed or flawless, nor should they contemplate the unsurpassed, perfect, and universal bodhi of the Buddhas as it is flawed or flawless. They should not contemplate all great bodhisattva actions as they are with arising or extinction, nor should they contemplate the unsurpassed, perfect, and universal bodhi of the Buddhas as it is with arising or extinction. They should not contemplate all great bodhisattva actions as they are virtuous or not virtuous, nor should they contemplate the unsurpassed, perfect, and universal bodhi of the Buddhas as it is virtuous or not virtuous. They should not contemplate all great bodhisattva actions as they are guilty or not guilty, nor should they contemplate the unsurpassed, perfect, and universal bodhi of the Buddhas as it is guilty or not guilty. They should not contemplate all great bodhisattva actions as they are with or without vexations, nor should they contemplate the unsurpassed, perfect, and universal bodhi of the Buddhas as it is with or without vexations. They should not contemplate all great bodhisattva actions as they are of the world or beyond the world, nor should they contemplate the unsurpassed, perfect, and universal bodhi of the Buddhas as it is of the world or beyond the world. They should not contemplate all great bodhisattva actions as they are contaminated or purified, nor should they contemplate the unsurpassed, perfect, and universal bodhi of the Buddhas as it is contaminated or purified. They should not contemplate all great bodhisattva actions as they belong to birth and death or to nirvana, nor should they contemplate the unsurpassed, perfect, and universal bodhi of the Buddhas as it belongs to birth and death or to nirvana. They should not contemplate all great bodhisattva actions as they are inside, outside, or in between, nor should they contemplate the unsurpassed, perfect, and universal bodhi of the Buddhas as it is inside, outside, or in between. They should not contemplate all great bodhisattva actions as they are attainable or unattainable, nor should they contemplate the unsurpassed, perfect, and universal bodhi of the Buddhas as it is attainable or unattainable.

"Furthermore, Well Appearing One, when cultivating prajna paramita, the great bodhisattvas do not see great bodhisattva, prajna paramita, the name of great bodhisattva, and the name of prajna paramita either in the conditioned realm or in the unconditioned realm. Why? Well Appearing One, when cultivating prajna paramita, the great bodhisattvas do not have differentiation arising in their minds. Well Appearing One, when cultivating prajna paramita, the great bodhisattvas dwell in nondifferentiation of all dharmas, therefore they are able to cultivate giving, pure precept, forbearance, diligence, meditation, and prajna paramitas. They are able to dwell in internal emptiness, external emptiness, internal-external emptiness, emptiness of emptiness, emptiness of space, emptiness of ultimate truth, emptiness of conditioned phenomena, emptiness of unconditioned reality, emptiness in the final analysis, emptiness of nontemporality, emptiness of deconstruction, emptiness of changelessness, emptiness of original nature, emptiness of particular characteristics, emptiness of common characteristics, emptiness of all dharmas, emptiness of nonattainment, emptiness of selflessness, emptiness of self-nature, and emptiness of selfless self-nature. They are able to dwell in realness, dharma realm, dharma nature, the nature of nonillusion, the nature of changelessness, the nature of equality, the nature of nonarising, dharma concentration, dharma dwelling, reality, the realm of empty space, and the realm of the inconceivable. They are able to cultivate the four bases of mindfulness, four correct endeavors, four bases of power, five roots, five powers, seven factors for enlightenment, and the noble eightfold path. They are able to dwell in the noble truths of suffering, the cause of suffering, the cessation of suffering, and the path for the cessation of suffering. They are able to cultivate the four meditations, four immeasurable minds, and four formless concentrations. They are able to cultivate the eight liberations, eight vexation-overcoming meditations, nine concentrations in sequence, and ten universal contemplations. They are able to cultivate the liberation gates of emptiness, formlessness, and nonaspiration. They are able to cultivate all dharani gates and all samadhi gates. They are able to cultivate the stages of ecstasy, freedom from defilements, emitting light, flaming wisdom, being extremely difficult to be surpassed, manifestation of pure realness, going far away, the unmovable, expedient wisdom, and dharma cloud. They are able to cultivate the five eyes and the six supernatural powers. They are able to cultivate the Buddha's ten abilities, four kinds of fearlessness, four unhindered understandings, great loving-kindness, great compassion, great joy, great equanimity, and eighteen distinctive features of Buddha's wisdom and power. They are able to cultivate staying in correct mindfulness and dwelling in equanimity at all times. They are able to cultivate the perfect knowledge of everything, the perfect knowledge of the forms of the paths, and the perfect knowledge of all phenomena.

"Well Appearing One, at that time the great bodhisattvas do not see the great bodhisattva and the name of great bodhisattva, nor do they see prajna paramita and the name of prajna paramita. They are but wholeheartedly dedicated to a correct and diligent pursuit of the perfect knowledge of all perfect knowledge. Why? Well Appearing One, when cultivating prajna paramita, these great bodhisattvas have well understood the real phenomena of all dharmas thoroughly and know that there is neither contamination nor purification in them.

"Furthermore, Well Appearing One, when cultivating prajna paramita, the great bodhisattvas should be aware that both the names and the dharmas are provisionally created. Well Appearing One, after being aware of the reality of both provisionally established names and dharmas, the great bodhisattvas will not be attached to matter, feeling, thinking, intention, and consciousness. They will not be attached to the eye, ear, nose, tongue, body, and conscious spheres. They will not be attached to the sight, sound, smell, taste, touch, and mental-image spheres. They will not be attached to the eye, ear, nose, tongue, body, and conscious realms. They will not be attached to the sight, sound, smell, taste, touch, and mental-image realms. They will not be attached to the eye, ear, nose, tongue, body, and conscious consciousness realms. They will not be attached to the eye, ear, nose, tongue, body, and conscious contacts. They will not be attached to the pleasant, painful, and neutral feelings produced by the eye, ear, nose, tongue, body, and conscious contacts. They will not be attached to the earth, water, fire, wind, space, and consciousness realms. They will not be attached to cause and condition, the consecutive sequence of thoughts, the conditions that stimulate one's mind, the conditions that reinforce main causes, and the dharmas produced by conditions. They will not be attached to ignorance, action, consciousness, name and form, six sense spheres, contact, reception, craving, grasping, existence, birth, old age, death, worry, sorrow, misery, anxiety, and upset. They will not be attached to the conditioned realm and the unconditioned realm. They will not be attached to the flawed realm and the flawless realm. They will not be attached to giving paramita, pure-precept paramita, forbearance paramita, diligence paramita, meditation paramita, prajna paramita, expedient skillfulness paramita, wonderful aspiration paramita, abilities paramita, and perfect knowledge paramitas. They will not be attached to internal emptiness, external emptiness, internal-external emptiness, emptiness of emptiness, emptiness of space, emptiness of ultimate truth, emptiness of conditioned phenomena, emptiness of unconditioned reality, emptiness in the final analysis, emptiness of nontemporality, emptiness of deconstruction, emptiness of changelessness, emptiness of original nature, emptiness of particular characteristics, emptiness of common characteristics, emptiness of all dharmas, emptiness of nonattainment, emptiness of selflessness, emptiness of self-nature, and emptiness of selfless self-nature. They will not be attached to realness, dharma realm, dharma nature, the nature of nonillusion, the nature of changelessness, the nature of equality, the nature of nonarising, dharma concentration, dharma dwelling, reality, the realm of empty space, and the realm of the inconceivable. They will not be attached to the four bases of mindfulness, four correct endeavors, four bases of power, five roots, five powers, seven factors for enlightenment, and the noble eightfold path. They will not be attached to the noble truths of suffering, the cause of suffering, the cessation of suffering, and the path for the cessation of suffering. They will not be attached to the four meditations, four immeasurable minds, and four formless concentrations. They will not be attached to the eight liberations, eight vexation-

Fascicle 13, Chapter 7, Section 3

overcoming meditations, nine concentrations in sequence, and the ten universal contemplations. They will not be attached to the liberation gates of emptiness, formlessness, and nonaspiration. They will not be attached to the dharani gates and the samadhi gates. They will not be attached to the stages of ecstasy, freedom from defilements, emitting light, flaming wisdom, being extremely difficult to be surpassed, manifestation of pure realness, going far away, the unmovable, expedient wisdom, and dharma cloud. They will not be attached to the five eyes and the six supernatural powers. They will not be attached to the Buddha's ten abilities, four kinds of fearlessness, four unhindered understandings, and the eighteen distinctive features of Buddha's wisdom and ability. They will not be attached to great loving-kindness, great compassion, great joy, and great equanimity. They will not be attached to the thirty-two perfect major marks and the eighty distinguishing minor features. They will not be attached to staying in correct mindfulness and dwelling in equanimity at all times. They will not be attached to the perfect knowledge of everything, the perfect knowledge of the forms of the paths, and the perfect knowledge of all phenomena. They will not be attached to stream-entry effect, once-return effect, nonreturn effect, arhat effect, and self-enlightenment bodhi. They will not be attached to all great bodhisattva actions and the unsurpassed, perfect, and universal bodhi of the Buddhas. They will not be attached to the 'I,' the sentient being, the living one, the one who gives birth, the one who raises others, the gentleperson, the individual in reincarnation, the mentally born one, the learned child, the maker, the receiver, the initiator, the knower, and the viewer. They will not be attached to the ordinary sentient being, the holy one, the bodhisattva, and the Thus-Comer. They will not be attached to the mind and the body. They will not be attached to dignifying and purifying the Buddha lands. They will not be attached to assisting the sentient to grow and mature; and they will not be attached to expedient skillfulness. Why? Because all dharmas are nonexistent; the one who will become attached, the things to which one will be attached, and the time when and the place where the attachment occurs are all unattainable.

"Therefore, Well Appearing One, because of not being attached to all dharmas when cultivating prajna paramita, the great bodhisattvas are able to foster giving, pure precept, forbearance, diligence, meditation, prajna, expedient skillfulness, wonderful aspiration, abilities, and perfect knowledge paramitas and dwell firmly in internal emptiness, external emptiness, internal-external emptiness, emptiness of emptiness, emptiness of space, emptiness of ultimate truth, emptiness of conditioned phenomena, emptiness of unconditioned reality, emptiness in the final analysis, emptiness of nontemporality, emptiness of deconstruction, emptiness of changelessness, emptiness of original nature, emptiness of particular characteristics, emptiness of common characteristics, emptiness of all dharmas, emptiness of nonattainment, emptiness of selflessness, emptiness of self-nature, and emptiness of selfless self-nature. They are also able to dwell firmly in realness, dharma realm, dharma nature, the nature of nonillusion, the nature of changelessness, the nature of equality, the nature of nonarising, dharma concentration, dharma dwelling, reality, the realm of empty space, and the realm of the inconceivable. They are also able to foster the cultivation of the four bases of mindfulness, four correct endeavors, four bases of power, five roots, five powers, seven factors for enlightenment, and the noble eightfold path. They are also able to dwell firmly in the noble truths of suffering, the cause of suffering, the cessation of suffering, and the path for the cessation of suffering. They are also able to foster the cultivation of the four meditations, four immeasurable minds, and four formless concentrations. They are also able to foster the cultivation of the eight liberations, eight vexation-overcoming meditations, nine concentrations in sequence, and ten universal contemplations. They are also able to foster the cultivation of the liberation gates of emptiness, formlessness, and nonaspiration. They are also able to enter the correct bodhisattva path of nonarising. They are also able to dwell firmly in the stage of bodhisattva with no regression.

"They are also able to fulfill all dharani gates and all samadhi gates perfectly. They are also able to fulfill the stages of ecstasy, freedom from defilements, emitting light, flaming wisdom, being extremely difficult to be surpassed, manifestation of pure realness,

Fascicle 13, Chapter 7, Section 3   303

going far away, the unmovable, expedient wisdom, and dharma cloud perfectly. They are also able to fulfill the Buddha's ten abilities, four kinds of fearlessness, four unhindered understandings, and the eighteen distinctive features of Buddha's wisdom and power perfectly. They are also able to fulfill great loving-kindness, great compassion, great joy, and great equanimity perfectly. They are also able to fulfill the thirty-two perfect major marks and the eighty distinguishing minor features perfectly. They are also able to fulfill staying in correct mindfulness and dwelling in equanimity at all times perfectly. They are also able to fulfill the perfect knowledge of everything, the perfect knowledge of the forms of the paths, and the perfect knowledge of all phenomena perfectly. They are also able to attain the most superior supernatural powers of bodhisattva. After attaining the supernatural powers, they are able to travel from one Buddha country to the other. In order to assist the sentient beings to mature and dignify and purify the Buddha lands, they visit with the Thus-Comers, Ones Worthy of Offerings, Perfectly and Universally Enlightened Ones, and make offerings to, esteem, and acclaim them so that their virtuous roots are well nurtured. As their virtuous roots grow, they will be able to go as they wish and listen to the correct dharma taught by the Buddhas. From that time on until finally sitting peacefully on the throne of the wonderful bodhi, when they realize and attain the unsurpassed, perfect, and universal bodhi, they will never forget what they have heard about correct dharma. In the meantime, they will be perfectly free in mastering all dharani gates and samadhi gates.

"Therefore, Well Appearing One, when cultivating prajna paramita, the great bodhisattvas should be awake to know what provisionally established names and dharmas really are.

"Furthermore, Well Appearing One, what do you think about great bodhisattva? Is great bodhisattva the same as matter?"

"No, I don't think so, World-Honored One!"

"Is great bodhisattva the same as feeling, thinking, action, and consciousness?"

"No, I don't think so, World-Honored One!"

"Is great bodhisattva different from matter?"

"No, I don't think so, World-Honored One!"

"Is great bodhisattva different from feeling, thinking, action, and consciousness?"

"No, I don't think so, World-Honored One!"

"Is there great bodhisattva in matter?"

"No, I don't think so, World-Honored One!"

"Is there great bodhisattva in feeling, thinking, action, and consciousness?"

"No, I don't think so, World-Honored One!"

"Is there matter in great bodhisattva?"

"No, I don't think so, World-Honored One!"

"Are there feeling, thinking, action, and consciousness in great bodhisattva?"

"No, I don't think so, World-Honored One!"

"Is there great bodhisattva apart from matter?"

"No, I don't think so, World-Honored One!"

"Is there great bodhisattva apart from feeling, thinking, action, and consciousness?"

"No, I don't think so, World-Honored One!"

"Furthermore, Well Appearing One, what do you think about great bodhisattva? Is great bodhisattva the same as the eye sphere?"

"No, I don't think so, World-Honored One!"

"Is great bodhisattva the same as the ear, nose, tongue, body, and conscious spheres?"

"No, I don't think so, World-Honored One!"

"Is great bodhisattva different from the eye sphere?"

"No, I don't think so, World-Honored One!"

"Is great bodhisattva different from the ear, nose, tongue, body, and conscious spheres?"

"No, I don't think so, World-Honored One!"

"Is there great bodhisattva in the eye sphere?"

"No, I don't think so, World-Honored One!"

"Is there great bodhisattva in the ear, nose, tongue, body, and conscious spheres?"

"No, I don't think so, World-Honored One!"

"Is there eye sphere in the great bodhisattva?"

"No, I don't think so, World-Honored One!"

Fascicle 13, Chapter 7, Section 3

"Are there ear, nose, tongue, body, and conscious spheres in the great bodhisattva?"

"No, I don't think so, World-Honored One!"

"Is there great bodhisattva apart from the eye sphere?"

"No, I don't think so, World-Honored One!"

"Is there great bodhisattva apart from the ear, nose, tongue, body, and conscious spheres?"

"No, I don't think so, World-Honored One!"

"Furthermore, Well Appearing One, what do you think about great bodhisattva? Is great bodhisattva the same as the sight sphere?"

"No, I don't think so, World-Honored One!"

"Is great bodhisattva the same as the sound, smell, taste, touch, and mental-image spheres?"

"No, I don't think so, World-Honored One!"

"Is great bodhisattva different from the sight sphere?"

"No, I don't think so, World-Honored One!"

"Is great bodhisattva different from the sound, smell, taste, touch, and mental-image spheres?"

"No, I don't think so, World-Honored One!"

"Is there great bodhisattva in the sight sphere?"

"No, I don't think so, World-Honored One!"

"Is there great bodhisattva in the sound, smell, taste, touch, and mental-image spheres?"

"No, I don't think so, World-Honored One!"

"Is there sight sphere in the great bodhisattva?"

"No, I don't think so, World-Honored One!"

"Are there sound, smell, taste, touch, and mental-image spheres in the great bodhisattva?"

"No, I don't think so, World-Honored One!"

"Is there great bodhisattva apart from the sight sphere?"

"No, I don't think so, World-Honored One!"

"Is there great bodhisattva apart from the sound, smell, taste, touch, and mental-image spheres?"

"No, I don't think so, World-Honored One!"

"Furthermore, Well Appearing One, what do you think about great bodhisattva? Is great bodhisattva the same as the eye realm?"

"No, I don't think so, World-Honored One!"

"Is great bodhisattva the same as the ear, nose, tongue, body, and conscious realms?"

"No, I don't think so, World-Honored One!"

"Is great bodhisattva different from the eye realm?"

"No, I don't think so, World-Honored One!"

"Is great bodhisattva different from the ear, nose, tongue, body, and conscious realms?"

"No, I don't think so, World-Honored One!"

"Is there great bodhisattva in the eye realm?"

"No, I don't think so, World-Honored One!"

"Is there great bodhisattva in the ear, nose, tongue, body, and conscious realms?"

"No, I don't think so, World-Honored One!"

"Is there eye realm in the great bodhisattva?"

"No, I don't think so, World-Honored One!"

"Are there ear, nose, tongue, body, and conscious realms in the great bodhisattva?"

"No, I don't think so, World-Honored One!"

"Is there great bodhisattva apart from the eye realm?"

"No, I don't think so, World-Honored One!"

"Is there great bodhisattva apart from the ear, nose, tongue, body, and conscious realms?"

"No, I don't think so, World-Honored One!"

"Furthermore, Well Appearing One, what do you think about the great bodhisattva? Is great bodhisattva the same as the sight realm?"

"No, I don't think so, World-Honored One!"

"Is great bodhisattva the same as the sound, smell, taste, touch, and mental-image realms?"

"No, I don't think so, World-Honored One!"

"Is great bodhisattva different from the sight realm?"

"No, I don't think so, World-Honored One!"

"Is great bodhisattva different from the sound, smell, taste, touch, and mental-image realms?"

"No, I don't think so, World-Honored One!"

"Is there great bodhisattva in the sight realm?"

"No, I don't think so, World-Honored One!"
"Is there great bodhisattva in the sound, smell, taste, touch, and mental-image realms?"
"No, I don't think so, World-Honored One!"
"Is there sight realm in the great bodhisattva?"
"No, I don't think so, World-Honored One!"
"Are there the sound, smell, taste, touch, and mental-image realms in great bodhisattva?"
"No, I don't think so, World-Honored One!"
"Is there great bodhisattva apart from the sight realm?"
"No, I don't think so, World-Honored One!"
"Is there great bodhisattva apart from the sound, smell, taste, touch, and mental-image realms?"
"No, I don't think so, World-Honored One!"
"Furthermore, Well Appearing One, what do you think about the great bodhisattva? Is great bodhisattva the same as the eye consciousness realm?"
"No, I don't think so, World-Honored One!"
"Is great bodhisattva the same as the ear, nose, tongue, body, and conscious consciousness realms?"
"No, I don't think so, World-Honored One!"
"Is great bodhisattva different from the eye consciousness realm?"
"No, I don't think so, World-Honored One!"
"Is great bodhisattva different from the ear, nose, tongue, body, and conscious consciousness realms?"
"No, I don't think so, World-Honored One!"
"Is there great bodhisattva in the eye consciousness realm?"
"No, I don't think so, World-Honored One!"
"Is there great bodhisattva in the ear, nose, tongue, body, and conscious consciousness realms?"
"No, I don't think so, World-Honored One!"
"Is there eye consciousness realm in the great bodhisattva?"
"No, I don't think so, World-Honored One!"
"Are there ear, nose, tongue, body, and conscious consciousness realms in the great bodhisattva?"

"No, I don't think so, World-Honored One!"

"Is there great bodhisattva apart from the eye consciousness realm?"

"No, I don't think so, World-Honored One!"

"Is there great bodhisattva apart from the ear, nose, tongue, body, and conscious consciousness realms?"

"No, I don't think so, World-Honored One!"

"Furthermore, Well Appearing One, what do you think about the great bodhisattva? Is great bodhisattva the same as the eye contact?"

"No, I don't think so, World-Honored One!"

"Is great bodhisattva the same as the ear, nose, tongue, body, and conscious contacts?"

"No, I don't think so, World-Honored One!"

"Is great bodhisattva different from the eye contact?"

"No, I don't think so, World-Honored One!"

"Is great bodhisattva different from the ear, nose, tongue, body, and conscious contacts?"

"No, I don't think so, World-Honored One!"

"Is there great bodhisattva in the eye contact?"

"No, I don't think so, World-Honored One!"

"Is there great bodhisattva in the ear, nose, tongue, body, and conscious contacts?"

"No, I don't think so, World-Honored One!"

"Is there eye contact in the great bodhisattva?"

"No, I don't think so, World-Honored One!"

"Are there ear, nose, tongue, body, and conscious contacts in the great bodhisattva?"

"No, I don't think so, World-Honored One!"

"Is there great bodhisattva apart from the eye contact?"

"No, I don't think so, World-Honored One!"

"Is there great bodhisattva apart from the ear, nose, tongue, body, and conscious contacts?"

"No, I don't think so, World-Honored One!"

"Furthermore, Well Appearing One, what do you think about the great bodhisattva? Is great bodhisattva the same as the feelings produced by eye contact?"

"No, I don't think so, World-Honored One!"
"Is great bodhisattva the same as the feelings produced by ear, nose, tongue, body, and conscious contacts?"
"No, I don't think so, World-Honored One!"
"Is great bodhisattva different from the feelings produced by eye contact?"
"No, I don't think so, World-Honored One!"
"Is great bodhisattva different from the feelings produced by ear, nose, tongue, body, and conscious contacts?"
"No, I don't think so, World-Honored One!"
"Is there great bodhisattva in the feelings produced by eye contact?"
"No, I don't think so, World-Honored One!"
"Is there great bodhisattva in the feelings produced by ear, nose, tongue, body, and conscious contacts?"
"No, I don't think so, World-Honored One!"
"Are there feelings produced by eye contact in the great bodhisattva?"
"No, I don't think so, World-Honored One!"
"Are there feelings produced by ear, nose, tongue, body, and conscious contacts in the great bodhisattva?"
"No, I don't think so, World-Honored One!"
"Is there great bodhisattva apart from the feelings produced by eye contact?"
"No, I don't think so, World-Honored One!"
"Is there great bodhisattva apart from the feelings produced by ear, nose, tongue, body, and conscious contacts?"
"No, I don't think so, World-Honored One!"
"Furthermore, Well Appearing One, what do you think about the great bodhisattva? Is great bodhisattva the same as the earth realm?"
"No, I don't think so, World-Honored One!"
"Is great bodhisattva the same as the water, fire, wind, empty space, and consciousness realms?"
"No, I don't think so, World-Honored One!"
"Is great bodhisattva different from the earth realm?"
"No, I don't think so, World-Honored One!"

"Is great bodhisattva different from the water, fire, wind, empty space, and consciousness realms?"

"No, I don't think so, World-Honored One!"

"Is there great bodhisattva in the earth realm?"

"No, I don't think so, World-Honored One!"

"Is there great bodhisattva in the water, fire, wind, empty space, and consciousness realms?"

"No, I don't think so, World-Honored One!"

"Is there earth realm in the great bodhisattva?"

"No, I don't think so, World-Honored One!"

"Are there water, fire, wind, empty space, and consciousness realms in the great bodhisattva?"

"No, I don't think so, World-Honored One!"

"Is there great bodhisattva apart from the earth realm?"

"No, I don't think so, World-Honored One!"

"Is there great bodhisattva apart from the water, fire, wind, empty space, and consciousness realms?"

"No, I don't think so, World-Honored One!"

"Furthermore, Well Appearing One, what do you think about the great bodhisattva? Is great bodhisattva the same as cause and condition?"

"No, I don't think so, World-Honored One!"

"Is great bodhisattva the same as the consecutive sequence of thoughts, the conditions that stimulate one's mind, and the conditions that reinforce main causes?"

"No, I don't think so, World-Honored One!"

"Is great bodhisattva different from cause and condition?"

"No, I don't think so, World-Honored One!"

"Is great bodhisattva different from the consecutive sequence of thoughts, the conditions that stimulate one's mind, and the conditions that reinforce main causes?"

"No, I don't think so, World-Honored One!"

"Is there great bodhisattva in cause and condition?"

"No, I don't think so, World-Honored One!"

"Is there great bodhisattva in the consecutive sequence of thoughts, the conditions that stimulate one's mind, and the conditions that reinforce main causes?"

"No, I don't think so, World-Honored One!"
"Is there cause and condition in the great bodhisattva?"
"No, I don't think so, World-Honored One!"
"Are the consecutive sequence of thoughts, the conditions that stimulate one's mind, and the conditions that reinforce main causes in the great bodhisattva?"
"No, I don't think so, World-Honored One!"
"Is there great bodhisattva apart from cause and condition?"
"No, I don't think so, World-Honored One!"
"Is there great bodhisattva apart from the consecutive sequence of thoughts, the conditions that stimulate one's mind, and the conditions that reinforce main causes?"
"No, I don't think so, World-Honored One!"
"Furthermore, Well Appearing One, what do you think about the great bodhisattva? Is great bodhisattva the same as the dharmas produced by conditions?"
"No, I don't think so, World-Honored One!"
"Is great bodhisattva different from the dharmas produced by conditions?"
"No, I don't think so, World-Honored One!"
"Is there great bodhisattva in the dharmas produced by conditions?"
"No, I don't think so, World-Honored One!"
"Are there the dharmas produced by conditions in the great bodhisattva?"
"No, I don't think so, World-Honored One!"
"Is there great bodhisattva apart from the dharmas produced by conditions?"
"No, I don't think so, World-Honored One!"

Fascicle 14

Chapter 7
The Cautions and the Teachings

Section 4

(In the First Assembly)

"Furthermore, Well Appearing One, what do you think about great bodhisattva? Is great bodhisattva the same as ignorance?"

"No, I don't think so, World-Honored One!"

"Is great bodhisattva the same as action, consciousness, name and form, six sense spheres, contact, reception, craving, grasping, existence, birth, old age, and death?"

"No, I don't think so, World-Honored One!"

"Is great bodhisattva different from ignorance?"

"No, I don't think so, World-Honored One!"

"Is great bodhisattva different from action, and so forth, as well as old age, and death?"

"No, I don't think so, World-Honored One!"

"Is there great bodhisattva in ignorance?"

"No, I don't think so, World-Honored One!"

"Is there great bodhisattva in action, and so forth, as well as old age and death?"

"No, I don't think so, World-Honored One!"
"Is there ignorance in great bodhisattva?"
"No, I don't think so, World-Honored One!"
"Is there action, and so forth, as well as old age and death in great bodhisattva?"
"No, I don't think so, World-Honored One!"
"Is there great bodhisattva apart from ignorance?"
"No, I don't think so, World-Honored One!"
"Is there great bodhisattva apart from action, and so forth, as well as old age and death?"
"No, I don't think so, World-Honored One!"
"Furthermore, Well Appearing One, what do you think about great bodhisattva? Is great bodhisattva the same as giving paramita?"
"No, I don't think so, World-Honored One!"
"Is great bodhisattva the same as pure precept, forbearance, diligence, meditation, and prajna paramitas?"
"No, I don't think so, World-Honored One!"
"Is great bodhisattva different from giving paramita?"
"No, I don't think so, World-Honored One!"
"Is great bodhisattva different from pure precept, forbearance, diligence, meditation, and prajna paramitas?"
"No, I don't think so, World-Honored One!"
"Is there great bodhisattva in giving paramita?"
"No, I don't think so, World-Honored One!"
"Is there great bodhisattva in pure precept, forbearance, diligence, meditation, and prajna paramitas?"
"No, I don't think so, World-Honored One!"
"Is there giving paramita in great bodhisattva?"
"No, I don't think so, World-Honored One!"
"Are there pure precept, forbearance, diligence, meditation, and prajna paramitas in great bodhisattva?"
"No, I don't think so, World-Honored One!"
"Is there great bodhisattva apart from giving paramita?"
"No, I don't think so, World-Honored One!"
"Is there great bodhisattva apart from pure precept, forbearance, diligence, meditation, and prajna paramitas?"
"No, I don't think so, World-Honored One!"

"Furthermore, Well Appearing One, what do you think about great bodhisattva? Is great bodhisattva the same as internal emptiness?"

"No, I don't think so, World-Honored One!"

"Is great bodhisattva the same as external emptiness, internal-external emptiness, emptiness of emptiness, emptiness of space, emptiness of ultimate truth, emptiness of conditioned phenomena, emptiness of unconditioned reality, emptiness in the final analysis, emptiness of nontemporality, emptiness of deconstruction, emptiness of changelessness, emptiness of original nature, emptiness of particular characteristics, emptiness of common characteristics, emptiness of all dharmas, emptiness of nonattainment, emptiness of selflessness, emptiness of self-nature, and emptiness of selfless self-nature?"

"No, I don't think so, World-Honored One!"

"Is great bodhisattva different from internal emptiness?"

"No, I don't think so, World-Honored One!"

"Is great bodhisattva different from external emptiness, and so forth, as well as emptiness of selfless self-nature?"

"No, I don't think so, World-Honored One!"

"Is there great bodhisattva in internal emptiness?"

"No, I don't think so, World-Honored One!"

"Is there great bodhisattva in external emptiness, and so forth, as well as emptiness of selfless self-nature?"

"No, I don't think so, World-Honored One!"

"Is there internal emptiness in great bodhisattva?"

"No, I don't think so, World-Honored One!"

"Is there external emptiness, and so forth, as well as emptiness of selfless self-nature in great bodhisattva?"

"No, I don't think so, World-Honored One!"

"Is there great bodhisattva apart from internal emptiness?"

"No, I don't think so, World-Honored One!"

"Is there great bodhisattva apart from external emptiness, and so forth, as well as emptiness of selfless self-nature?"

"No, I don't think so, World-Honored One!"

"Furthermore, Well Appearing One, what do you think about great bodhisattva? Is great bodhisattva the same as realness?"

Fascicle 14, Chapter 7, Section 4

"No, I don't think so, World-Honored One!"

"Is great bodhisattva the same as dharma realm, dharma nature, the nature of nonillusion, the nature of changelessness, the nature of equality, the nature of nonarising, dharma concentration, dharma dwelling, reality, the realm of empty space, and the realm of the inconceivable?"

"No, I don't think so, World-Honored One!"

"Is great bodhisattva different from realness?"

"No, I don't think so, World-Honored One!"

"Is great bodhisattva different from dharma realm, and so forth, as well as the realm of the inconceivable?"

"No, I don't think so, World-Honored One!"

"Is there great bodhisattva in realness?"

"No, I don't think so, World-Honored One!"

"Is there great bodhisattva in dharma realm, and so forth, as well as the realm of the inconceivable?"

"No, I don't think so, World-Honored One!"

"Is there realness in great bodhisattva?"

"No, I don't think so, World-Honored One!"

"Is there dharma realm, and so forth, as well as the realm of the inconceivable in great bodhisattva?"

"No, I don't think so, World-Honored One!"

"Is there great bodhisattva apart from realness?"

"No, I don't think so, World-Honored One!"

"Is there great bodhisattva apart from dharma realm, and so forth, as well as the realm of the inconceivable?"

"No, I don't think so, World-Honored One!"

"Furthermore, Well Appearing One, what do you think about great bodhisattva? Is great bodhisattva the same as the four bases of mindfulness?"

"No, I don't think so, World-Honored One!"

"Is great bodhisattva the same as the four correct endeavors, four bases of power, five roots, five powers, seven factors for enlightenment, and noble eightfold path?"

"No, I don't think so, World-Honored One!"

"Is great bodhisattva different from the four bases of mindfulness?"

"No, I don't think so, World-Honored One!"

"Is great bodhisattva different from the four correct endeavors, and so forth, as well as the noble eightfold path?"

"No, I don't think so, World-Honored One!"

"Is there great bodhisattva in the four bases of mindfulness?"

"No, I don't think so, World-Honored One!"

"Is there great bodhisattva in the four correct endeavors, and so forth, as well as the noble eightfold path?"

"No, I don't think so, World-Honored One!"

"Are the four bases of mindfulness in great bodhisattva?"

"No, I don't think so, World-Honored One!"

"Are there the four correct endeavors, and so forth, as well as the noble eightfold path in great bodhisattva?"

"No, I don't think so, World-Honored One!"

"Is there great bodhisattva apart from the four bases of mindfulness?"

"No, I don't think so, World-Honored One!"

"Is there great bodhisattva apart from the four correct endeavors, and so forth, as well as the noble eightfold path?"

"No, I don't think so, World-Honored One!"

"Furthermore, Well Appearing One, what do you think about great bodhisattva? Is great bodhisattva the same as the noble truth of suffering?"

"No, I don't think so, World-Honored One!"

"Is great bodhisattva the same as the noble truths of the cause of suffering, the cessation of suffering, and the path for the cessation of suffering?"

"No, I don't think so, World-Honored One!"

"Is great bodhisattva different from the noble truth of suffering?"

"No, I don't think so, World-Honored One!"

"Is great bodhisattva different from the noble truths of the cause of suffering, the cessation of suffering, and the path for the cessation of suffering?"

"No, I don't think so, World-Honored One!"

"Is there great bodhisattva in the noble truth of suffering?"

"No, I don't think so, World-Honored One!"

"Is there great bodhisattva in the noble truths of the cause of suffering, the cessation of suffering, and the path for the cessation of suffering?"

"No, I don't think so, World-Honored One!"

"Is there the noble truth of suffering in great bodhisattva?"

"No, I don't think so, World-Honored One!"

"Are there the noble truths of the cause of suffering, the cessation of suffering, and the path for the cessation of suffering in great bodhisattva?"

"No, I don't think so, World-Honored One!"

"Is there great bodhisattva apart from the noble truth of suffering?"

"No, I don't think so, World-Honored One!"

"Is there great bodhisattva apart from the noble truths of the cause of suffering, the cessation of suffering, and the path for the cessation of suffering?"

"No, I don't think so, World-Honored One!"

"Furthermore, Well Appearing One, what do you think about great bodhisattva? Is great bodhisattva the same as the four meditations?"

"No, I don't think so, World-Honored One!"

"Is great bodhisattva the same as the four immeasurable minds and the four formless concentrations?"

"No, I don't think so, World-Honored One!"

"Is great bodhisattva different from the four meditations?"

"No, I don't think so, World-Honored One!"

"Is great bodhisattva different from the four immeasurable minds and the four formless concentrations?"

"No, I don't think so, World-Honored One!"

"Is there great bodhisattva in the four meditations?"

"No, I don't think so, World-Honored One!"

"Is there great bodhisattva in the four immeasurable minds and the four formless concentrations?"

"No, I don't think so, World-Honored One!"

"Are there the four meditations in great bodhisattva?"

"No, I don't think so, World-Honored One!"

"Are there the four immeasurable minds and the four formless concentrations in great bodhisattva?"

"No, I don't think so, World-Honored One!"

"Is there great bodhisattva apart from the four meditations?"

"No, I don't think so, World-Honored One!"

"Is there great bodhisattva apart from the four immeasurable minds and the four formless concentrations?"

"No, I don't think so, World-Honored One!"

"Furthermore, Well Appearing One, what do you think about great bodhisattva? Is great bodhisattva the same as the eight liberations?"

"No, I don't think so, World-Honored One!"

"Is great bodhisattva the same as the eight vexation-overcoming meditations, nine concentrations in sequence, and the ten universal contemplations?"

"No, I don't think so, World-Honored One!"

"Is great bodhisattva different from the eight liberations?"

"No, I don't think so, World-Honored One!"

"Is great bodhisattva different from the eight vexation-overcoming meditations, nine concentrations in sequence, and the ten universal contemplations?"

"No, I don't think so, World-Honored One!"

"Is there great bodhisattva in the eight liberations?"

"No, I don't think so, World-Honored One!"

"Is there great bodhisattva in the eight vexation-overcoming meditations, nine concentrations in sequence, and the ten universal contemplations?"

"No, I don't think so, World-Honored One!"

"Are there the eight liberations in great bodhisattva?"

"No, I don't think so, World-Honored One!"

"Are there the eight vexation-overcoming meditations, nine concentrations in sequence, and the ten universal contemplations in great bodhisattva?"

"No, I don't think so, World-Honored One!"

"Is there great bodhisattva apart from the eight liberations?"

"No, I don't think so, World-Honored One!"

"Is there great bodhisattva apart from the eight vexation-overcoming meditations, nine concentrations in sequence, and the ten universal contemplations?"

"No, I don't think so, World-Honored One!"

"Furthermore, Well Appearing One, what do you think about great bodhisattva? Is great bodhisattva the same as the liberation gate of emptiness?"

"No, I don't think so, World-Honored One!"

"Is great bodhisattva the same as the liberation gates of formlessness and nonaspiration?"

"No, I don't think so, World-Honored One!"

"Is great bodhisattva different from the liberation gate of emptiness?"

"No, I don't think so, World-Honored One!"

"Is great bodhisattva different from the liberation gates of formlessness and nonaspiration?"

"No, I don't think so, World-Honored One!"

"Is there great bodhisattva in the liberation gate of emptiness?"

"No, I don't think so, World-Honored One!"

"Is there great bodhisattva in the liberation gates of formlessness and nonaspiration?"

"No, I don't think so, World-Honored One!"

"Is there the liberation gate of emptiness in great bodhisattva?"

"No, I don't think so, World-Honored One!"

"Are there the liberation gates of formlessness and nonaspiration in great bodhisattva?"

"No, I don't think so, World-Honored One!"

"Is there great bodhisattva apart from the liberation gate of emptiness?"

"No, I don't think so, World-Honored One!"

"Is there great bodhisattva apart from the liberation gates of formlessness and nonaspiration?"

"No, I don't think so, World-Honored One!"

"Furthermore, Well Appearing One, what do you think about great bodhisattva? Is great bodhisattva the same as the dharani gates?"

"No, I don't think so, World-Honored One!"

"Is great bodhisattva the same as the samadhi gates?"

"No, I don't think so, World-Honored One!"

"Is great bodhisattva different from the dharani gates?"

"No, I don't think so, World-Honored One!"

"Is great bodhisattva different from the samadhi gates?"

"No, I don't think so, World-Honored One!"

"Is there great bodhisattva in the dharani gates?"

"No, I don't think so, World-Honored One!"

"Is there great bodhisattva in the samadhi gates?"

"No, I don't think so, World-Honored One!"

"Are there dharani gates in great bodhisattva?"

"No, I don't think so, World-Honored One!"

"Are there samadhi gates in great bodhisattva?"

"No, I don't think so, World-Honored One!"

"Is there great bodhisattva apart from the dharani gates?"

"No, I don't think so, World-Honored One!"

"Is there great bodhisattva apart from the samadhi gates?"

"No, I don't think so, World-Honored One!"

"Furthermore, Well Appearing One, what do you think about great bodhisattva? Is great bodhisattva the same as the stage of ecstasy?"

"No, I don't think so, World-Honored One!"

"Is great bodhisattva the same as the stages of freedom from defilements, emitting light, flaming wisdom, being extremely difficult to be surpassed, manifestation of pure realness, going far away, the unmovable, expedient wisdom, and dharma cloud?"

"No, I don't think so, World-Honored One!"

"Is great bodhisattva different from the stage of ecstasy?"

"No, I don't think so, World-Honored One!"

"Is great bodhisattva different from the stage of freedom from defilements, and so forth, as well as the stage of dharma cloud?"

"No, I don't think so, World-Honored One!"

"Is there great bodhisattva in the stage of ecstasy?"

"No, I don't think so, World-Honored One!"

"Is there great bodhisattva in the stage of freedom from defilements, and so forth, as well as the stage of dharma cloud?"

"No, I don't think so, World-Honored One!"

"Is there the stage of ecstasy in great bodhisattva?"

"No, I don't think so, World-Honored One!"

"Is there the stage of freedom from defilements, and so forth, as well as the stage of dharma cloud in great bodhisattva?"

"No, I don't think so, World-Honored One!"
"Is there great bodhisattva apart from the stage of ecstasy?"
"No, I don't think so, World-Honored One!"
"Is there great bodhisattva apart from the stage of freedom from defilements, and so forth, as well as the stage of dharma cloud?"
"No, I don't think so, World-Honored One!"
"Furthermore, Well Appearing One, what do you think about great bodhisattva? Is great bodhisattva the same as the five eyes?"
"No, I don't think so, World-Honored One!"
"Is great bodhisattva the same as the six supernatural powers?"
"No, I don't think so, World-Honored One!"
"Is great bodhisattva different from the five eyes?"
"No, I don't think so, World-Honored One!"
"Is great bodhisattva different from the six supernatural powers?"
"No, I don't think so, World-Honored One!"
"Is there great bodhisattva in the five eyes?"
"No, I don't think so, World-Honored One!"
"Is there great bodhisattva in the six supernatural powers?"
"No, I don't think so, World-Honored One!"
"Are there the five eyes in great bodhisattva?"
"No, I don't think so, World-Honored One!"
"Are there the six supernatural powers in great bodhisattva?"
"No, I don't think so, World-Honored One!"
"Is there great bodhisattva apart from the five eyes?"
"No, I don't think so, World-Honored One!"
"Is there great bodhisattva apart from the six supernatural powers?"
"No, I don't think so, World-Honored One!"
"Furthermore, Well Appearing One, what do you think about great bodhisattva? Is great bodhisattva the same as the Buddha's ten abilities?"
"No, I don't think so, World-Honored One!"
"Is great bodhisattva the same as the four kinds of fearlessness, four unhindered understandings, and the eighteen distinctive features of Buddha's wisdom and power?"
"No, I don't think so, World-Honored One!"

"Is great bodhisattva different from the Buddha's ten abilities?"

"No, I don't think so, World-Honored One!"

"Is great bodhisattva different from the four kinds of fearlessness, four unhindered understandings, and the eighteen distinctive features of Buddha's wisdom and power?"

"No, I don't think so, World-Honored One!"

"Is there great bodhisattva in the Buddha's ten abilities?"

"No, I don't think so, World-Honored One!"

"Is there great bodhisattva in the four kinds of fearlessness, four unhindered understandings, and the eighteen distinctive features of Buddha's wisdom and power?"

"No, I don't think so, World-Honored One!"

"Are there the Buddha's ten abilities in great bodhisattva?"

"No, I don't think so, World-Honored One!"

"Are there the four kinds of fearlessness, four unhindered understandings, and the eighteen distinctive features of Buddha's wisdom and power in great bodhisattva?"

"No, I don't think so, World-Honored One!"

"Is there great bodhisattva apart from the Buddha's ten abilities?"

"No, I don't think so, World-Honored One!"

"Is there great bodhisattva apart from the four kinds of fearlessness, four unhindered understandings, and the eighteen distinctive features of Buddha's wisdom and power?"

"No, I don't think so, World-Honored One!"

"Furthermore, Well Appearing One, what do you think about great bodhisattva? Is great bodhisattva the same as great loving-kindness?"

"No, I don't think so, World-Honored One!"

"Is great bodhisattva the same as great compassion, great joy, and great equanimity?"

"No, I don't think so, World-Honored One!"

"Is great bodhisattva different from great loving-kindness?"

"No, I don't think so, World-Honored One!"

"Is great bodhisattva different from great compassion, great joy, and great equanimity?"

"No, I don't think so, World-Honored One!"

"Is there great bodhisattva in great loving-kindness?"
"No, I don't think so, World-Honored One!"
"Is there great bodhisattva in great compassion, great joy, and great equanimity?"
"No, I don't think so, World-Honored One!"
"Is there great loving-kindness in great bodhisattva?"
"No, I don't think so, World-Honored One!"
"Are there great compassion, great joy, and great equanimity in great bodhisattva?"
"No, I don't think so, World-Honored One!"
"Is there great bodhisattva apart from great loving-kindness?"
"No, I don't think so, World-Honored One!"
"Is there great bodhisattva apart from great compassion, great joy, and great equanimity?"
"No, I don't think so, World-Honored One!"
"Furthermore, Well Appearing One, what do you think about great bodhisattva? Is great bodhisattva the same as the thirty-two perfect major marks?"
"No, I don't think so, World-Honored One!"
"Is great bodhisattva the same as the eighty distinguishing minor features?"
"No, I don't think so, World-Honored One!"
"Is great bodhisattva different from the thirty-two perfect major marks?"
"No, I don't think so, World-Honored One!"
"Is great bodhisattva different from the eighty distinguishing minor features?"
"No, I don't think so, World-Honored One!"
"Is there great bodhisattva in the thirty-two perfect major marks?"
"No, I don't think so, World-Honored One!"
"Is there great bodhisattva in the eighty distinguishing minor features?"
"No, I don't think so, World-Honored One!"
"Are there the thirty-two perfect major marks in great bodhisattva?"
"No, I don't think so, World-Honored One!"

"Are there the eighty distinguishing minor features in great bodhisattva?"

"No, I don't think so, World-Honored One!"

"Is there great bodhisattva apart from the thirty-two perfect major marks?"

"No, I don't think so, World-Honored One!"

"Is there great bodhisattva apart from the eighty distinguishing minor features?"

"No, I don't think so, World-Honored One!"

"Furthermore, Well Appearing One, what do you think about great bodhisattva? Is great bodhisattva the same as staying in correct mindfulness?"

"No, I don't think so, World-Honored One!"

"Is great bodhisattva the same as dwelling in equanimity at all times?"

"No, I don't think so, World-Honored One!"

"Is great bodhisattva different from staying in correct mindfulness?"

"No, I don't think so, World-Honored One!"

"Is great bodhisattva different from dwelling in equanimity at all times?"

"No, I don't think so, World-Honored One!"

"Is there great bodhisattva in staying in correct mindfulness?"

"No, I don't think so, World-Honored One!"

"Is there great bodhisattva in dwelling in equanimity at all times?"

"No, I don't think so, World-Honored One!"

"Is there staying in correct mindfulness in great bodhisattva?"

"No, I don't think so, World-Honored One!"

"Is there dwelling in equanimity at all times in great bodhisattva?"

"No, I don't think so, World-Honored One!"

"Is there great bodhisattva apart from staying in correct mindfulness?"

"No, I don't think so, World-Honored One!"

"Is there great bodhisattva apart from dwelling in equanimity at all times?"

"No, I don't think so, World-Honored One!"

"Furthermore, Well Appearing One, what do you think about great bodhisattva? Is great bodhisattva the same as the perfect knowledge of everything?"

"No, I don't think so, World-Honored One!"

"Is great bodhisattva the same as the perfect knowledge of the forms of the paths and the perfect knowledge of all phenomena?"

"No, I don't think so, World-Honored One!"

"Is great bodhisattva different from the perfect knowledge of everything?"

"No, I don't think so, World-honored One!"

"Is great bodhisattva different from the perfect knowledge of the forms of the paths and the perfect knowledge of all phenomena?"

"No, I don't think so, World-Honored One!"

"Is there great bodhisattva in the perfect knowledge of everything?"

"No, I don't think so, World-Honored One!"

"Is there great bodhisattva in the perfect knowledge of the forms of the paths and the perfect knowledge of all phenomena?"

"No, I don't think so, World-Honored One!"

"Is there the perfect knowledge of everything in great bodhisattva?"

"No, I don't think so, World-Honored One!"

"Are there the perfect knowledge of the forms of the paths and the perfect knowledge of all phenomena in great bodhisattva?"

"No, I don't think so, World-Honored One!"

"Is there great bodhisattva apart from the perfect knowledge of everything?"

"No, I don't think so, World-Honored One!"

"Is there great bodhisattva apart from the perfect knowledge of the forms of the paths and the perfect knowledge of all phenomena?"

"No, I don't think so, World-Honored One!"

At that time, the Buddha asked the long-lived sage Well Appearing One, "Based on what reason do you say that the great bodhisattva is not the same as matter, feeling, thinking, action, and consciousness; that the great bodhisattva is not different from matter, feeling, thinking, action, and consciousness; that there is no great bodhisattva in matter, feeling, thinking, action, and consciousness; that there are no matter, feeling, thinking, action, and consciousness in great bodhisattva; and that there is no great bodhisattva apart from matter, feeling, thinking, action, and consciousness?"

The long-lived sage Well Appearing One replied, "World-Honored One, as bodhi [the awakening], sattva [sentient beings], matter, feeling, thinking, action, and consciousness are in the final analysis unattainable because they are without self-natures, how can we say that the great bodhisattva is existent? Given the truth that they are all nonexistent, how can we say that the great bodhisattva is the same as matter, feeling, thinking, action, and consciousness; that the great bodhisattva is different from matter, feeling, thinking, action, and consciousness; that there is great bodhisattva in matter, feeling, thinking, action, and consciousness; that there are matter, feeling, thinking, action, and consciousness in great bodhisattva; and that there is great bodhisattva apart from matter, feeling, thinking, action, and consciousness?"

"Furthermore, Well Appearing One, based on what reason do you say that the great bodhisattva is not the same as the eye, ear, nose, tongue, body, and conscious spheres; that the great bodhisattva is not different from the eye, ear, nose, tongue, body, and conscious spheres; that there is no great bodhisattva in the eye, ear, nose, tongue, body, and conscious spheres; that there are no eye, ear, nose, tongue, body, and conscious spheres in great bodhisattva; and that there is no great bodhisattva apart from the eye, ear, nose, tongue, body, and conscious spheres?"

"World-Honored One, as bodhi, sattva, and the eye, ear, nose, tongue, body, and conscious spheres are in the final analysis unattainable because they are without self-natures, how can we say that the great bodhisattva is existent? Given the truth that they are all nonexistent, how can we say that the great bodhisattva is the same as the eye, ear, nose, tongue, body, and conscious spheres; that the great bodhisattva is different from the eye, ear, nose, tongue, body, and conscious spheres; that there is great bodhisattva in the eye, ear, nose, tongue, body, and conscious spheres; that there are the eye, ear, nose, tongue, body, and conscious spheres in great bodhisattva; and that there is great bodhisattva apart from the eye, ear, nose, tongue, body, and conscious spheres?"

"Furthermore, Well Appearing One, based on what reason do you say that the great bodhisattva is not the same as the sight, sound, smell, taste, touch, and mental-image spheres; that the great bodhisattva is not different from the sight, sound, smell, taste, touch, and mental-image spheres; that there is no great bodhisattva in the sight, sound, smell, taste, touch, and mental-image spheres; that there are no sight, sound, smell, taste, touch, and mental-image spheres in great bodhisattva; and that there is no great bodhisattva apart from the sight, sound, smell, taste, touch, and mental-image spheres?"

"World-Honored One, as bodhi, sattva, and the sight, sound, smell, touch, and mental-image spheres are in the final analysis unattainable because they are without self-natures, how can we say that the great bodhisattva is existent? Given the truth that they are all nonexistent, how can we say that the great bodhisattva is the same as the sight, sound, smell, taste, touch, and mental-image spheres; that the great bodhisattva is different from the sight, sound, smell, taste, touch, and mental-image spheres; that there is great bodhisattva in the sight, sound, smell, taste, touch, and mental-image spheres; that there are the sight, sound, smell, taste, touch, and mental-image spheres in great bodhisattva; and that there is great bodhisattva apart from the sight, sound, smell, taste, touch, and mental-image spheres?"

"Furthermore, Well Appearing One, based on what reason do you say that the great bodhisattva is not the same as the eye, ear, nose, tongue, body, and conscious realms; that the great bodhisattva is not different from the eye, ear, nose, tongue, body, and conscious realms; that there is no great bodhisattva in the eye, ear, nose, tongue, body, and conscious realms; that there are no eye, ear, nose, tongue, body, and conscious realms in great bodhisattva; and that there is no great bodhisattva apart from the eye, ear, nose, tongue, body, and conscious realms?"

"World-Honored One, as bodhi, sattva, and the eye, ear, nose, tongue, body, and conscious realms are in the final analysis unattainable because they are without self-natures, how can we say that the great bodhisattva is existent? Given the truth that they are all nonexistent, how can we say that the great bodhisattva is the same as the eye, ear, nose, tongue, body, and conscious realms; that the great bodhisattva is different from the eye, ear, nose, tongue, body, and conscious realms; that there is great bodhisattva in the eye, ear, nose, tongue, body, and conscious realms; that there are the eye, ear, nose, tongue, body, and conscious realms in the great bodhisattva; and that there is great bodhisattva apart from the eye, ear, nose, tongue, body, and conscious realms?"

"Furthermore, Well Appearing One, based on what reason do you say that the great bodhisattva is not the same as the sight, sound, smell, touch, and mental-image realms; that the great bodhisattva is not different from the sight, sound, smell, taste, touch, and mental-image realms; that there is no great bodhisattva in the sight, sound, smell, taste, touch, and mental-image realms; that there are no sight, sound, smell, taste, touch, and mental-image realms in great bodhisattva; and that there is no great bodhisattva apart from the sight, sound, smell, taste, touch, and mental-image realms?"

"World-Honored One, as bodhi, sattva, and the sight realm, sound, smell, taste, touch, and mental-image realms are in the final analysis unattainable because they are without self-natures, how can we say that the great bodhisattva is existent? Given the truth that they are all nonexistent, how can we say that the great bodhisattva is the same as the sight, sound, smell, taste, touch, and mental-image realms; that the great bodhisattva is different from the sight, sound, smell, taste, touch, and mental-image realms; that there is great bodhisattva in the sight, sound, smell, taste, touch, and mental-image realms; that there are the sight, sound, smell, taste, touch, and mental-image realms in the great bodhisattva; and that there is the great bodhisattva apart from the sight, sound, smell, taste, touch, and mental-image realms?"

"Furthermore, Well Appearing One, based on what reason do you say that the great bodhisattva is not the same as the eye, ear, nose, tongue, body, and conscious consciousness realms; that the

Fascicle 14, Chapter 7, Section 4   329

great bodhisattva is not different from the eye, ear, nose, tongue, body, and conscious consciousness realms; that there is no great bodhisattva in the eye, ear, nose, tongue, body, and conscious consciousness realms; that there are no eye, ear, nose, tongue, body, and conscious consciousness realms in great bodhisattva; and that there is no great bodhisattva apart from the eye, ear, nose, tongue, body, and conscious consciousness realms?"

"World-Honored One, as bodhi, sattva, and the eye, ear, nose, tongue, body, and conscious consciousness realms are in the final analysis unattainable because they are without self-natures, how can we say that the great bodhisattva is existent? Given the truth that they are all nonexistent, how can we say that the great bodhisattva is the same as the eye, ear, nose, tongue, body, and conscious consciousness realms; that the great bodhisattva is different from the eye, ear, nose, tongue, body, and conscious consciousness realms; that there is great bodhisattva in the eye, ear, nose, tongue, body, and conscious consciousness realms; that there are the eye, ear, nose, tongue, body, and conscious consciousness realms in the great bodhisattva; and that there is great bodhisattva apart from the eye, ear, nose, tongue, body, and conscious consciousness realms?"

"Furthermore, Well Appearing One, based on what reason do you say that the great bodhisattva is not the same as the eye, ear, nose, tongue, body, and conscious contacts; that the great bodhisattva is not different from the eye, ear, nose, tongue, body, and conscious contacts; that there is no great bodhisattva in the eye, ear, nose, tongue, body, and conscious contacts; that there are no eye, ear, nose, tongue, body, and conscious contacts in the great bodhisattva; and that there is no great bodhisattva apart from the eye, ear, nose, tongue, body, and conscious contacts?"

"World-Honored One, as bodhi, sattva, and the eye, ear, nose, tongue, body, and conscious contacts are in the final analysis unattainable because they are without self-natures, how can we say that the great bodhisattva is existent? Given the truth that they are all nonexistent, how can we say that the great bodhisattva is the same as the eye, ear, nose, tongue, body, and conscious contacts; that the great bodhisattva is different from the eye, ear, nose, tongue, body, and conscious contacts; that there is great bodhisattva in the eye, ear, nose, tongue, body, and conscious contacts; that there are the eye, ear, nose, tongue, body, and conscious contacts in the great bodhisattva; and that there is great bodhisattva apart from the eye, ear, nose, tongue, body, and conscious contacts?"

"Furthermore, Well Appearing One, based on what reason do you say that the great bodhisattva is not the same as the feelings produced by the eye, ear, nose, tongue, body, and conscious contacts; that the great bodhisattva is not different from the feelings produced by the eye, ear, nose, tongue, body, and conscious contacts; that there is no great bodhisattva in the feelings produced by the eye, ear, nose, tongue, body, and conscious contacts; that there are no feelings produced by the eye, ear, nose, tongue, body, and conscious contacts in great bodhisattva; and that there is no great bodhisattva apart from the feelings produced by the eye, ear, nose, tongue, body, and conscious contacts?"

"World-Honored One, as bodhi, sattva, and the feelings produced by the eye, ear, nose, tongue, body, and conscious contacts are in the final analysis unattainable because they are without self-natures, how can we say that the great bodhisattva is existent? Given the truth that they are all nonexistent, how can we say that the great bodhisattva is the same as the feelings produced by the eye, ear, nose, tongue, body, and conscious contacts; that the great bodhisattva is different from the feelings produced by the eye, ear, nose, tongue, body, and conscious contacts; that there is great bodhisattva in the feelings produced by the eye, ear, nose, tongue, body, and conscious contacts; that there are the feelings produced by the eye, ear, nose, tongue, body, and conscious contacts in great bodhisattva; and that there is great bodhisattva apart from various feelings produced by the eye, ear, nose, tongue, body, and conscious contacts?"

"Furthermore, Well Appearing One, based on what reason do you say that the great bodhisattva is not the same as the earth, water, fire, wind, empty space, and consciousness realms; that the great bodhisattva is not different from the earth, water, fire, wind, empty space, and consciousness realms; that there is no great bodhisattva in the earth, water, fire, wind, empty space, and consciousness realms; that there are no earth, water, fire, wind, empty space, and consciousness realms in great bodhisattva; and that there is no

Fascicle 14, Chapter 7, Section 4

great bodhisattva apart from the earth, water, fire, wind, empty space, and consciousness realms?"

"World-Honored One, as bodhi, sattva, the earth realm, and the water, fire, wind, empty space, and consciousness realms are in the final analysis unattainable because they are without self-natures, how can we say that the great bodhisattva is existent? Given the truth that they are all nonexistent, how can we say that the great bodhisattva is the same as the earth, water, fire, wind, empty space, and consciousness realms; that the great bodhisattva is different from the earth, water, fire, wind, space, and consciousness realms; that there is great bodhisattva in the earth, water, fire, wind, empty space, and consciousness realms; that there are the earth, water, fire, wind, empty space, and consciousness realms in the great bodhisattva; and that there is great bodhisattva apart from the earth, water, fire, wind, empty space, and consciousness realms?"

"Furthermore, Well Appearing One, based on what reason do you say that the great bodhisattva is not the same as cause and condition, the consecutive sequence of thoughts, the conditions that stimulate one's mind, and the conditions that reinforce main causes; that the great bodhisattva is not different from cause and condition, the consecutive sequence of thoughts, conditions that stimulate one's mind, and the conditions that reinforce main causes; that there is no great bodhisattva in cause and condition, the consecutive sequence of thoughts, the conditions that stimulate one's mind, and the conditions that reinforce main causes; that there are no cause and condition, the consecutive sequence of thoughts, the conditions that stimulate one's mind, and the conditions that reinforce main causes in great bodhisattva; and that there is no great bodhisattva apart from cause and condition, the consecutive sequence of thoughts, the conditions that stimulate one's mind, and the conditions that reinforce main causes?"

"World-Honored One, as bodhi, sattva, cause and condition, the consecutive sequence of thoughts, the conditions that stimulate one's mind, and the conditions that reinforce main causes are in the final analysis unattainable because they are without self-natures, how can we say that the great bodhisattva is existent? Given the truth that they are all nonexistent, how can we say that the great bodhisattva is the same as cause and condition, the consecutive sequence of thoughts, the conditions that stimulate one's mind, and the conditions that reinforce main causes; that the great bodhisattva is different from cause and condition, the consecutive sequence of thoughts, the conditions that stimulate one's mind, and the conditions that reinforce main causes; that there is great bodhisattva in cause and condition, the consecutive sequence of thoughts, the conditions that stimulate one's mind, and the conditions that reinforce main causes; that there are cause and condition, the consecutive sequence of thoughts, the conditions that stimulate one's mind, and the conditions that reinforce main causes in great bodhisattva; and that there is great bodhisattva apart from cause and condition, the consecutive sequence of thoughts, the conditions that stimulate one's mind, and the conditions that reinforce main causes?"

"Furthermore, Well Appearing One, based on what reason do you say that the great bodhisattva is not the same as the dharmas produced by conditions; that the great bodhisattva is not different from the dharmas produced by conditions; that there is no great bodhisattva in the dharmas produced by conditions; that there are no dharmas produced by conditions in great bodhisattva; and that there is no great bodhisattva apart from the dharmas produced by conditions?"

"World-Honored One, as bodhi, sattva, and the dharmas produced by conditions are in the final analysis unattainable because they are without self-natures, how can we say that the great bodhisattva is existent? Given the truth that they are all nonexistent, how can we say that the great bodhisattva is the same as the dharmas produced by conditions; that the great bodhisattva is different from the dharmas produced by conditions; that there is great bodhisattva in the dharmas produced by conditions; that there are the dharmas produced by conditions in the great bodhisattva; and that there is great bodhisattva apart from the dharmas produced by conditions?"

"Furthermore, Well Appearing One, based on what reason do you say that the great bodhisattva is not the same as ignorance, action, consciousness, name and form, six sense spheres, contact, reception, craving, grasping, existence, birth, old age and death;

that the great bodhisattva is not different from ignorance, action, and so forth, as well as old age and death; that there is no great bodhisattva in ignorance, action, and so forth, as well as old age and death; that there are no ignorance, action, and so forth, as well as old age and death in great bodhisattva; and that there is no great bodhisattva apart from ignorance, action, and so forth, as well as old age and death?"

"World-Honored One, as bodhi, sattva, ignorance, action, and so forth, as well as old age and death are in the final analysis unattainable because they are without self-natures, how can we say that the great bodhisattva is existent? Given the truth that they are all nonexistent, how can we say that the great bodhisattva is the same as ignorance, action, and so forth, as well as old age and death; that the great bodhisattva is different from ignorance, action, and so forth, as well as old age and death; that there is great bodhisattva in ignorance, action, and so forth, as well as old age and death; that there are ignorance, action, and so forth, as well as old age and death in great bodhisattva; and that there is great bodhisattva apart from ignorance, action, and so forth, as well as old age and death?"

"Furthermore, Well Appearing One, based on what reason do you say that the great bodhisattva is not the same as giving, pure precept, forbearance, diligence, meditation, and prajna paramitas; that the great bodhisattva is not different from giving, pure precept, forbearance, diligence, meditation, and prajna paramitas; that there is no great bodhisattva in giving, pure precept, forbearance, diligence, meditation, and prajna paramitas; that there is no giving, pure precept, forbearance, diligence, meditation, and prajna paramitas in great bodhisattva; and that there is no great bodhisattva apart from giving, pure precept, forbearance, diligence, meditation, and prajna paramitas?"

"World-Honored One, as bodhi, sattva, and giving, pure precept, forbearance, diligence, meditation, and prajna paramitas are in the final analysis unattainable because they are without self-natures, how can we say that the great bodhisattva is existent? Given the truth that they are all nonexistent, how can we say that the great bodhisattva is the same as giving, pure precept, forbearance, diligence, meditation, and prajna paramitas; that the great bodhisattva is different from giving, pure precept, forbearance, diligence, meditation, and prajna paramitas; that there is great bodhisattva in giving, pure precept, forbearance, diligence, meditation, and prajna paramitas; that there are giving, pure precept, forbearance, diligence, meditation, and prajna paramitas in great bodhisattva; and that there is great bodhisattva apart from giving, pure precept, forbearance, diligence, meditation, and prajna paramitas?"

"Furthermore, Well Appearing One, based on what reason do you say that the great bodhisattva is not the same as internal emptiness, external emptiness, internal-external emptiness, emptiness of emptiness, emptiness of space, emptiness of ultimate truth, emptiness of conditioned phenomena, emptiness of unconditioned reality, emptiness in the final analysis, emptiness of nontemporality, emptiness of deconstruction, emptiness of changelessness, emptiness of original nature, emptiness of particular characteristics, emptiness of common characteristics, emptiness of all dharmas, emptiness of nonattainment, emptiness of selflessness, emptiness of self-nature, and emptiness of selfless self-nature; that the great bodhisattva is not different from internal emptiness, external emptiness, and so forth, as well as emptiness of selfless self-nature; that there is no great bodhisattva in internal emptiness, external emptiness, and so forth, as well as emptiness of selfless self-nature; that there are no internal emptiness, external emptiness, and so forth, as well as emptiness of selfless self-nature in great bodhisattva; and that there is no great bodhisattva apart from internal emptiness, external emptiness, and so forth, as well as emptiness of selfless self-nature?"

"World-Honored One, as bodhi, sattva, internal emptiness, external emptiness, and so forth, as well as emptiness of selfless self-nature are in the final analysis unattainable because they are without self-natures, how can we say that the great bodhisattva is existent? Given the truth that they are all nonexistent, how can we say that the great bodhisattva is the same as internal emptiness, external emptiness, and so forth, as well as emptiness of selfless self-nature; that the great bodhisattva is different from internal emptiness, external emptiness, and so forth, as well as emptiness of selfless self-nature; that there is great bodhisattva in internal emptiness, external emptiness, and so forth, as well as emptiness of selfless self-nature; that there are internal emptiness, external emptiness, and so forth, as well as emptiness of selfless self-nature in great bodhisattva; and that there is great bodhisattva apart from internal emptiness, external emptiness, and so forth, as well as emptiness of selfless self-nature?"

"Furthermore, Well Appearing One, based on what reason do you say that the great bodhisattva is not the same as realness, dharma realm, dharma nature, the nature of nonillusion, the nature of changelessness, the nature of equality, the nature of nonarising, dharma concentration, dharma dwelling, reality, the realm of empty space, and the realm of the inconceivable; that the great bodhisattva is not different from realness, dharma realm, and so forth, as well as the realm of the inconceivable; that there is no great bodhisattva in realness, dharma realm, and so forth, as well as the realm of the inconceivable; that there are no realness, dharma realm, and so forth, as well as the realm of the inconceivable in great bodhisattva; that there is no great bodhisattva apart from realness, dharma realm, and so forth, as well as the realm of the inconceivable?"

"World-Honored One, as bodhi, sattva, realness, the dharma realm, and so forth, as well as the realm of the inconceivable are in the final analysis unattainable because they are without self-natures, how can we say that the great bodhisattva is existent? Given the truth that they are all nonexistent, how can we say that the great bodhisattva is the same as realness, dharma realm, and so forth, as well as the realm of the inconceivable; that the great bodhisattva is different from realness, dharma realm, and so forth, as well as the realm of the inconceivable; that there is great bodhisattva in realness, dharma realm, and so forth, as well as the realm of the inconceivable; that there are realness, dharma realm, and so forth, as well as the realm of the inconceivable in great bodhisattva; and that there is great bodhisattva apart from realness, dharma realm, and so forth, as well as the realm of the inconceivable?"

"Furthermore, Well Appearing One, based on what reason do you say that the great bodhisattva is not the same as the four bases of mindfulness, four correct endeavors, four bases of power, five roots, five powers, seven factors for enlightenment, and noble eightfold path; that the great bodhisattva is not different from the four bases of mindfulness, four correct endeavors, and so forth, as well as the noble eightfold path; that there is no great bodhisattva in the four bases of mindfulness, four correct endeavors, and so forth, as well as the noble eightfold path; that there are no four bases of mindfulness, four correct endeavors, and so forth, as well as the noble eightfold path in great bodhisattva; and that there is no great bodhisattva apart from the four bases of mindfulness, four correct endeavors, and so forth, as well as the noble eightfold path?"

"World-Honored One, as bodhi, sattva, the four bases of mindfulness, four correct endeavors, and so forth, as well as the noble eightfold path are in the final analysis unattainable because they are without self-natures, how can we say that the great bodhisattva is existent? Given the truth that they are all nonexistent, how can we say that the great bodhisattva is the same as the four bases of mindfulness, four correct endeavors, and so forth, as well as the noble eightfold path; that the great bodhisattva is different from the four bases of mindfulness, four correct endeavors, and so forth, as well as the noble eightfold path; that there is great bodhisattva in the four bases of mindfulness, four correct endeavors, and so forth, as well as the noble eightfold path; that there are the four bases of mindfulness, four correct endeavors, and so forth, as well as the noble eightfold path in great bodhisattva; and that there is great bodhisattva apart from the four bases of mindfulness, four correct endeavors, and so forth, as well as the noble eightfold path?"

FASCICLE 15

Chapter 7
The Cautions and the Teachings

Section 5

(In the First Assembly)

"FURTHERMORE, WELL APPEARING ONE, BASED ON WHAT REASON do you say that the great bodhisattva is not the same as the noble truths of suffering, the cause of suffering, the cessation of suffering, and the path for the cessation of suffering; that the great bodhisattva is not different from the noble truths of suffering, the cause of suffering, the cessation of suffering, and the path for the cessation of suffering; that there is no great bodhisattva in the noble truths of suffering, the cause of suffering, the cessation of suffering, and the path for the cessation of suffering; that there are no noble truths of suffering, the cause of suffering, the cessation of suffering, and the path for the cessation of suffering in great bodhisattva; and that there is no great bodhisattva apart from the noble truths of suffering, the cause of suffering, the cessation of suffering, and the path for the cessation of suffering?"

"World-Honored One, as bodhi, sattva, and the noble truths of suffering, the cause of suffering, the cessation of suffering, and the path for the cessation of suffering are in the final analysis unattainable because they are without self-natures, how can we say that the great bodhisattva is existent? Given the truth that they are all nonexistent, how can we say that the great bodhisattva is the same as the noble truths of suffering, the cause of suffering, the cessation of suffering, and the path for the cessation of suffering; that the great bodhisattva is different from the noble truths of suffering, the cause of suffering, the cessation of suffering, and the path for the cessation of suffering; that there is great bodhisattva in the noble truths of suffering, the cause of suffering, the cessation of suffering, and the path for the cessation of suffering; that there are noble truths of suffering, the cause of suffering, the cessation of suffering, and the path for the cessation of suffering in great bodhisattva; and that there is great bodhisattva apart from the noble truths of suffering, the cause of suffering, the cessation of suffering, and the path for the cessation of suffering?"

"Furthermore, Well Appearing One, based on what reason do you say that the great bodhisattva is not the same as the four meditations, four immeasurable minds, and four formless concentrations; that the great bodhisattva is not different from the four meditations, four immeasurable minds, and four formless concentrations; that there is no great bodhisattva in the four meditations, four immeasurable minds, and four formless concentrations; that there are no four meditations, four immeasurable minds, and four formless concentrations in great bodhisattva; and that there is no great bodhisattva apart from the four meditations, four immeasurable minds, and four formless concentrations?"

"World-Honored One, as bodhi, sattva, the four meditations, four immeasurable minds, and four formless concentrations are in the final analysis unattainable because they are without self-natures, how can we say that the great bodhisattva is existent? Given the truth that they are all nonexistent, how can we say that the great bodhisattva is the same as the four meditations, four immeasurable minds, and four formless concentrations; that the great bodhisattva is different from the four meditations, four immeasurable minds, and four formless concentrations; that there is no great bodhisattva in the four meditations, four immeasurable minds, and four formless concentrations; that there are no four meditations, four immeasurable

Fascicle 15, Chapter 7, Section 5   339

minds, and four formless concentrations in the great bodhisattva; and that there is no great bodhisattva apart from the four meditations, four immeasurable minds, and four formless concentrations?"

"Furthermore, Well Appearing One, based on what reason do you say that the great bodhisattva is not the same as the eight liberations, eight vexation-overcoming meditations, nine concentrations in sequence, and the ten universal contemplations; that the great bodhisattva is not different from the eight liberations, eight vexation-overcoming meditations, nine concentrations in sequence, and the ten universal contemplations; that there is no great bodhisattva in the eight liberations, eight vexation-overcoming meditations, nine concentrations in sequence, and the ten universal contemplations; that there are no eight liberations, eight vexation-overcoming meditations, nine concentrations in sequence, and the ten universal contemplations in great bodhisattva; and that there is no great bodhisattva apart from the eight liberations, eight vexation-overcoming meditations, nine concentrations in sequence, and the ten universal contemplations?"

"World-Honored One, as bodhi, sattva, the eight liberations, eight vexation-overcoming meditations, nine concentrations in sequence, and the ten universal contemplations are in the final analysis unattainable because they are without self-natures, how can we say that the great bodhisattva is existent? Given the truth that they are all nonexistent, how can we say that the great bodhisattva is the same as the eight liberations, eight vexation-overcoming meditations, nine concentrations in sequence, and ten universal contemplations; that the great bodhisattva is different from the eight liberations, eight vexation-overcoming meditations, nine concentrations in sequence, and the ten universal contemplations; that there is great bodhisattva in the eight liberations, eight vexation-overcoming meditations, nine concentrations in sequence, and the ten universal contemplations; that there are the eight liberations, eight vexation-overcoming meditations, nine concentrations in sequence, and ten universal contemplations in the great bodhisattva; and that there is great bodhisattva apart from the eight liberations, eight vexation-overcoming meditations, nine concentrations in sequence, and the ten universal contemplations?"

"Furthermore, Well Appearing One, based on what reason do you say that the great bodhisattva is not the same as the liberation gates of emptiness, formlessness, and nonaspiration; that the great bodhisattva is not different from the liberation gates of emptiness, formlessness, and nonaspiration; that there is no great bodhisattva in the liberation gates of emptiness, formlessness, and nonaspiration; that there are no liberation gates of emptiness, formlessness, and nonaspiration in great bodhisattva; and that there is no great bodhisattva apart from the liberation gates of emptiness, formlessness, and nonaspiration?"

"World-Honored One, as bodhi, sattva, and the liberation gates of emptiness, formlessness, and nonaspiration are in the final analysis unattainable because they are without self-natures, how can we say that the great bodhisattva is existent? Given the truth that they are all nonexistent, how can we say that the great bodhisattva is the same as the liberation gates of emptiness, formlessness, and nonaspiration; that the great bodhisattva is not different from the liberation gates of emptiness, formlessness, and nonaspiration; that there is great bodhisattva in the liberation gates of emptiness, formlessness, and nonaspiration; that there are the liberation gates of emptiness, formlessness, and nonaspiration in the great bodhisattva; and that there is great bodhisattva apart from the liberation gates of emptiness, formlessness, and nonaspiration?"

"Furthermore, Well Appearing One, based on what reason do you say that the great bodhisattva is not the same as the dharani gates and the samadhi gates; that the great bodhisattva is not different from the dharani gates and the samadhi gates; that there is no great bodhisattva in the dharani gates and the samadhi gates; that there are no dharani gates and samadhi gates in great bodhisattva; and that there is no great bodhisattva apart from the dharani gates and the samadhi gates?"

"World-Honored One, as bodhi, sattva, the dharani gates, and the samadhi gates are in the final analysis unattainable because they are without self-natures, how can we say that the great bodhisattva is existent? Given the truth that they are all nonexistent, how can we say that the great bodhisattva is the same as the dharani gates and the samadhi gates; that the great bodhisattva is different

Fascicle 15, Chapter 7, Section 5

from the dharani gates and the samadhi gates; that there is great bodhisattva in the dharani gates and the samadhi gates; that there are dharani gates and samadhi gates in the great bodhisattva; and that there is great bodhisattva apart from the dharani gates and the samadhi gates?"

"Furthermore, Well Appearing One, based on what reason do you say that the great bodhisattva is not the same as the stages of ecstasy, freedom from defilements, emitting light, flaming wisdom, being difficult to be surpassed, manifestation of pure realness, going far away, the unmovable, expedient wisdom, and dharma cloud; that the great bodhisattva is not different from the stage of ecstasy, and so forth, as well as the stage of dharma cloud; that there is no great bodhisattva in the stage of ecstasy, and so forth, as well as the stage of dharma cloud; that there is no stage of ecstasy, and so forth, as well as the stage of dharma cloud in great bodhisattva; and that there is no great bodhisattva apart from the stage of ecstasy, and so forth, as well as the stage of dharma cloud?"

"World-Honored One, as bodhi, sattva, the stage of ecstasy, and so forth, as well as the stage of dharma cloud are in the final analysis unattainable because they are without self-natures, how can we say that the great bodhisattva is existent? Given the truth that they are all nonexistent, how can we say that the great bodhisattva is the same as the stage of ecstasy, and so forth, as well as the stage of dharma cloud; that the great bodhisattva is different from the stage of ecstasy, and so forth, as well as the stage of dharma cloud; that there is great bodhisattva in the stage of ecstasy, and so forth, as well as the stage of dharma cloud; that there is the stage of ecstasy, and so forth, as well as the stage of dharma cloud in great bodhisattva; and that there is great bodhisattva apart from the stage of ecstasy, and so forth, as well as the stage of dharma cloud?"

"Furthermore, Well Appearing One, based on what reason do you say that the great bodhisattva is not the same as the five eyes and the six supernatural powers; that the great bodhisattva is not different from the five eyes and the six supernatural powers; that there is no great bodhisattva in the five eyes and the six supernatural powers; that there are no five eyes and six supernatural powers in the great bodhisattva; and that there is no great bodhisattva apart from the five eyes and the six supernatural powers?"

"World-Honored One, as bodhi, sattva, the five eyes, and the six supernatural powers are in the final analysis unattainable because they are without self-natures, how can we say that the great bodhisattva is existent? Given the truth that they are all nonexistent, how can we say that the great bodhisattva is the same as the five eyes and the six supernatural powers; that the great bodhisattva is different from the five eyes and the six supernatural powers; that there is great bodhisattva in the five eyes and the six supernatural powers; that there are the five eyes and the six supernatural powers in the great bodhisattva; and that there is great bodhisattva apart from the five eyes and the six supernatural powers?"

"Furthermore, Well Appearing One, based on what reason do you say that the great bodhisattva is not the same as the Buddha's ten abilities, four kinds of fearlessness, four unhindered understandings, and the eighteen distinctive features of Buddha's wisdom and power; that the great bodhisattva is not different from the Buddha's ten abilities, four kinds of fearlessness, four unhindered understandings, and the eighteen distinctive features of Buddha's wisdom and power; that there is no great bodhisattva in the Buddha's ten abilities, four kinds of fearlessness, four unhindered understandings, and the eighteen distinctive features of Buddha's wisdom and power; that there are no Buddha's ten abilities, four kinds of fearlessness, four unhindered understandings, and eighteen distinctive features of Buddha's wisdom and power in great bodhisattva; and that there is no great bodhisattva apart from the Buddha's ten abilities, four kinds of fearlessness, four unhindered understandings, and the eighteen distinctive features of Buddha's wisdom and power?"

"World-Honored One, as bodhi, sattva, the Buddha's ten abilities, four kinds of fearlessness, four unhindered understandings, and the eighteen distinctive features of Buddha's wisdom and power are in the final analysis unattainable because they are without self-natures, how can we say that the great bodhisattva is existent? Given the truth that they are all nonexistent, how can we say that the great bodhisattva is the same as the Buddha's ten abilities, four kinds of fearlessness, four unhindered understandings, and the eighteen distinctive features of Buddha's wisdom and power; that the great bodhisattva is different from the Buddha's ten abilities, four kinds of fearlessness, four unhindered understandings, and the eighteen distinctive features of Buddha's wisdom and power; that there is great bodhisattva in the Buddha's ten abilities, four kinds of fearlessness, four unhindered understandings, and the eighteen distinctive features of Buddha's wisdom and power; that there are the Buddha's ten abilities, four kinds of fearlessness, four unhindered understandings, and the eighteen distinctive features of Buddha's wisdom and power in great bodhisattva; and that there is great bodhisattva apart from the Buddha's ten abilities, four kinds of fearlessness, four unhindered understandings, and the eighteen distinctive features of Buddha's wisdom and power?"

"Furthermore, Well Appearing One, based on what reason do you say that the great bodhisattva is not the same as great loving-kindness, great compassion, great joy, and great equanimity; that the great bodhisattva is not different from great loving-kindness, great compassion, great joy, and great equanimity; that there is no great bodhisattva in great loving-kindness, great compassion, great joy, and great equanimity; that there are no great loving-kindness, great compassion, great joy, and great equanimity in great bodhisattva; and that there is no great bodhisattva apart from great loving-kindness, great compassion, great joy, and great equanimity?"

"World-Honored One, as bodhi, sattva, great loving-kindness, great compassion, great joy, and great equanimity are in the final analysis unattainable because they are without self-natures, how can we say that the great bodhisattva is existent? Given the truth that they are all nonexistent, how can we say that the great bodhisattva is the same as great loving-kindness, great compassion, great joy, and great equanimity; that the great bodhisattva is different from great loving-kindness, great compassion, great joy, and great equanimity; that there is great bodhisattva in great loving-kindness, great compassion, great joy, and great equanimity; that there are great loving-kindness, great compassion, great joy, and great equanimity in great bodhisattva; and that there is great bodhisattva apart from great loving-kindness, great compassion, great joy, and great equanimity?"

"Furthermore, Well Appearing One, based on what reason do you say that the great bodhisattva is not the same as the thirty-two perfect major marks and the eighty distinguishing minor features; that the great bodhisattva is not different from the thirty-two perfect major marks and the eighty distinguishing minor features; that there is no great bodhisattva in the thirty-two perfect major marks and the eighty distinguishing minor features; that there are no thirty-two perfect major marks and the eighty distinguishing minor features in great bodhisattva; and that there is no great bodhisattva apart from the thirty-two perfect major marks and the eighty distinguishing minor features?"

"World-Honored One, as bodhi, sattva, the thirty-two perfect major marks, and the eighty distinguishing minor features are in the final analysis unattainable because they are without self-natures, how can we say that the great bodhisattva is existent? Given the truth that they are all nonexistent, how can we say that the great bodhisattva is the same as the thirty-two perfect major marks and the eighty distinguishing minor features; that the great bodhisattva is different from the thirty-two perfect major marks and the eighty distinguishing minor features; that there is great bodhisattva in the thirty-two perfect major marks and the eighty distinguishing minor features; that there are the thirty-two perfect major marks and the eighty distinguishing minor features in great bodhisattva; and that there is great bodhisattva apart from the thirty-two perfect major marks and the eighty distinguishing minor features?"

"Furthermore, Well Appearing One, based on what reason do you say that the great bodhisattva is not the same as staying in correct mindfulness and dwelling in equanimity at all times; that the great bodhisattva is not different from staying in correct mindfulness and dwelling in equanimity at all times; that there is no great bodhisattva in staying in correct mindfulness and dwelling in equanimity at all times; that there are no staying in correct mindfulness and dwelling in equanimity at all times in great bodhisattva; and that there is no great bodhisattva apart from staying in correct mindfulness and dwelling in equanimity at all times?"

"World-Honored One, as bodhi, sattva, staying in correct mindfulness and dwelling in equanimity at all times are in the final analysis unattainable because they are without self-natures, how can we say that the great bodhisattva is existent? Given the truth that they are all nonexistent, how can we say that the great bodhisattva is the same as staying in correct mindfulness and dwelling in equanimity at all times; that the great bodhisattva is different from staying in correct mindfulness and dwelling in equanimity at all times; that there is great bodhisattva in staying in correct mindfulness and dwelling in equanimity at all times; that there are staying in correct mindfulness and dwelling in equanimity at all times in the great bodhisattva; and that there is great bodhisattva apart from staying in correct mindfulness and dwelling in equanimity at all times?"

"Furthermore, Well Appearing One, based on what reason do you say that the great bodhisattva is not the same as the perfect knowledge of everything, the perfect knowledge of the forms of the paths, and the perfect knowledge of all phenomena; that the great bodhisattva is not different from the perfect knowledge of everything, the perfect knowledge of the forms of the paths, and the perfect knowledge of all phenomena; that there is no great bodhisattva in the perfect knowledge of everything, the perfect knowledge of the forms of the paths, and the perfect knowledge of all phenomena; that there are no perfect knowledge of everything, perfect knowledge of the forms of the paths, and the perfect knowledge of all phenomena in great bodhisattva; and that there is no great bodhisattva apart from the perfect knowledge of everything, the perfect knowledge of the forms of the paths, and the perfect knowledge of all phenomena?"

"World-Honored One, as bodhi, sattva, the perfect knowledge of everything, the perfect knowledge of the forms of the paths, and the perfect knowledge of all phenomena are in the final analysis unattainable because they are without self-natures, how can we say that the great bodhisattva is existent? Given the truth that they are all nonexistent, how can we say that the great bodhisattva is the same as the perfect knowledge of everything, the perfect knowledge of the forms of the paths, and the perfect knowledge of all phenomena; that the great bodhisattva is different from the perfect knowledge of everything, the perfect knowledge of the forms of the paths, and the perfect knowledge of all phenomena; that there is the great bodhisattva in the perfect knowledge of everything, the perfect knowledge of the forms of the paths, and the perfect knowledge of all phenomena; that there are the perfect knowledge of everything, the perfect knowledge of the forms of the paths, and the perfect knowledge of all phenomena in great bodhisattva; and that there is great bodhisattva apart from the perfect knowledge of everything, the perfect knowledge of the forms of the paths, and the perfect knowledge of all phenomena?"

"World-Honored One, given the truth that bodhi, sattva, matter, and so forth are unattainable, it is unreasonable to say that the great bodhisattva is the same as matter, and so forth; that the great bodhisattva is different from matter, and so forth; that there is the great bodhisattva in matter, and so forth; that there is matter, and so forth, in the great bodhisattva; and that there is the great bodhisattva apart from matter, and so forth."

The Buddha said to Well Appearing One, "Excellent, excellent! It is as you say. Well Appearing One, because matter, and so forth, are unattainable, great bodhisattva is also unattainable. Because the great bodhisattvas are unattainable, the prajna paramita that they practice is also unattainable. Well Appearing One, when cultivating prajna paramita, the great bodhisattvas should learn this way.

"Furthermore, Well Appearing One, what do you think about this: is great bodhisattva the same as the realness of matter?"

"No, I don't think so, World-Honored One!"

"Is great bodhisattva the same as the realness of feeling, thinking, action, and consciousness?"

"No, I don't think so, World-Honored One!"

"Is great bodhisattva different from the realness of matter?"

"No, I don't think so, World-Honored One!"

"Is great bodhisattva different from the realness of feeling, thinking, action, and consciousness?"

"No, I don't think so, World-Honored One!"

"Is there great bodhisattva in the realness of matter?"

"No, I don't think so, World-Honored One!"

"Is there great bodhisattva in the realness of feeling, thinking, action, and consciousness?"

Fascicle 15, Chapter 7, Section 5

"No, I don't think so, World-Honored One!"
"Is there the realness of matter in the great bodhisattva?"
"No, I don't think so, World-Honored One!"
"Is there the realness of feeling, thinking, action, and consciousness in the great bodhisattva?"
"No, I don't think so, World-Honored One!"
"Is there great bodhisattva apart from the realness of matter?"
"No, I don't think so, World-Honored One!"
"Is there great bodhisattva apart from the realness of feeling, thinking, action, and consciousness?"
"No, I don't think so, World-Honored One!"
"Furthermore, Well Appearing One, what do you think about this: is great bodhisattva the same as the realness of the eye sphere?"
"No, I don't think so, World-Honored One!"
"Is great bodhisattva the same as the realness of the ear, nose, tongue, body, and conscious spheres?"
"No, I don't think so, World-Honored One!"
"Is great bodhisattva different from the realness of the eye sphere?"
"No, I don't think so, World-Honored One!"
"Is great bodhisattva different from the realness of the ear, nose, tongue, body, and conscious spheres?"
"No, I don't think so, World-Honored One!"
"Is there great bodhisattva in the realness of the eye sphere?"
"No, I don't think so, World-Honored One!"
"Is there great bodhisattva in the realness of the ear, nose, tongue, body, and conscious spheres?"
"No, I don't think so, World-Honored One!"
"Is there the realness of the eye sphere in the great bodhisattva?"
"No, I don't think so, World-Honored One!"
"Is there the realness of the ear, nose, tongue, body, and conscious spheres in the great bodhisattva?"
"No, I don't think so, World-Honored One!"
"Is there great bodhisattva apart from the realness of the eye sphere?"
"No, I don't think so, World-Honored One!"

"Is there great bodhisattva apart from the realness of the ear, nose, tongue, body, and conscious spheres?"

"No, I don't think so, World-Honored One!"

"Furthermore, Well Appearing One, what do you think about this: is great bodhisattva the same as the realness of the sight sphere?"

"No, I don't think so, World-Honored One!"

"Is great bodhisattva the same as the realness of the sound, smell, taste, touch, and mental-image spheres?"

"No, I don't think so, World-Honored One!"

"Is great bodhisattva different from the realness of the sight sphere?"

"No, I don't think so, World-Honored One!"

"Is great bodhisattva different from the realness of the sound, smell, taste, touch, and mental-image spheres?"

"No, I don't think so, World-Honored One!"

"Is there great bodhisattva in the realness of the sight sphere?"

"No, I don't think so, World-Honored One!"

"Is there great bodhisattva in the realness of the sound, smell, taste, touch, and mental-image spheres?"

"No, I don't think so, World-Honored One!"

"Is there the realness of the sight sphere in the great bodhisattva?"

"No, I don't think so, World-Honored One!"

"Is there the realness of the sound, smell, taste, touch, and mental-image spheres in the great bodhisattva?"

"No, I don't think so, World-Honored One!"

"Is there great bodhisattva apart from the realness of the sight sphere?"

"No, I don't think so, World-Honored One!"

"Is there great bodhisattva apart from the realness of the sound, smell, taste, touch, and mental-image spheres?"

"No, I don't think so, World-Honored One!"

"Furthermore, Well Appearing One, what do you think about this: is great bodhisattva the same as the realness of the eye realm?"

"No, I don't think so, World-Honored One!"

"Is great bodhisattva the same as the realness of the ear, nose, tongue, body, and conscious realms?"

"No, I don't think so, World-Honored One!"
"Is great bodhisattva different from the realness of the eye realm?"
"No, I don't think so, World-Honored One!"
"Is great bodhisattva different from the realness of the ear, nose, tongue, body, and conscious realms?"
"No, I don't think so, World-Honored One!"
"Is there great bodhisattva in the realness of the eye realm?"
"No, I don't think so, World-Honored One!"
"Is there great bodhisattva in the realness of the ear, nose, tongue, body, and conscious realms?"
"No, I don't think so, World-Honored One!"
"Is there realness of the eye realm in the great bodhisattva?"
"No, I don't think so, World-Honored One!"
"Is there realness of the ear, nose, tongue, body, and conscious realms in the great bodhisattva?"
"No, I don't think so, World-Honored One!"
"Is there great bodhisattva apart from the realness of the eye realm?"
"No, I don't think so, World-Honored One!"
"Is there great bodhisattva apart from the realness of the ear, nose, tongue, body, and conscious realms?"
"No, I don't think so, World-Honored One!"
"Furthermore, Well Appearing One, what do you think about this: is great bodhisattva the same as the realness of the sight realm?"
"No, I don't think so, World-Honored One!"
"Is great bodhisattva the same as the realness of the sound, smell, taste, touch, and mental-image realms?"
"No, I don't think so, World-Honored One!"
"Is great bodhisattva different from the realness of the sight realm?"
"No, I don't think so, World-Honored One!"
"Is great bodhisattva different from the realness of the sound, smell, taste, touch, and mental-image realms?"
"No, I don't think so, World-Honored One!"
"Is there great bodhisattva in the realness of the sight realm?"
"No, I don't think so, World-Honored One!"

"Is there great bodhisattva in the realness of the sound, smell, taste, touch, and mental-image realms?"
"No, I don't think so, World-Honored One!"
"Is there realness of the sight realm in the great bodhisattva?"
"No, I don't think so, World-Honored One!"
"Is there realness of the sound, smell, taste, touch, and mental-image realms in the great bodhisattva?"
"No, I don't think so, World-Honored One!"
"Is there great bodhisattva apart from the realness of the sight realm?"
"No, I don't think so, World-Honored One!"
"Is there great bodhisattva apart from the realness of the sound, smell, taste, touch, and mental-image realms?"
"No, I don't think so, World-Honored One!"
"Furthermore, Well Appearing One, what do you think about this: is great bodhisattva the same as the realness of the eye consciousness realm?"
"No, I don't think so, World-Honored One!"
"Is great bodhisattva the same as the realness of the ear consciousness, nose consciousness, tongue consciousness, body consciousness, and conscious consciousness realms?"
"No, I don't think so, World-Honored One!"
"Is great bodhisattva different from the realness of the eye consciousness realm?"
"No, I don't think so, World-Honored One!"
"Is great bodhisattva different from the realness of the ear consciousness, nose consciousness, tongue consciousness, body consciousness, and conscious consciousness realms?"
"No, I don't think so, World-Honored One!"
"Is there great bodhisattva in the realness of the eye consciousness realm?"
"No, I don't think so, World-Honored One!"
"Is there great bodhisattva in the realness of the ear consciousness, nose consciousness, tongue consciousness, body consciousness, and conscious consciousness realms?"
"No, I don't think so, World-Honored One!"

Fascicle 15, Chapter 7, Section 5

"Is there realness of the eye consciousness realm in the great bodhisattva?"

"No, I don't think so, World-Honored One!"

"Is there realness of the ear consciousness, nose consciousness, tongue consciousness, body consciousness, and conscious consciousness realms in the great bodhisattva?"

"No, I don't think so, World-Honored One!"

"Is there great bodhisattva apart from the realness of the eye consciousness realm?"

"No, I don't think so, World-Honored One!"

"Is there great bodhisattva apart from the realness of the ear consciousness, nose consciousness, tongue consciousness, body consciousness, and conscious consciousness realms?"

"No, I don't think so, World-Honored One!"

"Furthermore, Well Appearing One, what do you think about this: is great bodhisattva the same as the realness of the eye contact?"

"No, I don't think so, World-Honored One!"

"Is great bodhisattva the same as the realness of the ear, nose, tongue, body, and conscious contacts?"

"No, I don't think so, World-Honored One!"

"Is great bodhisattva different from the realness of the eye contact?"

"No, I don't think so, World-Honored One!"

"Is great bodhisattva different from the realness of the ear, nose, tongue, body, and conscious contacts?"

"No, I don't think so, World-Honored One!"

"Is there great bodhisattva in the realness of the eye contact?"

"No, I don't think so, World-Honored One!"

"Is there great bodhisattva in the realness of the ear, nose, tongue, body, and conscious contacts?"

"No, I don't think so, World-Honored One!"

"Is there realness of the eye contact in the great bodhisattva?"

"No, I don't think so, World-Honored One!"

"Is there realness of the ear, nose, tongue, body, and conscious contacts in the great bodhisattva?"

"No, I don't think so, World-Honored One!"

"Is there great bodhisattva apart from the realness of the eye contact?"

"No, I don't think so, World-Honored One!"

"Is there great bodhisattva apart from the realness of the ear, nose, tongue, body, and conscious contacts?"

"No, I don't think so, World-Honored One!"

"Furthermore, Well Appearing One, what do you think about this: is great bodhisattva the same as the realness of the feelings produced by eye contact?"

"No, I don't think so, World-Honored One!"

"Is great bodhisattva the same as the realness of the feelings produced by ear, nose, tongue, body, and conscious contacts?"

"No, I don't think so, World-Honored One!"

"Is great bodhisattva different from the realness of the feelings produced by eye contact?"

"No, I don't think so, World-Honored One!"

"Is great bodhisattva different from the realness of the feelings produced by ear, nose, tongue, body, and conscious contacts?"

"No, I don't think so, World-Honored One!"

"Is there great bodhisattva in the realness of the feelings produced by eye contact?"

"No, I don't think so, World-Honored One!"

"Is there great bodhisattva in the realness of the feelings produced by ear, nose, tongue, body, and conscious contacts?"

"No, I don't think so, World-Honored One!"

"Is there realness of the feelings produced by eye contact in the great bodhisattva?"

"No, I don't think so, World-Honored One!"

"Is there realness of the feelings produced by ear, nose, tongue, body, and conscious contacts in the great bodhisattva?"

"No, I don't think so, World-Honored One!"

"Is there great bodhisattva apart from the realness of the feelings produced by eye contact?"

"No, I don't think so, World-Honored One!"

"Is there great bodhisattva apart from the realness of the feelings produced by ear, nose, tongue, body, and conscious contacts?"

"No, I don't think so, World-Honored One!"

"Furthermore, Well Appearing One, what do you think about this: is great bodhisattva the same as the realness of the earth realm?"

"No, I don't think so, World-Honored One!"

"Is great bodhisattva the same as the realness of the water, fire, wind, empty space, and consciousness realms?"

"No, I don't think so, World-Honored One!"

"Is great bodhisattva different from the realness of the earth realm?"

"No, I don't think so, World-Honored One!"

"Is great bodhisattva different from the realness of the water, fire, wind, space, and consciousness realms?"

"No, I don't think so, World-Honored One!"

"Is there great bodhisattva in the realness of the earth realm?"

"No, I don't think so, World-Honored One!"

"Is there great bodhisattva in the realness of the water, fire, wind, space, and consciousness realms?"

"No, I don't think so, World-Honored One!"

"Is there realness of the earth realm in the great bodhisattva?"

"No, I don't think so, World-Honored One!"

"Is there realness of the water, fire, wind, space, and consciousness realms in the great bodhisattva?"

"No, I don't think so, World-Honored One!"

"Is there great bodhisattva apart from the realness of the earth realm?"

"No, I don't think so, World-Honored One!"

"Is there great bodhisattva apart from the realness of the water, fire, wind, space, and consciousness realms?"

"No, I don't think so, World-Honored One!"

"Furthermore, Well Appearing One, what do you think about this: is great bodhisattva the same as the realness of cause and condition?"

"No, I don't think so, World-Honored One!"

"Is great bodhisattva the same as the realness of the consecutive thoughts in sequence, the conditions that stimulate one's mind, and the conditions that reinforce main causes?"

"No, I don't think so, World-Honored One!"

"Is great bodhisattva different from the realness of cause and condition?"

"No, I don't think so, World-Honored One!"

"Is great bodhisattva different from the realness of the consecutive thoughts in sequence, the conditions that stimulate one's mind, and the conditions that reinforce main causes?"

"No, I don't think so, World-Honored One!"

"Is there great bodhisattva in the realness of cause and condition?"

"No, I don't think so, World-Honored One!"

"Is there great bodhisattva in the realness of the consecutive thoughts in sequence, the conditions that stimulate one's mind, and the conditions that reinforce main causes?"

"No, I don't think so, World-Honored One!"

"Is there realness of cause and condition in the great bodhisattva?"

"No, I don't think so, World-Honored One!"

"Is there realness of the consecutive thoughts in sequence, the conditions that stimulate one's mind, and the conditions that reinforce main causes in the great bodhisattva?"

"No, I don't think so, World-Honored One!"

"Is there great bodhisattva apart from the realness of cause and condition?"

"No, I don't think so, World-Honored One!"

"Is there great bodhisattva apart from the realness of the consecutive thoughts in sequence, the conditions that stimulate one's mind, and the conditions that reinforce main causes?"

"No, I don't think so, World-Honored One!"

"Furthermore, Well Appearing One, what do you think about this: is great bodhisattva the same as the realness of the dharmas caused by conditions?"

"No, I don't think so, World-Honored One!"

"Is great bodhisattva different from the realness of the dharmas caused by conditions?"

"No, I don't think so, World-Honored One!"

"Is there great bodhisattva in the realness of the dharmas caused by conditions?"

"No, I don't think so, World-Honored One!"
"Is there realness of the dharmas caused by conditions in the great bodhisattva?"
"No, I don't think so, World-Honored One!"
"Is there great bodhisattva apart from the realness of the dharmas caused by conditions?"
"No, I don't think so, World-Honored One!"
"Furthermore, Well Appearing One, what do you think about this: is great bodhisattva the same as the realness of ignorance?"
"No, I don't think so, World-Honored One!"
"Is great bodhisattva the same as the realness of action, consciousness, name and form, six sense spheres, contact, reception, craving, grasping, existence, birth, old age, and death?"
"No, I don't think so, World-Honored One!"
"Is great bodhisattva different from the realness of ignorance?"
"No, I don't think so, World-Honored One!"
"Is great bodhisattva different from the realness of action, and so forth, as well as old age and death?"
"No, I don't think so, World-Honored One!"
"Is there great bodhisattva in the realness of ignorance?"
"No, I don't think so, World-Honored One!"
"Is there great bodhisattva in the realness of action, and so forth, as well as old age and death?"
"No, I don't think so, World-Honored One!"
"Is there realness of ignorance in the great bodhisattva?"
"No, I don't think so, World-Honored One!"
"Is there realness of action, and so forth, as well as old age and death in the great bodhisattva?"
"No, I don't think so, World-Honored One!"
"Is there great bodhisattva apart from the realness of ignorance?"
"No, I don't think so, World-Honored One!"
"Is there great bodhisattva apart from the realness of action, and so forth, as well as old age and death?"
"No, I don't think so, World-Honored One!"
"Furthermore, Well Appearing One, what do you think about this: is great bodhisattva the same as the realness of giving paramita?"
"No, I don't think so, World-Honored One!"

"Is great bodhisattva the same as the realness of pure precept, forbearance, diligence, meditation, and prajna paramitas?"

"No, I don't think so, World-Honored One!"

"Is great bodhisattva different from the realness of giving paramita?"

"No, I don't think so, World-Honored One!"

"Is great bodhisattva different from the realness of pure precept, forbearance, diligence, meditation, and prajna paramitas?"

"No, I don't think so, World-Honored One!"

"Is there great bodhisattva in the realness of giving paramita?"

"No, I don't think so, World-Honored One!"

"Is there great bodhisattva in the realness of pure precept, forbearance, diligence, meditation, and prajna paramitas?"

"No, I don't think so, World-Honored One!"

"Is there realness of giving paramita in the great bodhisattva?"

"No, I don't think so, World-Honored One!"

"Is there realness of pure precept, forbearance, diligence, meditation, and prajna paramitas in the great bodhisattva?"

"No, I don't think so, World-Honored One!"

"Is there great bodhisattva apart from the realness of giving paramita?"

"No, I don't think so, World-Honored One!"

"Is there great bodhisattva apart from the realness of pure precept, forbearance, diligence, meditation, and prajna paramitas?"

"No, I don't think so, World-Honored One!"

"Furthermore, Well Appearing One, what do you think about this: is great bodhisattva the same as the realness of internal emptiness?"

"No, I don't think so, World-Honored One!"

"Is great bodhisattva the same as the realness of external emptiness, internal-external emptiness, emptiness of emptiness, emptiness of space, emptiness of ultimate truth, emptiness of conditioned phenomena, emptiness of unconditioned reality, emptiness in the final analysis, emptiness of nontemporality, emptiness of deconstruction, emptiness of changelessness, emptiness of original nature, emptiness of particular characteristics, emptiness of common characteristics, emptiness of all dharmas, emptiness of nonattainment, emptiness of selflessness, emptiness of self-nature, and emptiness of selfless self-nature?"

"No, I don't think so, World-Honored One!"

"Is great bodhisattva different from the realness of internal emptiness?"

"No, I don't think so, World-Honored One!"

"Is great bodhisattva different from the realness of external emptiness, and so forth, as well as emptiness of selfless self-nature?"

"No, I don't think so, World-Honored One!"

"Is there great bodhisattva in the realness of internal emptiness?"

"No, I don't think so, World-Honored One!"

"Is there great bodhisattva in the realness of external emptiness, and so forth, as well as emptiness of selfless self-nature?"

"No, I don't think so, World-Honored One!"

"Is there realness of internal emptiness in the great bodhisattva?"

"No, I don't think so, World-Honored One!"

"Is there realness of external emptiness, and so forth, as well as emptiness of selfless self-nature in the great bodhisattva?"

"No, I don't think so, World-Honored One!"

"Is there great bodhisattva apart from the realness of internal emptiness?"

"No, I don't think so, World-Honored One!"

"Is there great bodhisattva apart from the realness of external emptiness, and so forth, as well as emptiness of selfless self-nature?"

"No, I don't think so, World-Honored One!"

"Furthermore, Well Appearing One, what do you think about this: is great bodhisattva the same as the realness of the four bases of mindfulness?"

"No, I don't think so, World-Honored One!"

"Is great bodhisattva the same as the realness of the four correct endeavors, four bases of power, five roots, five powers, seven factors for enlightenment, and noble eightfold path?"

"No, I don't think so, World-Honored One!"

"Is great bodhisattva different from the realness of the four bases of mindfulness?"

"No, I don't think so, World-Honored One!"

"Is great bodhisattva different from the realness of the four correct endeavors, and so forth, as well as the noble eightfold path?"

"No, I don't think so, World-Honored One!"

"Is there great bodhisattva in the realness of the four bases of mindfulness?"

"No, I don't think so, World-Honored One!"

"Is there great bodhisattva in the realness of the four correct endeavors, and so forth, as well as the noble eightfold path?"

"No, I don't think so, World-Honored One!"

"Is there realness of the four bases of mindfulness in the great bodhisattva?"

"No, I don't think so, World-Honored One!"

"Is there realness of the four correct endeavors, and so forth, as well as the noble eightfold path in the great bodhisattva?"

"No, I don't think so, World-Honored One!"

"Is there great bodhisattva apart from the realness of the four bases of mindfulness?"

"No, I don't think so, World-Honored One!"

"Is there great bodhisattva apart from the realness of the four correct endeavors, and so forth, as well as the noble eightfold path?"

"No, I don't think so, World-Honored One!"

"Furthermore, Well Appearing One, what do you think about this: is great bodhisattva the same as the realness of the noble truth of suffering?"

"No, I don't think so, World-Honored One!"

"Is great bodhisattva the same as the realness of the noble truths of the cause of suffering, the cessation of suffering, and the path for the cessation of suffering?"

"No, I don't think so, World-Honored One!"

"Is great bodhisattva different from the realness of the noble truth of suffering?"

"No, I don't think so, World-Honored One!"

"Is great bodhisattva different from the realness of the noble truths of the cause of suffering, the cessation of suffering, and the path for the cessation of suffering?"

"No, I don't think so, World-Honored One!"

"Is there great bodhisattva in the realness of the noble truth of suffering?"

"No, I don't think so, World-Honored One!"

"Is there great bodhisattva in the realness of the noble truths of the cause of suffering, the cessation of suffering, and the path for the cessation of suffering?"

"No, I don't think so, World-Honored One!"

"Is there realness of the noble truth of suffering in the great bodhisattva?"

"No, I don't think so, World-Honored One!"

"Is there realness of the noble truths of the cause of suffering, the cessation of suffering, and the path for the cessation of suffering in the great bodhisattva?"

"No, I don't think so, World-Honored One!"

"Is there great bodhisattva apart from the realness of the noble truth of suffering?"

"No, I don't think so, World-Honored One!"

"Is there great bodhisattva apart from the realness of the noble truths of the cause of suffering, the cessation of suffering, and the path for the cessation of suffering?"

"No, I don't think so, World-Honored One!"

"Furthermore, Well Appearing One, what do you think about this: is great bodhisattva the same as the realness of the four meditations?"

"No, I don't think so, World-Honored One!"

"Is great bodhisattva the same as the realness of the four immeasurable minds and the four formless concentrations?"

"No, I don't think so, World-Honored One!"

"Is great bodhisattva different from the realness of the four meditations?"

"No, I don't think so, World-Honored One!"

"Is great bodhisattva different from the realness of the four immeasurable minds and the four formless concentrations?"

"No, I don't think so, World-Honored One!"

"Is there great bodhisattva in the realness of the four meditations?"

"No, I don't think so, World-Honored One!"

"Is there great bodhisattva in the realness of the four immeasurable minds and the four formless concentrations?"

"No, I don't think so, World-Honored One!"

"Is there realness of the four meditations in the great bodhisattva?"

"No, I don't think so, World-Honored One!"

"Is there realness of the four immeasurable minds and the four formless concentrations in the great bodhisattva?"

"No, I don't think so, World-Honored One!"

"Is there great bodhisattva apart from the realness of the four meditations?"

"No, I don't think so, World-Honored One!"

"Is there great bodhisattva apart from the realness of the four immeasurable minds and the four formless concentrations?"

"No, I don't think so, World-Honored One!"

"Furthermore, Well Appearing One, what do you think about this: is great bodhisattva the same as the realness of the eight liberations?"

"No, I don't think so, World-Honored One!"

"Is great bodhisattva the same as the realness of the eight vexation-overcoming meditations, nine concentrations in sequence, and ten universal contemplations?"

"No, I don't think so, World-Honored One!"

"Is great bodhisattva different from the realness of the eight liberations?"

"No, I don't think so, World-Honored One!"

"Is great bodhisattva different from the realness of the eight vexation-overcoming meditations, nine concentrations in sequence, and ten universal contemplations?"

"No, I don't think so, World-Honored One!"

"Is there great bodhisattva in the realness of the eight liberations?"

"No, I don't think so, World-Honored One!"

"Is there great bodhisattva in the realness of the eight vexation-overcoming meditations, nine concentrations in sequence, and ten universal contemplations?"

"No, I don't think so, World-Honored One!"
"Is there realness of the eight liberations in the great bodhisattva?"
"No, I don't think so, World-Honored One!"
"Is there realness of the eight vexation-overcoming meditations, nine concentrations in sequence, and ten universal contemplations in the great bodhisattva?"
"No, I don't think so, World-Honored One!"
"Is there great bodhisattva apart from the realness of the eight liberations?"
"No, I don't think so, World-Honored One!"
"Is there great bodhisattva apart from the realness of the eight vexation-overcoming meditations, nine concentrations in sequence, and ten universal contemplations?"
"No, I don't think so, World-Honored One!"
"Furthermore, Well Appearing One, what do you think about this: Is great bodhisattva the same as the realness of the liberation gate of emptiness?"
"No, I don't think so, World-Honored One!"
"Is great bodhisattva the same as the realness of the liberation gates of formlessness and nonaspiration?"
"No, I don't think so, World-Honored One!"
"Is great bodhisattva different from the realness of the liberation gate of emptiness?"
"No, I don't think so, World-Honored One!"
"Is great bodhisattva different from the realness of the liberation gates of formlessness and nonaspiration?"
"No, I don't think so, World-Honored One!"
"Is there great bodhisattva in the realness of the liberation gate of emptiness?"
"No, I don't think so, World-Honored One!"
"Is there great bodhisattva in the realness of the liberation gates of formlessness and nonaspiration?"
"No, I don't think so, World-Honored One!"
"Is there realness of the liberation gate of emptiness in the great bodhisattva?"

"No, I don't think so, World-Honored One!"

"Is there realness of the liberation gates of formlessness and nonaspiration in the great bodhisattva?"

"No, I don't think so, World-Honored One!"

"Is there great bodhisattva apart from the realness of the liberation gate of emptiness?"

"No, I don't think so, World-Honored One!"

"Is there great bodhisattva apart from the realness of the liberation gates of formlessness and nonaspiration?"

"No, I don't think so, World-Honored One!"

"Furthermore, Well Appearing One, what do you think about this: is great bodhisattva the same as the realness of the dharani gates?"

"No, I don't think so, World-Honored One!"

"Is great bodhisattva the same as the realness of the samadhi gates?"

"No, I don't think so, World-Honored One!"

"Is great bodhisattva different from the realness of the dharani gates?"

"No, I don't think so, World-Honored One!"

"Is great bodhisattva different from the realness of the samadhi gates?"

"No, I don't think so, World-Honored One!"

"Is there great bodhisattva in the realness of the dharani gates?"

"No, I don't think so, World-Honored One!"

"Is there great bodhisattva in the realness of the samadhi gates?"

"No, I don't think so, World-Honored One!"

"Is there realness of the dharani gates in the great bodhisattva?"

"No, I don't think so, World-Honored One!"

"Is there realness of the samadhi gates in the great bodhisattva?"

"No, I don't think so, World-Honored One!"

"Is there great bodhisattva apart from the realness of the dharani gates?"

"No, I don't think so, World-Honored One!"

"Is there great bodhisattva apart from the realness of the samadhi gates?"

"No, I don't think so, World-Honored One!"

"Furthermore, Well Appearing One, what do you think about this: is great bodhisattva the same as the realness of the stage of ecstasy?"

"No, I don't think so, World-Honored One!"

"Is great bodhisattva the same as the realness of the stages of freedom from defilements, emitting light, flaming wisdom, being extremely difficult to be surpassed, manifestation of pure realness, going far away, the unmovable, expedient wisdom, and dharma cloud?"

"No, I don't think so, World-Honored One!"

"Is great bodhisattva different from the realness of the stage of ecstasy?"

"No, I don't think so, World-Honored One!"

"Is great bodhisattva different from the realness of the stage of freedom from defilements, and so forth, as well as the stage of dharma cloud?"

"No, I don't think so, World-Honored One!"

"Is there great bodhisattva in the realness of the stage of ecstasy?"

"No, I don't think so, World-Honored One!"

"Is there great bodhisattva in the realness of the stage of freedom from defilements, and so forth, as well as the stage of dharma cloud?"

"No, I don't think so, World-Honored One!"

"Is there realness of the stage of ecstasy in the great bodhisattva?"

"No, I don't think so, World-Honored One!"

"Is there realness of the stage of freedom from defilements, and so forth, as well as the stage of dharma cloud in the great bodhisattva?"

"No, I don't think so, World-Honored One!"

"Is there great bodhisattva apart from the realness of the stage of ecstasy?"

"No, I don't think so, World-Honored One!"

"Is there great bodhisattva apart from the realness of the stage of freedom from defilements, and so forth, as well as the stage of dharma cloud?"

"No, I don't think so, World-Honored One!"

"Furthermore, Well Appearing One, what do you think about this: is great bodhisattva the same as the realness of the five eyes?"

"No, I don't think so, World-Honored One!"

"Is great bodhisattva the same as the realness of the six supernatural powers?"

"No, I don't think so, World-Honored One!"

"Is great bodhisattva different from the realness of the five eyes?"

"No, I don't think so, World-Honored One!"

"Is great bodhisattva different from the realness of the six supernatural powers?"

"No, I don't think so, World-Honored One!"

"Is there great bodhisattva in the realness of the five eyes?"

"No, I don't think so, World-Honored One!"

"Is there great bodhisattva in the realness of the six supernatural powers?"

"No, I don't think so, World-Honored One!"

"Is there realness of the five eyes in the great bodhisattva?"

"No, I don't think so, World-Honored One!"

"Is there realness of the six supernatural powers in the great bodhisattva?"

"No, I don't think so, World-Honored One!"

"Is there great bodhisattva apart from the realness of the five eyes?"

"No, I don't think so, World-Honored One!"

"Is there great bodhisattva apart from the realness of the six supernatural powers?"

"No, I don't think so, World-Honored One!"

FASCICLE 16

Chapter 7
The Cautions and the Teachings

Section 6

(In the First Assembly)

"FURTHERMORE, WELL APPEARING ONE, WHAT DO YOU MEAN by great bodhisattva? Is great bodhisattva the same as the realness of the Buddha's ten abilities?"

"No, I don't think so, World-Honored One!"

"Is great bodhisattva the same as the realness of the four kinds of fearlessness, four unhindered understandings, and the eighteen distinctive features of Buddha's wisdom and power?"

"No, I don't think so, World-Honored One!"

"Is great bodhisattva different from the realness of the Buddha's ten abilities?"

"No, I don't think so, World-Honored One!"

"Is great bodhisattva different from the realness of the four kinds of fearlessness, four unhindered understandings, and the eighteen distinctive features of Buddha's wisdom and power?"

"No, I don't think so, World-Honored One!"

"Is there great bodhisattva in the realness of the Buddha's ten abilities?"

"No, I don't think so, World-Honored One!"

"Is there great bodhisattva in the realness of the four kinds of fearlessness, four unhindered understandings, and the eighteen distinctive features of Buddha's wisdom and power?"

"No, I don't think so, World-Honored One!"

"Is there realness of the Buddha's ten abilities in the great bodhisattva?"

"No, I don't think so, World-Honored One!"

"Is there realness of the four kinds of fearlessness, four unhindered understandings, and the eighteen distinctive features of Buddha's wisdom and power in the great bodhisattva?"

"No, I don't think so, World-Honored One!"

"Is there great bodhisattva apart from the realness of the Buddha's ten abilities?"

"No, I don't think so, World-Honored One!"

"Is there great bodhisattva apart from the realness of the four kinds of fearlessness, four unhindered understandings, and the eighteen distinctive features of Buddha's wisdom and power?"

"No, I don't think so, World-Honored One!"

"Furthermore, Well Appearing One, what do you mean by great bodhisattva? Is great bodhisattva the same as the realness of great loving-kindness?"

"No, I don't think so, World-Honored One!"

"Is great bodhisattva the same as the realness of great compassion, great joy, and great equanimity?"

"No, I don't think so, World-Honored One!"

"Is great bodhisattva different from the realness of great loving-kindness?"

"No, I don't think so, World-Honored One!"

"Is great bodhisattva different from the realness of great compassion, great joy, and great equanimity?"

"No, I don't think so, World-Honored One!"

"Is there great bodhisattva in the realness of great loving-kindness?"

"No, I don't think so, World-Honored One!"

"Is there great bodhisattva in the realness of great compassion, great joy, and great equanimity?"

Fascicle 16, Chapter 7, Section 6 367

"No, I don't think so, World-Honored One!"

"Is there realness of great loving-kindness in the great bodhisattva?"

"No, I don't think so, World-Honored One!"

"Is there realness of great compassion, great joy, and great equanimity in the great bodhisattva?"

"No, I don't think so, World-Honored One!"

"Is there great bodhisattva apart from the realness of great loving-kindness?"

"No, I don't think so, World-Honored One!"

"Is there great bodhisattva apart from the realness of great compassion, great joy, and great equanimity?"

"No, I don't think so, World-Honored One!"

"Furthermore, Well Appearing One, what do you mean by great bodhisattva? Is great bodhisattva the same as the realness of the thirty-two perfect major marks?"

"No, I don't think so, World-Honored One!"

"Is great bodhisattva the same as the realness of the eighty distinguishing minor features?"

"No, I don't think so, World-Honored One!"

"Is the great bodhisattva different from the realness of the thirty-two perfect major marks?"

"No, I don't think so, World-Honored One!"

"Is the great bodhisattva different from the realness of the eighty distinguishing minor features?"

"No, I don't think so, World-Honored One!"

"Is there the great bodhisattva in the realness of the thirty-two perfect major marks?"

"No, I don't think so, World-Honored One!"

"Is there the great bodhisattva in the realness of the eighty distinguishing minor features?"

"No, I don't think so, World-Honored One!"

"Is there the realness of the thirty-two perfect major marks in the great bodhisattva?"

"No, I don't think so, World-Honored One!"

"Is there the realness of the eighty distinguishing minor features in the great bodhisattva?"

"No, I don't think so, World-Honored One!"

"Is there the great bodhisattva apart from the realness of the thirty-two perfect major marks?"

"No, I don't think so, World-Honored One!"

"Is there the great bodhisattva apart from the realness of the eighty distinguishing minor features?"

"No, I don't think so, World-Honored One!"

"Furthermore, Well Appearing One, what do you mean by great bodhisattva? Is great bodhisattva the same as the realness of staying in correct mindfulness?"

"No, I don't think so, World-Honored One!"

"Is great bodhisattva the same as the realness of dwelling in equanimity at all times?"

"No, I don't think so, World-Honored One!"

"Is the great bodhisattva different from the realness of staying in correct mindfulness?"

"No, I don't think so, World-Honored One!"

"Is the great bodhisattva different from the realness of dwelling in equanimity at all times?"

"No, I don't think so, World-Honored One!"

"Is there the great bodhisattva in the realness of staying in correct mindfulness?"

"No, I don't think so, World-Honored One!"

"Is there the great bodhisattva in the realness of dwelling in equanimity at all times?"

"No, I don't think so, World-Honored One!"

"Is there the realness of staying in correct mindfulness in the great bodhisattva?"

"No, I don't think so, World-Honored One!"

"Is there the realness of dwelling in equanimity at all times in the great bodhisattva?"

"No, I don't think so, World-Honored One!"

"Is there the great bodhisattva apart from the realness of staying in correct mindfulness?"

"No, I don't think so, World-Honored One!"

"Is there the great bodhisattva apart from the realness of dwelling in equanimity at all times?"

"No, I don't think so, World-Honored One!"

"Furthermore, Well Appearing One, what do you mean by great bodhisattva? Is great bodhisattva the same as the realness of the perfect knowledge of everything?"

"No, I don't think so, World-Honored One!"

"Is great bodhisattva the same as the realness of the perfect knowledge of the forms of the paths and the perfect knowledge of all phenomena?"

"No, I don't think so, World-Honored One!"

"Is great bodhisattva different from the realness of the perfect knowledge of everything?"

"No, I don't think so, World-Honored One!"

"Is great bodhisattva different from the realness of the perfect knowledge of the forms of the paths and the perfect knowledge of all phenomena?"

"No, I don't think so, World-Honored One!"

"Is there the great bodhisattva in the realness of the perfect knowledge of everything?"

"No, I don't think so, World-Honored One!"

"Is there the great bodhisattva in the realness of the perfect knowledge of the forms of the paths and the perfect knowledge of all phenomena?"

"No, I don't think so, World-Honored One!"

"Is there the realness of the perfect knowledge of everything in the great bodhisattva?"

"No, I don't think so, World-Honored One!"

"Is there the realness of the perfect knowledge of the forms of the paths and the perfect knowledge of all phenomena in the great bodhisattva?"

"No, I don't think so, World-Honored One!"

"Is there the great bodhisattva apart from the realness of the perfect knowledge of everything?"

"No, I don't think so, World-Honored One!"

"Is there the great bodhisattva apart from the realness of the perfect knowledge of the forms of the paths and the perfect knowledge of all phenomena?"

"No, I don't think so, World-Honored One!"

At that time, the Buddha asked the long-lived sage Well Appearing One, "Based on what reasons do you say that being with the realness of matter, feeling, thinking, action, and consciousness is not the great bodhisattva; that being different from the realness of matter, feeling, thinking, action, and consciousness is not the great bodhisattva; that there is no great bodhisattva in the realness of matter, feeling, thinking, action, and consciousness; that there is no realness of matter, feeling, thinking, action, and consciousness in the great bodhisattva; and that there is no great bodhisattva apart from the realness of matter, feeling, thinking, action, and consciousness?"

The long-lived sage Well Appearing One replied, "World-Honored One! As the dharmas such as matter, feeling, thinking, action, and consciousness are all in the final analysis unattainable and without self-nature, how can we say that the realness of matter, feeling, thinking, action, or consciousness is attainable and with self-nature? Given the truth that the realness is not existent, how can we say that being with the realness of matter, feeling, thinking, action, and consciousness is the great bodhisattva; that being different from the realness of matter, feeling, thinking, action, and consciousness is the great bodhisattva; that there is the great bodhisattva in the realness of matter, feeling, thinking, action, and consciousness; that there is the realness of matter, feeling, thinking, action, and consciousness in the great bodhisattva; and that there is the great bodhisattva apart from the realness of matter, feeling, thinking, action, and consciousness?"

"Furthermore, Well Appearing One, based on what reasons do you say that being with the realness of the eye, ear, nose, tongue, body, and conscious spheres is not the great bodhisattva; that being different from the realness of the eye, ear, nose, tongue, body, and conscious spheres is not the great bodhisattva; that there is no great bodhisattva in the realness of the eye, ear, nose, tongue, body, and conscious spheres; that there is no realness of the eye, ear, nose, tongue, body, and conscious spheres in the great bodhisattva; and that there is no great bodhisattva apart from the realness of the eye, ear, nose, tongue, body, and conscious spheres?"

The long-lived sage Well Appearing One replied, "World-Hon-

Fascicle 16, Chapter 7, Section 6

ored One! As the dharmas such as the eye, ear, nose, tongue, body, and conscious spheres are all in the final analysis unattainable and are without self-nature, how can we say that the realness of the eye, ear, nose, tongue, body, or conscious sphere is attainable and with self-nature? Given the truth that the realness is not existent, how can we say that being with the realness of the eye, ear, nose, tongue, body, and conscious spheres is the great bodhisattva; that being different from the realness of the eye, ear, nose, tongue, body, and conscious spheres is the great bodhisattva; that there is the great bodhisattva in the realness of the eye, ear, nose, tongue, body, and conscious sphere; that there is the realness of the eye, ear, nose, tongue, body, and conscious spheres in the great bodhisattva; and that there is the great bodhisattva apart from the realness of the eye, ear, nose, tongue, body, and conscious spheres?"

"Furthermore, Well Appearing One, based on what reasons do you say that being with the realness of the sight, sound, smell, taste, touch, and mental-image spheres is not the great bodhisattva; that being different from the realness of the sight, sound, smell, taste, touch, and mental-image spheres is not the great bodhisattva; that there is no great bodhisattva in the realness of the sight, sound, smell, taste, touch, and mental-image spheres; that there is no realness of the sight, sound, smell, taste, touch, and mental-image spheres in the great bodhisattva; and that there is no great bodhisattva apart from the realness of the sight, sound, smell, taste, touch, and mental-image spheres?"

The long-lived sage Well Appearing One replied, "World-Honored One! As the dharmas such as the sound, smell, taste, touch, and mental-image spheres are all in the final analysis unattainable and are without self-nature, how can we say that the realness of the sight, sound, smell, taste, touch, or mental-image sphere is attainable and with self-nature? Given the truth that the realness is not existent, how can we say that being with the realness of the sight, sound, smell, taste, touch, and mental-image spheres is the great bodhisattva; that being different from the realness of the sight, sound, smell, taste, touch, and mental-image spheres is the great bodhisattva; that there is the great bodhisattva in the realness of the sight, sound, smell, taste, touch, and mental-image spheres;

that there is the realness of the sight, sound, smell, taste, touch, and mental-image spheres in the great bodhisattva; and that there is the great bodhisattva apart from the realness of the sight, sound, smell, taste, touch, and mental-image spheres?"

"Furthermore, Well Appearing One, based on what reasons do you say that being with the realness of the eye, ear, nose, tongue, body, and conscious realms is not the great bodhisattva; that being different from the realness of the eye, ear, nose, tongue, body, and conscious realms is not the great bodhisattva; that there is no great bodhisattva in the realness of the eye, ear, nose, tongue, body, and conscious realms; that there is no realness of the eye, ear, nose, tongue, body, and conscious realms in the great bodhisattva; and that there is no great bodhisattva apart from the realness of the eye, ear, nose, tongue, body, and conscious realms?"

The long-lived sage Well Appearing One replied, "World-Honored One! As the dharmas such as the eye, ear, nose, tongue, body, and the conscious realms are all in the final analysis unattainable and are without self-nature, how can we say that the realness of the eye, nose, tongue, body, or the conscious realm is attainable and with self-nature? Given the truth that the realness is nonexistent, how can we say that being with the realness of the eye, ear, nose, tongue, body, and conscious realms is the great bodhisattva; that being different from the realness of the eye, ear, nose, tongue, body, and conscious realms is the great bodhisattva; that there is the great bodhisattva in the realness of the eye, ear, nose, tongue, body, and conscious realms; that there is the realness of the eye, ear, nose, tongue, body, and conscious realms in the great bodhisattva; and that there is the great bodhisattva apart from the realness of the eye, ear, nose, tongue, body, and conscious realms?"

"Furthermore, Well Appearing One, based on what reasons do you say that being with the realness of the sight, sound, smell, taste, touch, and mental-image realms is not the great bodhisattva; that being different from the realness of the sight, sound, smell, taste, touch, and mental-image realms is not the great bodhisattva; that there is no great bodhisattva in the realness of the sight, sound, smell, taste, touch, and mental-image realms; that there is no realness of the sight realm, sound, smell, taste, touch, and mental-image realms in the great bodhisattva; and that there is no great bodhisattva apart from the realness of the sight, sound, smell, taste, touch, and mental-image realms?"

The long-lived sage Well Appearing One replied, "World-Honored One! As the dharmas such as the sight, sound, smell, taste, touch, and mental-image realms are all in the final analysis unattainable and are without self-nature, how can we say that the realness of the sight, sound, smell, taste, touch, or mental-image realm is attainable and with self-nature? Given the truth that the realness is nonexistent, how can we say that being with the realness of the sight, sound, smell, taste, touch, and mental-image realms is the great bodhisattva; that being different from the realness of the sight, sound, smell, taste, touch, and mental-image realms is the great bodhisattva; that there is the great bodhisattva in the realness of the sight, sound, smell, taste, touch, and mental-image realms; that there is the realness of the sight, sound, smell, taste, touch, and mental-image realms in the great bodhisattva; and that there is the great bodhisattva apart from the realness of the sight, sound, smell, taste, touch, and mental-image realms?"

"Furthermore, Well Appearing One, based on what reasons do you say that being with the realness of the eye, ear, nose, tongue, body, and the conscious consciousness realms is not the great bodhisattva; that being different from the realness of the eye, ear, nose, tongue, body, and the conscious consciousness realms is not the great bodhisattva; that there is no great bodhisattva in the realness of the eye, ear, nose, tongue, body, and conscious consciousness realms; that there is no realness of the eye, ear, nose, tongue, body, and conscious consciousness realms in the great bodhisattva; and that there is no great bodhisattva apart from the realness of the eye, ear, nose, tongue, body, and conscious consciousness realms?"

The long-lived sage Well Appearing One replied, "World-Honored One! as the dharmas such as the eye, ear, nose, tongue, body, and conscious consciousness realms are all in the final analysis unattainable and are without self-nature, how can we say that the realness of the eye consciousness, ear consciousness, nose consciousness, tongue consciousness, body consciousness, or conscious consciousness realm is attainable and with self-nature? Given the truth that the realness is nonexistent, how can we say that being with the realness of the eye, ear, nose, tongue, body, and conscious consciousness realms is the great bodhisattva; that being different from the realness of the eye, ear, nose, tongue, body, and conscious consciousness realms is the great bodhisattva; that there is the great bodhisattva in the realness of the eye, ear, nose, tongue, body, and conscious consciousness realms; that there is the realness of the eye, ear, nose, tongue, body, and conscious consciousness realms in the great bodhisattva; and that there is the great bodhisattva apart from the realness of the eye, ear, nose, tongue, body, and conscious consciousness realms?"

"Furthermore, Well Appearing One, based on what reasons do you say that being with the realness of the eye, ear, nose, tongue, body, and conscious contacts is not the great bodhisattva; that being different from the realness of the eye, ear, nose, tongue, body, and conscious contacts is not the great bodhisattva; that there is no great bodhisattva in the realness of the eye, ear, nose, tongue, body, and conscious contacts; that there is no realness of the eye, ear, nose, tongue, body, and conscious contacts in the great bodhisattva; and that there is no great bodhisattva apart from the realness of the eye, ear, nose, tongue, body, and conscious contacts?"

The long-lived sage Well Appearing One replied, "World-Honored One! As the dharmas such as the eye, ear, nose, tongue, body, and conscious contacts are all in the final analysis unattainable and are without self-nature, how can we say that the realness of the eye, ear, nose, tongue, body, or conscious contact is attainable and with self-nature? Given the truth that the realness is nonexistent, how can we say that being with the realness of the eye, ear, nose, tongue, body, and conscious contacts is the great bodhisattva; that being different from the realness of the eye, ear, nose, tongue, body, and conscious contacts is the great bodhisattva; that there is the great bodhisattva in the realness of the eye, ear, nose, tongue, body, and conscious contacts; that there is the realness of the eye, ear, nose, tongue, body, and conscious contacts in the great bodhisattva; and that there is the great bodhisattva apart from the realness of the eye, ear, nose, tongue, body, and conscious contacts?"

"Furthermore, Well Appearing One, based on what reasons

Fascicle 16, Chapter 7, Section 6

do you say that being with the realness of the feelings produced by the eye, ear, nose, tongue, body, and conscious contacts is not the great bodhisattva; that being different from the realness of the feelings produced by the eye, ear, nose, tongue, body, and conscious contacts is not the great bodhisattva; that there is no great bodhisattva in the realness of the feelings produced by the eye, ear, nose, tongue, body, and conscious contacts; that there is no realness of the feelings produced by the eye, ear, nose, tongue, body, and conscious contacts in the great bodhisattva; and that there is no great bodhisattva apart from the realness of the feelings produced by the eye, ear, nose, tongue, body, and conscious contacts?"

The long-lived sage Well Appearing One replied, "World-Honored One! As the dharmas such as the feelings produced by the eye, ear, nose, tongue, body, and conscious contacts are all in the final analysis unattainable and are without self-nature, how can we say that the realness of the feelings produced by the eye, nose, tongue, body, or conscious contact is attainable and with self-nature? Given the truth that the realness is nonexistent, how can we say that being with the realness of the feelings produced by the eye, ear, nose, tongue, body, and conscious contacts is the great bodhisattva; that being different from the realness of the feelings produced by the eye, ear, nose, tongue, body, and conscious contacts is the great bodhisattva; that there is the great bodhisattva in the realness of the feelings produced by the eye, ear, nose, tongue, body, and conscious contacts; that there is the realness of the feelings produced by the eye, ear, nose, tongue, body, and conscious contacts in the great bodhisattva; and that there is the great bodhisattva apart from the realness of the feelings produced by the eye, ear, nose, tongue, body, and conscious contacts?"

"Furthermore, Well Appearing One, based on what reasons do you say that being with the realness of the earth, water, fire, wind, space, and consciousness realms is not the great bodhisattva; that being different from the realness of the earth, water, fire, wind, space, and consciousness realms is not the great bodhisattva; that there is no great bodhisattva in the realness of the earth, water, fire, wind, space, and consciousness realms; that there is no realness of the earth, water, fire, wind, space, and consciousness realms in the great bodhisattva; and that there is no great bodhisattva apart from the realness of the earth, water, fire, wind, space, and consciousness realms?"

The long-lived sage Well Appearing One replied, "World-Honored One! As the dharmas such as the earth, water, fire, wind, space, and consciousness realms are all in the final analysis unattainable and are without self-nature, how can we say that the realness of the earth, water, fire, wind, space, or consciousness realm is attainable and with self-nature? Given the truth that the realness is nonexistent, how can we say that being with the realness of the earth, water, fire, wind, space, and consciousness realms is the great bodhisattva; that being different from the realness of the earth, water, fire, wind, space, and consciousness realms is the great bodhisattva; that there is the realness of the earth, water, fire, wind, space, and consciousness in the great bodhisattva; that there is the great bodhisattva in the realness of the earth, water, fire, wind, space, and consciousness realms; and that there is the great bodhisattva apart from the realness of the earth, water, fire, wind, space, and consciousness realms?"

"Furthermore, Well Appearing One, based on what reasons do you say that being with the realness of the cause and condition, consecutive thoughts in sequence, the conditions that stimulate one's mind, and the conditions that reinforce main causes is not the great bodhisattva; that being different from the realness of the cause and condition, consecutive thoughts in sequence, the conditions that stimulate one's mind, and the conditions that reinforce main causes is not the great bodhisattva; that there is no great bodhisattva in the realness of the cause and condition, consecutive thoughts in sequence, the conditions that stimulate one's mind, and the conditions that reinforce main causes; that there is no realness of the cause and condition, consecutive thoughts in sequence, the conditions that stimulate one's mind, and the conditions that reinforce main causes in the great bodhisattva; and that there is no great bodhisattva apart from the realness of the cause and condition, consecutive thoughts in sequence, the conditions that stimulate one's mind, and the conditions that reinforce main causes?"

The long-lived sage Well Appearing One replied, "World-Hon-

Fascicle 16, Chapter 7, Section 6

ored One! As the dharmas such as the cause and condition, consecutive thoughts in sequence, the conditions that stimulate one's mind, and the conditions that reinforce main causes are all in the final analysis unattainable and are without self-nature, how can we say that the realness of the cause and condition, consecutive thoughts in sequence, the conditions that stimulate one's mind, or the conditions that reinforce main causes is attainable and with self-nature? Given the truth that the realness is nonexistent, how can we say that being with the realness of the cause and condition, consecutive thoughts in sequence, the conditions that stimulate one's mind, and the conditions that reinforce main causes is the great bodhisattva; that being different from the realness of the cause and condition, consecutive thoughts in sequence, the conditions that stimulate one's mind, and the conditions that reinforce main causes is the great bodhisattva; that there is the great bodhisattva in the realness of the cause and condition, consecutive thoughts in sequence, the conditions that stimulate one's mind, and the conditions that reinforce main causes; and that there is the realness of the cause and condition, consecutive thoughts in sequence, the conditions that stimulate one's mind, and the conditions that reinforce main causes in the great bodhisattva; and that there is the great bodhisattva apart from the realness of the cause and condition, consecutive thoughts in sequence, the conditions that stimulate one's mind, and the conditions that reinforce main causes?"

"Furthermore, Well Appearing One, based on what reasons do you say that being with the realness of the dharmas produced by conditions is not the great bodhisattva; that being different from the realness of the dharmas produced by conditions is not the great bodhisattva; that there is no great bodhisattva in the realness of the dharmas produced by conditions; that there is no realness of the dharmas produced by conditions in the great bodhisattva; and that there is no great bodhisattva apart from the realness of the dharmas produced by conditions?"

The long-lived sage Well Appearing One replied, "World-Honored One! As the dharmas produced by conditions are in the final analysis unattainable and are without self-nature, how can we say that the realness of the dharmas produced by conditions is attainable and with self-nature? Given the truth that the realness is nonexistent, how can we say that being with the realness of the dharmas produced by conditions is great bodhisattva; that being different from the realness of the dharmas produced by conditions is the great bodhisattva; that there is the great bodhisattva apart from the realness of the dharmas produced by conditions; that there is the realness of the dharmas produced by conditions in the great bodhisattva; and that there is the great bodhisattva in the realness of the dharmas produced by conditions?"

"Furthermore, Well Appearing One, based on what reasons do you say that being with the realness of ignorance, action, consciousness, name and form, six sense spheres, contact, reception, craving, grasping, existence, birth, old age, and death is not the great bodhisattva; that being different from the realness of ignorance, and so forth, as well as old age and death is not the great bodhisattva; that there is no great bodhisattva in the realness of ignorance, and so forth, as well as old age and death; that there is no realness of ignorance, and so forth, as well as old age and death in the great bodhisattva; and that there is no great bodhisattva apart from the realness of ignorance, and so forth, as well as old age and death?"

The long-lived sage Well Appearing One replied, "World-Honored One! As ignorance, and so forth, as well as old age and death are in the final analysis unattainable and are without self-nature, how can we say that the realness of ignorance, and so forth, as well as old age and death is attainable and with self-nature? Given the truth that the realness is nonexistent, how can we say that being with the realness of ignorance, and so forth, as well as old age and death is the great bodhisattva; that being different from the realness of ignorance, and so forth, as well as old age and death is great bodhisattva; that there is the great bodhisattva in the realness of ignorance, and so forth, as well as old age and death; that there is the realness of ignorance, and so forth, as well as old age and death in the great bodhisattva; and that there is the great bodhisattva apart from the realness of ignorance, and so forth, as well as old age and death?"

"Furthermore, Well Appearing One, based on what reasons do

you say that being with the realness of giving, pure precept, forbearance, diligence, meditation, and prajna paramitas is not the great bodhisattva; that being different from the realness of giving, pure precept, forbearance, diligence, meditation, and prajna paramitas is not the great bodhisattva; that there is no great bodhisattva in the realness of giving, pure precept, forbearance, diligence, meditation, and prajna paramitas; that there is no realness of giving, pure precept, forbearance, diligence, meditation, and prajna paramitas in the great bodhisattva; and that there is no great bodhisattva apart from the realness of giving, pure precept, forbearance, diligence, meditation, and prajna paramitas?"

The long-lived sage Well Appearing One replied, "World-Honored One! As giving, pure precept, forbearance, diligence, meditation, and prajna paramitas are in the final analysis unattainable and are without self-nature, how can we say that the realness of giving, pure precept, forbearance, diligence, meditation, or prajna paramita is attainable and with self-nature? Given the truth that the realness is nonexistent, how can we say that being with the realness of giving, pure precept, forbearance, diligence, meditation, and prajna paramitas is the great bodhisattva; that being different from the realness of giving, pure precept, forbearance, diligence, meditation, and prajna paramitas is the great bodhisattva; that there is the great bodhisattva in the realness of giving, pure precept, forbearance, diligence, meditation, and prajna paramitas; that there is the realness of giving, pure precept, forbearance, diligence, meditation, and prajna paramitas in the great bodhisattva; and that there is the great bodhisattva apart from the realness of giving, pure precept, forbearance, diligence, meditation, and prajna paramitas?"

"Furthermore, Well Appearing One, based on what reasons do you say that being with the realness of internal emptiness, external emptiness, internal-external emptiness, emptiness of emptiness, emptiness of space, emptiness of ultimate truth, emptiness of conditioned phenomena, emptiness of unconditioned reality, emptiness in the final analysis, emptiness of nontemporality, emptiness of deconstruction, emptiness of changelessness, emptiness of original nature, emptiness of particular characteristics, emptiness of common characteristics, emptiness of all dharmas, emptiness of nonattainment, emptiness of selflessness, emptiness of self-nature, and emptiness of selfless self-nature is not the great bodhisattva; that being different from the realness of internal emptiness, and so forth, as well as emptiness of selfless self-nature is not the great bodhisattva; that there is no great bodhisattva in the realness of internal emptiness, and so forth, as well as emptiness of selfless self-nature; that there is no realness of internal emptiness, and so forth, as well as emptiness of selfless self-nature in the great bodhisattva; and that there is no great bodhisattva apart from the realness of internal emptiness, and so forth, as well as emptiness of selfless self-nature?"

The long-lived sage Well Appearing One replied, "World-Honored One! As internal emptiness, and so forth, as well as emptiness of selfless self-nature are in the final analysis unattainable and are without self-nature, how can we say that the realness of internal emptiness, and so forth, as well as emptiness of selfless self-nature is attainable and with self-nature? Given the truth that the realness is nonexistent, how can we say that being with the realness of internal emptiness, and so forth, as well as emptiness of selfless self-nature is great bodhisattva; that being different from the realness of internal emptiness, and so forth, as well as emptiness of selfless self-nature is great bodhisattva; that there is great bodhisattva in the realness of internal emptiness, and so forth, as well as emptiness of selfless self-nature; that there is the realness of internal emptiness, and so forth, as well as emptiness of selfless self-nature in the great bodhisattva; and that there is the great bodhisattva apart from the realness of internal emptiness, and so forth, as well as emptiness of selfless self-nature?"

"Furthermore, Well Appearing One, based on what reasons do you say that being with the realness of the four bases of mindfulness, four correct endeavors, four bases of power, five roots, five powers, seven factors for enlightenment, and the noble eightfold path is not the great bodhisattva; that being different from the realness of the four bases of mindfulness, and so forth, as well as the noble eightfold path is not the great bodhisattva; that there is no great bodhisattva in the realness of the four bases of mindfulness, and so forth, as well as the noble eightfold path; that there is

Fascicle 16, Chapter 7, Section 6   381

no realness of the four bases of mindfulness, and so forth, as well as the noble eightfold path in the great bodhisattva; and that there is no great bodhisattva apart from the realness of the four bases of mindfulness, and so forth, as well as the noble eightfold path?"

The long-lived sage Well Appearing One replied, "World-Honored One! As the dharmas such as the four bases of mindfulness, and so forth, as well as the noble eightfold path are in the final analysis unattainable and are without self-nature, how can we say that the realness of the four bases of mindfulness, and so forth, as well as the noble eightfold path is attainable and with self-nature? Given the truth that the realness is nonexistent, how can we say that being with the realness of the four bases of mindfulness, and so forth, as well as the noble eightfold path is the great bodhisattva; that being different from the realness of the four bases of mindfulness, and so forth, as well as the noble eightfold path is the great bodhisattva; that there is the great bodhisattva in the realness of the four bases of mindfulness, and so forth, as well as the noble eightfold path; that there is the realness of the four bases of mindfulness, and so forth, as well as the noble eightfold path in the great bodhisattva; and that there is the great bodhisattva apart from the realness of the four bases of mindfulness, and so forth, as well as the noble eightfold path?"

"Furthermore, Well Appearing One, based on what reasons do you say that being with the realness of the noble truths of suffering, the cause of suffering, the cessation of suffering, and the path for the cessation of suffering is not the great bodhisattva; that being different from the realness of the noble truths of suffering, the cause of suffering, the cessation of suffering, and the path for the cessation of suffering is not the great bodhisattva; that there is no great bodhisattva in the realness of the noble truths of suffering, the cause of suffering, the cessation of suffering, and the path for the cessation of suffering; that there is no realness of the noble truths of suffering, the cause of suffering, the cessation of suffering, and the path for the cessation of suffering in the great bodhisattva; and that there is no great bodhisattva apart from the realness of the noble truths of suffering, the cause of suffering, the cessation of suffering, and the path for the cessation of suffering?"

The long-lived sage Well Appearing One replied, "World-Honored One! As the dharmas such as the noble truths of suffering, the cause of suffering, the cessation of suffering, and the path for the cessation of suffering are in the final analysis unattainable and are without self-nature, how can we say that the realness of the noble truths of suffering, the cause of suffering, the cessation of suffering, and the path for the cessation of suffering is attainable and with self-nature? Given the truth that the realness is nonexistent, how can we say that being with the realness of the noble truths of suffering, the cause of suffering, the cessation of suffering, and the path for the cessation of suffering is the great bodhisattva; that being different from the realness of the noble truths of suffering, the cause of suffering, the cessation of suffering, and the path for the cessation of suffering is the great bodhisattva; that there is the great bodhisattva in the realness of the noble truths of suffering, the cause of suffering, the cessation of suffering, and the path for the cessation of suffering; that there is the realness of the noble truths of suffering, the cause of suffering, the cessation of suffering, and the path for the cessation of suffering in the great bodhisattva; and that there is the great bodhisattva apart from the realness of the noble truths of suffering, the cause of suffering, the cessation of suffering, and the path for the cessation of suffering?"

"Furthermore, Well Appearing One, based on what reasons do you say that being with the realness of the four meditations, four immeasurable minds, and four formless concentrations is not the great bodhisattva; that being different from the realness of the four meditations, four immeasurable minds, and four formless concentrations is not the great bodhisattva; that there is no great bodhisattva in the realness of the four meditations, four immeasurable minds, and four formless concentrations; that there is no realness of the four meditations, four immeasurable minds, and four formless concentrations in the great bodhisattva; and that there is no great bodhisattva apart from the realness of the four meditations, four immeasurable minds, and four formless concentrations?"

The long-lived sage Well Appearing One replied, "World-Honored One! As the dharmas such as the four meditations, four immeasurable minds, and four formless concentrations are in the final analysis unattainable and are without self-nature, how can we say that the realness of the four meditations, four immeasurable minds, or the four formless concentrations is attainable and with self-nature? Given the truth that the realness is nonexistent, how can we say that being with the realness of the four meditations, four immeasurable minds, and four formless concentrations is the great bodhisattva; that being different from the realness of the four meditations, four immeasurable minds, and four formless concentrations is the great bodhisattva; that there is the great bodhisattva in the realness of the four meditations, four immeasurable minds, and four formless concentrations; that there is the realness of the four meditations, four immeasurable minds, and four formless concentrations in the great bodhisattva; and that there is the great bodhisattva apart from the realness of the four meditations, four immeasurable minds, and four formless concentrations?"

"Furthermore, Well Appearing One, based on what reasons do you say that being with the realness of the eight liberations, eight vexation-overcoming meditations, nine concentrations in sequence, and the ten universal contemplations is not the great bodhisattva; that being different from the realness of the eight liberations, eight vexation-overcoming meditations, nine concentrations in sequence, and the ten universal contemplations is not the great bodhisattva; that there is no great bodhisattva in the realness of the eight liberations, eight vexation-overcoming meditations, nine concentrations in sequence, and the ten universal contemplations; that there is no realness of the eight liberations, eight vexation-overcoming meditations, nine concentrations in sequence, and the ten universal contemplations in the great bodhisattva; and that there is no great bodhisattva apart from the realness of the eight liberations, eight vexation-overcoming meditations, nine concentrations in sequence, and the ten universal contemplations?"

The long-lived sage Well Appearing One replied, "World-Honored One! as the dharmas such as the eight liberations, eight vexation-overcoming meditations, nine concentrations in sequence, and the ten universal contemplations are in the final analysis unattainable and are without self-nature, how can we say that the realness of the eight liberations, eight vexation-overcoming meditations, nine concentrations in sequence, or the ten universal contemplations is attainable and with self-nature? Given the truth that the realness is nonexistent, how can we say that being with the realness of the eight liberations, eight vexation-overcoming meditations, nine concentrations in sequence, and the ten universal contemplations is the great bodhisattva; that being different from the realness of the eight liberations, eight vexation-overcoming meditations, nine concentrations in sequence, and the ten universal contemplations is the great bodhisattva; that there is the great bodhisattva in the realness of the eight liberations, eight vexation-overcoming meditations, nine concentrations in sequence, and the ten universal contemplations; that there is the realness of the eight liberations, eight vexation-overcoming meditations, nine concentrations in sequence, and the ten universal contemplations in the great bodhisattva; and that there is the great bodhisattva apart from the realness of the eight liberations, eight vexation-overcoming meditations, nine concentrations in sequence, and the ten universal contemplations?"

"Furthermore, Well Appearing One, based on what reasons do you say that being with the realness of the liberation gates of emptiness, formlessness, and nonaspiration is not the great bodhisattva; that being different from the realness of the liberation gates of emptiness, formlessness, and nonaspiration is not the great bodhisattva; that there is no great bodhisattva in the realness of the liberation gates of emptiness, formlessness, and nonaspiration; that there is no realness of the liberation gates of emptiness, formlessness, and nonaspiration in the great bodhisattva; and that there is no great bodhisattva apart from the realness of the liberation gates of emptiness, formlessness, and nonaspiration?"

The long-lived sage Well Appearing One replied, "World-Honored One! As the dharmas such as the liberation gates of emptiness, formlessness, and nonaspiration are in the final analysis unattainable and are without self-nature, how can we say that the realness of the liberation gate of emptiness, the liberation gate of formlessness, or the liberation gate of nonaspiration is attainable and with self-nature? Given the truth that the realness is nonexistent, how can we say that being with the realness of the liberation gates of emptiness, formlessness, and nonaspiration is the great bodhisattva; that being different from the realness of the liberation gates of emptiness, formlessness, and nonaspiration is the great bodhisattva; that there is the great bodhisattva in the realness of the liberation gates of emptiness, formlessness, and nonaspiration; that there is the realness of the liberation gates of emptiness, formlessness, and nonaspiration in the great bodhisattva; and that there is the great bodhisattva apart from the realness of the liberation gates of emptiness, formlessness, and nonaspiration?"

"Furthermore, Well Appearing One, based on what reasons do you say that being with the realness of the dharani gates and the samadhi gates is not the great bodhisattva; that being different from the realness of the dharani gates and samadhi gates is not the great bodhisattva; that there is no great bodhisattva in the realness of the dharani gates and samadhi gates; that there is no realness of the dharani gates and samadhi gates in the great bodhisattva; and that there is no great bodhisattva apart from the realness of the dharani gates and samadhi gates?"

The long-lived sage Well Appearing One replied, "World-Honored One! As the dharmas such as the dharani gates and samadhi gates are in the final analysis unattainable and are without self-nature, how can we say that the realness of the dharani gates or the samadhi gates is attainable and with self-nature? Given the truth that the realness is nonexistent, how can we say that being with the realness of the dharani gates and samadhi gates is the great bodhisattva; that being different from the realness of the dharani gates and samadhi gates is the great bodhisattva; that there is the great bodhisattva in the realness of the dharani gates and samadhi gates; that there is the realness of the dharani gates and samadhi gates in the great bodhisattva; and that there is the great bodhisattva apart from the realness of the dharani gates and samadhi gates?"

FASCICLE 17

Chapter 7
The Cautions and the Teachings

Section 7

(In the First Assembly)

"FURTHERMORE, WELL APPEARING ONE, BASED ON WHAT REASONS do you say that being with the realness of the stages of ecstasy, freedom from defilements, emitting light, flaming wisdom, being extremely difficult to be surpassed, the manifestation of pure realness, going far away, the unmovable, expedient wisdom, and dharma cloud is the great bodhisattva; that being different from the realness of the stage of ecstasy, and so forth, as well as the stage of dharma cloud is not the great bodhisattva; that there is no great bodhisattva in the realness of the stage of ecstasy, and so forth, as well as the stage of dharma cloud; that there is no realness of the stage of ecstasy, and so forth, as well as the stage of dharma cloud in the great bodhisattva; and that there is no great bodhisattva apart from the realness of the stage of ecstasy, and so forth, as well as the stage of dharma cloud?"

The long-lived sage Well Appearing One replied, "World-Honored One! As the dharmas such as the stages of ecstasy, freedom from defilements, and so forth, as well as the stage of dharma cloud are in the final analysis unattainable and without self-nature, how can we say that the realness of the stage of ecstasy, and so forth, or the stage of dharma cloud is attainable and with self-nature? Given the truth that the realness is nonexistent, how can we say that being with the realness of the stage of ecstasy, and so forth, as well as the stage of dharma cloud is the great bodhisattva; that being different from the realness of the stage of ecstasy, and so forth, as well as the stage of dharma cloud is the great bodhisattva; that there is great bodhisattva in the realness of the stage of ecstasy, and so forth, as well as the stage of dharma cloud; that there is the realness of the stage of ecstasy, and so forth, as well as the stage of dharma cloud in the great bodhisattva; and that there is the great bodhisattva apart from the realness of the stage of ecstasy, and so forth, as well as the stage of dharma cloud?"

"Furthermore, Well Appearing One, based on what reasons do you say that being with the realness of the five eyes and the six supernatural powers is the great bodhisattva; that being different from the realness of the five eyes and the six supernatural powers is the great bodhisattva; that there is no great bodhisattva in the realness of the five eyes and the six supernatural powers; that there is no realness of the five eyes and the six supernatural powers in the great bodhisattva; and that there is no great bodhisattva apart from the realness of the five eyes and the six supernatural powers?"

The long-lived sage Well Appearing One replied, "World-Honored One! As the dharmas such as the five eyes and the six supernatural powers are in the final analysis unattainable and without self-nature, how can we say that the realness of the five eyes and the realness of the six supernatural powers are attainable and with self-nature? Given the truth that the realness is nonexistent, how can we say that being with the realness of the five eyes and the six supernatural powers is the great bodhisattva; that being different from the realness of the five eyes and the six supernatural powers is the great bodhisattva; that there is the great bodhisattva in the realness of the five eyes and the six supernatural powers; that there is the realness of the five eyes and the six supernatural powers in the great bodhisattva; and that there is the great bodhisattva apart from the realness of the five eyes and the six supernatural powers?"

"Furthermore, Well Appearing One, based on what reasons do you say that being with the realness of the Buddha's ten abilities, four kinds of fearlessness, four unhindered understandings, and the eighteen distinctive features of Buddha's wisdom and power is not the great bodhisattva; that being different from the realness of the Buddha's ten abilities, four kinds of fearlessness, four unhindered understandings, and the eighteen distinctive features of Buddha's wisdom and power is not the great bodhisattva; that there is no great bodhisattva in the realness of the Buddha's ten abilities, four kinds of fearlessness, four unhindered understandings, and the eighteen distinctive features of Buddha's wisdom and power; that there is no realness of the Buddha's ten abilities, four kinds of fearlessness, four unhindered understandings, and the eighteen distinctive features of Buddha's wisdom and power in the great bodhisattva; and that there is no great bodhisattva apart from the realness of the Buddha's ten abilities, four kinds of fearlessness, four unhindered understandings, and the eighteen distinctive features of Buddha's wisdom and power?"

The long-lived sage Well Appearing One replied, "World-Honored One! As the dharmas such as the Buddha's ten abilities, four kinds of fearlessness, four unhindered understandings, and the eighteen distinctive features of Buddha's wisdom and power are in the final analysis unattainable and without self-nature, how can we say that the realness of the Buddha's ten abilities, four kinds of fearlessness, four unhindered understandings, or the eighteen distinctive features of Buddha's wisdom and power is attainable and with self-nature? Given the truth that the realness is nonexistent, how can we say that being with the realness of the Buddha's ten abilities, four kinds of fearlessness, four unhindered understandings, and the eighteen distinctive features of Buddha's wisdom and power is the great bodhisattva; that being different from the realness of the Buddha's ten abilities, four kinds of fearlessness, four unhindered understandings, and the eighteen distinctive features of Buddha's wisdom and power is the great bodhisattva; that there is the great bodhisattva in the realness of the Buddha's ten abilities, four kinds of fearlessness, four unhindered understandings, and the eighteen distinctive features of Buddha's wisdom and power; that there is the realness of the Buddha's ten abilities, four kinds of fearlessness, four unhindered understandings, and the eighteen distinctive features of Buddha's wisdom and power in the great bodhisattva; and that there is the great bodhisattva apart from the realness of the Buddha's ten abilities, four kinds of fearlessness, four unhindered understandings, and the eighteen distinctive features of Buddha's wisdom and power?"

"Furthermore, Well Appearing One, based on what reasons do you say that being with the realness of great loving-kindness, great compassion, great joy, and great equanimity is not the great bodhisattva; that being different from the realness of great loving-kindness, great compassion, great joy, and great equanimity is not the great bodhisattva; that there is no great bodhisattva in the realness of great loving-kindness, great compassion, great joy, and great equanimity; that there is no realness of great loving-kindness, great compassion, great joy, and great equanimity in the great bodhisattva; and that there is no great bodhisattva apart from the realness of great loving-kindness, great compassion, great joy, and great equanimity?"

The long-lived sage Well Appearing One replied, "World-Honored One! As the dharmas such as great loving-kindness, great compassion, great joy, and great equanimity are in the final analysis unattainable and without self-nature, how can we say that the realness of great loving-kindness, great compassion, great joy, or great equanimity is attainable and with self-nature? Given the truth that the realness is nonexistent, how can we say that being with the realness of great loving-kindness, great compassion, great joy, and great equanimity is the great bodhisattva; that being different from the realness of great loving-kindness, great compassion, great joy, and great equanimity is the great bodhisattva; that there is the great bodhisattva in the realness of great loving-kindness, great compassion, great joy, and great equanimity; that there is the realness of great loving-kindness, great compassion, great joy, and great equanimity in the great bodhisattva; and that there is the great bodhisattva apart from the realness of great loving-kindness, great compassion, great joy, and great equanimity?"

"Furthermore, Well Appearing One, based on what reasons

do you say that being with the realness of the thirty-two perfect major marks and the eighty distinguishing minor features is not the great bodhisattva; that being different from the realness of the thirty-two perfect major marks and the eighty distinguishing minor features is not the great bodhisattva; that there is no great bodhisattva in the realness of the thirty-two perfect major marks and the eighty distinguishing minor features; that there is no realness of the thirty-two perfect major marks and the eighty distinguishing minor features in the great bodhisattva; and that there is no great bodhisattva apart from the thirty-two perfect major marks and the eighty distinguishing minor features?"

The long-lived sage Well Appearing One replied, "World-Honored One! As the dharmas such as the thirty-two perfect major marks and the eighty distinguishing minor features are in the final analysis unattainable and without self-nature, how can we say that the realness of the thirty-two perfect major marks or the eighty distinguishing minor features is attainable and with self-nature? Given the truth that the realness is nonexistent, how can we say that being with the realness of the thirty-two perfect major marks and the eighty distinguishing minor features is the great bodhisattva; that being different from the realness of the thirty-two perfect major marks and the eighty distinguishing minor features is the great bodhisattva; that there is the great bodhisattva in the realness of the thirty-two perfect major marks and the eighty distinguishing minor features; that there is the realness of the thirty-two perfect major marks and the eighty distinguishing minor features in the great bodhisattva; and that there is the great bodhisattva apart from the realness of the thirty-two perfect major marks and the eighty distinguishing minor features?"

"Furthermore, Well Appearing One, based on what reasons do you say that being with the realness of staying in correct mindfulness and dwelling in equanimity at all times is not the great bodhisattva; that being different from the realness of staying in correct mindfulness and dwelling in equanimity at all times is not the great bodhisattva; that there is no great bodhisattva in the realness of staying in correct mindfulness and dwelling in equanimity at all times; that there is no realness of staying in correct mindfulness

Fascicle 17, Chapter 7, Section 7

and dwelling in equanimity at all times in the great bodhisattva; and that there is no great bodhisattva apart from the realness of staying in correct mindfulness and dwelling in equanimity at all times?"

The long-lived sage Well Appearing One replied, "World-Honored One! As the dharmas such as staying in correct mindfulness and dwelling in equanimity at all times are in the final analysis unattainable and without self-nature, how can we say that the realness of staying in correct mindfulness or dwelling in equanimity at all times is attainable and with self-nature? Given the truth that the realness is nonexistent, how can we say that being with the realness of staying in correct mindfulness and dwelling in equanimity at all times is the great bodhisattva; that being different from the realness of staying in correct mindfulness and dwelling in equanimity at all times is the great bodhisattva; that there is the great bodhisattva in the realness of staying in correct mindfulness and dwelling in equanimity at all times; that there is the realness of staying in correct mindfulness and dwelling in equanimity at all times in the great bodhisattva; and that there is the great bodhisattva apart from the realness of staying in correct mindfulness and dwelling in equanimity at all times?"

"Furthermore, Well Appearing One, based on what reasons do you say that being with the realness of the perfect knowledge of everything, the perfect knowledge of the forms of the paths, and the perfect knowledge of all phenomena is not the great bodhisattva; that being different from the realness of the perfect knowledge of everything, the perfect knowledge of the forms of the paths, and the perfect knowledge of all phenomena is not the great bodhisattva; that there is no great bodhisattva in the realness of the perfect knowledge of everything, the perfect knowledge of the forms of the paths, and the perfect knowledge of all phenomena; that there is no realness of the perfect knowledge of everything, the perfect knowledge of the forms of the paths, and the perfect knowledge of all phenomena in the great bodhisattva; and that there is no great bodhisattva apart from the realness of the perfect knowledge of everything, the perfect knowledge of the forms of the paths, and the perfect knowledge of all phenomena?"

The long-lived sage Well Appearing One replied, "World-Honored One! As the dharmas such as the perfect knowledge of everything, the perfect knowledge of the forms of the paths, and the perfect knowledge of all phenomena are in the final analysis unattainable and without self-nature, how can we say that the realness of the perfect knowledge of everything, the perfect knowledge of the forms of the paths, or the perfect knowledge of all phenomena is attainable and with self-nature? Given the truth that the realness is nonexistent, how can we say that the realness of the perfect knowledge of everything, the perfect knowledge of the forms of the paths, and the perfect knowledge of all phenomena is the great bodhisattva; that being different from the realness of the perfect knowledge of everything, the perfect knowledge of the forms of the paths, and the perfect knowledge of all phenomena is the great bodhisattva; that there is the great bodhisattva in the realness of the perfect knowledge of everything, the perfect knowledge of the forms of the paths, and the perfect knowledge of all phenomena; that there is the realness of the perfect knowledge of everything, the perfect knowledge of the forms of the paths, and the perfect knowledge of all phenomena in the great bodhisattva; and that there is the great bodhisattva apart from the realness of the perfect knowledge of everything, the perfect knowledge of the forms of the paths, and the perfect knowledge of all phenomena?"

"World-Honored One, given the truth that the dharmas such as matter, and so forth, as well as the realness are all unattainable, it is unreasonable to say that being with the realness of matter, and so forth, is the great bodhisattva; that being different from the realness of matter, and so forth, is the great bodhisattva; that there is the great bodhisattva in the realness of matter, and so forth; that there is the realness of matter, and so forth, in the great bodhisattva; and that there is the great bodhisattva apart from the realness of matter, and so forth."

The Buddha said to Well Appearing One, "Very good. It is as you say, Well Appearing One, because matter and all other dharmas are unattainable, their realness is also unattainable. Because the dharmas and their realness are unattainable, the great bodhisattvas are also unattainable. Because the great bodhisattvas are unattain-

Fascicle 17, Chapter 7, Section 7 393

able, the prajna paramita that they practice is also unattainable. Well Appearing One! When cultivating prajna paramita, the great bodhisattvas should learn this way.

"Furthermore, Well Appearing One, what does the great bodhisattva mean? Is the designated name of matter the great bodhisattva?"

"No, I don't think so, World-Honored One!"

"Is the designated name of feeling, thinking, action, or consciousness the great bodhisattva?"

"No, I don't think so, World-Honored One!"

"Is the designated name of the permanent matter the great bodhisattva?"

"No, I don't think so, World-Honored One!"

"Is the designated name of the permanent feeling, thinking, action, or consciousness the great bodhisattva?"

"No, I don't think so, World-Honored One!"

"Is the designated name of the impermanent matter the great bodhisattva?"

"No, I don't think so, World-Honored One!"

"Is the designated name of the impermanent feeling, thinking, action, or consciousness the great bodhisattva?"

"No, I don't think so, World-Honored One!"

"Is the designated name of the pleasant matter the great bodhisattva?"

"No, I don't think so, World-Honored One!"

"Is the designated name of the pleasant feeling, thinking, action, or consciousness the great bodhisattva?"

"No, I don't think so, World-Honored One!"

"Is the designated name of the painful matter the great bodhisattva?"

"No, I don't think so, World-Honored One!"

"Is the designated name of the painful feeling, thinking, action, or consciousness the great bodhisattva?"

"No, I don't think so, World-Honored One!"

"Is the designated name of the matter with selfness the great bodhisattva?"

"No, I don't think so, World-Honored One!"

"Is the designated name of the feeling, thinking, action, or consciousness with selfness the great bodhisattva?"

"No, I don't think so, World-Honored One!"

"Is the designated name of the selfless matter the great bodhisattva?"

"No, I don't think so, World-Honored One!"

"Is the designated name of the selfless feeling, thinking, action, or consciousness the great bodhisattva?"

"No, I don't think so, World-Honored One!"

"Is the designated name of the pure matter the great bodhisattva?"

"No, I don't think so, World-Honored One!"

"Is the designated name of the pure feeling, thinking, action, or consciousness the great bodhisattva?"

"No, I don't think so, World-Honored One!"

"Is the designated name of the impure matter the great bodhisattva?"

"No, I don't think so, World-Honored One!"

"Is the designated name of the impure feeling, thinking, action, or consciousness the great bodhisattva?"

"No, I don't think so, World-Honored One!"

"Is the designated name of the empty matter the great bodhisattva?"

"No, I don't think so, World-Honored One!"

"Is the designated name of the empty feeling, thinking, action, or consciousness the great bodhisattva?"

"No, I don't think so, World-Honored One!"

"Is the designated name of the not empty matter the great bodhisattva?"

"No, I don't think so, World-Honored One!"

"Is the designated name of the not empty feeling, thinking, action, or consciousness the great bodhisattva?"

"No, I don't think so, World-Honored One!"

"Is the designated name of the matter with form the great bodhisattva?"

"No, I don't think so, World-Honored One!"

"Is the designated name of the feeling, thinking, action, or consciousness with form the great bodhisattva?"
"No, I don't think so, World-Honored One!"
"Is the designated name of the formless matter the great bodhisattva?"
"No, I don't think so, World-Honored One!"
"Is the designated name of the formless feeling, thinking, action, or consciousness the great bodhisattva?"
"No, I don't think so, World-Honored One!"
"Is the designated name of the matter with aspiration the great bodhisattva?"
"No, I don't think so, World-Honored One!"
"Is the designated name of the feeling, thinking, action, or consciousness with aspiration the great bodhisattva?"
"No, I don't think so, World-Honored One!"
"Is the designated name of the matter without aspiration the great bodhisattva?"
"No, I don't think so, World-Honored One!"
"Is the designated name of the feeling, thinking, action, or consciousness without aspiration the great bodhisattva?"
"No, I don't think so, World-Honored One!"
"Is the designated name of the tranquil matter the great bodhisattva?"
"No, I don't think so, World-Honored One!"
"Is the designated name of the tranquil feeling, thinking, action, or consciousness the great bodhisattva?"
"No, I don't think so, World-Honored One!"
"Is the designated name of the not tranquil matter the great bodhisattva?"
"No, I don't think so, World-Honored One!"
"Is the designated name of the not tranquil feeling, thinking, action, or consciousness the great bodhisattva?"
"No, I don't think so, World-Honored One!"
"Is the designated name of the matter getting far away the great bodhisattva?"
"No, I don't think so, World-Honored One!"

"Is the designated name of the feeling, thinking, action, or consciousness getting far away the great bodhisattva?"

"No, I don't think so, World-Honored One!"

"Is the designated name of the matter not getting far away the great bodhisattva?"

"No, I don't think so, World-Honored One!"

"Is the designated name of the feeling, thinking, action, or consciousness not getting far away the great bodhisattva?"

"No, I don't think so, World-Honored One!"

"Is the designated name of the conditioned matter the great bodhisattva?"

"No, I don't think so, World-Honored One!"

"Is the designated name of the conditioned feeling, thinking, action, or consciousness the great bodhisattva?"

"No, I don't think so, World-Honored One!"

"Is the designated name of the unconditioned matter the great bodhisattva?"

"No, I don't think so, World-Honored One!"

"Is the designated name of the unconditioned feeling, thinking, action, or consciousness the great bodhisattva?"

"No, I don't think so, World-Honored One!"

"Is the designated name of the flawed matter the great bodhisattva?"

"No, I don't think so, World-Honored One!"

"Is the designated name of the flawed feeling, thinking, action, or consciousness the great bodhisattva?"

"No, I don't think so, World-Honored One!"

"Is the designated name of the flawless matter the great bodhisattva?"

"No, I don't think so, World-Honored One!"

"Is the designated name of the flawless feeling, thinking, action, or consciousness the great bodhisattva?"

"No, I don't think so, World-Honored One!"

"Is the designated name of the arising matter the great bodhisattva?"

"No, I don't think so, World-Honored One!"

"Is the designated name of the arising feeling, thinking, action, or consciousness the great bodhisattva?"

"No, I don't think so, World-Honored One!"

"Is the designated name of the extinguishing matter the great bodhisattva?"

"No, I don't think so, World-Honored One!"

"Is the designated name of the extinguishing feeling, thinking, action, or consciousness the great bodhisattva?"

"No, I don't think so, World-Honored One!"

"Is the designated name of the virtuous matter the great bodhisattva?"

"No, I don't think so, World-Honored One!"

"Is the designated name of the virtuous feeling, thinking, action, or consciousness the great bodhisattva?"

"No, I don't think so, World-Honored One!"

"Is the designated name of the not virtuous matter the great bodhisattva?"

"No, I don't think so, World-Honored One!"

"Is the designated name of the not virtuous feeling, thinking, action, or consciousness the great bodhisattva?"

"No, I don't think so, World-Honored One!"

"Is the designated name of the guilty matter the great bodhisattva?"

"No, I don't think so, World-Honored One!"

"Is the designated name of the guilty feeling, thinking, action, or consciousness the great bodhisattva?"

"No, I don't think so, World-Honored One!"

"Is the designated name of the not guilty matter the great bodhisattva?"

"No, I don't think so, World-Honored One!"

"Is the designated name of the not guilty feeling, thinking, action, or consciousness the great bodhisattva?"

"No, I don't think so, World-Honored One!"

"Is the designated name of the matter with vexations the great bodhisattva?"

"No, I don't think so, World-Honored One!"

"Is the designated name of the feeling, thinking, action, or consciousness with vexations the great bodhisattva?"

"No, I don't think so, World-Honored One!"

"Is the designated name of the matter without vexations the great bodhisattva?"

"No, I don't think so, World-Honored One!"

"Is the designated name of the feeling, thinking, action, or consciousness without vexations the great bodhisattva?"

"No, I don't think so, World-Honored One!"

"Is the designated name of the worldly matter the great bodhisattva?"

"No, I don't think so, World-Honored One!"

"Is the designated name of the worldly feeling, thinking, action, or consciousness the great bodhisattva?"

"No, I don't think so, World-Honored One!"

"Is the designated name of the matter beyond the world the great bodhisattva?"

"No, I don't think so, World-Honored One!"

"Is the designated name of the feeling, thinking, action, or consciousness beyond the world the great bodhisattva?"

"No, I don't think so, World-Honored One!"

"Is the designated name of the contaminated matter the great bodhisattva?"

"No, I don't think so, World-Honored One!"

"Is the designated name of the contaminated feeling, thinking, action, or consciousness the great bodhisattva?"

"No, I don't think so, World-Honored One!"

"Is the designated name of the purified matter the great bodhisattva?"

"No, I don't think so, World-Honored One!"

"Is the designated name of the purified feeling, thinking, action, or consciousness the great bodhisattva?"

"No, I don't think so, World-Honored One!"

"Is the designated name of the matter belonging to birth and death the great bodhisattva?"

"No, I don't think so, World-Honored One!"

Fascicle 17, Chapter 7, Section 7

"Is the designated name of the feeling, thinking, action, or consciousness belonging to birth and death the great bodhisattva?"

"No, I don't think so, World-Honored One!"

"Is the designated name of the matter belonging to nirvana the great bodhisattva?"

"No, I don't think so, World-Honored One!"

"Is the designated name of the feeling, thinking, action, or consciousness belonging to nirvana the great bodhisattva?"

"No, I don't think so, World-Honored One!"

"Is the designated name of the matter that is inside the great bodhisattva?"

"No, I don't think so, World-Honored One!"

"Is the designated name of the feeling, thinking, action, or consciousness that is inside the great bodhisattva?"

"No, I don't think so, World-Honored One!"

"Is the designated name of the matter that is outside the great bodhisattva?"

"No, I don't think so, World-Honored One!"

"Is the designated name of the feeling, thinking, action, or consciousness that is outside the great bodhisattva?"

"No, I don't think so, World-Honored One!"

"Is the designated name of the matter that is in between the great bodhisattva?"

"No, I don't think so, World-Honored One!"

"Is the designated name of the feeling, thinking, action, or consciousness that is in between the great bodhisattva?"

"No, I don't think so, World-Honored One!"

"Is the designated name of attainable matter the great bodhisattva?"

"No, I don't think so, World-Honored One!"

"Is the designated name of attainable feeling, thinking, action, or consciousness the great bodhisattva?"

"No, I don't think so, World-Honored One!"

"Is the designated name of unattainable matter the great bodhisattva?"

"No, I don't think so, World-Honored One!"

"Is the designated name of unattainable feeling, thinking, action, or consciousness the great bodhisattva?"

"No, I don't think so, World-Honored One!"

"Furthermore, Well Appearing One, what does the great bodhisattva mean? Is the designated name of the eye sphere the great bodhisattva?"

"No, I don't think so, World-Honored One!"

"Is the designated name of the ear, nose, tongue, body, or conscious sphere the great bodhisattva?"

"No, I don't think so, World-Honored One!"

"Is the designated name of the permanent eye sphere the great bodhisattva?"

"No, I don't think so, World-Honored One!"

"Is the designated name of the permanent ear, nose, tongue, body, or conscious sphere the great bodhisattva?"

"No, I don't think so, World-Honored One!"

"Is the designated name of the impermanent eye sphere the great bodhisattva?"

"No, I don't think so, World-Honored One!"

"Is the designated name of the impermanent ear, nose, tongue, body, or conscious sphere the great bodhisattva?"

"No, I don't think so, World-Honored One!"

"Is the designated name of the pleasant eye sphere the great bodhisattva?"

"No, I don't think so, World-Honored One!"

"Is the designated name of the pleasant ear, nose, tongue, body, or conscious sphere the great bodhisattva?"

"No, I don't think so, World-Honored One!"

"Is the designated name of the painful eye sphere the great bodhisattva?"

"No, I don't think so, World-Honored One!"

"Is the designated name of the painful ear, nose, tongue, body, or conscious sphere the great bodhisattva?"

"No, I don't think so, World-Honored One!"

"Is the designated name of the eye sphere with selfness the great bodhisattva?"

Fascicle 17, Chapter 7, Section 7   401

"No, I don't think so, World-Honored One!"
"Is the designated name of the ear, nose, tongue, body, or conscious sphere with selfness the great bodhisattva?"
"No, I don't think so, World-Honored One!"
"Is the designated name of the eye sphere without selfness the great bodhisattva?"
"No, I don't think so, World-Honored One!"
"Is the designated name of the ear, nose, tongue, body, or conscious sphere without selfness the great bodhisattva?"
"No, I don't think so, World-Honored One!"
"Is the designated name of the pure eye sphere the great bodhisattva?"
"No, I don't think so, World-Honored One!"
"Is the designated name of the pure ear, nose, tongue, body, or conscious sphere the great bodhisattva?"
"No, I don't think so, World-Honored One!"
"Is the designated name of the impure eye sphere the great bodhisattva?"
"No, I don't think so, World-Honored One!"
"Is the designated name of the impure ear, nose, tongue, body, or conscious sphere the great bodhisattva?"
"No, I don't think so, World-Honored One!"
"Is the designated name of the empty eye sphere the great bodhisattva?"
"No, I don't think so, World-Honored One!"
"Is the designated name of the empty ear, nose, tongue, body, or conscious sphere the great bodhisattva?"
"No, I don't think so, World-Honored One!"
"Is the designated name of the not empty eye sphere the great bodhisattva?"
"No, I don't think so, World-Honored One!"
"Is the designated name of the not empty ear, nose, tongue, body, or conscious sphere the great bodhisattva?"
"No, I don't think so, World-Honored One!"
"Is the designated name of the eye sphere with the form the great bodhisattva?"

"No, I don't think so, World-Honored One!"

"Is the designated name of the ear, nose, tongue, body, or conscious sphere with the form the great bodhisattva?"

"No, I don't think so, World-Honored One!"

"Is the designated name of the formless eye sphere the great bodhisattva?"

"No, I don't think so, World-Honored One!"

"Is the designated name of the formless ear, nose, tongue, body, or conscious sphere the great bodhisattva?"

"No, I don't think so, World-Honored One!"

"Is the designated name of the eye sphere with aspiration the great bodhisattva?"

"No, I don't think so, World-Honored One!"

"Is the designated name of the ear, nose, tongue, body, or conscious sphere with aspiration the great bodhisattva?"

"No, I don't think so, World-Honored One!"

"Is the designated name of the eye sphere without aspiration the great bodhisattva?"

"No, I don't think so, World-Honored One!"

"Is the designated name of the ear, nose, tongue, body, or conscious sphere without aspiration the great bodhisattva?"

"No, I don't think so, World-Honored One!"

"Is the designated name of the eye sphere with tranquility the great bodhisattva?"

"No, I don't think so, World-Honored One!"

"Is the designated name of the ear, nose, tongue, body, or conscious sphere with tranquility the great bodhisattva?"

"No, I don't think so, World-Honored One!"

"Is the designated name of the eye sphere without tranquility the great bodhisattva?"

"No, I don't think so, World-Honored One!"

"Is the designated name of the ear, nose, tongue, body, or conscious sphere without tranquility the great bodhisattva?"

"No, I don't think so, World-Honored One!"

"Is the designated name of the eye sphere getting far away the great bodhisattva?"

"No, I don't think so, World-Honored One!"
"Is the designated name of the ear, nose, tongue, body, or conscious sphere getting far away the great bodhisattva?"
"No, I don't think so, World-Honored One!"
"Is the designated name of the eye sphere not getting far away the great bodhisattva?"
"No, I don't think so, World-Honored One!"
"Is the designated name of the ear, nose, tongue, body, or conscious sphere not getting far away the great bodhisattva?"
"No, I don't think so, World-Honored One!"
"Is the designated name of the conditioned eye sphere the great bodhisattva?"
"No, I don't think so, World-Honored One!"
"Is the designated name of the conditioned ear, nose, tongue, body, or conscious sphere the great bodhisattva?"
"No, I don't think so, World-Honored One!"
"Is the designated name of the unconditioned eye sphere the great bodhisattva?"
"No, I don't think so, World-Honored One!"
"Is the designated name of the unconditioned ear, nose, tongue, body, or conscious sphere the great bodhisattva?"
"No, I don't think so, World-Honored One!"
"Is the designated name of the flawed eye sphere the great bodhisattva?"
"No, I don't think so, World-Honored One!"
"Is the designated name of the flawed ear, nose, tongue, body, or conscious sphere the great bodhisattva?"
"No, I don't think so, World-Honored One!"
"Is the designated name of the flawless eye sphere the great bodhisattva?"
"No, I don't think so, World-Honored One!"
"Is the designated name of the flawless ear, nose, tongue, body, or conscious sphere the great bodhisattva?"
"No, I don't think so, World-Honored One!"
"Is the designated name of the arising eye sphere the great bodhisattva?"

"No, I don't think so, World-Honored One!"

"Is the designated name of the arising ear, nose, tongue, body, or conscious sphere the great bodhisattva?"

"No, I don't think so, World-Honored One!"

"Is the designated name of the extinguishing eye sphere the great bodhisattva?"

"No, I don't think so, World-Honored One!"

"Is the designated name of the extinguishing ear, nose, tongue, body, or conscious sphere the great bodhisattva?"

"No, I don't think so, World-Honored One!"

"Is the designated name of the virtuous eye sphere the great bodhisattva?"

"No, I don't think so, World-Honored One!"

"Is the designated name of the virtuous ear, nose, tongue, body, or conscious sphere the great bodhisattva?"

"No, I don't think so, World-Honored One!"

"Is the designated name of the not virtuous eye sphere the great bodhisattva?"

"No, I don't think so, World-Honored One!"

"Is the designated name of the not virtuous ear, nose, tongue, body, or conscious sphere the great bodhisattva?"

"No, I don't think so, World-Honored One!"

"Is the designated name of the guilty eye sphere the great bodhisattva?"

"No, I don't think so, World-Honored One!"

"Is the designated name of the guilty ear, nose, tongue, body, or conscious sphere the great bodhisattva?"

"No, I don't think so, World-Honored One!"

"Is the designated name of the not guilty eye sphere the great bodhisattva?"

"No, I don't think so, World-Honored One!"

"Is the designated name of the not guilty ear, nose, tongue, body, or conscious sphere the great bodhisattva?"

"No, I don't think so, World-Honored One!"

"Is the designated name of the eye sphere with vexations the great bodhisattva?"

"No, I don't think so, World-Honored One!"
"Is the designated name of the ear, nose, tongue, body, or conscious sphere with vexations the great bodhisattva?"
"No, I don't think so, World-Honored One!"
"Is the designated name of the eye sphere without vexations the great bodhisattva?"
"No, I don't think so, World-Honored One!"
"Is the designated name of the ear, nose, tongue, body, or conscious sphere without vexations the great bodhisattva?"
"No, I don't think so, World-Honored One!"
"Is the designated name of the worldly eye sphere the great bodhisattva?"
"No, I don't think so, World-Honored One!"
"Is the designated name of the worldly ear, nose, tongue, body, or conscious sphere the great bodhisattva?"
"No, I don't think so, World-Honored One!"
"Is the designated name of the eye sphere beyond the world the great bodhisattva?"
"No, I don't think so, World-Honored One!"
"Is the designated name of the ear, nose, tongue, body, or conscious sphere beyond the world the great bodhisattva?"
"No, I don't think so, World-Honored One!"
"Is the designated name of the contaminated eye sphere the great bodhisattva?"
"No, I don't think so, World-Honored One!"
"Is the designated name of the contaminated ear, nose, tongue, body, or conscious sphere the great bodhisattva?"
"No, I don't think so, World-Honored One!"
"Is the designated name of the purified eye sphere the great bodhisattva?"
"No, I don't think so, World-Honored One!"
"Is the designated name of the purified ear, nose, tongue, body, or conscious sphere the great bodhisattva?"
"No, I don't think so, World-Honored One!"
"Is the designated name of the eye sphere belonging to birth and death the great bodhisattva?"

"No, I don't think so, World-Honored One!"

"Is the designated name of the ear, nose, tongue, body, or conscious sphere belonging to birth and death the great bodhisattva?"

"No, I don't think so, World-Honored One!"

"Is the designated name of the eye sphere belonging to nirvana the great bodhisattva?"

"No, I don't think so, World-Honored One!"

"Is the designated name of the ear, nose, tongue, body, or conscious sphere belonging to nirvana the great bodhisattva?"

"No, I don't think so, World-Honored One!"

"Is the designated name of the eye sphere that is inside the great bodhisattva?"

"No, I don't think so, World-Honored One!"

"Is the designated name of the ear, nose, tongue, body, or conscious sphere that is inside the great bodhisattva?"

"No, I don't think so, World-Honored One!"

"Is the designated name of the eye sphere that is outside the great bodhisattva?"

"No, I don't think so, World-Honored One!"

"Is the designated name of the ear, nose, tongue, body, or conscious sphere that is outside the great bodhisattva?"

"No, I don't think so, World-Honored One!"

"Is the designated name of the eye sphere that is in between the great bodhisattva?"

"No, I don't think so, World-Honored One!"

"Is the designated name of the ear, nose, tongue, body, or conscious sphere that is in between the great bodhisattva?"

"No, I don't think so, World-Honored One!"

"Is the designated name of the attainable eye sphere the great bodhisattva?"

"No, I don't think so, World-Honored One!"

"Is the designated name of the ear, nose, tongue, body, or conscious sphere attainable the great bodhisattva?"

"No, I don't think so, World-Honored One!"

"Is the designated name of the unattainable eye sphere the great bodhisattva?"

"No, I don't think so, World-Honored One!"

"Is the designated name of the ear, nose, tongue, body, or conscious sphere unattainable the great bodhisattva?"

"No, I don't think so, World-Honored One!"

"Furthermore, Well Appearing One, what does the great bodhisattva mean? Is the designated name of the sight sphere the great bodhisattva?"

"No, I don't think so, World-Honored One!"

"Is the designated name of the sound, smell, taste, touch, or mental-image sphere the great bodhisattva?"

"No, I don't think so, World-Honored One!"

"Is the designated name of the permanent sight sphere the great bodhisattva?"

"No, I don't think so, World-Honored One!"

"Is the designated name of the permanent sound, smell, taste, touch, or mental-image sphere the great bodhisattva?"

"No, I don't think so, World-Honored One!"

"Is the designated name of the impermanent sight sphere the great bodhisattva?"

"No, I don't think so, World-Honored One!"

"Is the designated name of the impermanent sound, smell, taste, touch, or mental-image sphere the great bodhisattva?"

"No, I don't think so, World-Honored One!"

"Is the designated name of the pleasant sight sphere the great bodhisattva?"

"No, I don't think so, World-Honored One!"

"Is the designated name of the pleasant sound, smell, taste, touch, or mental-image sphere the great bodhisattva?"

"No, I don't think so, World-Honored One!"

"Is the designated name of the painful sight sphere the great bodhisattva?"

"No, I don't think so, World-Honored One!"

"Is the designated name of the painful sound, smell, taste, touch, or mental-image sphere the great bodhisattva?"

"No, I don't think so, World-Honored One!"

"Is the designated name of the sight sphere with selfness the great bodhisattva?"

"No, I don't think so, World-Honored One!"

"Is the designated name of the sound, smell, taste, touch, or mental-image sphere with selfness the great bodhisattva?"

"No, I don't think so, World-Honored One!"

"Is the designated name of the sight sphere without selfness the great bodhisattva?"

"No, I don't think so, World-Honored One!"

"Is the designated name of the sound, smell, taste, touch, or mental-image sphere without selfness the great bodhisattva?"

"No, I don't think so, World-Honored One!"

"Is the designated name of the pure sight sphere the great bodhisattva?"

"No, I don't think so, World-Honored One!"

"Is the designated name of the pure sound, smell, taste, touch, or mental-image sphere the great bodhisattva?"

"No, I don't think so, World-Honored One!"

"Is the designated name of the impure sight sphere the great bodhisattva?"

"No, I don't think so, World-Honored One!"

"Is the designated name of the impure sound, smell, taste, touch, or mental-image sphere the great bodhisattva?"

"No, I don't think so, World-Honored One!"

"Is the designated name of the empty sight sphere the great bodhisattva?"

"No, I don't think so, World-Honored One!"

"Is the designated name of the empty sound, smell, taste, touch, or mental-image sphere the great bodhisattva?"

"No, I don't think so, World-Honored One!"

"Is the designated name of the not empty sight sphere the great bodhisattva?"

"No, I don't think so, World-Honored One!"

"Is the designated name of the not empty sound, smell, taste, touch, or mental-image sphere the great bodhisattva?"

"No, I don't think so, World-Honored One!"

"Is the designated name of the sight sphere with the form the great bodhisattva?"

"No, I don't think so, World-Honored One!"

"Is the designated name of the sound, smell, taste, touch, or mental-image sphere with the form the great bodhisattva?"
"No, I don't think so, World-Honored One!"
"Is the designated name of the formless sight sphere the great bodhisattva?"
"No, I don't think so, World-Honored One!"
"Is the designated name of the formless sound, smell, taste, touch, or mental-image sphere the great bodhisattva?"
"No, I don't think so, World-Honored One!"
"Is the designated name of the sight sphere with aspiration the great bodhisattva?"
"No, I don't think so, World-Honored One!"
"Is the designated name of the sound, smell, taste, touch, or mental-image sphere with aspiration the great bodhisattva?"
"No, I don't think so, World-Honored One!"
"Is the designated name of the sight sphere without aspiration the great bodhisattva?"
"No, I don't think so, World-Honored One!"
"Is the designated name of the sound, smell, taste, touch, or mental-image sphere without aspiration the great bodhisattva?"
"No, I don't think so, World-Honored One!"
"Is the designated name of the sight sphere with tranquility the great bodhisattva?"
"No, I don't think so, World-Honored One!"
"Is the designated name of the sound, smell, taste, touch, or mental-image sphere with tranquility the great bodhisattva?"
"No, I don't think so, World-Honored One!"
"Is the designated name of the sight sphere without tranquility the great bodhisattva?"
"No, I don't think so, World-Honored One!"
"Is the designated name of the sound, smell, taste, touch, or mental-image sphere without tranquility the great bodhisattva?"
"No, I don't think so, World-Honored One!"
"Is the designated name of the sight sphere getting far away the great bodhisattva?"
"No, I don't think so, World-Honored One!"

"Is the designated name of the sound, smell, taste, touch, or mental-image sphere getting far away the great bodhisattva?"

"No, I don't think so, World-Honored One!"

"Is the designated name of the sight sphere not getting far away the great bodhisattva?"

"No, I don't think so, World-Honored One!"

"Is the designated name of the sound, smell, taste, touch, or mental-image sphere not getting far away the great bodhisattva?"

"No, I don't think so, World-Honored One!"

"Is the designated name of the conditioned sight sphere the great bodhisattva?"

"No, I don't think so, World-Honored One!"

"Is the designated name of the conditioned sound, smell, taste, touch, or mental-image sphere the great bodhisattva?"

"No, I don't think so, World-Honored One!"

"Is the designated name of the unconditioned sight sphere the great bodhisattva?"

"No, I don't think so, World-Honored One!"

"Is the designated name of the unconditioned sound, smell, taste, touch, or mental-image sphere the great bodhisattva?"

"No, I don't think so, World-Honored One!"

"Is the designated name of the flawed sight sphere the great bodhisattva?"

"No, I don't think so, World-Honored One!"

"Is the designated name of the flawed sound, smell, taste, touch, or mental-image sphere the great bodhisattva?"

"No, I don't think so, World-Honored One!"

"Is the designated name of the flawless sight sphere the great bodhisattva?"

"No, I don't think so, World-Honored One!"

"Is the designated name of the flawless sound, smell, taste, touch, or mental-image sphere the great bodhisattva?"

"No, I don't think so, World-Honored One!"

"Is the designated name of the arising sight sphere the great bodhisattva?"

"No, I don't think so, World-Honored One!"

"Is the designated name of the arising sound, smell, taste, touch, or mental-image sphere the great bodhisattva?"
"No, I don't think so, World-Honored One!"
"Is the designated name of the extinguishing sight sphere the great bodhisattva?"
"No, I don't think so, World-Honored One!"
"Is the designated name of the extinguishing sound, smell, taste, touch, or mental-image sphere the great bodhisattva?"
"No, I don't think so, World-Honored One!"
"Is the designated name of the virtuous sight sphere the great bodhisattva?"
"No, I don't think so, World-Honored One!"
"Is the designated name of the virtuous sound, smell, taste, touch, or mental-image sphere the great bodhisattva?"
"No, I don't think so, World-Honored One!"
"Is the designated name of the not virtuous sight sphere the great bodhisattva?"
"No, I don't think so, World-Honored One!"
"Is the designated name of the not virtuous sound, smell, taste, touch, or mental-image sphere the great bodhisattva?"
"No, I don't think so, World-Honored One!"
"Is the designated name of the guilty sight sphere the great bodhisattva?"
"No, I don't think so, World-Honored One!"
"Is the designated name of the guilty sound, smell, taste, touch, or mental-image sphere the great bodhisattva?"
"No, I don't think so, World-Honored One!"
"Is the designated name of the not guilty sight sphere the great bodhisattva?"
"No, I don't think so, World-Honored One!"
"Is the designated name of the not guilty sound, smell, taste, touch, or mental-image sphere the great bodhisattva?"
"No, I don't think so, World-Honored One!"
"Is the designated name of the sight sphere with vexations the great bodhisattva?"
"No, I don't think so, World-Honored One!"

"Is the designated name of the sound, smell, taste, touch, or mental-image sphere with vexations the great bodhisattva?"

"No, I don't think so, World-Honored One!"

"Is the designated name of the sight sphere without vexations the great bodhisattva?"

"No, I don't think so, World-Honored One!"

"Is the designated name of the sound, smell, taste, touch, or mental-image sphere without vexations the great bodhisattva?"

"No, I don't think so, World-Honored One!"

"Is the designated name of the worldly sight sphere the great bodhisattva?"

"No, I don't think so, World-Honored One!"

"Is the designated name of the worldly sound, smell, taste, touch, or mental-image sphere the great bodhisattva?"

"No, I don't think so, World-Honored One!"

"Is the designated name of the sight sphere beyond the world the great bodhisattva?"

"No, I don't think so, World-Honored One!"

"Is the designated name of the sound, smell, taste, touch, or mental-image sphere beyond the world the great bodhisattva?"

"No, I don't think so, World-Honored One!"

"Is the designated name of the contaminated sight sphere the great bodhisattva?"

"No, I don't think so, World-Honored One!"

"Is the designated name of the contaminated sound, smell, taste, touch, or mental-image sphere the great bodhisattva?"

"No, I don't think so, World-Honored One!"

"Is the designated name of the purified sight sphere the great bodhisattva?"

"No, I don't think so, World-Honored One!"

"Is the designated name of the purified sound, smell, taste, touch, or mental-image sphere the great bodhisattva?"

"No, I don't think so, World-Honored One!"

"Is the designated name of the sight sphere belonging to birth and death the great bodhisattva?"

"No, I don't think so, World-Honored One!"

"Is the designated name of the sound, smell, taste, touch, or mental-image sphere belonging to birth and death the great bodhisattva?"

"No, I don't think so, World-Honored One!"

"Is the designated name of the sight sphere belonging to nirvana the great bodhisattva?"

"No, I don't think so, World-Honored One!"

"Is the designated name of the sound, smell, taste, touch, or mental-image sphere belonging to nirvana the great bodhisattva?"

"No, I don't think so, World-Honored One!"

"Is the designated name of the sight sphere that is inside the great bodhisattva?"

"No, I don't think so, World-Honored One!"

"Is the designated name of the sound, smell, taste, touch, or mental-image sphere that is inside the great bodhisattva?"

"No, I don't think so, World-Honored One!"

"Is the designated name of the sight sphere that is outside the great bodhisattva?"

"No, I don't think so, World-Honored One!"

"Is the designated name of the sound, smell, taste, touch, or mental-image sphere that is outside the great bodhisattva?"

"No, I don't think so, World-Honored One!"

"Is the designated name of the sight sphere that is in between the great bodhisattva?"

"No, I don't think so, World-Honored One!"

"Is the designated name of the sound, smell, taste, touch, or mental-image sphere that is in between the great bodhisattva?"

"No, I don't think so, World-Honored One!"

"Is the designated name of the sight sphere attainable the great bodhisattva?"

"No, I don't think so, World-Honored One!"

"Is the designated name of the sound, smell, taste, touch, or mental-image sphere attainable the great bodhisattva?"

"No, I don't think so, World-Honored One!"

"Is the designated name of the sight sphere unattainable the great bodhisattva?"

"No, I don't think so, World-Honored One!"

"Is the designated name of the sound, smell, taste, touch, or mental-image sphere unattainable the great bodhisattva?"

"No, I don't think so, World-Honored One!"

FASCICLE 18

Chapter 7
The Cautions and the Teachings

Section 8

(In the First Assembly)

"FURTHERMORE, WELL APPEARING ONE, WHAT DOES THE GREAT bodhisattva mean? Is the designated name of the eye realm the great bodhisattva?"

"No, I don't think so, World-Honored One!"

"Is the designated name of the ear, nose, tongue, body, or conscious realm the great bodhisattva?"

"No, I don't think so, World-Honored One!"

"Is the designated name of the permanent eye realm the great bodhisattva?"

"No, I don't think so, World-Honored One!"

"Is the designated name of the permanent ear, nose, tongue, body, or conscious realm the great bodhisattva?"

"No, I don't think so, World-Honored One!"

"Is the designated name of the impermanent eye realm the great bodhisattva?"

"No, I don't think so, World-Honored One!"

"Is the designated name of the impermanent ear, nose, tongue, body, or conscious realm the great bodhisattva?"

"No, I don't think so, World-Honored One!"

"Is the designated name of the pleasant eye realm the great bodhisattva?"

"No, I don't think so, World-Honored One!"

"Is the designated name of the pleasant ear, nose, tongue, body, or conscious realm the great bodhisattva?"

"No, I don't think so, World-Honored One!"

"Is the designated name of the painful eye realm the great bodhisattva?"

"No, I don't think so, World-Honored One!"

"Is the designated name of the painful ear, nose, tongue, body, or conscious realm the great bodhisattva?"

"No, I don't think so, World-Honored One!"

"Is the designated name of the eye realm with selfness the great bodhisattva?"

"No, I don't think so, World-Honored One!"

"Is the designated name of the ear, nose, tongue, body, or conscious realm with selfness the great bodhisattva?"

"No, I don't think so, World-Honored One!"

"Is the designated name of the eye realm without selfness the great bodhisattva?"

"No, I don't think so, World-Honored One!"

"Is the designated name of the ear, nose, tongue, body, or conscious realm without selfness the great bodhisattva?"

"No, I don't think so, World-Honored One!"

"Is the designated name of the pure eye realm the great bodhisattva?"

"No, I don't think so, World-Honored One!"

"Is the designated name of the pure ear, nose, tongue, body, or conscious realm the great bodhisattva?"

"No, I don't think so, World-Honored One!"

"Is the designated name of the impure eye realm the great bodhisattva?"

"No, I don't think so, World-Honored One!"

"Is the designated name of the impure ear, nose, tongue, body, or conscious realm the great bodhisattva?"
"No, I don't think so, World-Honored One!"
"Is the designated name of the empty eye realm the great bodhisattva?"
"No, I don't think so, World-Honored One!"
"Is the designated name of the empty ear, nose, tongue, body, or conscious realm the great bodhisattva?"
"No, I don't think so, World-Honored One!"
"Is the designated name of the not empty eye realm the great bodhisattva?"
"No, I don't think so, World-Honored One!"
"Is the designated name of the not empty ear, nose, tongue, body, or conscious realm the great bodhisattva?"
"No, I don't think so, World-Honored One!"
"Is the designated name of the eye realm with form the great bodhisattva?"
"No, I don't think so, World-Honored One!"
"Is the designated name of the ear, nose, tongue, body, or conscious realm with form the great bodhisattva?"
"No, I don't think so, World-Honored One!"
"Is the designated name of the eye realm without form the great bodhisattva?"
"No, I don't think so, World-Honored One!"
"Is the designated name of the ear, nose, tongue, body, or conscious realm without form the great bodhisattva?"
"No, I don't think so, World-Honored One!"
"Is the designated name of the eye realm with aspiration the great bodhisattva?"
"No, I don't think so, World-Honored One!"
"Is the designated name of the ear, nose, tongue, body, or conscious realm with aspiration the great bodhisattva?"
"No, I don't think so, World-Honored One!"
"Is the designated name of the eye realm without aspiration the great bodhisattva?"
"No, I don't think so, World-Honored One!"

"Is the designated name of the ear, nose, tongue, body, or conscious realm without aspiration the great bodhisattva?"

"No, I don't think so, World-Honored One!"

"Is the designated name of the eye realm in tranquility the great bodhisattva?"

"No, I don't think so, World-Honored One!"

"Is the designated name of the ear, nose, tongue, body, or conscious realm in tranquility the great bodhisattva?"

"No, I don't think so, World-Honored One!"

"Is the designated name of the eye realm not in tranquility the great bodhisattva?"

"No, I don't think so, World-Honored One!"

"Is the designated name of the ear, nose, tongue, body, or conscious realm not in tranquility the great bodhisattva?"

"No, I don't think so, World-Honored One!"

"Is the designated name of the eye realm getting far away the great bodhisattva?"

"No, I don't think so, World-Honored One!"

"Is the designated name of the ear, nose, tongue, body, or conscious realm getting far away the great bodhisattva?"

"No, I don't think so, World-Honored One!"

"Is the designated name of the eye realm not getting far away the great bodhisattva?"

"No, I don't think so, World-Honored One!"

"Is the designated name of the ear, nose, tongue, body, or conscious realm not getting far away the great bodhisattva?"

"No, I don't think so, World-Honored One!"

"Is the designated name of the conditioned eye realm the great bodhisattva?"

"No, I don't think so, World-Honored One!"

"Is the designated name of the conditioned ear, nose, tongue, body, or conscious realm the great bodhisattva?"

"No, I don't think so, World-Honored One!"

"Is the designated name of the unconditioned eye realm the great bodhisattva?"

"No, I don't think so, World-Honored One!"

"Is the designated name of the unconditioned ear, nose, tongue, body, or conscious realm the great bodhisattva?"
"No, I don't think so, World-Honored One!"
"Is the designated name of the flawed eye realm the great bodhisattva?"
"No, I don't think so, World-Honored One!"
"Is the designated name of the flawed ear, nose, tongue, body, or conscious realm the great bodhisattva?"
"No, I don't think so, World-Honored One!"
"Is the designated name of the flawless eye realm the great bodhisattva?"
"No, I don't think so, World-Honored One!"
"Is the designated name of the flawless ear, nose, tongue, body, or conscious realm the great bodhisattva?"
"No, I don't think so, World-Honored One!"
"Is the designated name of the arising eye realm the great bodhisattva?"
"No, I don't think so, World-Honored One!"
"Is the designated name of the arising ear, nose, tongue, body, or conscious realm the great bodhisattva?"
"No, I don't think so, World-Honored One!"
"Is the designated name of the extinguishing eye realm the great bodhisattva?"
"No, I don't think so, World-Honored One!"
"Is the designated name of the extinguishing ear, nose, tongue, body, or conscious realm the great bodhisattva?"
"No, I don't think so, World-Honored One!"
"Is the designated name of the virtuous eye realm the great bodhisattva?"
"No, I don't think so, World-Honored One!"
"Is the designated name of the virtuous ear, nose, tongue, body, or conscious realm the great bodhisattva?"
"No, I don't think so, World-Honored One!"
"Is the designated name of the not virtuous eye realm the great bodhisattva?"
"No, I don't think so, World-Honored One!"

"Is the designated name of the not virtuous ear, nose, tongue, body, or conscious realm the great bodhisattva?"

"No, I don't think so, World-Honored One!"

"Is the designated name of the guilty eye realm the great bodhisattva?"

"No, I don't think so, World-Honored One!"

"Is the designated name of the guilty ear, nose, tongue, body, or conscious realm the great bodhisattva?"

"No, I don't think so, World-Honored One!"

"Is the designated name of the not guilty eye realm the great bodhisattva?"

"No, I don't think so, World-Honored One!"

"Is the designated name of the not guilty ear, nose, tongue, body, or conscious realm the great bodhisattva?"

"No, I don't think so, World-Honored One!"

"Is the designated name of the eye realm with vexations the great bodhisattva?"

"No, I don't think so, World-Honored One!"

"Is the designated name of the ear, nose, tongue, body, or conscious realm with vexations the great bodhisattva?"

"No, I don't think so, World-Honored One!"

"Is the designated name of the eye realm without vexations the great bodhisattva?"

"No, I don't think so, World-Honored One!"

"Is the designated name of the ear, nose, tongue, body, or conscious realm without vexations the great bodhisattva?"

"No, I don't think so, World-Honored One!"

"Is the designated name of the worldly eye realm the great bodhisattva?"

"No, I don't think so, World-Honored One!"

"Is the designated name of the worldly ear, nose, tongue, body, or conscious realm the great bodhisattva?"

"No, I don't think so, World-Honored One!"

"Is the designated name of the eye realm beyond the world the great bodhisattva?"

"No, I don't think so, World-Honored One!"

"Is the designated name of the ear, nose, tongue, body, or conscious realm beyond the world the great bodhisattva?"

"No, I don't think so, World-Honored One!"

"Is the designated name of the contaminated eye realm the great bodhisattva?"

"No, I don't think so, World-Honored One!"

"Is the designated name of the contaminated ear, nose, tongue, body, or conscious realm the great bodhisattva?"

"No, I don't think so, World-Honored One!"

"Is the designated name of the purified eye realm the great bodhisattva?"

"No, I don't think so, World-Honored One!"

"Is the designated name of the purified ear, nose, tongue, body, or conscious realm the great bodhisattva?"

"No, I don't think so, World-Honored One!"

"Is the designated name of the eye realm belonging to birth and death the great bodhisattva?"

"No, I don't think so, World-Honored One!"

"Is the designated name of the ear, nose, tongue, body, or conscious realm belonging to birth and death the great bodhisattva?"

"No, I don't think so, World-Honored One!"

"Is the designated name of the eye realm belonging to nirvana the great bodhisattva?"

"No, I don't think so, World-Honored One!"

"Is the designated name of the ear, nose, tongue, body, or conscious realm belonging to nirvana the great bodhisattva?"

"No, I don't think so, World-Honored One!"

"Is the designated name of the inside eye realm the great bodhisattva?"

"No, I don't think so, World-Honored One!"

"Is the designated name of the inside ear, nose, tongue, body, or conscious realm the great bodhisattva?"

"No, I don't think so, World-Honored One!"

"Is the designated name of the outside eye realm the great bodhisattva?"

"No, I don't think so, World-Honored One!"

"Is the designated name of the outside ear, nose, tongue, body, or conscious realm the great bodhisattva?"

"No, I don't think so, World-Honored One!"

"Is the designated name of the in-between eye realm the great bodhisattva?"

"No, I don't think so, World-Honored One!"

"Is the designated name of the in-between ear, nose, tongue, body, or conscious realm the great bodhisattva?"

"No, I don't think so, World-Honored One!"

"Is the designated name of the attainable eye realm the great bodhisattva?"

"No, I don't think so, World-Honored One!"

"Is the designated name of the attainable ear, nose, tongue, body, or conscious realm the great bodhisattva?"

"No, I don't think so, World-Honored One!"

"Is the designated name of the unattainable eye realm the great bodhisattva?"

"No, I don't think so, World-Honored One!"

"Is the designated name of the unattainable ear, nose, tongue, body, or conscious realm the great bodhisattva?"

"No, I don't think so, World-Honored One!"

"Furthermore, Well Appearing One, what does the great bodhisattva mean? Is the designated name of the sight realm the great bodhisattva?"

"No, I don't think so, World-Honored One!"

"Is the designated name of the sound, smell, taste, touch, or mental-image realm the great bodhisattva?"

"No, I don't think so, World-Honored One!"

"Is the designated name of the permanent sight realm the great bodhisattva?"

"No, I don't think so, World-Honored One!"

"Is the designated name of the permanent sound, smell, taste, touch, or mental-image realm the great bodhisattva?"

"No, I don't think so, World-Honored One!"

"Is the designated name of the impermanent sight realm the great bodhisattva?"

"No, I don't think so, World-Honored One!"
"Is the designated name of the impermanent sound, smell, taste, touch, or mental-image realm the great bodhisattva?"
"No, I don't think so, World-Honored One!"
"Is the designated name of the pleasant sight realm the great bodhisattva?"
"No, I don't think so, World-Honored One!"
"Is the designated name of the pleasant sound, smell, taste, touch, or mental-image realm the great bodhisattva?"
"No, I don't think so, World-Honored One!"
"Is the designated name of the painful sight realm the great bodhisattva?"
"No, I don't think so, World-Honored One!"
"Is the designated name of the painful sound, smell, taste, touch, or mental-image realm the great bodhisattva?"
"No, I don't think so, World-Honored One!"
"Is the designated name of the sight realm with selfness the great bodhisattva?"
"No, I don't think so, World-Honored One!"
"Is the designated name of the sound, smell, taste, touch, or mental-image realm with selfness the great bodhisattva?"
"No, I don't think so, World-Honored One!"
"Is the designated name of the sight realm without selfness the great bodhisattva?"
"No, I don't think so, World-Honored One!"
"Is the designated name of the sound, smell, taste, touch, or mental-image realm without selfness the great bodhisattva?"
"No, I don't think so, World-Honored One!"
"Is the designated name of the pure sight realm the great bodhisattva?"
"No, I don't think so, World-Honored One!"
"Is the designated name of the pure sound, smell, taste, touch, or mental-image realm the great bodhisattva?"
"No, I don't think so, World-Honored One!"
"Is the designated name of the impure sight realm the great bodhisattva?"

"No, I don't think so, World-Honored One!"

"Is the designated name of the impure sound, smell, taste, touch, or mental-image realm the great bodhisattva?"

"No, I don't think so, World-Honored One!"

"Is the designated name of the empty sight realm the great bodhisattva?"

"No, I don't think so, World-Honored One!"

"Is the designated name of the empty sound, smell, taste, touch, or mental-image realm the great bodhisattva?"

"No, I don't think so, World-Honored One!"

"Is the designated name of the not empty sight realm the great bodhisattva?"

"No, I don't think so, World-Honored One!"

"Is the designated name of the not empty sound, smell, taste, touch, or mental-image realm the great bodhisattva?"

"No, I don't think so, World-Honored One!"

"Is the designated name of the sight realm with form the great bodhisattva?"

"No, I don't think so, World-Honored One!"

"Is the designated name of the sound, smell, taste, touch, or mental-image realm with form the great bodhisattva?"

"No, I don't think so, World-Honored One!"

"Is the designated name of the sight realm without form the great bodhisattva?"

"No, I don't think so, World-Honored One!"

"Is the designated name of the sound, smell, taste, touch, or mental-image realm without form the great bodhisattva?"

"No, I don't think so, World-Honored One!"

"Is the designated name of the sight realm with aspiration the great bodhisattva?"

"No, I don't think so, World-Honored One!"

"Is the designated name of the sound, smell, taste, touch, or mental-image realm with aspiration the great bodhisattva?"

"No, I don't think so, World-Honored One!"

"Is the designation of the sight realm without aspiration the great bodhisattva?"

Fascicle 18, Chapter 7, Section 8 425

"No, I don't think so, World-Honored One!"
"Is the designated name of the sound, smell, taste, touch, or mental-image realm without aspiration the great bodhisattva?"
"No, I don't think so, World-Honored One!"
"Is the designated name of the sight realm in tranquility the great bodhisattva?"
"No, I don't think so, World-Honored One!"
"Is the designated name of the sound, smell, taste, touch, or mental-image realm in tranquility the great bodhisattva?"
"No, I don't think so, World-Honored One!"
"Is the designated name of the sight realm not in tranquility the great bodhisattva?"
"No, I don't think so, World-Honored One!"
"Is the designated name of the sound, smell, taste, touch, or mental-image realm not in tranquility the great bodhisattva?"
"No, I don't think so, World-Honored One!"
"Is the designated name of the sight realm getting far away the great bodhisattva?"
"No, I don't think so, World-Honored One!"
"Is the designated name of the sound, smell, taste, touch, or mental-image realm getting far away the great bodhisattva?"
"No, I don't think so, World-Honored One!"
"Is the designated name of the sight realm not getting far away the great bodhisattva?"
"No, I don't think so, World-Honored One!"
"Is the designated name of the sound, smell, taste, touch, or mental-image realm not getting far away the great bodhisattva?"
"No, I don't think so, World-Honored One!"
"Is the designated name of the conditioned sight realm the great bodhisattva?"
"No, I don't think so, World-Honored One!"
"Is the designated name of the conditioned sound, smell, taste, touch, or mental-image realm the great bodhisattva?"
"No, I don't think so, World-Honored One!"
"Is the designated name of the unconditioned sight realm the great bodhisattva?"

"No, I don't think so, World-Honored One!"

"Is the designated name of the unconditioned sound, smell, taste, touch, or mental-image realm the great bodhisattva?"

"No, I don't think so, World-Honored One!"

"Is the designated name of the flawed sight realm the great bodhisattva?"

"No, I don't think so, World-Honored One!"

"Is the designated name of the flawed sound, smell, taste, touch, or mental-image realm the great bodhisattva?"

"No, I don't think so, World-Honored One!"

"Is the designated name of the flawless sight realm the great bodhisattva?"

"No, I don't think so, World-Honored One!"

"Is the designated name of the flawless sound, smell, taste, touch, or mental-image realm the great bodhisattva?"

"No, I don't think so, World-Honored One!"

"Is the designated name of the arising sight realm the great bodhisattva?"

"No, I don't think so, World-Honored One!"

"Is the designated name of the arising sound, smell, taste, touch, or mental-image realm the great bodhisattva?"

"No, I don't think so, World-Honored One!"

"Is the designated name of the extinguishing sight realm the great bodhisattva?"

"No, I don't think so, World-Honored One!"

"Is the designated name of the extinguishing sound, smell, taste, touch, or mental-image realm the great bodhisattva?"

"No, I don't think so, World-Honored One!"

"Is the designated name of the virtuous sight realm the great bodhisattva?"

"No, I don't think so, World-Honored One!"

"Is the designated name of the virtuous sound, smell, taste, touch, or mental-image realm the great bodhisattva?"

"No, I don't think so, World-Honored One!"

"Is the designated name of the not virtuous sight realm the great bodhisattva?"

Fascicle 18, Chapter 7, Section 8

"No, I don't think so, World-Honored One!"

"Is the designated name of the not virtuous sound, smell, taste, touch, or mental-image realm the great bodhisattva?"

"No, I don't think so, World-Honored One!"

"Is the designated name of the guilty sight realm the great bodhisattva?"

"No, I don't think so, World-Honored One!"

"Is the designated name of the guilty sound, smell, taste, touch, or mental-image realm the great bodhisattva?"

"No, I don't think so, World-Honored One!"

"Is the designated name of the not guilty sight realm the great bodhisattva?"

"No, I don't think so, World-Honored One!"

"Is the designated name of the not guilty sound, smell, taste, touch, or mental-image realm the great bodhisattva?"

"No, I don't think so, World-Honored One!"

"Is the designated name of the sight realm with vexations the great bodhisattva?"

"No, I don't think so, World-Honored One!"

"Is the designated name of the sound, smell, taste, touch, or mental-image realm with vexations the great bodhisattva?"

"No, I don't think so, World-Honored One!"

"Is the designated name of the sight realm without vexations the great bodhisattva?"

"No, I don't think so, World-Honored One!"

"Is the designated name of the sound, smell, taste, touch, or mental-image realm without vexations the great bodhisattva?"

"No, I don't think so, World-Honored One!"

"Is the designated name of the worldly sight realm the great bodhisattva?"

"No, I don't think so, World-Honored One!"

"Is the designated name of the worldly sound, smell, taste, touch, or mental-image realm the great bodhisattva?"

"No, I don't think so, World-Honored One!"

"Is the designated name of the sight realm beyond the world the great bodhisattva?"

"No, I don't think so, World-Honored One!"

"Is the designated name of the sound, smell, taste, touch, or mental-image realm beyond the world the great bodhisattva?"

"No, I don't think so, World-Honored One!"

"Is the designated name of the contaminated sight realm the great bodhisattva?"

"No, I don't think so, World-Honored One!"

"Is the designated name of the contaminated sound, smell, taste, touch, or mental-image realm the great bodhisattva?"

"No, I don't think so, World-Honored One!"

"Is the designated name of the purified sight realm the great bodhisattva?"

"No, I don't think so, World-Honored One!"

"Is the designated name of the purified sound, smell, taste, touch, or mental-image realm the great bodhisattva?"

"No, I don't think so, World-Honored One!"

"Is the designated name of the sight realm belonging to birth and death the great bodhisattva?"

"No, I don't think so, World-Honored One!"

"Is the designated name of the sound, smell, taste, touch, or mental-image realm belonging to birth and death the great bodhisattva?"

"No, I don't think so, World-Honored One!"

"Is the designated name of the sight realm belonging to nirvana the great bodhisattva?"

"No, I don't think so, World-Honored One!"

"Is the designated name of the sound, smell, taste, touch, or mental-image realm belonging to nirvana the great bodhisattva?"

"No, I don't think so, World-Honored One!"

"Is the designated name of the inside sight realm the great bodhisattva?"

"No, I don't think so, World-Honored One!"

"Is the designated name of the inside sound, smell, taste, touch, or mental-image realm inside the great bodhisattva?"

"No, I don't think so, World-Honored One!"

"Is the designated name of the outside sight realm the great bodhisattva?"

"No, I don't think so, World-Honored One!"
"Is the designated name of the outside sound, smell, taste, touch, or mental-image realm the great bodhisattva?"
"No, I don't think so, World-Honored One!"
"Is the designated name of the in-between sight realm the great bodhisattva?"
"No, I don't think so, World-Honored One!"
"Is the designated name of the in-between sound, smell, taste, touch, or mental-image realm the great bodhisattva?"
"No, I don't think so, World-Honored One!"
"Is the designated name of the attainable sight realm the great bodhisattva?"
"No, I don't think so, World-Honored One!"
"Is the designated name of the attainable sound, smell, taste, touch, or mental-image realm the great bodhisattva?"
"No, I don't think so, World-Honored One!"
"Is the designated name of the unattainable sight realm the great bodhisattva?"
"No, I don't think so, World-Honored One!"
"Is the designated name of the unattainable sound, smell, taste, touch, or mental-image realm the great bodhisattva?"
"No, I don't think so, World-Honored One!"
"Furthermore, Well Appearing One, what does the great bodhisattva mean? Is the designated name of the eye consciousness realm the great bodhisattva?"
"No, I don't think so, World-Honored One!"
"Is the designated name of the ear, nose, tongue, body, or conscious consciousness realm the great bodhisattva?"
"No, I don't think so, World-Honored One!"
"Is the designated name of the permanent eye consciousness realm the great bodhisattva?"
"No, I don't think so, World-Honored One!"
"Is the designated name of the permanent ear, nose, tongue, body, or conscious consciousness realm the great bodhisattva?"
"No, I don't think so, World-Honored One!"
"Is the designated name of the impermanent eye consciousness realm the great bodhisattva?"

"No, I don't think so, World-Honored One!"

"Is the designated name of the impermanent ear, nose, tongue, body, or conscious consciousness realm the great bodhisattva?"

"No, I don't think so, World-Honored One!"

"Is the designated name of the pleasant eye consciousness realm the great bodhisattva?"

"No, I don't think so, World-Honored One!"

"Is the designated name of the pleasant ear, nose, tongue, body, or conscious consciousness realm the great bodhisattva?"

"No, I don't think so, World-Honored One!"

"Is the designated name of the painful eye consciousness realm the great bodhisattva?"

"No, I don't think so, World-Honored One!"

"Is the designated name of the painful ear, nose, tongue, body, or conscious consciousness realm the great bodhisattva?"

"No, I don't think so, World-Honored One!"

"Is the designated name of the eye consciousness realm with selfness the great bodhisattva?"

"No, I don't think so, World-Honored One!"

"Is the designated name of the ear, nose, tongue, body, or conscious consciousness realm with selfness the great bodhisattva?"

"No, I don't think so, World-Honored One!"

"Is the designated name of the eye consciousness realm without selfness the great bodhisattva?"

"No, I don't think so, World-Honored One!"

"Is the designated name of the ear, nose, tongue, body, or conscious consciousness realm without selfness the great bodhisattva?"

"No, I don't think so, World-Honored One!"

"Is the designated name of the pure eye consciousness realm the great bodhisattva?"

"No, I don't think so, World-Honored One!"

"Is the designated name of the pure ear, nose, tongue, body, or conscious consciousness realm the great bodhisattva?"

"No, I don't think so, World-Honored One!"

"Is the designated name of the impure eye consciousness realm the great bodhisattva?"

"No, I don't think so, World-Honored One!"

"Is the designated name of the impure ear, nose, tongue, body, or conscious consciousness realm the great bodhisattva?"
"No, I don't think so, World-Honored One!"
"Is the designated name of the empty eye consciousness realm the great bodhisattva?"
"No, I don't think so, World-Honored One!"
"Is the designated name of the empty ear, nose, tongue, body, or conscious consciousness realm the great bodhisattva?"
"No, I don't think so, World-Honored One!"
"Is the designated name of the not empty eye consciousness realm the great bodhisattva?"
"No, I don't think so, World-Honored One!"
"Is the designated name of the not empty ear, nose, tongue, body, or conscious consciousness realm the great bodhisattva?"
"No, I don't think so, World-Honored One!"
"Is the designated name of the eye consciousness realm with form the great bodhisattva?"
"No, I don't think so, World-Honored One!"
"Is the designated name of the ear, nose, tongue, body, or conscious consciousness realm with form the great bodhisattva?"
"No, I don't think so, World-Honored One!"
"Is the designated name of the eye consciousness realm without form the great bodhisattva?"
"No, I don't think so, World-Honored One!"
"Is the designated name of the ear, nose, tongue, body, or conscious consciousness realm without form the great bodhisattva?"
"No, I don't think so, World-Honored One!"
"Is the designated name of the eye consciousness realm with aspiration the great bodhisattva?"
"No, I don't think so, World-Honored One!"
"Is the designated name of the ear, nose, tongue, body, or conscious consciousness realm with aspiration the great bodhisattva?"
"No, I don't think so, World-Honored One!"
"Is the designated name of the eye consciousness realm without aspiration the great bodhisattva?"
"No, I don't think so, World-Honored One!"
"Is the designated name of the ear, nose, tongue, body, or con-

scious consciousness realm without aspiration the great bodhisattva?"

"No, I don't think so, World-Honored One!"

"Is the designated name of the eye consciousness realm in tranquility the great bodhisattva?"

"No, I don't think so, World-Honored One!"

"Is the designated name of the ear, nose, tongue, body, or conscious consciousness realm in tranquility the great bodhisattva?"

"No, I don't think so, World-Honored One!"

"Is the designated name of the eye consciousness realm not in tranquility the great bodhisattva?"

"No, I don't think so, World-Honored One!"

"Is the designated name of the ear, nose, tongue, body, or conscious consciousness realm not in tranquility the great bodhisattva?"

"No, I don't think so, World-Honored One!"

"Is the designated name of the eye consciousness realm getting far away the great bodhisattva?"

"No, I don't think so, World-Honored One!"

"Is the designated name of the ear, nose, tongue, body, or conscious consciousness realm getting far away the great bodhisattva?"

"No, I don't think so, World-Honored One!"

"Is the designated name of the eye consciousness realm not getting far away the great bodhisattva?"

"No, I don't think so, World-Honored One!"

"Is the designated name of the ear, nose, tongue, body, or conscious consciousness realm not getting far away the great bodhisattva?"

"No, I don't think so, World-Honored One!"

"Is the designated name of the conditioned eye consciousness realm the great bodhisattva?"

"No, I don't think so, World-Honored One!"

"Is the designated name of the conditioned ear, nose, tongue, body, or conscious consciousness realm the great bodhisattva?"

"No, I don't think so, World-Honored One!"

"Is the designated name of the unconditioned eye consciousness realm the great bodhisattva?"

Fascicle 18, Chapter 7, Section 8

"No, I don't think so, World-Honored One!"
"Is the designated name of the unconditioned ear, nose, tongue, body, or conscious consciousness realm the great bodhisattva?"
"No, I don't think so, World-Honored One!"
"Is the designated name of the flawed eye consciousness realm the great bodhisattva?"
"No, I don't think so, World-Honored One!"
"Is the designated name of the flawed ear, nose, tongue, body, or conscious consciousness realm the great bodhisattva?"
"No, I don't think so, World-Honored One!"
"Is the designated name of the flawless eye consciousness realm the great bodhisattva?"
"No, I don't think so, World-Honored One!"
"Is the designated name of the flawless ear, nose, tongue, body, or conscious consciousness realm the great bodhisattva?"
"No, I don't think so, World-Honored One!"
"Is the designated name of the arising eye consciousness realm the great bodhisattva?"
"No, I don't think so, World-Honored One!"
"Is the designated name of the arising ear, nose, tongue, body, or conscious consciousness realm the great bodhisattva?"
"No, I don't think so, World-Honored One!"
"Is the designated name of the extinguishing eye consciousness realm the great bodhisattva?"
"No, I don't think so, World-Honored One!"
"Is the designated name of the extinguishing ear, nose, tongue, body, or conscious consciousness realm the great bodhisattva?"
"No, I don't think so, World-Honored One!"
"Is the designated name of the virtuous eye consciousness realm the great bodhisattva?"
"No, I don't think so, World-Honored One!"
"Is the designated name of the virtuous ear, nose, tongue, body, or conscious consciousness realm the great bodhisattva?"
"No, I don't think so, World-Honored One!"
"Is the designated name of the not virtuous eye consciousness realm the great bodhisattva?"

"No, I don't think so, World-Honored One!"

"Is the designated name of the not virtuous ear, nose, tongue, body, or conscious consciousness realm the great bodhisattva?"

"No, I don't think so, World-Honored One!"

"Is the designated name of the guilty eye consciousness realm the great bodhisattva?"

"No, I don't think so, World-Honored One!"

"Is the designated name of the guilty ear, nose, tongue, body, or conscious consciousness realm the great bodhisattva?"

"No, I don't think so, World-Honored One!"

"Is the designated name of the not guilty eye consciousness realm the great bodhisattva?"

"No, I don't think so, World-Honored One!"

"Is the designated name of the not guilty ear, nose, tongue, body, or conscious consciousness realm the great bodhisattva?"

"No, I don't think so, World-Honored One!"

"Is the designated name of the eye consciousness realm with vexations the great bodhisattva?"

"No, I don't think so, World-Honored One!"

"Is the designated name of the ear, nose, tongue, body, or conscious consciousness realm with vexations the great bodhisattva?"

"No, I don't think so, World-Honored One!"

"Is the designated name of the eye consciousness realm without vexations the great bodhisattva?"

"No, I don't think so, World-Honored One!"

"Is the designated name of the ear, nose, tongue, body, or conscious consciousness realm without vexations the great bodhisattva?"

"No, I don't think so, World-Honored One!"

"Is the designated name of the worldly eye consciousness realm the great bodhisattva?"

"No, I don't think so, World-Honored One!"

"Is the designated name of the worldly ear, nose, tongue, body, or conscious consciousness realm the great bodhisattva?"

"No, I don't think so, World-Honored One!"

"Is the designated name of the eye consciousness realm beyond the world the great bodhisattva?"

"No, I don't think so, World-Honored One!"
"Is the designated name of the ear, nose, tongue, body, or conscious consciousness realm beyond the world the great bodhisattva?"
"No, I don't think so, World-Honored One!"
"Is the designated name of the contaminated eye consciousness realm the great bodhisattva?"
"No, I don't think so, World-Honored One!"
"Is the designated name of the contaminated ear, nose, tongue, body, or conscious consciousness realm the great bodhisattva?"
"No, I don't think so, World-Honored One!"
"Is the designated name of the purified eye consciousness realm the great bodhisattva?"
"No, I don't think so, World-Honored One!"
"Is the designated name of the purified ear, nose, tongue, body, or conscious consciousness realm the great bodhisattva?"
"No, I don't think so, World-Honored One!"
"Is the designated name of the eye consciousness realm belonging to birth and death the great bodhisattva?"
"No, I don't think so, World-Honored One!"
"Is the designated name of the ear, nose, tongue, body, or conscious consciousness realm belonging to birth and death the great bodhisattva?"
"No, I don't think so, World-Honored One!"
"Is the designated name of the eye consciousness realm belonging to nirvana the great bodhisattva?"
"No, I don't think so, World-Honored One!"
"Is the designated name of the ear, nose, tongue, body, or conscious consciousness realm belonging to nirvana the great bodhisattva?"
"No, I don't think so, World-Honored One!"
"Is the designated name of the inside eye consciousness realm the great bodhisattva?"
"No, I don't think so, World-Honored One!"
"Is the designated name of the inside ear, nose, tongue, body, or conscious consciousness realm the great bodhisattva?"
"No, I don't think so, World-Honored One!"

"Is the designated name of the outside eye consciousness realm the great bodhisattva?"

"No, I don't think so, World-Honored One!"

"Is the designated name of the outside ear, nose, tongue, body, or conscious consciousness realm the great bodhisattva?"

"No, I don't think so, World-Honored One!"

"Is the designated name of the in-between eye consciousness realm the great bodhisattva?"

"No, I don't think so, World-Honored One!"

"Is the designated name of the in-between ear, nose, tongue, body, or conscious consciousness realm the great bodhisattva?"

"No, I don't think so, World-Honored One!"

"Is the designated name of the attainable eye consciousness realm the great bodhisattva?"

"No, I don't think so, World-Honored One!"

"Is the designated name of the attainable ear, nose, tongue, body, or conscious consciousness realm the great bodhisattva?"

"No, I don't think so, World-Honored One!"

"Is the designated name of the unattainable eye consciousness realm the great bodhisattva?"

"No, I don't think so, World-Honored One!"

"Is the designated name of the unattainable ear, nose, tongue, body, or conscious consciousness realm the great bodhisattva?"

"No, I don't think so, World-Honored One!"

"Furthermore, Well Appearing One, what do you mean by the great bodhisattva? Is the designated name of the eye contact the great bodhisattva?"

"No, I don't think so, World-Honored One!"

"Is the designated name of the ear, nose, tongue, body, or conscious contact the great bodhisattva?"

"No, I don't think so, World-Honored One!"

"Is the designated name of the permanent eye contact the great bodhisattva?"

"No, I don't think so, World-Honored One!"

"Is the designated name of the permanent ear, nose, tongue, body, or conscious contact the great bodhisattva?"

"No, I don't think so, World-Honored One!"
"Is the designated name of the impermanent eye contact the great bodhisattva?"
"No, I don't think so, World-Honored One!"
"Is the designated name of the impermanent ear, nose, tongue, body, or conscious contact the great bodhisattva?"
"No, I don't think so, World-Honored One!"
"Is the designated name of the pleasant eye contact the great bodhisattva?"
"No, I don't think so, World-Honored One!"
"Is the designated name of the pleasant ear, nose, tongue, body, or conscious contact the great bodhisattva?"
"No, I don't think so, World-Honored One!"
"Is the designated name of the painful eye contact the great bodhisattva?"
"No, I don't think so, World-Honored One!"
"Is the designated name of the painful ear, nose, tongue, body, or conscious contact the great bodhisattva?"
"No, I don't think so, World-Honored One!"
"Is the designated name of the eye contact with selfness the great bodhisattva?"
"No, I don't think so, World-Honored One!"
"Is the designated name of the ear, nose, tongue, body, or conscious contact with selfness the great bodhisattva?"
"No, I don't think so, World-Honored One!"
"Is the designated name of the eye contact without selfness the great bodhisattva?"
"No, I don't think so, World-Honored One!"
"Is the designated name of the ear, nose, tongue, body, or conscious contact without selfness the great bodhisattva?"
"No, I don't think so, World-Honored One!"
"Is the designated name of the pure eye contact the great bodhisattva?"
"No, I don't think so, World-Honored One!"
"Is the designated name of the pure ear, nose, tongue, body, or conscious contact the great bodhisattva?"

"No, I don't think so, World-Honored One!"

"Is the designated name of the impure eye contact the great bodhisattva?"

"No, I don't think so, World-Honored One!"

"Is the designated name of the impure ear, nose, tongue, body, or conscious contact the great bodhisattva?"

"No, I don't think so, World-Honored One!"

"Is the designated name of the empty eye contact the great bodhisattva?"

"No, I don't think so, World-Honored One!"

"Is the designated name of the empty ear, nose, tongue, body, or conscious contact the great bodhisattva?"

"No, I don't think so, World-Honored One!"

"Is the designated name of the not empty eye contact the great bodhisattva?"

"No, I don't think so, World-Honored One!"

"Is the designated name of the not empty ear, nose, tongue, body, or conscious contact the great bodhisattva?"

"No, I don't think so, World-Honored One!"

"Is the designated name of the eye contact with form the great bodhisattva?"

"No, I don't think so, World-Honored One!"

"Is the designated name of the ear, nose, tongue, body, or conscious contact with form the great bodhisattva?"

"No, I don't think so, World-Honored One!"

"Is the designated name of the eye contact without form the great bodhisattva?"

"No, I don't think so, World-Honored One!"

"Is the designated name of the ear, nose, tongue, body, or conscious contact without form the great bodhisattva?"

"No, I don't think so, World-Honored One!"

"Is the designated name of the eye contact with aspiration the great bodhisattva?"

"No, I don't think so, World-Honored One!"

"Is the designated name of the ear, nose, tongue, body, or conscious contact with aspiration the great bodhisattva?"

"No, I don't think so, World-Honored One!"
"Is the designated name of the eye contact without aspiration the great bodhisattva?"
"No, I don't think so, World-Honored One!"
"Is the designated name of the ear, nose, tongue, body, or conscious contact without aspiration the great bodhisattva?"
"No, I don't think so, World-Honored One!"
"Is the designated name of the eye contact in tranquility the great bodhisattva?"
"No, I don't think so, World-Honored One!"
"Is the designated name of the ear, nose, tongue, body, or conscious contact in tranquility the great bodhisattva?"
"No, I don't think so, World-Honored One!"
"Is the designated name of the eye contact not in tranquility the great bodhisattva?"
"No, I don't think so, World-Honored One!"
"Is the designated name of the ear, nose, tongue, body, or conscious contact not in tranquility the great bodhisattva?"
"No, I don't think so, World-Honored One!"
"Is the designated name of the eye contact getting far away the great bodhisattva?"
"No, I don't think so, World-Honored One!"
"Is the designated name of the ear, nose, tongue, body, or conscious contact getting far away the great bodhisattva?"
"No, I don't think so, World-Honored One!"
"Is the designated name of the eye contact not getting far away the great bodhisattva?"
"No, I don't think so, World-Honored One!"
"Is the designated name of the ear, nose, tongue, body, or conscious contact not getting far away the great bodhisattva?"
"No, I don't think so, World-Honored One!"
"Is the designated name of the conditioned eye contact the great bodhisattva?"
"No, I don't think so, World-Honored One!"
"Is the designated name of the conditioned ear, nose, tongue, body, or conscious contact the great bodhisattva?"

"No, I don't think so, World-Honored One!"

"Is the designated name of the unconditioned eye contact the great bodhisattva?"

"No, I don't think so, World-Honored One!"

"Is the designated name of the unconditioned ear, nose, tongue, body, or conscious contact the great bodhisattva?"

"No, I don't think so, World-Honored One!"

"Is the designated name of the flawed eye contact the great bodhisattva?"

"No, I don't think so, World-Honored One!"

"Is the designated name of the flawed ear, nose, tongue, body, or conscious contact the great bodhisattva?"

"No, I don't think so, World-Honored One!"

"Is the designated name of the flawless eye contact the great bodhisattva?"

"No, I don't think so, World-Honored One!"

"Is the designated name of the flawless ear, nose, tongue, body, or conscious contact the great bodhisattva?"

"No, I don't think so, World-Honored One!"

"Is the designated name of the arising eye contact the great bodhisattva?"

"No, I don't think so, World-Honored One!"

"Is the designated name of the arising ear, nose, tongue, body, or conscious contact the great bodhisattva?"

"No, I don't think so, World-Honored One!"

"Is the designated name of the extinguishing eye contact the great bodhisattva?"

"No, I don't think so, World-Honored One!"

"Is the designated name of the extinguishing ear, nose, tongue, body, or conscious contact the great bodhisattva?"

"No, I don't think so, World-Honored One!"

"Is the designated name of the virtuous eye contact the great bodhisattva?"

"No, I don't think so, World-Honored One!"

"Is the designated name of the virtuous ear, nose, tongue, body, or conscious contact the great bodhisattva?"

Fascicle 18, Chapter 7, Section 8

"No, I don't think so, World-Honored One!"

"Is the designated name of the not virtuous eye contact the great bodhisattva?"

"No, I don't think so, World-Honored One!"

"Is the designated name of the not virtuous ear, nose, tongue, body, or conscious contact the great bodhisattva?"

"No, I don't think so, World-Honored One!"

"Is the designated name of the guilty eye contact the great bodhisattva?"

"No, I don't think so, World-Honored One!"

"Is the designated name of the guilty ear, nose, tongue, body, or conscious contact the great bodhisattva?"

"No, I don't think so, World-Honored One!"

"Is the designated name of the not guilty eye contact the great bodhisattva?"

"No, I don't think so, World-Honored One!"

"Is the designated name of the not guilty ear, nose, tongue, body, or conscious contact the great bodhisattva?"

"No, I don't think so, World-Honored One!"

"Is the designated name of the eye contact with vexations the great bodhisattva?"

"No, I don't think so, World-Honored One!"

"Is the designated name of the ear, nose, tongue, body, or conscious contact with vexations the great bodhisattva?"

"No, I don't think so, World-Honored One!"

"Is the designated name of eye contact without vexations the great bodhisattva?"

"No, I don't think so, World-Honored One!"

"Is the designated name of the ear, nose, tongue, body, or conscious contact without vexations the great bodhisattva?"

"No, I don't think so, World-Honored One!"

"Is the designated name of the worldly eye contact the great bodhisattva?"

"No, I don't think so, World-Honored One!"

"Is the designated name of the worldly ear, nose, tongue, body, or conscious contact the great bodhisattva?"

"No, I don't think so, World-Honored One!"

"Is the designated name of the eye contact beyond the world the great bodhisattva?"

"No, I don't think so, World-Honored One!"

"Is the designated name of the ear, nose, tongue, body, or conscious contact beyond the world the great bodhisattva?"

"No, I don't think so, World-Honored One!"

"Is the designated name of the contaminated eye contact the great bodhisattva?"

"No, I don't think so, World-Honored One!"

"Is the designated name of the contaminated ear, nose, tongue, body, or conscious contact the great bodhisattva?"

"No, I don't think so, World-Honored One!"

"Is the designated name of the purified eye contact the great bodhisattva?"

"No, I don't think so, World-Honored One!"

"Is the designated name of the purified ear, nose, tongue, body, or conscious contact the great bodhisattva?"

"No, I don't think so, World-Honored One!"

"Is the designated name of the eye contact belonging to birth and death the great bodhisattva?"

"No, I don't think so, World-Honored One!"

"Is the designated name of the ear, nose, tongue, body, or conscious contact belonging to birth and death the great bodhisattva?"

"No, I don't think so, World-Honored One!"

"Is the designated name of the eye contact belonging to nirvana the great bodhisattva?"

"No, I don't think so, World-Honored One!"

"Is the designated name of the ear, nose, tongue, body, or conscious contact belonging to nirvana the great bodhisattva?"

"No, I don't think so, World-Honored One!"

"Is the designated name of the inside eye contact the great bodhisattva?"

"No, I don't think so, World-Honored One!"

"Is the designated name of the inside ear, nose, tongue, body, or conscious contact the great bodhisattva?"

"No, I don't think so, World-Honored One!"

Fascicle 18, Chapter 7, Section 8

"Is the designated name of the outside eye contact the great bodhisattva?"

"No, I don't think so, World-Honored One!"

"Is the designated name of the outside ear, nose, tongue, body, or conscious contact the great bodhisattva?"

"No, I don't think so, World-Honored One!"

"Is the designated name of the in-between eye contact the great bodhisattva?"

"No, I don't think so, World-Honored One!"

"Is the designated name of the in-between ear, nose, tongue, body, or conscious contact the great bodhisattva?"

"No, I don't think so, World-Honored One!"

"Is the designated name of the attainable eye contact the great bodhisattva?"

"No, I don't think so, World-Honored One!"

"Is the designated name of the attainable ear, nose, tongue, body, or conscious contact the great bodhisattva?"

"No, I don't think so, World-Honored One!"

"Is the designated name of the unattainable eye contact the great bodhisattva?"

"No, I don't think so, World-Honored One!"

"Is the designated name of the unattainable ear, nose, tongue, body, or conscious contact the great bodhisattva?"

"No, I don't think so, World-Honored One!"

"Furthermore, Well Appearing One, what do you mean by the great bodhisattva? Is the designated name of the feelings produced by eye contact the great bodhisattva?"

"No, I don't think so, World-Honored One!"

"Is the designated name of the feelings produced by ear, nose, tongue, body, or conscious contact the great bodhisattva?"

"No, I don't think so, World-Honored One!"

"Is the designated name of the permanent feelings produced by eye contact the great bodhisattva?"

"No, I don't think so, World-Honored One!"

"Is the designated name of the permanent feelings produced by ear, nose, tongue, body, or conscious contact the great bodhisattva?"

"No, I don't think so, World-Honored One!"

"Is the designated name of the impermanent feelings produced by eye contact the great bodhisattva?"

"No, I don't think so, World-Honored One!"

"Is the designated name of the impermanent feelings produced by ear, nose, tongue, body, or conscious contact the great bodhisattva?"

"No, I don't think so, World-Honored One!"

"Is the designated name of the pleasant feelings produced by eye contact the great bodhisattva?"

"No, I don't think so, World-Honored One!"

"Is the designated name of the pleasant feelings produced by ear, nose, tongue, body, or conscious contact the great bodhisattva?"

"No, I don't think so, World-Honored One!"

"Is the designated name of the painful feelings produced by eye contact the great bodhisattva?"

"No, I don't think so, World-Honored One!"

"Is the designated name of the painful feelings produced by ear, nose, tongue, body, or conscious contact the great bodhisattva?"

"No, I don't think so, World-Honored One!"

"Is the designated name of the feelings with selfness produced by eye contact the great bodhisattva?"

"No, I don't think so, World-Honored One!"

"Is the designated name of the feelings with selfness produced by ear, nose, tongue, body, or conscious contact the great bodhisattva?"

"No, I don't think so, World-Honored One!"

"Is the designated name of the feelings without selfness produced by eye contact the great bodhisattva?"

"No, I don't think so, World-Honored One!"

"Is the designated name of the feelings without selfness produced by ear, nose, tongue, body, or conscious contact the great bodhisattva?"

"No, I don't think so, World-Honored One!"

"Is the designated name of the pure feelings produced by eye contact the great bodhisattva?"

"No, I don't think so, World-Honored One!"

"Is the designated name of the pure feelings produced by ear, nose, tongue, body, or conscious contact the great bodhisattva?"

"No, I don't think so, World-Honored One!"

"Is the designated name of the impure feelings produced by eye contact the great bodhisattva?"

"No, I don't think so, World-Honored One!"

"Is the designated name of the impure feelings produced by ear, nose, tongue, body, or conscious contact the great bodhisattva?"

"No, I don't think so, World-Honored One!"

"Is the designated name of the empty feelings produced by eye contact the great bodhisattva?"

"No, I don't think so, World-Honored One!"

"Is the designated name of the empty feelings produced by ear, nose, tongue, body, or conscious contact the great bodhisattva?"

"No, I don't think so, World-Honored One!"

"Is the designated name of the not empty feelings produced by eye contact the great bodhisattva?"

"No, I don't think so, World-Honored One!"

"Is the designated name of the not empty feelings produced by ear, nose, tongue, body, or conscious contact the great bodhisattva?"

"No, I don't think so, World-Honored One!"

"Is the designated name of the feelings with form produced by eye contact the great bodhisattva?"

"No, I don't think so, World-Honored One!"

"Is the designated name of the feelings with form produced by ear, nose, tongue, body, or conscious contact the great bodhisattva?"

"No, I don't think so, World-Honored One!"

"Is the designated name of the feelings without form produced by eye contact the great bodhisattva?"

"No, I don't think so, World-Honored One!"

"Is the designated name of the feelings without form produced by ear, nose, tongue, body, or conscious contact the great bodhisattva?"

"No, I don't think so, World-Honored One!"

"Is the designated name of the feelings with aspiration produced by eye contact the great bodhisattva?"

"No, I don't think so, World-Honored One!"

"Is the designated name of the feelings with aspiration produced by ear, nose, tongue, body, or conscious contact the great bodhisattva?"

"No, I don't think so, World-Honored One!"

"Is the designated name of the feelings without aspiration produced by eye contact the great bodhisattva?"

"No, I don't think so, World-Honored One!"

"Is the designated name of the feelings without aspiration produced by ear, nose, tongue, body, or conscious contact the great bodhisattva?"

"No, I don't think so, World-Honored One!"

"Is the designated name of the tranquil feelings produced by eye contact the great bodhisattva?"

"No, I don't think so, World-Honored One!"

"Is the designated name of the tranquil feelings produced by ear, nose, tongue, body, or conscious contact the great bodhisattva?"

"No, I don't think so, World-Honored One!"

"Is the designated name of the not tranquil feelings produced by eye contact the great bodhisattva?"

"No, I don't think so, World-Honored One!"

"Is the designated name of the not tranquil feelings produced by ear, nose, tongue, body, or conscious contact the great bodhisattva?"

"No, I don't think so, World-Honored One!"

"Is the designated name of the faraway feelings produced by eye contact the great bodhisattva?"

"No, I don't think so, World-Honored One!"

"Is the designated name of the faraway feelings produced by ear, nose, tongue, body, or conscious contact the great bodhisattva?"

"No, I don't think so, World-Honored One!"

"Is the designated name of the not faraway feelings produced by eye contact the great bodhisattva?"

"No, I don't think so, World-Honored One!"

"Is the designated name of the not faraway feelings produced by ear, nose, tongue, body, or conscious contact the great bodhisattva?"

"No, I don't think so, World-Honored One!"

"Is the designated name of the conditioned feelings produced by eye contact the great bodhisattva?"
"No, I don't think so, World-Honored One!"
"Is the designated name of the conditioned feelings produced by ear, nose, tongue, body, or conscious contact the great bodhisattva?"
"No, I don't think so, World-Honored One!"
"Is the designated name of the unconditioned feelings produced by eye contact the great bodhisattva?"
"No, I don't think so, World-Honored One!"
"Is the designated name of the unconditioned feelings produced by ear, nose, tongue, body, or conscious contact the great bodhisattva?"
"No, I don't think so, World-Honored One!"
"Is the designated name of the flawed feelings produced by eye contact the great bodhisattva?"
"No, I don't think so, World-Honored One!"
"Is the designated name of the flawed feelings produced by ear, nose, tongue, body, or conscious contact the great bodhisattva?"
"No, I don't think so, World-Honored One!"
"Is the designated name of the flawless feelings produced by eye contact the great bodhisattva?"
"No, I don't think so, World-Honored One!"
"Is the designated name of the flawless feelings produced by ear, nose, tongue, body, or conscious contact the great bodhisattva?"
"No, I don't think so, World-Honored One!"
"Is the designated name of the arising feelings produced by eye contact the great bodhisattva?"
"No, I don't think so, World-Honored One!"
"Is the designated name of the arising feelings produced by ear, nose, tongue, body, or conscious contact the great bodhisattva?"
"No, I don't think so, World-Honored One!"
"Is the designated name of the extinguishing feelings produced by eye contact the great bodhisattva?"
"No, I don't think so, World-Honored One!"
"Is the designated name of the extinguishing feelings produced

by ear, nose, tongue, body, or conscious contact the great bodhisattva?"

"No, I don't think so, World-Honored One!"

"Is the designated name of the virtuous feelings produced by eye contact the great bodhisattva?"

"No, I don't think so, World-Honored One!"

"Is the designated name of the virtuous feelings produced by ear, nose, tongue, body, or conscious contact the great bodhisattva?"

"No, I don't think so, World-Honored One!"

"Is the designated name of the not virtuous feelings produced by eye contact the great bodhisattva?"

"No, I don't think so, World-Honored One!"

"Is the designated name of the not virtuous feelings produced by ear, nose, tongue, body, or conscious contact the great bodhisattva?"

"No, I don't think so, World-Honored One!"

"Is the designated name of the guilty feelings produced by eye contact the great bodhisattva?"

"No, I don't think so, World-Honored One!"

"Is the designated name of the guilty feelings produced by ear, nose, tongue, body, or conscious contact the great bodhisattva?"

"No, I don't think so, World-Honored One!"

"Is the designated name of the not guilty feelings produced by eye contact the great bodhisattva?"

"No, I don't think so, World-Honored One!"

"Is the designated name of the not guilty feelings produced by ear, nose, tongue, body, or conscious contact the great bodhisattva?"

"No, I don't think so, World-Honored One!"

"Is the designated name of the feelings with vexations produced by eye contact the great bodhisattva?"

"No, I don't think so, World-Honored One!"

"Is the designated name of the feelings with vexations produced by ear, nose, tongue, body, or conscious contact the great bodhisattva?"

"No, I don't think so, World-Honored One!"

"Is the designated name of the feelings without vexations produced by eye contact the great bodhisattva?"

"No, I don't think so, World-Honored One!"

"Is the designated name of the feelings without vexations produced by ear, nose, tongue, body, or conscious contact the great bodhisattva?"

"No, I don't think so, World-Honored One!"

"Is the designated name of the worldly feelings produced by eye contact the great bodhisattva?"

"No, I don't think so, World-Honored One!"

"Is the designated name of the worldly feelings produced by ear, nose, tongue, body, or conscious contact the great bodhisattva?"

"No, I don't think so, World-Honored One!"

"Is the designated name of the feelings beyond the world produced by eye contact the great bodhisattva?"

"No, I don't think so, World-Honored One!"

"Is the designated name of the feelings beyond the world produced by ear, nose, tongue, body, or conscious contact the great bodhisattva?"

"No, I don't think so, World-Honored One!"

"Is the designated name of the contaminated feelings produced by eye contact the great bodhisattva?"

"No, I don't think so, World-Honored One!"

"Is the designated name of the contaminated feelings produced by ear, nose, tongue, body, or conscious contact the great bodhisattva?"

"No, I don't think so, World-Honored One!"

"Is the designated name of the purified feelings produced by eye contact the great bodhisattva?"

"No, I don't think so, World-Honored One!"

"Is the designated name of the purified feelings produced by ear, nose, tongue, body, or conscious contact the great bodhisattva?"

"No, I don't think so, World-Honored One!"

"Is the designated name of the feelings produced by eye contact belonging to birth and death the great bodhisattva?"

"No, I don't think so, World-Honored One!"

"Is the designated name of the feelings produced by ear, nose, tongue, body, or conscious contact belonging to birth and death the great bodhisattva?"

"No, I don't think so, World-Honored One!"

"Is the designated name of the feelings produced by eye contact belonging to nirvana the great bodhisattva?"

"No, I don't think so, World-Honored One!"

"Is the designated name of the feelings produced by ear, nose, tongue, body, or conscious contact belonging to nirvana the great bodhisattva?"

"No, I don't think so, World-Honored One!"

"Is the designated name of the feelings produced by eye contact from inside the great bodhisattva?"

"No, I don't think so, World-Honored One!"

"Is the designated name of the feelings produced by ear, nose, tongue, body, or conscious contact from inside the great bodhisattva?"

"No, I don't think so, World-Honored One!"

"Is the designated name of the feelings produced by eye contact from outside the great bodhisattva?"

"No, I don't think so, World-Honored One!"

"Is the designated name of the feelings produced by ear, nose, tongue, body, or conscious contact from outside the great bodhisattva?"

"No, I don't think so, World-Honored One!"

"Is the designated name of the feelings produced by eye contact in between the great bodhisattva?"

"No, I don't think so, World-Honored One!"

"Is the designated name of the feelings produced by ear, nose, tongue, body, or conscious contact in between the great bodhisattva?"

"No, I don't think so, World-Honored One!"

"Is the designated name of the attainable feelings produced by eye contact the great bodhisattva?"

"No, I don't think so, World-Honored One!"

"Is the designated name of the attainable feelings produced by ear, nose, tongue, body, or conscious contact the great bodhisattva?"

"No, I don't think so, World-Honored One!"

"Is the designated name of the unattainable feelings produced by eye contact the great bodhisattva?"

"No, I don't think so, World-Honored One!"

"Is the designated name of the unattainable feelings produced by ear, nose, tongue, body, or conscious contact the great bodhisattva?"

"No, I don't think so, World-Honored One!"

FASCICLE 19

Chapter 7
The Cautions and the Teachings

Section 9

(In the First Assembly)

"Furthermore, Well Appearing One, what do you mean by great bodhisattva? Is the designated name of the earth realm the great bodhisattva?"

"No, I don't think so, World-Honored One!"

"Is the designated name of the water, fire, wind, space, or consciousness realm the great bodhisattva?"

"No, I don't think so, World-Honored One!"

"Is the designated name of the permanent earth realm the great bodhisattva?"

"No, I don't think so, World-Honored One!"

"Is the designated name of the permanent water, fire, wind, space, or consciousness realm the great bodhisattva?"

"No, I don't think so, World-Honored One!"

"Is the designated name of the impermanent earth realm the great bodhisattva?"

"No, I don't think so, World-Honored One!"

"Is the designated name of the impermanent water, fire, wind, space, or consciousness realm the great bodhisattva?"

"No, I don't think so, World-Honored One!"

"Is the designated name of the pleasant earth realm the great bodhisattva?"

"No, I don't think so, World-Honored One!"

"Is the designated name of the pleasant water, fire, wind, space, or consciousness realm the great bodhisattva?"

"No, I don't think so, World-Honored One!"

"Is the designated name of the painful earth realm the great bodhisattva?"

"No, I don't think so, World-Honored One!"

"Is the designated name of the painful water, fire, wind, space, or consciousness realm the great bodhisattva?"

"No, I don't think so, World-Honored One!"

"Is the designated name of the earth realm with selfness the great bodhisattva?"

"No, I don't think so, World-Honored One!"

"Is the designated name of the water, fire, wind, space, or consciousness realm with selfness the great bodhisattva?"

"No, I don't think so, World-Honored One!"

"Is the designated name of the earth realm without selfness the great bodhisattva?"

"No, I don't think so, World-Honored One!"

"Is the designated name of the water, fire, wind, space, or consciousness realm without selfness the great bodhisattva?"

"No, I don't think so, World-Honored One!"

"Is the designated name of the pure earth realm the great bodhisattva?"

"No, I don't think so, World-Honored One!"

"Is the designated name of the pure water, fire, wind, space, or consciousness realm the great bodhisattva?"

"No, I don't think so, World-Honored One!"

"Is the designated name of the impure earth realm the great bodhisattva?"

"No, I don't think so, World-Honored One!"

"Is the designated name of the impure water, fire, wind, space, or consciousness realm the great bodhisattva?"

"No, I don't think so, World-Honored One!"

"Is the designated name of the empty earth realm the great bodhisattva?"

"No, I don't think so, World-Honored One!"

"Is the designated name of the empty water, fire, wind, space, or consciousness realm the great bodhisattva?"

"No, I don't think so, World-Honored One!"

"Is the designated name of the not empty earth realm the great bodhisattva?"

"No, I don't think so, World-Honored One!"

"Is the designated name of the not empty water, fire, wind, space, or consciousness realm the great bodhisattva?"

"No, I don't think so, World-Honored One!"

"Is the designated name of the earth realm with form the great bodhisattva?"

"No, I don't think so, World-Honored One!"

"Is the designated name of the water, fire, wind, space, or consciousness realm with form the great bodhisattva?"

"No, I don't think so, World-Honored One!"

"Is the designated name of the earth realm without form the great bodhisattva?"

"No, I don't think so, World-Honored One!"

"Is the designated name of the water, fire, wind, space, or consciousness realm without form the great bodhisattva?"

"No, I don't think so, World-Honored One!"

"Is the designated name of the earth realm with aspiration the great bodhisattva?"

"No, I don't think so, World-Honored One!"

"Is the designated name of the water, fire, wind, space, or consciousness realm with aspiration the great bodhisattva?"

"No, I don't think so, World-Honored One!"

"Is the designated name of the earth realm without aspiration the great bodhisattva?"

"No, I don't think so, World-Honored One!"

"Is the designated name of the water, fire, wind, space, or consciousness realm without aspiration the great bodhisattva?"
"No, I don't think so, World-Honored One!"
"Is the designated name of the tranquil earth realm the great bodhisattva?"
"No, I don't think so, World-Honored One!"
"Is the designated name of the tranquil water, fire, wind, space, or consciousness realm the great bodhisattva?"
"No, I don't think so, World-Honored One!"
"Is the designated name of the not tranquil earth realm the great bodhisattva?"
"No, I don't think so, World-Honored One!"
"Is the designated name of the not tranquil water, fire, wind, space, or consciousness realm the great bodhisattva?"
"No, I don't think so, World-Honored One!"
"Is the designated name of the faraway earth realm the great bodhisattva?"
"No, I don't think so, World-Honored One!"
"Is the designated name of the faraway water, fire, wind, space, or consciousness realm the great bodhisattva?"
"No, I don't think so, World-Honored One!"
"Is the designated name of the not faraway earth realm the great bodhisattva?"
"No, I don't think so, World-Honored One!"
"Is the designated name of the not faraway water, fire, wind, space, or consciousness realm the great bodhisattva?"
"No, I don't think so, World-Honored One!"
"Is the designated name of the conditioned earth realm the great bodhisattva?"
"No, I don't think so, World-Honored One!"
"Is the designated name of the conditioned water, fire, wind, space, or consciousness realm the great bodhisattva?"
"No, I don't think so, World-Honored One!"
"Is the designated name of the unconditioned earth realm the great bodhisattva?"
"No, I don't think so, World-Honored One!"

"Is the designated name of the unconditioned water, fire, wind, space, or consciousness realm the great bodhisattva?"

"No, I don't think so, World-Honored One!"

"Is the designated name of the flawed earth realm the great bodhisattva?"

"No, I don't think so, World-Honored One!"

"Is the designated name of the flawed water, fire, wind, space, or consciousness realm the great bodhisattva?"

"No, I don't think so, World-Honored One!"

"Is the designated name of the flawless earth realm the great bodhisattva?"

"No, I don't think so, World-Honored One!"

"Is the designated name of the flawless water, fire, wind, space, or consciousness realm the great bodhisattva?"

"No, I don't think so, World-Honored One!"

"Is the designated name of the arising earth realm the great bodhisattva?"

"No, I don't think so, World-Honored One!"

"Is the designated name of the arising water, fire, wind, space, or consciousness realm the great bodhisattva?"

"No, I don't think so, World-Honored One!"

"Is the designated name of the extinguishing earth realm the great bodhisattva?"

"No, I don't think so, World-Honored One!"

"Is the designated name of the extinguishing water, fire, wind, space, or consciousness realm the great bodhisattva?"

"No, I don't think so, World-Honored One!"

"Is the designated name of the virtuous earth realm the great bodhisattva?"

"No, I don't think so, World-Honored One!"

"Is the designated name of the virtuous water, fire, wind, space, or consciousness realm the great bodhisattva?"

"No, I don't think so, World-Honored One!"

"Is the designated name of the not virtuous earth realm the great bodhisattva?"

"No, I don't think so, World-Honored One!"

"Is the designated name of the not virtuous water, fire, wind, space, or consciousness realm the great bodhisattva?"
"No, I don't think so, World-Honored One!"
"Is the designated name of the guilty earth realm the great bodhisattva?"
"No, I don't think so, World-Honored One!"
"Is the designated name of the guilty water, fire, wind, space, or consciousness realm the great bodhisattva?"
"No, I don't think so, World-Honored One!"
"Is the designated name of the not guilty earth realm the great bodhisattva?"
"No, I don't think so, World-Honored One!"
"Is the designated name of the not guilty water, fire, wind, space, or consciousness realm the great bodhisattva?"
"No, I don't think so, World-Honored One!"
"Is the designated name of the earth realm with vexations the great bodhisattva?"
"No, I don't think so, World-Honored One!"
"Is the designated name of the water, fire, wind, space, or consciousness realm with vexations the great bodhisattva?"
"No, I don't think so, World-Honored One!"
"Is the designated name of the earth realm without vexations the great bodhisattva?"
"No, I don't think so, World-Honored One!"
"Is the designated name of the water, fire, wind, space, or consciousness realm without vexations the great bodhisattva?"
"No, I don't think so, World-Honored One!"
"Is the designated name of the worldly earth realm the great bodhisattva?"
"No, I don't think so, World-Honored One!"
"Is the designated name of the worldly water, fire, wind, space, or consciousness realm the great bodhisattva?"
"No, I don't think so, World-Honored One!"
"Is the designated name of the earth realm beyond the world the great bodhisattva?"
"No, I don't think so, World-Honored One!"

"Is the designated name of the water, fire, wind, space, or consciousness realm beyond the world the great bodhisattva?"
"No, I don't think so, World-Honored One!"
"Is the designated name of the contaminated earth realm the great bodhisattva?"
"No, I don't think so, World-Honored One!"
"Is the designated name of the contaminated water, fire, wind, space, or consciousness realm the great bodhisattva?"
"No, I don't think so, World-Honored One!"
"Is the designated name of the purified earth realm the great bodhisattva?"
"No, I don't think so, World-Honored One!"
"Is the designated name of the purified water, fire, wind, space, or consciousness realm the great bodhisattva?"
"No, I don't think so, World-Honored One!"
"Is the designated name of the earth realm belonging to birth and death the great bodhisattva?"
"No, I don't think so, World-Honored One!"
"Is the designated name of the water, fire, wind, space, or consciousness realm belonging to birth and death the great bodhisattva?"
"No, I don't think so, World-Honored One!"
"Is the designated name of the earth realm belonging to nirvana the great bodhisattva?"
"No, I don't think so, World-Honored One!"
"Is the designated name of the water, fire, wind, space, or consciousness realm belonging to nirvana the great bodhisattva?"
"No, I don't think so, World-Honored One!"
"Is the designated name of the inside earth realm the great bodhisattva?"
"No, I don't think so, World-Honored One!"
"Is the designated name of the inside water, fire, wind, space, or consciousness realm the great bodhisattva?"
"No, I don't think so, World-Honored One!"
"Is the designated name of the outside earth realm the great bodhisattva?"
"No, I don't think so, World-Honored One!"

Fascicle 19, Chapter 7, Section 9   459

"Is the designated name of the outside water, fire, wind, space, or consciousness realm the great bodhisattva?"

"No, I don't think so, World-Honored One!"

"Is the designated name of the in-between earth realm the great bodhisattva?"

"No, I don't think so, World-Honored One!"

"Is the designated name of the in-between water, fire, wind, space, or consciousness realm the great bodhisattva?"

"No, I don't think so, World-Honored One!"

"Is the designated name of the attainable earth realm the great bodhisattva?"

"No, I don't think so, World-Honored One!"

"Is the designated name of the attainable water, fire, wind, space, or consciousness realm the great bodhisattva?"

"No, I don't think so, World-Honored One!"

"Is the designated name of the unattainable earth realm the great bodhisattva?"

"No, I don't think so, World-Honored One!"

"Is the designated name of the unattainable water, fire, wind, space, or consciousness realm the great bodhisattva?"

"No, I don't think so, World-Honored One!"

"Furthermore, Well Appearing One, what do you mean by great bodhisattva? Is the designated name of cause and condition the great bodhisattva?"

"No, I don't think so, World-Honored One!"

"Is the designated name of consecutive thoughts in sequence, the conditions that stimulate one's mind, or the conditions that reinforce main causes the great bodhisattva?"

"No, I don't think so, World-Honored One!"

"Is the designated name of the permanent cause and condition the great bodhisattva?"

"No, I don't think so, World-Honored One!"

"Is the designated name of the permanent consecutive thoughts in sequence, conditions that stimulate one's mind, or conditions that reinforce main causes the great bodhisattva?"

"No, I don't think so, World-Honored One!"

"Is the designated name of the impermanent cause and condition the great bodhisattva?"

"No, I don't think so, World-Honored One!"

"Is the designated name of the impermanent consecutive thoughts in sequence, conditions that stimulate one's mind, or conditions that reinforce main causes the great bodhisattva?"

"No, I don't think so, World-Honored One!"

"Is the designated name of the pleasant cause and condition the great bodhisattva?"

"No, I don't think so, World-Honored One!"

"Is the designated name of the pleasant consecutive thoughts in sequence, conditions that stimulate one's mind, or conditions that reinforce main causes the great bodhisattva?"

"No, I don't think so, World-Honored One!"

"Is the designated name of the painful cause and condition the great bodhisattva?"

"No, I don't think so, World-Honored One!"

"Is the designated name of the painful consecutive thoughts in sequence, conditions that stimulate one's mind, or conditions that reinforce main causes the great bodhisattva?"

"No, I don't think so, World-Honored One!"

"Is the designated name of the cause and condition with selfness the great bodhisattva?"

"No, I don't think so, World-Honored One!"

"Is the designated name of consecutive thoughts in sequence, the conditions that stimulate one's mind, or the conditions that reinforce main causes with selfness the great bodhisattva?"

"No, I don't think so, World-Honored One!"

"Is the designated name of the cause and condition without selfness the great bodhisattva?"

"No, I don't think so, World-Honored One!"

"Is the designated name of consecutive thoughts in sequence, the conditions that stimulate one's mind, or the conditions that reinforce main causes without selfness the great bodhisattva?"

"No, I don't think so, World-Honored One!"

"Is the designated name of the pure cause and condition the great bodhisattva?"

"No, I don't think so, World-Honored One!"
"Is the designated name of the pure consecutive thoughts in sequence, conditions that stimulate one's mind, or conditions that reinforce main causes the great bodhisattva?"
"No, I don't think so, World-Honored One!"
"Is the designated name of the impure cause and condition the great bodhisattva?"
"No, I don't think so, World-Honored One!"
"Is the designated name of the impure consecutive thoughts in sequence, conditions that stimulate one's mind, or conditions that reinforce main causes the great bodhisattva?"
"No, I don't think so, World-Honored One!"
"Is the designated name of the empty cause and condition the great bodhisattva?"
"No, I don't think so, World-Honored One!"
"Is the designated name of the empty consecutive thoughts in sequence, conditions that stimulate one's mind, or conditions that reinforce main causes the great bodhisattva?"
"No, I don't think so, World-Honored One!"
"Is the designated name of the not empty cause and condition the great bodhisattva?"
"No, I don't think so, World-Honored One!"
"Is the designated name of the not empty consecutive thoughts in sequence, conditions that stimulate one's mind, or conditions that reinforce main causes the great bodhisattva?"
"No, I don't think so, World-Honored One!"
"Is the designated name of the cause and condition with form the great bodhisattva?"
"No, I don't think so, World-Honored One!"
"Is the designated name of consecutive thoughts in sequence, the conditions that stimulate one's mind, or the conditions that reinforce main causes with form the great bodhisattva?"
"No, I don't think so, World-Honored One!"
"Is the designated name of the cause and condition without form the great bodhisattva?"
"No, I don't think so, World-Honored One!"
"Is the designated name of consecutive thoughts in sequence,

conditions that stimulate one's mind, or the conditions that reinforce main causes without form the great bodhisattva?"

"No, I don't think so, World-Honored One!"

"Is the designated name of the cause and condition with aspiration the great bodhisattva?"

"No, I don't think so, World-Honored One!"

"Is the designated name of consecutive thoughts in sequence, the conditions that stimulate one's mind, or the conditions that reinforce main causes with aspiration the great bodhisattva?"

"No, I don't think so, World-Honored One!"

"Is the designated name of the cause and condition without aspiration the great bodhisattva?"

"No, I don't think so, World-Honored One!"

"Is the designated name of consecutive thoughts in sequence without aspiration, the conditions that stimulate one's mind without aspiration, or the conditions that reinforce main causes without aspiration the great bodhisattva?"

"No, I don't think so, World-Honored One!"

"Is the designated name of the tranquil cause and condition the great bodhisattva?"

"No, I don't think so, World-Honored One!"

"Is the designated name of the tranquil consecutive thoughts in sequence, conditions that stimulate one's mind, or conditions that reinforce main causes the great bodhisattva?"

"No, I don't think so, World-Honored One!"

"Is the designated name of the not tranquil cause and condition the great bodhisattva?"

"No, I don't think so, World-Honored One!"

"Is the designated name of the not tranquil consecutive thoughts in sequence, conditions that stimulate one's mind, or conditions that reinforce main causes the great bodhisattva?"

"No, I don't think so, World-Honored One!"

"Is the designated name of the faraway cause and condition the great bodhisattva?"

"No, I don't think so, World-Honored One!"

"Is the designated name of the faraway consecutive thoughts in sequence, conditions that stimulate one's mind, or conditions that reinforce main causes the great bodhisattva?"

"No, I don't think so, World-Honored One!"

"Is the designated name of the not faraway cause and condition the great bodhisattva?"

"No, I don't think so, World-Honored One!"

"Is the designated name of the not faraway consecutive thoughts in sequence, conditions that stimulate one's mind, or conditions that reinforce main causes the great bodhisattva?"

"No, I don't think so, World-Honored One!"

"Is the designated name of the conditioned cause and condition the great bodhisattva?"

"No, I don't think so, World-Honored One!"

"Is the designated name of the conditioned consecutive thoughts in sequence, conditions that stimulate one's mind, or conditions that reinforce main causes the great bodhisattva?"

"No, I don't think so, World-Honored One!"

"Is the designated name of the unconditioned cause and condition the great bodhisattva?"

"No, I don't think so, World-Honored One!"

"Is the designated name of the unconditioned consecutive thoughts in sequence, conditions that stimulate one's mind, or conditions that reinforce main causes the great bodhisattva?"

"No, I don't think so, World-Honored One!"

"Is the designated name of the flawed cause and condition the great bodhisattva?"

"No, I don't think so, World-Honored One!"

"Is the designated name of the flawed consecutive thoughts in sequence, conditions that stimulate one's mind, or conditions that reinforce main causes the great bodhisattva?"

"No, I don't think so, World-Honored One!"

"Is the designated name of the flawless cause and condition the great bodhisattva?"

"No, I don't think so, World-Honored One!"

"Is the designated name of the flawless consecutive thoughts in sequence, conditions that stimulate one's mind, or conditions that reinforce main causes the great bodhisattva?"

"No, I don't think so, World-Honored One!"

"Is the designated name of the arising cause and condition the great bodhisattva?"

"No, I don't think so, World-Honored One!"

"Is the designated name of the arising consecutive thoughts in sequence, conditions that stimulate one's mind, or conditions that reinforce main causes the great bodhisattva?"

"No, I don't think so, World-Honored One!"

"Is the designated name of the extinguishing cause and condition the great bodhisattva?"

"No, I don't think so, World-Honored One!"

"Is the designated name of the extinguishing consecutive thoughts in sequence, conditions that stimulate one's mind, or conditions that reinforce main causes the great bodhisattva?"

"No, I don't think so, World-Honored One!"

"Is the designated name of the virtuous cause and condition the great bodhisattva?"

"No, I don't think so, World-Honored One!"

"Is the designated name of the virtuous consecutive thoughts in sequence, conditions that stimulate one's mind, or conditions that reinforce main causes the great bodhisattva?"

"No, I don't think so, World-Honored One!"

"Is the designated name of the not virtuous cause and condition the great bodhisattva?"

"No, I don't think so, World-Honored One!"

"Is the designated name of the not virtuous consecutive thoughts in sequence, conditions that stimulate one's mind, or conditions that reinforce main causes the great bodhisattva?"

"No, I don't think so, World-Honored One!"

"Is the designated name of the guilty cause and condition the great bodhisattva?"

"No, I don't think so, World-Honored One!"

"Is the designated name of the guilty consecutive thoughts in sequence, conditions that stimulate one's mind, or conditions that reinforce main causes the great bodhisattva?"

"No, I don't think so, World-Honored One!"

"Is the designated name of the not guilty cause and condition the great bodhisattva?"

"No, I don't think so, World-Honored One!"

"Is the designated name of the not guilty consecutive thoughts in sequence, conditions that stimulate one's mind, or conditions that reinforce main causes the great bodhisattva?"

"No, I don't think so, World-Honored One!"

"Is the designated name of the cause and condition with vexations the great bodhisattva?"

"No, I don't think so, World-Honored One!"

"Is the designated name of consecutive thoughts in sequence, the conditions that stimulate one's mind, or the conditions that reinforce main causes with vexations the great bodhisattva?"

"No, I don't think so, World-Honored One!"

"Is the designated name of the cause and condition without vexations the great bodhisattva?"

"No, I don't think so, World-Honored One!"

"Is the designated name of consecutive thoughts in sequence, the conditions that stimulate one's mind, or the conditions that reinforce main causes without vexations the great bodhisattva?"

"No, I don't think so, World-Honored One!"

"Is the designated name of the worldly cause and condition the great bodhisattva?"

"No, I don't think so, World-Honored One!"

"Is the designated name of the worldly consecutive thoughts in sequence, conditions that stimulate one's mind, or conditions that reinforce main causes the great bodhisattva?"

"No, I don't think so, World-Honored One!"

"Is the designated name of the cause and condition beyond the world the great bodhisattva?"

"No, I don't think so, World-Honored One!"

"Is the designated name of consecutive thoughts in sequence, conditions that stimulate one's mind, or the conditions that reinforce main causes beyond the world the great bodhisattva?"

"No, I don't think so, World-Honored One!"

"Is the designated name of the contaminated cause and condition the great bodhisattva?"

"No, I don't think so, World-Honored One!"

"Is the designated name of the contaminated consecutive thoughts in sequence, conditions that stimulate one's mind, or conditions that reinforce main causes the great bodhisattva?"

"No, I don't think so, World-Honored One!"

"Is the designated name of the purified cause and condition the great bodhisattva?"

"No, I don't think so, World-Honored One!"

"Is the designated name of the purified consecutive thoughts in sequence, conditions that stimulate one's mind, or conditions that reinforce main causes the great bodhisattva?"

"No, I don't think so, World-Honored One!"

"Is the designated name of the cause and condition belonging to birth and death the great bodhisattva?"

"No, I don't think so, World-Honored One!"

"Is the designated name of consecutive thoughts in sequence, the conditions that stimulate one's mind, or the conditions that reinforce main causes belonging to birth and death the great bodhisattva?"

"No, I don't think so, World-Honored One!"

"Is the designated name of the cause and condition belonging to nirvana the great bodhisattva?"

"No, I don't think so, World-Honored One!"

"Is the designated name of consecutive thoughts in sequence, the conditions that stimulate one's mind, or the conditions that reinforce main causes belonging to nirvana the great bodhisattva?"

"No, I don't think so, World-Honored One!"

"Is the designated name of the inside cause and condition the great bodhisattva?"

"No, I don't think so, World-Honored One!"

"Is the designated name of the inside consecutive thoughts in sequence, conditions that stimulate one's mind, or conditions that reinforce main causes the great bodhisattva?"

"No, I don't think so, World-Honored One!"

"Is the designated name of the outside cause and condition the great bodhisattva?"

"No, I don't think so, World-Honored One!"

"Is the designated name of the outside consecutive thoughts in sequence, conditions that stimulate one's mind, or conditions that reinforce main causes, outside, the great bodhisattva?"
"No, I don't think so, World-Honored One!"
"Is the designated name of the in-between cause and condition the great bodhisattva?"
"No, I don't think so, World-Honored One!"
"Is the designated name of the in-between consecutive thoughts in sequence, conditions that stimulate one's mind, or conditions that reinforce main causes the great bodhisattva?"
"No, I don't think so, World-Honored One!"
"Is the designated name of the attainable cause and condition the great bodhisattva?"
"No, I don't think so, World-Honored One!"
"Is the designated name of the attainable consecutive thoughts in sequence, conditions that stimulate one's mind, or conditions that reinforce main causes the great bodhisattva?"
"No, I don't think so, World-Honored One!"
"Is the designated name of the unattainable cause and condition the great bodhisattva?"
"No, I don't think so, World-Honored One!"
"Is the designated name of the unattainable consecutive thoughts in sequence, conditions that stimulate one's mind, or conditions that reinforce main causes the great bodhisattva?"
"No, I don't think so, World-Honored One!"
"Furthermore, Well Appearing One, what do you mean by great bodhisattva? Is the designated name of the dharmas produced by conditions the great bodhisattva?"
"No, I don't think so, World-Honored One!"
"Is the designated name of the permanent dharmas produced by conditions the great bodhisattva?"
"No, I don't think so, World-Honored One!"
"Is the designated name of the impermanent dharmas produced by conditions the great bodhisattva?"
"No, I don't think so, World-Honored One!"
"Is the designated name of the pleasant dharmas produced by conditions the great bodhisattva?"

468　　　*The Great Prajna Paramita Sutra*

"No, I don't think so, World-Honored One!"
"Is the designated name of the painful dharmas produced by conditions the great bodhisattva?"
"No, I don't think so, World-Honored One!"
"Is the designated name of the dharmas produced by conditions with selfness the great bodhisattva?"
"No, I don't think so, World-Honored One!"
"Is the designated name of the dharmas produced by conditions without selfness the great bodhisattva?"
"No, I don't think so, World-Honored One!"
"Is the designated name of the pure dharmas produced by conditions the great bodhisattva?"
"No, I don't think so, World-Honored One!"
"Is the designated name of the impure dharmas produced by conditions the great bodhisattva?"
"No, I don't think so, World-Honored One!"
"Is the designated name of the empty dharmas produced by conditions the great bodhisattva?"
"No, I don't think so, World-Honored One!"
"Is the designated name of the not empty dharmas produced by conditions the great bodhisattva?"
"No, I don't think so, World-Honored One!"
"Is the designated name of the dharmas with form produced by conditions the great bodhisattva?"
"No, I don't think so, World-Honored One!"
"Is the designated name of the dharmas without form produced by conditions the great bodhisattva?"
"No, I don't think so, World-Honored One!"
"Is the designated name of the dharmas with aspiration produced by conditions the great bodhisattva?"
"No, I don't think so, World-Honored One!"
"Is the designated name of the dharmas without aspiration produced by conditions the great bodhisattva?"
"No, I don't think so, World-Honored One!"
"Is the designated name of the tranquil dharmas produced by conditions the great bodhisattva?"

"No, I don't think so, World-Honored One!"
"Is the designated name of the not tranquil dharmas produced by conditions the great bodhisattva?"
"No, I don't think so, World-Honored One!"
"Is the designated name of the faraway dharmas produced by conditions the great bodhisattva?"
"No, I don't think so, World-Honored One!"
"Is the designated name of the not faraway dharmas produced by conditions the great bodhisattva?"
"No, I don't think so, World-Honored One!"
"Is the designated name of the conditioned dharmas produced by conditions the great bodhisattva?"
"No, I don't think so, World-Honored One!"
"Is the designated name of the unconditioned dharmas produced by conditions the great bodhisattva?"
"No, I don't think so, World-Honored One!"
"Is the designated name of the flawed dharmas produced by conditions the great bodhisattva?"
"No, I don't think so, World-Honored One!"
"Is the designated name of the flawless dharmas produced by conditions the great bodhisattva?"
"No, I don't think so, World-Honored One!"
"Is the designated name of the arising dharmas produced by conditions the great bodhisattva?"
"No, I don't think so, World-Honored One!"
"Is the designated name of the extinguishing dharmas produced by conditions the great bodhisattva?"
"No, I don't think so, World-Honored One!"
"Is the designated name of the virtuous dharmas produced by conditions the great bodhisattva?"
"No, I don't think so, World-Honored One!"
"Is the designated name of the not virtuous dharmas produced by conditions the great bodhisattva?"
"No, I don't think so, World-Honored One!"
"Is the designated name of the guilty dharmas produced by conditions the great bodhisattva?"

"No, I don't think so, World-Honored One!"

"Is the designated name of the not guilty dharmas produced by conditions the great bodhisattva?"

"No, I don't think so, World-Honored One!"

"Is the designated name of the dharmas with vexations produced by conditions the great bodhisattva?"

"No, I don't think so, World-Honored One!"

"Is the designated name of the dharmas without vexations produced by conditions the great bodhisattva?"

"No, I don't think so, World-Honored One!"

"Is the designated name of the worldly dharmas produced by conditions the great bodhisattva?"

"No, I don't think so, World-Honored One!"

"Is the designated name of the dharmas beyond the world produced by conditions the great bodhisattva?"

"No, I don't think so, World-Honored One!"

"Is the designated name of the contaminated dharmas produced by conditions the great bodhisattva?"

"No, I don't think so, World-Honored One!"

"Is the designated name of the purified dharmas produced by conditions the great bodhisattva?"

"No, I don't think so, World-Honored One!"

"Is the designated name of the dharmas produced by conditions belonging to birth and death the great bodhisattva?"

"No, I don't think so, World-Honored One!"

"Is the designated name of the dharmas produced by conditions belonging to nirvana the great bodhisattva?"

"No, I don't think so, World-Honored One!"

"Is the designated name of the inside dharmas produced by conditions the great bodhisattva?"

"No, I don't think so, World-Honored One!"

"Is the designated name of the outside dharmas produced by conditions the great bodhisattva?"

"No, I don't think so, World-Honored One!"

"Is the designated name of the in-between dharmas produced by conditions the great bodhisattva?"

"No, I don't think so, World-Honored One!"

"Is the designated name of the dharmas produced by attainable conditions the great bodhisattva?"

"No, I don't think so, World-Honored One!"

"Is the designated name of the dharmas produced by unattainable conditions the great bodhisattva?"

"No, I don't think so, World-Honored One!"

"Furthermore, Well Appearing One, what do you mean by great bodhisattva? Is the designated name of ignorance the great bodhisattva?"

"No, I don't think so, World-Honored One!"

"Is the designated name of action, consciousness, name and form, six sense spheres, contact, reception, craving, grasping, existence, birth, old age, and death the great bodhisattva?"

"No, I don't think so, World-Honored One!"

"Is the designated name of the permanent ignorance the great bodhisattva?"

"No, I don't think so, World-Honored One!"

"Is the designated name of the permanent action, and so forth, as well as old age and death the great bodhisattva?"

"No, I don't think so, World-Honored One!"

"Is the designated name of the impermanent ignorance the great bodhisattva?"

"No, I don't think so, World-Honored One!"

"Is the designated name of the impermanent action, and so forth, as well as old age and death the great bodhisattva?"

"No, I don't think so, World-Honored One!"

"Is the designated name of the pleasant ignorance the great bodhisattva?"

"No, I don't think so, World-Honored One!"

"Is the designated name of the pleasant action, and so forth, as well as old age and death the great bodhisattva?"

"No, I don't think so, World-Honored One!"

"Is the designated name of the painful ignorance the great bodhisattva?"

"No, I don't think so, World-Honored One!"

"Is the designated name of the painful action, and so forth, as well as old age and death the great bodhisattva?"

"No, I don't think so, World-Honored One!"

"Is the designated name of ignorance with selfness the great bodhisattva?"

"No, I don't think so, World-Honored One!"

"Is the designated name of action, and so forth, as well as old age and death with selfness the great bodhisattva?"

"No, I don't think so, World-Honored One!"

"Is the designated name of ignorance without selfness the great bodhisattva?"

"No, I don't think so, World-Honored One!"

"Is the designated name of action, and so forth, as well as old age and death without selfness the great bodhisattva?"

"No, I don't think so, World-Honored One!"

"Is the designated name of the pure ignorance the great bodhisattva?"

"No, I don't think so, World-Honored One!"

"Is the designated name of the pure action, and so forth, as well as old age and death the great bodhisattva?"

"No, I don't think so, World-Honored One!"

"Is the designated name of the impure ignorance the great bodhisattva?"

"No, I don't think so, World-Honored One!"

"Is the designated name of the impure action, and so forth, as well as old age and death the great bodhisattva?"

"No, I don't think so, World-Honored One!"

"Is the designated name of the empty ignorance the great bodhisattva?"

"No, I don't think so, World-Honored One!"

"Is the designated name of the empty action, and so forth, as well as old age and death the great bodhisattva?"

"No, I don't think so, World-Honored One!"

"Is the designated name of the not empty ignorance the great bodhisattva?"

"No, I don't think so, World-Honored One!"

"Is the designated name of the not empty action, and so forth, as well as old age and death the great bodhisattva?"

"No, I don't think so, World-Honored One!"

"Is the designated name of ignorance with form the great bodhisattva?"

"No, I don't think so, World-Honored One!"

"Is the designated name of action, and so forth, as well as old age and death with form the great bodhisattva?"

"No, I don't think so, World-Honored One!"

"Is the designated name of ignorance without form the great bodhisattva?"

"No, I don't think so, World-Honored One!"

"Is the designated name of action, and so forth, as well as old age and death without form the great bodhisattva?"

"No, I don't think so, World-Honored One!"

"Is the designated name of ignorance with aspiration the great bodhisattva?"

"No, I don't think so, World-Honored One!"

"Is the designated name of action and, so forth, as well as old age and death with aspiration the great bodhisattva?"

"No, I don't think so, World-Honored One!"

"Is the designated name of ignorance without aspiration the great bodhisattva?"

"No, I don't think so, World-Honored One!"

"Is the designated name of action, and so forth, as well as old age and death without aspiration the great bodhisattva?"

"No, I don't think so, World-Honored One!"

"Is the designated name of the tranquil ignorance the great bodhisattva?"

"No, I don't think so, World-Honored One!"

"Is the designated name of the tranquil action, and so forth, as well as old age and death the great bodhisattva?"

"No, I don't think so, World-Honored One!"

"Is the designated name of the not tranquil ignorance the great bodhisattva?"

"No, I don't think so, World-Honored One!"

"Is the designated name of the not tranquil action, and so forth, as well as old age and death the great bodhisattva?"

"No, I don't think so, World-Honored One!"

"Is the designated name of the faraway ignorance the great bodhisattva?"

"No, I don't think so, World-Honored One!"

"Is the designated name of the faraway action, and so forth, as well as old age and death the great bodhisattva?"

"No, I don't think so, World-Honored One!"

"Is the designated name of the not faraway ignorance the great bodhisattva?"

"No, I don't think so, World-Honored One!"

"Is the designated name of the not faraway action, and so forth, as well as old age and death the great bodhisattva?"

"No, I don't think so, World-Honored One!"

"Is the designated name of the conditioned ignorance the great bodhisattva?"

"No, I don't think so, World-Honored One!"

"Is the designated name of the conditioned action, and so forth, as well as old age and death the great bodhisattva?"

"No, I don't think so, World-Honored One!"

"Is the designated name of the unconditioned ignorance the great bodhisattva?"

"No, I don't think so, World-Honored One!"

"Is the designated name of the unconditioned action, and so forth, as well as old age and death the great bodhisattva?"

"No, I don't think so, World-Honored One!"

"Is the designated name of the flawed ignorance the great bodhisattva?"

"No, I don't think so, World-Honored One!"

"Is the designated name of the flawed action, and so forth, as well as old age and death the great bodhisattva?"

"No, I don't think so, World-Honored One!"

"Is the designated name of the flawless ignorance the great bodhisattva?"

"No, I don't think so, World-Honored One!"

"Is the designated name of the flawless action, and so forth, as well as old age and death the great bodhisattva?"

"No, I don't think so, World-Honored One!"
"Is the designated name of the arising ignorance the great bodhisattva?"
"No, I don't think so, World-Honored One!"
"Is the designated name of the arising action, and so forth, as well as old age and death the great bodhisattva?"
"No, I don't think so, World-Honored One!"
"Is the designated name of the extinguishing ignorance the great bodhisattva?"
"No, I don't think so, World-Honored One!"
"Is the designated name of the extinguishing action, and so forth, as well as old age and death the great bodhisattva?"
"No, I don't think so, World-Honored One!"
"Is the designated name of the virtuous ignorance the great bodhisattva?"
"No, I don't think so, World-Honored One!"
"Is the designated name of the virtuous action, and so forth, as well as old age and death the great bodhisattva?"
"No, I don't think so, World-Honored One!"
"Is the designated name of the not virtuous ignorance the great bodhisattva?"
"No, I don't think so, World-Honored One!"
"Is the designated name of the not virtuous action, and so forth, as well as old age and death the great bodhisattva?"
"No, I don't think so, World-Honored One!"
"Is the designated name of the guilty ignorance the great bodhisattva?"
"No, I don't think so, World-Honored One!"
"Is the designated name of the guilty action, and so forth, as well as old age and death the great bodhisattva?"
"No, I don't think so, World-Honored One!"
"Is the designated name of the not guilty ignorance the great bodhisattva?"
"No, I don't think so, World-Honored One!"
"Is the designated name of the not guilty action, and so forth, as well as old age and death the great bodhisattva?"

"No, I don't think so, World-Honored One!"

"Is the designated name of the ignorance with vexations the great bodhisattva?"

"No, I don't think so, World-Honored One!"

"Is the designated name of the action, and so forth, as well as old age and death with vexations the great bodhisattva?"

"No, I don't think so, World-Honored One!"

"Is the designated name of the ignorance without vexations the great bodhisattva?"

"No, I don't think so, World-Honored One!"

"Is the designated name of the action, and so forth, as well as old age and death without vexations the great bodhisattva?"

"No, I don't think so, World-Honored One!"

"Is the designated name of the worldly ignorance the great bodhisattva?"

"No, I don't think so, World-Honored One!"

"Is the designated name of the worldly action, and so forth, as well as old age and death the great bodhisattva?"

"No, I don't think so, World-Honored One!"

"Is the designated name of the ignorance beyond the world the great bodhisattva?"

"No, I don't think so, World-Honored One!"

"Is the designated name of the action, and so forth, as well as old age and death beyond the world the great bodhisattva?"

"No, I don't think so, World-Honored One!"

"Is the designated name of the contaminated ignorance the great bodhisattva?"

"No, I don't think so, World-Honored One!"

"Is the designated name of the contaminated action, and so forth, as well as old age and death the great bodhisattva?"

"No, I don't think so, World-Honored One!"

"Is the designated name of the purified ignorance the great bodhisattva?"

"No, I don't think so, World-Honored One!"

"Is the designated name of the purified action, and so forth, as well as old age and death the great bodhisattva?"

"No, I don't think so, World-Honored One!"
"Is the designated name of the ignorance belonging to birth and death the great bodhisattva?"
"No, I don't think so, World-Honored One!"
"Is the designated name of action, and so forth, as well as old age and death belonging to birth and death the great bodhisattva?"
"No, I don't think so, World-Honored One!"
"Is the designated name of the ignorance belonging to nirvana the great bodhisattva?"
"No, I don't think so, World-Honored One!"
"Is the designated name of action, and so forth, as well as old age and death belonging to nirvana the great bodhisattva?"
"No, I don't think so, World-Honored One!"
"Is the designated name of the inside ignorance the great bodhisattva?"
"No, I don't think so, World-Honored One!"
"Is the designated name of the inside action, and so forth, as well as old age and death the great bodhisattva?"
"No, I don't think so, World-Honored One!"
"Is the designated name of the outside ignorance the great bodhisattva?"
"No, I don't think so, World-Honored One!"
"Is the designated name of the outside action, and so forth, as well as old age and death the great bodhisattva?"
"No, I don't think so, World-Honored One!"
"Is the designated name of the in-between ignorance the great bodhisattva?"
"No, I don't think so, World-Honored One!"
"Is the designated name of the in-between action, and so forth, as well as old age and death the great bodhisattva?"
"No, I don't think so, World-Honored One!"
"Is the designated name of the attainable ignorance the great bodhisattva?"
"No, I don't think so, World-Honored One!"
"Is the designated name of the attainable action, and so forth, as well as old age and death the great bodhisattva?"

"No, I don't think so, World-Honored One!"

"Is the designated name of the unattainable ignorance the great bodhisattva?"

"No, I don't think so, World-Honored One!"

"Is the designated name of the unattainable action, and so forth, as well as old age and death the great bodhisattva?"

"No, I don't think so, World-Honored One!"

"Furthermore, Well Appearing One, what do you mean by great bodhisattva? Is the designated name of giving paramita the great bodhisattva?"

"No, I don't think so, World-Honored One!"

"Is the designated name of pure precept, forbearance, diligence, meditation, or prajna paramita the great bodhisattva?"

"No, I don't think so, World-Honored One!"

"Is the designated name of the permanent giving paramita the great bodhisattva?"

"No, I don't think so, World-Honored One!"

"Is the designated name of the permanent pure precept, forbearance, diligence, meditation, or prajna paramita the great bodhisattva?"

"No, I don't think so, World-Honored One!"

"Is the designated name of the impermanent giving paramita the great bodhisattva?"

"No, I don't think so, World-Honored One!"

"Is the designated name of the impermanent pure precept, forbearance, diligence, meditation, or prajna paramita the great bodhisattva?"

"No, I don't think so, World-Honored One!"

"Is the designated name of the pleasant giving paramita the great bodhisattva?"

"No, I don't think so, World-Honored One!"

"Is the designated name of the pleasant pure precept, forbearance, diligence, meditation, or prajna paramita the great bodhisattva?"

"No, I don't think so, World-Honored One!"

"Is the designated name of the painful giving paramita the great bodhisattva?"

"No, I don't think so, World-Honored One!"

"Is the designated name of the painful pure precept, forbearance, diligence, meditation, or prajna paramita the great bodhisattva?"

"No, I don't think so, World-Honored One!"

"Is the designated name of giving paramita with selfness the great bodhisattva?"

"No, I don't think so, World-Honored One!"

"Is the designated name of pure precept, forbearance, diligence, meditation, or prajna paramita with selfness the great bodhisattva?"

"No, I don't think so, World-Honored One!"

"Is the designated name of giving paramita without selfness the great bodhisattva?"

"No, I don't think so, World-Honored One!"

"Is the designated name of pure precept, forbearance, diligence, meditation, or prajna paramita without selfness the great bodhisattva?"

"No, I don't think so, World-Honored One!"

"Is the designated name of the pure giving paramita the great bodhisattva?"

"No, I don't think so, World-Honored One!"

"Is the designated name of the pure pure precept, forbearance, diligence, meditation, or prajna paramita the great bodhisattva?"

"No, I don't think so, World-Honored One!"

"Is the designated name of the impure giving paramita the great bodhisattva?"

"No, I don't think so, World-Honored One!"

"Is the designated name of the impure pure precept, forbearance, diligence, meditation, or prajna paramita the great bodhisattva?"

"No, I don't think so, World-Honored One!"

"Is the designated name of the empty giving paramita the great bodhisattva?"

"No, I don't think so, World-Honored One!"

"Is the designated name of the empty pure precept, forbearance, diligence, meditation, or prajna paramita the great bodhisattva?"

"No, I don't think so, World-Honored One!"

"Is the designated name of the not empty giving paramita the great bodhisattva?"

"No, I don't think so, World-Honored One!"

"Is the designated name of the not empty pure precept, forbearance, diligence, meditation, or prajna paramita the great bodhisattva?"

"No, I don't think so, World-Honored One!"

"Is the designated name of giving paramita with form the great bodhisattva?"

"No, I don't think so, World-Honored One!"

"Is the designated name of pure precept, forbearance, diligence, meditation, or prajna paramita with form the great bodhisattva?"

"No, I don't think so, World-Honored One!"

"Is the designated name of giving paramita without form the great bodhisattva?"

"No, I don't think so, World-Honored One!"

"Is the designated name of pure precept, forbearance, diligence, meditation, or prajna paramita without form the great bodhisattva?"

"No, I don't think so, World-Honored One!"

"Is the designated name of giving paramita with aspiration the great bodhisattva?"

"No, I don't think so, World-Honored One!"

"Is the designated name of pure precept, forbearance, diligence, meditation, or prajna paramita with aspiration the great bodhisattva?"

"No, I don't think so, World-Honored One!"

"Is the designated name of giving paramita without aspiration the great bodhisattva?"

"No, I don't think so, World-Honored One!"

"Is the designated name of pure precept, forbearance, diligence, meditation, or prajna paramita without aspiration the great bodhisattva?"

"No, I don't think so, World-Honored One!"

"Is the designated name of the tranquil giving paramita the great bodhisattva?"

"No, I don't think so, World-Honored One!"
"Is the designated name of the tranquil pure precept, forbearance, diligence, meditation, or prajna paramita the great bodhisattva?"
"No, I don't think so, World-Honored One!"
"Is the designated name of the not tranquil giving paramita the great bodhisattva?"
"No, I don't think so, World-Honored One!"
"Is the designated name of the not tranquil pure precept, forbearance, diligence, meditation, or prajna paramita the great bodhisattva?"
"No, I don't think so, World-Honored One!"
"Is the designated name of the faraway giving paramita the great bodhisattva?"
"No, I don't think so, World-Honored One!"
"Is the designated name of the faraway pure precept, forbearance, diligence, meditation, or prajna paramita the great bodhisattva?"
"No, I don't think so, World-Honored One!"
"Is the designated name of the not faraway giving paramita the great bodhisattva?"
"No, I don't think so, World-Honored One!"
"Is the designated name of the not faraway pure precept, forbearance, diligence, meditation, or prajna paramita the great bodhisattva?"
"No, I don't think so, World-Honored One!"
"Is the designated name of the conditioned giving paramita the great bodhisattva?"
"No, I don't think so, World-Honored One!"
"Is the designated name of the conditioned pure precept, forbearance, diligence, meditation, or prajna paramita the great bodhisattva?"
"No, I don't think so, World-Honored One!"
"Is the designated name of the unconditioned giving paramita the great bodhisattva?"
"No, I don't think so, World-Honored One!"
"Is the designated name of the unconditioned pure precept, for-

bearance, diligence, meditation, or prajna paramita the great bodhisattva?"

"No, I don't think so, World-Honored One!"

"Is the designated name of the flawed giving paramita the great bodhisattva?"

"No, I don't think so, World-Honored One!"

"Is the designated name of the flawed pure precept, forbearance, diligence, meditation, or prajna paramita the great bodhisattva?"

"No, I don't think so, World-Honored One!"

"Is the designated name of the flawless giving paramita the great bodhisattva?"

"No, I don't think so, World-Honored One!"

"Is the designated name of the flawless pure precept, forbearance, diligence, meditation, or prajna paramita the great bodhisattva?"

"No, I don't think so, World-Honored One!"

"Is the designated name of the arising giving paramita the great bodhisattva?"

"No, I don't think so, World-Honored One!"

"Is the designated name of the arising pure precept, forbearance, diligence, meditation, or prajna paramita the great bodhisattva?"

"No, I don't think so, World-Honored One!"

"Is the designated name of the extinguishing giving paramita the great bodhisattva?"

"No, I don't think so, World-Honored One!"

"Is the designated name of the extinguishing pure precept, forbearance, diligence, meditation, or prajna paramita the great bodhisattva?"

"No, I don't think so, World-Honored One!"

"Is the designated name of the virtuous giving paramita the great bodhisattva?"

"No, I don't think so, World-Honored One!"

"Is the designated name of the virtuous pure precept, forbearance, diligence, meditation, or prajna paramita the great bodhisattva?"

Fascicle 19, Chapter 7, Section 9   483

"No, I don't think so, World-Honored One!"
"Is the designated name of the not virtuous giving paramita the great bodhisattva?"
"No, I don't think so, World-Honored One!"
"Is the designated name of the not virtuous pure precept, forbearance, diligence, meditation, or prajna paramita the great bodhisattva?"
"No, I don't think so, World-Honored One!"
"Is the designated name of the guilty giving paramita the great bodhisattva?"
"No, I don't think so, World-Honored One!"
"Is the designated name of the guilty pure precept, forbearance, diligence, meditation, or prajna paramita the great bodhisattva?"
"No, I don't think so, World-Honored One!"
"Is the designated name of the not guilty giving paramita the great bodhisattva?"
"No, I don't think so, World-Honored One!"
"Is the designated name of the not guilty pure precept, forbearance, diligence, meditation, or prajna paramita the great bodhisattva?"
"No, I don't think so, World-Honored One!"
"Is the designated name of the giving paramita with vexations the great bodhisattva?"
"No, I don't think so, World-Honored One!"
"Is the designated name of the pure precept, forbearance, diligence, meditation, or prajna paramita with vexations the great bodhisattva?"
"No, I don't think so, World-Honored One!"
"Is the designated name of the giving paramita without vexations the great bodhisattva?"
"No, I don't think so, World-Honored One!"
"Is the designated name of the pure precept, forbearance, diligence, meditation, or prajna paramita without vexations the great bodhisattva?"
"No, I don't think so, World-Honored One!"
"Is the designated name of the worldly giving paramita the great bodhisattva?"

"No, I don't think so, World-Honored One!"

"Is the designated name of the worldly pure precept, forbearance, diligence, meditation, or prajna paramita the great bodhisattva?"

"No, I don't think so, World-Honored One!"

"Is the designated name of the giving paramita beyond the world the great bodhisattva?"

"No, I don't think so, World-Honored One!"

"Is the designated name of the pure precept, forbearance, diligence, meditation, or prajna paramita beyond the world the great bodhisattva?"

"No, I don't think so, World-Honored One!"

"Is the designated name of the contaminated giving paramita the great bodhisattva?"

"No, I don't think so, World-Honored One!"

"Is the designated name of the contaminated pure precept, forbearance, diligence, meditation, or prajna paramita the great bodhisattva?"

"No, I don't think so, World-Honored One!"

"Is the designated name of the purified giving paramita the great bodhisattva?"

"No, I don't think so, World-Honored One!"

"Is the designated name of the purified pure precept, forbearance, diligence, meditation, or prajna paramita the great bodhisattva?"

"No, I don't think so, World-Honored One!"

"Is the designated name of giving paramita belonging to birth and death the great bodhisattva?"

"No, I don't think so, World-Honored One!"

"Is the designated name of pure precept, forbearance, diligence, meditation, or prajna paramita belonging to birth and death the great bodhisattva?"

"No, I don't think so, World-Honored One!"

"Is the designated name of giving paramita belonging to nirvana the great bodhisattva?"

"No, I don't think so, World-Honored One!"

"Is the designated name of pure precept, forbearance, diligence, meditation, or prajna paramita belonging to nirvana the great bodhisattva?"

"No, I don't think so, World-Honored One!"

"Is the designated name of the inside giving paramita the great bodhisattva?"

"No, I don't think so, World-Honored One!"

"Is the designated name of the inside pure precept, forbearance, diligence, meditation, or prajna paramita the great bodhisattva?"

"No, I don't think so, World-Honored One!"

"Is the designated name of the outside giving paramita the great bodhisattva?"

"No, I don't think so, World-Honored One!"

"Is the designated name of the outside pure precept, forbearance, diligence, meditation, or prajna paramita the great bodhisattva?"

"No, I don't think so, World-Honored One!"

"Is the designated name of the in-between giving paramita the great bodhisattva?"

"No, I don't think so, World-Honored One!"

"Is the designated name of the in-between pure precept, forbearance, diligence, meditation, or prajna paramita the great bodhisattva?"

"No, I don't think so, World-Honored One!"

"Is the designated name of the attainable giving paramita the great bodhisattva?"

"No, I don't think so, World-Honored One!"

"Is the designated name of the attainable pure precept, forbearance, diligence, meditation, or prajna paramita the great bodhisattva?"

"No, I don't think so, World-Honored One!"

"Is the designated name of the unattainable giving paramita the great bodhisattva?"

"No, I don't think so, World-Honored One!"

"Is the designated name of the unattainable pure precept, forbearance, diligence, meditation, or prajna paramita the great bodhisattva?"

"No, I don't think so, World-Honored One!"

Fascicle 20

Chapter 7
The Cautions and the Teachings

Section 10

(In the First Assembly)

"Furthermore, Well Appearing One, what do you mean by great bodhisattva? Is the designated name of internal emptiness the great bodhisattva?"

"No, I don't think so, World-Honored One!"

"Is the designated name of external emptiness, internal-external emptiness, emptiness of emptiness, emptiness of space, emptiness of ultimate truth, emptiness of conditioned phenomena, emptiness of unconditioned reality, emptiness in the final analysis, emptiness of nontemporality, emptiness of deconstruction, emptiness of changelessness, emptiness of original nature, emptiness of particular characteristics, emptiness of common characteristics, emptiness of all dharmas, emptiness of nonattainment, emptiness of selflessness, emptiness of self-nature, or emptiness of selfless self-nature the great bodhisattva?"

"No, I don't think so, World-Honored One!"

"Is the designated name of the permanent internal emptiness the great bodhisattva?"

"No, I don't think so, World-Honored One!"
"Is the designated name of the permanent external emptiness, and so forth, as well as emptiness of selfless self-nature the great bodhisattva?"
"No, I don't think so, World-Honored One!"
"Is the designated name of the impermanent internal emptiness the great bodhisattva?"
"No, I don't think so, World-Honored One!"
"Is the designated name of the impermanent external emptiness, and so forth, as well as emptiness of selfless self-nature the great bodhisattva?"
"No, I don't think so, World-Honored One!"
"Is the designated name of the pleasant internal emptiness the great bodhisattva?"
"No, I don't think so, World-Honored One!"
"Is the designated name of the pleasant external emptiness, and so forth, as well as emptiness of selfless self-nature the great bodhisattva?"
"No, I don't think so, World-Honored One!"
"Is the designated name of the painful internal emptiness the great bodhisattva?"
"No, I don't think so, World-Honored One!"
"Is the designated name of the painful external emptiness, and so forth, as well as emptiness of selfless self-nature the great bodhisattva?"
"No, I don't think so, World-Honored One!"
"Is the designated name of the internal emptiness with selfness the great bodhisattva?"
"No, I don't think so, World-Honored One!"
"Is the designated name of the external emptiness, and so forth, as well as emptiness of selfless self-nature with selfness the great bodhisattva?"
"No, I don't think so, World-Honored One!"
"Is the designated name of internal emptiness without selfness the great bodhisattva?"
"No, I don't think so, World-honored One!"
"Is the designated name of external emptiness, and so forth, as

well as emptiness of selfless self-nature without selfness the great bodhisattva?"

"No, I don't think so, World-Honored One!"

"Is the designated name of the pure internal emptiness the great bodhisattva?"

"No, I don't think so, World-Honored One!"

"Is the designated name of the pure external emptiness, and so forth, as well as emptiness of selfless self-nature the great bodhisattva?"

"No, I don't think so, World-Honored One!"

"Is the designated name of the impure internal emptiness the great bodhisattva?"

"No, I don't think so, World-Honored One!"

"Is the designated name of the impure external emptiness, and so forth, as well as emptiness of selfless self-nature the great bodhisattva?"

"No, I don't think so, World-Honored One!"

"Is the designated name of the empty internal emptiness the great bodhisattva?"

"No, I don't think so, World-Honored One!"

"Is the designated name of the empty external emptiness, and so forth, as well as emptiness of selfless self-nature the great bodhisattva?"

"No, I don't think so, World-Honored One!"

"Is the designated name of the not empty internal emptiness the great bodhisattva?"

"No, I don't think so, World-Honored One!"

"Is the designated name of the not empty external emptiness, and so forth, as well as emptiness of selfless self-nature the great bodhisattva?"

"No, I don't think so, World-Honored One!"

"Is the designated name of internal emptiness with form the great bodhisattva?"

"No, I don't think so, World-Honored One!"

"Is the designated name of external emptiness, and so forth, as well as emptiness of selfless self-nature with form the great bodhisattva?"

"No, I don't think so, World-Honored One!"

Fascicle 20, Chapter 7, Section 10

"Is the designated name of internal emptiness without form the great bodhisattva?"

"No, I don't think so, World-Honored One!"

"Is the designated name of external emptiness, and so forth, as well as emptiness of selfless self-nature without form the great bodhisattva?"

"No, I don't think so, World-Honored One!"

"Is the designated name of internal emptiness with aspiration the great bodhisattva?"

"No, I don't think so, World-Honored One!"

"Is the designated name of external emptiness, and so forth, as well as emptiness of selfless self-nature with aspiration the great bodhisattva?"

"No, I don't think so, World-Honored One!"

"Is the designated name of internal emptiness without aspiration the great bodhisattva?"

"No, I don't think so, World-Honored One!"

"Is the designated name of external emptiness, and so forth, as well as emptiness of selfless self-nature without aspiration the great bodhisattva?"

"No, I don't think so, World-Honored One!"

"Is the designated name of the tranquil internal emptiness the great bodhisattva?"

"No, I don't think so, World-Honored One!"

"Is the designated name of the tranquil external emptiness, and so forth, as well as emptiness of selfless self-nature the great bodhisattva?"

"No, I don't think so, World-Honored One!"

"Is the designated name of the not tranquil internal emptiness the great bodhisattva?"

"No, I don't think so, World-Honored One!"

"Is the designated name of the not tranquil external emptiness, and so forth, as well as emptiness of selfless self-nature the great bodhisattva?"

"No, I don't think so, World-Honored One!"

"Is the designated name of the faraway internal emptiness the great bodhisattva?"

"No, I don't think so, World-Honored One!"

"Is the designated name of the faraway external emptiness, and so forth, as well as emptiness of selfless self-nature the great bodhisattva?"

"No, I don't think so, World-Honored One!"

"Is the designated name of the not faraway internal emptiness the great bodhisattva?"

"No, I don't think so, World-Honored One!"

"Is the designated name of the not faraway external emptiness, and so forth, as well as emptiness of selfless self-nature the great bodhisattva?"

"No, I don't think so, World-Honored One!"

"Is the designated name of the conditioned internal emptiness the great bodhisattva?"

"No, I don't think so, World-Honored One!"

"Is the designated name of the conditioned external emptiness, and so forth, as well as emptiness of selfless self-nature the great bodhisattva?"

"No, I don't think so, World-Honored One!"

"Is the designated name of the unconditioned internal emptiness the great bodhisattva?"

"No, I don't think so, World-Honored One!"

"Is the designated name of the unconditioned external emptiness, and so forth, as well as emptiness of selfless self-nature the great bodhisattva?"

"No, I don't think so, World-Honored One!"

"Is the designated name of the flawed internal emptiness the great bodhisattva?"

"No, I don't think so, World-Honored One!"

"Is the designated name of the flawed external emptiness, and so forth, as well as emptiness of selfless self-nature the great bodhisattva?"

"No, I don't think so, World-Honored One!"

"Is the designated name of the flawless internal emptiness the great bodhisattva?"

"No, I don't think so, World-Honored One!"

"Is the designated name of the flawless external emptiness, and so forth, as well as emptiness of selfless self-nature the great bodhisattva?"

"No, I don't think so, World-Honored One!"

"Is the designated name of the hidden internal emptiness the great bodhisattva?"

"No, I don't think so, World-Honored One!"

"Is the designated name of the hidden external emptiness, and so forth, as well as emptiness of selfless self-nature the great bodhisattva?"

"No, I don't think so, World-Honored One!"

"Is the designated name of the significant internal emptiness the great bodhisattva?"

"No, I don't think so, World-Honored One!"

"Is the designated name of the significant external emptiness, and so forth, as well as emptiness of selfless self-nature the great bodhisattva?"

"No, I don't think so, World-Honored One!"

"Is the designated name of the virtuous internal emptiness the great bodhisattva?"

"No, I don't think so, World-Honored One!"

"Is the designated name of the virtuous external emptiness, and so forth, as well as emptiness of selfless self-nature the great bodhisattva?"

"No, I don't think so, World-Honored One!"

"Is the designated name of the not virtuous internal emptiness the great bodhisattva?"

"No, I don't think so, World-Honored One!"

"Is the designated name of the not virtuous external emptiness, and so forth, as well as emptiness of selfless self-nature the great bodhisattva?"

"No, I don't think so, World-Honored One!"

"Is the designated name of the guilty internal emptiness the great bodhisattva?"

"No, I don't think so, World-Honored One!"

"Is the designated name of the guilty external emptiness, and so forth, as well as emptiness of selfless self-nature the great bodhisattva?"

"No, I don't think so, World-Honored One!"

"Is the designated name of the not guilty internal emptiness the great bodhisattva?"

"No, I don't think so, World-Honored One!"

"Is the designated name of the not guilty external emptiness, and so forth, as well as emptiness of selfless self-nature the great bodhisattva?"

"No, I don't think so, World-Honored One!"

"Is the designated name of internal emptiness with vexations the great bodhisattva?"

"No, I don't think so, World-Honored One!"

"Is the designated name of external emptiness, and so forth, as well as emptiness of selfless self-nature with vexations the great bodhisattva?"

"No, I don't think so, World-Honored One!"

"Is the designated name of internal emptiness without vexations the great bodhisattva?"

"No, I don't think so, World-Honored One!"

"Is the designated name of external emptiness, and so forth, as well as emptiness of selfless self-nature without vexations the great bodhisattva?"

"No, I don't think so, World-Honored One!"

"Is the designated name of internal emptiness of the world the great bodhisattva?"

"No, I don't think so, World-Honored One!"

"Is the designated name of external emptiness, and so forth, as well as emptiness of selfless self-nature of the world the great bodhisattva?"

"No, I don't think so, World-Honored One!"

"Is the designated name of internal emptiness beyond the world the great bodhisattva?"

"No, I don't think so, World-Honored One!"

"Is the designated name of external emptiness, and so forth, as well as emptiness of selfless self-nature beyond the world the great bodhisattva?"

"No, I don't think so, World-Honored One!"

"Is the designated name of the contaminated internal emptiness the great bodhisattva?"

"No, I don't think so, World-Honored One!"

"Is the designated name of the contaminated external emptiness, and so forth, as well as emptiness of selfless self-nature the great bodhisattva?"

"No, I don't think so, World-Honored One!"

"Is the designated name of the purified internal emptiness the great bodhisattva?"

"No, I don't think so, World-Honored One!"

"Is the designated name of the purified external emptiness, and so forth, as well as emptiness of selfless self-nature the great bodhisattva?"

"No, I don't think so, World-Honored One!"

"Is the designated name of internal emptiness belonging to birth and death the great bodhisattva?"

"No, I don't think so, World-Honored One!"

"Is the designated name of external emptiness, and so forth, as well as emptiness of selfless self-nature belonging to birth and death the great bodhisattva?"

"No, I don't think so, World-Honored One!"

"Is the designated name of internal emptiness belonging to nirvana the great bodhisattva?"

"No, I don't think so, World-Honored One!"

"Is the designated name of external emptiness, and so forth, as well as emptiness of selfless self-nature belonging to nirvana the great bodhisattva?"

"No, I don't think so, World-Honored One!"

"Is the designated name of the inside internal emptiness the great bodhisattva?"

"No, I don't think so, World-Honored One!"

"Is the designated name of the inside external emptiness, and so forth, as well as emptiness of selfless self-nature the great bodhisattva?"

"No, I don't think so, World-Honored One!"

"Is the designated name of the outside internal emptiness the great bodhisattva?"

"No, I don't think so, World-Honored One!"

"Is the designated name of the outside external emptiness, and so forth, as well as emptiness of selfless self-nature the great bodhisattva?"

"No, I don't think so, World-Honored One!"

"Is the designated name of the in-between internal emptiness the great bodhisattva?"

"No, I don't think so, World-Honored One!"

"Is the designated name of the in-between external emptiness, and so forth, as well as emptiness of selfless self-nature the great bodhisattva?"

"No, I don't think so, World-Honored One!"

"Is the designated name of the attainable internal emptiness the great bodhisattva?"

"No, I don't think so, World-Honored One!"

"Is the designated name of the attainable external emptiness, and so forth, as well as emptiness of selfless self-nature the great bodhisattva?"

"No, I don't think so, World-Honored One!"

"Is the designated name of the unattainable internal emptiness the great bodhisattva?"

"No, I don't think so, World-Honored One!"

"Is the designated name of the unattainable external emptiness, and so forth, as well as emptiness of selfless self-nature the great bodhisattva?"

"No, I don't think so, World-Honored One!"

"Furthermore, Well Appearing One, what do you mean by great bodhisattva? Is the designated name of realness the great bodhisattva?"

"No, I don't think so, World-Honored One!"

"Is the designated name of dharma realm, dharma nature, the nature of nonillusion, the nature of changelessness, the nature of equality, the nature of nonarising, dharma concentration, dharma dwelling, reality, the realm of empty space, and the realm of the inconceivable the great bodhisattva?"

"No, I don't think so, World-Honored One!"
"Is the designated name of the permanent realness the great bodhisattva?"
"No, I don't think so, World-Honored One!"
"Is the designated name of the permanent dharma realm, and so forth, as well as the permanent realm of the inconceivable the great bodhisattva?"
"No, I don't think so, World-Honored One!"
"Is the designated name of the impermanent realness the great bodhisattva?"
"No, I don't think so, World-Honored One!"
"Is the designated name of the impermanent dharma realm, and so forth, as well as the impermanent realm of the inconceivable the great bodhisattva?"
"No, I don't think so, World-Honored One!"
"Is the designated name of the pleasant realness the great bodhisattva?"
"No, I don't think so, World-Honored One!"
"Is the designated name of the pleasant dharma realm, and so forth, as well as the pleasant realm of the inconceivable the great bodhisattva?"
"No, I don't think so, World-Honored One!"
"Is the designated name of the painful realness the great bodhisattva?"
"No, I don't think so, World-Honored One!"
"Is the designated name of the painful dharma realm, and so forth, as well as the painful realm of the inconceivable the great bodhisattva?"
"No, I don't think so, World-Honored One!"
"Is the designated name of the realness with selfness the great bodhisattva?"
"No, I don't think so, World-Honored One!"
"Is the designated name of the dharma realm, and so forth, as well as the realm of the inconceivable with selfness the great bodhisattva?"

"No, I don't think so, World-Honored One!"

"Is the designated name of the realness without selfness the great bodhisattva?"

"No, I don't think so, World-Honored One!"

"Is the designated name of the dharma realm, and so forth, as well as the realm of the inconceivable without selfness the great bodhisattva?"

"No, I don't think so, World-Honored One!"

"Is the designated name of the pure realness the great bodhisattva?"

"No, I don't think so, World-Honored One!"

"Is the designated name of the pure dharma realm, and so forth, as well as the pure realm of the inconceivable the great bodhisattva?"

"No, I don't think so, World-Honored One!"

"Is the designated name of the impure realness the great bodhisattva?"

"No, I don't think so, World-Honored One!"

"Is the designated name of the impure dharma realm, and so forth, as well as the impure realm of the inconceivable the great bodhisattva?"

"No, I don't think so, World-Honored One!"

"Is the designated name of the empty realness the great bodhisattva?"

"No, I don't think so, World-Honored One!"

"Is the designated name of the empty dharma realm, and so forth, as well as the empty realm of the inconceivable the great bodhisattva?"

"No, I don't think so, World-Honored One!"

"Is the designated name of the not empty realness the great bodhisattva?"

"No, I don't think so, World-Honored One!"

"Is the designated name of the not empty dharma realm, and so forth, as well as the not empty realm of the inconceivable the great bodhisattva?"

"No, I don't think so, World-Honored One!"

"Is the designated name of the realness with form the great bodhisattva?"

"No, I don't think so, World-Honored One!"

"Is the designated name of the dharma realm, and so forth, as well as the realm of the inconceivable with form the great bodhisattva?"

"No, I don't think so, World-Honored One!"

"Is the designated name of the realness without form the great bodhisattva?"

"No, I don't think so, World-Honored One!"

"Is the designated name of the dharma realm, and so forth, as well as the realm of the inconceivable without form the great bodhisattva?"

"No, I don't think so, World-Honored One!"

"Is the designated name of the realness with aspiration the great bodhisattva?"

"No, I don't think so, World-Honored One!"

"Is the designated name of the dharma realm, and so forth, as well as the realm of the inconceivable with aspiration the great bodhisattva?"

"No, I don't think so, World-Honored One!"

"Is the designated name of the realness without aspiration the great bodhisattva?"

"No, I don't think so, World-Honored One!"

"Is the designated name of the dharma realm, and so forth, as well as the realm of the inconceivable without aspiration the great bodhisattva?"

"No, I don't think so, World-Honored One!"

"Is the designated name of the tranquil realness the great bodhisattva?"

"No, I don't think so, World-Honored One!"

"Is the designated name of the tranquil dharma realm, and so forth, as well as the tranquil realm of the inconceivable the great bodhisattva?"

"No, I don't think so, World-Honored One!"

"Is the designated name of the not tranquil realness the great bodhisattva?"

"No, I don't think so, World-Honored One!"

"Is the designated name of the not tranquil dharma realm, and so forth, as well as the not tranquil realm of the inconceivable the great bodhisattva?"

"No, I don't think so, World-Honored One!"

"Is the designated name of the faraway realness the great bodhisattva?"

"No, I don't think so, World-Honored One!"

"Is the designated name of the faraway dharma realm, and so forth, as well as the faraway realm of the inconceivable the great bodhisattva?"

"No, I don't think so, World-Honored One!"

"Is the designated name of the not faraway realness the great bodhisattva?"

"No, I don't think so, World-Honored One!"

"Is the designated name of the not faraway dharma realm, and so forth, as well as the not faraway realm of the inconceivable the great bodhisattva?"

"No, I don't think so, World-Honored One!"

"Is the designated name of the conditioned realness the great bodhisattva?"

"No, I don't think so, World-Honored One!"

"Is the designated name of the conditioned dharma realm, and so forth, as well as the conditioned realm of the inconceivable the great bodhisattva?"

"No, I don't think so, World-Honored One!"

"Is the designated name of the unconditioned realness the great bodhisattva?"

"No, I don't think so, World-Honored One!"

"Is the designated name of the unconditioned dharma realm, and so forth, as well as the unconditioned realm of the inconceivable the great bodhisattva?"

"No, I don't think so, World-Honored One!"

"Is the designated name of the flawed realness the great bodhisattva?"

"No, I don't think so, World-Honored One!"

"Is the designated name of the flawed dharma realm, and so forth, as well as the flawed realm of the inconceivable the great bodhisattva?"

"No, I don't think so, World-Honored One!"

"Is the designated name of the flawless realness the great bodhisattva?"

"No, I don't think so, World-Honored One!"

"Is the designated name of the flawless dharma realm, and so forth, as well as the flawless realm of the inconceivable the great bodhisattva?"

"No, I don't think so, World-Honored One!"

"Is the designated name of the hidden realness the great bodhisattva?"

"No, I don't think so, World-Honored One!"

"Is the designated name of the hidden dharma realm, and so forth, as well as the hidden realm of the inconceivable the great bodhisattva?"

"No, I don't think so, World-Honored One!"

"Is the designated name of the significant realness the great bodhisattva?"

"No, I don't think so, World-Honored One!"

"Is the designated name of the significant dharma realm, and so forth, as well as the significant realm of the inconceivable the great bodhisattva?"

"No, I don't think so, World-Honored One!"

"Is the designated name of the virtuous realness the great bodhisattva?"

"No, I don't think so, World-Honored One!"

"Is the designated name of the virtuous dharma realm, and so forth, as well as the virtuous realm of the inconceivable the great bodhisattva?"

"No, I don't think so, World-Honored One!"

"Is the designated name of the not virtuous realness the great bodhisattva?"

"No, I don't think so, World-Honored One!"

"Is the designated name of the not virtuous dharma realm, and so forth, as well as the not virtuous realm of the inconceivable the great bodhisattva?"

"No, I don't think so, World-Honored One!"
"Is the designated name of the guilty realness the great bodhisattva?"
"No, I don't think so, World-Honored One!"
"Is the designated name of the guilty dharma realm, and so forth, as well as the guilty realm of the inconceivable the great bodhisattva?"
"No, I don't think so, World-Honored One!"
"Is the designated name of the not guilty realness the great bodhisattva?"
"No, I don't think so, World-Honored One!"
"Is the designated name of the not guilty dharma realm, and so forth, as well as the not guilty realm of the inconceivable the great bodhisattva?"
"No, I don't think so, World-Honored One!"
"Is the designated name of the realness with vexations the great bodhisattva?"
"No, I don't think so, World-Honored One!"
"Is the designated name of the dharma realm, and so forth, as well as the realm of the inconceivable with vexations the great bodhisattva?"
"No, I don't think so, World-Honored One!"
"Is the designated name of the realness without vexations the great bodhisattva?"
"No, I don't think so, World-Honored One!"
"Is the designated name of the dharma realm, and so forth, as well as the realm of the inconceivable without vexations the great bodhisattva?"
"No, I don't think so, World-Honored One!"
"Is the designated name of the realness of the world the great bodhisattva?"
"No, I don't think so, World-Honored One!"
"Is the designated name of the dharma realm, and so forth, as well as the realm of the inconceivable of the world the great bodhisattva?"
"No, I don't think so, World-Honored One!"

Fascicle 20, Chapter 7, Section 10

"Is the designated name of the realness beyond the world the great bodhisattva?"

"No, I don't think so, World-Honored One!"

"Is the designated name of the dharma realm, and so forth, as well as the realm of the inconceivable beyond the world the great bodhisattva?"

"No, I don't think so, World-Honored One!"

"Is the designated name of the contaminated realness the great bodhisattva?"

"No, I don't think so, World-Honored One!"

"Is the designated name of the contaminated dharma realm, and so forth, as well as the contaminated realm of the inconceivable the great bodhisattva?"

"No, I don't think so, World-Honored One!"

"Is the designated name of the purified realness the great bodhisattva?"

"No, I don't think so, World-Honored One!"

"Is the designated name of the purified dharma realm, and so forth, as well as the purified realm of the inconceivable the great bodhisattva?"

"No, I don't think so, World-Honored One!"

"Is the designated name of the realness belonging to birth and death the great bodhisattva?"

"No, I don't think so, World-Honored One!"

"Is the designated name of the dharma realm, and so forth, as well as the realm of the inconceivable belonging to birth and death the great bodhisattva?"

"No, I don't think so, World-Honored One!"

"Is the designated name of the realness belonging to nirvana the great bodhisattva?"

"No, I don't think so, World-Honored One!"

"Is the designated name of the dharma realm, and so forth, as well as the realm of the inconceivable belonging to nirvana the great bodhisattva?"

"No, I don't think so, World-Honored One!"

"Is the designated name of the inside realness the great bodhisattva?"

"No, I don't think so, World-Honored One!"

"Is the designated name of the inside dharma realm, and so forth, as well as the inside realm of the inconceivable the great bodhisattva?"

"No, I don't think so, World-Honored One!"

"Is the designated name of the outside realness the great bodhisattva?"

"No, I don't think so, World-Honored One!"

"Is the designated name of the outside dharma realm, and so forth, as well as the outside realm of the inconceivable the great bodhisattva?"

"No, I don't think so, World-Honored One!"

"Is the designated name of the in-between realness the great bodhisattva?"

"No, I don't think so, World-Honored One!"

"Is the designated name of the in-between dharma realm, and so forth, as well as the in-between realm of the inconceivable the great bodhisattva?"

"No, I don't think so, World-Honored One!"

"Is the designated name of the attainable realness the great bodhisattva?"

"No, I don't think so, World-Honored One!"

"Is the designated name of the attainable dharma realm, and so forth, as well as the attainable realm of the inconceivable the great bodhisattva?"

"No, I don't think so, World-Honored One!"

"Is the designated name of the unattainable realness the great bodhisattva?"

"No, I don't think so, World-Honored One!"

"Is the designated name of the unattainable dharma realm, and so forth, as well as the unattainable realm of the inconceivable the great bodhisattva?"

"No, I don't think so, World-Honored One!"

"Furthermore, Well Appearing One, what do you mean by great bodhisattva? Is the designated name of the four bases of mindfulness the great bodhisattva?"

"No, I don't think so, World-Honored One!"

"Is the designated name of the four correct endeavors, four bases of power, five roots, five powers, seven factors for enlightenment, or the noble eightfold path the great bodhisattva?"

"No, I don't think so, World-Honored One!"

"Is the designated name of the permanent four bases of mindfulness the great bodhisattva?"

"No, I don't think so, World-Honored One!"

"Is the designated name of the permanent four correct endeavors, and so forth, as well as the permanent noble eightfold path the great bodhisattva?"

"No, I don't think so, World-Honored One!"

"Is the designated name of the impermanent four bases of mindfulness the great bodhisattva?"

"No, I don't think so, World-Honored One!"

"Is the designated name of the impermanent four correct endeavors, and so forth, as well as the impermanent noble eightfold path the great bodhisattva?"

"No, I don't think so, World-Honored One!"

"Is the designated name of the pleasant four bases of mindfulness the great bodhisattva?"

"No, I don't think so, World-Honored One!"

"Is the designated name of the pleasant four correct endeavors, and so forth, as well as the pleasant noble eightfold path the great bodhisattva?"

"No, I don't think so, World-Honored One!"

"Is the designated name of the painful four bases of mindfulness the great bodhisattva?"

"No, I don't think so, World-Honored One!"

"Is the designated name of the painful four correct endeavors, and so forth, as well as the painful noble eightfold path the great bodhisattva?"

"No, I don't think so, World-Honored One!"

"Is the designated name of the four bases of mindfulness with selfness the great bodhisattva?"

"No, I don't think so, World-Honored One!"

"Is the designated name of the four correct endeavors, and so forth, as well as the noble eightfold path with selfness the great bodhisattva?"

"No, I don't think so, World-Honored One!"

"Is the designated name of the four bases of mindfulness without selfness the great bodhisattva?"

"No, I don't think so, World-Honored One!"

"Is the designated name of the four correct endeavors, and so forth, as well as the noble eightfold path without selfness the great bodhisattva?"

"No, I don't think so, World-Honored One!"

"Is the designated name of the pure four bases of mindfulness the great bodhisattva?"

"No, I don't think so, World-Honored One!"

"Is the designated name of the pure four correct endeavors, and so forth, as well as the pure noble eightfold path the great bodhisattva?"

"No, I don't think so, World-Honored One!"

"Is the designated name of the impure four bases of mindfulness the great bodhisattva?"

"No, I don't think so, World-Honored One!"

"Is the designated name of the impure four correct endeavors, and so forth, as well as the impure noble eightfold path the great bodhisattva?"

"No, I don't think so, World-Honored One!"

"Is the designated name of the empty four bases of mindfulness the great bodhisattva?"

"No, I don't think so, World-Honored One!"

"Is the designated name of the empty four correct endeavors, and so forth, as well as the empty noble eightfold path the great bodhisattva?"

"No, I don't think so, World-Honored One!"

"Is the designated name of the not empty four bases of mindfulness the great bodhisattva?"

"No, I don't think so, World-Honored One!"

"Is the designated name of the not empty four correct endeavors, and so forth, as well as the not empty noble eightfold path the great bodhisattva?"

"No, I don't think so, World-Honored One!"

"Is the designated name of the four bases of mindfulness with form the great bodhisattva?"
"No, I don't think so, World-Honored One!"
"Is the designated name of the four correct endeavors, and so forth, as well as the noble eightfold path with form the great bodhisattva?"
"No, I don't think so, World-Honored One!"
"Is the designated name of the four bases of mindfulness without form the great bodhisattva?"
"No, I don't think so, World-Honored One!"
"Is the designated name of the four correct endeavors, and so forth, as well as the noble eightfold path without form the great bodhisattva?"
"No, I don't think so, World-Honored One!"
"Is the designated name of the four bases of mindfulness with aspiration the great bodhisattva?"
"No, I don't think so, World-Honored One!"
"Is the designated name of the four correct endeavors, and so forth, as well as the noble eightfold path with aspiration the great bodhisattva?"
"No, I don't think so, World-Honored One!"
"Is the designated name of the four bases of mindfulness without aspiration the great bodhisattva?"
"No, I don't think so, World-Honored One!"
"Is the designated name of the four correct endeavors, and so forth, as well as the noble eightfold path without aspiration the great bodhisattva?"
"No, I don't think so, World-Honored One!"
"Is the designated name of the tranquil four bases of mindfulness the great bodhisattva?"
"No, I don't think so, World-Honored One!"
"Is the designated name of the tranquil four correct endeavors, and so forth, as well as the tranquil noble eightfold path the great bodhisattva?"
"No, I don't think so, World-Honored One!"
"Is the designated name of the not tranquil four bases of mindfulness the great bodhisattva?"

"No, I don't think so, World-Honored One!"

"Is the designated name of the not tranquil four correct endeavors, and so forth, as well as the not tranquil noble eightfold path the great bodhisattva?"

"No, I don't think so, World-Honored One!"

"Is the designated name of the faraway four bases of mindfulness the great bodhisattva?"

"No, I don't think so, World-Honored One!"

"Is the designated name of the faraway four correct endeavors, and so forth, as well as the faraway noble eightfold path the great bodhisattva?"

"No, I don't think so, World-Honored One!"

"Is the designated name of the not faraway four bases of mindfulness the great bodhisattva?"

"No, I don't think so, World-Honored One!"

"Is the designated name of the not faraway four correct endeavors, and so forth, as well as the not faraway noble eightfold path the great bodhisattva?"

"No, I don't think so, World-Honored One!"

"Is the designated name of the conditioned four bases of mindfulness the great bodhisattva?"

"No, I don't think so, World-Honored One!"

"Is the designated name of the conditioned four correct endeavors, and so forth, as well as the conditioned noble eightfold path the great bodhisattva?"

"No, I don't think so, World-Honored One!"

"Is the designated name of the unconditioned four bases of mindfulness the great bodhisattva?"

"No, I don't think so, World-Honored One!"

"Is the designated name of the unconditioned four correct endeavors, and so forth, as well as the unconditioned noble eightfold path the great bodhisattva?"

"No, I don't think so, World-Honored One!"

"Is the designated name of the flawed four bases of mindfulness the great bodhisattva?"

"No, I don't think so, World-Honored One!"

"Is the designated name of the flawed four correct endeavors, and so forth, as well as the flawed noble eightfold path the great bodhisattva?"

"No, I don't think so, World-Honored One!"

"Is the designated name of the flawless four bases of mindfulness the great bodhisattva?"

"No, I don't think so, World-Honored One!"

"Is the designated name of the flawless four correct endeavors, and so forth, as well as the flawless noble eightfold path the great bodhisattva?"

"No, I don't think so, World-Honored One!"

"Is the designated name of the arising four bases of mindfulness the great bodhisattva?"

"No, I don't think so, World-Honored One!"

"Is the designated name of the arising four correct endeavors, and so forth, as well as the arising noble eightfold path the great bodhisattva?"

"No, I don't think so, World-Honored One!"

"Is the designated name of the extinguishing four bases of mindfulness the great bodhisattva?"

"No, I don't think so, World-Honored One!"

"Is the designated name of the extinguishing four correct endeavors, and so forth, as well as the extinguishing noble eightfold path the great bodhisattva?"

"No, I don't think so, World-Honored One!"

"Is the designated name of the virtuous four bases of mindfulness the great bodhisattva?"

"No, I don't think so, World-Honored One!"

"Is the designated name of the virtuous four correct endeavors, and so forth, as well as the virtuous noble eightfold path the great bodhisattva?"

"No, I don't think so, World-Honored One!"

"Is the designated name of the not virtuous four bases of mindfulness the great bodhisattva?"

"No, I don't think so, World-Honored One!"

"Is the designated name of the not virtuous four correct endeavors, and so forth, as well as the not virtuous noble eightfold path the great bodhisattva?"

"No, I don't think so, World-Honored One!"

"Is the designated name of the guilty four bases of mindfulness the great bodhisattva?"

"No, I don't think so, World-Honored One!"

"Is the designated name of the guilty four correct endeavors, and so forth, as well as the guilty noble eightfold path the great bodhisattva?"

"No, I don't think so, World-Honored One!"

"Is the designated name of the not guilty four bases of mindfulness the great bodhisattva?"

"No, I don't think so, World-Honored One!"

"Is the designated name of the not guilty four correct endeavors, and so forth, as well as the not guilty noble eightfold path the great bodhisattva?"

"No, I don't think so, World-Honored One!"

"Is the designated name of the four bases of mindfulness with vexations the great bodhisattva?"

"No, I don't think so, World-Honored One!"

"Is the designated name of the four correct endeavors, and so forth, as well as the noble eightfold path with vexations the great bodhisattva?"

"No, I don't think so, World-Honored One!"

"Is the designated name of the four bases of mindfulness without vexations the great bodhisattva?"

"No, I don't think so, World-Honored One!"

"Is the designated name of the four correct endeavors, and so forth, as well as the noble eightfold path without vexations the great bodhisattva?"

"No, I don't think so, World-Honored One!"

"Is the designated name of the four bases of mindfulness of the world the great bodhisattva?"

"No, I don't think so, World-Honored One!"

"Is the designated name of the four correct endeavors, and so forth, as well as the noble eightfold path of the world the great bodhisattva?"

"No, I don't think so, World-Honored One!"

Fascicle 20, Chapter 7, Section 10

"Is the designated name of the four bases of mindfulness beyond the world the great bodhisattva?"

"No, I don't think so, World-Honored One!"

"Is the designated name of the four correct endeavors, and so forth, as well as the noble eightfold path beyond the world the great bodhisattva?"

"No, I don't think so, World-Honored One!"

"Is the designated name of the contaminated four bases of mindfulness the great bodhisattva?"

"No, I don't think so, World-Honored One!"

"Is the designated name of the contaminated four correct endeavors, and so forth, as well as the noble eightfold path the great bodhisattva?"

"No, I don't think so, World-Honored One!"

"Is the designated name of the purified four bases of mindfulness the great bodhisattva?"

"No, I don't think so, World-Honored One!"

"Is the designated name of the purified four correct endeavors, and so forth, as well as the purified noble eightfold path the great bodhisattva?"

"No, I don't think so, World-Honored One!"

"Is the designated name of the four bases of mindfulness belonging to birth and death the great bodhisattva?"

"No, I don't think so, World-Honored One!"

"Is the designated name of the four correct endeavors, and so forth, as well as the noble eightfold path belonging to birth and death the great bodhisattva?"

"No, I don't think so, World-Honored One!"

"Is the designated name of the four bases of mindfulness belonging to nirvana the great bodhisattva?"

"No, I don't think so, World-Honored One!"

"Is the designated name of the four correct endeavors, and so forth, as well as the noble eightfold path belonging to nirvana the great bodhisattva?"

"No, I don't think so, World-Honored One!"

"Is the designated name of the inside four bases of mindfulness the great bodhisattva?"

"No, I don't think so, World-Honored One!"

"Is the designated name of the inside four correct endeavors, and so forth, as well as the inside noble eightfold path the great bodhisattva?"

"No, I don't think so, World-Honored One!"

"Is the designated name of the outside four bases of mindfulness the great bodhisattva?"

"No, I don't think so, World-Honored One!"

"Is the designated name of the outside four correct endeavors, and so forth, as well as the outside noble eightfold path the great bodhisattva?"

"No, I don't think so, World-Honored One!"

"Is the designated name of the in-between four bases of mindfulness the great bodhisattva?"

"No, I don't think so, World-Honored One!"

"Is the designated name of the in-between four correct endeavors, and so forth, as well as the in-between noble eightfold path the great bodhisattva?"

"No, I don't think so, World-Honored One!"

"Is the designated name of the attainable four bases of mindfulness the great bodhisattva?"

"No, I don't think so, World-Honored One!"

"Is the designated name of the attainable four correct endeavors, and so forth, as well as the attainable noble eightfold path the great bodhisattva?"

"No, I don't think so, World-Honored One!"

"Is the designated name of the unattainable four bases of mindfulness the great bodhisattva?"

"No, I don't think so, World-Honored One!"

"Is the designated name of the unattainable four correct endeavors, and so forth, as well as the unattainable noble eightfold path the great bodhisattva?"

"No, I don't think so, World-Honored One!"

"Furthermore, Well Appearing One, what do you mean by great bodhisattva? Is the designated name of the noble truth of suffering the great bodhisattva?"

"No, I don't think so, World-Honored One!"
"Is the designated name of the noble truths of the cause of suffering, the cessation of suffering, and the path for the cessation of suffering the great bodhisattva?"
"No, I don't think so, World-Honored One!"
"Is the designated name of the permanent noble truth of suffering the great bodhisattva?"
"No, I don't think so, World-Honored One!"
"Is the designated name of the permanent noble truths of the cause of suffering, the cessation of suffering, and the path for the cessation of suffering the great bodhisattva?"
"No, I don't think so, World-Honored One!"
"Is the designated name of the impermanent noble truth of suffering the great bodhisattva?"
"No, I don't think so, World-Honored One!"
"Is the designated name of the impermanent noble truths of the cause of suffering, the cessation of suffering, and the path for the cessation of suffering the great bodhisattva?"
"No, I don't think so, World-Honored One!"
"Is the designated name of the pleasant noble truth of suffering the great bodhisattva?"
"No, I don't think so, World-Honored One!"
"Is the designated name of the pleasant noble truths of the cause of suffering, the cessation of suffering, and the path for the cessation of suffering the great bodhisattva?"
"No, I don't think so, World-Honored One!"
"Is the designated name of the painful noble truth of suffering the great bodhisattva?"
"No, I don't think so, World-Honored One!"
"Is the designated name of the painful noble truths of the cause of suffering, the cessation of suffering, and the path for the cessation of suffering the great bodhisattva?"
"No, I don't think so, World-Honored One!"
"Is the designated name of the noble truth of suffering with selfness the great bodhisattva?"
"No, I don't think so, World-Honored One!"
"Is the designated name of the noble truths of the cause of suf-

fering, the cessation of suffering, and the path for the cessation of suffering with selfness the great bodhisattva?"

"No, I don't think so, World-Honored One!"

"Is the designated name of the noble truth of suffering without selfness the great bodhisattva?"

"No, I don't think so, World-Honored One!"

"Is the designated name of the noble truths of the cause of suffering, the cessation of suffering, and the path for the cessation of suffering without selfness the great bodhisattva?"

"No, I don't think so, World-Honored One!"

"Is the designated name of the pure noble truth of suffering the great bodhisattva?"

"No, I don't think so, World-Honored One!"

"Is the designated name of the pure noble truths of the cause of suffering, the cessation of suffering, and the path for the cessation of suffering the great bodhisattva?"

"No, I don't think so, World-Honored One!"

"Is the designated name of the impure noble truth of suffering the great bodhisattva?"

"No, I don't think so, World-Honored One!"

"Is the designated name of the impure noble truths of the cause of suffering, the cessation of suffering, and the path for the cessation of suffering the great bodhisattva?"

"No, I don't think so, World-Honored One!"

"Is the designated name of the empty noble truth of suffering the great bodhisattva?"

"No, I don't think so, World-Honored One!"

"Is the designated name of the empty noble truths of the cause of suffering, the cessation of suffering, and the path for the cessation of suffering the great bodhisattva?"

"No, I don't think so, World-Honored One!"

"Is the designated name of the not empty noble truth of suffering the great bodhisattva?"

"No, I don't think so, World-Honored One!"

"Is the designated name of the not empty noble truths of the cause of suffering, the cessation of suffering, and the path for the

cessation of suffering the great bodhisattva?"
"No, I don't think so, World-Honored One!"
"Is the designated name of the noble truth of suffering with form the great bodhisattva?"
"No, I don't think so, World-Honored One!"
"Is the designated name of the noble truths of the cause of suffering, the cessation of suffering, and the path for the cessation of suffering with form the great bodhisattva?"
"No, I don't think so, World-Honored One!"
"Is the designated name of the noble truth of suffering without form the great bodhisattva?"
"No, I don't think so, World-Honored One!"
"Is the designated name of the noble truths of the cause of suffering, the cessation of suffering, and the path for the cessation of suffering without form the great bodhisattva?"
"No, I don't think so, World-Honored One!"
"Is the designated name of the noble truth of suffering with aspiration the great bodhisattva?"
"No, I don't think so, World-Honored One!"
"Is the designated name of the noble truths of the cause of suffering, the cessation of suffering, and the path for the cessation of suffering with aspiration the great bodhisattva?"
"No, I don't think so, World-Honored One!"
"Is the designated name of the noble truth of suffering without aspiration the great bodhisattva?"
"No, I don't think so, World-Honored One!"
"Is the designated name of the noble truths of the cause of suffering, the cessation of suffering, and the path for the cessation of suffering without aspiration the great bodhisattva?"
"No, I don't think so, World-Honored One!"
"Is the designated name of the tranquil noble truth of suffering the great bodhisattva?"
"No, I don't think so, World-Honored One!"
"Is the designated name of the tranquil noble truths of the cause of suffering, the cessation of suffering, and the path for the cessation of suffering the great bodhisattva?"

"No, I don't think so, World-Honored One!"
"Is the designated name of the not tranquil noble truth of suffering the great bodhisattva?"
"No, I don't think so, World-Honored One!"
"Is the designated name of the not tranquil noble truths of the cause of suffering, the cessation of suffering, and the path for the cessation of suffering the great bodhisattva?"
"No, I don't think so, World-Honored One!"
"Is the designated name of the faraway noble truth of suffering the great bodhisattva?"
"No, I don't think so, World-Honored One!"
"Is the designated name of the faraway noble truths of the cause of suffering, the cessation of suffering, and the path for the cessation of suffering the great bodhisattva?"
"No, I don't think so, World-Honored One!"
"Is the designated name of the not faraway noble truth of suffering the great bodhisattva?"
"No, I don't think so, World-Honored One!"
"Is the designated name of the not faraway noble truths of the cause of suffering, the cessation of suffering, and the path for the cessation of suffering the great bodhisattva?"
"No, I don't think so, World-Honored One!"
"Is the designated name of the conditioned noble truth of suffering the great bodhisattva?"
"No, I don't think so, World-Honored One!"
"Is the designated name of the conditioned noble truths of the cause of suffering, the cessation of suffering, and the path for the cessation of suffering the great bodhisattva?"
"No, I don't think so, World-Honored One!"
"Is the designated name of the unconditioned noble truth of suffering the great bodhisattva?"
"No, I don't think so, World-Honored One!"
"Is the designated name of the unconditioned noble truths of the cause of suffering, the cessation of suffering, and the path for the cessation of suffering the great bodhisattva?"
"No, I don't think so, World-Honored One!"

Fascicle 20, Chapter 7, Section 10

"Is the designated name of the flawed noble truth of suffering the great bodhisattva?"

"No, I don't think so, World-Honored One!"

"Is the designated name of the flawed noble truths of the cause of suffering, the cessation of suffering, and the path for the cessation of suffering the great bodhisattva?"

"No, I don't think so, World-Honored One!"

"Is the designated name of the flawless noble truth of suffering the great bodhisattva?"

"No, I don't think so, World-Honored One!"

"Is the designated name of the flawless noble truths of the cause of suffering, the cessation of suffering, and the path for the cessation of suffering the great bodhisattva?"

"No, I don't think so, World-Honored One!"

"Is the designated name of the arising noble truth of suffering the great bodhisattva?"

"No, I don't think so, World-Honored One!"

"Is the designated name of the arising noble truths of the cause of suffering, the cessation of suffering, and the path for the cessation of suffering the great bodhisattva?"

"No, I don't think so, World-Honored One!"

"Is the designated name of the extinguishing noble truth of suffering the great bodhisattva?"

"No, I don't think so, World-Honored One!"

"Is the designated name of the extinguishing noble truths of the cause of suffering, the cessation of suffering, and the path for the cessation of suffering the great bodhisattva?"

"No, I don't think so, World-Honored One!"

"Is the designated name of the virtuous noble truth of suffering the great bodhisattva?"

"No, I don't think so, World-Honored One!"

"Is the designated name of the virtuous noble truths of the cause of suffering, the cessation of suffering, and the path for the cessation of suffering the great bodhisattva?"

"No, I don't think so, World-Honored One!"

"Is the designated name of the not virtuous noble truth of suffering the great bodhisattva?"

"No, I don't think so, World-Honored One!"

"Is the designated name of the not virtuous noble truths of the cause of suffering, the cessation of suffering, and the path for the cessation of suffering the great bodhisattva?"

"No, I don't think so, World-Honored One!"

"Is the designated name of the guilty noble truth of suffering the great bodhisattva?"

"No, I don't think so, World-Honored One!"

"Is the designated name of the guilty noble truths of the cause of suffering, the cessation of suffering, and the path for the cessation of suffering the great bodhisattva?"

"No, I don't think so, World-Honored One!"

"Is the designated name of the not guilty noble truth of suffering the great bodhisattva?"

"No, I don't think so, World-Honored One!"

"Is the designated name of the not guilty noble truths of the cause of suffering, the cessation of suffering, and the path for the cessation of suffering the great bodhisattva?"

"No, I don't think so, World-Honored One!"

"Is the designated name of the noble truth of suffering with vexations the great bodhisattva?"

"No, I don't think so, World-Honored One!"

"Is the designated name of the noble truths of the cause of suffering, the cessation of suffering, and the path for the cessation of suffering with vexations the great bodhisattva?"

"No, I don't think so, World-Honored One!"

"Is the designated name of the noble truth of suffering without vexations the great bodhisattva?"

"No, I don't think so, World-Honored One!"

"Is the designated name of the noble truths of the cause of suffering, the cessation of suffering, and the path for the cessation of suffering without vexations the great bodhisattva?"

"No, I don't think so, World-Honored One!"

"Is the designated name of the worldly noble truth of suffering the great bodhisattva?"

Fascicle 20, Chapter 7, Section 10

"No, I don't think so, World-Honored One!"
"Is the designated name of the worldly noble truths of the cause of suffering, the cessation of suffering, and the path for the cessation of suffering the great bodhisattva?"
"No, I don't think so, World-Honored One!"
"Is the designated name of the noble truth of suffering beyond the world the great bodhisattva?"
"No, I don't think so, World-Honored One!"
"Is the designated name of the noble truths of the cause of suffering, the cessation of suffering, and the path for the cessation of suffering beyond the world the great bodhisattva?"
"No, I don't think so, World-Honored One!"
"Is the designated name of the contaminated noble truth of suffering the great bodhisattva?"
"No, I don't think so, World-Honored One!"
"Is the designated name of the contaminated noble truths of the cause of suffering, the cessation of suffering, and the path for the cessation of suffering the great bodhisattva?"
"No, I don't think so, World-Honored One!"
"Is the designated name of the purified noble truth of suffering the great bodhisattva?"
"No, I don't think so, World-Honored One!"
"Is the designated name of the purified noble truths of the cause of suffering, the cessation of suffering, and the path for the cessation of suffering the great bodhisattva?"
"No, I don't think so, World-Honored One!"
"Is the designated name of the noble truth of suffering belonging to birth and death the great bodhisattva?"
"No, I don't think so, World-Honored One!"
"Is the designated name of the noble truths of the cause of suffering, the cessation of suffering, and the path for the cessation of suffering belonging to birth and death the great bodhisattva?"
"No, I don't think so, World-Honored One!"
"Is the designated name of the noble truth of suffering belonging to nirvana the great bodhisattva?"
"No, I don't think so, World-Honored One!"

"Is the designated name of the noble truths of the cause of suffering, the cessation of suffering, and the path for the cessation of suffering belonging to nirvana the great bodhisattva?"

"No, I don't think so, World-Honored One!"

"Is the designated name of the inside noble truth of suffering the great bodhisattva?"

"No, I don't think so, World-Honored One!"

"Is the designated name of the inside noble truths of the cause of suffering, the cessation of suffering, and the path for the cessation of suffering the great bodhisattva?"

"No, I don't think so, World-Honored One!"

"Is the designated name of the outside noble truth of suffering the great bodhisattva?"

"No, I don't think so, World-Honored One!"

"Is the designated name of the outside noble truths of the cause of suffering, the cessation of suffering, and the path for the cessation of suffering the great bodhisattva?"

"No, I don't think so, World-Honored One!"

"Is the designated name of the in-between noble truth of suffering the great bodhisattva?"

"No, I don't think so, World-Honored One!"

"Is the designated name of the in-between noble truths of the cause of suffering, the cessation of suffering, and the path for the cessation of suffering the great bodhisattva?"

"No, I don't think so, World-Honored One!"

"Is the designated name of the attainable noble truth of suffering the great bodhisattva?"

"No, I don't think so, World-Honored One!"

"Is the designated name of the attainable noble truths of the cause of suffering, the cessation of suffering, and the path for the cessation of suffering the great bodhisattva?"

"No, I don't think so, World-Honored One!"

"Is the designated name of the unattainable noble truth of suffering the great bodhisattva?"

"No, I don't think so, World-Honored One!"

"Is the designated name of the unattainable noble truths of the cause of suffering, the cessation of suffering, and the path for the cessation of suffering the great bodhisattva?"

"No, I don't think so, World-Honored One!"

"Furthermore, Well Appearing One, what do you mean by great bodhisattva? Is the designated name of the four meditations the great bodhisattva?"

"No, I don't think so, World-Honored One!"

"Is the designated name of the four immeasurable minds or four formless concentrations the great bodhisattva?"

"No, I don't think so, World-Honored One!"

"Is the designated name of the permanent four meditations the great bodhisattva?"

"No, I don't think so, World-Honored One!"

"Is the designated name of the permanent four immeasurable minds or four formless concentrations the great bodhisattva?"

"No, I don't think so, World-Honored One!"

"Is the designated name of the impermanent four meditations the great bodhisattva?"

"No, I don't think so, World-Honored One!"

"Is the designated name of the impermanent four immeasurable minds or four formless concentrations the great bodhisattva?"

"No, I don't think so, World-Honored One!"

"Is the designated name of the pleasant four meditations the great bodhisattva?"

"No, I don't think so, World-Honored One!"

"Is the designated name of the pleasant four immeasurable minds or four formless concentrations the great bodhisattva?"

"No, I don't think so, World-Honored One!"

"Is the designated name of the painful four meditations the great bodhisattva?"

"No, I don't think so, World-Honored One!"

"Is the designated name of the painful four immeasurable minds or four formless concentrations the great bodhisattva?"

"No, I don't think so, World-Honored One!"

"Is the designated name of the four meditations with selfness the great bodhisattva?"

"No, I don't think so, World-Honored One!"
"Is the designated name of the four immeasurable minds or four formless concentrations with selfness the great bodhisattva?"
"No, I don't think so, World-Honored One!"
"Is the designated name of the four meditations without selfness the great bodhisattva?"
"No, I don't think so, World-Honored One!"
"Is the designated name of the four immeasurable minds or four formless concentrations without selfness the great bodhisattva?"
"No, I don't think so, World-Honored One!"
"Is the designated name of the pure four meditations the great bodhisattva?"
"No, I don't think so, World-Honored One!"
"Is the designated name of the pure four immeasurable minds or the pure four formless concentrations the great bodhisattva?"
"No, I don't think so, World-Honored One!"
"Is the designated name of the impure four meditations the great bodhisattva?"
"No, I don't think so, World-Honored One!"
"Is the designated name of the impure four immeasurable minds or the impure four formless concentrations the great bodhisattva?"
"No, I don't think so, World-Honored One!"
"Is the designated name of the empty four meditations the great bodhisattva?"
"No, I don't think so, World-Honored One!"
"Is the designated name of the empty four immeasurable minds or the empty four formless concentrations the great bodhisattva?"
"No, I don't think so, World-Honored One!"
"Is the designated name of the not empty four meditations the great bodhisattva?"
"No, I don't think so, World-Honored One!"
"Is the designated name of the not empty four immeasurable minds or four formless concentrations the great bodhisattva?"
"No, I don't think so, World-Honored One!"
"Is the designated name of the four meditations with form the great bodhisattva?"
"No, I don't think so, World-Honored One!"

Fascicle 20, Chapter 7, Section 10

"Is the designated name of the four immeasurable minds or the four formless concentrations with form the great bodhisattva?"

"No, I don't think so, World-Honored One!"

"Is the designated name of the four meditations without form the great bodhisattva?"

"No, I don't think so, World-Honored One!"

"Is the designated name of the four immeasurable minds or the four formless concentrations without form the great bodhisattva?"

"No, I don't think so, World-Honored One!"

"Is the designated name of the four meditations with aspiration the great bodhisattva?"

"No, I don't think so, World-Honored One!"

"Is the designated name of the four immeasurable minds or the four formless concentrations with aspiration the great bodhisattva?"

"No, I don't think so, World-Honored One!"

"Is the designated name of the four meditations without aspiration the great bodhisattva?"

"No, I don't think so, World-Honored One!"

"Is the designated name of the four immeasurable minds or the four formless concentrations without aspiration the great bodhisattva?"

"No, I don't think so, World-Honored One!"

"Is the designated name of the tranquil four meditations the great bodhisattva?"

"No, I don't think so, World-Honored One!"

"Is the designated name of the tranquil four immeasurable minds or four formless concentrations the great bodhisattva?"

"No, I don't think so, World-Honored One!"

"Is the designated name of the not tranquil four meditations the great bodhisattva?"

"No, I don't think so, World-Honored One!"

"Is the designated name of the not tranquil four immeasurable minds or four formless concentrations the great bodhisattva?"

"No, I don't think so, World-Honored One!"

"Is the designated name of the faraway four meditations the great bodhisattva?"

"No, I don't think so, World-Honored One!"

"Is the designated name of the faraway four immeasurable minds or four formless concentrations the great bodhisattva?"

"No, I don't think so, World-Honored One!"

"Is the designated name of the not faraway four meditations the great bodhisattva?"

"No, I don't think so, World-Honored One!"

"Is the designated name of the not faraway four immeasurable minds or four formless concentrations the great bodhisattva?"

"No, I don't think so, World-Honored One!"

"Is the designated name of the conditioned four meditations the great bodhisattva?"

"No, I don't think so, World-Honored One!"

"Is the designated name of the conditioned four immeasurable minds or four formless concentrations the great bodhisattva?"

"No, I don't think so, World-Honored One!"

"Is the designated name of the unconditioned four meditations the great bodhisattva?"

"No, I don't think so, World-Honored One!"

"Is the designated name of the unconditioned four immeasurable minds or four formless concentrations the great bodhisattva?"

"No, I don't think so, World-Honored One!"

"Is the designated name of the flawed four meditations the great bodhisattva?"

"No, I don't think so, World-Honored One!"

"Is the designated name of the flawed four immeasurable minds or four formless concentrations the great bodhisattva?"

"No, I don't think so, World-Honored One!"

"Is the designated name of the flawless four meditations the great bodhisattva?"

"No, I don't think so, World-Honored One!"

"Is the designated name of the flawless four immeasurable minds or four formless concentrations the great bodhisattva?"

"No, I don't think so, World-Honored One!"

"Is the designated name of the arising four meditations the great bodhisattva?"

"No, I don't think so, World-Honored One!"

"Is the designated name of the arising four immeasurable minds or four formless concentrations the great bodhisattva?"

"No, I don't think so, World-Honored One!"

"Is the designated name of the extinguishing four meditations the great bodhisattva?"

"No, I don't think so, World-Honored One!"

"Is the designated name of the extinguishing four immeasurable minds or four formless concentrations the great bodhisattva?"

"No, I don't think so, World-Honored One!"

"Is the designated name of the virtuous four meditations the great bodhisattva?"

"No, I don't think so, World-Honored One!"

"Is the designated name of the virtuous four immeasurable minds or four formless concentrations the great bodhisattva?"

"No, I don't think so, World-Honored One!"

"Is the designated name of the not virtuous four meditations the great bodhisattva?"

"No, I don't think so, World-Honored One!"

"Is the designated name of the not virtuous four immeasurable minds or four formless concentrations the great bodhisattva?"

"No, I don't think so, World-Honored One!"

"Is the designated name of the guilty four meditations the great bodhisattva?"

"No, I don't think so, World-Honored One!"

"Is the designated name of the guilty four immeasurable minds or four formless concentrations the great bodhisattva?"

"No, I don't think so, World-Honored One!"

"Is the designated name of the not guilty four meditations the great bodhisattva?"

"No, I don't think so, World-Honored One!"

"Is the designated name of the not guilty four immeasurable minds or four formless concentrations the great bodhisattva?"

"No, I don't think so, World-Honored One!"

"Is the designated name of the four meditations with vexations the great bodhisattva?"

"No, I don't think so, World-Honored One!"

"Is the designated name of the four immeasurable minds or four formless concentrations with vexations the great bodhisattva?"

"No, I don't think so, World-Honored One!"

"Is the designated name of the four meditations without vexations the great bodhisattva?"

"No, I don't think so, World-Honored One!"

"Is the designated name of the four immeasurable minds or four formless concentrations without vexations the great bodhisattva?"

"No, I don't think so, World-Honored One!"

"Is the designated name of the worldly four meditations the great bodhisattva?"

"No, I don't think so, World-Honored One!"

"Is the designated name of the worldly four immeasurable minds or worldly four formless concentrations the great bodhisattva?"

"No, I don't think so, World-Honored One!"

"Is the designated name of the four meditations beyond the world the great bodhisattva?"

"No, I don't think so, World-Honored One!"

"Is the designated name of the four immeasurable minds or four formless concentrations beyond the world the great bodhisattva?"

"No, I don't think so, World-Honored One!"

"Is the designated name of the contaminated four meditations the great bodhisattva?"

"No, I don't think so, World-Honored One!"

"Is the designated name of the contaminated four immeasurable minds or four formless concentrations the great bodhisattva?"

"No, I don't think so, World-Honored One!"

"Is the designated name of the purified four meditations the great bodhisattva?"

"No, I don't think so, World-Honored One!"

"Is the designated name of the purified four immeasurable minds or four formless concentrations the great bodhisattva?"

"No, I don't think so, World-Honored One!"

"Is the designated name of the four meditations belonging to birth and death the great bodhisattva?"

"No, I don't think so, World-Honored One!"

"Is the designated name of the four immeasurable minds or four formless concentrations belonging to birth and death the great bodhisattva?"

"No, I don't think so, World-Honored One!"

"Is the designated name of the four meditations belonging to nirvana the great bodhisattva?"

"No, I don't think so, World-Honored One!"

"Is the designated name of the four immeasurable minds or four formless concentrations belonging to nirvana the great bodhisattva?"

"No, I don't think so, World-Honored One!"

"Is the designated name of the inside four meditations the great bodhisattva?"

"No, I don't think so, World-Honored One!"

"Is the designated name of the inside four immeasurable minds or four formless concentrations the great bodhisattva?"

"No, I don't think so, World-Honored One!"

"Is the designated name of the outside four meditations the great bodhisattva?"

"No, I don't think so, World-Honored One!"

"Is the designated name of the outside four immeasurable minds or four formless concentrations the great bodhisattva?"

"No, I don't think so, World-Honored One!"

"Is the designated name of the in-between four meditations the great bodhisattva?"

"No, I don't think so, World-Honored One!"

"Is the designated name of the in-between four immeasurable minds or four formless concentrations the great bodhisattva?"

"No, I don't think so, World-Honored One!"

"Is the designated name of the attainable four meditations the great bodhisattva?"

"No, I don't think so, World-Honored One!"

"Is the designated name of the attainable four immeasurable minds or four formless concentrations the great bodhisattva?"

"No, I don't think so, World-Honored One!"

"Is the designated name of the unattainable four meditations the great bodhisattva?"

"No, I don't think so, World-Honored One!"

"Is the designated name of the unattainable four immeasurable minds or four formless concentrations the great bodhisattva?"

"No, I don't think so, World-Honored One!"

Glossary of Terms

Ananda: Ananda, meaning "joyfully celebrating one," was one of the ten principal disciples of Sakyamuni Buddha. As Buddha's younger cousin, he served as his attendant for more than twenty years until Buddha entered into nirvana. He was famous for being able to remember what he heard from the Buddha. Because the Buddha himself did not write down what he said, Ananda served to recite the sutras from memory in the first convention for compiling the Buddhist scriptures, held soon after Buddha's passing away in the Vaibhara cave in Magadha, India, and presided over by Mahakasyapa. As the second patriarch in the Chan lineage succeeding Mahakasyapa, Ananda survived the Buddha by twenty to twenty-five years.

anuttara-samyak-sambodhi: The unsurpassed, perfect, and universal bodhi; the perfect and universal wisdom for enlightenment attained by the Thus-Comers only, unattainable by voice-hearers, self-enlightened ones, bodhisattvas, or ordinary sentient beings. The ultimate goal a Buddhist practitioner aspires to achieve.

aranya: A quiet and distant place, usually in a forest, where one meditates and practices ascetic cultivations.

arhat: As the highest stage of voice-hearing cultivation, arhat refers to the one worthy of offerings, the one who has eliminated all vexations; removed attachment to desires, form, and formlessness; and has been liberated from the bondage of birth and death.

arrogance: Various kinds of arrogance are mentioned by the Buddha in the sutras:
1. Arrogance of overstating one's strength
2. Arrogance of highly exaggerating one's strength
3. Arrogance caused by an attachment to selfness
4. Arrogance of overstating one's achievement in cultivation
5. Not being humble as one should be
6. Claiming that one is morally good although one is not

Barely Tolerable World: The world in which we live is difficult and unpleasant. What one can do is accept its imperfection and learn to adjust to or change and improve it with great patience and skillfulness. On the other hand, this is where the bodhisattvas are able to learn the six paramitas and other Buddha dharma in order to become more mature and bring benefits to all sentient beings.

Bhadrakalpa, the Kalpa of the Sages: The present eon is named the Kalpa of the Sages and is when many Buddhas and bodhisattvas appear. The past eon is the Kalpa of Dignity, while the future one is the Kalpa of Stellar.

Bhagavat: One of the ten names of the Buddha, meaning that the Buddha is the most honored and respected one in the world, the World-Honored One, because of his unsurpassed merits, virtues, loving-kindness, compassion, knowledge, wisdom, and powers.

bhiksu: The Buddhist monk.

bhiksuni: The Buddhist nun.

bliss-inviting practice of giving: Virtues and merits and other happy effects caused by practicing giving to ones in need or making offerings to revered ones.

bliss-inviting practice of observing precepts: Virtues and merits and other happy effects caused by observing pure precepts.

bliss-inviting cultivation: Virtues and merits and other happy effects caused by practicing meditation.

bodhi: *Bodhi* means wisdom, but not exactly as the word "wisdom" is commonly understood. The wisdom for the voice-hearers is the voice-hearing bodhi; the wisdom for the self-enlightened ones is the self-enlightenment bodhi. The subtlest and most exquisite knowledge and wisdom that the Thus-Comers realize is the great bodhi, the unsurpassed, perfect, and universal bodhi that the great bodhisattvas aspire to.

bodhisattva, great bodhisattva: The bodhisattvas pursue the unsurpassed, perfect, and universal bodhi to bring benefits, peace, and happiness to all sentient beings. Their minds are broad, their aspirations are widespread, and their loving-kindness and compassion for all sentient beings is immeasurable, so they are also named *great bodhisattvas*. While the voice-hearers and self-enlightened ones seek self-enlightenment and self-liberation, the bodhisattvas pursue the unsurpassed great bodhi in order to liberate all sentient beings. The bodhisattva actions are indispensable for one to become a Buddha.

bodhisattva actions: The actions that great bodhisattvas practice to attain the unsurpassed, perfect, and universal bodhi; the actions not shared by the voice-hearers and the self-enlightened ones. The bodhisattva path learners should practice the bodhisattva actions in correspondence with the emptiness of all dharmas.

bodhi tree: Sakyamuni Buddha attained the unsurpassed, perfect, and universal enlightenment under the bodhi tree. The term is therefore used as a symbol of attaining enlightenment with perfect knowledge, wisdom, and liberation.

Brahma: One of the lords of the heavens in the realm of form in Buddhist cosmology.

Brahman: The highest of the four castes in ancient India, consisting of priests who were responsible for religious rituals and scriptures interpretation. Also used as a general term for Hindu priests.

Buddha: The fully enlightened one who has achieved perfection in knowledge, wisdom, and actions and possesses exceptional virtues, abilities, and powers not shared by the voice-hearers, self-enlightened ones, and the rest of sentient beings. The most recent Buddha is Sakyamuni, who was born in India about 2,500 years ago. The Buddha who will appear in the upcoming kalpa is Maitreya Buddha.

To become a Buddha signifies the complete actualization of one's Buddha nature, which is said to be inherent in every sentient being. One needs to fulfill perfectly all learning and cultivation in order to fulfill Buddhahood. There are countless Buddhas in the past, future, and present. The bodhisattva path is necessary for one to become a Buddha; that is a process of combining self-education and educating others expediently and skillfully. The Buddha is awakened to the meaning of the reality and knows the dharmas thoroughly as they really are. He is awakened to the particular characteristics, common characteristics, form, and formlessness of all dharmas in the three phases of time. The Buddha is able to enlighten all sentient beings so they will stay away from the suffering caused by upside-down karmas. Please refer to fascicle 365.

Buddha eye: Please see *five eyes*.

Buddha's ten abilities: According to *The Great Prajna Paramita Sutra* (fascicles 53, 415, and 469), the Buddha's ten abilities are:

1. The ability to know the laws of cause and effect, and so forth, and to tell right from wrong.
2. The ability to know about the karmic causes and effects of sentient beings in the past, future, and present as they really are.
3. The ability to know about the characteristics of numberless realms of sentient beings as they really are.
4. The ability to know the definitive beliefs and understandings of all sentient beings as they really are.
5. The ability to know the strengths and weaknesses of all sentient beings as they really are.
6. The ability to know the characteristics of the five universal functions concomitant at all times with perceptive activities of the sentient beings as they really are.
7. The ability to know the samadhi and the samapatti of meditations and liberations that are either impure or pure of the sentient beings as they really are.
8. The ability to know previous lives of the sentient beings as they really are.
9. The ability to know the birth and death of sentient beings as they really are.
10. The ability to know that one's flaws and defilements have been completely removed.

Candala: One of the lowest social classes in the ancient Indian caste system; they work as prison guards, butchers, fishers, and hunters. It also refers to violent or rude people.

cause and condition: The Buddha discovered that all dharmas (existent beings) of the world arise because of the combination of causes and conditions; nothing arises alone. The human world is a complicated articulation of causes and conditions and thus is very difficult to understand; only the Buddhas and the very highly developed bodhisattvas can really know the origins and the interactive effects of causes and conditions in each case as well as in general.

concentration of extinction: The state of concentration when all conscious activities cease as one reaches the stage of the Buddha and arhat; the highest state of concentration in which tranquility and nirvana without remainder prevail, and ego, feeling, and perception perish. The concentration of nonthinking and not nonthinking is also a stage in which all conscious activities cease, but ego is still active. It is only in this highest stage of concentration that ego no longer exists.

conditioned dharma: These are the dharmas that are dependently originated, in change, and caused by the integration or disintegration of causes and conditions. The conditioned dharmas definitely will go through the process of arising, duration, decay, and extinction.

consecutive sequence of thoughts: The uninterrupted connection between prior and subsequent thoughts, with the former ones always serving, all or partially, as the incessant causes of the latter thoughts

contemplation of impure body: See also *four bases of mindfulness*. The mindfulness of the impurity of the body is one of the four bases of mindfulness. As the great bodhisattvas cultivate prajna paramita, they should adopt nonattainment as expedience to investigate their own bodies to know and be mindful of the fact that the whole body, from head to toe, is filled with various impure things, all wrapped in a thin layer of skin. These include hairs and furs, fingernails and teeth, skin, blood and flesh, tendons and veins, bones and marrow, and so forth. Please refer to fascicle 53.

continent of Aparagodaniya: One of the four continents, according to the Buddhist cosmology in ancient India, located in the west of Mount Sumeru. It is surrounded by seven golden mountains and Mahacakravala, the great circular iron enclosure. This is a land with many cows, sheep, jade, and pearls; the inhabitants there trade these products for living.

Glossary of Terms 533

continent of Purvavideha: One of the four continents located in the east of Mount Sumeru, standing in the salty ocean between the seven golden mountains and Mahacakravala, the great circular iron enclosure; a vast and beautiful land.

continent of Jambudvipa: One of the four continents located in the south of Mount Sumeru, a land with many jambu trees and jambu gold. The continent where human beings live; they are smart and with good memory; they work hard and learn fast; and they are privileged to be able to hear, learn, and practice the Buddha dharma because the Buddha is present there.

continent of Uttarakuru: One of the four continents located in the north of Mount Sumeru and surrounded by seven golden mountains and the great circular iron enclosure. It is a bright, peaceful, and tranquil land, in which the sentient beings enjoy a happy life without bondage. Because the Buddha does not appear in that land, the sentient beings there are not privileged to learn the Buddhist dharma. Their lifespan is one thousand years. There are no fights, vicious conduct, or theft in that land; it is a place where hell does not exist either. The sentient beings in that land will be reborn in the Heaven of Thirty-Three Smaller Heavens or the Heaven of Enjoying Other-Made Changes.

correct path of nonarising: For the voice-hearing practitioners, this is the stage of stream-entry aspiration; for the bodhisattva practitioners, the stage of ecstasy.

Because of practicing giving, observing precepts, and cultivating concentration, wisdom, liberation, and the knowledge and views of liberation, the great bodhisattvas will be able to transcend the stages of the voice-hearer and self-enlightened one and approach the bodhisattva path of nonarising. Once they enter onto this path, they will not regress from the pursuit of the great bodhi; rather, they will be able to dignify and purify the Buddha lands and assist the sentient beings to grow and mature. They will realize the unsurpassed, perfect, and universal bodhi step by step, and turn the dharma wheel (fascicle 372).

dependent origination: One of the natural laws that the Buddha discovered is that all existent beings arise owing to the combination of causes and conditions and extinguish when causes and conditions disintegrate. The world and all existent beings are not created, according to Buddhist teachings, nor are they permanent. They are always in change because causes and conditions and their relations change at all times.

dharani: A term widely used in Buddhism as a summary of essential Buddhist teachings; it is easy for Buddhist practitioners to repeat, memorize, uphold, and master when they learn, teach, and practice. There are several kinds of dharani mentioned in the sutra:
1. Dharani for hearing Buddha dharma and upholding it without losing it.
2. Dharani for discerning right from wrong.
3. Voice dharani.
4. Letter dharani.
5. Spell dharani for removing evil spirits or calamities.
6. Forbearance dharani for realizing the reality of the dharmas.

dharani gate of letters and words: The gate to understand the various gates of alphabetical letters based on the nature of the equality of letters, languages, and the meanings of the statements. In fascicle 53 of *The Great Prajna Paramita Sutra*, the Buddha said to his disciple Well Appearing One, "Well Appearing One, in practicing prajna paramita, the great bodhisattvas adopt nonattainment as expedience to enter the letter gate of *a* and realize that all beings are intrinsically without arising; enter the letter gate of *ra* and realize that all beings are apart from dirty dusts; enter the letter gate of *pa* and realize the ultimate meaning of all beings; enter the letter gate of *ca* and realize that all beings are without birth and death; enter the letter gate of *na* and realize that all beings stay far away from terminology without loss and gain..." and so forth.

dharma gates: The ways, approaches, and methods used in practic-

Glossary of Terms 535

ing Buddha's teachings for self-relief and for bringing relief to all sentient beings. The dharma gates provide Buddha practitioners with correct paths to perfect enlightenment. There are numberless dharma gates, according to the Buddha.

dharma: Dharma refers to the reality of all dharmas, the rules and principles of all existent beings of this world, the truth of the worldly phenomena, the way of correct thinking and behavior, and the ultimate meanings of the truths taught by the Buddha.

Dharma also means all kinds of existent beings in the world and their particular phenomena. There are conditioned and unconditioned dharmas, material and immaterial dharmas, visible and invisible dharmas, substantial and unsubstantial dharmas, flawed and flawless dharmas, contaminated and purified dharmas, dharmas in the world and beyond the world, the dharmas belonging to the birth and death, the dharmas belonging to nirvana, and so forth.

dharma beyond the world: Dharmas that transcend worldly experiences and the physical laws of the world; the dharmas that are not conditioned by the law of dependent origination; and the dharmas that avoid the flawed world and become flawless and liberated. The dharmas of birth and death are those in the world, while the dharmas belonging to nirvana are beyond the world. The knowledge that ordinary sentient beings possess is the knowledge of the world; the knowledge owned by the voice-hearers and self-enlightened ones is the knowledge beyond the world; and the knowledge possessed by great bodhisattvas and Thus-Comers is the unsurpassed knowledge beyond the world.

dharma body: To know and see accurately that the dharmas do not arise; realness is unmovable although the dharmas arise; and realness does not arise although it gives birth to all dharmas. Realness is the dharma body.

dharma concentration: See *realness*.

dharma dwelling: See *realness*.

dharma forbearance: To understand and accept the laws of the world, such as cause and effect and dependent origination; grasp the reality and the phenomena of the sensual world.

dharma nature: Pure, changeless, and unequaled equal, it is free from defilements, and originally uncontaminated. It permeates the entire realm of empty space and sentient beings, but remains immeasurable, boundless, and without differentiation and separation. It is neither being with nor apart from the dharmas (fascicle 569).

The unconditioned and the conditioned are two kinds of dharma nature. The unconditioned dharma nature means that all dharmas do not arise or extinguish, stay, or decay; they are neither contaminated nor purified; they do not increase or decrease; they are without form and action; and their self-natures are without natures. The conditioned dharma nature is the innumerable gates of knowledge of the phenomenal existents (fascicle 129).

dharma realm: See *realness*.

dharma of the world: The dharmas regulated and confined by the physical laws of the world; the existent beings that have arising, decay, extinction, changes, flaws, and contaminations. They are the phenomena of the world; they are like illusions, dreams, and so forth, as well as the transformed things and mirages. See *dharma beyond the world*.

diamond-like concentration: The state of concentration that is as solid and firm as a diamond, capable of destroying all kinds of worries and vexations.

different maturation: The effects of karmas appear at different times and in different ways from that of the causes of the karmas.

Glossary of Terms

eight factors for great person awakening: Eight virtues that the Buddha teaches his disciples are: having fewer desires, being easily satisfied, staying away from incorrect ideas and evil conduct, being diligent, dwelling in correct mindfulness, staying in correct concentration, staying with correct wisdom, and staying away from nonsensical arguments.

eight kinds of heavenly beings: The eight kinds of heavenly beings dedicated to the protection of Buddha dharma are: the deities of the heavens (deva), dragons (naga), flying spirits of the dead (yaksa), perfume-eating spirits of music (gandharva), golden-winged birds (garuda), demigods fond of fighting (asura), heavenly singers and dancers who look human but are not human (kiṃnara), and snake spirits (mahoraga).

eight liberations: The eight kinds of liberation attained through the meditations that eliminate the bondages in the realms of desire, form, and formlessness are:
1. Contemplation of the phenomena of inner body.
2. Contemplation of the phenomena of the outer objects.
3. Experiencing pure and superior liberation of the body.
4. Liberation of boundless emptiness, transcending all kinds of differentiation and thinking.
5. Liberation of boundless consciousness, transcending the level of boundless emptiness.
6. Liberation of nothingness, transcending the boundless consciousness.
7. Liberation of nonthinking and not nonthinking, transcending the level of nothingness.
8. Liberation of the extinction of all mental activities, transcending the level of nonthinking and not nonthinking. (Fascicles 46, 53, 380, and 469.)

Fascicle 531 says that to contemplate the inner phenomena is the first liberation for the great bodhisattvas. To contemplate the outer phenomena is the second liberation for the great bodhisattvas. To contemplate and realize definitively the purity of inner body is the third liberation for the great bodhisattvas. To fully dwell in the concentration of boundless emptiness is the fourth liberation for the great bodhisattvas. To fully dwell in the sphere of boundless consciousness is the fifth liberation for the great bodhisattvas. To fully dwell in the sphere of nothingness is the sixth liberation for the great bodhisattvas. To fully dwell in the sphere of nonthinking and not nonthinking is the seventh liberation for the great bodhisattvas. To fully dwell in the concentration of the extinction of thinking and feeling is the eighth liberation for the great bodhisattvas.

eight vexation-overcoming meditations: The meditations based on equanimity, achieved only when the desires and defilements of the three realms are removed. While the eight liberations emphasize the effort of removing defilements, the eight vexation-overcoming meditations, cultivated through the same way as the eight liberations, focus on the practice of equanimity for overcoming one's vexations.

eighteen distinctive features of the Buddha's wisdom and power: The eighteen features are achieved only by the Buddhas; they are not shared by the voice-hearers, self-enlightened ones, bodhisattvas, or other sentient beings. They are:
1. Actions are flawless
2. Speeches are flawless
3. Thoughts are flawless
4. Always treating all beings equally
5. Always staying in concentration
6. Always staying in equanimity
7. Aspirations never diminish
8. Diligence never diminishes
9. Correct mindfulness never diminishes
10. Wisdom never diminishes
11. Liberation never diminishes
12. The knowledge and views of liberation never diminish
13. Always acting in compliance with wisdom
14. Always speaking in compliance with wisdom
15. Always thinking in compliance with wisdom

Glossary of Terms 539

16. Knowing the past without hindrance
17. Knowing the present without hindrance
18. Knowing the future without hindrance
(Fascicles 53, 381, 415, 469, and 531.)

eighteen realms: Six internal spheres, six external spheres, and six consciousness realms make the eighteen realms. These realms comprise all cognitive activities and elements.

The six internal spheres, the perceiving organs, include eye sphere, ear sphere, nose sphere, tongue sphere, body sphere, and conscious sphere.

The six external spheres, the perceived objects, include sight sphere, sound sphere, smell sphere, taste sphere, touch sphere, and mental-image sphere.

The six consciousness realms, the effects of perception, include eye consciousness realm, ear consciousness realm, nose consciousness realm, tongue consciousness realm, body consciousness realm, and conscious consciousness realm.

eighth pudgala: The eighth stage of voice-hearing cultivation; the arhat effect.

eighty distinguishing minor features: While the thirty-two perfect major marks indicate the obvious and observable perfect signs of physical body, voice, appearance, and demeanor, the eighty distinguishing features, on the other hand, indicate the relatively hidden features. The thirty-two marks are possessed by the Buddhas, highly cultivated bodhisattvas, and wheel-turning kings, while the eighty features are possessed by the Buddhas and very highly developed bodhisattvas only. They are not shared by the wheel-turning kings. According to fascicle 381, *The Great Prajna Paramita Sutra*, the eighty characteristics of the Buddha are:
1. His fingernails are long, narrow, smooth, bright, fresh, pure, and clean and are of copper color.
2. His fingers are round, fine, and long, and the joints are concealed.

3. All his limbs are of the same length; no space is left between the fingers.
4. His limbs are round, dexterous, free, soft, and clean; they look bright and colorful as a lotus.
5. The sinews, arteries, and veins are well connected, but concealed.
6. Both his ankles are concealed.
7. When moving straight forward, his gait resembles a dragon king or an elephant king.
8. His gait is neat and solemn, which resembles a lion king.
9. His peaceful and moderate gait is like an ox king.
10. His graceful gait is like a swan king.
11. He looks back by turning his body around, resembling what a dragon king or elephant king does.
12. His limbs and their parts are well proportioned.
13. His joints fit together nicely, like a dragon coiling itself up.
14. His knees are firm and round and well proportioned.
15. His sex organs are pure and complete.
16. His body and limbs are moist, soft, and shining without dust.
17. His looking is solemn and fearless; it never is timid.
18. His body and limbs are thick, with strength, and well proportioned.
19. His body and limbs are steady, heavy, and complete, and never become loose.
20. His appearance is like a king of celestial beings, surrounded by solemn and pure light.
21. His body is surrounded by a light circle that shines at all times.
22. His abdomen is square, upright, soft, complete, and hidden.
23. His navel looks like a clockwise spiral, which is deep, round, pretty, pure, and brilliant.
24. He has a thick navel, neither bulging nor hollow, with a pretty periphery.
25. His skin is free from scabs, freckles, and black spots.
26. His palms are full and soft; his soles are flat.

Glossary of Terms

27. His hands are long, straight, moist, and bright.
28. His lips are as bright and red as a bimba fruit; his upper and lower lips are well proportioned.
29. His face is neither too long nor too short, neither too big nor too small, but is just the right size.
30. His tongue is soft, broad, thin, and long, and it is copper in color.
31. His voice is clear and bright and can spread far away like a roaring elephant king.
32. His wonderful voice has a rhythm that sounds like an echo in a deep valley.
33. His nose is tall, prominent, and thin; his nostrils are concealed.
34. His teeth are square, even, and fresh white.
35. His teeth are round, white, and sharp.
36. His eyes are clear and bright.
37. His eyes are long and broad, resembling the petals of a green lotus.
38. His eyelashes are trim and thick and are not white in color.
39. His eyebrows are slender, thin, and soft, but not white.
40. His eyebrows are beautiful, smooth, and neat, and are dark-red glazed in color.
41. His eyebrows are high, prominent, bright, and moist, shining like a new moon.
42. He has large, slender, and thick ears with perfect lobes.
43. His ears are beautiful, neat, and without any defect.
44. His appearance and demeanor will never disappoint or defile any viewer; they are pure, perfect, and attractive, and always invite respect and admiration.
45. His forehead is broad, full, even, and neat, and the shape is uniquely wonderful.
46. His upper body is perfectly composed; it is incomparably perfect, resembling a lion king.
47. His hair is slender and thick, dark purple in color, but not white.
48. His hair is fragrant, clean, soft, thin, pliable, and coiled.
49. His hair is even and neat, not twisted or messy.

50. His hair is strong, not broken or falling.
51. His hair is bright and smooth, with no dust on it.
52. His body is sturdy and full, even stronger than Narayana, the powerful god.
53. His body is tall and upright.
54. All his organs are pure and perfect.
55. His body and limbs are incomparably superior and powerful.
56. His body and appearance always attract people; they always want to look at him.
57. His face has a perfectly proportioned length and width; it looks as bright, clear, and pure as a full moon.
58. He has a bright, easy, and peaceful face; he always smiles before he speaks; and he looks at people when he speaks.
59. His face is bright, easy, and pleasant; he never knits his brows, and no colors such as green indicating illness or red ever appear on his face.
60. His body and skin are pure and clean, having no bad smell or filthy things.
61. In all his pores there is always a kind of sweet and gratifying fragrance.
62. His face smells of the most pleasant fragrance.
63. His head is rounded and in perfect shape, like a canopy or a madana fruit.
64. His hair is purple, bright, and pure, resembling the beautiful iridescent hair on a peacock's neck.
65. His voice reaches the listeners just loud enough to make each one satisfied.
66. The top of his head has never been overlooked.
67. His finger and toe webs are clear, solemn, and good looking; they are a beautiful copper-red color.
68. He walks with his feet off the ground, and a four-finger wide imprint is left on the ground when he passes.
69. He walks steadily, not staggering, and no guard is needed.
70. His powers and virtues are far-reaching but always keep people from fear and worry and make them happy and carefree.

71. His voice pitch always pleases sentient beings when talking with them.
72. His lectures can always gratify the sentient beings' needs and favors.
73. Although he speaks in one voice, listeners can each gain the understanding they need.
74. His lectures are given in a reasonable order, and whatever he says is always good and based on causes and conditions.
75. He treats all sentient beings equally, admires good conduct and blames bad conduct, but has no love or hatred.
76. He watches and makes a perfect plan before taking actions. His own actions are a good model and purify the sentient beings' minds.
77. Sentient beings do not tire of looking at his good appearance.
78. His skull is solid and complete.
79. His appearance always looks young; he likes to visit the places he used to live previously.
80. His palms, soles, and chest are marked with auspicious and pleasant symbols in a red color.

eleven kinds of knowledge: According to fascicle 53 of *The Great Prajna Paramita Sutra*, there are eleven kinds of perfect knowledge:
1. The knowledge of the dharma: To know accurately various characteristics of the five aggregates by adopting nonattainment as expedience.
2. The knowledge of the categories: To know accurately the impermanence, and so forth, of the aggregates, realms, perception spheres, and various kinds of dependent origination, in general and in particular, by adopting nonattainment as expedience.
3. The knowledge of the secular world: To know accurately the provisional names of all dharmas by adopting nonattainment as expedience.
4. The knowledge of others' minds: To know others' minds, the associated images, their cultivations, what they have

realized and attained, and what they have extinguished by adopting nonattainment as expedience.
5. The knowledge of suffering: To know accurately the suffering of all sentient beings by adopting nonattainment as expedience.
6. The knowledge of the cause of suffering: To know accurately the cause of suffering by adopting nonattainment as expedience.
7. The knowledge of the cessation of suffering: To know accurately that suffering can be and should be ended by adopting nonattainment as expedience.
8. The knowledge of the path for the cessation of suffering: To know accurately the path of ceasing suffering by adopting nonattainment as expedience.
9. The knowledge of vexations termination: To know accurately how greed, anger, and ignorance can be terminated forever by adopting nonattainment as expedience.
10. The knowledge of nonarising: To know accurately the destinies of rebirth so one will not be reborn again by adopting nonattainment as expedience.
11. The knowledge of the reality: The perfect knowledge of everything and the perfect knowledge of all phenomena as possessed by the Buddha.

emptiness looked at from twenty perspectives: These include internal emptiness, external emptiness, internal-external emptiness (emptiness of perceiving process), emptiness of emptiness, emptiness of space, emptiness of ultimate truth, emptiness of conditioned phenomena, emptiness of unconditioned reality, emptiness in the final analysis, emptiness of nontemporality, emptiness of deconstruction, emptiness of changelessness, emptiness of original nature, emptiness of particular characteristics, emptiness of common characteristics, emptiness of all dharmas, emptiness of nonattainment, emptiness of selflessness, emptiness of self-nature, and emptiness of selfless self-nature (fascicle 413).
1. Internal emptiness: The six sense organs (the eye, ear, nose,

Glossary of Terms 545

tongue, body, and the conscious organs) are empty because they are formed conditionally dependent on causes and conditions; they are in change and will finally perish. Their original natures are neither permanent nor in decay.

2. External emptiness: The six perceived objects (sight, sound, smell, taste, touch, and mental-image spheres) are empty because they are also dependently originated; their original natures are neither permanent nor in decay.
3. Internal-external emptiness: The perceiving subjects, perceived objects, and the process of perception are all empty. Because the internal and external factors are empty, the process in which both parties interact is empty too.
4. Emptiness of emptiness: While using the concept of emptiness to replace attachment, the concept itself should not become a new object of attachment. Any concept, including emptiness, is provisional and instrumental. Its original nature is neither permanent nor in decay.
5. Emptiness of space: The nature of any space is empty. Anything can be called a space if it can be filled with something, and that possibility presupposes an empty space.
6. Emptiness of ultimate truth: Both ultimate truth and phenomenal truth are created provisionally as an expedient way for teaching the truth so that ordinary people can understand the complicated, worldly phenomena. This dualism is nonexistent if one's contemplation of all beings is enlightened. The so-called ultimate truth is empty and unattainable. Ultimate meaning is nirvana; it is empty because its original nature is neither permanent nor in decay.
7. Emptiness of conditioned phenomena: Conditioned phenomena indicate the realms of desire, form, and formlessness. They are empty because their original natures are neither permanent nor in decay. Phenomena arise because of the combination of causes and conditions. They will extinguish when the combination falls apart.
8. Emptiness of unconditioned reality: Unconditioned reality means nonarising, nonduration, nondecay, and nonextinction. The unconditioned reality is empty because its

original nature is neither permanent nor in decay. The unconditioned is created as an antithesis of the conditioned. Correct understanding of the existents and their phenomena awakens us the fact that the change of causes and conditions necessitates a change of the phenomena. While conditioned phenomena are impermanent and empty, the so-called unconditioned one, created as its antithesis, is also empty.

9. Emptiness in the final analysis: In ultimate analysis, all dharmas are empty, whether they are material or immaterial, substantial or nominal, worldly or transcendental. "In the final analysis" means that various dharmas are unattainable in an ultimate investigation. This final analysis is empty because its original nature is neither permanent nor in decay.

10. Emptiness of nontemporality: Nontemporality means that nothing in the past, present, and future is attainable, and nothing in coming and going is attainable either. This nontemporality is empty because its original nature is neither permanent nor in decay.

11. Emptiness of deconstruction: Deconstruction means that the possibility of letting go, discarding, and renunciation is attainable. Deconstruction is empty because its original nature is neither permanent nor in decay.

12. Emptiness of changelessness: Changelessness means letting go, discarding, or renunciation are not attainable. Changelessness is empty because its original nature is neither permanent nor in decay.

13. Emptiness of original nature: The original nature refers to the original nature of all dharmas. It connotes that the natures of the conditioned dharma and the natures of the unconditioned dharma are not created by voice-hearers, self-enlightened ones, bodhisattvas, Thus-Comers, or anyone else. The original nature is empty because the original nature is neither permanent nor in decay.

14. Emptiness of particular characteristics: Particular characteristics indicate the characteristics of individual dharma.

For instance, one particular characteristic of matter is its changing substance; one characteristic of feeling is receiving messages; one characteristic of thinking is forming images; one characteristic of action is making; and one characteristic of consciousness is cognition. All conditioned and unconditioned dharmas have their particular characteristics. The particular characteristics are empty because they are particular characteristics. Why? Because their original natures are neither permanent nor in decay.

15. Emptiness of common characteristics: Common characteristics are the characteristics all dharmas share. For instance, suffering is a common characteristic of all flawed dharmas; impermanence is a common characteristic of the conditioned dharmas; and emptiness and selflessness are common characteristics of all dharmas. So there are numberless common characteristics. Common characteristics are empty because they are common characteristics. Why? It is because their original natures are neither permanent nor in decay.

16. Emptiness of all dharmas: The so-called all dharmas consists of the five aggregates, twelve spheres, eighteen realms, the dharmas with and without forms, the material and immaterial dharmas, the visible and the invisible dharmas, the substantial and unsubstantial dharmas, the flawed and flawless dharmas, and the conditioned and the unconditioned dharmas. All dharmas are empty because their original natures are neither permanent nor in decay.

17. Emptiness of nonattainment: Nonattainment means all dharmas are unattainable. For instance, the past is unattainable, the future is unattainable, and the present is unattainable. In the past, neither the future nor the present is attainable. In the future, neither the past nor the present is attainable. In the present, neither the past nor the future is attainable. This nonattainment is empty because its original nature is neither permanent nor in decay.

18. Emptiness of selflessness: Selflessness means no selfness is attainable. Selflessness is empty because it is the selflessness.

Why? It is because its original nature is neither permanent nor in decay. Selflessness means 'the unconditioned,' so it is empty.

19. Emptiness of self-nature: Self-nature refers to the five aggregates. The nature of the arising of the five aggregates is unattainable. All dharmas are without self-natures. This emptiness is not made by knowledge, views, or others. Self-nature is empty because its original nature is neither permanent nor in decay.

20. Emptiness of selfless self-nature: Selfless self-nature means that various dharmas have no nature of combining causes and conditions, but have a self-nature of being combined. This selfless self-nature is empty because its original nature is neither permanent nor in decay. (Fascicle 51).

enduring disposition: Enduring dispositions are not vexations. Voice-hearers and the self-enlightened ones have terminated their vexations, but a few factors of greed, anger, and ignorance remain and affect their body, speech, and conscious actions, and these are the enduring dispositions. Such dispositions will cause unjust and improper consequences for the ordinary sentient beings, but not for the voice-hearers and the self-enlightened ones. Only the Buddhas have eliminated such dispositions forever (fascicle 363).

even-headed individuals in reincarnation: Those whose vexations are not removed until the end of reincarnation; because of the lack of good causes and conditions, they are unable to terminate vexations early.

external giving: To give ones' property, and so forth, to others (fascicle 404).

five aggregates: The five categories cover both the physical and mental aspects of all sentient beings: matter (form), feeling (reception, sensation), thinking, action (motivation, volition), and consciousness.

five contemplations:
1. Contemplation of impurity
2. Contemplation of loving-kindness and compassion
3. Contemplation of dependent origination
4. Contemplation of the emptiness of the eighteen realms
5. Contemplation of counting breathing

Refer to fascicle 394.

five covers: The five mental and moral hindrances that will hinder wisdom and bring about vexations: desire, hatred and anger, dullness and drowsiness, restless mind and repentance, and doubt.

five desires: Desires arise from the perceived objects of the five senses, including sight, sound, smell, taste, and physical touch; or the desires for wealth, sex, food and drink, reputation, and sleep. Please refer to fascicles 398.

five eyes:
1. Physical eye, possessed by human beings.
2. Heavenly eye, possessed by heavenly beings, caused by meditations. With heavenly eye, the heavenly beings can see very far and clearly; better than human eyes do; they can see things in the past also.
3. Wisdom eye, the insightful eye possessed by both great and small vehicle practitioners, who can see the emptiness of all dharmas.
4. Dharma eye, possessed by the bodhisattvas, who can see all dharma gates clearly with this eye.
5. Buddha eye, only possessed by the Buddhas, who can see insightfully the reality of all dharmas and illumine all sentient beings with great loving-kindness and compassion. As the physical, heavenly, and wisdom eyes merge into the

Buddha eye, the Buddha can see, hear, and know everything. Refer to fascicle 404.

five lower bonds: When one fulfills the third stage of voice-hearing cultivation, he or she will not be reborn in this world, and so is named as attaining the nonreturn effect. At this stage, the five lower bonds in the realm of desire, including greedy craving, hatred and anger, upside-down thinking that the self is permanent and real, incorrect thinking that some invalid and unreasonable "precepts" will lead one to liberation and enlightenment, and skepticism about the truth are completely terminated forever. Refer to fascicle 36.

five powers: The power caused by belief, the power caused by diligence, the power caused by mindfulness, the power caused by concentration, and the power caused by wisdom are the five powers for the great bodhisattvas. The five powers are listed in the thirty-seven aids to enlightenment.

Fascicle 53: "In practicing prajna paramita, the bodhisattvas should adopt nonattainment as expedience and aspire to the practice of the powers of belief, diligence, mindfulness, concentration, and wisdom." Also see fascicles 380 and 531.

five precepts for lay believers: No killing, no stealing, no adultery, no lying, and no alcoholic intoxication.

five roots: The five bases for developing one's abilities in the pursuit of great bodhi: the roots of faith, diligence, correct mindfulness, concentration, and wisdom. The five roots are listed as part of the thirty-seven factors for enlightenment. Refer to fascicles 53 and 531.

five upper bonds: They are the craving for the form, craving for formlessness, ignorance, arrogance, and wandering and restless mind. One will achieve the stage of arhat, the highest stage of voice-hearer, after removing these five upper bonds forever. Refer to fascicle 36.

Glossary of Terms 551

following the craving for the dharmas: When cultivating prajna paramita, the great bodhisattvas are attached to the thinking that they should or should not do this or that; that such dharma should or should not dwell in emptiness, formlessness, and so forth; that this is contamination, and that is purification; that this should be kept in close contact, and that should not be kept in close contact; that this should be done, and that should not be done; that this is the path, and that is not the path; that this should be learned, and that should not be learned. Refer to fascicle 36.

forbearance of nonarising: The insight that in the final analysis, all beings are selfless and tranquil and nothing really has arising and extinction.

four approaches of absorption: The four approaches that bodhisattvas use expediently and efficiently to get along with people and guide them toward the Buddha path: unconditioned giving, speaking good and kind words, acting in a way that is beneficial for others, and getting along with others in harmony and empathy (fascicles 3, 48, 300, 380, 402, 438, and 508).

four bases of mindfulness: Being mindful at all times of the four basic contemplations: the body is impure, the feeling is painful, the mind is impermanent, and all dharmas are without selfness (fascicle 380).

The great bodhisattvas will adopt nonattainment as expedience to cultivate prajna paramita and dwell in and investigate their inner and outer bodies, feelings, minds, and dharmas without attainment. These are the phenomena of the large vehicle for the great bodhisattvas. For instance, in order to contemplate the body, they will go to the graveyard to look at the corpses there, thinking that no one's physical body will be exempt from this natural law except being fully liberated; no wise, but only ignorant, ones will treasure their own bodies and be attached to them (fascicle 53).

Also, the great bodhisattvas will dwell in and contemplate

the dharmas inside the body, the dharmas outside the body, and the interaction of them. Fully equipped with correct diligence, knowledge, and mindfulness, they will remove greed and worries of the world and contemplate the causes of the bodily activities and the cessation of the causes, then they will rely on and be attached to nothing. This is the first base of mindfulness, the mindfulness of the body. The same is true with the mindfulness of feeling, mind, and the dharma (fascicle 531).

four bases of power: The four factors that cause supernatural powers to activate, nurture, and fulfill perfect concentration are:
1. Powerful motivation and determination to achieve a perfect concentration; aspiration-samadhi practice.
2. Concentration practice to rest a wandering mind; mind-samadhi practice.
3. Tireless effort to persevere in concentration practice; effort-samadhi practice.
4. Contemplation practice; contemplation-samadhi practice (fascicles 53, 380, and 469).

Fascicle 531: "The great bodhisattvas will cultivate the four bases: samadhi of motives related to the negative karma termination, samadhi of diligence related to the negative karma termination, samadhi of concentrative mind related to the negative karma termination, and samadhi of contemplation related to the negative karma termination in order to increase their powers to fulfill perfectly wisdom and meditation that they pursue."

four bondages: The bondages of desire, anger, believing in invalid disciplines and precepts, and being attached to the existence of all dharmas (beings).

four correct endeavors: Working diligently and correctly to
1. discontinue evil things,
2. prevent new evil things from occurring,
3. bring the virtuous things into existence, and

Glossary of Terms

4. develop and proliferate existing virtuous things.

The four correct endeavors are listed as the elements among the thirty-seven factors for enlightenment (fascicles 53 and 380).

Also, in fascicle 531, "The great bodhisattvas initiate incentives to work delightedly, diligently, and continuously, so that the evil, not virtuous dharmas that have not arisen yet will never arise, while the evil, not virtuous dharmas that have arisen will be eliminated immediately; the virtuous dharmas that have not arisen yet will arise, and the virtuous dharmas that have arisen will increase and expand. These are the four correct endeavors."

four continents: The components of the universe. In the cosmology of ancient India, the four continents, surrounded by Mount Sumeru and standing in a salty ocean between seven golden mountains and a great circular iron enclosure, consist of the continents of Purvavideha, Jambudvipa, Aparagodaniya, and Uttarakuru.

four dwellings in the Heaven of Brahma: Dwelling in the mind of immeasurable loving-kindness, the mind of immeasurable compassion, the mind of immeasurable joy, and the mind of immeasurable equanimity (fascicle 380).

four formless concentrations: The four concentrations in the realm of formlessness are the concentrations of boundless emptiness, boundless consciousness, nothingness, and nonthinking and not nonthinking.

four fundamental components: The four basic elements forming the world and all existent beings are the earth, water, fire, and wind. Very often *empty space* and *consciousness* are added to make the six fundamental components of the world and all dharmas in it.

four groups of Buddhist disciples: The monks (bhiksus), nuns (bhiksunis), layman believers (upasakas), and laywoman believers (upasikas).

four immeasurable minds: Great loving-kindness, great compassion, great joy, and great equanimity are immeasurable because they are unconditioned giving without requesting anything in return. These are the minds that the great bodhisattvas should learn to embrace.

four inverted understandings of reality: When reflecting on all dharmas, one incorrectly thinks that they are permanent instead of impermanent, pleasant instead of painful, with selfness instead of selfless and pure instead of impure.

four kinds of enlightenment: Four steps in the development of enlightenment are:
1. The original intrinsic pure mind that needs to be activated from its long-term contaminated reincarnation.
2. The initial awakening obtained through the cultivation of the ten dwellings, ten actions, and ten transferences.
3. The progressive awakening that occurs in the first stage of bodhisattva and above and will correctly lead one to final enlightenment.
4. The ultimate awakening, the stage of the Thus-Comer.

four kinds of fearlessness: The fearlessness possessed by the Buddhas only, not shared by voice-hearers, self-enlightened ones, bodhisattvas, and other sentient beings (Fascicles 53, 381, 451, and 469):
1. As the Buddha declares that he is the fully enlightened one, some sramanas (monks of various religions), Brahmans, heavenly demon kings, or other ordinary sentient beings will stand up to challenge and argue against him, saying that his attainment of perfect enlightenment is not true. But he will not be scared, because he can see clearly that their arguments are wrong. Instead, he will stay calm and

in comfort and again will declare that he is already a great immortal being of the highest position.
2. As the Buddha declares that his flaws and afflictions have been completely eliminated, some sramanas, Brahmans, and so forth will stand up to challenge and argue against him, saying that his flaws and afflictions are not completely removed. But he will not be scared at all, because he can see clearly that their arguments are wrong. Instead, he will stay calm and in comfort and declare again that he is already a great immortal being of the highest position.
3. As the Buddha teaches the methods for removing obstacles in pursuing the truth, some sramanas, Brahmans, and so forth will stand up to challenge and argue against him, saying that his methods do not work for removing obstacles to pursuing the truth. But he will not be scared at all, because he can see clearly that their arguments are wrong. Instead, he will stay calm and in comfort and declare again that he is already a great immortal being of the highest position.
4. As the Buddha teaches the methods for ceasing suffering, some sramanas, Brahmans, and so forth will stand up to challenge and argue against him, saying that his methods do not work for ceasing suffering. But he will not be scared at all, because he can see clearly that their arguments are wrong. Instead, he will stay calm and in comfort and declare again that he is already a great immortal being of the highest position.

four kinds of food: The food for physical body; the food for sensation; the food for thinking; and the food for consciousness (fascicles 36 and 408).

four meditations: The four stages of meditations (dhyana) in the realm of form are:
1. In the first stage of meditation, there are no more perceptions of smell or taste, while the perceptive activities of the

eye, ear, body and the conscious remain active. The joy and delight derived from the four perceptions dominate in this stage, and the cognition of insightful investigation is active too. This is the stage in which joy and delight arise because of getting far away from defilements.

2. In the second stage of meditation, all cognitive activities cease; joy and delight are caused by concentration, in which tranquility dominates, and cognition is now at rest.
3. In the third stage of meditation, both joy and delight are at rest, and the mind abides in correct mindfulness, serenity, and detachment, which is called a stage of wonderful happiness without joy and delight.
4. In the fourth stage of meditation, both suffering and happiness are terminated, purity and equanimity dominate, while inhalation and exhalation cease.

four noble truths: The truths that the Buddha teaches to guide sentient beings to reflect on human suffering, face it, believe that the suffering can be and should be relieved, and finally follow the correct path to cultivate and become liberated from suffering.

1. The noble truth of suffering: Realizing that all sentient beings suffer from greed, hatred, ignorance, arrogance, and skepticism. They suffer because they do not know the truth of the world, of themselves, and of all sentient beings. They suffer because they have craving and attachment, incorrect understanding and views, and because what they do and think are flawed. This is the truth that everyone should get to know and face.
2. The noble truth of the cause of suffering: Realizing that suffering is caused by a combination of negative causes and conditions. Learn to find out what they really are.
3. The noble truth of the cessation of suffering: Realizing that it is definitely possible to eliminate suffering if people do the correct things and are determined to do so.
4. The noble truth of the path for the cessation of suffering: The correct ways for relieving suffering have already been

Glossary of Terms 557

taught by the Buddha. What one needs to do is to follow the path and practice it diligently.

four raging currents: The four things that will disturb one's feelings and emotions and make them as violent as raging currents are desire, existence, ignorance, and false views.

four superior dwellings: They are the heavenly beings dwelling in giving, precepts, and virtuous mind; the Brahma dwelling in the four immeasurable minds; the holy ones dwelling in the samadhi of emptiness, samadhi of formlessness, and samadhi of nonaction; and the Buddha dwelling in immeasurable samadhi.

four types of birth: Sentient beings are born from an egg, a womb, moisture, or transformation.

four unhindered understandings: The unhindered ability to understand the meanings of teachings, to understand the principles of the world, to understand and use various languages, and to lecture and debate (fascicles 53, 381, and 469).

four upside-down views: The four incorrect views are mistaking impermanence for permanence, suffering for happiness, selflessness for selfness, and impurity for purity (fascicle 484).

four yokes (four fetters): The fetters that impede virtuous nature are desire, attachment to existence, incorrect views, and ignorance.

good destinies of rebirth: Two realms into which one is reborn resulting from positive karma are the human realm and the heavenly realm.

Great Prajna Paramita Sutra: The largest Buddhist canon ever published recording the Buddha's teachings about prajna, the perfect wisdom. The teachings were given during a period of twenty years in sixteen assemblies at Mount Vulture Peak near

Rajagriha, Anathapindika garden of jeta grove in Sravasti, the palace of the Heaven of Enjoying Other-Made Changes (Paranirmitavasavartin), and the Bamboo Garden near Rajagriha.

Before teaching prajna paramita, the Buddha had given teaching on *Hua Yen Sutra* (*The Magnificent and Dignified Flowers Sutra*) for three weeks, *Agamas* at Deer Park for twelve years mainly for voice-hearing pursuers, and the great vehicle sutras for eight years for the bodhisattva path practitioners.

In this gigantic sutra of six hundred fascicles, the dialogues between Buddha and his disciples unfold gradually and extensively, yet systematically and comprehensively. The Buddha elaborates the ideas of prajna paramita and the other five paramitas: giving, pure precept, forbearance, diligence, and meditation paramitas. With the Buddha's skillful guidance, his disciples and other pure Buddha dharma pursuers explore and demonstrate for bodhisattva path practitioners the unsurpassed and perfect wisdom. The answers to these questions are comprehensively given:

What is the superior and flawless life?

What makes great bodhisattvas unique?

What makes the great bodhisattvas different from and superior to the voice-hearers and the self-enlightened ones?

What is the emptiness of all dharmas?

Why are expedient skillfulness and nonattainment important for great bodhisattva?

What are the great bodhisattva actions?

What is the Buddha?

Why is the great vehicle superior to the small vehicle?

What is great bodhisattva cultivation?

In regard to the world, their dialogues, with the support of the Buddha's supernatural powers, show a new horizon as vast and boundless as empty space and a tranquil and fathomless sphere where all heavy burdens and differentiations vanish. As to the phenomena of human life, all are like the dreams, illusions, mirages, images, and echoes. They look real, yet they are unreal.

The Chinese version was rendered from Sanskrit about

Glossary of Terms 559

1,350 years ago (from AD 660 through 663) by Xuanzang (Hsüan-tsang, c. AD 602–664), from which the present English translation is made.
1. Fascicles 1 through 400 cover the teachings the Buddha gave in the first assembly; the title "Upper Prajna" is given to this section of teachings.
2. Fascicles 401 through 537 cover the teachings the Buddha taught in the second and third assemblies; the title "Middle Prajna" is given to this section of teachings.
3. Fascicles 538 through 565 cover the teachings the Buddha gave in the fourth and fifth assemblies; the title "Lower Prajna" is given to this section of teachings.
4. Fascicles 566 through 573 cover the teachings the Buddha gave in the sixth assembly; the title "Heavenly King Prajna" is given to these teachings.
5. Fascicles 574 through 575 cover the teachings the Buddha gave in the seventh assembly; the title "Manjusri (Manjusri Bodhisattva) Prajna" is given to these teachings.
6. Fascicle 576 covers the teaching the Buddha gave in the eighth assembly; the title "Nagasri (dragon the auspicious) Prajna" is given to this teaching.
7. Fascicle 577 covers the teaching the Buddha gave in the ninth assembly; the title "Diamond Prajna" is given to this teaching. This is also the archetype of the *Diamond Sutra*.
8. Fascicle 578 covers the teaching the Buddha gave in the tenth assembly; the title "Essential Meanings of Prajna" is given to this teaching.
9. Fascicles 579 through 600 cover the teachings the Buddha gave in the eleventh through sixteen assemblies; the title "Six Divisions of Prajna" is given to this section of teachings.

Great Circular Iron Enclosure: Mount Sumeru is surrounded by eight circles of mountains and oceans, among which the eighth circle of mountains is named Cakravada-parvata, circular iron enclosure, or great circular iron enclosure.

heavens in the realm of desire: The realm of desire is one of the three realms in heaven; the other two are the realm of form and the realm of formlessness. Six heavens are comprised in this realm: the Heaven of Four Great Kings, the Heaven of Thirty-Three Smaller Heavens, the Heaven of Wonderful Times (the Heaven of Yama), the Heaven of Joyful Satisfaction (the Heaven of Tusita), the Heaven of Enjoying Self-Made Changes, and the Heaven of Enjoying Other-Made Changes.

Heaven of Four Great Kings: As the first level in the realm of desire, there are four kings in this heaven. One day and one night in this heaven equal fifty years in earthly time. The average lifespan of sentient beings in this heaven is five hundred years.

Heaven of Thirty-Three Smaller Heavens: As the second level of the realm of desire, this heaven is located at the summit of Mount Sumeru. In its central palace, the lord of the heaven, Heavenly Emperor Indra, one of the major protectors of Buddhism, is said to live. There are four quarters in this heaven, and in each quarter there are eight gods who are sovereign over thirty-two smaller heavens. The average lifespan in this heaven is one thousand years, and one day of this heaven is equivalent to a hundred years on earth.

Heaven of Wonderful Times or the Heaven of Yama: This is the third-level heaven of the realm of desire. The Sanskrit word *Yama* means "wonderful times." Sentient beings are reborn to this heaven when observing pure precepts of no killing, no stealing, and no adultery. There is only daytime in this heaven; nighttime never appears. The living environment is so beautiful and comfortable that the heavenly beings have experienced incredible pleasure at all times. Unlike the Heaven of Thirty-Three Smaller Heavens, the heavenly beings in this heaven are peace-lovers, so they do not battle with the asuras. They have sexual contacts by hugging or touching each other. Whenever they wish to have a child, they just imagine it, and then a three- or four-year-old child will appear on their laps. This heaven was later referred to as the place where King Yama (Yama-raja) is judging all the deaths.

Heaven of Tusita or the Heaven of Joyful Satisfaction: This is the fourth-level heaven of the desire realm. The lord of this heaven is named Sajtusita-devaraja. One day and night in this heaven is equivalent to five hundred years on earth, and the lifespan of sentient beings there is four thousand years. This heaven is divided into two districts. One is the exterior area in which ordinary heavenly beings live and enjoy a life of desire. The other is the interior area in which Bodhisattva Maitreya, the future Buddha of our Buddha land in the next era, is lecturing on Buddha dharma; it is therefore also named Maitreya Pure Land.

Heaven of Enjoying Self-Made Changes: This is the fifth heaven of the realm of desire in which sentient beings enjoy self-created pleasant things. They have sexual contacts through staring at another's eyes and smiling.

Heaven of Enjoying Other-Made Changes: This is the sixth heaven of the realm of desire, in which all sentient beings enjoy pleasant changes created by others. The lord of this heaven, a demonic king, also reigns over the dark side of the realm and does many things to disturb and hinder the spreading of the Buddha's teachings.

Heavens in the realm of form: In the realm of form, eighteen heavens are included. They are divided into four stages of meditation heaven: three heavens in each of the first three stages of meditation and nine heavens in the fourth stage of meditation. The desires of the sentient beings in this realm are very slight. In contrast to the realm of desire, the forms of the existent beings in this realm are relatively very thin. The heavens in the first meditation heaven are the Heaven of Brahma Followers, the Heaven of Brahma Subordinates, and the Heaven of Great Brahma. The heavens in the second meditation heaven are the Heaven of Lesser Light, the Heaven of Infinite Light, and the Heaven of Extremely Great Brightness and Purity. The heavens in the third meditation heaven are the Heaven of Lesser Purity, the Heaven of Infinite Purity, and the Heaven of Universal Purity. There are nine heavens in the fourth meditation heaven: the Cloudless Heaven, the Heaven of Merits, the Heaven of Lesser Expansion, the Heaven of Extensive Rewards, the Heaven of No Affliction, the Heaven of No Aspiration, the Heaven of Good Appearance, the Heaven of Good Sight, and the Heaven of Ultimate Form.

Heaven of Brahma Followers: The first heaven of the first meditation heaven in the realm of form, where the followers of the Brahma live.

Heaven of Brahma Subordinates: The second heaven of the first meditation heaven, in which the inhabitants serve as the assistants to the Great Brahma, the lord of the first meditation heaven.

Heaven of Great Brahma: The third heaven of the first meditation heaven in the realm of form. Great Brahma, in Hinduism, is regarded as the lord who created the world. In Buddhism, he is a god with mighty supernatural power who protects and supports Buddha dharma.

Heaven of Brahma Family: The general name for all heavens in the Brahma family.

Heaven of Light: The general name for the Heaven of Lesser Light, the Heaven of Infinite Light, and the Heaven of Extremely Great Brightness and Purity.

Heaven of Lesser Light: The first of the three heavens in the second meditation heaven in the realm of form, the one with least light in this meditation heaven.

Glossary of Terms 563

Heaven of Infinite Light: The second of the three heavens in the second meditation heaven of the realm of form. The light in this heaven is very bright. The heavenly beings of this heaven speak with their mouths emitting lights.

Heaven of Extremely Great Brightness and Purity: The third heaven of the second meditation heaven in the realm of form. Sentient beings in this heaven do not speak; they communicate through emitting light. They enjoy "eating" meditative tranquility as their "food." They live in peace and brightness, possess supernatural powers, and can fly. It is said that the beings in this heaven once came down to the earth a long time ago, and as they started to eat the food grown in the ground, they gained weight and gradually they lost all supernatural powers and became the human beings.

Heaven of Pure Residence: This includes the five heavens in the highest level of the form realm, namely the fourth meditation heaven, in which the highly spiritually developed beings live. These five heavens are the Heaven of No Aspiration, Heaven of No Affliction, Heaven of Good Sight, Heaven of Good Appearance, and the Heaven of Ultimate Form.

Heaven of Purity: A general name for all the Heavens of Lesser Purity, Infinite Purity, and Universal purity, where the voice-hearers and the self-enlightened ones who have attained carefree easiness and removed all defilements live.

Heaven of Lesser Purity: The first of the three heavens in the third meditation heaven in the realm of form in which the heavenly beings are proud of the purity of their minds, although it is not as pure as other heavens in the third meditation heaven.

Heaven of Infinite Purity: The second of the three heavens in the third meditation heaven of the realm of form in which the heavenly beings enjoy a greater tranquility and purer delight than those in the Heaven of Lesser Purity.

Heaven of Universal Purity: The highest level of the third meditation heaven of the realm of form in which the heavenly beings enjoy overwhelming tranquility and pure delight of concentration.

Heaven of Expansion: The general name for the Heaven of Lesser Expansion, Heaven of Infinite Expansion, and the Heaven of Extensive Rewards.

Heaven, cloudless: The first of the nine heavens in the fourth meditation heaven of the realm of form in which the sentient beings have no feeling of pain, pleasure, worry, or joy; they live in serenity and equanimity.

Heaven of Merits: The second of the nine heavens in the fourth meditation heaven of the realm of form. Sentient beings are born into this heaven because they have amassed a large amount of merit owing to their cultivation of wisdom, mindfulness, equanimity, and serenity.

Heaven of Lesser Expansion: Also named the Heaven of Nonthinking, this is the third of the nine heavens in the fourth meditation heaven in the realm of form. Sentient beings are born into this heaven owing to a perfect practice of nonthinking meditation. This level is regarded by Brahman practitioners as the highest stage of nirvana, where they live in a form without desires and thinking, while some elements, neither mental nor material, remain active. These elements are acquisition and achievement, the root of life, the common characteristics of sentient beings, the nature of ordinary sentient being, the concentration of nonthinking, the concentration of extinction, rebirth in the heaven of nonthinking as a consequence of practicing concentration of nonthinking, names, sentences, words, birth, old age, duration, impermanence, transmigration or drifting, the definitive differences caused by different causes and conditions, correspondence and association, quick action or change, sequence,

Glossary of Terms 565

direction in space, time, number, nature of combination, and the nature of noncombination.

Heaven of Extensive Rewards: The fourth of the nine heavens in the fourth meditation heaven of the realm of form. When the wind-disaster at the end of this kalpa happens, the earth will be destroyed, but humans who have achieved the fourth level of meditation will be reborn to this heaven and escape the disaster.

Heaven of No Affliction: The fifth of the nine heavens in the fourth meditation heaven in the realm of form. Sentient beings in this heaven have become pliable from meditation practice, and their worries and afflictions are also removed.

Heaven of No Aspiration: The sixth of the nine heavens in the fourth meditation heaven in the realm of form. Sentient beings in this heaven do not aspire to be reborn into the realm of formlessness.

Heaven of Good Appearance: The seventh of the nine heavens in the fourth meditation heaven in the realm of form. The heavenly beings in this heaven have developed good virtues and behavior because of practicing high-level meditation.

Heaven of Good Sight: The eighth heaven in the fourth meditation heaven in the realm of form. The sentient beings in this heaven have attained good sight from practicing concentration.

Heaven of Ultimate Form: The highest of the nine heavens in the fourth meditation heaven in the realm of form. Those who have achieved the highest stage of practice in the fourth meditation heaven are reborn to this heaven.

heavens in the realm of formlessness: This is one of the three realms. Sentient beings in this realm experience neither physical existence nor space directions. There are four formless concentrations in this realm:

1. The concentration of boundless emptiness, a meditation without physical form and limited space, in which the ideas of forms are terminated.
2. The concentration of boundless consciousness, in which the ideas of limitless space cease.
3. The concentration of nothingness, in which the ideas of limitless consciousness cease and all beings are viewed as empty.
4. The concentration of nonthinking and not nonthinking, the highest stage of meditation of this realm in which all kinds of thinking and perception stop.

Heavenly Emperor Indra: Originally a god in ancient Hinduism who was regarded in Buddhism as the heavenly emperor, the lord of the Heaven of Thirty-Three Smaller Heavens in the realm of desire, an enthusiastic protector of Buddha dharma. One of his names, "Kausika," appears very often in *The Great Prajna Paramita Sutra*; he plays the role of a challenger in the dialogues between Buddha and his disciples (fascicle 77).

heavenly sons: In ancient China, emperors asserted that they were the sons of heaven, the so-called heavenly sons. In Buddhist sutras, heavenly sons indicates heavenly beings in general (fascicle 81).

Heaven of Longevity: The heavens in the realm of form and the realm of formlessness where the lifespan of heavenly beings is very long (fascicle 394).

heavy bondages: There are three kinds of heavy bondages. Killing, stealing, and adultery are the heavy bondages of the body; lying, divisive words, rude and vicious words, and filthy words are the heavy bondages of speech; while greed, anger, and incorrect views are the heavy bondages of the mind (fascicles 393, 476, and 535).

hidden roots of vexations: The subtle and hidden roots of vexa-

Glossary of Terms 567

tions continuously affect one's thinking and behavior in a way difficult to be aware of. These roots amass in one's long-term life history, resulting from mutual permeation between one's consciousness and the phenomenal world, and contribute to forging one's disposition and personality.

indestructible form: The stage of cultivation in which bodhisattvas are able to see the emptiness of all dharma without destroying their existential forms

individual existents in reincarnation: The terms often used in Buddhist texts to describe the forms of individual existence: I, the sentient being, the living one, the one who gives birth, the one who raises others, the gentleperson (purusa), the individual in reincarnation (pudgala), the mentally born one (mano-maya-kaya), the learned child (manava), the maker, the one who makes others make, the elicitor (the one who creates rewards or punishments), the one who makes others elicit (the one who makes others create rewards and punishments), the receiver (the one who receives rewards or punishments in a future life), the one who makes others receive rewards or punishments in a future life, the knower, and the viewer.

inferior one: The one who is able or intends to liberate only himself or herself.

inferior destinies of rebirth: These are the hells, the realm of animals, and the realm of the hungry ghosts. They are also called *the three bad destinies.*

internal giving: To give one's life, body, or organs to others (fascicle 404).

illusory world: The illusions, dreams, echoes, images, shadows, images of water under sunlight, flowers in the sky, mirages, and transformed things are terms often used in Buddhist texts to describe the illusory and changing world and the beings in it.

They imply that both the nature and the forms of beings are empty.

jambu gold: The gold extracted from the river passing through jambu forest in the continent of Jambudvipa (fascicle 77).

jivaj-jivaka: A bird of two heads; a sweet songster singing with wonderful and auspicious voice (fascicle 398).

kalavinka: A bird found in the valleys of the Himalayas. It has the most exquisite and pleasing voice, superior to other species of birds. They also are the birds in the Buddha's pure lands; they "sing" the truth of the dharma beautifully and wonderfully (fascicle 381).

Kalpa of the Sages: See *bhadrakalpa*.

karma: One's action and its effect.
1. Happy karma or positive karma in the realm of desire.
2. Unhappy karma or negative karma in the realm of desire.
3. Unmovable good karma in the realm of form and the realm of formlessness.
4. Three kinds of karma: the positive, negative, and unmovable positive karmas.
5. White karma: good karma.
6. Black karma: bad karma (fascicle 395).

Kausika: Lord of the Heaven of Thirty-Three Smaller Heavens; the name of the Heavenly Emperor Indra (fascicle 77).

King Prasenajit of Kosala: Living in Sravasti of Kosala, he was born in the same year as Sakyamuni Buddha. He, his wife, and his son (the crown prince Jeta) became important lay members of the earliest Buddhist community.

konghou: An ancient Chinese plucked stringed musical instrument (fascicle 400).

Glossary of Terms 569

koti: Ten million, one million, or one hundred thousand, in Sanskrit.

koti nayuta: A quantity too large to be calculated or imagined. On the other hand, an extremely small quantity is expressed in Buddhist texts like this: *less than one hundredth, one thousandth, one hundred thousandth, one kotith, one hundred kotith, one thousand kotith, and one hundred thousand kotith; too little to be counted, reckoned, measured, and demonstrated; as little as one upanisadam-api.*

kulajkula: The voice-hearing vehicle practitioners who will be reborn from one family to another and finally enter into nirvana; they are the once-returners, twice-returners, or thrice-returners.

krosa: An ancient Indian scale equaling the distance a cow's voice or the sound of drums can be heard. But it differs depending on the height of the lands and the loudness of the sound or voice (fascicles 398 and 444).

kumuda: The red lotus (fascicles 10, 398, 405, and 446).

living forbearance: As one looks at the world and human life with compassion and empathic understanding, it will be easier for him or her to accept the existing human or personal conditions. This is a good starting point to improve the situation.

large threefold thousand-world: One large, threefold thousand-world comprises one thousand medium thousand-worlds; one medium thousand-world (medium chilocosm) comprises one thousand small thousand-worlds; while one small thousand-world (small chilocosm) comprises one thousand smaller worlds, in which mountains, heavens, oceans, and continents are found. A large threefold thousand-world therefore consists of one billion smaller worlds. This is a way to express the hugeness of the universe. These terms originated in ancient India and have been adopted by Buddhist texts.

length of two arms at full stretch: A measurement used in ancient India (fascicle 398).

liberation gates, three: The liberation gates of emptiness, formlessness, and nonaspiration.

As the great bodhisattvas cultivate prajna paramita, they adopt nonattainment as expedience to contemplate the particular characteristics of all dharmas and get to know that they are empty, so their minds dwell in that emptiness firmly and peacefully. This is the liberation gate of emptiness, which is also named the Samadhi of Emptiness.

As the great bodhisattvas cultivate prajna paramita, they adopt nonattainment as expedience to contemplate the particular characteristics of all dharmas and get to know that they are empty. Because they are empty, they are formless, so their minds will dwell in that formlessness firmly and peacefully. This is the liberation gate of formlessness, which is also named the Samadhi of Formlessness.

As the great bodhisattvas cultivate prajna paramita, they adopt nonattainment as expedience to contemplate the particular characteristics of all dharmas and get to know that they are empty. Because all dharmas are empty, they have no more aspirations, so their minds dwell in that nonaspiration firmly and peacefully. This is named the liberation gate of nonaspiration and also is named the Samadhi of Nonaspiration. Also see fascicles 380 and 531.

long-lived sage: A complimentary title the Buddha gave to his highly enlightened senior disciples, meaning that they had long life both in physical body and dharma wisdom.

lotus position of sitting: A typical posture of sitting in meditation achieved by placing the right foot on the left thigh and the left foot on the right thigh; this position has been practiced by Buddhists since ancient India.

Mahamaudgalyayana: One of the Sakyamuni Buddha's ten principal disciples, regarded as the best one in mastering supernatural power. A very good friend of Sariputras; both became the followers of Sakyamuni Buddha along with their groups of 250 persons each. In order to rescue his mother from the realm of hungry ghosts, he started to make offerings to all sanghas in the ten directions on the fifteenth day of the seventh lunar month each year, which was the origin of Ullambana service held to relieve all souls in suffering.

Mahakasyapa: One of Sakyamunis Buddha's ten principal disciples, considered the best one in ascetic cultivation. He organized and convened the first council for compiling Buddhist texts immediately after Buddha's passing away. He also has been regarded as the first patriarch in the lineage of Chan practice. It is said that he has not entered into nirvana because he is waiting at Cock's Foot Mountain, following Sakyamuni Buddha's direction, for the arrival of the future Buddha Maitreya to pass the Sakyamuni Buddha's cassock and alms bowl to him.

Manjusuri: The prince of Buddha dharma. The name literally means "wonderful virtues" or "wonderful auspice." He is one of the four most popular great bodhisattvas in China; a symbol of wisdom in Buddhism. The lion he is riding is a symbol of bravery and power (fascicle 401).

mahapadma: The great yellow lotus, a symbol of purity and fragrance, or the great red lotus, after which the eighth cold hell is named.

Makapajapadai: Madame Maya's younger sister, aunt of Gautama (Sakyamuni Buddha's name). Seven days after Gautama's birth, his mother, Madame Maya, died. Her sister, Makapajapadai, took the responsibility of raising Gautama until he grew up. Decades later she became the first nun (bhiksuni) in the history of Buddhist order.

Mara: The lord of the sixth heaven in the realm of desire.

merit transfer: To transfer one's merits earned by cultivation of virtues and good conduct to others or to a certain noble objective, such as attainment of the unsurpassed, perfect, and universal bodhi, so that the one who makes the transfer and the one who receives it both will be benefited in the pursuit of ultimate wisdom and enlightenment.

Mount Sumeru: According to Buddhist cosmology, in the center of each small world there is one Mount Sumeru. So in one small thousand-world, which consists of one thousand small worlds, there are one thousand mountains. The Heaven of Four Great Kings and the Heaven of Thirty-Three Smaller Heavens are located at the peak of this mountain, while the Heaven of Yama and others are floating in the upper regions of the air.

nature of noncombination: One of the twenty-four elements not concomitant with the mind in Yogacara theory; contrasted to combination, it is a provisionally established element referring to the capability of all dharmas for separation, opposition, and interference by hindering the combination of causes and conditions and thus hindering the arising of the dharmas (fascicle 314).

nayuta or niyuta: A very large quantity in the ancient Indian numerical system, but its reckonings vary in different texts; usually it is a bigger number than *koti*.

nine ways of thinking about the human body:
1. Thinking that the body is swelling.
2. Thinking about the pus and festering wounds.
3. Thinking that skin and flesh are eaten and peeled off.
4. Thinking that the appearance turns blue because of bruises.
5. Thinking that the body is eaten by pecking.
6. Thinking that the body is separated and scattered.
7. Thinking that only bones and skeletons remain.
8. Thinking that the body is burned.
9. Thinking that nothing in the world can endure forever.

Glossary of Terms 573

nirvana without remainder: A state of nirvana in which no remainder of karma exists. There is no physical body that one may rely on the way one is used to, so there is no more hindrance of one's liberation.

noble eightfold path: The noble eightfold path consists of right view, right thinking, right speech, right action, right livelihood, right diligence, right mindfulness, and right concentration; the great bodhisattvas cultivate these by adopting nonattainment as an expedience focused on getting far away, noncontamination, extinction, and transference toward equanimity when practicing and learning prajna paramita (fascicle 53; also see fascicles 351, 380, and 415).

noble family of Ksatriya: The second most powerful of the four castes in ancient India (but ranked the first in Buddhist texts), consisting of kings and warriors. Sakyamuni Buddha, whose father was a king, was born into this caste.

noble family of Brahman: Brahman, the most powerful caste in ancient India, consists of priests and is responsible for religious rituals and Hindu scripture interpretation.

noble family of elders: The elders in ancient India were recognized and respected by other people and the community because of their virtues, reputation, and devotion to the protection of the Buddhist order.

noble family of laypersons or the noble Vaisya family: The noble family of laypersons. The Vaisya is the third of the four castes in ancient India and consists of merchants, farmers, engineers, and lay religious believers.

nine concentrations in sequence: These concentrations consist of:
1. The four levels of concentration in the realm of form: the first, second, third, and the fourth meditations.
2. The four levels of concentration in the realm of formless-

ness: the concentration of boundless emptiness, the concentration of boundless consciousness, the concentration of nothingness, and the concentration of nonthinking and not nonthinking.

3. The highest, ninth level, of all concentrations: the concentration of extinction.

In the first stage of concentration, one stays away from desire, evil, and the not virtuous dharmas, while the conscious functions, such as general investigation and specific contemplation, remain active. When one stays away from defilements, joy and pleasure arise.

In the second stage, tranquility without general investigation and specific contemplation dominates, the pure mind of equality permeates, and joy and pleasure are active.

In the third stage, one stays away from joy and dwells in equanimity and correct views, while physical pleasure remains. This is a state of mind staying in equanimity with wonderful happiness.

In the fourth stage, the feeling of pleasure or pain ceases and joy and worry disappear. Practitioners discard mindfulness and stay in pure equanimity without pain and pleasure.

In the fifth stage of concentration, one enters into and stays in boundless emptiness, and all kinds of thinking disappear.

In the sixth stage, one enters into and stays in boundless consciousness and transcends all boundless emptiness.

In the seventh stage, one enters into and stays in nothingness and transcends boundless consciousness.

In the eighth stage, one enters into and stays in nonthinking and not nonthinking and transcends nothingness.

In the ninth stage, one enters into and stays in the extinction of mental activities, and transcends the state of nonthinking and not nonthinking (fascicles 46, 48, and 380).

Fascicle 531: Leaving desires and the evil and not virtuous dharmas behind, the great bodhisattvas, with general contemplation and specific investigation as well as the joys caused by getting far away, enter into and fully dwell in the first meditation. This is the first concentration. And so on. They will

Glossary of Terms 575

transcend the sphere of nonthinking and not nonthinking and enter into and dwell fully in the concentration of the extinction of thinking and feeling. These are the nine concentrations in sequence.

nonreturn aspiration and effect: The stage when one aspires to the third stage of voice-hearing cultivation. Cultivation in this stage focuses on completely removing greed and anger. When one fulfills the third stage of voice-hearing cultivation, he or she will not be reborn in this world and so is said to have attained the nonreturn effect. At this stage, all problems in the realm of desire or the five lower bonds, including greed, anger, mistaking the self for real, attachment to unreasonable and invalid precepts, and skepticism about the truth, are completely terminated forever.

obstacle (two kinds): The first kind of obstacle is produced by incorrect thinking that the "I" and sentient beings are real. Such an obstacle will hinder one from removing vexations and attaining nirvana. The other kind of obstacle is produced by the incorrect view that all dharmas are real. Such an obstacle will hinder one from attaining the perfect knowledge of all perfect knowledge (fascicle 393).

once-return aspiration: After attaining stream-entry effect, the voice-hearing practitioner now aspires to the second stage, the stage of once-returner. The three incorrect views are eliminated in the first-stage cultivation; now the second-stage practitioner focuses on improving the disposition by resolving inherited problems and removing the vexations caused by greed, anger, and ignorance.

once-return effect: The effect one attains when completing the second stage of voice-hearing cultivation. The one fulfilling this practice will be reborn one more time because his or her greed, anger, and ignorance now has become very slight.

One Worthy of Offerings: This is one of the names of the Buddha. When one has reached a very high level of cultivation, such as the stage of arhat, he or she becomes worthy of respect and offerings made by other sentient beings. The Buddha has attained the highest level of achievement and is definitely worthy of offerings made by all heavenly and human beings.

One Perfect in Wisdom and Actions: One of the names of the Buddha; it means that the Buddha's wisdom, abilities, virtues, and merits are all complete and perfect.

One Who Knows the World: One of the ten names of the Buddha; it means that the Buddha knows everything in all worlds, in general and in particular: the natural world, the human world, the world of the sentient beings, and the world of nonsentient beings.

Ones Who Need No More Learning: Those who have successfully removed all vexations and attained perfect freedom need no more learning and cultivation. They are the arhats, the self-enlightened ones, and the Buddhas.

Ones Who Need More Learning: Ones who need more cultivation and learning in order to attain complete liberation from bondages of vexations and suffering.

One With One More Rebirth before Nirvana: The holy one who needs one more rebirth to totally get rid of all vexations; a non-return practitioner (fascicles 425 and 499).

other nature: The nature formed or created through environmental influences. It is not the original nature (fascicle 413).

padma: The yellow lotus (fascicles 10, 398, and 405).

paramita: Sanskrit, meaning to be ferried from the mortal life of suffering and afflictions on this shore to the complete freedom,

Glossary of Terms 577

tranquility, and happiness of nirvana on the other shore. Paramita also means a perfect and flawless condition that will bring about transcendental cultivation. For bodhisattva way cultivation, six paramitas are particularly stressed.

1. Giving paramita: The cultivation of giving to perfection without attachment to the giver, the receiver, and the thing given, and it is based on prajna paramita.
2. Pure-precept paramita: The cultivation of observing pure precepts to its perfection without attachment to the violation or nonviolation of the precepts, the ones who observe the precepts, and the precepts per se, and it is based on prajna paramita.
3. Forbearance paramita: The cultivation of forbearance to its perfection without attachment to the one who practices forbearance, the things one refrains from, and forbearance per se, and it is based on prajna paramita.
4. Diligence paramita: The cultivation of diligence to its perfection without attachment to the one who practices diligence, the purpose of diligence, and diligence per se, and it is based on prajna paramita.
5. Meditation paramita: The cultivation of meditation to its perfection without attachment to the one who practices meditations, samadhi and samapatti, and the levels that practitioners have achieved, and it is based on prajna paramita.
6. Prajna paramita: Prajna paramita is immaterial, invisible, and unsubstantial; it has only one form, namely the formlessness. Prajna paramita will lead one to the other shore of all dharmas; because of prajna paramita, all voice-hearers, self-enlightened ones, bodhisattvas, and the Thus-Comers, Ones Worthy of Offerings, Perfectly and Universally Enlightened Ones are able to reach the other shore. Prajna paramita comprises realness, reality, and dharma realm. Prajna paramita can give birth to all superior virtuous dharmas; it can elicit and activate wisdom and the talent of debate; it can bring about all pleasures in and beyond the world. Such prajna paramita is profound, solid, and firm;

it cannot be moved or destroyed. If the great bodhisattvas practice prajna paramita, all demons and their followers, and so forth, cannot do harm to them (fascicle 363).

The fathomless prajna paramita can give birth to all Buddha dharma and manifest the real phenomena of all dharmas in the world; it can give birth to all merit and virtues of the Thus-Comers and manifest the real phenomena of all dharmas in the world. Meditation paramita, and so forth, as well as giving paramita and the perfect knowledge of all phenomena, arise because of the fathomless prajna paramita. All stream-entry effect, once-return effect, nonreturn effect, arhat effect, and self-enlightenment bodhi arise because of the fathomless prajna paramita; all bodhisattva actions and the unsurpassed, perfect, and universal bodhi of the Buddhas arise because of the fathomless prajna paramita; and all stream-enterers, and so forth, as well as the Buddhas appear because of the fathomless prajna paramita. It is also because of the fathomless prajna paramita that all Thus-Comers, Ones Worthy of Offerings, Perfectly and Universally Enlightened Ones in the past, future, and the present attain the unsurpassed, perfect, and universal bodhi (fascicle 510).

Meanings correspondent with the fathomless prajna paramita are expressed by designated statements such as emptiness, formlessness, nonaspiration, nondoing, nonextinction, nonexistence, noncontamination, and nirvana, while the rest of dharmas are also correspondent with prajna paramita (fascicle 562).

The great bodhisattvas have stayed in a mind correspondent with the perfect knowledge of all perfect knowledge under the guidance of great compassion. They then adopt nonattainment as expedience to give their bodies and lives as well as all their properties to others; dwell in the path of the ten virtuous karmas; foster forbearance; cultivate the six paramitas diligently; skillfully enter into various meditations, immeasurable minds, and the formless concentrations without being reborn under the influence of those powers; and contemplate accurately all dharma natures without being attached to them. They will also encourage others to do so. They will further transfer these virtuous roots along with all sentient beings toward the unsurpassed, perfect, and universal bodhi. These are the six paramitas for the great bodhisattvas (fascicle 51).

perfect knowledge of everything: This includes perfect knowledge of the five aggregates, twelve spheres, eighteen realms, and so forth, in the past, future, and present. Voice-hearers and self-enlightened ones also can realize it, but they cannot realize the perfect knowledge of the forms of the paths and the perfect knowledge of all phenomena (fascicle 363).

perfect knowledge of the forms of the paths: The great bodhisattvas should learn the forms of all paths, namely the forms of the voice-hearing path, the forms of the self-enlightenment path, the forms of the bodhisattva path, and the forms of the Thus-Comer path. The great bodhisattvas should cultivate and learn all these paths in order to fulfill them perfectly; they should do what should be done, but they should not seek to dwell in the reality. This perfect knowledge is not shared by the voice-hearers and the self-enlightened ones (fascicle 363).

perfect knowledge of all phenomena: Knowing that all dharmas have only one form: the form of tranquil extinction. The dharmas are manifested by actions, characteristics, and phenomena; the Thus-Comers know them all universally and comprehensively so it is named the perfect knowledge of all phenomena. This knowledge is possessed by the Thus-Comers only; it is not shared by the voice-hearers, self-enlightened ones, and great bodhisattvas (fascicle 363).

perfect knowledge of various subtle phenomena: Perfect knowledge of the phenomena, specifically on subtle sameness, differences, relationship, and the context of various phenomena.

perfect knowledge of all perfect knowledge: The perfect knowledge of everything, the perfect knowledge of the forms of the paths, and the perfect knowledge of all phenomena, but it transcends all of them. This is the perfect knowledge possessed only by the Buddhas, surpassing the perfect knowledge possessed by the voice-hearers, self-enlightened ones, and bodhisattvas.

people in borderland: Lower-class people who live far away from cities and know nothing of the Buddha dharma. This also indicates people who live in the edge of pure land and are skeptical about the Buddha dharma (fascicles 341 and 520).

pudgala: Individuals who are still bound in reincarnation.

Purna: One of the Sakyamuni Buddha's ten principal disciples; he is well known for having great talent of teaching Buddha dharma.

Pulkasa: Originally a Sanskrit term, it refers to the lowest class inferior to Candala in ancient India. They collected droppings and carried and moved dead bodies. It also refers to those who are attached to incorrect views and do not believe in the law of cause and effect.

pundarika: The snow-white lotus (fascicles 10, 398, 405, and 446).

Rajagriha: Rajagriha was the capital of a large and powerful country, Magadha, in Sakyamuni Buddha's age. Located in central India, it was ruled by the well-known king, Bimbisara, and his son Ajatasatru, whose names appear frequently in Buddhist texts. This was one of the cities where the Buddha visited and stayed frequently; the renowned Vulture Mountain, where the Buddha gave teachings, was nearby. The first council of Buddhist sutras was convened here.

realness: There are eleven names used in *The Great Prajna Paramita Sutra* to designate the realness of all existent beings (dharmas): dharma realm, dharma nature, nature of nonillusion, nature of changelessness, nature of equality, nature of nonarising, dharma concentration, dharma dwelling, reality, realm of empty space, and the realm of the inconceivable. There are also twenty-three names used in the sutra to designate realness: realness, dharma realm, dharma nature, nature of nonillusion, nature of changelessness, realm of the inconceivable, realm of space, realm of cessation, realm of departure, realm of extinction, nature of equality, nature of nonarising, dharma concentration, dharma dwelling, realm of selflessness, realm of formlessness, realm of effortlessness, realm of nonaction, realm of equanimity, realm of tranquility, original nothingness, reality, and ultimate nirvana.

Realness is the essence of all existent beings; the fundamental absorption of all humans, physical things, and spiritual beings; and a paradigm of patterns, and the rule of all operations of the world. It is therefore named *reality*. It spreads over all realms and spheres evenly, so it is named the dharma realm, dharma nature, or the nature of equality. It comprises and transcends the beings in space and time. It changes and arises, but in the final analysis it does not change or arise at all, and it is therefore named the nature of changelessness or the nature of nonarising. It is as vast as boundless space and spreads and fills all of it, so it is named the realm of empty space. It is the basis of peace and tranquility upon which all beings rely and all sentient beings rest; it is therefore named dharma concentration or dharma dwelling. It is beyond human logical understanding and imagination, so it is also named the realm of the inconceivable. It is without difference, changelessness, arising, and extinction; it is the reality of the self-nature; and it does not invite controversial arguments (fascicle 569).

regression from the top stage of bodhisattva: If the great bodhisattvas practice prajna paramita and dwell in the three liberation gates without expedient skillfulness, they will fall back to the stage of voice-hearing or the stage of self-enlightenment bodhi; they will be unable to enter the correct bodhisattva path of nonarising. This is named regressing from the top stage of bodhisattva; it also is named "arising" because it is a craving for the dharmas, and those who follow this craving will be named in arising. Refer to fascicle 36.

safranin: A plant used as an essence of red dye.

Sakyamuni Buddha, Sakyamuni Thus-Comer: The founder of Buddhism and Buddhist Order, born as a son to king of Kapilavastu in a place now named Tilaurakot in north India, a part of Nepal, east of the river Rapti. The years of his life vary among historians. According to modern Buddhist scholar Venerable Yin Shun in Taiwan, the Buddha was born between 464 and 467 BCE and died between 387 and 384 BCE. Sakyamuni literally means "the sage of the Sakya clan," a wise and compassionate person who assists others to become wise and compassionate too. His family name was Gautama and given name was Siddhartha, which means to live an auspicious future. His lifetime can be divided into three phases. In the first phase from birth until nineteen years of age, he received the best nurture and carefully designed education in the palace. His education was comprehensive in content, with an attempt to make him a mature and qualified worldly king. The second phase started with his discovering the truth about the outside world, which was so different from his living environment. Renouncing all he had as a wealthy prince and the promising career of a king, he left home and wandered around for quite a while in order to look for the path to relieving suffering of all sentient beings and bringing peace and joy to them. After a long, frustrated, and diligent ascetic practice, he drew himself back to observe the middle path of cultivation, and at the age of twenty-nine, he finally attained the unsurpassed, universal, and perfect bodhi and became a Buddha. In the third phase of his life, from this time until he passed into nirvana at age of eighty, he taught Buddha dharma to his disciples and laypersons.

samadhi: A calm, stable, and concentrative state of mind; a state of equanimity and correct mindfulness caused by the practice of

Glossary of Terms 583

samatha and vipasyana. Among numberless kinds of samadhi, there are the samadhi with both general examination and in-depth investigation, the samadhi with in-depth investigation only, and the samadhi without both general examination and in-depth investigation.

1. Samadhi with general examination and specific in-depth investigation means getting rid of the not virtuous dharmas, such as greedy desire and hatred, to stay in joy and pleasure caused by nonarising, and to enter the first meditation and fully dwell in it.
2. Samadhi with in-depth investigation only is the concentration that occurs between the first and second meditations.
3. Samadhi without general examination and in-depth investigation includes the concentrations from the second meditation up to the stage of nonthinking and not nonthinking.

There are actually countless kinds of samadhi, and they are included in the phrase "all samadhi gates."

samadhi gates, all: Among numberless samadhi gates, one hundred and fifty-seven samadhi gates are listed and explicated in fascicle 52 of *The Great Prajna Paramita Sutra*. Some of them are the Samadhi of Steady Walk, Samadhi of Treasured Seal, Samadhi of Lion's Play, Samadhi of Wonderful Moon, Samadhi of the Flow of All Dharma, Diamond-like Samadhi, Samadhi of Emitting Light, Samadhi without Forgetting, Samadhi of Mindfulness through Emitting Light, Samadhi of Diligence Power, Samadhi of Glorious Power, Samadhi of Evenly Flowing, Samadhi of Definitively Understanding All Language, Samadhi of Definitively Understanding All Names, Samadhi of Taking Care of All Directions, Samadhi of Covering Empty Space, Samadhi of Diamond Wheel, Samadhi without Attachment and Obstacles, and so forth.

In fascicle 36, these samadhi gates also are mentioned: Samadhi with the Factors For Enlightenment, Samadhi of Lion's Play, Samadhi of Lion's Powerful Quickness, Samadhi of Lion Stretching Limbs, Samadhi of Lion at Yawning,

Samadhi of Steady Walk, Samadhi of Treasured Seal, Samadhi of Wonderful Moon, Samadhi of Moon Streamer, Samadhi of All Dharma Seals, Samadhi of Pouring Water on the Head, Samadhi of Definitive Dharma Realm, Samadhi of Definitive Streamer Form, Samadhi of Solid Diamond, Samadhi of Entering All Dharma Seals, Samadhi of the King Dwelling in Concentration, Samadhi of King's Seal, Samadhi of Diligence Power, Samadhi of Evenly Flowing, Samadhi of Definitely Understanding Various Speeches, Samadhi of Definitely Understanding Various Names, Samadhi of Seeing All Directions, Samadhi of Dharani Seal, Samadhi of Staying in Mindfulness, Samadhi of Various Dharmas Equally Reaching Ocean Seal, Samadhi of Covering All Empty Spaces, Samadhi of Pure Three-Wheel, Samadhi of Attaining Nonretreat Supernatural Powers, Samadhi of Flowing from Containers, Samadhi of Most Superior Streamer, Samadhi of Burning Up Afflictions, Samadhi of Conquering Four Devils, Samadhi of Great Wisdom Torch, Samadhi of Producing Ten Powers, and other hundreds of thousands of samadhi.

samahita: Physical and mental peace and equanimity brought about by superior concentration (fascicles 366, 592).

samapatti: One's mind in balance and tranquility, a state regarded as higher than samadhi. According to *Abhidharma Mahavibhasa Sastra*, samapatti includes eight levels of concentration. While samadhi aims at one object, samapatti aims at the five aggregates; samadhi lasts for a brief instant and samapatti lasts for much longer; some kinds of samadhi are included in samapatti, some kinds of samapatti are also included in samadhi. However, samapatti is not equivalent to samadhi.

samatha: A state of mind in which reflection and restlessness cease and stability, concentration, calmness, easiness, and equilibrium dominate; the basis for in-depth investigation and thorough contemplation (vipasyana).

Glossary of Terms 585

sands of the Ganges River, as many as the: Very often used in the Buddhist texts to indicate a very large number of something, even beyond what one may measure and imagine. The Ganges River in India long has been relied upon by inhabitants for multiple purposes, including agriculture, transportation, drinking, bathing, and religious rituals.

sangha: Literally means to live and work together in harmony, observe precepts in agreement, and share the same beliefs, correct views, and understanding of the truth; a general name for Buddhist monks, nuns, male and female novices; the monastic community.

sapphire: A large blue gemstone.

Sariputra: One of Sakyamuni Buddha's ten principal disciples, recognized as the one with the highest wisdom. He sometimes gave teachings in Buddha's absence. He often appeared in prajna texts to converse with the Buddha.

sarvajna: The perfect knowledge of dharma nature; the unhindered awakening that surpasses all attachments (fascicle 559).

self-enlightened one (pratyekabuddha): One learns to become awakened and attain the bodhi by himself alone when the Buddha's teachings are not available. This also means that one has attained insightful understanding of dependent origination without aspiring to assist sentient beings as the bodhisattvas do. The term *pratyekabuddha* is rendered in Chinese as "being enlightened by realizing insightfully the law of dependent origination," meaning that one has become enlightened by realizing the twelve chains of arising based on the law of dependent origination. Both the voice-hearers (sravaka) and the self-enlightened one (pratyekabuddha) are considered the holy ones in the two small vehicles who pursue self-liberation but are not sufficiently motivated to relieve the suffering of all sentient beings.

Glossary of Terms

self-enlightenment bodhi: The wisdom of enlightenment that self-enlightened ones attain based on the understanding of dependent origination, mainly the twelve chains of cause and condition origination.

seven factors for enlightenment: The factor of mindfulness, the factor of intelligent decision, the factor of diligence, the factor of joy, the factor of ease and freedom, the factor of concentration, and the factor of equanimity are those the great bodhisattvas cultivate by adopting nonattainment as expedience focused on getting far away, noncontamination, extinction, and transference toward equanimity when practicing and learning prajna paramita (fascicles 53 and 380).

Fascicle 531: "The universal enlightenment of mindfulness, the universal enlightenment of intelligent choice, the universal enlightenment of diligence, the universal enlightenment of joy, the universal enlightenment of easiness and peace, the universal enlightenment of concentration, and the universal enlightenment of equanimity are the seven factors for enlightenment for the great bodhisattvas."

seven sacred treasures: The practice of seven virtues: faith, the precepts, shame, repentance, hearing, giving, and wisdom (fascicles 3 and 402).

shallow-minded people: Those who have only superficial understanding of Buddhist teachings (fascicle 341).

sitting on the seat of wonderful bodhi: Metaphorically indicating the one who has attained the unsurpassed, perfect, and universal wisdom of enlightenment.

stage of cultivation: In the second and third stages of voice-hearing cultivation, one's defiled desire, anger, hatred, ignorance, and so forth, are cut off.

six changes: These changes or movements of the earth, the auspi-

Glossary of Terms 587

cious signs, appear right before the Buddha gives lectures on the great vehicle sutras. The six ways of change are move, powerful move, most powerful move; rise, powerful rise, most powerful rise; shake, powerful shake, most powerful shake; beat, powerful beat, most powerful beat; roar, powerful roar, most powerful roar; explosion, powerful explosion, most powerful explosion. The change rises in the east and sinks in the west; rises in the west and sinks in the east; rises in the south and sinks in the north; rises in the north and sinks in the south; rises in the middle and sinks in the border, and rises in the border and sinks in the middle (fascicles 1, 76, 413, 424, 447, and 513).

six contacts: Eye contact, ear contact, nose contact, tongue contact, body contact, and conscious contact.

six paramitas: The distinctive content of bodhisattva cultivation includes six paramitas, one of the major paths leading to becoming a Buddha. They are giving, pure precept, forbearance, diligence, meditation, and prajna paramitas. Paramita, in Sanskrit, literally means "the other shore of the river" in which freedom and bliss are implied. It also refers to the perfection that one may achieve in cultivation.

six realms: The earth realm, water realm, fire realm, wind realm, space realm, and consciousness realm are the six fundamental elements that make up the world.

six supernatural powers: The supernatural powers of transformation, heavenly ear, knowing other's minds, knowing previous lives, heavenly eye, and flawlessness are the six supernatural powers for the great bodhisattvas (fascicle 531). Also see fascicles 9, 380, 404, and 405.

sramana: This Sanskrit word means the one who has renounced the family and other worldly connections, vowing to pursue wholeheartedly the truth of the world and the path leading to liberation and enlightenment.

stage of perfection: The stage of arhat; the highest stage of voice-hearing cultivation when the practitioner's thinking and emotions are purified, delusion and afflictions are completely eliminated and no more learning is needed.

stage of seeing the truth: The first stage of voice-hearing cultivation when the practitioner is regarded as having seen the truth and his or her incorrect views are eliminated; the stage of stream-entry. See *stream-entry aspiration and effect*.

stream-entry aspiration and effect: The first stage of voice-hearing cultivation is "stream-entry," and one who aspires to the pursuit of stream-entry has stream-entry aspiration.

One who has completed stream-entry cultivation and attained the stage of stream-entry gains "stream-entry effect." In this stage, problems resulting from incorrect views are terminated forever. It is said that there are eighty-eight kinds of problems, but they can be summed up in three incorrect views: mistaking the self for permanent and real existence, mistaking erroneous percepts for pure precepts, and being skeptical about the truth. The effect of stream-entry is a complete elimination of these three bonds. Once the three bonds are eliminated, the seizure of birth and death will loosen and finally will be untied.

Sudra: The lowest caste of the four-caste system in ancient India; the caste of slaves.

Superior One: One who always is pleased to assist others and do as bodhisattvas do.

tala tree: *Tala* means "starry" or "scintillation". It is an edible fruit resembling the pomegranate; its fan-palm leaves are used for writing. (*A Dictionary of Chinese Buddhist Terms*, compiled by William Edward Soothill and Lewis Hodous, London and New York: Routledge, 2006 (1937), p. 209) (fascicle 398).

Teacher of Heavenly and Human Beings: One of the ten names of the Buddha, meaning he is a great teacher of human beings and heavenly beings who have the greatest potential to learn from the Buddha and attain enlightenment quickly among all sentient beings.

ten actions: The ten stages of cultivation, from the twenty-first through the thirtieth among the fifty-two stages of the bodhisattva path, in which the actions beneficial to others are particularly emphasized:
1. Selfless giving with joy.
2. Observing pure precepts in order to benefit others.
3. Practicing tolerance and forbearance.
4. Practicing courageous diligence.
5. Staying away from restless and incorrect mindfulness.
6. Manifestation of formlessness, selflessness, and nonarising of all dharmas through expedient skillfulness based on the purity of body, speech, and conscious karmas.
7. Practicing all kinds of positive actions without attachment.
8. Practicing various difficult but beneficial things for the sake of sentient beings.
9. Dwelling in and disseminating the wonderful dharma.
10. Assisting all sentient beings to attain the ultimate truth.

ten not virtuous karmas: The actions contrary to the ten virtuous karmas, the causes of rebirth in negative destinies: killing, stealing, adultery, lying, divisive speech, harsh speech and slander, nonsensical speech, greed, anger, and ignorance.

ten contemplations: The contemplations of impermanence, suffering, selflessness, impurity, death, undesirability of all worldly beings, disgust of food, extinction of negative disposition and actions, freedom from desire, and freedom from arising.

ten dharma realms: The worlds of the Buddhas, bodhisattvas, self-enlightened ones, voice-hearers, deities and heavenly beings, humans, asuras, animals, hungry ghosts, and denizens of hell.

ten dwellings: The stages from the eleventh through the twentieth of the fifty-two stages of bodhisattva-path cultivation:

1. Dwelling in an aspiration to bodhisattva enlightenment. Through listening to Buddha's teachings, seeing Buddha's thirty-two perfect marks and eighty distinguishing features, watching transformations made by supernatural powers, experiencing the suffering of sentient beings, or other causes and conditions, the bodhisattvas aspire to the bodhi in order to assist all sentient beings so they begin to learn the Buddha dharma and practice the Buddha's teachings.
2. Dwelling in an earnest motivation for learning. During this stage, the bodhisattvas focus developing the mind of great loving-kindness, great compassion, and great joy; assist and protect all sentient beings; and stay in mindfulness of the Buddha. They learn diligently as much correct dharma as possible and stay in close contact with virtuous teachers and friends. This is a period of preparation, nurtured by dharma cultivation, for becoming a well-developed bodhisattva.
3. Dwelling in diligent cultivation without hindrance. The bodhisattvas during this stage learn to contemplate the transience, emptiness, and selflessness of all dharmas. They also learn various realms of all sentient beings, the world, dharma realm, the fundamental components, and the three realms in order to enrich their knowledge and deepen their thinking.
4. Being ready to be born in the family of the Buddha. The bodhisattvas during this stage should cultivate contemplation of the Buddhas, the worlds, karma, cause and effect, birth and death, and nirvana; they should continue to learn the Buddha dharma in the past, future, and the present.
5. Dwelling in expedient cultivation. The bodhisattvas during this stage know that all the practices of virtuous roots are for these purposes: to protect, benefit, soothe, relieve, comfort, and assist sentient beings; be eager to see that they will become mature; bring them happiness; and lead them to nirvana. Therefore the bodhisattvas must learn to know

Glossary of Terms 591

sentient beings well and how to guide them with expedient skills.

6. Dwelling in correct mindfulness of prajna paramita. This is the stage for concentration cultivation in which bodhisattvas learn to remain unmoved by admiration or slander. They will also learn that all beings are empty, formless, unreal, selfless, illusory, and unattainable.
7. Dwelling in the three liberation gates without regression. During this stage the bodhisattvas learn not to regress in their pursuit of the Buddha dharma no matter how the circumstances change. They should further learn that "one is many and many is one," to be existent is to be nonexistent and to be nonexistent is to be existent, formlessness is form, and the form is formlessness, and so forth.
8. Dwelling in purity like a Buddha-child. During this stage the bodhisattvas learn to purify their actions of body, speech, and mind. They learn various characteristics of sentient beings, their strengths, weaknesses, and all their karmas. They further learn about the Buddhas, the Buddha lands, the wonderful dharma, and the supernatural powers of the Buddhas.
9. Dwelling in the dharma in accordance with the Buddha's teachings as a dharma prince. After diligent learning and cultivation, the bodhisattvas during this stage know well the destinations, vexations, and the dispositions of the sentient beings and how to use expedient skills to assist them and relieve their suffering. They further learn to know well the Dharma King and all his subtle methods so they will be ready to become the successors to the Dharma King.
10. Dwelling in dharma water and being ready to do as a bodhisattva should do. During this stage the bodhisattvas learn the abilities to cause the numberless worlds to move, illuminate the numberless worlds, influence the numberless worlds, travel all over the numberless worlds, and glorify and dignify the numberless worlds. They learn about the sentient beings and how to expediently and skillfully tame

and guide them. The bodhisattvas at this stage should also learn the perfect knowledge in the three phases of time, Buddha dharma, dharma realms, sentient beings, and the worlds.

ten directions: The four cardinal points (east, west, south, and north), four intermediary points (northeast, southeast, southwest, and northwest), the zenith, and the nadir.

ten forbearances:
1. Listening to Buddha's teachings with joy and understanding.
2. Contemplating all dharmas as they really are with equanimity and pure mind.
3. Knowing that all dharmas are without arising and extinction.
4. Knowing that all dharmas are like illusions.
5. Knowing that all dharmas are like the illusory images of water under sunlight.
6. Knowing that all dharmas are like dreams.
7. Knowing that all dharmas are like echoes.
8. Knowing that all dharmas are like shadows.
9. Knowing that all dharmas are like transformed things.
10. Knowing that all dharmas are like empty space.

ten virtuous karmas, the path of: The path leading to good effects, including rebirth in good destinies:
1. No killing
2. No stealing
3. No adultery
4. No lying
5. Do not drive a wedge between people
6. No harsh speech or slander
7. No nonsensical speech
8. No greed
9. No hatred and anger
10. No erroneous views or ignorance

Glossary of Terms 593

ten kinds of mindfulness: The mindfulness in compliance with the Buddha, the dharma, the sangha, the precepts, equanimity, the heaven, tranquility and getting away, inhalation and exhalation, the body, and death. These ten kinds of mindfulness based on nonattainment as expedience are included in the phenomena of the large vehicle for the great bodhisattvas (fascicles 53, 408, 456, 484, and 489).

ten paramitas: The ten paramitas are the six paramitas (giving, pure precept, forbearance, diligence, meditation, and prajna paramitas) and the following four paramitas: expedient skillfulness, wonderful aspiration, power, and knowledge.

ten principal disciples of Sakyamuni Buddha: Ananda, Aniruddha, Mahakasyapa, Mahakatyayana, Mahamaudgalyayana, Purna, Rahula, Sariputra, Subhuti, and Upali.

ten stages of cultivation common to the three vehicles:
1. The stage of ordinary sentient beings, when worldly wisdom is unfertilized by meditation. This is also named the stage of pure contemplation.
2. The stage of embryonic Buddha nature, in which virtuous roots are in the embryo and the views are channeled into a correct direction, although attachment remains.
3. The stage of eight-forbearance: the stage of stream-entry aspiration and the stage of nonarising forbearance of a bodhisattva.
4. The stage of insight: the stage of stream-entry and the stage of the bodhisattva without regression.
5. The stage of slight vexation: the stage of once-return and the stage of the bodhisattva when most vexations are terminated.
6. The stage of eliminating all desires: where nonreturn practitioners and the bodhisattva practitioners have acquired the five supernatural powers.
7. The stage of arhat.
8. The stage of self-enlightenment bodhi.

9. The stage of bodhisattva.
10. The stage of Thus-Comer.

ten stages of bodhisattva: The great bodhisattvas practice these stages, step by step, in order to become the Buddhas:
1. The stage of ecstasy. After doing many virtuous actions, making offerings respectfully to the Buddhas, and vowing to aspire to the unsurpassed bodhi with an attempt to relieve all sentient beings from suffering, the great bodhisattvas enter and dwell in the stage of ecstasy. They are joyful and fearless when dwelling in this stage; their anger and hatred diminish too.
2. The stage of freedom from defilements. Because the bodhisattvas have developed straightforward, fair, soft, bearable, tamed, tranquil, pure, virtuous, uncontaminated, detached, broad, and great mind, they enter the stage of freedom from defilements. They stay far away from killing and anger; they treat all sentient beings compassionately. They also teach others how to practice the ten virtuous actions and stay away from the not virtuous ones.
3. The stage of emitting light. The bodhisattvas have developed the ten minds: pure mind, peacefully dwelling mind, mind of renunciation, mind of nongreed, mind of nonregression, stable mind, bright and powerful mind, brave mind, broad mind, and great mind, and enter the stage of emitting light. Dwelling in this stage, the bodhisattvas can contemplate all conditioned phenomena as they really are and see clearly the conditions of human beings. They continue to work hard in order to benefit more sentient beings.
4. The stage of flaming wisdom. The bodhisattvas have observed and contemplated various dharma realms and enter the fourth stage of flaming wisdom. These bodhisattvas have deep faith in the triple gem and know well the essence of human life and the universe; they can do self-reflection very well. They cultivate the four correct endeavors, four bases of power, five roots, five

powers, seven factors for enlightenment, and the noble eightfold path diligently with an attempt to attain the perfect knowledge of all perfect knowledge so that they can dignify and purify the Buddha lands for the sake of all sentient beings.
5. The stage of being difficult to be surpassed. The bodhisattvas have developed well the ten pure equal minds of the Buddha dharma in the past; the Buddha dharma in the future; the Buddha dharma in the present; the precepts; the mind; removing incorrect view, skepticism, and regrets; the perfect knowledge of path and nonpath; the knowledge and the views of cultivation; contemplating all factors for enlightenment; and teaching the sentient beings and enter the fifth stage of being difficult to be surpassed. They master the cultivation of the seven factors for enlightenment very well, and their minds are very pure in the pursuit of the unsurpassed truth. They are very compassionate to all sentient beings and know well the noble truths of suffering, the cause of suffering, the cessation of suffering, and the path for the cessation of suffering.
6. The stage of the manifestation of pure realness. After contemplating the equality of all dharmas, the bodhisattvas enter the sixth stage of the manifestation of pure realness. They realize that all dharmas are equal because they are formless, without entity, without arising, without formation, originally pure, without nonsensical arguments, without grasping and renunciation, tranquil, illusionary, like dreams, like shadows, like echoes, like the moon in the water, like images in the mirror, like the illusory images of water under sunlight, and like transformed things. Because all dharmas are not dualistic, they are equal. They have contemplated and realized the twelve chains of causes and conditions in origination; they have attained the liberation samadhi of emptiness, formlessness, and nonaspiration and understand insightfully the prajna paramita well. They are always compassionate to all sentient beings, hoping that

they will finally stay away from the two vehicles and be dedicated to the Buddha vehicle.
7. The stage of going far away. After cultivating various kinds of expedient wisdom, the bodhisattvas enter the seventh stage of going far away. Although having cultivated formlessness and emptiness, they are loving, kind, and compassionate and never allow themselves to turn away from the sentient beings. Although having attained the law of equality of the Buddhas, they love to make offerings respectfully to the Buddhas. Although they contemplate and understand the wisdom of emptiness, they work diligently to accumulate merits and virtues. Although they are far away from the three realms, they work to dignify the three realms. Although they know that the vexations are tranquil in the final analysis, they still work hard to eliminate vexations for the sake of the sentient beings. Although they know all dharmas are illusory, they can recognize and tell the differences of existing phenomena accurately. Although they understand that all lands are like the illusions and are not real, they work hard to dignify the lands and purify human minds.
8. The stage of the unmovable. The bodhisattvas continue to practice the Buddha dharma and are awakened by the insight that everything is inherently without arising, formless, and equal. After getting away from differentiation and attachment, they enter the eighth stage of the unmovable. The distinctive features of this stage are that they do all things without effort; they have no more attainment even in practicing all bodhisattva actions, let alone other worldly concerns.
9. The stage of expedient wisdom. In order to pursue the higher level of tranquility and liberation, the bodhisattvas continue to learn the wisdom of the Buddha and other hidden paths and enter the ninth stage of expedient wisdom. The bodhisattvas who dwell in this stage can know the dharmas virtuous and not virtuous, flawed and flawless, in and beyond the world, the conditioned and the

Glossary of Terms

unconditioned; they also know the paths of voice-hearing, self-enlightenment, bodhisattva, and the Buddha as they really are. They know sentient beings very well and can use expedient skills to teach them and assist them. They are fluent in giving lectures and can debate without hindrance. They stay in correct mindfulness at all times.

10. The stage of dharma cloud. The bodhisattvas in this stage are ready to receive the position of Buddha. They have done many difficult things; they have accumulated many merits, virtues, and wisdom in countless kalpas; they have gained perfect knowledge and are able to know everything and every being in subtle detail; they know time and space and the mutual absorption between them; they have entered the Buddha's mind and know what the Buddha knows; and they can absorb numberless dharma of great wisdom and brightness. This stage is named dharma cloud.

ten universal contemplations: In concentration, one contemplates these ten spheres: earth, water, fire, wind, green, yellow, red, white, emptiness, and consciousness.

The Taming and Guiding One: One of the ten names of the Buddha; the Buddha is expediently skillful in counseling, guiding, and helping people. What the Buddha does is always based on great loving-kindness, compassion, equanimity, and great wisdom.

thirty-seven aids to enlightenment: This comprises four bases of mindfulness, four correct endeavors, four bases of power, five roots, five powers, seven factors for enlightenment, and the noble eightfold path.

thirty-two major marks: The Buddha's extraordinary features of body and demeanors as described in the Buddhist texts:
1. The Buddha's feet have flat and full soles, which are exquisite and are as firm and stable as the bottom of a solid

makeup case; wherever he walks, his soles touch the ground evenly and completely.
2. There are perfect thousand-spoke wheel signs on his soles.
3. His hands and feet are flexible and soft.
4. His fingers and toes are webbed, resembling those of the wild goose king.
5. He has slender and round fingers and toes.
6. He has wide, long, and perfect heels, matching the insteps very well.
7. He has slender, high, and full insteps, matching the heels very well.
8. He has slender and round shins in good proportion, like that of the deer king.
9. His slender and long arms extend past the knees like the trunk of the elephant king.
10. His male sex organ is concealed, resembling that of a dragon, a horse, or the elephant king.
11. There is one hair in each of his pores.
12. All his hair stands straight up in a right-handed rotation.
13. His skin is delicate and moisturized.
14. All his skin is a golden color and is clean and bright.
15. His legs, palms, shoulders, and neck are delicate and full, and the muscles are soft.
16. He has perfect and wonderful shoulders and neck.
17. His shoulder blades and armpits are full and round.
18. His face and manner are perfect, proper, and upright.
19. The shape of his body is slender, wide, solemn, and upright.
20. The span of his arms equals the height of his body; the profile of his body is as perfect as a nyagrodha tree.
21. His upper body, chin, and chest are big and wide, resembling that of the lion king.
22. Bright light always radiates from his face.
23. He has forty neat and white teeth.
24. He has four white canine teeth.
25. He has flavored saliva, swallows smoothly, and always has the most delicious taste when eating.

26. His tongue is long, slender, pure, and broad and can reach the edge of his hair.
27. His voice is as loud and powerful as the heavenly drum. When he recites, his voice is so graceful and far-reaching that all listeners can hear him clearly and evenly. When he speaks, his voice vibrates with resonance.
28. His eyelashes are deep blue and neat, like that of a bull king.
29. His eyes are deep blue and bright.
30. His face is like a full moon, and his eyebrows are like the bows used by the heavenly gods.
31. There are white hairs between his eyebrows.
32. He has a bump on the top of the head.

(Fascicles 381 and 469.)

three bonds: The three knots of mind caused by the wrong views:
1. Mistakenly thinking that the self is permanent and real
2. Mistakenly thinking that practicing some invalid and erroneous precepts will lead to liberation and enlightenment
3. Skepticism about the truth.

Greedy craving and hatred with anger are added to make the five bonds (fascicle 36).

three different destinies decided by cultivation:
1. The holy ones will definitely attain the unsurpassed, perfect, and universal enlightenment because of the correct cultivation.
2. The evil ones will definitely fall in the inferior destinies.
3. Some are not certain whether they will stay on the correct path of cultivation; their destinies are uncertain.

three flaws: The flaws caused by desires, incorrect view of existence, and ignorance.

three flawless roots:
1. The knowledge about the four noble truths that one should know but has not yet known. All the roots of belief, diligence, mindfulness, concentration, and wisdom for the "needing more learning" practitioners who have not yet intuitively understood the noble truths or attained the holy effects.
2. The knowledge that one has fully known about the four noble truths. All the roots of belief, diligence, mindfulness, concentration, and wisdom for the "needing more learning" practitioners who have attained an intuitive understanding of the noble truths and the holy effects.
3. An insightful understanding of the four noble truths and complete removal of all vexations. The roots of belief, diligence, mindfulness, concentration, and wisdom possessed by the ones who need no more learning, such as the arhats, the self-enlightened ones, the great bodhisattvas who have achieved the tenth stage, and the Thus-Comers, Ones Worthy of Offerings, Perfectly and Universally Enlightened Ones. They have insightfully understood the noble truths and have also removed all vexations.

These three roots will free one from defilements and vexations through the practice of will, joy, delight, equanimity, faith, diligence, mindfulness, concentration, and wisdom (fascicles 3, 46, 53, 402, and 415).

three negative roots: The roots of greed, anger, and ignorance.

three supernatural powers: Three kinds of insightful awareness:
1. Knowing the previous lives and their traits of all sentient beings
2. Knowing where each of the sentient beings comes from and where and how each of them will go after death
3. The wisdom of getting rid of all vexations (fascicles 3 and 402)

three vehicles: They are the voice-hearing vehicle, self-enlightenment vehicle, and the bodhisattva vehicle. The first two vehicles are the small ones, while the bodhisattva vehicle is the great one. Among them, the great or large vehicle is capable of ferrying as large a number of sentient beings as possible across the river of birth and death to the other shore of nirvana. The first two vehicles focus on self-liberation, while the large one aims at liberating all sentient beings, and that is the path of bodhisattva.

three paths of bodhi: Three approaches for cultivating the wisdom of enlightenment, including the voice-hearing path, self-enlightenment path, and the bodhisattva path.

three wheels, the purity of: The almsgiving practitioner who realizes the emptiness of all dharmas and becomes unattached to the three wheels: the giver, the receiver, and the things given.

Thus-Comer (Tathagata): The fully developed one, the perfect one, the one who comes as he or she does in such a natural and spontaneous way, and the one who neither comes nor doesn't come.

The Thus-Comers know the phenomena of all dharmas as they really show without misunderstanding and speak of the phenomena of all dharmas as they really show without distortion or deception.

The Thus-Comers come through a stable and peaceful path as the Buddhas do. They come through the real path. The Buddha has become a Buddha because he has insightfully understood realness.

The Buddha comes by riding "as it is" as a vehicle. He realizes the truth as it is. He accomplishes ultimate nirvana based on the unsurpassed, perfect, and universal bodhi as it is. He is the one who has fulfilled perfectly all virtuous karmas and fully and permanently eliminated all bad karmas. He has lectured on the fundamental path of liberation; he leads sentient beings to stay away from negative paths and stay on correct path; and he comes from the realness of the self-natures. So he is named Thus-Comer.

triple gem: The Buddha, the dharma, and the sangha (fascicle 394).

turning the dharma wheel: A symbolic term indicating that the Buddha and the great bodhisattvas propagate the dharma tirelessly, expediently, and skillfully to relieve the sentient beings from suffering.

twelve divisions of Buddha's teachings: Buddha's teachings were given in different styles; they were later recorded and compiled under twelve canonical divisions: the texts (sutra), short verses (geya), prophecy (vyakarana), long verses (gatha), self-statement (udana), origins (nidana), anecdotes (itivrttaka), past lives (jataka), broad teaching (vaipulya), unusual ways (abdhuta-dharma), similes (avadana), and discourses (upadesa).
  1. Sutra: The general name for the recorded texts of the teachings given by the Buddha.
  2. Geya: A partial repeat of sutra in verse style.
  3. Vyakarana: The stories that record the Buddha's prophecies about his disciples or followers who will become a Buddha in the future, including when, where, and with what names.
  4. Gatha: The Buddha's teachings, given in verse style.
  5. Udana: Lectures initiated by the Buddha himself, not upon his disciples' request.
  6. Nidana: The origin and background of how and why the Buddha's teachings are given.
  7. Itivrttaka: What the Buddha and his disciples did in their past lives, but no exact times and places of the events were indicated.
  8. Jataka: The stories of the Buddha's compassionate deeds in previous lives when he was still a bodhisattva.
  9. Vaipulya: The teachings of the ultimate truth with elaborated interpretation and in-depth analysis.
  10. Adbhuta-dharma: The record of the Buddha and his disciples' mystic and unusual conducts.
  11. Avadana: The similes and the celebrated stories of ancient sages given in Buddha's teachings.

12. Upadesa: The Buddha's teachings given in discursive way.

twelve forms in three steps for turning the dharma wheel: The Buddha teaches the four noble truths each in three steps:
1. Demonstrating what the four noble truths are.
2. Teaching what suffering should be aware of and that the cause of suffering should be terminated, the cessation of suffering should be realized, and the path for the cessation of suffering should be cultivated.
3. Showing how suffering can be aware of, the cause of suffering can be terminated, the cessation of suffering can be realized, and the path for the cessation of suffering can be cultivated (fascicle 341).

twelve chains of dependent arising: The Buddha became awakened to the truth of the twelve chains of dependent arising at the moment of attaining the unsurpassed, perfect, and universal bodhi. For ordinary sentient beings, the chains make a circle of reincarnation based on karmas, while the enlightened holy ones are able to trace the circle back to the cause of all suffering and untie the chains of life. For the former ones, the flow of the three modes of time is shown as a successive cause-and-effect connection in the change of one's life-form. The core of this life-drifting is consciousness, the alaya, which is viewed as a storage of one's karmas.
1. Ignorance: Because of ignorance, one will not know the past and future, the relationship between them, cause and effect, causes and conditions, the triple gem, the four noble truths, dependent origination, the virtuous and the not virtuous, the pure and the contaminated, and so forth.
2. Action: Because of ignorance, one's actions will be flawed and imperfect and will give rise to all kinds of suffering.
3. Consciousness: Actions come from consciousness, while the karmas of one's actions affect consciousness; they will be stored in it and integrated with previously existing seeds as causes for further actions.
4. Name and form or mind and body: Human beings and

other things come into existence because of the combination of mental factors and physical factors and based on one's consciousness and the related disposition and ideas.
5. Six sense spheres, namely eye, ear, nose, tongue, body, and conscious spheres.
6. Contact.
7. Feeling or reception.
8. Craving.
9. Grasping.
10. Existence, becoming existent.
11. Birth, arising.
12. Old age, death, worry, sorrow, misery, anxiety, and upset.

twelve ways of ascetic practice: The twelve ways are:
1. Living alone in a quiet place far away from people.
2. Begging for food.
3. Always begging in order; do not skip anyone in order to receive or not receive alms from someone else.
4. One meal a day.
5. Do not eat much.
6. Do not drink juice, juicy food, or dense soup after noon.
7. Wearing ragged clothes.
8. Owning only three pieces of clothes.
9. Living in graveyards.
10. Living under the trees.
11. Sleeping in the open.
12. Sleeping when sitting instead of lying down.

Unsurpassed Great Person: This is one of the ten names of the Buddha. The great bodhisattvas should surpass the fifty-first stage of equal awakening and achieve the last stage of bodhisattva cultivation, the fifty-second stage of exquisite awakening to become a Buddha. Therefore, the Buddha is a great person unequaled and unsurpassed in knowledge, wisdom, abilities, and virtues.

**unsurpassed, perfect, and universal bodhi (wisdom of enlightenment): The perfect and universal wisdom for enlightenment, unsurpassed and incomparable, attained by the Buddhas only, not by voice-hearers, self-enlightened ones, bodhisattvas, or ordinary sentient beings. The ultimate goal for a Buddhist practitioner.

Unsurpassed, Perfectly and Universally Enlightened One: One of the ten names of the Buddha, indicating one who has attained the unsurpassed, perfect, and universal bodhi; one who has been fully enlightened; one who has fully realized the perfect and universal bodhi.

upanisadam-api: Upanisadam, a Sanskrit term from ancient India, indicates an extremely large quantity. On the contrary, upanisadam-api is an extremely small quantity; it means the smallest unit of matter into which anything can be divided.

upasaka: A Buddhist layman.

upasika: A Buddhist laywoman.

utpala: The blue lotus, one kind of water lily (fascicles 10, 398, 405).

view of discontinuation: One of two extreme points of view apart from the middle way; ones who hold this view believe that the cause-and-effect connection is invalid and unreal; they believe that one's life ends at death and no future rebirth is possible. This is in contrast with another extreme point of view that believes that the self and the existent beings of the world are permanent.

view of permanence: A belief that the self and existent beings of the world are permanent; one of the two extreme points of view that deviates from the middle way.

vinaya: Behavioral rules for the monastics that were established by the Buddha (fascicles 395, 435, 439).

vipasyana: Originally a Sanskrit term meaning one's inner investigation, observation, analysis, and contemplation that aims at one or several objects in samatha in order to see things as they really are.

voice-hearer (sravaka): Literally referring to the Buddha's disciples who directly heard teachings from the Buddha, the Sanskrit word *sravaka* indicates one who pursues self-liberation through arhat effect instead of the bodhisattva path. The voice-hearers and the self-enlightened ones (pratyekabuddha) belong to the "small vehicles," while the bodhisattvas belong to the "large vehicle" and are dedicated to assisting other sentient beings in order to alleviate their suffering.

The voice-hearing path includes:
1. Contemplating the four noble truths
2. Cultivating the four bases of mindfulness, four correct endeavors, four bases of power, five roots, five powers, seven factors for enlightenment, and noble eightfold path
3. Learning to eliminate the puzzles caused by incorrect views and incomplete knowledge
4. Learning to eliminate the puzzles caused by flawed character and immature personality that have not fully developed in the process of self-cultivation

There are four stages of voice-hearing cultivation: stream-entry aspiration and effect, once-return aspiration and effect, nonreturn aspiration and effect, and arhat aspiration and effect.

Vulture Peak Mountain: The mountain located near Rajagriha in ancient India. It was well known because the Buddha gave many teachings there, including *The Lotus Sutra*, *The Great Prajna Paramita Sutra*, and others.

Well Appearing One (Subhuti): One of Sakyamuni Buddha's ten most distinguished disciples, Subhuti was recognized by

Glossary of Terms 607

Buddha as the best in understanding the truth of emptiness and frequently appears in the prajna sutras conversing with the Buddha.

Well Gone One: One of the ten names of the Buddha, meaning the Buddha teaches the truth in a perfect and wonderful way; the Buddha progresses very well in the process of becoming a Buddha; the Buddha comes to this world and ferries across the river of vexations to the other shore of liberation in a wonderful way; and the Buddha comes and goes in complete freedom.

wheel-turning king: The most blessed kings who usually appear in an age when the human lifespan is longer than eighty-four thousand years and the world is in peace, prosperity, and happiness. The wheel-turning kings have tremendous wealth and the thirty-two perfect major marks. Because they have cultivated and accumulated many merits and virtues, they become the wealthiest, healthiest, and happiest kings of the world.

They are always followed and surrounded by seven gems, the big family, and the big crowd of associates. They are always ready to give food, drinks, clothes, vehicles, spreading fragrances, incense powders, burning incenses, wreaths, houses, beddings, lamps, candles, medicines, gold, silvers, pearls, corals, jades, and all other necessities for living to those in need. Then they will teach them the dharma correspondent with the six paramitas (fascicle 49).

World-Honored One: One of the ten names of the Buddha. Please see *Bhagavat*.

Xuanzang (Hsüan-tsang) (602?–664 CE): Xuanzang is one of the most important translators of Buddhist texts in Chinese history. He rendered seventy-five volumes (1,335 fascicles) of Sanskrit Buddhist scriptures into Chinese during a period of nineteen years. One of them is *The Great Prajna Paramita Sutra* in six hundred fascicles. He is also one of the most outstanding logicians, epistemologists, and psychologists in Buddhist history, both in India and China.

Xuanzang's family name was Chen. It was under his elder brother's guidance and encouragement that he began to learn Buddhist, Confucian, and Taoist classics when he was a child. In 622 CE, Xuanzang followed his brother and became a fully ordained monk. He then wholeheartedly devoted himself to learning and cultivating Buddhist sutras, precepts, and treatises and became a learned and renowned young monastic.

But at the same time, he strongly felt that the existing Chinese texts could not solve all of his puzzles about Buddhist theories. So he decided that he should go to India, where Buddhism originated, to learn the Sanskrit Buddhist classics. Regardless of the order banning travel to India issued by the government, he left China for India in 629. After struggling against cruel weather, perilous roads, and loneliness for years, he finally arrived in India.

He went to study at Nalanda, the most famous and the oldest university in India and fortunately encountered Master Silabhadra, who was over 100 years old at that time. As the greatest Buddhist logician in that age, he still worked hard to serve as the president and the prime mentor of the university. Xuanzang learned yogacara and Buddhist epistemology from him. The master adored Xuanzang very much and was happy to become his advisor. Xuanzang was eager to learn from whatever disciplines he could and studied extensively the theories of all denominations of Buddhism. He also traveled around India to visit with scholars and sought and acquired as many Sanskrit texts as possible. When he finished all studies, his knowledge, insightful wisdom, and personality had fully developed; he was esteemed by the monastics, lay believers, scholars, and the kings in India. He was invited by his master to teach Consciousness-Only theory at Nalanda.

After staying abroad for seventeen years, he decided that it was time to bring the Sanskrit Buddhist scriptures home and began the next phase of his career: translating these scriptures into Chinese to fulfill his original aspiration to benefit Chinese

Glossary of Terms 609

Buddhist believers by giving them faithful and readable translated texts. He was forty-one years old then. Being aware of his decision, the king invited eighteen kings in the five states of India, seven thousand Buddhist monks from great and small vehicles, and Brahmans to attend a conference in which Xuanzang was the keynote speaker. His paper was posted on the main gate of the meeting for eighteen days, and no one was able to challenge him. Xuanzang returned to China (The Tang-Dynasty) in 646. He brought 657 volumes of Sanskrit Buddhist texts, Buddha's portraits and statues, and one hundred and fifty pieces of Buddha's relics back to China. He then started the important work of translating Sanskrit texts into Chinese until he entered into nirvana in 664.

yojana: The distance an ox carrying a yoke walks in a day; according to Xuanzang's *Journey to the West Frontiers in Great Tang Dynasty*, a yojana indicates the distance a king's army walks in a day (fascicle 398).

Lightning Source UK Ltd.
Milton Keynes UK
UKHW010438020621
384770UK00011B/56